BUSINESS WEEK

Guide to Mutual Funds

BUSINESS WEEK

Guide to Mutual Funds

Eighth Annual Edition

Jeffrey M. Laderman
Senior Writer, BUSINESS WEEK

McGraw-Hill

New York   San Francisco   Washington, D.C.   Auckland   Bogotá
Caracas   Lisbon   London   Madrid   Mexico City   Milan
Montreal   New Delhi   San Juan   Singapore
Sydney   Tokyo   Toronto

International Standard Serial Number:
BUSINESS WEEK Guide to Mutual Funds
ISSN 1060-975x

McGraw-Hill

A Division of The McGraw·Hill Companies

1 2 3 4 5 6 7 8 9 0   MAL/MAL   9 0 3 2 1 0 9 8

ISBN 0-07-038200-X

The editor for this book was Susan Barry, the editing supervisor was Jane Palmieri, and the production supervisor was Pamela Pelton. It was set in Century Expanded by North Market Street Graphics.

Printed and bound by Malloy Lithographers, Inc.

McGraw-Hill books are available at special quantity discounts to use as premiums and sales promotions, or for use in corporate training programs. For more information, please write to the Director of Special Sales, McGraw-Hill, 11 West 19th Street, New York, NY 10011. Or contact your local bookstore.

CONTENTS

Preface   ix

1 Mutual Funds: The People's Choice   1

What's a Mutual Fund?   4
First Encounters with a Mutual Fund   5
The Joys of Compound Growth   6
Be Realistic About Your Expectations   8

2 The World of Mutual Funds   11

Determining Style   13
Equity Funds   16
    Large-Cap Value Funds   16
    Large-Cap Blend Funds   18
    Large-Cap Growth Funds   19
    Mid-Cap Value Funds   21
    Mid-Cap Blend Funds   22
    Mid-Cap Growth Funds   23
    Small-Cap Value Funds   24
    Small-Cap Blend Funds   26
    Small-Cap Growth Funds   27
    Hybrid Funds—Domestic and International   28
    International Funds   32
    Precious Metals Funds   36
    Specialty Funds   38
    Index and Social Investing Funds   40
Bond Funds   43
    Long-Term Funds   49
    Intermediate-Term Funds   50
    Short-Term Funds   51
    Ultrashort Funds   51
    Long-Term Government Funds   52
    Intermediate-Term Government Funds   54
    Short-Term Government Funds   56
    High-Yield Funds   57
    Convertible Funds   60
    International Funds   61
    Multisector Funds   63
    Municipal Funds   63
Money-Market Funds   66
    Taxable Funds   67
    Tax-Exempt Funds   71
Closed-End Funds   72

3 Buying and Selling: The Essentials   79

What You Need to Know About Loads   79
    No-Load Funds   80
    Back-End Loads   80
    "Hidden Loads"   81
To Load or Not to Load?   83
Mutual Fund Networks   85
Advisers and "Wraps"   86
Buying on Margin   88

Prospecting the Prospectus   88
   Statement of Additional Information   89
   Taking a Closer Look   89
   Investment Policy   93
   Shareholder Services   93
Redemptions   94

4 Building an Investment Portfolio   95

Determining Your Financial Goals   95
   Do You Need Current Income from Your Investments?   96
   How Soon Will You Need the Proceeds of Your Investments?   97
   How Will Inflation Affect You?   97
   How Much Risk Are You Willing to Take?   97
   How Will Taxes Affect Your Investments?   98
   What Kind of Temperament Do You Have for Investing?   99
Putting It All Together   100
   Your Asset Allocation Plan   101
   Achieving Your Financial Goals   102
   Savings for Retirement   102
   Look to Your Horizon   103
Using the Scoreboard Ratings   105
   Load or No-Load?   106
   A Minimum Investment?   106
   Taxable or Tax-Deferred Account?   106
Building and Rebuilding Fund Portfolios   108
   Funds for a 401(k)   108
   The Rollover IRA   109
   Equity Funds for Retirement   110
   Restructuring a Portfolio   110
Making Your First Investment   112
Dollar-Cost Averaging   113
Switch Funds! The Timing Game   115

5 Monitoring Your Mutual Funds   119

Tracking Funds in the Financial Pages   119
   Interpreting the Fund Tables   120
Keeping Score   122
Let the Computer Do It   123
Mutual Funds Online   124
When Your Fund Is Ailing   126
Keep in Touch with Your Fund   127
When the Fund Manager Changes   130
Mutual Fund Mergers   133
Change Objectives, Change Funds   134

6 Taxes and Record-Keeping   135

Mutual Funds' Special Tax Status   135
Ducking the Distribution   137
Tax Swapping   138
What's My "Cost Basis"?   139

Tax-Deferred Investing   141
  IRAs   141
  Keogh Plans   143
  401(k) Plans   143
  Variable Annuities   143

7 Using the BW Scoreboard   **147**

Ratings   147
Size   149
Fees   151
Total Return: Pretax and Aftertax   153
History   154
Portfolio Data   154
Risk   157

8 Are Four Great Years in a Row Really Possible?   **161**

Equity Funds   162
  New Faces Among the Top-Rated Funds   165
  Top-Rated Holdovers   166
  Category Ratings Give Funds Another Look   166
  Specialty Funds: Financial, Real Estate, and Utilities Shine   169
  International Sectors   170
  Big Is Beautiful   171
Bond Funds   171
  High Yield and Converts Look Great, But . . .   173
  International Bonds Bite Back   175
  Muni Funds Party—But Nobody Shows   175
Closed-End Funds   176

The BUSINESS WEEK Mutual Fund Scoreboard   **179**

PREFACE

Each and every year, BUSINESS WEEK's annual Mutual Fund Scoreboard issue, *The Best Mutual Funds*, is one of the best-selling single issues of the magazine. It's easy to understand why. Mutual fund assets now stand at $4.5 trillion, up $1 trillion in one year alone. Heck, mutual fund assets just hit the $1 trillion mark in 1990.

Of course, BUSINESS WEEK isn't the only publication that reports on and rates mutual funds. But we think we're the best. So do the mutual fund executives who were asked by *Securities Industry Management* magazine a few years ago to rate those who rate mutual funds. SIM's survey awarded BW's Mutual Fund Scoreboard an A–, the highest grade of seven publications rated. In its comments, SIM gave BW "high marks for being an innovator and for solid editorial comment." The best grade any of the competitors received was a B.

Now the magazine with the best mutual fund scoreboard is proud to bring you the best mutual fund book on the market, BUSINESS WEEK *Guide to Mutual Funds*, Eighth Annual Edition. This slim, easy-to-read volume is your passport into the dynamic world of mutual fund investing. We tell you all you want to know about mutual funds—which funds are beating the market and their competitors, which funds are delivering the highest returns with the least risk, and which funds have

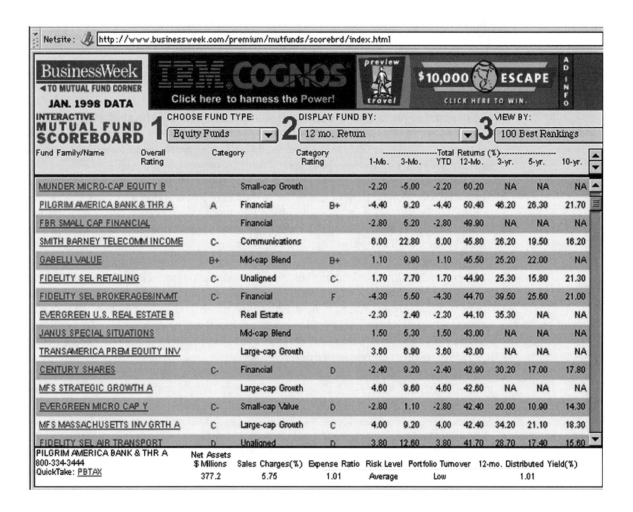

the highest and lowest costs. And we also feature the BUSINESS WEEK ratings. These ratings assess the risk-adjusted returns of each fund with at least five years of performance history against all other funds (three years for closed-end funds). The new edition's Scoreboard, in the back of the book, has the latest information on 885 equity, 653 bond, and 470 closed-end funds.

But now there's even more to BW's fund coverage than what's in the back. We're pleased to bring you the Interactive Mutual Fund Scoreboard, now available at BUSINESS WEEK's site on the World Wide Web (www.businessweek.com).

The Interactive Scoreboard is not confined by the printed page. There's data on 4000 equity and bond funds and, better yet, it's updated monthly—we recalculate returns and BW ratings. This book draws on that trove of information. You can use the online site in many ways: to screen the database for funds in which to invest or to keep tabs on funds you already own. If you want information that goes beyond what's in the Scoreboard, with one click you can jump to a Morningstar page. Another click will take you to the fund's website.

The book is basically composed of two parts. In the first part, we pull together the essentials you need to know about mutual funds: how they work and how you can use them. The second part is the print version of the BUSINESS WEEK Mutual Fund Scoreboard. The Scoreboard provides a wealth of information about mutual fund performance, costs, and risks that helps you to keep track of your own holdings—and prospect for new ones. The ratings are the highlight of the Scoreboard. Funds are rated on the basis of their returns—and their risk.

The book's first chapter is an introduction to mutual funds: why they're popular, what kinds of returns they can provide, and how investors can harness their earning power. Chapter 2 takes a close-up look at the world of mutual funds and discusses how they invest your money. We'll also look into the closed-end funds, the manic first cousins of mutual funds. They often have higher highs and lower lows than their mutual fund kin.

In Chapter 3 we examine how you buy and sell mutual funds. That includes all you need to know about commissions, or the "load." There are funds that are sold with front-end loads, back-end loads, low-loads, hidden loads, and no-loads. And if you're going to pay a load, we'll help you determine which is the most cost-effective way of doing so. And we also explore new ways for investors to buy funds, such as networks or fund marketplaces developed by Charles Schwab & Co. and others and the increasingly popular adviser-based "wrap" programs.

When you've completed Chapters 2 and 3, you will know about the variety of funds and how you buy them. Then the question is what to buy. Chapter 4 asks you the questions you need to answer to help you build your own investment portfolio of mutual funds. And, of course, once you have your funds you can't just forget about them. So in Chapter 5 we cover how to monitor your funds—making sure they do what you want them to do—and using some online tools to do it.

If you've made the right moves, you're making money. And if you're making money, you will have to pay taxes. Chapter 6 explains the special tax rules that apply to how mutual funds report their income to you and how you, the shareholder, report to the Internal Revenue Service. We'll show you how to minimize the tax bite when you're cashing in your gains, and how to make the most of your losses by turning them into tax deductions.

In Chapter 7 we take a closer look at the Scoreboard and how to interpret the information in it. Chapter 8 looks at the most recent Scoreboard: which funds are in ascendancy, which are in decline, and what it means for the coming years. What follows is the Scoreboard itself—a cornucopia of information on 2000 funds. Once you have the basics of mutual funds investing under your belt, the Scoreboard is the perfect place to start your search for the funds that will help you reach your financial goals.

Acknowledgments

The Scoreboard itself is produced for BUSINESS WEEK by Morningstar, Inc. This company takes care of gathering the vast amounts of data from the funds—organizing it and analyzing it in a way that allows us to assign ratings to funds. We'd like to thank the folks at Morningstar, especially Kelly Messman, for their advice and assistance in preparing the Guide.

At BUSINESS WEEK, Senior Writer Jeffrey M. Laderman took charge of writing the book and coordinating the project. Laderman, a Chartered Financial Analyst, has covered mutual funds for over 15 years. He helped to launch the first Mutual Fund Scoreboard in February 1986, and has written the accompanying stories every year since.

Also contributing to the book is Senior Editor Seymour Zucker, who lent his skillful editing and much valued advice. Without his enthusiastic support, and that of Stephen B. Shepard, BW's editor-in-chief, and Mark Morrison, the managing editor, this project would not have been possible.

Mutual Funds: The People's Choice

Over the last several years, investors have embraced mutual funds with a fervor that even the most optimistic fund executive could not have predicted. Since the beginning of 1991, investors have poured nearly $1 trillion into mutual funds that invest in stocks and bonds. In the record-setting year 1997 alone, equity funds took in a record $231 billion; bond funds, nearly $45 billion.

Why are people putting billions into mutual funds? Well, nothing sells like success, and for the most part investors have been enormously successful. In 1991, 1992, and 1993, they earned plump returns as interest rates fell, vastly increasing the value of stocks and bonds. In 1994, interest rates shot up, causing losses in bond funds that have stopped the flood of new money for years. But investors never wavered in their support for equity funds, even when the stock market teetered that year.

Investors who stuck it out during tough 1994 were paid off wonderfully in 1995, 1996, and 1997. During that three-year period, perhaps the best three years ever for the U.S. stock market, the average U.S. equity fund delivered a total return of 24.5 percent, including appreciation, dividends, and capital gains distributions. That's a rate at which money doubles every three years.

And though many investment strategists did not have high hopes for 1997, that too, turned out to be an excellent year for equity funds. The BUSINESS WEEK Mutual Fund Scoreboard shows that U.S. diversified equity funds earned an average 24.1 percent total return; all equity funds, 17.5 percent. The 25 funds with the highest returns earned at least 45.6 percent (Table 1-1). The average bond fund earned 8.3 percent. But the top 25 bond funds came in with impressive results—the best was up 30.1 percent (Table 1-2).

Investors have also seen some of the foibles of mutual funds. Several portfolio managers faced disciplinary actions from regulators for making personal investments that conflicted with their professional duties. One was even dismissed from his job. The actions prompted most companies to tighten up their personnel trading policies, and the fund industry itself developed guidelines about what fund personnel should and should not do with personal trading.

Fund shareholders also learned a new 4-letter word with 11 letters: "derivatives." These derivatives—financially-engineered investment instruments whose value is "derived" from some other security or index—helped sink two government-mortgage funds and erode principal in dozens more. Money-market mutual funds, which are supposed to be the most risk-averse funds of all, were not untouched by the derivatives mess, either. However, in all but one instance, the funds' management companies absorbed the losses of the handful of money funds adversely affected by derivatives. In early 1997, another fund management company stepped in to bail out a money-market mutual fund that had erred the old-fashioned way—it had made an investment that turned out bad because of "financial irregularities" at the company.

By and large, investors have a lot of confidence in mutual funds. In a summer 1994 BUSINESS WEEK/Harris Poll of mutual fund investors, after much of the year's damage had been done, fully 94 percent said they're somewhat or very confident that their investments are safe and only 24 percent said they planned to scale back their

TABLE 1-1

EQUITY FUNDS
1997'S TOP RETURNS

Fund	Total return*
AMERICAN HERITAGE	75.0%
MUNDER MICRO-CAP EQUITY B	71.3
LEXINGTON TROIKA RUSSIA	67.4
PILGRIM AMERICA BANK & THRIFT A	64.2
FIDELITY SEL. BROKERAGE & INVST. MGT.	62.3
FBR SMALL CAP FINANCIAL	58.4
TITAN FINANCIAL SERVICES	55.6
HARTFORD CAPITAL APPRECIATION A	55.1
OAKMARK SELECT	55.0
BRAZOS/JMIC SMALL CAP GROWTH	54.5
EVERGREEN U.S. REAL ESTATE	53.9
HANCOCK REGIONAL BANK B	52.8
FIDELITY SEL. ENERGY SERVICE	51.9
MFS STRATEGIC GROWTH A	50.4
CENTURY SHARES	50.1
SAFECO GROWTH NO LOAD	50.0
MFS MASSACHUSETTS INV. GROWTH A	48.3
GABELLI VALUE	48.2
DELAWARE AGGRESSIVE GROWTH A	48.1
FBR FINANCIAL SERVICES	47.7
EVERGREEN MICRO CAP Y	47.6
TRANSAMERICA PREM. EQUITY INV.	47.5
JANUS SPECIAL SITUATIONS	46.0
FIDELITY SEL. HOME FINANCE	45.9
TEXAS CAPITAL VALUE & GROWTH	45.6

*Appreciation plus reinvestment of dividends and capital gains, before taxes

DATA: MORNINGSTAR INC.

holdings. In addition, the poll's respondents showed they had a fairly realistic view of the risks that go with investing. Asked who is to blame if a mutual fund loses money, 60 percent said "no one." Asked what they would expect if one of their funds lost money, 80 percent said they did not expect anyone to make up the losses.

The sentiments expressed in that poll were certainly borne out in the subsequent three years. Investors continue to stash their savings in mutual funds. With more than one out of four U.S. households owning mutual funds, funds have established their place in family finance alongside the savings account, the checkbook, and the credit cards.

And those not familiar with funds are learning about them at the workplace. Mutual funds are fast becoming a mainstay of a type of pension program called the 401(k) plan. In these sorts of plans, employees—often matched in part by employers—make regular pretax contributions to the plan, which in turn are invested in any one of several choices which may include mutual funds. In 1995, for instance, General Motors Corp. added 38 Fidelity mutual funds to its 401(k) plan, a figure that's since been increased to 50. A large percentage of the monthly inflows to mutual funds comes through the workplace.

Sure, novice investors have learned through experience that markets—and mutual fund prices—don't always go up. But taking a longer-term view, investors have been rewarded for taking the higher risks of investing. Indeed, over the long haul, the greater risk to investors is in playing it too safe. Investors who keep long-term funds in CDs and U.S. Treasury bills may be taking a big risk that they won't meet their long-term financial objectives, like a college education for their children or a comfortable retirement for themselves.

Mutual funds are not new. They've been a part of the investment world since the 1920s. For most of that time, funds offered one sort of investment—stocks. Bond funds were few, and tax-free bond and money-market mutual funds didn't come along until the 1970s. Even equity mutual funds were only a sideshow on Wall Street. First, individual investors and, later, pension funds held much more sway.

Today, because individuals have put their dollars in the hands of mutual fund managers, mutual funds dominate the stock market. They don't dominate in the sense that they "control" companies. But right now the funds are the most active investors, with the most new money to put to work. Market participants follow the funds' moves very closely. Just consider all the publicity surrounding the trading in the gargantuan Fidelity Magellan Fund. In late 1995, portfolio manager Jeffrey Vinik, in shareholder reports and in press interviews, made complimentary remarks about technology stocks around the same time he was selling them. In November 1995, Magellan sold an estimated $5 billion in tech stocks—and other Fidelity funds likely sold a few billion more. Fidelity critics howled, saying Vinik was trying to talk up the stocks to get a better price on his sales. Fidelity officials said Vinik's statements were his honest opinion at the time they were made but portfolio managers have to be free to change their minds. Indeed, that's what they're paid for. Certainly, portfolio managers must play by the rules, but that doesn't include telling everybody what their next move is going to be. That would be detrimental to fund shareholders to whom every portfolio manager has a fiduciary responsibility.

TABLE 1-2

BOND FUNDS

1997'S TOP RETURNS

Fund ▼	Total return* ▼
AMERICAN CENTURY–BENHAM TARGET MAT. 2025	30.1%
DAVIS CONVERTIBLE SECURITIES A	28.7
AMERICAN CENTURY–BENHAM TARGET MAT. 2020	28.6
CALAMOS GROWTH & INCOME	23.3
AMERICAN CENTURY–BENHAM TARGET MAT. 2015	22.9
PACIFIC HORIZON CAPITAL INCOME A	22.0
NICHOLAS-APPLEGATE INCOME & GROWTH C	21.8
NORTHERN INCOME EQUITY	20.8
CALAMOS CONVERTIBLE A	20.4
FRANKLIN CONVERTIBLE SECURITIES I	20.3
PUTNAM CONVERTIBLE INCOME-GROWTH A	19.6
BATTERY PARK HIGH-YIELD A	18.0
OPPENHEIMER BOND FOR GROWTH B	17.9
SUMMIT HIGH-YIELD RET.	17.6
RESERVE CONVERTIBLE SECURITIES	17.5
FIDELITY NEW MARKETS INCOME	17.4
INVESCO HIGH-YIELD	17.1
VALUE LINE CONVERTIBLE	17.0
FIDELITY ADVISOR HIGH-YIELD T	17.0
VAN KAMPEN AMER. CAP. HARBOR A	16.9
HANCOCK HIGH-YIELD BOND B	16.9
FIDELITY SPARTAN HIGH-INCOME	16.9
T. ROWE PRICE EMERGING MARKETS BOND	16.9
AMERICAN CENTURY–BENHAM TARGET MAT. 2010	16.8
DREYFUS HIGH-YIELD SECURITIES	16.7

*Appreciation plus reinvestment of dividends and capital gains, before taxes

DATA: MORNINGSTAR INC.

Mutual funds play a critical role in the fixed-income markets as well. State and local governments increasingly turn to the mutual funds to buy their bonds and provide the financing needed to operate public services and rebuild the aging infrastructure. Through investment in U.S. Treasury securities, mutual funds help to finance the U.S. government. Funds bring fresh capital to the home mortgage market through their purchases of mortgage-backed securities, making it easier and a little cheaper for families to buy homes. And, with investments in high-yield bonds and commercial paper, mutual funds are helping to lower the borrowing costs for corporations.

Mutual funds would still be a financial backwater if not for the millions of individuals who now entrust their hard-earned money to mutual fund companies. It's not always an easy trust to give. Savers who move their money out of a bank or thrift give up federal deposit insurance. Mutual funds have no guarantees.

The growth of the mutual fund industry has even surprised industry officials. In 1990, for instance, an industry-sponsored study estimated the funds would have $2 trillion in assets by 1995 or 1996, and at least $3 trillion by 2000. At year-end 1997, fund assets were nearly at the $4.5 trillion mark; the number of funds stood at 6809; the number of shareholder accounts, 149 million (Figure 1-1). The popularity of the funds is more than a bull market phenomenon. After all, many fund investors could just as easily buy stocks and bonds directly, but choose funds instead. Funds are convenient and efficient investment vehicles that give all individuals—even those with small sums to invest—access to a splendid array of opportunities. Mutual funds are uniquely democratic institutions. They can take a portfolio of giant blue-chip companies like Exxon, General Electric, and Philip Morris, and slice it into small enough pieces that most anyone can buy.

Mutual funds allow investors to participate in foreign stock and bond markets which they couldn't do on their own—or would find to be a costly, time-consuming, and logistical quagmire if they tried. International equity funds make investing across national borders no more difficult than investing across state lines. Closed-end funds, which, like mutual funds, are pools of professionally managed investments, allow investors to target their investments into individual nations like Chile, Indonesia, Thailand, and Turkey. (Closed-end funds also offer more conventional stock and bond investments.)

Mutual funds have opened up a world of fixed-income investing to people who not too many years ago had few choices other than passbook accounts and savings bonds. Through bond funds individuals can tap into the interest payments from any kind of fixed-income security you can imagine and many you can't. The range goes from U.S. Treasury bonds to collateralized mortgage obligations, adjustable-rate preferred stock, floating rate notes, and even other countries' debt—denominated both in U.S. dollars and in other currencies.

After the bond market volatility investors experienced in 1994 and, to a lesser degree, in 1996, a boring old bank account may look pretty good to a yield-oriented investor. Funds are not the same as bank deposits. No one guarantees that your assets will remain intact, let alone grow. Some legislators and regulators have pointed to surveys of bank customers who bought mutual funds at the bank—and think they're insured. The only fund that can be considered as safe as a bank

FIGURE 1-1

THE EXPLOSIVE GROWTH IN MUTUAL FUNDS

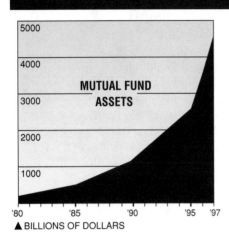

MUTUAL FUND ASSETS

▲ BILLIONS OF DOLLARS

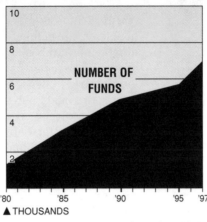

NUMBER OF FUNDS

▲ THOUSANDS

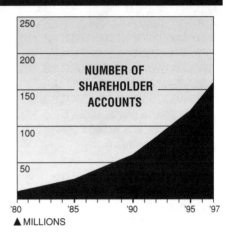

NUMBER OF SHAREHOLDER ACCOUNTS

▲ MILLIONS

DATA: INVESTMENT COMPANY INSTITUTE, STRATEGIC INSIGHT

deposit is one investing solely in U.S. Treasury bills. No one should use equity funds for money that they're going to need to buy a house or a car in the near future. But the longer the investment horizon, the lower the risk of losses. Money stashed away for many years instead of months could well go into a mutual fund, or a properly constructed portfolio of funds.

How do you find the right funds? BUSINESS WEEK's *Guide to Mutual Funds*, Eighth Annual Edition, will make it easy for you. In one volume we survey the world of funds, tell you what you need to know about them, help you tailor your own investment plan, and choose the funds that will best fulfill it. Perhaps you would rather invest through a broker or financial planner, relying on their advice. That's fine, too. But don't turn to a salesperson without a solid grasp of mutual funds yourself. If you enter the world of mutual funds as an educated consumer and avoid the common mistakes (Table 1-3), you can become a successful investor.

What's a Mutual Fund?

A mutual fund is an investment company that pools the money of many individual investors. When the fund takes in money from investors, it issues shares. The price of a mutual fund share is the total net assets—the fund's assets less liabilities—divided by the number of shares outstanding. This figure is also called the fund's net asset value, commonly referred to as "NAV."

Unlike stocks, whose prices are subject to change at each trade, mutual fund NAVs are calculated at the end of each day. To figure their NAVs, the funds use the closing prices of each of the securities in their portfolios. (Bond funds often own securities that trade infrequently and daily prices are hard to come by. These funds use outside services that estimate the bonds' prices.)

A mutual fund is also an "open-end" vehicle. That means the fund doesn't have a fixed number of shares, but issues new shares as it takes in money and redeems them as investors withdraw. This liquidity—the ability for investors to get in and out of the funds easily and at little or no cost—is one of the most important features the funds bring to the financial system. A smaller number of funds are "closed-end" funds. They raise their capital during offering periods, and after that, investors can only get into the fund or out of it by buying or selling the shares on a stock exchange or in the over-the-counter market.

Open-end or closed-end, both types of funds are highly regulated entities, governed by a federal law—the Investment Company Act of 1940. Regulators don't dictate investment policy, but they make sure investment managers adhere to prescribed standards of disclosure, record-keeping, and administration.

As a practical matter, the fund companies police themselves. The U.S. Securities and Exchange Commission (SEC) has several hundred examiners to check up on thousands of funds. For the most part, the mutual funds have avoided the kind of financial scandals seen on Wall Street and in the thrift business in the 1980s and have a fairly clean record.

The mutual fund format is especially good for those just getting started in the investment game. If you only have $1000 or $2000 to invest, very few stockbrokers or professional money managers are going to bother with you. Those who do will not give you the attention and research support afforded to their more well-heeled clients—nor should you expect it. They have to make a living, and the commission on a small nest egg isn't worth much of their time.

But if you put your money in a mutual fund, the first-string portfolio managers will be working on your mutual fund account. The $1000 investor gets the same attention as the $100,000 investor. That's because the fund's performance is the manager's calling card. Its successes will be chronicled in the media—and so will its failures. That's a powerful incentive for the portfolio manager to give the fund his or her very best efforts.

You might be one of those people who thinks of a mutual fund as an investment for small and unsophisticated investors; that it's okay for investors who are still building their assets, but anyone with an appreciable amount of money moves into direct investment in stocks and bonds. That's not so. Today many investors who could well afford stockbrokers and professional money managers prefer mutual funds. Over the last decade, a few fund companies have developed "sector funds," nondiversified funds that invest in a particular industry or group of industries. Such investment vehicles are designed to look more like stocks than mutual funds and to appeal to investors who might otherwise choose to invest in individual stocks.

Service, convenience, and efficiency all help to explain the growth of mutual funds. But no one would invest in mutual funds if they didn't think they would make money. And, indeed, mutual funds have made huge sums of money for those wise enough to have invested in them.

First Encounters with a Mutual Fund

Many investors first encountered a mutual fund when they bought a money-market fund. In the late 1970s and early 1980s, the interest rates that banks and thrifts could pay savers were set by bank regulators—and they were kept artificially low. Those with $10,000 could pull their money out of the bank and buy Treasury bills, but there was no high-interest vehicle for individuals with less money—until the money-market mutual fund.

The money-market funds revolutionized savings in America. They pooled investors' money and bought the kind of higher-yielding money-market investments that individuals could not get on their own. When short-term interest rates soared to almost 20 percent, the money funds made it possible for anyone to take advantage of the enormous yield. Before the advent of these funds, the only choice a small investor had was a passbook account paying 5 percent.

The money-market funds also resuscitated the mutual fund industry, which for years had been suffering from liquidation—investors taking more money out of the funds than they were putting in. By 1982, money-market funds had commandeered about $200 billion in assets. When the great bull market in stocks and bonds got underway, the mutual fund companies had millions of new customers to whom they could pitch their stock and bond funds.

Fund investors were not disappointed. During the 1980s equity mutual funds earned on average an annual total return of 14.9 percent. In one sense, that's terrific. A $1000 investment in the average equity fund at the start of the decade would have grown to a little more than $4000 by the end. But relative to the Standard & Poor's

TABLE 1-3

FUND INVESTORS' BIGGEST MISTAKES

- ▶ Buying last year's or last quarter's hottest performer only because it did well.
- ▶ Ignoring the prospectus—especially the parts on fees and investment policy.
- ▶ Choosing funds inappropriate for investment goals.
- ▶ Selecting highest yields without regard for risks.
- ▶ Losing track of fund performance.
- ▶ Failure to keep records for investment evaluation and taxes.

500 stock index, the yardstick by which money managers are measured, the return is a little thin. The S&P 500, in fact, delivered an average annual total return of 17.5 percent during the decade.

But examine those returns more closely. The S&P 500 is an index, "managed" by a computer. A mutual fund is a portfolio of stocks that needs a manager, who is usually backed up by analysts and some support staff. The fund must keep meticulous records of its own transactions and those of its thousands of shareholders. Account statements need to be prepared and mailed to each of them. There's also the cost of staffing those toll-free phone lines and fees for the auditing and regulatory filings. All this service costs, on average, about 1.21 percent a year of fund assets, or $1.21 per $100 invested. And that comes out of a fund's returns.

Next, consider that most equity mutual funds keep about 5 percent of their assets in cash. In a bull market, cash (Treasury bills and other money-market instruments) has lower returns than stocks. Over the decade, the cash accounted for another half a percentage point in the underperformance.

Finally, remember that the S&P 500 is dominated by large companies—and the average mutual fund owns companies that are much smaller than the General Motors and Exxons of the world. In the 1980s, the stock price performance of the larger companies beat the small-to-medium-sized companies. So there was no way that the average fund could top the S&P 500.

This "underperformance" doesn't seem to have dampened investor enthusiasm for mutual funds. Nor should it. The performance of equity funds still beat money-market and bond funds over the decade and probably gave investors a better return than if they had done nothing with their money. In addition, the average return is just that. Hundreds of funds fared better and 64 even beat the S&P during the decade.

And, even better for mutual fund investors is the fact that the tide seems to have shifted toward small-to-medium-sized companies. From 1991 through 1993, the average U.S. diversified fund, which has more small and midsized stocks than the S&P 500, beat S&P by an average of 3 percentage points a year. Since 1994, those smaller companies have had periods of strong performance, but in each of the three calendar years, the S&P 500 topped the average fund.

Moreover, you don't have to settle for average

returns. If you choose your mutual funds carefully and keep abreast of your funds' progress by tracking net asset values, reading shareholder reports, and using the BUSINESS WEEK ratings, you can improve your portfolio performance.

One academic study pondered the question, "Do winners repeat?" The academics examined monthly mutual fund returns over a 12-year period and found that they do indeed, as do losers, and concluded that a review of past performance is useful in differentiating one mutual fund from another. Although it may not be wise to buy only the No. 1 performer in any one year, it is indeed advisable to select from funds that have been among the best year after year.

Another study looked at equity mutual funds over a 14-year period and concluded that there is some "persistence" of performance. The researchers found that funds that excelled during one year continued to excel for as long as eight quarters, or two years, more. More important, they concluded that there are ways to identify these mutual funds so investors can put their money into the funds and enjoy the benefit of the funds' expertise.

One way to find the best funds, the ones that exhibit this persistence of performance, is in the BUSINESS WEEK Mutual Fund Scoreboard. The BW ratings take into account a mutual fund's risk as well as its total return over a five-year period. This longer view of performance screens out the one-year wonders. The funds that rise to the top do so with consistently strong risk-adjusted returns.

The Joys of Compound Growth

I f you're ever cornered by a mutual fund salesperson, he or she will whip out the "mountain" chart (Figure 1-2). What's really important is not the mountain, but the top line, which depicts the growth of a one-time investment in a mutual fund. The line rises slowly at first, but soon accelerates and appears to jump off the page. The Templeton funds, for instance, show what would have happened if you had invested $10,000 in the Templeton Growth Fund when it opened for business in November 1954 and instructed the fund to reinvest all dividends and capital gains distributions. Over four decades later, your original

> Do winners repeat? Some say they do.

FIGURE 1-2

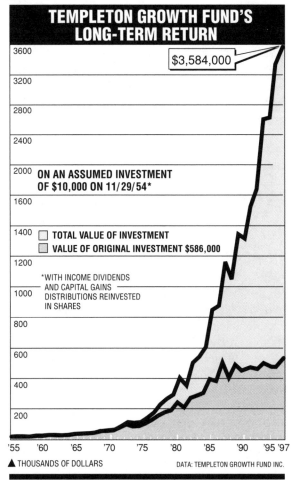

TEMPLETON GROWTH FUND'S LONG-TERM RETURN

$3,584,000

ON AN ASSUMED INVESTMENT OF $10,000 ON 11/29/54*

☐ TOTAL VALUE OF INVESTMENT
☐ VALUE OF ORIGINAL INVESTMENT $586,000

*WITH INCOME DIVIDENDS AND CAPITAL GAINS DISTRIBUTIONS REINVESTED IN SHARES

▲ THOUSANDS OF DOLLARS   DATA: TEMPLETON GROWTH FUND INC.

$10,000 alone would be worth over $532,479. But with reinvestment of dividends and capital gains, your investment is worth $3.6 million, more than six times as much.

Sales hype? Well, the track record is real. Templeton Growth Fund, which was one of the first international funds (that is, funds that invest in non-U.S. stocks), has had an average annual return of 14.6 percent. What is a little exaggerated is the $10,000 investment. The equivalent in today's dollars is more than $50,000. Even today, that's hardly your average initial mutual fund investment.

The example may be a bit fanciful, but the principle demonstrated in this sort of sales material is simple—the power of compound rates of return. You earn a return on your investment and, if you don't take it out of the fund, you begin to earn returns on your returns. You're probably familiar with a bank certificate of deposit. If you leave the interest in the CD, you earn interest on your interest. Mutual funds don't pay a fixed rate

of interest. But if you reinvest profits in more fund shares, you're compounding your returns.

Look at Table 1-4. If you invest $10,000 now, hold on to the investment for 20 years, reinvest your returns, and earn, on average, 11 percent, your nest egg grows more than eightfold—to $80,623. Now look at the return in another way. An 11 percent return on $10,000 is $1100. Over 20 years that totals $22,000. So, after two decades you can account for $32,000—your $10,000 initial investment and the annual return earned on it. The other $48,000 is the return on your returns.

Mutual funds don't guarantee a rate of return. The portfolio managers do their best to deliver the highest rate of return they can and live within their investment objectives. And if a fund does earn, on average, 12 percent a year, it's not earning that every year. Some years the fund might earn twice that amount and other years actually lose money. It's only in retrospect that you come up with nice round numbers like a 12 percent or 14 percent annual rate of return. It's simply an average.

If you want to harness the power of compound rates of return, investing in mutual funds is a convenient and efficient way to do it. Suppose you own some bonds and collect $389 in interest twice a year. You want to reinvest the money, but what can you do with it? You can't buy more bonds because it's an odd amount. You can stash it away in a money-market mutual fund until you have enough to buy another bond. But while the money is sitting in a money-market fund, it's probably not earning what it could in a bond.

A mutual fund makes this process much simpler. If a bond fund pays you $389, or any other such amount, you can (in advance) direct the fund to reinvest the money immediately. You don't have to worry about odd amounts of money. There is no check stuck in the mail. Your money is at work all the time. The mutual fund will take whatever the amount is, divide it by the current price per share, and give you that many shares. If it's 17.693 shares, so be it, since the fund can sell you fractional shares down to one-thousandth of a decimal place.

The ability to invest odd sums and buy fractional shares makes mutual funds ideal vehicles for savings programs. Millions of mutual fund shareholders, in fact, invest regularly through automatic investment plans. Suppose you want to save $200 a month and invest it in equities. It's not practical to buy $200 worth of stock at a time. Commissions are high on small orders, and

TABLE 1-4

THE WONDERFUL WORLD OF COMPOUND INTEREST

Invest $10,000 in year 1

Rate of return	What your investment would be worth at the end of year...					
	5	10	15	20	25	305
7%	$14,026	$19,672	$27,950	$38,697	$52,274	$76,123
8	14,693	21,589	31,722	46,610	68,485	100,627
9	15,386	23,674	36,425	56,044	86,231	132,677
10	16,105	25,937	41,772	67,275	108,347	174,494
11	16,851	28,394	47,846	80,623	135,855	228,923
12	17,623	31,058	54,736	96,463	170,001	299,599

Invest $2,000 a year

Rate of return	What your investment would be worth at the end of year...					
	5	10	15	20	25	30
7%	$12,307	$29,567	$53,776	$87,730	$135,353	$202,146
8	12,672	31,291	58,649	98,846	157,909	244,692
9	13,047	33,121	64,007	111,529	184,648	297,150
10	13,431	35,062	69,899	126,005	216,364	361,887
11	13,826	37,123	76,380	142,530	253,998	441,826
12	14,230	39,309	83,507	161,398	298,668	540,585

Invest $200 a month

Rate of return	What your investment would be worth at the end of year...					
	5	10	15	20	25	30
7%	$14,402	$34,819	$63,762	$104,793	$162,959	$245,417
8	14,793	36,833	69,669	118,589	191,473	300,059
9	15,198	38,993	76,249	134,579	225,906	368,895
10	15,616	41,310	83,585	153,139	267,578	455,865
11	16,049	43,797	91,772	174,715	318,116	566,046
12	16,497	46,468	100,915	199,830	379,527	705,983

DATA: BUSINESS WEEK

there's no way to invest odd amounts that are left over and buy fractional shares of stock on any exchange.

With a regular savings program the compound growth tables look even more alluring. Remember, the numbers are greater because you periodically invest new money in the fund. Put $200 a month into a mutual fund and you can really see the money build up. After 20 years you've put in $48,000. If that money earns an 11 percent average annual return for 20 years, your stake grows to about $174,715. That's nearly $127,000 more than you put in.

The ease and efficiency with which investments compound make mutual funds perfect investments for long-term savings programs like college funds or retirement accounts. That's why mutual funds are the investment vehicle of choice for Individual Retirement Accounts (IRAs). According to figures compiled by the Investment Company Institute, at the end of 1996 mutual fund IRAs held about $410.8 billion in assets, 35 percent of all IRA money. Banks and thrifts together had only a little more than half that amount. In 1985 mutual funds had only 12.5 percent of the IRA pie; banks and thrifts together had over 60 percent of the IRA assets.

Be Realistic About Your Expectations

Remember the Templeton Growth Fund, with the mythical investor whose $10,000 investment of 40 years earlier made him a millionaire? He didn't become a millionaire instantaneously. Invest $10,000, and even if you earn 20 percent a year, it would still take 26 years to turn it into a million. Mutual funds won't get you rich quick, but if you persist in investing, and you invest with funds that are persistently good, your wealth will grow.

Whatever funds you choose for your investment program, you should be realistic in your expectations. Mutual funds are organized to invest in a specific kind of security or a particular market. So if you choose an equity fund that invests in large capitalization stocks, you hope it's going to perform better than the S&P 500. But if the S&P is down 20 percent, you can't realistically expect your fund to be up. If your fund was down only 10 percent, you might still be hopping mad at the fund manager, but, in fact, among peers, he or she would be considered a hero. Likewise, if you're investing in a money-market fund when Treasury bill rates are 5 percent, you shouldn't expect a 10 percent return. The returns generated by the fund won't be terribly different from what happens in the market in which it invests. If you did get 10 percent from that very fund, it would be a sure bet that the fund was not living up to the investment guidelines that all money-market mutual funds must follow.

You also need a little perspective on expectations. The last three years, 1995, 1996, and 1997, were extraordinary years for the U.S. stock market, a period when the market more than doubled. The S&P 500 gained an average 31.1 percent a year, nearly three times the long-term average price gain for large-capitalization U.S. stocks. Many market commentators have argued for the last several years that the stock market is overpriced and bound for a crash, or at least a serious correction. We at BUSINESS WEEK believe there are solid fundamental economic reasons for the stock market's advance, and that even with the Dow Jones industrial average well over 8000, stocks and mutual funds can offer good long-term investment opportunities. However, we recognize—and you should too—that rate of gain in the last three years cannot continue indefinitely. More important, it doesn't have to to make investing pay off.

As an investor, you have no control over the stock or bond markets. But you do have control over your own portfolio of mutual funds. We don't advocate buying and selling funds frequently, trying to catch the ups and avoid the downs of the market (what's known as market-timing, see Chapter 4). But if you select funds with the help of the BUSINESS WEEK ratings, monitor their performance, and keep investments matched to your financial objectives, your long-term investment program will be rewarding.

CHAPTER 2

The World of Mutual Funds

You may know you want to invest in mutual funds, but where do you start? At one time, funds pretty much invested in big U.S. corporations. Period. Today, there are funds that specialize in everything from biotechnology to small Asian companies to municipal bonds issued within the boundaries of a single state. The number of funds is so large and investment programs so varied that investors would be overwhelmed without some way to organize the offerings.

This chapter will help you make sense of the thousands of funds—and how they invest your money. To accomplish this, we've broken the chapter into several sections: equity funds, bond funds, and money-market funds. We follow with a section on closed-end funds—a predecessor of the mutual fund that is usually overshadowed by mutual funds and overlooked by investors.

Let's look first at equity funds, those funds that invest in equities, or common stocks. Many of the companies most widely held by equity funds are household names—Philip Morris, General Electric, Intel, IBM, Citicorp, and Microsoft (Table 2-1). Find the column, "Percent of net assets." Philip Morris, the stock most commonly found in equity mutual fund portfolios, amounts to less than 1 percent of the net assets of all equity fund holdings. Even the 25 largest holdings amount to only 12 percent of equity funds' net assets. That's a sign of the diversity and variety within mutual fund portfolios.

To get a better understanding of equity funds, you have to look closer. The mutual fund industry has traditionally categorized funds by the fund's investment objective as stated in the prospectus, a legal document required by securities law. These are the investment objectives you will find in most mutual fund publications and advertising: "growth," "growth and income," and "small company."

But now, mutual funds have become so diverse in their strategies that the old nomenclature doesn't work anymore. For example, what is a "growth" fund anyway? It's a fund whose "primary aim is to provide capital appreciation (a rise in share price) rather than steady income," according to the 1997 *Mutual Fund Fact Book* (which is published by the Investment Company

TABLE 2-1

EQUITY FUNDS

LARGEST HOLDINGS

Stock ▼	Percent of net assets ▼
PHILIP MORRIS	0.93%
GENERAL ELECTRIC	0.82
INTEL	0.72
FANNIE MAE	0.63
IBM	0.60
BRISTOL-MYERS SQUIBB	0.57
CITICORP	0.52
MERCK	0.50
MICROSOFT	0.49
PFIZER	0.48
BANKAMERICA	0.45
E.I. DUPONT DE NEMOURS	0.43
COMPAQ COMPUTER	0.42
CHASE MANHATTAN	0.41
SCHLUMBERGER	0.41
EXXON	0.41
WAL-MART STORES	0.39
ALLSTATE	0.39
WARNER-LAMBERT	0.37
AMERICAN EXPRESS	0.36
AMERICAN HOME PRODUCTS	0.35
AMERICAN INTERNATIONAL GROUP	0.35
AT&T	0.34
PROCTER & GAMBLE	0.33
JOHNSON & JOHNSON	0.33

DATA: MORNINGSTAR INC.

Institute, the fund industry's principal trade association). The problem with that definition is that it's so vague it can be applied to hundreds, if not thousands, of funds.

The truth is that this definition gives an investor little guidance on exactly how the fund actually "grows" the value of your investment. The Vanguard U.S. Growth Fund takes a fairly traditional growth route, buying stocks in blue-chip growth companies such as Intel, Microsoft, Coca-Cola, Hewlett-Packard, Philip Morris, and Procter & Gamble. The median market capitalization (total market value of a company's shares) of all the stocks in the portfolio is $55.9 billion.

At the other end of the growth-fund spectrum is Lindner Growth Investors, which, judged by its portfolio, has little in common with Vanguard U.S. Growth Fund. Among the largest holdings are Alliant Techsystems, Charming Shoppes, Minorco, and Noram Energy. Recognize any of these names? Probably not. They're not household names, and they're much, much smaller companies. The median market capitalization is only $513 million, less than 1 percent of that of Vanguard U.S. Growth Fund.

Are these two funds at all alike? Other than the fact that both are growth funds that invest in equities, no. It's not even that one invests in very large companies, the other in very small companies. The companies the funds choose differ in more than size. Vanguard U.S. Growth's companies sell, on average, at 8.8 times their "book" value, which, simply put, is the value of the company's assets that are "on the books" less the liabilities. It's what the accountants say the company's worth. That may seem high, but the key here is earnings growth, not book value. On that side, Vanguard U.S. Growth's companies are well above average for large companies—an average 23 percent growth in earnings a year over the last three.

Lindner Growth's companies, on the other hand, sell for just 2.5 times book value. Why so low? Well, these companies are often out of favor with investors. Look at the three-year earnings growth rate—in this case, just 11.5 percent—and you can understand why these stocks are out of favor. So why do the managers of the Lindner Growth fund want to invest in them? They believe that the stocks are undervalued and certain changes are going on in the companies that will result in the market's ultimately recognizing that value. These changes might be an upturn in earnings, an exciting new product, a corporate restructuring, or perhaps even a merger.

In the investment world, Vanguard's stocks would be considered a "growth" portfolio; Lindner's, a "value" portfolio. We can also characterize the funds by the median market capitalization of the stocks they hold. Vanguard U.S. Growth is definitely large-cap, the Lindner fund, small-cap. Use the two characteristics to describe each fund and you get large-cap growth and small-cap value. Those are two very distinct "investment styles," both of which, when executed well, have the capability to make money.

Of course, not all investment styles do equally well all the time. For instance, Vanguard U.S. Growth bested Lindner Growth every year since 1994, but the Lindner fund beat the Vanguard fund in 1992 and 1993. That's one of the reasons it's important to examine mutual funds by their styles. Properly categorized, style tells you more about how the fund invests than the "investment objective."

Investment style also tells you more about what to expect from your fund. Consider the widely varying performances of large-cap growth and small-cap growth funds, many of which are nonetheless categorized as growth funds. Small-cap growth stocks woefully underperformed large-cap growth stocks since mid-1996, so you would expect a small-cap growth fund to have underperformed as well.

These categories are not entirely new. Several years ago, BW started to report investment style in the Scoreboard while still using the old investment objectives for grouping funds. Now we are categorizing funds in the Scoreboard and in this chapter by style. That means it will be easier for investors to compare funds with like investment programs. For example, an investor might have thought a switch from Growth Fund A to Growth Fund B was warranted, since the two were growth funds and B was performing a whole lot better than A. But a stylistic approach reveals that there's a reasonable explanation for disparities in performance: Fund A is a small-cap growth fund, Fund B a large-cap growth, and large-caps have been trouncing the small-cap stocks.

There are other good reasons for looking at funds through this stylistic filter. For instance, most fund investors today own more than one fund, with the idea that some diversification among funds is a good idea. Suppose an investor owned the Kaufmann, Janus Enterprise, Baron Growth & Income, and Robertson Stephens Emerging Growth funds. Using investment objectives to categorize funds, the investor would

How exactly does a fund "grow" your investment?

have a maximum growth, a growth, a growth and income, and a small company fund and think she's getting some diversification. Yet, in a stylistic analysis, all are small-cap growth funds, and it's likely they're making many similar investments. Is that the diversification the fund investor was seeking? A fund investor who is trying to build a diversified portfolio of funds will have an easier time doing it by using stylistic categories than by using the traditional investment objectives.

One more good reason for using market cap/investment style analysis on funds is that it levels the playing field. For instance, fund companies sometimes give their funds names that track one investment objective when the funds actually pursue another. Look at Robertson Stephens Growth & Income Fund. Most growth and income funds strive to produce some dividend payout, so they must invest a good portion of the fund assets in stocks that pay dividends. Such stocks are less volatile than growth stocks that don't pay dividends. Yet the fund's portfolio plummeted more like a growth fund than a growth and income fund. The reason: portfolio manager John Wallace does not invest like the majority of growth and income managers. He puts most of the fund's money into high-octane growth stocks that don't pay dividends. For the income component, he invests in convertible bonds and eschews the conservative dividend-paying stocks commonly found in his competitors' funds. Most of the time, this strategy allows him to outshine the other growth and income fund managers.

Is it right for Robertson Stephens & Co. to call this a "growth and income" fund? Well, the definition of that investment objective is broad enough and vague enough to allow the Robertson Stephens fund to fit within it. But to call it a growth and income fund might stretch credibility a bit, since it neither invests like most of those funds nor produces returns that look like most of the other growth and income funds. When it outperforms other growth and income funds, do investors really understand it's doing so because it's taking greater risks and investing like a growth fund?

One way of compensating for this sort of unexpected behavior is to ignore the objective listed in the fund's prospectus and put the fund into a different objective group. Morningstar, for instance, has done this on occasion to better describe a fund's behavior. For the last several years, the fund research firm has put Warburg

Pincus Growth and Income Common Shares into its growth fund category, even though "income" is in the name. And it seems appropriate. During 1997, the fund paid out only 1 percent in yield, which is less than what would be expected in a growth and income fund, even when yields on equities are at record lows.

But moving errant funds into different objectives categories isn't enough if the objective categories themselves are inadequate for today's investment world. Suppose Robertson Stephens Growth & Income Fund were reclassified as a growth fund. An investor still runs into the same kind of problem described earlier with Vanguard U.S. Growth and Lindner Growth Investors—growth funds themselves encompass a myriad of investment styles. So, comparing growth funds to growth funds isn't always a fair comparison, either. Robertson Stephens Growth & Income is a growth fund investing in midsized companies, while Lindner Growth Investors invests in small-cap value stocks.

Style-based categories give investors much better descriptive information about funds than the traditional investment objectives. The style analysis comes right out of the fund's portfolio. Investment objectives come out of a document written by marketing executives and lawyers. Which would you rather trust?

Determining Style

Y ou don't need an MBA to look at the holdings of a mutual fund and tell whether they're large or small companies. But Morningstar analysts don't rely just on eyeballing the portfolios to determine their median market caps or whether the stocks fall into the growth or value camp. There's a methodology to it.

To determine the appropriate capitalization, the analysts calculate the median market capitalization for all the stocks in the portfolio. Suppose there are 75 stocks in a fund. The analysts will calculate the market cap for each of the companies, and then rank them from high to low. The market cap of stock No. 38 is the median market cap for the fund. It's right in the middle, with an equal number of stocks (Nos. 1 through 37 and 39 through 75) above and below it. Morningstar uses the median rather than the mean (or what we know as an average) because having a few very

Investment "style" tells the story.

large stocks (Microsoft, Intel, or Coca-Cola, for instance) can significantly skew the results. If the median market cap of the companies in the portfolio is greater than $5 billion, it's a large-cap fund; $1 billion to $5 billion, a mid-cap fund; and less than $1 billion, a small-cap fund.

The second part of designating style is to determine whether the fund practices a growth or value approach to investing. Again, the Morningstar analysts go back to the fund portfolio to crunch numbers. First, they calculate a price-to-earnings (p–e) ratio for each stock in the fund. That's the price divided by the most recent 12 months' per-share earning. Then, they weight the p–e by holdings, so that the p–e of a stock that comprises 2 percent of the fund counts twice as much as the p–e of a stock that makes up only 1 percent of the fund. Then they go through the same process to calculate and weight price-to-book value (p–b) ratios for the stocks. A company's book value is its assets less liabilities, or what the accountants would say the company is worth. But few stocks sell at book value, and in a bull market, most sell well in excess of book value. When comparing price-to-book value, the lower the ratio, the cheaper the stock; the higher the ratio, the more expensive the stock. Then, as with p–e's, the p–b's are weighted.

The next step is to compare the fund's p–e ratio and p–b ratio to a benchmark. For funds investing in the United States, it's the S&P 500. Here's how it works. Suppose a fund has an 18 p–e and a 2.5 p–b ratio compared to the S&P's 21 p–e ratio and 3.7 p–b ratio. (Remember, the S&P's p–e and p–b ratios rise and fall depending on the health of the stock market and the level of interest rates. Thus, in a bull market, a fund with a p–e of 15 ends up as a value portfolio, while in a bear market, the same p–e would be associated with a growth-stock portfolio.) The style calculation first divides the fund's p–e by S&P's p–e and gets 0.857; then divides the fund's p–b by S&P's p–b, the result of which is 0.675. Morningstar adds the two quotients, the sum of which in this case is 1.532. Since the sum is less than 1.75, the fund is tagged a value fund; above 2.25, it would be a growth fund. Should it fall between 1.75 and 2.25, it's a blend of the two, suggesting some characteristics of both value and growth. Since each diversified domestic equity fund is classified in one of three categories of size and style, there are now nine categories (Figure 2-1).

One problem with style-based categories is that some funds temporarily change style. This may not be a deliberate move by the fund managers, just market dynamics. For instance, a successful value manager might find his fund has gone from the value column to the blend column because some of the stocks he bought have appreciated handsomely and are no longer as cheap as value stocks. The manager might still consider himself a value investor, and eventually sell those stocks and replace them with more traditional value investments. That's why Morningstar looks at the fund's stylistic history as well as its current practices when determining which style category to place a fund into.

The BUSINESS WEEK Scoreboard applies this stylistic grouping to diversified funds that invest primarily in the United States. Essentially, all the funds that in the past were categorized as maximum growth, growth, growth and income, equity-income, and small company have been reclassified as one of the following: large-cap value, large-cap blend, large-cap growth; mid-cap value, mid-cap blend, mid-cap growth; or small-cap value, small-cap blend, small-cap growth. Generally speaking, the large-cap value funds are expected to be the least risky, or volatile; the small-cap growth funds are expected to be the most risky.

There's more to these categories. The three investment objectives that combine stocks and bonds—asset allocation, balanced, and multiasset global—are in two categories: domestic hybrid and international hybrid (Table 2-2). And whether they are domestic or international, hybrids must have on average no less than 20 percent and no more than 70 percent of their

FIGURE 2-1

A BETTER LOOK AT YOUR FUNDS

BUSINESS WEEK now categorizes U.S. diversified equity funds in two ways: by the median market capitalization of the stocks it owns and by the relative valuation or "style" of those stocks. It's a system developed by Morningstar Inc.

Funds whose stocks have a median market cap of $5 billion or more are considered large-cap funds, $1 billion or less are small-cap, and those in between, mid-cap. To determine each fund's style, the average price–earnings ratios and price-to-book ratios are calculated and compared with the S&P 500. Those with significantly lower-than-average p–e's and p–b's are "value" funds, those higher than average "growth," and those in the middle "blend."

Median Market Capitalization	Investment Style		
	VALUE	BLEND	GROWTH
LARGE	LARGE-CAP VALUE	LARGE-CAP BLEND	LARGE-CAP GROWTH
MEDIUM	MID-CAP VALUE	MID-CAP BLEND	MID-CAP GROWTH
SMALL	SMALL-CAP VALUE	SMALL-CAP BLEND	SMALL-CAP GROWTH

assets in equities. Fidelity Puritan Fund, for instance, is now a domestic hybrid. Merrill Lynch Global Allocation B is an international hybrid.

Morningstar has also refined what is considered a domestic portfolio and what is considered an international portfolio. Funds can have up to 40 percent non-U.S. holdings and still be considered domestic, then slotted into one of the nine categories of domestic funds. A fund must be more than 40 percent non-U.S. to be considered an international fund. Thus, SmallCap World Fund, which you might surmise is an international fund investing in small companies, is now considered a domestic small-cap growth fund since it has only 40 percent of its assets abroad.

There's a new line-up among international funds as well. There's a Latin America category, and what was formerly the Pacific investment objective is split into three categories: Diversified Pacific, Pacific ex-Japan, and Japan. For a fund to be categorized by region, at least 75 percent of its assets much be invested in that region. The other international classifications remain the same. A foreign fund invests almost entirely in non-U.S. markets, though it can have up to 10 percent of its assets in the United States. A world fund is just the opposite, it can invest anywhere and has no less than 10 percent of its money in the United States. Diversified emerging markets funds must have at least 50 percent of their assets in the emerging markets.

What doesn't change in the new fund classifications are the specialty or sector funds. The sector fund categories are communications, financial, health care, natural resources, precious metals, real estate, technology, utilities, and unaligned (the few funds that don't fit into any of the other categories).

Morningstar has reorganized its bond fund line-up as well. The conventional bond fund objectives categorize funds mainly by the kinds of bonds they buy—government, corporates, or municipals. We have adopted the new Morningstar system, which looks at both the type of bonds and the average maturity or duration of the fund's bonds. Long-term bond funds are those with durations (a more refined measure of maturity that we'll discuss later in this chapter) of greater than 6 years; intermediate-term funds have durations of greater than 3.5 years and less than 6 years; short-term funds are those with durations of less than 3.5 years but greater than 1. There's one ultrashort category that encompasses both government and corporate bonds and has a duration of less than a year. Municipal funds

are organized into national and single-state long- and intermediate-term categories, but all short-term muni funds, whether national or single-state, are in the same category. With muni funds, the definition of long-term, intermediate-term, and short-term are a little different. Long-term funds

TABLE 2-2

THE NEW MUTUAL FUND CATEGORIES VS. THE OLD INVESTMENT OBJECTIVES

New ▼	Old ▼
EQUITY FUNDS*	
Large-cap Value	Maximum Growth
Large-cap Blend	Growth
Large-cap Growth	Growth and Income
Mid-cap Value	Equity-Income
Mid-cap Blend	Small Company
Mid-cap Growth	
Small-cap Value	
Small-cap Blend	
Small-cap Growth	
Domestic Hybrid	Balanced
International Hybrid	Asset Allocation
	Multiasset Global
Diversified Emerging Markets	Diversified Emerging Markets
Foreign	Foreign
World	World
Europe	Europe
Diversified Pacific	Pacific Basin
Pacific ex-Japan	
Japan	
Latin America	
BOND FUNDS	
Long Bonds (Gen.)	Corporate—General
Intermediate Bonds (Gen.)	Corporate—High-Quality
Short Bonds (Gen.)	Corporate—High-Yield
Ultrashort	Government—General
Long Government	Government—Adjustable-Rate Mortgages
Intermediate Government	Government—Mortgage
Short Government	Government—Treasury
Municipal National Long	Municipal—National
Municipal National Intermediate	Municipal—Single-State
Municipal Single-State Long	Municipal—California
Municipal Single-State Intermediate	Municipal—New York
Municipal Short	Convertibles
High-Yield	World Bond
Convertibles	Short-Term World Income
International	
Multisector	

*No change in the specialty equity funds.
DATA: MORNINGSTAR INC., BUSINESS WEEK

are those with durations greater than 7 years; intermediate, between 4.5 and 7 years; and short, less than 4.5 years.

Shuffling the bond fund categories makes selecting bond funds and tracking their returns much simpler. It's much easier to see how well funds are performing if you compare them to funds with like maturities or durations. On this count, bond funds have always been a little easier to understand than stock equity funds since many have "long-term" or "intermediate" in their titles. Still, by rating funds in their own categories, investors will be able to see more quickly which long-term U.S. government fund has not only the best return but also the best risk-adjusted return as well.

Not all bond funds fit into these categories. Convertible bonds and high-yield bonds, which in many ways have as much to do with the equity market as interest rates, retain their own categories. There's no further differentiation for intermediate or long-term bonds. Most high-yields (and convertibles, too, since most of them are less than investment grade) fall in the short-to-intermediate-term range. The world bond fund category also remains. It picks up the leavings of the short-term world income category, which has too few funds and assets to keep it alive as a separate classification.

Equity Funds

We'll start with equity funds and look first at the larger, lower-risk diversified sorts, such as the large-cap value funds, and eventually work our way to the more aggressive small-cap growth funds. Then we'll examine the hybrid and specialty funds.

LARGE-CAP VALUE FUNDS

You know you should invest in equity mutual funds, but somehow the volatility of the stock market and the possibility of losing your money scares the daylights out of you. If this describes you, try a fund that invests in large-cap value stocks. Of the nine categories of domestic equity funds, these funds are the least risky and perhaps the most palatable for the anxious investor. Most of the funds in this category were formerly in the growth and income and equity-income investment objectives. They keep one eye on downside

TABLE 2-3

LARGE-CAP VALUE FUNDS		
BEST RETURNS		
Period ▼	Fund ▼	Total return* ▼
1997	SEQUOIA	42.3%
1995-97	LEGG MASON VALUE PRIMARY SHARES	38.7
1993-97	LEGG MASON VALUE PRIMARY SHARES	24.7
1988-97	VISTA GROWTH & INCOME A	24.1

*Average annual, pretax   DATA: MORNINGSTAR INC.

risk and the other on a stock's upside potential. Some of the larger and better-known funds in this category are Fidelity Equity-Income, Fidelity Equity-Income II, Fidelity Destiny I, Fidelity Destiny II, Vanguard/Windsor, Vanguard/Windsor II, and Washington Mutual Investors. The best-performing large-cap value fund of 1997 was the Sequoia Fund, with a 42.3 percent total return (Table 2-3). (Don't rush to buy it because you can't. It's been closed to new investors for 15 years.)

Just because they're cautious doesn't mean these funds can't perform well. During 1997, the funds earned an average 26.7 percent total return—nearly 10 percentage points better than the average fund. In 1996, for instance, the two large-cap value funds among the 20 largest equity funds beat the S&P 500. Legg Mason Value Primary Shares has an exceptionally strong three-year and five-year performance because it has had, on average, over 40 percent of its assets in financial stocks during a period in which they recovered from near-death prices.

Still, two factors are what make these funds relatively conservative. One is the nature of the stocks they buy. No high-flying semiconductor or software stocks here, but some of the biggest names in American business: Philip Morris, IBM, Federal National Mortgage Assn., and Citicorp (Table 2-4). To most value investors, what makes a stock attractive is that it's cheap. Don't confuse cheap with a low price, like $5 or $10 a share. A share of stock is said to be cheap only when it's measured by some valuation criteria such as the p–e ratio and/or p–b ratio and then compared to a benchmark, like the p–e or the p–b of the S&P 500.

That a stock is cheap—suppose it has a lower-than-average p–e ratio—is no guarantee against losing money, since a cheap stock can always get cheaper. But think of it this way: If the market gets hit with a downdraft, cheap stocks can fall, but usually not as far or as hard as expensive stocks. Chances are, you're going to lose more money if an expensive stock becomes cheap than if a cheap stock gets cheaper.

Another important attribute of large-cap value funds is the emphasis on dividend-paying stocks. Some of the funds, like the two Fidelity Equity-Income offerings, stipulate that at least 65 percent of the stocks in the fund must be dividend payers. There's a reason for this: that a company is able to pay a dividend suggests that it is generating cash above and beyond its needs and is not likely to go broke. That doesn't mean that investing in dividend-paying companies is a cinch. These companies still require monitoring. Sometimes dividend payers fail to recognize their problems, refuse to cut dividends when they should, and get into trouble. Since these are large, highly visible companies, investment analysts usually detect the trouble right away. They advise their clients to sell, and the stock starts to fall in anticipation of a dividend cut.

In recent years, neither investors nor companies themselves have paid much attention to dividends. Investors preferred to buy stocks that had greater growth potential than is available in most dividend-paying stocks. And companies themselves responded to the market's appetite for share appreciation by deploying excess cash to buy back shares rather than hike dividends. Some investors argue it's not a bad thing to do. Dividends are considered ordinary income and are taxed at the same rate investors pay on their salary and interest income, which can be as high as 39.6 percent (and that's just the federal tax). When companies buy back shares instead of boosting their dividends, the only shareholders that get taxed are those who sell their shares. If

TABLE 2-4

LARGE-CAP VALUE FUNDS
LARGEST HOLDINGS

Stock ▼	Percent of net assets ▼
PHILIP MORRIS	1.68%
IBM	1.28
FANNIE MAE	1.19
CITICORP	1.01
ALLSTATE	1.00
AT&T	0.95
CHASE MANHATTAN	0.88
FORD MOTOR	0.87
ATLANTIC RICHFIELD	0.86
E.I. DUPONT DE NEMOURS	0.85

DATA: MORNINGSTAR INC.

those shares were held for longer than a year, any profits would be taxed at the more favorable long-term capital gains rate, a maximum of 20 percent.

Since these large-cap value funds generate fully taxable dividend income, many advisers counsel high-income investors to use them only in tax-deferred accounts like 401(k)s and IRAs. In such accounts, there's no tax liability until the investor retires and starts drawing the money out.

Be forewarned that many veteran investors don't take a casual view of dividends. In bear markets, a situation that many of today's investors have not experienced, a steady dividend stream becomes a primary support of a stock or a portfolio of stocks. After all, the only way to make money in stocks is through capital appreciation and dividends. When the appreciation part is in doubt, the security of a dividend payout starts to look a whole lot better.

Even though they buy many of the same big, cheap, dividend-paying stocks, some funds in this category stand out with their own particular quirks. Vanguard/Windsor (which is closed to new investors) is not afraid to concentrate its positions. Its 10 largest holdings amount to some 33 percent of the $20.8 billion portfolio. Oppenheimer Quest Opportunity Value Fund A, which is slightly under $2 billion, has half of its portfolio in its top 10 holdings. The $1.4 billion Babson Value Fund takes a somewhat different tack, keeping the portfolio to 40 stocks and trying to keep an equal weighting in each. If portfolio manager Nick Whitridge wants to add a new stock, he must sell one—presumably the weakest, or the one that went up the most and is no longer a value.

Some analysts interpret such huge concentrations as risky, since there are more eggs in fewer baskets. Managers of these risk-shy funds see it differently. Good value investments are hard to come by, so when you find them, you have to make the most of them. This buy-and-hold tendency is reflected in the low turnover ratios that are not much more than half the average for equity funds.

A-rated Washington Mutual Investors, part of the American Funds family, has a low turnover as well, perhaps because there aren't that many stocks it can invest in. That's because the fund follows the "Prudent Man Rule," a rule for fiduciaries that means every investment in the fund must pass certain quality standards and pay a dividend. According to Morningstar analysts, fewer than 300 stocks are even eligible for investment by the fund.

Lexington Corporate Leaders, another large-cap value fund, also has a rather select portfolio. In fact, it's almost a static portfolio. The fund goes back to 1935 and was set up to invest in 30 stocks its founders thought would prosper for years to come. The portfolio manager has the ability to sell a stock, but cannot add a new name. Still, 23 of the original 30 survive, and they include such companies as Mobil, Procter & Gamble, General Electric, DuPont, and Exxon. Even more amazing, the fund has been a strong performer in its category over the last 5- and 10-year periods.

LARGE-CAP BLEND FUNDS

Some investment managers call themselves "value" investors, and others "growth" investors. But you'd be hard pressed to find investment managers who call themselves "blend" investors. The blend fund, however, is sort of the vast middle—the huge category into which fall all the funds that don't strongly gravitate to either side of the investment world. The blend funds have attributes of both the growth and value styles. What makes them a blend is that when the portfolio statistics are calculated, the numbers fall in the middle. According to Morningstar's criteria, the combined p–e and p–b ratios of these funds can be no more than 12.5 percent greater than or 12.5 percent less than the combined p–e and p–b ratios for the S&P 500. The best performer of 1997 was Heritage Capital Appreciation A, with a 42.7 percent total return (Table 2-5).

Blend does not have to be bland. Large-cap blend is a huge category (the largest of the nine categories of U.S. diversified equity funds), and it includes many highly regarded funds: Fidelity Growth & Income, Investment Company of America, Janus, and T. Rowe Price Equity-Income. That Fidelity offering has long been a winner, with high returns and below-average risk scores. Compared to most of Fidelity's mega-funds, it had a strong performance in 1996 and 1997. With $35.8 billion in assets, portfolio manager Steven Kaye can't be too nimble, but it's far easier to manage a fund of this size in large-cap rather than small or mid-sized stocks. The largest stocks in this universe include General Electric, Philip Morris, Intel, and IBM (Table 2-6).

Though it's a large-cap blend fund, T. Rowe Price Equity–Income still manages to produce a dividend stream that puts most large-cap value funds to shame. Brian Rogers, portfolio manager for more than a decade, often goes against the conventional wisdom, such as buying electric and telephone utilities when few pros had a good word for them. But more often than not, Rogers's moves pay off. Two other Price offerings in this category, too new to be rated, still bear watching—T. Rowe Price Blue Chip Growth Fund and T. Rowe Price Dividend Growth Fund. Dividend Growth Fund, in fact, has a similar risk profile to Equity–Income, but a much smaller asset base.

Another large-cap blend with an admirable long-term record is the Guardian Park Avenue A Fund. The $2.2 billion fund beat the S&P 500 during the last 1-, 5-, and 10-year periods by using a quantitative stock selection system that chooses stocks through both macroeconomic data and fundamental factors like earnings and valuation. One qualitative factor that may make the fund attractive to some: it's had the same portfolio manager, Charles Albers, for nearly 25 years. One drawback is that the fund has the ability to invest in almost any style, and, indeed, three years ago, it was a small-cap value. So if you're a demon for style consistency, the fund is probably not for you.

But perhaps the most compelling—and sometimes controversial—of the large-cap blend funds is the Vanguard Index Trust 500 Portfolio, which is a fund that invests in such a way as to replicate the S&P 500 index. It's an "index" fund and, in a way, it's an unfund-like fund. Its critics call it "guaranteed mediocrity." Why? Unlike the vast majority of mutual funds, the Vanguard Index Trust 500 Portfolio does not attempt to beat a benchmark, only to match it. (The fund is usually off by no more than one-tenth of a percentage point.) Expenses are ridiculously low, less than one-sixth that of the average equity fund. That's because, since the fund does not pick stocks, there's no need for an army of analysts or on-site visits with corporate executives. And, in effect, the fund is managed by a computer. The irony of all this is that over the last three years this "pas-

TABLE 2-5

LARGE-CAP BLEND FUNDS		
BEST RETURNS		
Period ▼	Fund ▼	Total return* ▼
1997	**HERITAGE CAPITAL APPRECIATION A**	42.7%
1995–97	**RYDEX NOVA**	39.0
1993–97	**TORRAY**	23.7
1988–97	**FIDELITY CONTRAFUND**	23.0
*Average annual, pretax		DATA: MORNINGSTAR INC.

TABLE 2-6

LARGE-CAP BLEND FUNDS

LARGEST HOLDINGS

Stock ▼	Percent of net assets ▼
GENERAL ELECTRIC	1.69%
PHILIP MORRIS	1.51
INTEL	1.31
IBM	1.03
BRISTOL-MYERS SQUIBB	1.00
MERCK	0.96
EXXON	0.96
FANNIE MAE	0.92
PFIZER	0.88
MICROSOFT	0.84

DATA: MORNINGSTAR INC.

sive" fund—so called because its managers just follow the S&P 500—has beaten over 90 percent of active managers. Part of the reason is the low expenses, but even with expenses excluded, the fund has been a winner.

There's a more fundamental reason for the index fund's strong performance. In recent years, while small and mid-sized stocks generally did well, the large-cap stocks performed even better. For most of that time, Wall Street had fears of a recession and bear market, and big investors shifted money out of the smaller stocks and into the bigger. The reason: In a recession, larger companies have more resources and staying power, and in a bear market, larger company stocks are far more liquid and easier to sell than smaller, lesser-known names.

Another reason for the index fund's success is the index fund phenomenon itself. Indexing is far more popular among multi-billion-dollar pension funds than it is among individual investors, who still have a little difficulty grasping the notion that matching a benchmark can give you a superior result. But most of the individuals coming to indexing are coming via pension plans, like the employer-sponsored 401(k) plans. In some respects, index funds perform well just because more and more people are choosing to index. In the case of an S&P index fund, every dollar is spent the same way. The more money that goes into indexing, the more money that gets spent investing in those very stocks that make up the index. Is it any surprise they perform so well?

Does this make an S&P index fund a must-buy investment? It's hard to argue against it. Certainly, many investors can benefit by having some portion of their equity portfolio in an index

fund. But viewing the index fund over the last five years alone is a little misleading. The stock market has had an extraordinarily good run during that period.

But if the market fell badly, the index would not look so good. For starters, there's no safety net. Index funds don't carry cash, which cushions a fall, and unlike active managers, they can't redeploy more of their assets to "defensive" sectors like utilities or food stocks. While these actions by active managers can hold a fund back during a bull market, properly deployed, such actions can soften a downturn. So remember when you are considering index funds, there is that drawback.

Indexing itself does not have to be boring. Look at the Rydex Nova Fund. Though designed for market-timers, Rydex will open the door for anyone with a relatively steep $25,000 minimum investment. By design, the Nova fund seeks investment returns that correspond to 150 percent of the performance of the S&P 500. So if the S&P is up 20 percent, this fund should go up 30 percent. Likewise, if the S&P goes down 20 percent, this fund should go down 30 percent. The fund doesn't always reach that 150 percent goal; in 1997, for instance, its return was just 126 percent that of the S&P 500. For the three years, it's about the same. Rydex runs the fund without a share of stock. It's managed with a combination of cash, bonds, and call options.

Rydex Ursa Fund is an index fund in reverse. It's managed to move in the opposite direction of the S&P 500, so its big fat 21 percent loss in 1997 is neither unexpected nor a sign of portfolio ineptitude. Ursa, the Latin word for "bear," is designed to win in a bear market. Its mission is to move in the opposite direction of the S&P 500. (It's run with a combination of cash, options, and futures.) So if the stock market takes a dive, Ursa should shine.

LARGE-CAP GROWTH FUNDS

For the last several years, Wall Streeters dabbled with small-cap and mid-cap stocks but ultimately fled to the safety of large-cap growth stocks. There was good reason for this. At every hint of a slowing economy, these companies—with a clearly defined, "visible" earnings outlook—seemed more and more attractive in an uncertain economic environment. The major stocks in these funds tended to be larger high-tech companies and defensive consumer stocks like food, drugs, and beverages. In 1997, the best fund in this category, MFS Strategic Growth A,

TABLE 2-7

LARGE-CAP GROWTH FUNDS		
BEST RETURNS		
Period ▼	Fund ▼	Total return* ▼
1997	MFS STRATEGIC GROWTH A	50.4%
1995-97	WHITE OAK GROWTH	35.9
1993-97	SPECTRA	23.8
1988-97	AMER. CENT.–20TH CENT. ULTRA INV.	21.9
*Average annual, pretax		DATA: MORNINGSTAR INC.

earned an enviable 50.4 percent total return versus 26.9 percent for the average large-cap growth fund (Table 2-7).

The question to consider when investing in these funds is, how long can these large-cap growth stocks continue their winning streak? The conventional wisdom about successful large companies is that inertia will eventually overtake them. Rapidly growing companies become above-average growers, above-average turns out to be average. The slowdown in growth is predictable—in theory. The art of investing in these companies is getting the timing of that growth right, to buy at a p–e ratio that's fair relative to the growth rate.

Look at Cisco Systems, a principal manufacturer of servers and related equipment that tie together computer networks. It's one of the top holdings of the large-cap growth funds (Table 2-8). The company has gone from annual sales of nearly $70 million in fiscal 1990 to $6 billion in the most recent fiscal year. That's about a 90 percent a year gain; during the same time, average annual earnings grew 43 percent. Cisco is still chugging along, but it's no longer growing at the same torrid pace of five years ago. (At that time, you would not have found Cisco in a large-cap growth portfolio, but in a small or mid-size fund.) Now, the earnings growth rate is forecast to be about 30 percent. That's a far cry from what it was, but 30 percent annual earnings growth is nearly four times that of the average big-company stock. At the end of 1997, Cisco sold for about 45 times estimated 1998 earnings. In a slow growth, low-interest rate environment, a 45 p–e may not be too expensive for a company with earnings growing at a 30 percent pace. Still, it's a valuation that leaves little room for disappointment.

The apparent risks notwithstanding, there's a reason why the market values these companies highly. They are superb companies. Many of these companies, though based in the United States, are world-class leaders with substantial operations outside the United States. Coca-Cola, for instance, has no equal anywhere on the planet, and most of its profits are generated outside the United States. Nor does any semiconductor company even approach Intel. Mutual funds that identify and invest in these sorts of companies early on can make a bundle for their investors.

The exceptionally strong returns earned by these funds may be masking some unrealized risks. These large-cap growth stocks are the most closely watched on Wall Street (they're the so-called "institutional favorites" you hear about in stock market reports), and they're said to be the most efficiently priced. To stand out in this category, a fund manager has to make some serious "sector" bets, concentrating holdings in a few areas that he or she thinks will do a lot better than the large growth stocks in general. During 1997, for instance, MFS Massachusetts Growth Stock Investors A had about 33 percent of its assets in technology stocks versus 23 percent for the large-cap growth funds and just 13 percent for the S&P 500. Fortunately, that bet paid off, but it could have been a big depressant on the fund had it not.

Of course, sector weightings aren't everything either. American Century–20th Century Ultra Investors, the giant in this category, had an even larger allocation to technology, 36 percent. But while the fund did not collapse in 1997, it still lagged the S&P 500 by a healthy margin. One explanation may be that this fund is playing out of its league. Until five years ago, it was a small company fund. When it hit paydirt and shot up 86 percent in 1991, the assets ballooned—and the managers were forced to move up to larger and

TABLE 2-8

LARGE-CAP GROWTH FUNDS	
LARGEST HOLDINGS	
Stock ▼	Percent of net assets ▼
INTEL	2.41%
GENERAL ELECTRIC	2.23
PFIZER	1.98
MICROSOFT	1.96
CISCO SYSTEMS	1.62
MERCK	1.61
PHILIP MORRIS	1.48
ELI LILLY	1.41
CITICORP	1.30
SCHLUMBERGER	1.14
DATA: MORNINGSTAR INC.	

larger stocks. There's nothing wrong with that, except that the fund built its reputation on a much smaller asset base and much smaller stocks than it now owns.

Other noteworthy funds in this category include Gabelli Growth, Putnam Investors A, Vanguard U.S. Growth, and Vanguard Index Growth. Perhaps one of the most interesting of the large company growth funds is Stein Roe Young Investor Fund, a fund with a mission to invest in securities issued by companies that affect the lives of children and teenagers. The idea is perhaps more marketing oriented than market oriented. No doubt Stein Roe marketers thought the fund would be a natural for parents and grandparents to buy for their kids. And, in fact, the company developed sales literature and shareholder reports that even a kid could understand.

The reality is that the fund can invest in almost anything. Its second largest holding is Intel. The connection? Well, Intel chips power nearly all the PCs and lots of kids and teenagers use or own their PCs, no? As a practical matter, it's hard to think of a company with a business that couldn't in some way be linked to kids. (A steel company? This company is a supplier to the automakers, who use it to build cars and mini-vans that parents use to chauffeur their children.) You don't have to be a young investor to invest in or profit from this fund. The fact is, this fund would have admirable returns under any name.

MID-CAP VALUE FUNDS

It's difficult to generalize about mid-cap value funds, or, for that matter, any kind of mid-cap fund. Funds that fit in one of the corners of the nine-category box—large-cap value, large-cap growth, small-cap value, and small-cap growth—are the most distinctive about how they invest. Look inside the portfolio of a small-cap growth or large-cap value fund, and you won't mistake it for anything else.

Many mid-cap value funds have long used "value" in their names, but only in the last few years have some funds started to call themselves "mid-cap" or even "mid-cap value." Pioneer Three Fund changed its name to Pioneer Mid-Cap Fund in 1996. A few months later, Lord Abbett Value Appreciation Fund was renamed Lord Abbett Mid-Cap Value Fund. What's behind the name changes? One reason is the recognition of investor interest in funds that define their investment style. The other reason

may be marketing. Neither the Pioneer nor the Lord Abbett fund had distinguished track records, so there was nothing to lose in changing the names. If nothing else, it might attract money that's looking for a mid-cap home.

Still, many mid-cap funds—including value, blend, and growth varieties—didn't set out to be mid-caps, but they sort of backed into it. Take, for instance, Oakmark Select Fund, the best performer of 1997 (Table 2-9). The fund says nothing about mid-caps in its prospectus, but nearly all the holdings of the fund are unambiguously mid-cap in nature. One explanation for this is that the Oakmark Fund, the Select's big brother, was a mid-cap value fund until 1997, when it became large enough to move into large-cap value. Since the Oakmark family already had a small-cap fund, it made sense for the newest member, Oakmark Select, to troll in mid-cap waters. The other explanation: the fund became a mid-cap value fund as a result of the investments it made, not because it sought to make specifically mid-cap investments.

Mid-cap funds often become mid-cap because mid-caps represents the median market cap—the funds have holdings that are both far larger and far smaller, and perhaps few holdings would qualify as mid-cap on their own. That's much the case of the Sound Shore Fund, one of the better-performing mid-cap value funds. Among the holdings are Wal-Mart Stores, with a whopping $89 billion in market capitalization; Fannie Mae, with $61.4 billion; and Banc One, with $32.6 billion. But there's also relatively small Albany International, which supplies machinery to the paper industry, at $578 million, and Polaris Industries, recreational vehicle company, at $795 million. All told, Sound Shore's median market cap comes out to $3.6 billion.

Sound Shore is not at all unusual for a mid-cap value fund. Very often, these funds buy a wide range of stocks, and for these managers, capitalization is not as important as what they consider

TABLE 2-9

MID-CAP VALUE FUNDS		
BEST RETURNS		
Period ▼	Fund ▼	Total return* ▼
1997	OAKMARK SELECT	55.0%
1995–97	SOUND SHORE	33.2
1993–97	FPA CAPITAL	23.7
1988–97	FPA CAPITAL	22.1

*Average annual, pretax   DATA: MORNINGSTAR INC.

TABLE 2-10

MID-CAP VALUE FUNDS

LARGEST HOLDINGS

Stock ▼	Percent of net assets ▼
CHASE MANHATTAN	1.68%
SUNBEAM (144A)	0.94
US WEST MEDIA GROUP	0.82
INVESTOR CL. B	0.71
RJR NABISCO HOLDINGS	0.68
GENERAL MOTORS	0.68
PHILIP MORRIS	0.64
MORGAN STANLEY DEAN WITTER DIS.	0.58
IBM	0.57
IBP	0.54

DATA: MORNINGSTAR INC.

to be a good investment idea. That's pretty much what you see in Michael F. Price's enormously successful Mutual Series funds—now known as Mutual Shares Z, Mutual Qualified Z, and Mutual Beacon Z. They're three of the five largest funds in this category. Like many mid-cap value funds, Price's funds include a wide range of investments chosen more for their attractiveness as value plays than to meet any market capitalization target. One of Price's big successes of recent years was to take a big stake in the large but undervalued Chase Manhattan Corp. and lobby the management, the board of directors, and, if necessary, other big shareholders into taking action to improve "shareholder value." That's the buzz word for "get the stock price up—or else." In several months' time, Chase agreed to a merger with rival Chemical Banking Corp. to create a bank holding company larger than Citicorp. Even while participating in the megabanking play, the portfolios remained mid-cap in character.

Price's funds still own a good chunk of Chase Manhattan stock, and because of those funds' size, Chase is the No. 1 holding of the mid-cap value funds, comprising 1.68 percent of total net assets (Table 2-10). Several other of Price's largest holdings also appear on this list: U.S. West Media Group, RJR Nabisco Holdings, and Investor Cl.B. (a Swedish holding company). None of them are particularly mid-cap, but they definitely are value plays.

MID-CAP BLEND FUNDS

Many funds will call themselves mid-cap value or mid-cap growth, but it's unlikely a fund company will ever market a fund as a mid-cap blend. Mid-dle of the road in market cap without a distinct value or growth bent? Sounds like a big yawner—or a marketing challenge.

But consider this: the supersized Fidelity Contrafund looks like a large-cap fund at the moment, but since Morningstar began tracking investment style, Contrafund has behaved more like a mid-cap blend. Still, Fidelity marketing department has never presented this fund as a mid-cap, only as a "contrarian" in nature. With over $30 billion in assets, it's hard to even imagine this as a contrarian. Still, it's 10-year performance makes it best in its category (Table 2-11). What's more, 7 of those 10 years have been under the leadership of the same portfolio manager, Will Danoff. Seven years is an eternity at Fidelity, where the portfolio manager changes almost as frequently as George Steinbrenner used to change managers.

Until last year, the giant Fidelity Magellan Fund was also a mid-cap blend fund. After all, the fund's reputation had been built on savvy stock-picking, not stylistic purity. It makes a lot of sense that many of the funds run by star stock-pickers wind up in this category—they'll go to all corners of the stock market for a good investment. And when the compositions of those portfolios are calculated, they wind up smack in the middle of the pack.

The largest holdings of the mid-cap blend funds certainly don't look very mid-cap at all. That's because the mid-caps are often a blend of large and small, and those large ones tend to dominate such listings. The smallest company of the top 10 holdings is Freddie Mac at $7 billion market cap, still a little too large to be a mid-cap stock by Morningstar's definitions (Table 2-12).

Another long-standing mid-cap player is the Nicholas II Fund, a $1 billion fund run by the man whose name is on the door, Albert Nicholas. By charter, it's supposed to invest in small-cap and mid-cap companies, and it does. Many years ago, the fund had more of a small-cap cast, but with

TABLE 2-11

MID-CAP BLEND FUNDS

BEST RETURNS

Period ▼	Fund ▼	Total return* ▼
1997	GABELLI VALUE	48.2%
1995-97	MAIRS & POWER GROWTH	34.4
1993-97	EXCELSIOR VALUE & RESTRUCTURING A	27.2
1988-97	FIDELITY CONTRAFUND	23.0

*Average annual, pretax   DATA: MORNINGSTAR INC.

TABLE 2-12

MID-CAP BLEND FUNDS

LARGEST HOLDINGS

Stock ▼	Percent of net assets ▼
INTEL	0.90%
TEXAS INSTRUMENTS	0.89
FANNIE MAE	0.78
FEDERAL EXPRESS	0.59
FREDDIE MAC	0.56
AMERICAN INTERNATIONAL GROUP	0.56
MICROSOFT	0.56
PHILIP MORRIS	0.55
COMPAQ COMPUTER	0.53
SCHLUMBERGER	0.53

DATA: MORNINGSTAR INC.

the growth in assets, the fund has tended to own some larger stocks. The older, and much larger Nicholas Fund, also run by Albert Nicholas, is also a mid-cap blend, but it's pushing the upper limit of mid-cap. It's a good bet that it will soon be moved to large-cap.

The two Nicholas funds have an attribute that's a little more common in this category than in most others—portfolio managers with lots of longevity. Nicholas has been running the Nicholas Fund since 1969 and Nicholas II since 1983. George Mairs has been calling the shots for Mairs & Powers Growth Fund since 1980. Donald Yacktman started the fund that bears his name in 1992. But that came after a long career running other funds, and he was no babe in the business. Mario Gabelli, whose Gabelli Value Fund was the best performer in this category in 1997, is another veteran stockpicker who was a portfolio manager for years before branching out into mutual funds about 10 years ago.

Another marathoner in this category is Kenneth Heebner of CGM Capital Development Fund. He's been running that fund for 20 years. Heebner, known for making bold bets on particular stocks and industry sectors, has an excellent 15-year record. But interspersed in those years are some nasty single-year surprises. In four of those years, he lagged the S&P 500 by more than 10 percentage points, and in 1994, the fund was actually down nearly 23 percent.

MID-CAP GROWTH FUNDS

Scratch beneath the surface of a mid-cap growth fund, and you may just find a successful small-cap growth fund. Many funds, of course, have long plowed the sometimes neglected area of mid-cap stocks, but they never presented themselves as such. Brian W. H. Berghuis, portfolio manager of T. Rowe Price Mid-Cap Growth Fund, recalls that when his fund started in 1992, the term "mid-cap investing" was barely on Wall Street's radar screen. Berghuis seized the ground because, he felt, investors could earn nearly as much money with mid-caps as small-caps but take on a lot less stock-price volatility. Berghuis's strategy is to buy the growth stocks when they are in the $500 million-to-$1.5 billion market cap range and let them roll. If this strategy is successful, they'll grow into mid-caps. If you start with mid-caps, the successful ones eventually graduate to the big leagues.

There have always been mid-cap growth funds, though, even if they didn't explicitly present themselves that way. The William Blair Growth Fund, for instance, invests in growth stocks of all market capitalizations, but has always balanced the mix so that it falls smack in the middle. The New Economy Fund does not specifically mention mid-cap companies in its prospectus objective, but it's long been a mid-cap investor.

Some of the better-known mid-cap growth funds certainly didn't start out that way. Look at PBHG Growth Fund. The prospectus allows the fund to invest in companies with either revenues or market capitalizations of up to $2 billion. That's the limit. Until 1995, the fund always managed to keep its median market cap well within the small-cap limits. And, of course, the fund excelled in that tough field, especially in the 1990s. In 1991 and 1995, the fund earned a little better than 50 percent returns.

Success brings in money, and more money can lead to the inevitable "market cap creep." With more and more money, fund managers are simply forced to buy larger- and larger-cap stocks to fill the portfolio. Among the other better-known mid-caps that grew into this category are Alger Small

TABLE 2-13

MID-CAP GROWTH FUNDS

BEST RETURNS

Period ▼	Fund ▼	Total return* ▼
1997	DELAWARE AGGRESSIVE GROWTH A	48.1%
1995-97	DELAWARE AGGRESSIVE GROWTH A	33.2
1993-97	FRANKLIN CA GROWTH A	25.0
1988-97	MFS EMERGING GROWTH B	21.3

*Average annual, pretax   DATA: MORNINGSTAR INC.

TABLE 2-14

MID-CAP GROWTH FUNDS

LARGEST HOLDINGS

Stock ▼	Percent of net assets ▼
MICROSOFT	0.90%
HFS	0.89
COMPUTER ASSOCIATES INTL.	0.87
BMC SOFTWARE	0.82
CISCO SYSTEMS	0.79
EMC	0.71
COMPAQ COMPUTER	0.70
INTEL	0.69
WORLDCOM	0.63
HBO & CO.	0.57

DATA: MORNINGSTAR INC.

Capitalization, American Century–20th Century Vista Investors, Fidelity OTC, and MFS Emerging Growth B, the fund with the best 10-year record (Table 2-13). Delaware Aggressive Growth A, the fund with the best 1- and 3-year returns, is a tiny fund with less than $30 million in all its share classes. The fund scored big returns even though it had more than half its assets in technology stocks in a period when tech stocks came under enormous selling pressure.

At PBHG Growth, the fund assets grew so much it was remarkable that fund manager Gary Pilgrim could keep the fund focused on small-cap stocks as long as he did. PBHG Growth swelled to $187 million at the end of 1993 from $3 million at the end of 1992. By the end of 1995, the fund had $2 billion in assets, already a sizeable fund for one with a small-cap mission. The fund had been closed for awhile in 1995, but reopened at the start of 1996, and the money rushed in again. By year-end, assets were up to $5.9 billion. Coincidentally, in 1996 PBHG Growth could only muster a 9.8 percent total return, and in 1997 the fund actually lost money—down 3.3 percent, its worst showing in eight years. Perhaps the amount of money has finally overwhelmed the fund's ability to earn the superior returns.

Of course, even if a successful small-cap growth fund is closed to new investors, it still can become a mid-cap fund by virtue of its successes. If enough small-cap stocks flourish, they eventually become mid-caps. Some managers will sell them out of the portfolio at that point, but not all. If you have enough of them, the fund will evolve into a mid-cap investor. That's a result of successful investing.

As is much the case with the other mid-cap

fund categories, most of the largest holdings are not mid-cap companies themselves (Table 2-14). None of the 10 largest holdings is a true mid-cap. No. 4, BMC Software, with a market capitalization of $6.5 billion, comes closest. No. 10, HBO & Co. (a health-care management firm, not a cable TV operator), is the only other major holding below $10 billion in market cap.

The mid-cap growth category also contains several quirky funds worth mentioning. One, Merrill Lynch Growth B, earned good returns even while carrying a sizeable cash hoard. While the cash cushions the downswings, the fund manager must work extra hard with the invested assets to overcome the drag of cash in a bull market. So far, portfolio manager Stephen Johnes has been able to pull it off, mainly by concentrating the holdings in sectors which he thinks will outperform.

SMALL-CAP VALUE FUNDS

When you mention investing in small companies, many people think of an Internet start-up or biotech research firms or faddish specialty retailers or fast-food chains. Now look at the major holdings of Oakmark Small Cap, one of the better performing small-cap value funds of the last few years. There's a manufacturing conglomerate, a machine tool maker, a real estate development company, a cable TV operator, and a community bank. Doesn't sound real sexy or cutting edge, does it?

That doesn't mean you can't make money in these stocks. Indeed, a well-run company in a prosaic business can be a big money-maker. These companies don't usually have to worry too much that their new technology will become obsolete in six months or that new competitors are opening their doors every day. That's usually not the case.

Small-cap value stocks—and the funds that invest in them—often run counter to the faster-paced, highfliers that usually make the headlines. When those "momentum" stocks sputter, as they

TABLE 2-15

SMALL-CAP VALUE FUNDS

BEST RETURNS

Period ▼	Fund ▼	Total return* ▼
1997	EVERGREEN MICRO-CAP Y	47.6%
1995-97	WEITZ HICKORY	38.3
1993-97	FIDELITY LOW-PRICED STOCK	20.4
1988-97	SKYLINE SPECIAL EQUITIES	22.3

*Average annual, pretax   DATA: MORNINGSTAR INC.

TABLE 2-16

SMALL-CAP VALUE FUNDS
LARGEST HOLDINGS

Stock ▼	Percent of net assets ▼
PXRE	0.33%
COLE NATIONAL CL. A	0.28
US INDUSTRIES	0.26
BANCTEC	0.26
DALLAS SEMICONDUCTOR	0.25
UNIVERSAL HEALTH SVCS. CL. B	0.24
ICN PHARMACEUTICALS	0.24
IMATION	0.23
CATELLUS DEVELOPMENT	0.23
FREMONT GENERAL	0.22

DATA: MORNINGSTAR INC.

did in the second half of 1996 and first quarter of 1997, and again late in 1997, the small-cap value stocks usually pick up steam. The stock market tends to swing back and forth between favoring value stocks and growth stocks. Over the last 10-year and 15-year periods, small-cap growth beat small-cap value. But largely because of the sluggish small-cap growth performance in 1996 and 1997, small-cap value beat small-cap growth over the 1-, 3-, and 5-year periods.

There's another advantage to owning small-cap value funds. Because the stocks they buy are already "cheap" when measured by traditional yardsticks like p–e ratios, p–b ratios, and dividend yields, the funds tend to be less volatile than the funds that buy the more traditional emerging growth stocks. In effect, these funds are a way to play the small-cap market without wild price swings, a more palatable way to play small-cap stocks for nervous investors.

As a result, small-cap value funds fare a lot better in risk-adjusted ratings than the small-cap growth. In the 1998 BUSINESS WEEK Mutual Fund Scoreboard, six small-cap value funds earned A's, the highest rating for risk-adjusted returns. No small-cap growth or small-cap blend funds made it onto the overall top performers' list.

Small-cap value funds can be a pretty diverse lot, if only because there are so many more companies they can invest in. Large-cap growth funds pretty much all choose from among the same 200 to 300 companies. Even small-cap growth funds tend to be duplicative in their holdings because the managers are mainly seeking the same lightning-like emerging growth companies. But in small-cap value, there are literally thousands of possible investments.

That doesn't mean it's easy to invest in these companies. Many of the stocks are illiquid. That is, there's little day-to-day trading in the stocks because there are not that many shares to start with. And many of them are "closely held," that is, in the hands of a founder, some family members, or managers. Because of the limitations of this corner of the market, small-cap value funds sometimes face the choice of closing to new investors or moving up the capitalization ladder. Babson Enterprise, Franklin Balance Sheet Investment, Heartland Value, and T. Rowe Price Small-Cap Value have dealt with size by closing to new investors. As a result, this category has few megafunds. The giant is Fidelity Low-Priced Stock Fund, which is a strong performer despite its $10.5 billion girth. It still has the best five-year record in the group (Table 2-15). From time to time, flows have been so heavy that Fidelity has had to close it to give the portfolio manager time to invest the cash. The next largest small-cap value fund is Heartland Value, about one-quarter the size.

Small-cap is a huge universe of stocks, so many managers find it useful to break it into even smaller segments. Consider the Royce Micro-Cap and Royce Premier Funds. Portfolio manager Charles Royce takes distinctly different approaches to the two. Royce Premier chooses its investments from among 1400 or so small-cap companies with market capitalizations of $300 million to $1 billion. Most small-cap funds and institutional investors stalk that prey, he says, and so it's a fairly efficient market. So with Royce Premier he makes bigger bets, limiting his holdings to about 50 companies and concentrating them in several sectors. For Royce Micro-Cap, he looks to a universe of some 6500 companies, with market caps of between $5 million and $300 million. Since this micro-market is much less liquid, he owns many more stocks—about 150—in a broadly diversified portfolio. Another Royce-run fund, Pennsylvania Mutual Fund, has a mix of the two strategies.

Perhaps because this universe is so diverse, there is far less concentration in the funds' largest holdings (Table 2-16). For instance, the largest holding of the small-cap value funds is PXRE, a reinsurance company (they insure insurance companies), but it's 0.33 percent of the category's collective holdings. Compare that to the top name in mid-cap value, Chase Manhattan Corp., which commands 1.78 percent of the category's holding. What's more, these major holdings really are, for these markets, small companies. The two largest holdings in the category, PXRE and Cole National, are companies with market caps below $500 million. The other two below $1 billion in market cap are Banctec and Imation.

SMALL-CAP BLEND FUNDS

If you are only going to invest in one small-cap fund, you may want to go up the middle with a small-cap blend fund. Dreyfus New Leaders, for instance, builds its portfolio with two managers who mix value and growth plays. The value manager buys financial and energy stocks, the growth manager, consumer products and health-care companies. But taken as a whole, the blended funds tend to behave a little more like growth funds than value. So they're not exactly the same as buying 50 percent each of a small-cap growth and a small-cap value fund. Still, these funds can give investors much of the taste of small-cap growth without quite as much hair-raising volatility.

The best performer in 1997, Hartford Capital Appreciation A, was up 55.1 percent (Table 2-17). Although it was a relatively new offering as a mutual fund, portfolio manager Saul Pannell of Wellington Management Co. has run a similar fund for years for some of Hartford Life's variable annuity and variable life insurance products. (Usually, successful funds are cloned for insurance products, not the other way around.)

Other funds in this category are less specific in their investment objectives. Basically, their portfolio managers are just looking for money-making opportunities in small-cap stocks. The largest holdings in this category truly are a blend of growth and value stocks (Table 2-18). There's America Online, of course, which isn't even a small-cap company anymore (it's about $9.5 billion in market cap). It's here most likely because

TABLE 2-18

SMALL-CAP BLEND FUNDS	
LARGEST HOLDINGS	
Stock ▼	Percent of net assets ▼
AMERICA ONLINE	0.40%
QUANTUM	0.29
CMAC INVESTMENT	0.26
SUN HEALTHCARE GROUP	0.24
INPUT/OUTPUT	0.24
AMERIN	0.23
ORION CAPITAL	0.22
WESTERN DIGITAL	0.21
MAGELLAN HEALTH SERVICES	0.20
AIR EXPRESS INTERNATIONAL	0.20
DATA: MORNINGSTAR INC.	

a small-cap manager purchased the stock when it was a much smaller company, and rode up on the company's successes. Remember, even in a small-cap fund, managers have a lot of leeway about the companies they will hold. Some just require that the companies be small when purchased; others boot them when they reach a particular size. No. 2, Quantum Corp., a manufacturer of disk drives and other information storage devices, is a $3 billion company, but the others are pretty much solidly small-cap.

Of course, there are some excellent small-cap blend funds in which the manager is not required to buy small-cap stocks. If they invest in this sector, it's because that's where they think the opportunities are. A good example of this approach to small-caps is the top-performing Safeco No Load Growth Fund. The prospectus makes no mention of market capitalization. It only states that the fund will invest primarily in common stocks. For the eight years that Thomas Maguire has run the fund, he's found the good opportunities in small-cap stocks, but says he would go up the market capitalization scale if that was what it took to get good investments. The fund does have about 15 percent of its assets in large-cap stocks—the most notable are RJR Nabisco Holdings and Philip Morris.

The small-cap blend category is where you will find small-cap index funds. The Vanguard Group, the largest manager of indexed mutual funds, has several in this category—Vanguard Index Small Cap Stock, which tracks the Russell 2000 stock index, and Vanguard Index Extended Market, which tracks the Wilshire 4500 (which is roughly the 5000 largest U.S. stocks without the 500 at the top of the list). Vanguard Index Small Cap

TABLE 2-17

SMALL-CAP BLEND FUNDS		
BEST RETURNS		
Period ▼	Fund ▼	Total return* ▼
1997	HARTFORD CAPITAL APPRECIATION A	55.1%
1995-97	HUDSON CAPITAL APPRECIATION A**	33.7
1993-97	SAFECO GROWTH NO-LOAD	22.8
1988-97	NICHOLAS LIMITED EDITION	18.5

*Average annual, pretax
**800-800-9169, or see Business Week Online

DATA: MORNINGSTAR INC.

Stock is the "smaller" of the two. The median market capitalization is $706 million, well within the small-cap parameters. The median market cap on Extended Market is $1.3 billion, which, if it continues to grow, may well become a mid-cap fund. Over the last one- and three-year periods, the Extended Market outperformed Small Cap. For the last five years, the returns are the same.

While index funds have made mincemeat of stockpicking fund managers in the large-cap arena, the case for indexing among small-cap stocks is not so clear cut. Active managers argue that these stocks are less efficient than big-caps and they can exploit these inefficiencies through good stock selection. The index funds say the higher costs of operating in the small-cap arena wipe out any gains from stockpicking. New research from Morningstar Inc. comes to two conclusions about small-cap index funds. During bull markets, they edge out actively run small-company funds using the same investment style. During bear markets, they lag, and their overall risk-return profiles are equal to or slightly worse than those of actively managed rivals.

SMALL-CAP GROWTH FUNDS

Strap on your seat belt, put on a crash helmet. Small-cap growth funds are the most volatile of the nine U.S. diversified fund categories. In theory, this should be the most rewarding kind of fund. The fund managers are investing in small, rapidly growing companies. When these high-octane stocks work, they can make big, big bucks for fund investors. When they flop, by failing to meet an expected profit forecast or bungling a new product, look out below. There are few buyers for those busted emerging growth stocks when all the small-cap growth managers want to sell. So they sell what they can and mark down the rest of their holdings.

Still, there's plenty of potential in these stocks and these funds because of some of the simple laws of percentages. There's no limit on how much a successful company can earn or gain in stock value. Just look at Microsoft, which went public in March 1986 at $21 per share—58 cents, adjusted for all the splits since. At the recent price of $130, that's a 22,000 percent gain. Had Microsoft bombed, the maximum loss would have been 100 percent—and fund managers hold on to a losing situation to that point. A few stocks with even one-tenth of Microsoft's gain can make a powerful impact on these funds. A small-cap growth fund doesn't have to hit a home run with every stock; a handful will more than carry the

rest of the portfolio to fund stardom in any one year.

This is a category where rookie funds often turn in stellar results. That's because they have relatively few assets, and a few choice small-cap stocks can really make them run. That was certainly the case with Munder Micro-Cap Equity B, a fund run by a team at a well-respected institutional money management firm, Munder Capital Management. With only $24 million in its four share classes, the fund, with a median market cap of only $123 million, really does troll the waters for undiscovered gems long before Wall Street finds them. The fund came close to the finish line in 1997, but in the end, was nudged out by the American Heritage Fund (Table 2-19).

Micro-cap stocks—generally speaking, companies with market capitalizations of less than $100 million—were barely on investors' radar screens a few years ago. But in 1996 they appeared like jumbo jets. From January through May, the micro-cap funds racked up year-to-date returns in excess of 40 percent. But then that balloon was pricked and the micro-cap growth stocks, perhaps the riskiest of the riskiest fund category, plummeted. The funds were pummeled again early in 1997 and in the fourth quarter as well.

With such volatility, investors in these funds have to be able to ride out the downdrafts or forget about investing in them altogether. Otherwise, investors end up buying after the fund has already done very well—and come to their attention—and selling out at a loss.

Whether micro-cap funds ultimately pay off remains to be seen. There haven't been enough of them in operation long enough to make any judgments. Several of the older micro-caps, Babson Enterprise and Royce Micro-Cap, work the value side of Wall Street. They do not invest in IPOs or hot Internet software companies and do not show a lot of volatility. Capital market theory argues

TABLE 2-19

SMALL-CAP GROWTH FUNDS		
BEST RETURNS		
Period ▼	Fund ▼	Total return* ▼
1997	**AMERICAN HERITAGE****	75.0%
1995-97	**BARON GROWTH & INCOME**	36.7
1993-97	**BARON ASSET**	24.0
1988-97	**BARON ASSET**	19.9

*Average annual, pretax
**800-828-5050, or see Business Week Online

DATA: MORNINGSTAR INC.

TABLE 2-20

SMALL-CAP GROWTH FUNDS

LARGEST HOLDINGS

Stock ▼	Percent of net assets ▼
CEDANT	0.44%
CBT GROUP (ADR)	0.39
EVI	0.38
AES	0.33
ALTERA	0.32
SUNBURST HOSPITALITY	0.31
HEFTEL BROADCASTING CL. A	0.31
BRIGHTPOINT	0.30
HBO & CO.	0.30
ROBERT HALF INTERNATIONAL	0.29

DATA: MORNINGSTAR INC.

that the highest returns go to those who take the highest risks. By that reckoning, the volatile small-cap growth funds should make money for investors over the long haul.

Most investors, however, may feel more comfortable with more mainstream small-cap growth funds. Sure, at times they can be heavy investors in volatile market sectors, like technology. But as a group, it pays to shop around. PBHG Emerging Growth, a one-time star in this category, has at times had nearly half the portfolio in tech stocks. But Alliance Quasar A, another long-term notable in this category, has not had more than 20 percent in technology anytime in the last three years. And Baron Growth & Income, with the best three-year record, is almost technology free. The list of the category's largest holdings includes technology, but also health-care, franchisers, broadcasters, cellular communications, and even an electric power company (Table 2-20).

Still, these funds are not for the faint of heart. Many of the funds practice an investment strategy called "momentum investing"—buying the stocks of companies with a high earnings growth rate and great prospects that this will continue, companies with "momentum."

Practitioners of this strategy don't believe in buying cheap stocks and selling them when they move up. Their game is to buy what's moving up and sell it when it moves up higher. In other words, "buy high, sell higher." The distinguishing characteristics of the stocks these funds traffic in is their high price-to-earnings ratios. Three funds in this category have average p–e ratios of 50. About one-third of the rated funds in this category have a risk rating of "very high" compared to less than 10 percent of all equity funds.

Among the momentum funds are AIM Aggressive Growth A Fund and the Kaufmann Fund. They were the top return funds for the last 5- and 10-year periods ending in 1996. But in 1997, there was no momentum to be had. The AIM fund could only earn 12.2 percent, and Kaufmann, just 12.6 percent. American Century–20th Century Giftrust Investors had long been a successful momentum player, but in 1996, like many other momentum players, it lost the "mo" and has yet to find it since. This unusual fund, which demands a long-term perspective because it locks shareholders in for a minimum of 10 years, earned only 5.8 percent in 1996 and actually lost a little money in 1997.

It's important to note that not all small-cap growth funds take their investors on these wild rides. Baron Asset Fund, for instance, has an enviable 24 percent average annual total return for the last five years with only average risk. It earns a B+ rating against all equity funds and an A against other small-cap growth funds. It's got a higher return than either of the other two funds rated A in the small-cap growth category: Manager Special Equity Fund has a five-year average annual return of 19.1 percent; SmallCap World's five-year average is just 15.7 percent.

HYBRID FUNDS—DOMESTIC AND INTERNATIONAL

Introduced in 1997, domestic and international hybrid funds are also relatively new investment categories. There's really nothing new here, just reorganization of the funds formerly classified as balanced, asset allocation, or multiasset global. Basically, they are funds that regularly own equities, but may also mix them with bonds, cash, and sometimes gold. Among the leading domestic hybrid funds are Heartland Value Plus, Waddell & Reed Growth, AIM Balanced A, and the upstart, Transamerica Premier Balanced Investors (Table 2-21).

TABLE 2-21

DOMESTIC HYBRID FUNDS

BEST RETURNS

Period ▼	Fund ▼	Total return* ▼
1997	TRANSAMERICA PREMIER BALANCED INV.**	35.4%
1995-97	HEARTLAND VALUE PLUS	29.5
1993-97	WADDELL & REED GROWTH B	18.1
1988-97	AIM BALANCED A	15.4

*Average annual, pretax
**800-892-7587, or see Business Week Online

DATA: MORNINGSTAR INC.

Because hybrids offer diversification among types of assets as well as diversification among securities, they have become popular vehicles for retirement plans such as individual retirement accounts (IRAs) and employer-sponsored plans like 401(k)s. An asset allocation option can make an appealing choice, both for retirement plans that don't offer a wide variety of funds or for investors who don't want to go through the trouble of stitching together a program from a lot of funds.

Outside the retirement plan, investors don't really need the hybrid funds. If fact, if all you want is a fairly straightforward mix of U.S. stocks and U.S. bonds, you can probably get better performance and lower costs from putting 60 percent of your money in a large-cap blend fund and 40 percent in an investment-grade bond fund. If you want a richer asset mix, one that includes foreign stocks and bonds, and perhaps real estate and gold, then you need more funds and more money (to meet initial investment hurdles). In that case, a well-diversified hybrid might be a better option. With many of these hybrids, you can get the diversification and breadth of investment with just a minimum investment of a few thousand dollars.

Before investing in some of these retirement-oriented hybrids, investors are asked to complete a questionnaire that helps to determine their risk-taking ability. Then, depending on the score, investors are pointed toward an aggressive, moderate, or conservative asset allocation fund, with the most aggressive usually taking the most risk. Those most aggressive funds are usually recommended to the younger investors. Fidelity is the leader in this product, with its Asset Manager series of funds. Putnam, T. Rowe Price, and Vanguard have also introduced their own versions of the Asset Manager approach. Obviously, over time, the investor is going to have to move from the growth to the middle of the road and, eventually, to the most conservative portfolio. Stagecoach Funds, the mutual fund arm of Wells Fargo Bank, takes a different approach. Stagecoach LifePath Funds have different "target maturities" starting with the year 2000. Investors who will be retiring around 2020, for instance, would choose the 2020 fund, which would gradually adjust its portfolio toward a more conservative mix as its shareholders age. Stagecoach also has a 2040 Retirement Fund, which might make a good choice for someone just getting out of college now.

The majority of domestic hybrid funds are the old "balanced" funds, which are the "sensible shoes" of the mutual fund business—prudent, practical, and, yes, boring. With these funds you get stocks for growth and bonds for income—and a portfolio manager who gets paid to figure out how much of each you need. There's nothing trendy about balanced funds, either. They are among the oldest funds. Vanguard/Wellington Fund opened up shop in 1928, and about a dozen more date back to the 1930s. But new balanced funds keep opening up all the time.

The balanced fund is based on the principle that stock prices and bond prices go in opposite directions. In a booming economy, for instance, stocks rise because of improving corporate profitability. The boom creates increasing demand for credit, so interest rates rise and bond prices fall. Then, in a recession, the opposite is supposed to happen: Stocks fall and bonds rise. But in the recession of 1990, both stocks and bonds tumbled. And in 1991, 1993, 1995, and 1997, both stocks and bonds went up together; in 1990 and 1994, they fell side by side. So much for the theory behind balanced funds: the assets move in opposite directions.

As a class, domestic hybrid funds are quite diverse in their results. Their returns depend on how the portfolio managers fill in the stock and bond portions of their portfolios. In 1997, the funds that had large-cap stocks in the equity portion and cash or short-term bonds in the fixed-income portion did best. Of course, these funds are usually pitched to investors as conservative investments and tend to own blue-chip stocks in most cases. Among the largest holdings are familiar blue-chips like Philip Morris, General Electric, and Fannie Mae, as well as U.S. Treasury securities (Table 2-22).

TABLE 2-22

DOMESTIC HYBRID FUNDS
LARGEST HOLDINGS

Security ▼	Percent of net assets ▼
PHILIP MORRIS	1.14%
GENERAL ELECTRIC	0.82
U.S. TREASURY NOTE 6.25% 8/15/23	0.81
U.S. TREASURY NOTE 5.875% 10/31/98	0.79
FANNIE MAE	0.74
ALLSTATE	0.62
CITICORP	0.61
BANKAMERICA	0.59
BRISTOL-MYERS SQUIBB	0.58
U.S. TREASURY NOTE 6.5% 05/15/05	0.51

DATA: MORNINGSTAR INC.

The balanced funds, with their long histories, may give comfort to investors. Over the last few years, they don't look all that appealing compared to all-equity funds that rode the crest of the bull market. But over the long haul these funds have provided respectable returns with relatively low risk. That's because they tend to live circumscribed lives. For instance, one typical common rule is that the fund have no more than 65 percent of its assets in stocks. It's a good discipline. If rising prices push the stock portfolio up against the limit, the portfolio managers must start unloading stocks in order to balance the holdings. This fits well with an old Wall Street adage, "You can't go broke taking a profit."

While the balanced funds have a long history, the asset allocation funds are relative upstarts. They're sort of hyperactive balanced funds. While balanced funds are generally stocks and bonds, asset allocation funds may add other assets into the mix, including gold, real estate, or commodity-linked securities. What's more, many of the asset allocation funds have the ability to boost a particular class of asset up to 100 percent of the fund. Balanced funds by definition can't take that extreme a position.

Exactly how much of each asset goes into the fund is determined by the fund manager using a sophisticated computer-driven program, and they're not all the same. While equity fund results largely depend on stock selection, the success of asset allocation programs relies on how much of the fund goes into each asset class. Security selection does not play as much of a role in these funds' returns.

To understand the asset allocation fund, look at Fidelity Asset Manager, with $11.9 billion in assets. Two sister funds, Fidelity Asset Manager: Growth and Fidelity Asset Manager: Income together claim another $5.2 billion in assets. In the early 1990s, the funds pushed the frontiers away from traditional asset classes like U.S. stocks, U.S. bonds, and money-market funds to include global stocks and bonds from both developed countries and emerging markets. Then portfolio manager Robert A. Beckwitt developed the computer models that set asset allocations for the fund. Once the allocations were set, Beckwitt would usually leave stockpicking to the equity specialists at the firm.

But in reinventing the asset allocation fund, Beckwitt also ventured out into areas relatively new for mutual funds. For instance, he put money in "structured notes"—bonds with interest payments tied to commodity prices. These derivatives—yes, they are derivatives—make good investment sense. They allow a fund to profit from a rise in commodity prices without investing in commodities or futures contracts, which a fund usually cannot do. For several years, Asset Manager earned sensational returns, even while spreading the money around the globe. But all that came unraveled in 1994. Prices for emerging market debt started to topple in January, and after the Federal Reserve started to raise rates in February, the rest of the bond markets—and eventually the stock markets—skidded as well. By April, this wunderfund was down some 7 percent. Beckwitt managed to recoup some of the losses, but the fund was pummeled again late in the year when the Mexican peso crashed. That scotched any hope for getting back in the black, and the fund finished 1994 with a –6.6 percent total return. Despite a change in managers—it's now run by a team instead of a solo practitioner—the fund has never recovered its former luster. Under the new regime the Asset Manager funds have shed most of their foreign holdings and are classified as domestic hybrids.

In recent years, international hybrid funds haven't appeared all that appealing, mainly because overseas stock markets have either headed south or generally lagged U.S. stocks in their gains. Still, there's a strong case to be made for the additional diversification that international securities bring to a fund or to a portfolio.

If the average international hybrid was nothing to sing about, individual funds certainly managed to rise above the crowd. Consider GAM Global A, the best performer for the last one-, three-, and five-year periods (Table 2-23). The fund jumps around between stocks, bonds, and cash—both U.S. and foreign—to take advantage of broad economic and market trends. Unlike the managers of many hybrids, GAM's John Horseman feels no need to keep minimum allocations anywhere. In 1997, for instance, he eschewed

TABLE 2-23

INTERNATIONAL HYBRID FUNDS
BEST RETURNS

Period ▼	Fund ▼	Total return* ▼
1997	**GAM GLOBAL A**	35.0%
1995-97	**GAM GLOBAL A**	27.5
1993-97	**GAM GLOBAL A**	24.9
1988-97	**GAM INTERNATIONAL A**	17.1

*Average annual, pretax   DATA: MORNINGSTAR INC.

bonds and went heavily for U.S. stocks—especially financial stocks. While the strengthening dollar hurt many international funds (a stronger dollar means stocks denominated in other currencies are worth less in dollars) Horseman gave up little on that count because he had also successfully hedged currencies. His GAM International A, though far behind Global, was the second best performer for 1997 and the international hybrid with the best 10-year record. The main difference between the two funds is Global can include U.S. securities, International cannot.

The GAM funds stood out, perhaps, because they made big bets on stocks and currencies that paid off, while the rest of the group tended to place more money in bonds. As a group, the largest holdings of the international hybrids were mainly bonds—and U.S. ones at that (Table 2-24). The others were Argentine, German, and British bonds, and one stock—the Japanese electronics firm, Canon.

Although Horseman's funds dominate the field by performance, they are not giants—GAM International A has $1.7 billion. Merrill Lynch Global Allocation B, on the other hand, has $9.8 billion. The Merrill fund, while lower in return, is a well-regarded, conservatively run fund that still earns top ratings from BUSINESS WEEK—and has for some time. The Merrill fund tends to keep more money in bonds and cash than the average international hybrid, which dampens price volatility. And because of the fund's heft, it owns more than 500 stocks in over 30 countries.

Though the Fidelity and Merrill funds loom large in the relatively small number of international hybrid funds, there are a few others worth noting. Perhaps the fund in this category admired by most investment advisers is SoGen International, the very low-risk but usually rewarding fund managed for nearly 20 years by Jean-Marie Eveillard. The fund has an excellent long-term record, but in the short term, it's been a laggard, and that has cost it its usually top-drawer rating.

The New York-based Frenchman runs an eclectic portfolio. There's no elaborate computer model here. Eveillard is an old-fashioned value investor, and he'll go anywhere in the world to find value. He's not afraid to make unorthodox investments, either. For many years, one of his fund's largest holdings was the Bank of International Settlements, an institution in Switzerland that serves as a clearinghouse for all the central banks (you know, the Federal Reserve, the Bank of England, the Bundesbank). Its shares sell for

TABLE 2-24

INTERNATIONAL HYBRID FUNDS	
LARGEST HOLDINGS	
Security ▼	Percent of net assets ▼
U.S. TREASURY NOTE 5.875% 11/15/99	3.99%
U.S. TREASURY NOTE 5.75% 12/31/98	0.78
REPUBLIC OF ARGENTINA FRN 03/31/05	0.74
U.S. TREASURY NOTE 6.125% 12/31/01	0.69
U.S. TREASURY NOTE 8.875% 11/15/98	0.53
U.S. TREASURY NOTE 3.625% 07/15/02	0.51
REPUBLIC OF GERMANY 7.375% 01/03/05	0.51
CANON	0.48
U.S. TREASURY NOTE 3.375% 01/15/07	0.48
UNITED KINGDOM TREASURY 10% 09/08/03	0.43

DATA: MORNINGSTAR INC.

far less than the amount of cash and gold bullion that backs each share. The bank is still in the portfolio, but it's now a minor investment.

There are clunkers in all fund categories, but in this category you will find two of the real clunkers of the fund universe: the Comstock Partners Capital Value A and Comstock Partners Strategy O funds. Both funds have been prepared for a bear market for 10 years—and the returns show it. The funds play the bearish game through gold stocks, short sales, and put options. Those are good tools, but used at the wrong time, they make for a woeful performance. For instance, Capital Value gained 13 percent in 1990's third quarter, when we were really having a bear market and the average fund lost 15.8 percent. That's because at the beginning of the quarter the portfolio manager had lots of cash, little in stocks, and even had 2 percent of the fund in put options that shot up in value as the Japanese stock market tanked. It really made its mark in 1987, when it dodged Black Monday and managed to turn in a 29 percent return for the year.

Perhaps the point of these funds is to be permanently bearish, giving investors a contrarian holding for their portfolios. But if that's the mission, the funds have not really performed that role, either. If that were the case, the funds would at least have made a modest amount of money in 1994, when bond markets worldwide plunged and stock markets swung wildly. Yet they did not. Nor did Comstock Capital Value Fund or Comstock Partners Strategy Fund stand out in the stormy fourth quarter of 1997. They suffered losses of 12.0 and 10.2 percent, respectively.

International funds help diversify a portfolio.

INTERNATIONAL FUNDS

We pay up for German-made sports cars and luxury sedans. We sip French and Italian wines and bottled water. Many of our favorite electronic toys like compact disc players, video game machines, and camcorders come from the Pacific rim. We Americans are worldly as consumers but, until a few years ago, we've been parochial as investors. United States stocks make up only about one-third of the market value of world equities, but U.S. investors have, at most, only about one-sixth of their equity assets abroad.

That's changing thanks to mutual funds that make it easy and convenient to invest abroad. Heck, with funds, buying a portfolio of French, Brazilian, and Chinese stocks is no more difficult than buying a portfolio of U.S. blue-chips. In 1993, international equity funds captured the imaginations—and the money—of millions of U.S. investors who sent billions abroad. In one year, the number of international equity funds investing abroad shot up from 210 to 344. More important, the assets in those funds rocketed from $42 billion to $104 billion. For many months, one out of every two dollars flowing into equity funds was going international. Today, there are some 1300 U.S.-based international mutual funds with some $360 billion in assets.

Because international funds reach into the far corners of the globe, even many sophisticated investors who pick and choose at home opt for mutual funds when investing abroad. Many international funds are associated with organizations having global investment capabilities, and that gives the funds first-hand information on, say, Japanese banks or German machine-tool companies or Spanish utilities. That's awfully hard to get from your desk in Pittsburgh, Peoria, or Paramus—even with a computer, a modem, and the World Wide Web.

Then, too, accounting standards and tax treatments vary across borders, so the financial reports of Germany's Siemens or Sweden's ABB Brown Boveri and General Electric are not going to be comparable, even if their businesses are. Good equity analysis of non-U.S. companies takes some specialized knowledge most U.S. investors just don't have. Finally, the logistics of buying and selling abroad are daunting—and expensive—and may require several brokers, banks, and other services to process trades. That can be vastly simplified by leaving it all to a fund, where the processes are well-established and performed at institutional rates.

One particular type of international fund that really galloped to the forefront during this decade is the so-called "emerging markets" fund—a mutual fund that invests in developing stock markets such as those in Latin America, the Pacific Basin (excluding Japan, Australia, and New Zealand), and even the nascent markets of Eastern Europe. During 1993, for instance, Fidelity Emerging Markets Fund earned an 81.3 percent total return. (Fidelity could not keep up with the demand for prospectuses.) In 1997, that same fund lost 40.8 percent of its value.

But in the markets, risk and reward are intertwined. Relatively large gains in some years can be expected to result in relatively large losses in others. That's because such funds take large risks just by the nature of the markets they invest in. Investing in developing economies is risky; the skills of corporate managers are usually lacking by U.S. standards; business and politics are hard to separate; corruption and nepotism, while hardly rare in the more mature economies, is often the norm here. Nonetheless, as long as these countries are growing and attempting to develop economic and financial institutions like those of the more developed nations, the stocks of these nations can make alluring investments. Okay, maybe "investment" is a little strong. "Speculation" is better.

While mutual funds have made it cheap and easy to access these emerging markets, the very presence of the funds has changed their nature. The inflows of foreign capital can send stocks to valuations far beyond the level that could be achieved if the stocks were only purchased by local investors. But the influence of outside money cuts both ways. When the foreign investor—that's you or the portfolio manager of an emerging markets fund—wants to sell out, there are precious few buyers for the stock. That causes prices to fall even farther. And once a problem develops in these markets, it spreads quickly.

In 1997, a currency crisis in Thailand spread to neighboring Malaysia, Indonesia, and the Philippines. When the once rock solid Hong Kong market plunged, emerging markets like Brazil and Russia, which had been faring well all year, skidded as well. Fearing redemptions by shareholders and unable to sell many of their Asian stocks, portfolio managers sold holdings elsewhere.

Right now, the emerging markets funds are the newsiest, but they're a relatively small and recent phenomenon. International mutual funds are hardly a new idea. The Templeton Growth

Fund, for instance, started in 1954 and has posted an average annual return of 14.6 percent over its four decades. Templeton started investing in Japan in the 1950s when the whole notion that it would become the world's second largest stock market (for a period in the late 1980s, it was the largest) seemed absurd. But for many years, the mutual fund industry left international investing to Templeton and a few others. Today, most fund families have at least one international fund and many have multiple offerings.

In fact, international funds have become so diverse that we've split the group into eight categories: two broader groups, foreign and world; diversified emerging markets; two regional groups, Europe and Latin America; and three sorts of funds for the Pacific Basin (Table 2-25). Those categories are Diversified Pacific, Pacific ex-Japan, and one just for Japan.

If you don't own any international fund, your first should come from the foreign or world categories. Sound the same, don't they? Foreign funds invest mainly in the more industrialized countries and mature capital markets, though some do spice the portfolios with emerging markets securities. What's more, they usually specifically exclude U.S. stocks.

World funds, on the other hand, usually have some of their portfolios in U.S. stocks. (One fund, SmallCap World, has 60 percent of its portfolio in the United States and has historically kept its U.S. component so high that Morningstar classifies it as a domestic small-cap growth fund.) In fact, 5 of the 20 largest equity holdings in this category are Philip Morris, Ford Motor, General Motors, Time-Warner, and Pfizer. They're all U.S. companies, but they all have significant operations around the globe as well. To be a large U.S. company today, you have to be global.

Whether you choose a world fund that includes the United States or a foreign fund that excludes the United States depends on how you construct your portfolio of funds. Suppose you decide you want to invest 25 percent of your total portfolio outside the United States. You should steer clear of the "world" funds, since such funds may have about one-third of their assets in U.S. stocks. So instead of getting 25 percent of your money abroad, you may get only 16 percent. If you don't mind having the U.S. stocks or you don't care about a precise asset allocation, then don't exclude these investment vehicles. World funds have one advantage over foreign funds. If the U.S. stocks look better to the portfolio manager than foreign markets, he or she can take

TABLE 2-25

INTERNATIONAL FUNDS
BEST RETURNS

Period ▼	Fund ▼	Total return* ▼
DIVERSIFIED EMERGING MARKETS		
1997	OPPENHEIMER DEVELOPING MARKETS A	14.1%
1995-97	NICHOLAS-APPLEGATE EMRG. CNTY. A	14.1
1993-97	TEMPLETON DEVELOPING MARKETS I	14.1
1988-97	LEXINGTON WORLDWIDE EMRG. MKTS.	7.0
FOREIGN		
1997	DRESDNER RCM GLOBAL SMALL-CAP**	25.5%
1995-97	BT INVSTMNT. INTERNATIONAL EQ.	18.8
1993-97	HARBOR INTERNATIONAL	19.8
1988-97	HARBOR INTERNATIONAL	17.7
WORLD		
1997	INVESCO WORLDWIDE CAPITAL GOODS	27.8%
1995-97	MUTUAL DISCOVERY Z	25.5
1993-97	MUTUAL DISCOVERY Z	22.7
1988-97	TEMPLETON GROWTH I	15.5
EUROPE		
1997	LEXINGTON TROIKA RUSSIA	67.4%
1995-97	SCUDDER GREATER EUROPE GROWTH	26.1
1993-97	DEAN WITTER EUROPEAN GROWTH B	22.1
1988-97	FIDELITY EUROPE	12.9
LATIN AMERICA		
1997	WRIGHT EQUIFUND-MEXICO	42.4%
1995-97	MORGAN STANLEY LATIN AMERICA A	17.9
1993-97	SCUDDER LATIN AMERICA	19.1
1988-97	NOT APPLICABLE	
DIVERSIFIED PACIFIC		
1997	MERRILL LYNCH PACIFIC B	-7.3%
1995-97	MERRILL LYNCH PACIFIC B	1.5
1993-97	PUTNAM ASIA/PACIF. GROWTH A	8.6
1988-97	GAM PACIFIC BASIN A	8.3
JAPAN		
1997	VISTA JAPAN	1.6%
1995-97	GAM JAPAN CAPITAL	1.3
1993-97	G.T. GLOBAL JAPAN GROWTH A	4.3
1988-97	G.T. GLOBAL JAPAN GROWTH A	2.8
PACIFIC EX-JAPAN		
1997	EATON VANCE GREATER INDIA B	5.4%
1995-97	GUINNESS FLIGHT CHINA	8.9
1993-97	CAPSTONE NEW ZEALAND**	2.1
1988-97	G.T. GLOBAL NEW PACIFIC A	5.6

*Average annual, pretax
**Dresdner, 800-726-7240; Capstone, 800-262-6631; or see Business Week Online

DATA: MORNINGSTAR INC.

advantage of those opportunities. That was certainly the case in 1995, 1996, and 1997 when U.S. stocks far outpaced the foreign markets.

With international investing, fund managers usually take one of two basic approaches. First, there's the "top-down" method. Portfolio managers look first at the countries, the local economies, and macroeconomic data like growth in Gross Domestic Product, inflation, and employment. Then they look at how that stacks up with the local stock market—is it cheap or dear given the economic backdrop? The funds usually use an international index as a guide and overweight or underweight countries according to their estimation of the stock market prospects. The managers decide on a country allocation—so much percent of the portfolio to Germany, so much to Japan, and fill in the stocks accordingly, or turn that job over to other managers or analysts. The idea is to get the markets right and all else will follow. Some of the practitioners of this method are Fidelity Diversified International, T. Rowe Price International Stock, and the Scudder International Fund.

The opposite tack is, of course, the "bottom-up" method, one favored by the Templeton Funds. In bottom-up, the portfolio managers first use various stock selection methods to come up with the companies they want to invest in. The resulting country allocation is the result of stock selection. Thus, the returns of these funds can be quite different from the indexes. For instance, Artisan International Fund, with a 34.4 percent total return in 1996 had 11 percent of its assets in Sweden and 10 percent in Norway. The two Scandinavian countries together make up only a few percentage points of any international index. Had the fund stayed close to an index, it would never have earned those kinds of outsized returns. Had the manager been wrong about Scandinavian stocks, the fund would have been near the bottom of the pack.

The sorts of investments made by European, Pacific, and Latin American funds are self-evident. These funds are not substitutes for foreign funds, but supplements. These regional funds are the sector funds of the international equity world. Each category has a different investment story to tell. Europe, for instance, is developing into one megamarket, with economic barriers falling across the continent. That should make it nearly as easy, for instance, for a Spanish company to sell its products in France and Germany as it is for a New Jersey company to sell in Pennsylvania and New York. Perhaps even more

significant is the currency union. In 1999, Germany, France, and a number of other Western European nations will exchange their local currencies into a common European one.

Eventually, this one-market Europe should be a bonanza for businesses and their shareholders. Many of the European funds started up a few years ago, hoping to be reaping those riches by now. But Germany's high interest rates sent rates soaring all over Europe in the early 1990s. That depressed business and was deadly for European stocks.

The last three years have been much better for European funds. In 1995, currency turmoil and slowing economies on the Continent held these markets in check, but the markets still made gains and the European funds, on average, gained 18 percent. The only markets to thrive were Britain's and Switzerland's. In 1996, the Europe funds put on their best show since 1993, climbing 24.7 percent and even beating the S&P 500. In 1997, all the major European markets made significant double-digit gains, riding a mergers and acquisition boom not unlike that in the United States. Even after adjusting for the strong dollar, funds investing in Europe delivered 17.8 percent to U.S. investors.

On the other side of the globe, Pacific funds have historically had some of the world's worst- and best-performing stock markets. Look at the Japanese stock market. During the 1980s, the market soared, with the Nikkei stock average going from less than 10,000 in 1980 to nearly 40,000 at the end of 1989. But that's not all. Starting in 1985, the value of the dollar versus the Japanese yen has fallen by nearly two-thirds. That means, even if there had been no appreciation in the price of a Japanese stock denominated in yen, it still would have soared for dollar-based shareholders.

But since 1990, the yen price of stocks has more than halved. In the last year, the losses became even worse as the value of the yen sank against the U.S. dollar. The bear market in Japan has been devastating for such one-time highfliers as the Japan Fund and G.T. Global Japan Growth Fund. (Both funds had good returns in 1993 and 1994, more because of the stronger yen than because of a bull market in stocks.) In 1997, the best-performing fund in the Japan category was Vista Japan A, up a whopping 1.6 percent. The average Japan fund was down 16.8 percent.

For most of this decade, the rest of Asia was quite another story. Spurred by economic and market reforms in China, the entire region underwent a strong burst of economic growth in the early 1990s. That made a star of the Hong Kong stock market in 1992 and 1993, as Western investors saw it as the door to China. But the China boom spread throughout the region to such nations as Thailand, Indonesia, Singapore, and Malaysia. In 1993, nearly all the stock markets around China's perimeter doubled in local currency terms.

All these markets corrected in 1994, but while Hong Kong rebounded strongly in 1995 and 1996, the other developing Asian markets turned in spotty returns. Then in 1997, these markets melted down, a combination of investor loss of faith in the currency and a sharp economic slowdown. International bankers extended loan packages to South Korea, Thailand, and Indonesia, demanding stiff economic and market reforms in return for loans. The reforms would require big sacrifices—shutting down and merging many banks as well as high local interest rates that would slow down economic growth and increase unemployment—politically unpopular moves. In January of 1998, the situation became so bad in Indonesia that the people lost faith in the government and the economy, dumping their currency for dollars, hoarding goods against feared shortages and future price increases, and, at times, rioting in the streets. That crisis rocked the U.S. stock market, which slid over 4 percent in the first week of January.

Your money does not have to travel halfway around the world to get a wild ride. There's always the Latin America funds, which have opened for business over the last several years as many neighboring nations in our hemisphere started to fight inflation, privatize their economies, and invite foreign investment. In 1997, the average Latin America fund earned a snappy 26 percent atop 24.3 percent in 1996. Even so, the three-year average for these funds is 9.7 percent and the five-year average, 11.3 percent. That tells you 1994 and 1995 were some pretty difficult years.

Indeed, at the end of 1994, the Mexican government devalued the peso after promising investors it wouldn't and set off a near panic in Mexican markets and throughout Latin America. Investors fled Mexico and also pulled money out of Argentina and Brazil, pushing all these emerging markets into a funk, as well as all the diversified emerging markets funds. Latin stocks comprise a large proportion of those funds, and, along with some successes in the nascent markets of Eastern Europe, were largely responsible for the improvement in the returns of diversified emerging markets funds in 1996.

Sure, international funds may seem risky. But when they're combined with U.S. funds, they actually lower the riskiness, at least as measured by volatility. That's because U.S. funds have a high degree of correlation. When one goes up or down, they all do, though not to the same extent. But non-U.S. markets and funds that invest in them do not have a high degree of correlation. They're more likely to zig when the U.S. funds zag. So if U.S. funds are in a slump, chances are some non-U.S. funds will be doing well. That's why even when the foreign markets were eclipsed by the United States, mutual fund companies were launching new international funds.

International investing makes sense for another fundamental reason. If other countries are enjoying faster economic growth than the United States, it stands to reason that corporate profits are going to be stronger than in the United States. So by investing abroad you get a chance to capture some of that other growth. And you still have the opportunity to invest in industries that have all but disappeared in the United States, such as consumer electronics.

For some investors, the chief worry about international investing is currency risk. That's an important question to ask when shopping for international funds. Some funds do hedge currencies; some don't. You have to read the prospectus for the fund's hedging policy. Here's how a hedge works: Suppose a fund owned $100 million worth of Japanese stocks and the manager believed the yen would decline against the dollar. One way to protect the yen-denominated investment would be to sell $100 million worth of yen in the currency market. That move has the effect of "neutralizing" the yen in the fund. Then, the fund gains or loses on the stock price movement of the Japanese stock—just as it would with a U.S. stock.

But hedging has a cost, even if it's done right. It can be especially costly if it's done wrong. What if, against the forecasts of the currency experts, the yen went up instead of down against the dollar? (That's exactly what happened in 1994.) That hedge, which is supposed to protect the portfolio, would become a money-loser. That's why many funds—such as Templeton, one of the most experienced in overseas investing—don't explicitly hedge. But they will factor a depreciating foreign currency into their portfolio by investing in companies that benefit from the cheaper currency, like exporters.

"Bottoms-up" funds choose stocks without regard to country.

Sure, there will be times when investors wish they had hedged the currency, like the Mexican currency crisis that began on December 20, 1994. Unable to support the peso at its then level of 3.5 pesos to the dollar, about 29 cents, the Mexican government devalued the currency 15 percent—the first major devaluation in seven years and the first since the international investors and U.S. mutual fund investors sent billions south of the border. Then the currency speculators rushed in and drove the peso down even further in the foreign exchange market. Unable to prop up the currency, the government just let the peso seek its own level. Three weeks later, the peso had dropped to about 17 cents, or 41 percent of its original value.

At first, most of the damage came from currency. But then the Mexican stock market was hit, and other Latin American markets were hit as well because investors feared a repeat of the Mexican situation. By March 1995, Mexico's stock market and the Latin funds had hit their lows and slowly began to rebound. Still, nearly all finished 1995 with huge losses, ranging from –9 percent for Scudder Latin America Growth to –24.6 for Merrill Lynch Latin America B.

Even with currency risk—that the value of your investments will fluctuate because of currency fluctuations—it's still advisable for U.S. investors to place some international funds in their portfolios. Even if you have all your assets in dollars, you're not without risk. What if the dollar is falling in relation to other currencies? You may have to kiss off that European vacation, but you can live without that. A weak dollar could mean you spend more for foreign-made goods, some of which have no domestic substitutions. And a weak dollar can even push up prices for U.S.-made goods. Although you're shopping for a Chevy, your cost for the car can still be affected by currency fluctuations. If the dollar falls against the yen, that would probably lead to higher prices for Japanese cars that compete with Chevrolet. If its competitors' prices are going up, General Motors may try to profit by raising prices too. Putting a portion of your assets abroad is as American as baseball, hot dogs, apple pie, and the 4th of July.

PRECIOUS METALS FUNDS

Incredible. Astounding. Mindboggling. No adjectives really do justice to the 1993 performance of the funds specializing in precious metals, or gold funds. Lexington Strategic Investments, the leading gold fund of the group and the leading

mutual fund of the year, blasted out a 264.9 percent return. That's probably an all-time record for a mutual fund. United Services Gold Shares, at 123.9 percent, was no slouch either, with a double. The top 25 funds of the year were all gold funds, and the average gold fund delivered a whopping 97 percent return.

But the subsequent years were not so spectacular. Lexington Strategic Investments was still the leader of the pack in 1994, though it was up only 11.3 percent—the only gold fund to make money that year. By 1995, when the average precious metals fund earned a 1.4 percent return, it lost 14.7 percent. By 1996, it lost another 11 percent. And in 1997, the fund dropped 45.7 percent. U.S. Global Investors Gold Shares, also a hot shot in 1993, took a 24.9 percent dive in 1995, another 25.5 percent loss in 1996, and a 38.7 percent loss in 1997. The long-term results are dismal. A dollar invested in U.S. Global Investors Gold Shares five years ago is now worth about 50 cents. Even Oppenheimer Gold & Special Minerals A, the best-performing precious metals fund for the past decade, is a pretty sorry sight (Table 2-26). If you had been able to invest 10 years ago without paying the 5.75 percent load, every dollar would be worth $1.04; if you paid the load, you'd still be in the red.

So why would anyone invest in precious metals funds? For years, the conventional wisdom argued that every investor should place a small portion of his or her assets into gold or gold mutual funds, which mainly buy gold-mining stocks. Gold was seen as a hedge against inflation, a safe haven in times of international upheaval or economic strife. But the conventional wisdom hasn't seemed to work for quite some time. Gold traded for $370 right before Iraq's 1990 invasion of Kuwait. Ten weeks later, after oil prices had nearly doubled, gold sold at about the same price. For the third quarter of 1990, pre-

TABLE 2-26

PRECIOUS METALS FUNDS

Period	Fund	Total return*
	BEST RETURNS	
1997	LEXINGTON STRATEGIC SILVER	-8.1%
1995-97	LEXINGTON STRATEGIC SILVER	1.9
1993-97	LEXINGTON STRATEGIC SILVER	11.3
1988-97	OPPENHEIMER GOLD & SPEC. MNLS. A	0.4

*Average annual, pretax

DATA: MORNINGSTAR INC.

cious metals funds were the best-performing fund category, but they still returned only 4 percent. And for the year, precious metals funds plunged 23.6 percent. Nor did gold prices react much in August 1991, at the time of the abortive Soviet coup. And during the meltdowns of the Asian markets in 1997 and early 1998, investors demanded U.S. dollars, not gold, and prices for the yellow metal remained stuck at 18-year lows. So much for "crisis" protection.

An inflation hedge? Perhaps. But for many years real interest rates—that is, interest rates after inflation—have been high. An investor who put money in short-term fixed-income securities could earn a rate of return well in excess of the inflation rate. Compare that to owning gold bullion, which must be insured and stored while it produces no income to offset those out-of-pocket expenses.

Gold prices finally started to move up in 1993, from nearly $300 an ounce toward $400. This was the move that helped to spark the tremendous move in gold mutual funds, and that was a period when global inflation was relatively subdued. Since then, gold has rallied to the $400 level several times, but could never sustain it. By early 1997, the price was below $350, and by the end of the year, around $285. The new depressant on gold prices: another wave of gold sales by central banks. Even Switzerland, one of the most economically conservative nations in the world, is considering selling off about half its gold reserves.

The case for having a little money in gold funds is that it's nearly impossible to predict when they're going to zoom. Certainly, the gold market is so beaten up now, a small amount of good news could always spark a rebound. At the end of 1992, on the eve of their spectacular 1993 bull market, the gold funds had a little more than $2 billion in assets, less than half of 1 percent of all money in equity mutual funds. Clearly, those who profited most in the gold rush of 1993 were investors who had a contrarian bent. They had invested in the doggiest of investments on the chance that the pendulum would swing back the other way.

The best explanation for gold's 17.3 percent rise in 1993 was a rather elementary one—supply and demand. For many years, foreign central banks, which are big owners of gold, sold millions of ounces of gold bullion to help shore up their currencies. That supply swamped the market in 1991 and 1992, but the selling abated in 1993. Demand picked up as well, especially in the

TABLE 2-27

PRECIOUS METALS FUNDS	
LARGEST HOLDINGS	
Stock ▼	Percent of net assets ▼
NEWMONT MINING	7.36%
BARRICK GOLD	5.95
PLACER DOME	4.60
EURO-NEVADA MINING	3.72
GETCHELL GOLD	3.60
FRANCO-NEVADA MINING	2.92
HOMESTAKE MINING	2.60
FREEPORT-MCMORAN COPPER/GOLD A	2.38
NORMANDY MINING	2.01
TVX GOLD	1.81

DATA: MORNINGSTAR INC.

rapidly growing economies of Asia, where the newly wealthy convert excess cash into gold.

But how does an increase of less than 20 percent in the price of gold translate into a near double for gold mutual funds? For one reason: Gold-mining shares have operating leverage; that is, a little increase in the price of gold can increase their profits handsomely. Here's why. Suppose a mining company can produce gold at a cost of $325 an ounce, and gold sells at $350 an ounce. That's a profit of $25 an ounce. If gold goes to $375 an ounce, the company's cost is still $325, but the profit is $50 an ounce. That's a 100 percent increase in profits on a 7 percent increase in the price of gold (from $350 to $375). That's why, when gold prices are rising, many traders prefer to play the rally via gold-mining shares. Of course, the same principle works on the way down. If gold is falling, mining company profits can melt away quickly.

But rising gold prices don't explain all of 1993's gold-fund returns. For that, you have to look at the unfolding political developments in South Africa, a major gold-producing nation, as the white-controlled government agreed to cede power to the black majority. That touched off a huge rally in the South African stock market, where many of the gold-mining companies are traded, as well as a surge in the value of the South African currency. While many precious metals funds own a mixture of South African, North American, and Australian gold stocks, Lexington Strategic Investments and United Services Gold Shares own exclusively South African stocks.

Many thought the remarkable political changes in South Africa would help to narrow the rift in the gold-shares market because many institutional and individual investors have long refused to put money into South African companies, lest it be seen as approval of the former government's racial policies. Now, the South African mining companies are largely ignored because they are high-cost producers.

Indeed, investors are starting to view gold stocks less as inflation plays and more as potential money-making vehicles, the same way they would approach another natural resource like oil, copper, or forest products. In 1996 Bre-X Minerals, a tiny Canadian company that reputedly struck it big in Indonesia, soared 300 percent—and was a major holding of many gold funds. But in 1997, Bre-X stock plunged as serious doubts were raised about its gold find, and regulators launched fraud investigations. But all the junior gold-mining stocks plunged as well, as investors lost faith in a broad swath of the industry.

The largest holdings of the gold funds are larger North American producers, such as Barrick Gold, Newmont Mining, and Placer Dome (Table 2-27). As restrictions against South African investments fade away, the striking valuation differences between the South African and non–South African stocks should also narrow.

Putting a little money in precious metals funds is not a bad idea. Most diversified equity funds don't own any gold shares at all, so a precious metals fund helps your total portfolio diversification. And while they are the most volatile of equity funds, precious metals funds live a life of their own. The fluctuations in NAVs have little to do with the ups and downs of the Dow, the S&P 500, or any other stock market indicator. That attribute also improves a portfolio's diversification and lowers its overall risk. It's not easy to find gold funds that shine among the overall universe. But BUSINESS WEEK's category ratings now show Lexington Strategic Silver as the best of the precious metals funds. It's main attribute is that it's not a gold fund. The next best ratings belong to Franklin Gold, Scudder Gold, and Oppenheimer Gold & Special Minerals A. Any takers for these funds?

SPECIALTY FUNDS

Specialty funds are essentially nondiversified mutual funds. They may invest in dozens of companies, but they're all in the same industry or group of industries. When their underlying sectors do well, these funds rise to the top. For a few years, health-care funds led the performance derby. Then it was financial funds, precious met-

als, technology funds, and, now, real estate and financial funds. (We've separated precious metals from the other specialty funds because they have very different investment characteristics from most specialized portfolios.) Our specialty group also includes a catchall "unaligned" category, which includes such diverse and unrelated sectors as food and agriculture, environmental services, media, and retailing. They're all in the miscellaneous category because there aren't yet enough of any one of them (Table 2-28).

Investment advisers and mutual fund experts often debate whether fund investors should use specialty funds. After all, if you choose a specialty fund, you are making a choice that's left to professional portfolio managers in the more diversified funds. Are you qualified to make that decision? It's a decision that's more typically made by investors who choose stocks for themselves.

Specialty funds are the middle ground between investing in funds and investing in stocks. In fact, in setting up the vast array of sector funds, Fidelity Investments designed the program to appeal to investors who might otherwise trade stocks. The sector funds are priced every hour during the trading day, and investors can buy or sell at the next hour's prices. (Most mutual funds are priced only after the close of trading, and transactions made before 4 p.m. are executed at the end of the day.)

Though many fund families have some specialty funds in their line-up, none even approaches Fidelity's large menu. For instance, not only is there a financial services fund, but there's a roster of single-industry funds within that: brokerage and investment management, insurance, regional banks, and home finance (savings and loans). There's a fairly broadly chartered technology fund, but Fidelity also manages more narrowly defined funds. Fidelity has separate funds for computers, software, and electronics as well. Fidelity Select Electronics was the best-performing tech fund for the 1995–97 and 1993–97 periods.

If the fund managers are doing their jobs right, the specialty funds should have the same characteristics as the market sectors they represent. Natural resources funds primarily invest in energy and look the best when energy prices are rising. They're often considered a hedge against inflation, though they didn't look that way during 1994, when inflation was a concern in the financial markets. Utilities funds should be safe and boring, since they buy stocks to collect the divi-

TABLE 2-28

SPECIALTY FUNDS
BEST RETURNS

Period ▼	Fund ▼	Total return* ▼
COMMUNICATION		
1997	SMITH BARNEY TELECOMM INCOME	44.8%
1995-97	FLAG INVESTORS TELEPHONE INC. A	27.4
1993-97	FIDELITY SELECT MULTIMEDIA	20.5
1988-97	FIDELITY SEL. TELECOMMUNICATIONS	18.9
FINANCIAL		
1997	PILGRIM AMERICA BANK & THRIFT A	64.2%
1995-97	PILGRIM AMERICA BANK & THRIFT A	45.2
1993-97	FIDELITY SELECT HOME FINANCE	32.0
1988-97	FIDELITY SELECT HOME FINANCE	27.6
HEALTH		
1997	PUTNAM HEALTH SCIENCES A	32.4%
1995-97	VANGUARD SPEC. HEALTH CARE	31.3
1993-97	VANGUARD SPEC. HEALTH CARE	22.6
1988-97	FIDELITY SEL. HEALTH CARE	23.2
NATURAL RESOURCES		
1997	FIDELITY SELECT ENERGY SERVICE	51.9%
1995-97	FIDELITY SELECT ENERGY SERVICE	47.2
1993-97	FIDELITY SELECT ENERGY SERVICE	31.2
1988-97	FIDELITY SELECT ENERGY SERVICE	17.4
TECHNOLOGY		
1997	MUNDER NETNET**	30.4%
1995-97	INTERACTIVE INV. TECH. VALUE**	40.2
1993-97	FIDELITY SELECT ELECTRONICS	33.5
1988-97	FIDELITY SELECT ELECTRONICS	23.4
UNALIGNED		
1997	FIDELITY SELECT RETAILING	41.7%
1995-97	FIDELITY SEL. AEROSPACE & DEFENSE	31.5
1993-97	FIDELITY SEL. AEROSPACE & DEFENSE	24.4
1988-97	FIDELITY SELECT RETAILING	21.9
REAL ESTATE		
1997	EVERGREEN U.S. REAL ESTATE B	53.2%
1995-97	EVERGREEN U.S. REAL ESTATE B	35.5
1993-97	TEMPLETON GLOBAL REAL ESTATE I	19.1
1988-97	FIDELITY REAL ESTATE INVESTMENT	14.9
UTILITIES		
1997	AMERICAN CENTURY UTILITIES	35.7%
1995-97	MFS UTILITIES B	27.0
1993-97	FRANKLIN GLOBAL UTILITIES I	17.4
1988-97	FIDELITY SEL. UTILITIES GROWTH	16.1

*Average annual, pretax
**Munder, 800-438-5789; Interactive, 888-883-3863; or see Business Week Online

DATA: MORNINGSTAR INC.

dends. But in 1994, they were anything but safe and boring. Rising interest rates and increased competition in the utility industry wreaked havoc on the utilities—and funds that invest in them. In 1997, lower interest rates sent them climbing anew.

Specialty funds can only perform as well as the sectors in which they must invest. In 1997, all financial service funds soared, riding the crest of a takeover boom in banks, brokerage firms, and insurance. The companies also climbed on strong profits, the result of a strong economy and buoyant markets, and on lower interest rates. But these specialty-fund performance returns swing around. Just look at the health-care sector. Funds specializing in health-care stocks were up 22.5 percent in 1990 and 78.3 percent in 1991. Then, the stocks and the funds took to their sickbeds. Health funds slid and earned only an 11.2 percent return in 1992 and 1.7 percent for all 1993. Over the last five years, an investor would have fared nearly as well in a diversified U.S. equity fund as in the average health-care fund. Are they worth the additional risks of sector investing?

Even within specialty funds, the strategies can vary. Consider the T. Rowe Price Science & Technology Fund. The fund is mainly high-tech and some medical technology. But it invests not only in the creators and producers of technology, but also in companies that employ technology to their benefit. In 1996, one of its largest holdings was First Data, a provider of data processing services that relies heavily on the application of computer technology.

The Merrill Lynch Technology Fund takes an unorthodox approach to sector investing. Unlike nearly all specialty funds, which remain fully invested in their sectors at all times, portfolio manager James Renck will sell stocks and raise cash if he thinks that's the prudent thing to do. And when he does choose stocks, Renck focuses on a few rather than a broad selection of stocks. The fund has had its moments of brilliance, but the three-year results are poor, an average annual return of 1.1 percent versus the category average of 23.5 percent.

Technology funds have all the hot companies, but one of the best-performing specialty categories of the last several years is real estate. These funds invest mainly in real estate investment trusts (REITs), which are not unlike mutual funds. They pool investors' money to invest in real estate. Some REITs are diversified in the kind of property they buy, but others are specialized—shopping centers, multifamily housing, office buildings, or even nursing homes. Real estate funds may also invest in construction or homebuilding companies, but their principal holdings are REITs.

The real estate fund is one sort of specialty fund that investors could comfortably tuck away in their portfolios as a core holding. They really do add diversification to a portfolio. Most diversified equity funds do not invest in REITs, nor do index funds. (In 1996, Vanguard launched a REIT index fund.)

REITs represent a distinctly different asset class from stocks or bonds. Real estate is, of course, cyclical, but it does not have a high correlation with stocks. So a tumble in the stock market does not necessarily presage a fall in REITs. In fact, early in the summer of 1996, when the stock market was going down at a rapid pace, REITs were climbing.

The other striking characteristic of REITs and the funds that invest in them is that they are mainly income-oriented vehicles. As such, many fund investors would do well to use them in their tax-deferred retirement accounts rather than in taxable accounts where they'll produce taxable income. The difference between REITs and bonds is that REITs are not fixed-payment instruments. An economic boom that would cause interest rates to rise and bond prices to fall would probably also increase rental income, money that ultimately flows back to REIT owners. So REIT funds can be viewed as an inflation hedge for a fixed-income portfolio.

Whether it's technology funds or health-care funds or financial funds, one thing is clear. When specialty funds are on a hot streak, they attract "hot money." Many professional traders track sector-fund prices, just as they keep tabs on individual stocks, looking for the funds with "momentum." When they spot it, they can really pile into a fund. For instance, at the start of 1992, Fidelity Savings & Loan Fund (since renamed Fidelity Home Finance) had $10 million in assets—it was not even large enough to get into the Scoreboard. But the fund was up 15 percent in the first quarter, while the stock market was down 2.5 percent. By March 31, the fund totaled $134 million in assets. Five very profitable years later, the fund has $800 million in assets, suggesting this sort of fund has limited rather than widespread appeal. If it had wide appeal, the fund would have several billion dollars.

With these specialty funds, the more specific the investment mission, the more risk is in the fund. But there's obviously more potential for big gains. If you think health-care funds have

excelled, look at the purely biotech funds. Oppenheimer Global Bio-Tech was up 121.1 percent in 1991, the single best fund for the year. (In 1994, Oppenheimer folded the fund and merged it with Oppenheimer Global Emerging Growth Fund.) Fidelity Select Biotechnology Fund was up over 40 percent in 1989 and 1990 and 99 percent in 1991. The same forces that can bring about big gains can take them away, too. Biotech funds were pummeled in 1992 and 1994 and broke even in 1993. The Fidelity fund gained 49.1 percent in 1995, but even so, the five-year average annual return was a paltry 3.1 percent, about a third of the return earned by the average health-care funds.

Still, specialty funds can be a good alternative to trying to pick stocks in hard-to-understand industries. For instance, only a handful of biotechnology companies are real operating companies with marketable products and real sales. For those companies, the tools of financial analysis can work. But most biotechnology companies are research and development operations that don't make any money. To find the winners among those, an investor would have to have a Ph.D. in molecular biology to figure out which companies were pursuing the research that would be most likely to result in marketable drugs.

This more specialized service may come at a higher price. Specialized funds tend to have somewhat higher expenses, in part because they're smaller and in part because the fund companies can charge them. Fidelity Select portfolios charge combined loads and redemption fees of 3.75 percent. That's not onerous if it's a long-term investment, but it's a high price if you're looking to capitalize on a short-term move. Watch out. This is one area where fees and expenses can really get you.

INDEX AND SOCIAL INVESTING FUNDS

Index mutual funds have been around for some 20 years, but only in 1996 did they all of a sudden become hot properties. The Vanguard Index Trust 500 Portfolio, which tracks the Standard & Poor's 500-stock index, took in $8 billion in fresh cash, finished the year with $30.3 billion in assets, and climbed the ladder of size to become the third largest fund. Now, with $48.3 billion, it's second in size only to the Fidelity Magellan Fund and sometime in the next few years will likely surpass it.

Indexing is a method for managing investments, not an investment style in itself. The Mutual Fund Scoreboard categorizes index funds

TABLE 2-29

INDEX AND SOCIAL INVESTING FUNDS

INDEX FUNDS

AMERICAN CENTURY GLOBAL GOLD	ONE GROUP EQUITY INDEX B
AMERICAN CENTURY GLOBAL NATURAL RESOURCES*	PEGASUS EQUITY INDEX A
ASM INDEX 30	PORTICO EQUITY INDEX RET.*
BT ADVISOR EAFE EQUITY INDEX ADV.	PORTICO SHORT-TERM BOND RET.*
BT ADVISOR SMALL CAP INDEX ADV.*	PRINCIPAL PRES. PSE TECH 100*
BT INVESTMENT EQUITY INDEX	SCHWAB 1000
CALIFORNIA INVST. S&P 500*	SCHWAB INTERNATIONAL INDEX INV.
CALIFORNIA INVST. S&P MIDCAP*	SCHWAB S&P 500 INV.
CALIFORNIA INVST. S&P SMALLCAP*	SSGA S&P 500 INDEX
CITIZENS INDEX	STAGECOACH EQUITY INDEX
COMPASS INDEX EQUITY INV. B*	STI CLASSIC INTL. EQUITY INDEX*
COMPOSITE NORTHWEST A	T. ROWE PRICE EQUITY INDEX
COREFORE EQUITY INDEX Y	TRANSAMERICAN PREM. INDEX INV.*
DEVCAP SHARED RETURN*	U.S. GLOBAL INV. ALL-AMERICA EQ.*
DOMINI SOCIAL EQUITY	USAA S&P 500 INDEX
DREYFUS BOND MARKET INDEX INV.*	VANGUARD BALANCED INDEX
DREYFUS MIDCAP INDEX	VANGUARD BOND INDEX INTERM.-TERM
DREYFUS S&P 500 INDEX	VANGUARD BOND INDEX LONG-TERM
FEDERATED MAX-CAP INSTL.	VANGUARD BOND INDEX SHORT-TERM
FEDERATED MID-CAP	VANGUARD BOND INDEX TOTAL MARKET
FEDERATED MINI-CAP*	VANGUARD INDEX 500
FIRST AMERICAN EQUITY INDEX B*	VANGUARD INDEX EXTENDED MARKET
GALAXY II LARGE CO. INDEX RET.	VANGUARD INDEX GROWTH
GALAXY II SMALL CO. INDEX RET.	VANGUARD INDEX SMALL CAP STOCK
GALAXY II U.S. TREASURY INDEX RET.*	VANGUARD INDEX TOTAL STOCK MARKET
GATEWAY MID-CAP INDEX*	VANGUARD INDEX VALUE
GATEWAY SMALL CAP INDEX*	VANGUARD INDEX INTL. EQ. EMRG. MKTS.
GRANDVIEW S&P REIT INDEX*	VANGUARD INDEX INTL. EQ. EUROPEAN
GREEN CENTURY EQUITY*	VANGUARD INDEX INTL. EQ. PACIFIC
HARRIS INS. INDEX A*	VANGUARD INDEX SPECIAL REIT INDEX
IDS SMALL COMPANY INDEX A*	VICTORY STOCK INDEX
KENT INDEX EQUITY INVEST.*	WACHOVIA EQUITY INDEX A*
KEY STOCK INDEX	WILSHIRE TARGET LARGE GROWTH INV.*
MAINSTAY EQUITY INDEX A	WILSHIRE TARGET LARGE VALUE INV.*
MUNDER INDEX 500 A*	WILSHIRE TARGET SMALL GROWTH INV.*
NATIONS EQUITY-INDEX INV. A*	WILSHIRE TARGET SMALL VALUE INV.*
NORTHERN STOCK INDEX*	

SOCIAL INVESTING FUNDS

AMANA GROWTH*	DREYFUS THIRD CENTURY
AMANA INCOME*	GREEN CENTURY BALANCED*
AQUINAS BALANCED*	GREEN CENTURY EQUITY*
AQUINAS EQUITY GROWTH*	MMA PRAXIS GROWTH*
AQUINAS EQUITY INCOME*	MMA PRAXIS INTERM. INCOME*
AQUINAS FIXED-INCOME*	NEUBERGER & BERMAN SOCIAL RESP.*
ARIEL APPRECIATION	NEW ALTERNATIVES*
ARIEL GROWTH	NOAH*
BRIDGEWAY SOCIAL RESPONSIBILITY*	PARNASSUS
CALVERT CAPITAL ACCUMULATE A*	PARNUSSUS INCOME BALANCED*
CALVERT SOCIAL INV. EQUITY A*	PARNASSUS INCOME CA T-E*
CALVERT SOCIAL INV. MANAGED A	PARNASSUS INCOME FIXED-INC.*
CALVERT WORLD VALUE INTL. A	PAX WORLD
CITIZENS EMERGING GROWTH*	RIGHTIME SOCIAL AWARENESS*
CITIZENS GLOBAL EQUITY*	SMITH BARNEY CONCERT SOC. AWR. A
CITIZENS INCOME*	TIMOTHY PLAN A*
CITIZENS INDEX	WOMEN'S EQUITY*
DEVCAP SHARED RETURN*	

*For further information, see Business Week Online

DATA: MORNINGSTAR INC.

Index funds try to match, not beat, the market.

like any other funds, by the nature of the portfolio. The Vanguard Index 500 is a large-cap blend fund; Vanguard Index Small Capitalization Stock, a small-cap blend; American Century Global Gold (formerly Benham Gold Equities Index), a precious metals fund. Most of the time, index funds are easy to spot. They either have "index" in their title, or very low expenses, or both (Table 2-29).

Index funds are mutual funds designed to replicate, rather than beat, the performance of a market index. That's why they're low cost, too. They can be managed by computers. But, isn't accepting an index's return the same as settling for average? Not at all. It's better than not beating the index. And every year many funds fail to beat the indexes. The Vanguard Index 500, which copies the S&P 500, beat the average large-cap blend fund in the one-, three-, and five-year periods ending in 1997. During the same periods, it also beat the average U.S. diversified fund and the average equity fund. Is it any wonder that index funds are so popular?

In part, the Vanguard index fund's edge comes from low expenses. The Vanguard fund has an expense ratio of 0.20, or 20 cents per $100. The average large-cap blend fund takes $1.25 per $100 in expenses. Right off the bat, the S&P index fund has nearly a 1 percentage point edge. But be forewarned. While all S&P 500 index funds have the same stocks, they don't all own the same return. The difference is expenses. Vanguard charges only the cost of running the funds; others charge much higher rates. The comparable index funds offered by others charge 0.20 to 0.30 percentage points more for the same service.

Index funds also have another advantage that works especially well in bull markets. They are always fully invested in stocks. In fact, one of an index fund manager's main responsibilities at the end of the day is to make sure the net new cash (inflows less outflows) is invested in the index stocks all in the right proportions. That's the only way to insure that all the fund shareholders' money is earning the index returns.

Conventional equity funds don't run fully invested. There's always 4 or 5 percent of their assets in cash, as it sometimes takes awhile to find places for the new money. This is especially a problem with value funds that are picky about where they put the money.

Of course, the main reason index funds look so good now is that the U.S. stock market has been in a bull market for over seven years. In a bear market, cash is a cushion against declining prices.

Since index funds don't carry cash, there is no downside protection. If the S&P 500 were to undergo a serious correction, many investors—some of whom have come to think the S&P 500 is "riskless"—will have a shocking revelation about the dark side of index funds.

Index funds, though they have average returns, actually have above-average BW ratings. That's because, to get a positive rating, a fund must beat the S&P on a risk-adjusted basis. Since many funds fail to do that, they drop to the C or "average" rating. If enough of them do that, the index funds get pushed up to B, an above-average rating. That plus the low cost factor make a compelling case for index-fund investing.

But fund analysts question whether all index funds have such an advantage over managed funds. The S&P 500 fund is successful because the market for big-cap U.S. stocks is very efficient. It's hard for portfolio managers and analysts to add value to an S&P-like fund. Away from the 500, though, markets are far less efficient, and smart stock picking can pay off. Thus, indexing may not be as good an idea in other investment categories, such as small-cap stocks or foreign markets.

In emerging markets, for instance, good stock picking should outperform an index. But in 1995, Vanguard International Equity Index Emerging Markets Portfolio was slightly in the black, up 0.5 percent. That made it the best diversified emerging markets fund of the year. In 1996, the fund earned a 15.8 percent return, easily beating the 11.1 percent category average. How could that be? George U. Sauter, the chief of Vanguard's index funds, says that while it's true that the smaller markets are less efficient, the trading and management costs are much higher. That means the cost of exploiting those inefficiencies wipes out any excess return from those investments.

Bear markets show the ugly side of indexing. Active managers can take some steps to mitigate losses or soften the impact of falling stock prices. Not so an index fund, which must remain fully invested and slavishly adhere to its pertinent index. That same Vanguard emerging markets index fund that did so well in 1996 had losses in 1997 that were three times as great as its actively-managed competitors. Vanguard International Index Equity Pacific Portfolio has been a poor performer among the Asian funds because some 75 percent of it, like the Morgan Stanley Capital International Pacific Index, is invested in Japan. Most "managed" Pacific funds beat it by underplaying or ignoring Japanese stocks.

"Social investing" or "socially responsible" funds, like index funds, cut across a number of categories. The Dreyfus Third Century Fund is a large-cap growth fund; Parnassus Fund is small-cap value; and Pax World Fund, despite its name, is a domestic hybrid. What characterizes these funds is not so much what they do, but what they don't do: They don't invest in defense, tobacco, alcohol, or gaming industries.

And that's not all. Many of these funds screen potential investments for their labor relations, minority employment practices, and attitudes toward women. Companies with questionable track records are also excluded. The same principles carry over to fixed-income investments as well. Pax World won't even invest in U.S. Treasury bonds because the proceeds could be used for military purposes.

In recent years, some of the social investing funds have done well. Pax World and Dreyfus Third Century were top-rated in the early 1990s. That doesn't mean social investing is a superior method of stock picking. It's just that in the 1987–1991 period, drug and health-care companies, which are naturals for social investing funds, performed much better than steel and oil companies, which are much less likely to be part of social investing funds. In recent years, the returns have been all over the lot, suggesting it's more a case of stock selection than social philosophy. Dreyfus Third Century did well in 1995 and 1996, but Parnassus Fund fared relatively poorly in both years despite a strong market. Indeed, social investing screens were never meant to enhance returns, but to assure investors who care about it that their money would not be used to support industries or practices they don't like.

For years, social investing funds were "South Africa free." Because of the country's apartheid policies and white minority rule, they certainly did not make any direct investments in South Africa nor would they invest in any company that had business there. Now, with apartheid abolished and blacks able to participate in political life, it's no longer taboo to invest in that country or in companies that do business there.

Bond Funds

When interest rates go up, bond prices go down. When rates decline, bond prices shoot up. Understand that, and you're well on your way to understanding bond, or fixed-income, mutual funds.

Look at Table 2-30. Consider a bond that pays a 7 percent coupon and matures in 10 years. If rates go down 1 percentage point to 6 percent, the price of the bond climbs to 7.44 percent. Should rates rise by a like amount, the bond declines 6.80 percent in value. As you can see from the table, the longer the maturity, the more sensitive the bond is to changes in interest rates. If rates on a 30-year bond were to rise 1 percentage point, the bond would drop 11.31 percent in price. The five-year bond would only be nicked by a 4.06 percent drop.

The relationship between interest rates and bond prices is one of the most fundamental in all of finance. Yet how many of the millions of investors who flocked into bond funds in the 1991–1993 period really understand that? For instance, an investor who purchased Vanguard Fixed-Income Long-Term U.S. Treasury Portfolio at the beginning of October 1993 suffered a 17 percent decline in net asset value over the next year. That was softened somewhat by the fund's 7 percent yield, but the bottom line was ugly—a –10 percent total return. Investors may not like it, but will accept that kind of behavior from stocks. But from bonds?

If understanding the inverse relationship between interest rates and bond prices (and bond fund NAVs) isn't hard enough, now the bond-fund investors also have to grapple with the "D" word, derivatives. These have been around for years but hit the headlines during 1994 when their quickly sinking prices caused big trouble for

TABLE 2-30

HOW CHANGES IN INTEREST RATES AFFECT BOND PRICES				RATES FALL 1%, PRICES RISE BY... / RATES RISE 1%, PRICES FALL...
MATURITY ▶ COUPON	1 YEAR	5 YEARS	10 YEARS	30 YEARS
5%	0.97% / −0.96	4.49% / −4.27	8.18% / −7.79	17.38% / −13.80
6%	0.96% / −0.95	4.38 / −4.16	7.79 / −7.11	15.45 / −12.47
7%	0.96% / −0.94	4.27 / −4.06	7.44 / −6.80	13.84 / −11.31
8%	0.95% / −0.94	4.16 / −3.96	7.11 / −6.50	12.47 / −10.32

DATA: T. ROWE PRICE ASSOCIATES

some corporations, public investment funds, and, yes, a few mutual funds.

Simply put, a derivative is a financial instrument the value of which is derived from some other source. Take, for instance, a "structured note" with an interest payment tied to the price of copper. To price the note you have to know the interest-rate formula, and that's dependent on the price of copper. If the price of copper goes up, so will the interest payments and the price an investor would pay for the note. If copper slides, so will the note. There's nothing especially risky or suspicious about that.

Derivatives can be used to speculate in stocks, bonds, or commodity-market movements. Options limit the potential loss; futures do not. But most derivatives can be used in a way to hedge portfolio risk. Selling Treasury bond futures, for instance, can protect a bond-fund portfolio from losses related to rising interest rates.

The problem with derivatives comes when they're used to speculate on the direction of the financial markets rather than to hedge against adverse moves—and the portfolio manager's bet turns out wrong. And if the derivative is leveraged, too, the loss is further magnified.

The leverage might work like this. During the three years of falling interest rates, many large investors—mutual funds included—bought "inverse floaters," bonds structured so that their interest payments actually increased as rates went down. But because of the way these bonds were engineered, the inverse floater's interest rate may go up 3 or 4 percentage points for every 1 percentage point drop in the regular rate. Naturally, as short-term rates dropped 4 percentage points over the period, some of these bonds were paying out very juicy yields—sometimes in excess of 20 percent. But the flip side is that when interest rates started to rise—as they did in 1994—the bond's payout started to decline, also 3 or 4 percentage points down for every percentage point the regular rates went up. Since such securities are priced based on their payout, the prices for such leveraged derivatives just melted away.

The derivative debacle of 1994 underscored another problem. Many of the derivatives created in the early 1990s from mortgage-backed securities did not behave as the financial engineers' computer models had predicted. For instance, Piper Jaffray Institutional Government Income Fund and Managers Intermediate Mortgage Fund—both managed by Piper's Worth Bruntjen—plunged and racked up a 25 percent

decline in total return in 1994's first quarter. The two funds, chock full of mortgage-backed derivatives, fell, in part, because many of the unusual securities did not behave as expected. For instance, Bruntjen's financial models predicted that the interest-only and principal-only securities would neutralize each other. If one went down, the other would go up in value. Instead, in the chaotic, declining market, both sorts of securities went down in price. The Piper fund ended the year with a –28.8 percent total return, the Managers fund, nearly as bad, went down 25 percent.

Computer models can "value" a security, but at the end of the day, when a mutual fund has to price its portfolio, what counts is the market price. When the bond market rout began, market prices were far below theoretical prices—and for good reason. There were hordes of investors who wanted to unload these mortgage derivatives, but scant few buyers willing to step up. Losses were so bad in the PaineWebber Short-Term U.S. Government Fund that to preserve its credibility with investors and brokers, Paine Webber spent some $268 million to buy unmarketable securities—known on the Street as "kitchen sink" bonds—from the fund. That, incidentally, did not make the shareholders whole, but simply lightened their losses. For the year, the fund had a –4.9 percent total return.

What is so daunting to bond-fund investors is that even if they do their homework and study the portfolio, it's hard to spot the derivatives. No portfolio manager is going to point to a security— often the underlying issuer is a government-affiliated issuer like Fannie Mae or Freddie Mac—and say, "This is a derivative security, the price of which can be extremely volatile under rapidly changing market conditions." Usually, investors will look at the credit quality of the issue—which is excellent with these two issuers—and figure the investment is secure. With these derivatives, there's no question that in the end they will pay off at maturity. But the problem is that a portfolio manager may have paid a price figuring on a five-year payback, but after rates rose, the estimated payback period might have shot up to 25 years. So the security takes a double price hit because it's now a longer maturity and it's paying a less-than-market interest rate.

Of course the derivative minefield can be treacherous for an investor who, until a few years ago, kept most of his or her money in the bank. Fortunately, most bond funds do not—and never

Derivatives can enhance returns.

have—used the exotic derivatives. But to be sure, Randall Merk of American Century Benham Funds suggests that an investor quiz the broker or fund's sales agent about the use of derivatives in the fund (Table 2-31).

For all the brouhaha over derivatives, most bond funds don't invest in derivatives and, in 1994 and 1996, lost money the old-fashioned way. Interest rates rose, and the price of the bonds went down accordingly. How much they declined depended on the average maturity of the portfolio, a figure that you can find in the BUSINESS WEEK Mutual Fund Scoreboard. But you can also obtain that figure from bond-fund shareholder reports, or just by calling the fund company. The average maturity is nothing more than the weighted average of the maturities of all the bonds held by the fund. And the maturity of the bond is merely the number of years left until the bond will be redeemed by its issuer for its full, principal value.

Maturity is a revealing piece of information. The longer the maturity, the more sensitive the bond prices are to changes in interest rates. And buying the golden credit of the U.S. Treasury is no safe haven from fluctuating bond prices. U.S. Treasury bonds, in fact, are considered to have no credit risk, so their values are solely a function of the changes in rates. (High-yield, or junk bond, funds are also affected by interest rates, but less so. When the economy is strong, corporate cash flows increase, and so does the ability for companies to pay their debt. So high-yield bonds usually take a little less of a hit from rising rates than do highly rated investment grade bonds.)

As a rule, the net asset value of a fund comprised of long-term bonds will fluctuate more than a fund of intermediate-term bonds. And a short-term bond fund is the least volatile of the three. Table 2-32, for instance, which comes from the Vanguard Group, sums up how changes in interest rates would affect some of its bond funds. In general, short-term funds like the Vanguard Short-Term Corporate Bond Portfolio keep their average maturities below 3 years; intermediate funds like the Vanguard Bond Index fund, in the 3- to 10-year range; long-term funds have maturities over 10 years; and many, like the Vanguard Fixed-Income Long-Term U.S. Treasury Bond Portfolio, keep the average in the 20- to 25-year range.

Maturity is a good measure of the potential price volatility of a government or general bond fund. But it doesn't tell the whole story. Two bonds, or bond funds, with the same maturity

TABLE 2-31

WHAT TO ASK A MUTUAL FUND MANAGER ABOUT DERIVATIVES

What percentage of the fund is in derivatives?
Be wary if it's any more than five percent. Most of the funds that ran into trouble had anywhere from 15 to 40 percent.

How are the derivatives used?
Ideally, they're used for hedging. Be wary if the fund is using them to juice the yield. Watch out if interest-only (IO) and principal-only (PO) derivatives are paired off and declared to be perfectly hedged. Experience shows that may not be the case.

Is anyone paying attention to what the fund manager is doing?
The fund management company and the fund's board of directors should be aware of what the portfolio manager is doing and monitoring the use of derivatives.

How are the derivatives priced?
The fund should be using an impartial, third-party service to price derivative securities for purposes of calculating the day's net asset value.

How have the derivatives benefited or hurt the fund in the past?
If the fund hasn't used them before, you might avoid that fund. Do you want the fund manager to get his education in derivatives using your money?

DATA: AMERICAN CENTURY BENHAM FUNDS, BUSINESS WEEK

may not necessarily have the same duration, and as such they won't react to interest rate changes in the same way. Bond fund managers pay close attention to duration in running their funds, but the concept is not well-known or understood among lay investors. Most bond fund managers will give shareholders information on yields and maturities in their funds, but ask a shareholder representative about duration and you might just stump them.

The calculation of duration is complex, but the principle behind it is not. Duration looks at a bond as a series of cash payments (interest payments and the bond redemption at maturity are considered payments). The duration formula calculates a "present value" for each payment, adds them up, and estimates how long it would take the bondholder to recover his or her entire investment in today's dollars.

Suppose Bond Fund A and Bond Fund B have portfolio maturities of 15 years and they yield 6 percent. But Fund A owns bonds issued when rates were lower: they have lower interest payments and they sell at a discount to their redemption value, say 90 cents on the dollar. Fund B has bonds that were issued when rates were higher and now sell for 110 cents on the dollar. Fund A has the higher duration because, since it has lower cash payments, it will take longer for the

TABLE 2-32

HOW INTEREST RATES AFFECT BOND FUNDS

VANGUARD PORTFOLIO ▼	EST. IMPACT OF INTEREST RATE CHANGE ON NET ASSET VALUE				
	AVERAGE MATURITY ▼	–1% ▼	–2% ▼	+1% ▼	+2% ▼
SHORT-TERM CORPORATE BOND	2.6 yrs.	2.2%	4.4%	–2.1%	–4.1%
TOTAL BOND MARKET INDEX	8.6 yrs.	4.3	8.4	–4.5	–9.2
LONG-TERM U.S. TREASURY	20.2 yrs.	11.0	23.6	–9.6	–17.0

DATA: VANGUARD GROUP OF INVESTMENT COS.

investor to recover his or her money. Fund B, whose bonds pay out more income, has a lower duration.

Is low duration better than high? That depends on your market outlook. When interest rates are falling, high duration bonds and bond funds will do better. The lower interest rate gives all the future cash flows a higher present value. When rates are rising, lower duration is less vulnerable to loss.

Sometimes investors who worry a lot about fluctuations in net asset value choose to keep their money in short-term bond funds or stick with money-market funds. In a money-market fund the principal is steady, but the yield, or interest rate, is very volatile. That's just the opposite of the long-term fund, where the NAV can be volatile, but the interest is steadier. If you depend on your investments to generate a certain amount of income, you will need to use intermediate- or long-term funds. The returns from shorter-term funds may be too unpredictable.

When investing in bond funds, it's also important to note the difference between owning, say, a bond fund and owning bonds directly. Most bonds pay interest twice a year, at predetermined dates and at a predetermined amount. A 20-year, $1000 bond with a 7 percent interest rate will make a $35 payment every six months for the next 20 years. That's not the case with a managed bond fund.

Most bond funds make an income distribution monthly, and it may or may not be the same every month. The funds don't earn the same amount of money every month because they rarely have the interest coming in in 12 equal payments. And many bond funds just pass on whatever they've earned during the month, after taking out fund expenses.

But some funds have shareholders who take the income in cash rather than reinvest it. And many of those shareholders like a steady payout. So in those cases, the fund managers attempt to smooth out the income distributions and pay a set amount. Suppose the fund managers settle on a payout of 10 cents per share per month, which may be reasonable given the interest earnings on the portfolio. Some months the fund earns more, some months less, but on average the fund can afford to pay out $1.20 over the year.

Now suppose interest rates fall. Thousands of new shareholders are buying into the fund because they heard about the 10 cents per share per month distribution. But the fund can't invest the new money at as high a rate as before, and the earnings of the fund drop. Inevitably, the income payout must drop too. A mutual fund must pay out its earnings, but it can't pay what it doesn't earn. If, in a period of falling interest rates, someone tries to sell you a bond fund with an unusually high monthly payout, beware. The payout may not be sustainable—or the fund is making the payment out of capital, not income. If that's the case, the fund is chipping away at its net asset value.

This loss of net asset value can be significant. To test just how much, the analysts at Morningstar Inc. looked at the change in fund NAVs for 181 government and high-quality corporate bond funds from November 1, 1986 to September 30, 1994. The significance of those two dates is that the interest-rate environments at the two points were nearly identical, with the long-term interest rate on U.S. government bonds at about 8 percent. If bond funds behaved like bonds, the net asset values in 1994 should have been around the same as in 1986.

But that was not the case at all. The average fund was down 7.6 percent, and with 14 funds, the NAV loss exceeded 15 percent. The reason, concluded Morningstar, was that the funds were stretching to pay the highest possible yields. And in doing that, they emphasized premium bonds—those are bonds whose interest payments were set when rates were higher. So a 20-year government bond with an 11.25 percent coupon will, in a period when a new bond with the same maturity fetches about 8 percent, sell at a "premium"—in this case, $1294 for a bond with a $1000 face value. Even so, the bond pays $112.50 a year, and even on a $1294 investment, that's an 8.7 percent current yield ($112.50 divided by $1294). But here's the catch: Every year, the value of the bond will decline as it gets closer to maturity. So the yield to maturity is much closer to 8 percent—the current rate of interest.

The high-coupon strategy allows a higher current payout, and that's very important to bond funds that are sold by brokers and salespersons, because, as they say in the business, yield sells. Those same bond funds often have much higher than average expenses and so must seek higher yields to be able to pay them and also provide their shareholders a competitive rate of return. And some portfolio managers defend the practice, especially if it has delivered a good total return.

A fund that overachieves on the income side may be okay if it's in an individual retirement account or other tax-sheltered plan. But it doesn't make much sense for many taxpaying investors. The interest is taxable in the year it's paid and at ordinary income tax rates. If the high-yield strategy has also delivered capital losses (remember the average 7.6 percent NAV loss over eight years), investors will eventually be able to deduct them. But the future tax savings from long-term capital losses will be worth far less than the current tax bite from the higher-yield funds.

There's another major difference between direct ownership of bonds and owning shares in a bond fund. If you own a 10-year bond, you know that next year it will be a 9-year bond; in 2 years, an 8-year; and so forth. In 10 years, it will mature. Though interest rates may go up and down in the interim, the maturity of your portfolio of bonds gets shorter every year. The price volatility should decrease with the shortening of the portfolio's maturity. Bond funds, on the other hand, never "mature." If a fund's policy is to keep its maturity around 10 years, it will keep trading the bonds in the portfolio to do just that. Investors can't "shorten" their maturities without switching to another fund. And that could trigger capital gains taxes, even if the investments are in municipal bond funds.

The basic relationship between average maturity and volatility of bond funds holds true no matter whether your fund is taxable or tax-free, government or corporate. The net asset values of funds that invest in U.S. government securities are almost entirely dependent on interest rate movements.

The creditworthiness of the issuer comes into play—but in a small way—with investment-grade corporate and municipal bonds. Investment-grade corporate and municipal bonds are those rated AAA, AA, A, or BBB by Standard & Poor's, or Aaa, Aa, A, or Baa by Moody's Investor Services (Table 2-33).

Anything less than investment grade is "junk" debt, more charitably known as "high-yield" debt. The junk segment of the bond market is where credit considerations may even overwhelm interest rate movements in the pricing of securities. The highest ratings in the junk sector, sometimes also referred to by the oxymoron "quality junk," are BB and B. Some of the quality junk companies are formerly blue-chips that have taken on enormous amounts of debt in leveraged buyouts, takeovers, or other financial restructurings. Then there's CCC and on down to D for default, or bonds no longer making interest payments. That would include the bonds of companies in bankruptcy.

TABLE 2-33

A GUIDE TO BOND CREDIT RATINGS

RATING		
S&P	**MOODY'S**	
AAA	Aaa	Amoco, BellSouth, Exxon, and General Electric are a few of the dwindling number of borrowers in this very exclusive club.
AA	Aa	Here's where you'll find AT&T and many other phone companies. Also Coca-Cola, McDonald's, and Wal-Mart Stores.
A	A	Tough times a few years ago sent IBM's credit rating down along with its stock price. The quality is still high.
BBB	Baa	The lowest rating a bond can receive and still be considered an investment-grade security.
BB	Ba	The highest ranking for junk bonds, sometimes known by the oxymoron, "quality junk."
B	B	Many highly leveraged companies are in this category, which suggests some doubt about borrower's ability to pay.
CCC	Caa	"Currently vulnerable," company's ability to pay is subject to current business conditions.
CC	Ca	Just another rung down the credit ladder, with increasing possibility for default.
C	C	The pits. At Moody's this means default.
D	na	Interest and/or principal is in arrears.

DATA: BUSINESS WEEK

Since interest rates are the driving force in the bond market, the variations in returns from bond funds are not as dramatic as those from equities. Take, for instance, the municipal bond funds. During 1994, the single worst year in the bond market in 60 years, the best muni fund delivered a total return of 2.4 percent; the worst, −20.4 percent. That's a range of nearly 23 percentage points. By contrast, equity funds are far more heterogeneous. Interest rates, though they play a role, are only one of many fundamental forces that affect stocks. So returns from equity funds have a much greater variation. During 1994 the best equity fund delivered a 35.3 percent return; the worst, −50.3 percent—a range of nearly 86 percentage points.

Although these statements are generalizations, they become even more true when you hone in on funds with similar goals. True, Vanguard Fixed-Income Long-Term U.S. Treasury Fund, with an average maturity of 20.2 years, is going to get nailed if interest rates rise. But so will the net asset values of all long-term government bond funds.

So, in a sense, bond funds are much more targeted in their mission than equity funds. Portfolio managers for equity funds typically have far more choice of what stocks to invest in than bond fund managers have choice of bonds. And even in declining stock markets, there are always a few industries or companies that will run counter to the trend. A dramatic breakthrough with a genetically engineered drug will send a biotechnology stock climbing, no matter what's happening to the Dow Jones industrial average. Find enough of the winners and equity fund managers can still buck a downtrend.

But bond fund managers work from a pool of securities that are far more homogeneous. If you manage the Merrill Lynch Federal Securities Fund, you have to invest in U.S. government debt or government-backed debt. How different are the results going to be from other government bond funds?

Bonds and bond funds entail some other risks as well. First, there's call risk. Most corporate and municipal bonds give the issuer the right to redeem the bonds or "call" them after about 5 years in the case of corporates, 10 in the case of long-term municipal bonds. If interest rates have dropped by the time a bond becomes callable, issuers will call the bonds and refinance them at a lower rate. (It's basically the same idea as refinancing your home mortgage to take advantage of lower interest rates.)

Calls are bad news for bondholders. True, the bondholders collect a premium for their bonds: The issuer may pay $1030 or $1050 for a $1000 bond. But that's small consolation to the bondholders who will have to reinvest the proceeds at a lower rate of interest. A mutual fund with a large number of callable bonds might find itself in that quandary. Part of a bond fund manager's job is to steer around such obstacles. One way around the call problem is to buy bonds whose coupons are so low that they're unlikely to be called. The easiest solution, of course, is U.S. government bonds, which can't be called.

Whether or not a bond is callable, the bond or bond fund investor also faces reinvestment risk. Remember, a bond provides the investor a series of interest payments over a set number of years, and the reinvestment of that money is part of the total return from investing in bonds. (If you take the money out when it's paid, there is no reinvestment.) The risk in reinvestment risk is that rates will decline over the life of the bond, and the cash from the periodic interest payments will be reinvested at lower and lower rates. The antidote to reinvestment risk is to invest in zero coupon bonds. These bonds don't pay interest. Instead they are sold at discount to face value. The difference between the purchase price and the maturity value is the interest. Since there is no cash to reinvest, there is no reinvestment risk.

Another sort of risk is "event risk." There's not too much heard about it nowadays, but it was big back in the 1980s. Event risk was the danger that an investment grade bond would turn into a lower quality bond through an event like a hostile takeover or a management-led leveraged buyout.

In trying to understand bond funds, it helps to think of them as similar to specialty or "sector" funds found among equity mutual funds. Diversified equity funds have wide latitude in what they can invest in. Specialty funds target particular investments. Bond funds tend to "specialize" in a certain sector, like a long-term government securities fund or a short-term municipals. This specialization puts more responsibility on the investor. If you choose to invest in a long-term bond fund and interest rates shoot up, there isn't much the portfolio manager can do to keep the NAV from falling. The best he or she can do is try to contain the damage.

What's also important to remember when looking at bond funds is the difference between a fund's yield and its total return. Total return includes the yield plus or minus changes in net asset value. Suppose a fund has a 12 percent yield but only a 2 percent total return. You can surmise that the fund lost 10 percent of its asset value during the year. Likewise, in an up market, a fund's total return should exceed the yield owing to an upturn in bond prices. If you're comparing bond funds, be sure to compare yields with yields and total returns with total returns.

Given these caveats, let's look at categories of bond funds in the BUSINESS WEEK Mutual Fund Scoreboard. As with equity funds, we've overhauled many of the categories, organizing them by maturity as well as the issuers of the bonds in the portfolio. The funds in the general bond category mainly invest in investment-grade and government debt. We break them down into four groups by maturity: long, intermediate, short, and ultrashort. U.S. government bond funds are classified as long, intermediate, or short. Among the municipal bond funds, there's one short-term category. Long-term and intermediate-term municipal funds are divided into national (with bonds from all across the country) and single-state (with bonds from a single state, usually of interest only to taxpayers of that state).

The more specialized categories are largely the same as before: high-yield, convertibles, and multisector. International bond funds now incorporate the short-term world income funds.

As with the equity funds, the new categories are meant to sort the funds into groups by the way they invest, not necessarily what they say about themselves. As such, you will find funds that, judged by their names, seem to be in the wrong category. For instance, Strong Government Securities is in the general bond intermediate category because it fails to meet the intermediate government fund hurdle of having at least 80 percent of the portfolio in government securities. Despite its name, Fidelity Intermediate Bond Fund falls in the short-term category. That's because its average duration is less than the 3.5 year-minimum for intermediate funds.

LONG-TERM FUNDS

If you choose to invest in a general long-term bond fund, you're probably putting your money into one of the most volatile sorts of bond funds. Only long-term government funds are more risky. The risk here, of course, is not credit risk, which comes to mind when most people think about borrowers and lenders. It's interest-rate or market risk, the chance that the fund's net asset value will slide around with fluctuations in interest rates. Funds in this category have an average

maturity in excess of 10 years and an average duration of 6 or more years. Roughly speaking, the NAV of a fund whose bonds have an average duration of 6 years will fall 6 percent for a 1 percentage point rise in interest rates, and rise 6 percent for a 1 percentage point decline. But most of these funds have durations in excess of 10 years.

That said, why do investors choose these funds? In general, the longer the maturity of a bond, the higher the interest rate. That's one of the underlying principles of investing in bonds. Indeed, though it does not happen every year, over the last five years, the average long-term bond fund topped the intermediates and short-terms.

These funds certainly maintain a high credit quality, so they should hold up relatively well in an economic slowdown or recession. Better than one-quarter of their holdings are U.S. government or government-backed securities. Another sort of blue-chip investment is "sovereign" bonds, or dollar bonds issued by foreign governments with high credit ratings and interest payments in dollars. Only about 10 percent of the holdings are below investment grade. On the other hand, the ability of a general bond fund to dabble in the lower-quality issues can help prop a fund's results when interest rates are rising.

The real superstar of this category is the Loomis Sayles Bond Fund. No, you'll no longer find it in the Scoreboard. Loomis Sayles, the management company, converted its funds into institutional funds, and they are no longer available to individual investors. As such, we no longer cover it in the Scoreboard. If you have it, or if you work with an adviser who can get it for you, take it. Smith Barney Investment Grade Bond is the performance leader in this category (Table 2-34). The fund led its peers in total return for the last one-, three-, and five-year periods. But it's a disaster in risk-adjusted returns, earning an F rating both when compared to all funds and when compared to other long-term funds. A

TABLE 2-34

LONG-TERM FUNDS (GEN.)		
BEST RETURNS		
Period ▼	Fund ▼	Total return* ▼
1997	SMITH BARNEY INV. GRADE BOND B	16.4%
1995-97	SMITH BARNEY INV. GRADE BOND B	15.8
1993-97	SMITH BARNEY INV. GRADE BOND B	10.7
*Average annual, pretax		DATA: MORNINGSTAR INC.

better choice would be Invesco Select Income, one of two long-term funds with an A category rating. The Invesco fund also rates a B+ in the overall bond fund ratings.

Invesco's Jerry Paul keeps the fund's duration shorter than most long-term funds. He prefers to make money through good credit research and savvy trading rather than betting on interest rates. In 1997, he scored big with utility bonds as many beleaguered electric utility companies worked to improve their finances. Paul also uses his expertise in the high-yield market to the extent he can without compromising the fund's credit standards. Paul manages the Invesco High-Yield Fund as well.

INTERMEDIATE-TERM FUNDS

The general corporate intermediate bond fund category is a broad one, encompassing a wide variety of bond-picking investment styles. What ties these funds together is their focus on a portfolio with an investment-grade credit rating, an average maturity between 4 and 10 years, and average durations of between 3.5 and 6 years. Those duration figures give you a way to assess risk. Simply put, an intermediate fund with an average duration of 5 years has half the interest rate sensitivity as one with a 10-year duration. Since intermediate funds generate yields that are 80 to 90 percent those of the long-term funds, it's no wonder that many more investors opt for intermediate maturities. You get most of the yield with much less of the risk.

Intermediate funds don't usually make big bets. Their portfolios tend to revolve around a benchmark, the Lehman Brothers Aggregate Bond Index. That index has a duration of around 5 years, so the portfolio managers who really expect a fall in rates might buy longer-term, higher-yield bonds in order to push their duration out to 6 years. Those who anticipate higher rates might sell longer-term bonds in order to shorten the maturity to 4.5 or even 4 years.

In late 1997, judging these funds by their largest holdings might have suggested they were government bond funds. That's because, after a long economic expansion, the yield on investment-grade corporate debt is not much greater than that of Treasuries. In such situations, bond managers might say corporates are "rich" and Treasuries "cheap." What that means is that investors can switch into Treasuries—which have no credit risk—from corporates, without having to give up much yield in return. In a recession, when investors fear corporations may not have the means to pay their debts, that gap is much wider.

Bond fund managers pay close attention to those gaps (in bond parlance, they're quality spreads). They track the yield differentials between many kinds of bonds and often make trades when the historical relationship gets out of whack. To stock market investors, that's like betting on grass growing. But in the bond fund world, a manager's compensation can depend on beating the next guy or an index by a couple of one-hundredths of a percentage point. In that context, those trades can be worthwhile.

Strong Corporate Bond Fund, the fund with the highest returns over the last three- and five-year periods, rarely gets far away from its duration benchmark (Table 2-35). Instead, the managers add value to the portfolio by paying close attention to those differentials between sectors of the bond market and even unusual gaps between individual issuers. This results in perhaps three times the amount of trading that takes place in the average intermediate fund, but it's been profitable trading nonetheless. The fund earns an A category rating when compared to other intermediate funds.

Federated Bond F also earns the highest category rating. But it does so with bigger bets. When the portfolio manager anticipates a faster economic growth, he shortens the duration and lowers the credit quality. When he anticipates slower growth, he lengthens duration and upgrades credits. The returns are strong because, over the last five years, the manager has managed to make the right calls at the right times. But if he doesn't, the fund might get a nasty double whammy, both from the wrong interest rate and the wrong credit quality calls.

If you don't want to worry about managers making the right call, this category also includes the Vanguard Bond Index Fund Total Bond Market Portfolio. That mouthful is a bond index fund managed to replicate the return of the Lehman

TABLE 2-35

INTERMEDIATE-TERM FUNDS (GEN.)
BEST RETURNS

Period ▼	Fund ▼	Total return* ▼
1997	DREYFUS LIFETIME INCOME	11.9%
1995-97	STRONG CORPORATE BOND	13.4
1993-97	STRONG CORPORATE BOND	11.3

*Average annual, pretax   DATA: MORNINGSTAR INC.

Bros. Aggregate Bond Index. The fund employs the same indexing approach as with equity funds and earns its keep by not trying to second-guess the market and keeping expenses to a minimum.

Indexed bond funds have not caught on in the bond market as in the equity market. Part of the reason is that investors just aren't interested in bond funds these days. The other reason, perhaps, is that these funds haven't so convincingly beaten the managed bond funds. For the last one-, three-, and five-year periods, the Vanguard Bond Index Fund Total Bond Market Portfolio beat the average taxable bond fund, and it beat the average intermediate funds as well. Vanguard also has separate intermediate-term and short-term bond index funds.

SHORT-TERM FUNDS

As bond funds go, short-term funds are not very volatile. To qualify for this category, the maturities usually must be between 1 and 5 years, and the durations between 1 and 3.5 years. But in absolute terms, they're still pretty safe. Sure, a 1 percentage point increase in interest rates could knock 3 percent off a fund with a duration of 3 years. But in the short maturities, such movements are infrequent.

Since these funds are fairly restricted regarding what they can do with maturities, they try to make their mark through bond selection. These funds generally invest in a wide variety of fixed-income instruments—from Treasuries and investment-grade corporates to high-yield and emerging markets debt. In most cases, the funds are restricted as to the portion of their assets that can go into the less creditworthy issues.

At a time when longer-term bonds are falling in price, these funds can deliver relatively attractive returns. In 1996, for instance, a year that experienced several sharp swings in long-term rates, the short-term funds turned in some attractive returns. The average short-term general bond fund earned a 5 percent total return, which handily beat the intermediate's 3.7 percent return and the long-term's 3.3 percent return. That was the reverse order of 1995 and 1997, both bullish years for bonds in which the longest maturities made the most money.

The best short-term bond fund for the last one- and three-year periods was BT Investment Lifecycle Short-Term, with a fat 13.7 percent return (Table 2-36). Before you rush to buy it, be forewarned that it's an atypical short-term fund, with a small slug of equities in the portfolio that

TABLE 2-36

SHORT-TERM FUNDS (GEN.)

BEST RETURNS

Period	Fund	Total return*
1997	BT INVEST. LIFECYCLE SHORT-TERM	13.7%
1995-97	BT INVEST. LIFECYCLE SHORT-TERM	12.0
1993-97	DREYFUS SHORT-TERM INCOME	6.9

*Average annual, pretax   DATA: MORNINGSTAR INC.

gives it some extra kick in a year when equities did very well.

Far more conventional choices in this category are Dreyfus Short-Term Income, Harbor Short Duration Fund, and Strong Short-Term Bond, all of which earned the highest category ratings. The Strong fund keeps an investment grade credit quality, but has the ability to put up to 25 percent of the assets in bonds rated BB. For most of the last few years, the ability to buy the higher yield, lesser credits has helped boost the returns of the fund.

ULTRASHORT FUNDS

The ultrashort category is the newest addition to the bond fund portion of the BUSINESS WEEK Mutual Fund Scoreboard. This relatively small category takes in ultrashort corporate funds, like Strong Advantage Fund and Neuberger & Berman Ultra-Short Bond, and the adjustable-rate mortgage funds that were previously in the government category. The two types of funds have very different investment programs but they share an important common characteristic—a portfolio duration of less than one year. The idea behind these funds is to earn a higher return than a money-market fund without taking a whole lot more risk.

Strong Advantage Fund, the best performer of the last five-year period, is one of the oldest of the ultrashort funds (Table 2-37). With $1.4 billion in assets, it's also the largest of the funds. Volatility is kept to a minimum. Portfolio manager Jeffrey A. Koch, who's run the fund since 1991, keeps the duration at 6 months. That's not a whole lot more than a money-market fund. He seeks the extra yield by venturing out into the lesser credits where money-market funds typically don't go. That's because money-market funds are managed to keep their net asset values (NAVs) constant at $1 per share. Strong Advantage does not have a lot of variation in NAV, but it's not obliged to stay at a fixed rate. During

TABLE 2-37

ULTRASHORT FUNDS		
BEST RETURNS		
Period ▼	Fund ▼	Total return* ▼
1997	FRANKLIN ADJUSTABLE RATE SECS.	7.1%
1995-97	ASSET MANAGEMENT ADJ. RATE	7.2
1993-97	STRONG ADVANTAGE	6.5
*Average annual, pretax		DATA: MORNINGSTAR INC.

1997, the fund earned a total return of 6.5 percent and paid out income distributions of 6.2 percent, which means the fund actually went up a little bit in NAV.

The other members of this group are the funds that invest in adjustable-rate mortgages. In theory, a mutual fund that owns nothing but adjustable-rate mortgages (ARMs) should be a pretty safe, conservative offering. Most of the ARMs are issued by government-sponsored enterprises like Fannie Mae and Ginnie Mae, so credit is not an issue. And since most ARMs reset their interest rates at least once a year, the effective maturity is no more than a year. So even though the net asset values of ARMs funds fluctuate, they shouldn't fluctuate much—and ARMs still provide a higher rate of interest than a money-market mutual fund.

In reality, many of these funds have been disappointments. If anything, these short-maturity funds should have distinguished themselves in 1994's bear market by at least completing the year with a positive total return. But the average ARMs fund fell far short, and, in fact, only 5 of the 12 ARMs funds in the Scoreboard had positive results.

The bear market disappointment might have been more palatable if the funds really outperformed during the bull markets. But in the three-year period of falling interest rates, only in 1991 did the funds—and there were only six at the time—really stand out, earning 10.5 percent total return and beating the average taxable money-market fund by 5 percentage points. Spotting sharp 1991 returns, fund-management companies rolled out new ARMs funds, and by the end of 1992 the number of funds had risen to 32 and assets more than doubled to $20 billion; the total return wound up being less than half that of the year before.

The culprit then was falling interest rates. Because ARM securities have higher yields than, say, short-term Treasuries, they typically sell at a premium. So an ARM with a 6 percent yield may sell for $1050, or 105 in bond parlance. But then interest rates go down, and at the next reset, the yield falls to 5 percent. Now the ARM may sell for only $1030, or 103. The fund's shareholders lose that $20 out of net asset value.

But that's not the only problem posed by the ARMs funds. Like conventional mortgage funds, falling rates often encourage homeowners to refinance. That means every ARM purchased at 103 or 105 is paid off at 100. Fund shareholders have to eat the losses, too. Not surprisingly, rising interest rates proved problematic as well. In 1994, for instance, short-term rates ran up so fast and so far that the built-in adjustments did not bring the yields of many ARMs up to competitive rates of interest. The result—sagging prices for ARMs securities.

Although ARMs funds are not the magic investment that many had hoped for, they still can offer a decent return with a modest amount of risk. Whether they delight or disappoint depends on what investor expectations are. Investors who are concerned about stability of NAV should seek out the "purest" ARMs funds they can find—those that invest in government-backed ARMs only. Stay clear of those that mix in other privately issued ARMs securities. If trouble sets in, there is no market for them.

Even when ARMs funds stick to top-drawer issuers, it's not certain they are a great deal for the investor. Given that most of these funds have been through an entire interest-rate cycle (down and then back up to the starting point), it has become clear that there still remains a big gap between the theory and the practice of ARMs investing. Rather than put, say, $10,000 in an ARMs fund, an investor might achieve better results by putting $5000 each in a money-market fund and a short-term U.S. government bond fund (a plain vanilla fund without derivatives). Or better yet, put the entire amount in a well-seasoned ultrashort bond fund like Strong Advantage Fund.

LONG-TERM GOVERNMENT FUNDS

Long-term government bond funds are not for the faint of heart. Sure, the U.S. government guarantee may comfort the investor worried about the creditworthiness of borrowers. But because government bonds have no credit risk, they are totally creatures of changes in interest rates. And since the long government funds own bonds with average maturities in excess of 10 years and durations of more than 6 years, they are the most sensitive to changes in interest rates. When rates fell in 1995, these funds earned an average 24.4 percent total return; in 1997, rates fell again and they gained an average 13 percent. In 1994 and 1996, when rates rose, the total returns were –7.1 percent and –1.9 percent, respectively. In 1997, the best performer in this category was American Century-Benham Target Maturities 2025, a zero-coupon bond fund (Table 2-38).

American Century-Benham runs a series of these funds and they are the most volatile in what is a potentially volatile category of fund. These bonds sell at a fraction of their par value, $1000, and mature in their target year at $1000. There are no interest payments in the interim. The "interest" from a zero-coupon bond is just the difference between the purchase price and $1000. There are six of these funds, with maturities in 2000, 2005, 2010, 2015, 2020, and 2025. The last three belong to the long-term government category.

There's no bond more sensitive to changes in interest rates than a zero-coupon bond. Go back to the idea of duration. A 30-year bond with a 7 percent coupon has a duration of around 11 or 12 years. A 30-year zero-coupon bond has a duration of 30 years. There are no interest payments between now and year 30, so the value of the bond is determined by the present value of that redemption payment of so many years away. In 1993, a year in which long-term interest rates declined to the lowest level in decades, the fund maturing in 2020 had gained as much as 40 percent by October, but then declined to finish the year with a still sharp 35.6 percent gain. In 1994, when interest rates shot up quickly, that same fund lost 17.7 percent in net asset value. In 1995, the fund shot up an amazing 61.3 percent.

In periods of falling interest rates, the zero-coupon funds will invariably be the best performers. Of course, they'll likely be the worst when interest rates rise. As short-term trading vehicles, these funds make some sense. They're no-load and can be bought and sold with a telephone call. But as long-term investments, even Benham management admits you're better off in a regular zero-coupon bond.

Suppose you're going to be 65 in 2020, nearly 25 years away. You decide to put your individual retirement account funds into zero-coupon bonds that mature that year, a reasonable thing to do. The best bet would be to pay the broker's commission, for once you do, you won't pay another nickel for the next 25 years. But if you buy the zero-coupon mutual fund, you'll be hit for 0.50 to 0.65 percent in expenses each year.

(Zero-coupon bonds or bond funds only make sense in a tax-deferred account. Though they pay no cash interest, the Internal Revenue Service says the zero earnings "accrete" interest every year as they get closer to maturity. So you have to pay taxes on the interest every year, though you don't collect it for years to come. Some people use them for children's accounts, and invest in the series that matures when the child is college age. If a child is paying tax at his or her parents' rate—and many now do—the zeros may not be worthwhile for him or her, either. Right now, only minors 14 and older have their income taxed at their own tax rates.)

The fate of the more conventional long-term government funds, those that buy coupon-bearing bonds, is largely determined by the course of interest rates. Still, there is some room for portfolio managers to maneuver. If the manager believes that interest rates will decline, he or she can move fund assets into longer maturity bonds with higher duration. If it looks like interest rates are heading higher, the manager can sell bonds to "shorten" the maturity and duration. Managers can't avoid declining bond prices altogether, but can take steps to lessen the damage, such as investing in "premium" bonds. Those are bonds that sell at a price in excess of their value at maturity because their coupons or interest payments are higher than those of the current rates. When rates go up, such bonds tend to hold their value better.

If the fund is a general government bond fund instead of one restricted to Treasuries, the manager has the ability to pick up some extra return by investment in government-backed mortgages or government-agency issued bonds. As a practical matter, the government stands behind them, but because they're not Treasuries, they tend to pay somewhat higher interest rates.

Not surprisingly, this long-term government fund category is a relatively small one in number of funds and assets under management. Most

TABLE 2-38

LONG-TERM GOVERNMENT FUNDS

BEST RETURNS

Period	Fund	Total return*
1997	AMER. CENT.–BENHAM TARGET MATURITY 2025	30.1%
1995-97	AMER. CENT.–BENHAM TARGET MATURITY 2025	23.7
1993-97	AMER. CENT.–BENHAM TARGET MATURITY 2020	15.4

*Average annual, pretax   DATA: MORNINGSTAR INC.

bond investors are risk-averse anyway, so why invest in bonds that at times can exhibit the same volatility as equity funds? General long-term bonds are risky, too, but they can moderate a little of the interest-rate sensitivity by investing in lower-grade corporates or non-U.S. issues, which also respond to changes in credit quality. Not so for long-term government funds.

INTERMEDIATE-TERM GOVERNMENT FUNDS

If you listen to the business and financial news on television and radio, the announcers will, along with the Dow Jones industrial average, give the bond market a mention: "The interest rate on the benchmark 30-year U.S. Treasury bond declined one-tenth of 1 percent today. . . ." Investors pay a lot of attention to the 30-year government bond, but that's no more the bond market than the price of Coca-Cola or General Electric is the stock market. The government bond market is by and large a market of intermediate-term securities.

There's another good reason for investors to choose intermediate-term over long-term bond funds. They provide nearly as much return for about one-third to one-half less risk. That's certainly the case in the bond market, in which the yield on a 10-year bond is usually around 90 percent or more of that of the 30-year bond. Much the same goes for mutual fund returns. For the five years ending in 1997, the intermediate-term government funds earned nearly 80 percent of the return earned by long-term government funds.

Some of these government funds rely mainly on Treasuries and U.S. agency issues, others emphasize mortgage-backed securities. The advantage of those that have only Treasury and U.S. agency issues is that the income produced by those bonds is exempt from state and local income taxes. Mortgage-backed securities have no such exemption, even those issued by government agencies like Fannie Mae or Freddie Mac.

Mortgage-related funds tend to dominate this category. Many are recognizable as such, with "GNMA" or "Mortgage Securities" in their titles. But not all. The $9.3 billion Franklin U.S. Government Securities I invests solely in government-guaranteed mortgages. But aren't mortgages mainly long-term, like 15 or 30 years?

Indeed they are, but rare is the person who sticks with one mortgage for 30 years and pays it off in its entirety. Most people pay much sooner, either when they sell the house or refinance. Most mortgage-backed securities issued by the Ginnie Mae, for instance, are backed by pools of individual mortgages, and the "average life" of a GNMA is about 12 years.

Intermediate-term government funds may sound fairly generic, but they take different approaches to investing. Note, for instance, State Street Research Government Income A does not have "U.S." in front of the word "government." The fund's prospectus says it will usually have at least 65 percent of its assets in U.S. government securities. What about the rest? For part of 1997, at least, it was Australian and Israeli government debt. In all, 25 percent of the portfolio was in something other than U.S. government securities.

An investor would also expect a government income fund to preserve capital, but that's not necessarily the case. Some funds say their objective is preservation of capital and current income, or current income consistent with preservation of capital. Some say current income alone, with no mention of capital preservation. There is a difference. To maximize current income, a fund can take steps that put a part of its capital at risk.

That's certainly the case with Franklin U.S. Government Securities I. It's a popular fund because it has one of the highest yields in the bond fund universe, even when compared to high-yield corporate issues with far higher coupons. (The yield in 1997 was 6.9 percent.) The fund achieves this by investing in current coupon GNMA securities (those whose mortgages pay at the going rate at the time of purchase). Most investors recognize that higher interest rates will damage the NAVs. But if mortgage holders prepay higher-rate mortgages too quickly, the fund suffers capital losses, and the NAV drops. During 1996, the fund paid out 7.3 percent in cash, but the total return was only 4.6 percent. That comes out to about a 2.7 percent loss in net asset value.

Fidelity Mortgage Securities Initial Shares, which earned the best returns over the five-year period, doesn't make bets on the direction of rates (Table 2-39). The fund's duration is usually that of the Salomon Bros. Mortgage Index. The manager tries to earn extra returns by investing in sectors of the mortgage market he thinks are undervalued, like balloon-note mortgages or securities backed by commercial properties. (The initial share class is now closed. This fund is now part of the Fidelity Advisor Group, whose funds are sold by brokers and financial advisers and charge a load. A good alternative would be Fidelity Spartan Ginnie Mae Fund.)

Over time, mortgage funds beat Treasuries.

TABLE 2-39

INTERMEDIATE-TERM GOVERNMENT FUNDS

BEST RETURNS

Period ▼	Fund ▼	Total return* ▼
1997	PACIFIC ADVISORS GOVERNMENT SECS. A**	11.7%
1995-97	MONITOR MORTGAGE SECURITIES INVEST.**	14.8
1993-97	FIDELITY MORTGAGE SECURITIES INIT.	7.9

*Average annual, pretax
**Pacific Advisors, 800-989-6693; Monitor, 800-253-0412;
or see Business Week Online

DATA: MORNINGSTAR INC.

To understand how mortgage securities work, think of your own situation. Most of these funds invest in home mortgages, just like yours. You make a mortgage payment every month to a bank, thrift, or mortgage company. You don't send your payment to a mutual fund. But it's likely that the original lender has sold your mortgage and is now merely collecting payments and forwarding the proceeds—less a small service charge, of course.

Your mortgage, along with hundreds of others, might be pooled together into a mortgage-backed security—and such investments are the principal holdings of the government–mortgage funds. Mutual funds are among the major buyers of mortgage-backed securities. In that sense, they have a role to play in supporting home ownership. Who knows? You may invest in a mutual fund that owns a security that includes your mortgage.

Either way, Fannie's, Freddie's, and Ginnie's mortgage-backed securities are prized by investors. Their credit quality is considered just a shade under that of pure Treasury securities. If borrowers default, the federal agencies guarantee interest and principal. And the federal government stands behind the agencies. Yet the yields are about 1 percentage point higher than Treasury bonds. In 1989, the yield advantage went as high as 1.7 percentage points, as the ailing thrift industry dumped billions into mortgages to raise capital.

Some mortgage-backed securities are bonds, with pools of mortgages serving as collateral. Many are mortgage pass-through certificates and they're like owning the mortgages themselves. A growing segment of this market is collateralized mortgage obligations, better known as CMOs. In a broad sense, all CMOs are derivatives. But not all CMOs are volatile securities that can blow a big hole in a fund's net asset value. However, to understand the mortgage derivatives, you should first understand how the underlying mortgages work.

Despite the sometimes odd behavior of mortgage-backed securities, the mortgage funds are still governed by the immutable laws of fixed-income investing. When interest rates go up, the value of existing mortgages goes down. But there's another dynamic at work, too. The interest and a small part of the principal is paid monthly and is predictable. But mortgages can pay off their principal at any time. A certain amount of prepayment is always figured into the price of a mortgage security. However, what is unsettling to the mortgage market—and to funds that invest in mortgage securities—is when the expectations about principal repayment suddenly change.

Here's why. The mortgage-backed market operates on the assumption that a pool of 30-year mortgages will have an "average life" of 12 years. Most people move or refinance their homes well before they pay off a mortgage. But a change in interest rates also alters the expected life of a mortgage-backed security. If that life expectancy drops to 10 years—or lengthens to 15 years—the price of the securities can change dramatically.

Suppose you buy a house and finance the deal with an 8 percent mortgage. And that mortgage, in turn, is owned by some investors through a mortgage-backed security with an 8 percent coupon. You plan to trade up to a larger house in five years, but that doesn't change anything because other mortgages have no plans to move at all.

Five years go by and you're ready to move, but interest rates shoot up to 10 percent. Your plans are now on hold. You can't sell your house, because the higher interest rates have depressed the housing market. In addition, you are reluctant to take on a mortgage at 10 percent. Instead of selling your home and paying back the mortgage, you stay in the house for a few more years.

At the same time, the investors who hold your mortgage are also hurt. Like all fixed-income instruments, the higher interest rate lowers its value. But in addition, you and many others have delayed your moving plans. That means you will be holding on to your 8 percent mortgages longer. So this security, originally assumed to have a 12-year expected life, now has a 15-year expected life. Higher rates and a longer life make the security less desirable.

But suppose interest rates had dropped to 6 percent. The owners of your mortgage are happy because they're getting 8 percent from you while new mortgages are fetching only 6 percent. But then you sell your house, pay off the 8 percent mortgage, and buy another house with a 6 percent mortgage. Other homeowners in your mortgage pool also sell or refinance their homes to take advantage of the 6 percent rate.

That means the principal gets repaid faster than originally expected, and the security with a 12-year life expectancy now looks like a 10-year. If rates were going up, the mortgage holders would like the faster payback. But with rates heading down, the last thing they want is principal coming back to them. That principal was earning 8 percent. Reinvested in a new mortgage-backed security, the principal would fetch only 6 percent. As mortgage rates come down, one of the major problems for mortgage-fund managers is minimizing prepayment risks.

Got it so far? Now let's look at CMOs and mortgage derivatives. To understand this, go back to how CMOs are created. Investment bankers start with a pool of underlying mortgage securities, like GNMAs. Suppose an underwriter has $200 million worth of mortgages. That represents two cash flows. One is a predictable one, the interest and partial principal payment that homeowners make each month. The other cash flow is the prepayments, or principal that gets paid back early, either from homeowners' selling their homes or refinancing their mortgages. The sponsor of the CMO will look at all the cash flows the mortgages produce and then carve them up to suit different investors.

For those investors who want the more predictable stream of payments, the CMO bankers will take half the mortgage pool, or $100 million, and create a series of "planned amortization class" bonds (PACs). These bonds will behave much like conventional bonds, with regular cash flows. Such bonds will work fine for most bond funds. Generally, these funds also carry a lower interest rate than the underlying mortgages. That's the price these investors pay for predictability. Two-to-three year PACs will work fine in bond funds with two-to-three-year maturities. Seven-year PACs are fine for long-term bond funds.

Then come the PAC II and PAC III bonds. Their cash flows are far less certain (II's are more certain than III's) since they get paid after all the PACs are paid. That makes them inherently more risky than PACs, and as such they have higher interest rates (some of the yield held back from the PAC bonds is assigned to the PAC II's and III's). But PAC II's or PAC III's are also far

more volatile than PACs, and probably should be shunned by most bond funds.

Risk-averse investors should also avoid the funds that invest heavily in interest-only securities (IOs) or principal-only securities (POs). Those are mortgage-backed securities which pay either interest from a pool of underlying mortgages or principal from a pool of underlying mortgages, but not both. Both are volatile in periods of rapidly changing interest rates. In addition, the risk-shy should avoid funds that are heavy investors in inverse floaters, which are floating rate securities whose payouts go up when rates go down. Their main problem is that when rates go up, their payouts—and prices—melt away. Finally, cautious fund investors should be wary of "Z" bonds, which have the most erratic payout schedule of all the mortgage-backed securities.

Many of those derivatives—inverse floaters, POs, and Z bonds—were responsible for several of the worst bond fund wrecks of 1994: Piper Jaffray Institutional Government Income, with an ugly 28.8 percent loss for the year, and Managers Intermediate Income Fund, with an almost as ugly 25.1 percent loss. The basic problem was that those derivatives plunged in value when interest rates shot up, far faster than conventional mortgages and bonds would have. Added to that was the fact that many of these securities had been leveraged—purchased with borrowed money—meaning the funds were even more susceptible to higher rates and falling bond prices.

How good are mortgage funds as investments? That depends on other market conditions. Millions of shareholders poured into government mortgage funds in the mid-1980s as interest rates tumbled. Their government imprimatur and higher yields were appealing. But high-coupon mortgage securities usually lag behind bond market rallies because investors are reluctant to pay up for high-yielding mortgages when the conditions are ripe for homeowners to pay them off. On the other hand, when the bonds are beginning to falter, mortgages often hold up better than bonds because what principal does come back gets reinvested at higher rates. Held over an "interest-rate cycle"—a period when rates go up, down, and return to the starting point—the mortgage funds should outperform the pure Treasury funds by about 1 percentage point a year.

SHORT-TERM GOVERNMENT FUNDS

Short-term government bond funds fill the gap between the inviolable safety of the money-market fund and the calculated risk-taking of the intermediate-term fund. By and large, the market risk of these funds is roughly half that of the intermediates, and a lot less than that of the long-terms. Not a whole lot of market risk, but not a whole lot of reward, either. During 1996, a difficult year for the bond market, they earned a 4.3 percent total return, beating the intermediates and trouncing the long-term government funds. But the yield paid out was over 5 percent, suggesting that even in these low-risk vehicles, you can suffer a capital loss. In 1997, a strong year for the bond market, these funds returned about 6.5 percent, about half as much as the average long-term fund.

To qualify for this category, the maturities usually must be between 1 and 5 years, and the durations, between 1 and 3.5 years. That, plus the constraints of a government fund, doesn't leave room for funds to differentiate themselves. But leave it to the fund managers. There's a lot more diversity in investment approach than you might think. The Vanguard Group even has two entries in this category: Vanguard Fixed-Income Short-Term U.S. Treasury Securities and Vanguard Fixed-Income Short-Term Federal Securities. The difference? The Treasury fund invests only in Treasury securities, the Federal, in all U.S.-issued securities except Treasuries. The Federal portfolio has a slightly higher yield and total return.

Some funds earn extra returns by searching for the more out-of-the-way government securities. Look at the Sit U.S. Government Securities, the best performer for the five years ending in 1997 (Table 2-40). It's a pipsqueak of a bond fund, less than $100 million, but this gives the portfolio manager more flexibility than the managers of a $10 billion fund. In 1997, for instance, the managers picked up GNMA-backed mobile-home mortgage bonds, which pay 0.80 to 1.5 more percentage points in yield than Treasuries with very little additional risk.

TABLE 2-40

SHORT-TERM GOVERNMENT FUNDS
BEST RETURNS

Period	Fund	Total return*
1997	HANCOCK INTERM. MAT. GOVERNMENT A	18.8%
1995-97	BAIRD ADJUSTABLE RATE INCOME**	9.7
1993-97	SIT U.S. GOVERNMENT SECURITIES	6.7

*Average annual, pretax
**Baird, 800-792-2473, or see Business Week Online

DATA: MORNINGSTAR INC.

IDS Federal Income takes an approach that's fairly unusual for a short-term fund. The manager doesn't confine himself to the short end of the spectrum, but chooses from a variety of U.S. agency and mortgage-related securities, some with decades to go to maturity. From these securities, he gets a higher yield than he would from a strictly short-term portfolio but he also gets the duration of an intermediate fund, about 4.5 years. To bring the duration down, he uses futures and options. Those derivatives have a "negative duration" of 2.3 years. The result is a fund with a duration around 2.2 years, well in the range of a short-term fund.

Yet another approach, practiced by AIM Limited Maturity Treasury Retail Shares, is what's called "laddering." (Actually, this strategy can be and is done with intermediate- and long-term bonds as well.) The fund buys two-year Treasury notes and sells them off after owning them for about a year. Then it buys more two-year notes. The duration ends up around 1.4 years and changes little. The net asset value remains fairly steady, and the fund usually earns good risk-adjusted returns.

The laddering approach is so simple that many investment advisers say there's no point to doing it within the confines of a mutual fund, especially a U.S. Treasury fund. The portfolio manager isn't performing any credit analysis or interest-rate forecasting. Why pay a management fee? Investors can buy the Treasuries themselves—they're easily purchased through frequent Treasury auctions—and do much the same as the portfolio manager is doing. With $5000 or less to invest, a short-term government fund might make more sense. But if you would put $20,000 or more into a short-term government fund, you could ladder a portfolio yourself. Divide your money into thirds, buy a one-year, a two-year, and a three-year note. One year from now, replace the note that's about to mature with a new three-year note. A mutual fund is not always the best way to fill an investment need.

HIGH-YIELD FUNDS

High-yield bonds and the mutual funds that invest in them make most other sorts of bonds look like pikers. Since 1991, they have trounced investment grade bonds by a wide margin. Even looking at 10- and 15-year records, which include a vicious bear market in 1989 and 1990, the high-yield funds still look significantly better. You have to wonder why anyone would ever invest in a government or investment-grade security.

Well, here's the rub. High-yield bonds are legally bonds. The issuer, or borrower, promises to pay interest at particular times and at a particular interest rate. And because of those fixed-rate payments, these bonds have some sensitivity to changes in interest rates. But the truth is, even if these securities look like bonds, they behave more like stocks. Every year in this decade when the stock market has been strong, so has the high-yield bond market. And even in 1994, when the stock market was barely profitable, the high-yield bonds beat stocks by a few percentage points. Martin Fridson, chief of high-yield research at Merrill Lynch & Co., confirmed our suspicions about the true nature of high-yield bonds. He looked at the monthly returns of high-yield bonds from 1985 through 1996 and found that the returns on high-yield bonds correlate with the stock market about 52 percent of the time versus a 41 percent correlation with the 10-year U.S. Treasury bond.

If it's not a stock, but doesn't really behave like a bond, what is a high-yield security? It's evolving almost as a separate and distinct asset, the inclusion of which in a portfolio can help to diversify risks and enhance returns. In short, many investors should consider adding one of these funds to their portfolios. Who wouldn't like to have owned Northeast Investors Trust? Over the last five years, the fund earned an average annual total return of 15.2 percent (Table 2-41).

How high are the yields? That's a moving target, depending on the general level of interest rates. When the high-yield, or "junk," bond market was flat on its back in 1990, many big issues traded at yields 10 or more percentage points higher than the comparable Treasury rates. In early 1998, the yields were perhaps 2-to-3 percentage points higher, and high-yield bond funds had yields (after expenses) of about 8 percent. Many investors argue that high-yields are too low to make them attractive. Perhaps so, but

TABLE 2-41

HIGH-YIELD FUNDS

BEST RETURNS

Period ▼	Fund ▼	Total return* ▼
1997	**BATTERY PARK HIGH-YIELD A****	18.0%
1995-97	**SUMMIT HIGH-YIELD****	16.8
1993-97	**NORTHEAST INVESTORS**	15.2

*Average annual, pretax
**Battery Park, 888-244-2874; Summit, 800-272-3442;
or see Business Week Online

DATA: MORNINGSTAR INC.

they are also a lot safer securities now than they were then. It's somewhat analogous to the people who, when the Dow Jones hit 5000, said the stock market was overpriced. When the Dow hit 7000, those who declined to invest paid a heavy opportunity cost.

One thing is for certain: The returns from high-yield bond funds from here on out cannot match those earned over the last decade. Ernest Monrad, portfolio manager of Northeast Investors Trust, recalls that in 1990 he snapped up R.J. Reynolds bonds at 20 percent yields. So he collected a fat coupon payment to start with, and the bonds eventually appreciated in price as well, giving a substantial total return. But now, rates have fallen considerably and credit quality is much improved. A bond with an 8.5 percent coupon still might go up in value, but it's probably not going to make the gains that can be had when a bond is selling to yield at twice that rate. But investors might still consider putting some money in these sorts of funds. Says Monrad: "All things being equal, you start off with an 8 percent or 9 percent return. With stocks, the dividend yield is less than 2 percent. You have to depend on appreciation to do better. And income is more reliable than stock price appreciation."

High-yield bond funds were originally pitched to income-oriented investors, who still own large amounts of them. But they should be equally, if not more, attractive to stock market investors as "high-yield equity." At least equity fund buyers would probably take their sometimes volatile performance more in stride. Since these funds pay out a large portion of their profit as income, most investors would probably fare better if they held high-yield bond funds in their tax-deferred accounts, such as IRAs or 401(k)s.

So why do these bonds behave a lot like stocks? They're responding to many of the same forces in the economy. Since the 1990–1991 recession, the economy has been on a relatively slow but steady upward climb. Business conditions improved. Companies got leaner and meaner. Productivity increased. Corporate cash flow and profits zoomed.

All of that is great for stocks, and it's great for high-yield bonds, too. Here's why: The issuers of high-yield bonds are often less mature companies or those with a lot of debt. They pay higher interest rates because they are riskier borrowers. There's a greater chance with these companies that they'll default—or fail to make their interest payments. But when business is good and the companies make money, they become stronger financially and more creditworthy borrowers. Fewer issuers default on their bonds. (The average default rate is about 3 percent a year. For the last several years, the rate was about 1 percent—another reason this market has performed so well.) With better credit ratings, the prices of their bonds will also go up. The investors win two ways—bond prices go up and they collect a very healthy interest payment to boot.

A good economy is good for high-yield bonds. It's not always good for investment-grade bonds, because interest rates often go up. Higher rates do hurt the high-yield bonds somewhat, but that can be offset by improved credit quality. What would really derail the high-yield bond market is a recession (it would be hard on stocks, too). That's when business goes into a tailspin, and that's especially rough on less mature, debt-heavy companies. The reason high-yields have looked so strong in recent years is that we haven't had a recession. But that doesn't mean we won't in the future, either. The last recession hit just as the high-yield market was imploding from the excesses of the 1980s. It wasn't pretty.

The character of the high-yield market has changed a lot over the last 20 years—and it's still evolving. Until the late 1970s nearly all junk bonds were "fallen angels," bonds of once investment-grade companies that had fallen upon hard times. But then, investment banker Michael R. Milken of Drexel Burnham Lambert pioneered the idea of original-issue junk bonds. First, Milken used the bonds to raise money for capital-hungry emerging growth companies. Later, corporate raiders tapped the junk bond market to raise funds to take over big companies or to finance leveraged buyouts—purchases of companies that are made with mostly borrowed money. In the 1990s, there's been little takeover or LBO-related junk bond issuance. Instead, many of the new bonds come from new companies borrowing for the first time or established borrowers refinancing high-interest-rate debt.

The original premise behind junk bond investing is simple. Though these securities were riskier than high-quality bonds, the vast majority continued to make interest payments. So, although investing in a few junk bonds may be a dicey proposition, a well-diversified portfolio of junk bonds would be a tempting dish. In such a portfolio the regular income would more than make up for the losses from the occasional default. So mutual funds made a natural vehicle for investing in junk bonds.

The high-yield funds captured investors' attention—and their dollars—in the mid-1980s when interest rates on government and investment-grade bonds fell into the single digits. While the yields in junk bond funds averaged 3 to 4 percentage points higher than those from high-quality funds, the difference between the total returns on junk funds and investment-grade funds was less striking: 22 percent total return (yield plus capital appreciation) for junk funds in 1985 versus 20.6 percent for high-quality funds. In 1986 and 1987, the total returns were nearly identical. The high-yield funds were paying out more in interest, but the investment-grade funds did a better job of maintaining their net asset values.

Those numbers suggest that investors bought junk bond funds for their yields and were not really looking at total return. Only in 1988 did the total returns from junk bonds beat investment-grade bonds decisively—12.6 percent versus 7.6 percent. That was more than reversed in the junk bond debacle. In 1989, for instance, junk funds had an average return of 1.5 percent versus 11.9 percent for high grades. In 1990, junk bonds had a −12.3 percent return versus 17.4 percent for high-quality funds.

What happened to the junk bond market? For starters, Drexel Burnham Lambert—the investment bank that controlled nearly half the market—started to falter in 1989. The firm and Milken, its junk bond chieftain, were under investigation by federal authorities for securities laws violations stemming from the insider trading scandals of the 1980s. (Milken ultimately pleaded guilty to some securities laws violations and spent time in a federal penitentiary.) Drexel's powers and prowess faded, and the firm finally went into bankruptcy in early 1990. The empires of some big junk bond issuers teetered or collapsed under mountains of debt. Finally, new federal laws prevented savings and loans from buying junk bonds and forced those that already owned them to divest. That further depressed demand for the bonds and increased supply.

An investor exodus from high-yield funds exacerbated the junk market's woes. To meet redemptions, fund managers often sold their "quality" junk because it *could* be sold. That left portfolios in even worse shape. After Drexel's demise, some funds had virtually untradeable bonds. As an underwriter, Drexel agreed to make a market for the bonds it brought public. But other brokers didn't have any such obligation to Drexel clients. They could choose which bonds

High-yield funds can diversify any portfolio.

59

they wanted to trade and ignore the others. As a defensive measure, those funds that had the flexibility added some U.S. Treasury securities. Though lower in yield, managers hoped they would help stem the erosion in net asset value. And if the fund needed to sell bonds to meet redemptions, Treasuries are the most marketable securities in the world.

Junk bond investing was a good idea carried to speculative and dangerous excesses. Not every investor in junk funds got creamed in the bear market. Some high-yield bond funds, such as Invesco High-Yield, Phoenix High-Yield, and Value Line Aggressive Income, managed to keep an even keel, and their shareholders suffered little on a total return basis.

While high-yield bond funds can deliver equity-like returns, they can also have some equity-like changes in their NAVs. For instance, on November 22, 1995, Harrah's Jazz company filed for Chapter 11 bankruptcy, causing bond prices to plunge. Keystone High-Income (B-4) Fund lost 2.6 percent in NAV that day; Paine Webber High-Income Fund, 2.2 percent; and Fidelity Spartan High Income Fund and Fidelity Capital & Income Fund, 1.9 percent each. (That was not severe enough to cost either Fidelity fund its high BW rating.)

Junk bond funds, like equity funds, encompass many investment styles. As a result, their portfolios—and their returns—are far more varied than, say, government or municipal funds. Most high-yield funds now have the lion's share of their assets in "B"-rated bonds. Some, like Phoenix High-Yield, have also gone into global emerging markets—bonds of such countries as Mexico, Argentina, Morocco, and Thailand—in their search for a high yield. That paid off handsomely in 1993 when the fund earned a 21.5 percent total return. But the fund stayed abroad too long in 1994, and the fund's return sank to –28 percent. At least two other junk bond funds damaged by emerging market debt were Keystone America Strategic Income B, down 10.3 percent, and T. Rowe Price High-Yield, down 8 percent.

Then there's the more conservative sort, like Nicholas Income and Vanguard Fixed-Income High-Yield Corporate Portfolio, which stress higher-rated bonds and have lower highs and higher lows than the Phoenix fund. The Vanguard fund, by charter, must have 80 percent of its assets in bonds rated B or better. Northeast Investors Trust takes yet another path. It invests in the junkiest junk—the fund is invested almost entirely in credit B or below, or unrated.

The fund can also boost its income by leveraging the fund, borrowing money to buy bonds on margin, thereby increasing the income.

A more conservative approach isn't necessarily less risky. For instance, when the junk bond market like most bond markets, fell in October 1992, the total return for Fidelity Capital & Income was –1 percent. The higher-quality Vanguard fund had a 2.5 percent fall. Why the difference? The prices for the Fidelity fund's bonds are dependent on each company's situation. The prices for higher-quality junk bonds are more interest-rate sensitive. Each approach to junk fund investing carries its own risks. They're not all the same.

CONVERTIBLE FUNDS

If you think the high-yield bonds are really stocks in disguise, consider convertible bonds. They are issued as bonds, with a set interest payment schedule and a promise to redeem by a certain date. The interest rate is a lower rate than you might expect the issuer to pay. But there is a sweetener here that should more than compensate for that lower rate—the bondholder has the option to convert the bonds into a specified amount of stock in the issuing company at a specified price. So when stocks do really well, convertibles do too. And if the stock of the issuing company doesn't reach its conversion price, the investor always has some interest income from the investment.

The 1995 through 1997 period, strong years for the stock market, was a sweet time for convertibles. Convertible bond funds were the best-performing category of bond fund—and they were best in three-year and five-year performance as well. And Davis Convertible Securities A was the best performer for 1997, and also for the three- and five-year periods ending in 1997 (Table 2-42). Yet even when convertible funds do well, they usually don't attract much investor attention. The funds are rather small, and new start-ups are rare. They suffer perhaps because

TABLE 2-42

CONVERTIBLE FUNDS
BEST RETURNS

Period	Fund	Total return*
1997	DAVIS CONVERTIBLE SECURITIES A	28.7%
1995-97	DAVIS CONVERTIBLE SECURITIES A	28.3
1993-97	DAVIS CONVERTIBLE SECURITIES A	18.2

*Average annual, pretax DATA: MORNINGSTAR INC.

convertibles, which have attributes of both stocks and bonds, are little appreciated by pure stock or pure bond investors. Yet they seem to have a role to play in an equity portfolio. With dividend yields on stocks so low, they make a good addition to the portfolio of a more conservative equity investor, perhaps supplanting the role once played by equity–income funds. For the bond investor, the convertibles can actually smooth out the volatility of a portfolio that's overly sensitive to interest rates. Convertible bonds have only a 20 percent correlation with investment-grade bonds, so they definitely do bring diversification to an income-oriented portfolio.

While both high-yield bond funds and convertible bond funds seem to take more of their cues from stocks than from bonds, the two sorts of funds are not really duplicative. In theory, at least, the conversion feature to equity gives convertibles an unlimited return. High-yield bonds, on the other hand, are still fixed-income instruments—and the gains are limited by the interest payment and the difference between your purchase price and the bond's redemption value.

The issuers are not the same, either. The companies that issue convertible bonds are smaller, more rapidly growing concerns, often in growth industries like high technology and health-care. They are looking to keep borrowing costs down because they need money for growth. Those that issue high-yield debt tend to be more mature companies that are not growing fast enough to need to expand their shareholder base. So, in effect, an investor bringing convertible funds and high-yield funds into his or her portfolio is adding a lot of diversification.

The convertible bond market is not a large one. In fact, it's only about one-quarter the size of the high-yield bond market. Sometimes, even the portfolio managers of the relatively few convertible bond funds have a hard time finding the right bonds. So under certain market conditions, some funds create "synthetic convertibles" by pairing straight debt and call options on the issuer stock. (After all, a convertible bond is merely the combination of a straight bond and a call option on the issuer's stock.) And some funds just park their money in straight debt or equity when they don't like what's happening in the converts market.

INTERNATIONAL FUNDS

Just a dozen years ago, it wasn't too hard to guess which international bond fund would be the best of the year. There were only two, and they both invested in investment-grade foreign debt. Emerging markets debt mutual funds had not yet been invented. Nor had short-term world income funds, a sort of fund that tried—and ultimately failed—to earn high short-term yields without currency risk.

Today, you will find all three sorts of funds within the international bond fund category, a new grouping that marries the former world bond and short-term world income fund classifications. What all of these funds have in common is that they must have at least 40 percent of their assets in foreign-issued bonds. But that's it. There's a wide variety of investment strategies, ranging across the risk spectrum. American Century-Benham International Bond Fund used to invest only in the bonds of the major European nations. Since they're heading toward a common currency, the fund recently expanded its charter (and changed its name from European to International) and decided to expand the list of nations to Canada, Australia, and, on a limited basis, Japan. It rarely hedges currencies. Goldman Sachs Global Income A, on the other hand, goes heavy on hedging. Franklin Templeton Hard Currency Fund is really a foreign money-market fund. The portfolio's average maturity is always around six months, and the fund never hedges currency exposure. The idea behind the portfolio is to invest in the currencies of low-inflation countries as a hedge against inflation in the United States. Nowadays, the fund holds lots of U.S. securities, which says a lot about inflation in the United States and the strength of the dollar.

Of course, the most alluring funds nowadays are the emerging market debt funds. Not surprisingly, the best-performing international fund of 1997 was Fidelity New Markets Income Fund, with a 17.4 percent total return (Table 2-43). Only about 9.5 percent of that return was income. Most came from capital gains. That was no easy feat, given the chaos in the emerging markets, especially in Southeast Asia. But the Fidelity fund

TABLE 2-43

INTERNATIONAL FUNDS		
BEST RETURNS		
Period ▼	Fund ▼	Total return* ▼
1997	**FIDELITY NEW MARKETS INCOME**	17.4%
1995-97	**T. ROWE PRICE EMERGING MARKETS BOND**	26.2
1993-97	**G.T. GLOBAL HIGH-INCOME B**	16.9
*Average annual, pretax		DATA: MORNINGSTAR INC.

went into the crisis with about 75 percent of its assets in emerging market Brady bonds (denominated in dollars, and backed by U.S. Treasuries). The fund had very little money in any of the currencies that melted down.

The reason the 1997 returns were so high—far surpassing emerging markets equity funds—was that the funds were rebounding from a bear market that started in 1994 and ran through early 1995. That bear market hit these young funds hard. First came the hit from the rapidly rising interest rate environment. Later came the Mexican peso crisis. In just three weeks, the Fidelity New Markets Income Fund dropped 23.2 percent and G.T. Global High-Income A, 19.6 percent, and they're geographically diversified funds. Alliance North American Government Income Fund B, with a heavy weighting in Mexico, dropped a whopping 28.6 percent. Even though the currency devaluation was contained to Mexico, investors lost their nerve and fled many other markets, driving down prices for emerging market debt everywhere.

You probably have a sneaking suspicion that "emerging markets" is a 1990s euphemism for Third World debt, the scourge of lenders in the 1980s. You're right. Most of the debtors are indeed former deadbeats, and many emerging markets bonds are actually repackaged and restructured bank loans.

The idea behind investing in emerging markets debt is that these countries have cleaned up their acts economically. They've restructured their economies, allowed for privatization of state-owned industries, lowered trade barriers, and welcomed foreign capital. In short, they became much better borrowers than they had been. Indeed, portfolio managers who run these funds hone in on such factors as inflation, unemployment, and government fiscal and monetary policy before buying only those countries or "credits" that are clearly on the road to economic reform. The profit for emerging markets debt funds is not only in the higher interest rates, but also in price appreciation of the bonds as other investors recognize the improved credit quality and pay up for the bonds. In that sense, they're somewhat analogous to junk bond funds, and, indeed, many junk bond funds also invest in these markets.

Currency changes play a part in these funds, too, but usually not as much as you think. Many emerging nations peg their currencies to the U.S. dollar or issue dollar-denominated debt, so currency-induced fluctuations in the fund may well be less than in traditional world bond funds. But when a Third World currency collapses, like many of those in East Asia did in 1997, watch out below.

With the more conventional international bond funds, currencies count for more than credit quality. The argument for international bond investing is the same as it is for investing in foreign stocks—diversification. But non-U.S. bonds do not always zig while the other markets zag. The 1994 bear market in bonds was a global, not just a U.S., bear market. As such, it was hard to find any short-term world income or world bond funds that excelled in 1994, when a U.S. investor would really have appreciated it. Likewise, in 1995, these funds went up along with U.S. bond funds, but nobody complains about that.

What sometimes makes foreign fixed-income securities alluring is when interest rates are higher abroad than they are at home. That makes the yields attractive in themselves. But you have to factor in whether the dollar is appreciating against British pounds and German marks. What if your fund is earning 9 percent on its German bonds and the mark appreciates 9 percent against the dollar? Your total return is 18 percent.

But what happens if the dollar appreciates or the other countries' currencies depreciate? That's what happened in 1992. U.S. investors in world bond funds earned, on average, total returns of only 2.8 percent—that's after the yield. PaineWebber Global Income Fund, for instance, paid out a yield of nearly 7 percent, but wound up the year with a total return of 1.3 percent. Investors lost nearly 5 percent of their net asset value during the year.

Or, what happens when the dollar falls, making foreign bonds more valuable, yet the international bond fund you own is plodding along because of a hedging strategy? Indeed, that's what happened in early 1995, when the dollar plunged, especially against the German mark and the Japanese yen, yet very few international bond funds were able to profit on that. That's because they had used the foreign exchange market to "convert" their marks into dollars, a strategy that pays off when the dollar goes up against the mark. But if the mark goes up against the dollar, and the fund has sold its marks, there's no money to be made. Yet most world bond funds employ strategies that do just that.

Why? Most international bond funds are sold as low-risk yield vehicles, not as total return investments. And one way to keep the risk low is to neutralize the foreign currency exposure. But a fund that does that is also undercutting much of the diversification advantage investors get from going global.

MULTISECTOR FUNDS

Can't decide what kind of bond fund you want? Maybe you don't have to. Try a multisector bond fund. By their charters, they are supposed to keep their money in three types of fixed-income investments: U.S. government bonds or government-backed mortgage securities; foreign debt, both government and private issue; and high-yield corporates, or "junk" bonds. Most of the funds have a benchmark or "neutral" allocation of one-third of assets to each of the three sectors. Then, the portfolio manager is permitted to diverge from that depending on the investment opportunities in each.

The mix makes a lot of sense. U.S. government bonds are high in credit quality, but are the most sensitive to interest-rate risk, or the changes in bond prices that come from changes in interest rates. High-yield corporates are less interest-rate sensitive, but more credit-sensitive. A strong economy might send interest rates up on government bonds, but should also improve the cash flow, and, hence, credit quality, of high-yield bonds. Foreign bonds, even if they are dollar denominated, bring diversification to the mix, since the movements of many foreign economies and bond markets do not correlate to that of the United States.

Though these funds try to maintain somewhat of a balance among the bond sectors, the managers do tilt them to take advantage of perceived market opportunities. During 1997, the best opportunities were in high-yield and foreign bonds—especially those with emerging markets debt. The best multisector performer of 1997, Alliance Global Strategic Income B (Table 2-44), earned its high return with a generous helping of Latin American debt. Franklin Strategic Income,

TABLE 2-44

MULTISECTOR FUNDS		
BEST RETURNS		
Period ▼	Fund ▼	Total return* ▼
1997	ALLIANCE GLOBAL STRATEGIC INCOME B	13.8%
1995-97	FRANKLIN STRATEGIC INCOME	15.2
1993-97	HANCOCK STRATEGIC INCOME	10.5

*Average annual, pretax   DATA: MORNINGSTAR INC.

the best performer for the last three-year period, has generated top returns by leaning heavily on junk bonds.

AIM Income A has a different take on the multisector bond fund. It tends to own longer-term securities with higher durations. The average multisector fund looks to earn its money from sector allocations, not interest-rate bets. Most keep their durations around 4 or 5 years, giving them volatility characteristics of intermediate funds. If funds are going to make interest-rate bets, they'd better be on the right side. In 1995, when U.S. interest rates plummeted, AIM Income A took the top spot because it had a heavy slug of long-term U.S. securities. On the other hand, Janus Flexible Income Fund started 1996 with a duration of 7, which proved troublesome in the first quarter when interest rates jumped up. The manager quickly shortened the duration to 4, but the damage was largely done. The fund finished the year with a 6.4 percent return, well below the sector's 9.8 percent average.

One interesting note about the multisector funds: nearly all of them are sold and managed by load-fund companies. The reason is that the funds' investment pitch is more sophisticated than just a government bond or a straight muni fund. So fund executives thought that, to sell the fund, they would need the help of salespeople to explain the product to investors. There are only three pure no-loads in this category: Janus Flexible Income, Strong Short-Term Global Bond, and T. Rowe Price Spectrum Income. The Price fund is actually a fund that invests in other T. Rowe Price bond funds. It's a B+ fund when compared to all bond funds, and an A compared to other multisectors.

MUNICIPAL FUNDS

No one likes higher taxes. No one, that is, except the people who sell and manage municipal bond funds. When Bill Clinton was first elected, the "muni" market cheered. His tax hikes for upper-income taxpayers make the muni alternative look better than ever. The income from muni bond funds can't be touched by the Internal Revenue Service as long as the interest income comes from tax-exempt securities issued by state and local governments and authorities. Right after the Republican sweep of Congress in the 1994 elections, muni bond prices slumped. One explanation: the GOP's campaign promises to lower taxes. Lower taxes make munis less attractive. Just about the time munis started to recover from that GOP Congress, millionaire publisher Steve Forbes started campaigning for the Republican presidential nomination. His chief rallying cry was the "flat tax," a "one rate fits all" plan that's anathema to the municipal bond crowd. The lower tax rates go, the higher yields tax-exempt bonds have to pay to attract investors.

A tax-exempt security typically sports a lower yield than a taxable security of comparable maturity and credit quality. All things being equal, their returns are lower than those on comparable taxable funds, though at times, muni funds can outperform taxable funds (Table 2-45). That's because investors will accept a lower rate in return for the tax exemption. In deciding whether to invest in a muni or taxable bond fund, the key question to ask is, "What is the taxable equivalent of the yield on a muni fund?" The answer to that question depends on your marginal tax rate. The higher the rate, the better a muni looks compared to a taxable fund. (If you're talking about a tax-deferred retirement account, always choose the higher yielding taxable bonds.)

When marginal tax rates were first slashed in 1982, some predicted that tax-exempt bonds would lose their attraction. Prior to that, the top tax rate on individual income was 50 percent, so a 7 percent muni bond payout was the same as a 14 percent taxable bond. But after the 1986 tax act, which introduced a 28 percent top rate, the 7 percent coupon was worth only 9.72 percent in a taxable bond.

But the muni never lost its appeal to investors. The 1986 tax bill that cut rates also scotched many of the tax shelters high-income individuals used to cut their tax bills. The muni was the one tax haven left. More important, shelters only delay paying taxes. The interest income generated by municipal bonds is always tax-free, and so is interest income that an investor receives from a muni bond fund. However, not all the income generated by the fund is tax-exempt. If the fund is adept at trading bonds, and earns some capital gains, those gains (net of losses) will be passed on to investors as a capital gains distribution, taxable at the capital gains rate.

It's possible that muni funds may start to generate fully-taxable ordinary income as well. That's because the 1993 tax act changed the law so that the money earned when bonds bought at discount to par are redeemed at par will be considered ordinary income—taxable at the investor's highest rate. Before the changes, that difference would have been considered capital gains, taxed at a lower rate. Not surprisingly, Wall Street and mutual fund lobbyists are trying to change that law.

Even so, muni bond funds make sense for many investors. The top federal tax bracket is 36 percent, and for an elite few, a millionaire's surcharge raises it to 39.6 percent. Municipal bonds almost always beat taxables for investors in the highest brackets. But muni yields have been so high at times that muni funds are attractive to investors in lower tax brackets too. To get the maximum return, investors need to compare muni and taxable funds, adjusting for the tax exemption. For instance, in December 1997, the Vanguard Fixed-Income Long-Term U.S. Treasury Fund was yielding 6.02 percent, while the Vanguard Municipal Bond Long-Term Fund was yielding 4.83 percent. What's the better buy? Suppose you're in the 31 percent marginal tax bracket. You merely subtract 31 percent of the yield from 6.02 percent and you get a 4.15 percent

TABLE 2-45

MUNICIPAL FUNDS

BEST RETURNS

Period ▼	Fund ▼	Total return* ▼
MUNICIPAL NATIONAL LONG		
1997	FUNDAMENTAL F/I HIGH-YIELD MUNI**	15.7%
1995-97	FUNDAMENTAL F/I HIGH-YIELD MUNI**	14.8
1993-97	SMITH BARNEY MANAGED MUNIS A	9.3
MUNICIPAL NATIONAL INTERMEDIATE		
1997	STRONG MUNICIPAL BOND	12.1%
1995-97	AMERICAN HIGH INCOME MUNI. B	11.8
1993-97	VAN KAMPEN AM. CAP. H/Y MUNI A	8.1
MUNICIPAL SINGLE-STATE LONG		
1997	SMITH BARNEY MUNI. GA A	12.7%
1995-97	SAFECO CA T/F INCOME NO LOAD	13.0
1993-97	EVERGREEN FL HIGH INCOME MUNI A	11.5
MUNICIPAL SINGLE-STATE INTERMEDIATE		
1997	LORD ABBETT TAX-FREE INCOME GA	10.4%
1995-97	LORD ABBETT TAX-FREE INCOME WA	10.8
1993-97	COLORADO BONDSHARES**	8.3
MUNICIPAL SHORT		
1997	SIT TAX-FREE INCOME	9.7%
1995-97	SIT TAX-FREE INCOME	9.4
1993-97	SIT TAX-FREE INCOME	7.5

*Average annual, pretax
**Fundamental, 800-322-6864; Colorado, 800-572-0069;
or see Business Week Online

DATA: MORNINGSTAR INC.

yield after taxes. Obviously, the muni fund offers a better yield.

There's another way to look at this. Start with the number 1 and subtract your marginal tax bracket from it: 1 minus 0.31 (31 percent is also expressed as 0.31) equals 0.69. Next, divide that number into the tax-exempt yield. Divide 4.92 percent by 0.69 and you get 7 percent. So, unless you can get a return of at least 7 percent in a taxable investment of like quality, the muni is the better deal.

Though muni bond income is free from federal taxes, states tax muni income from bonds issued in other states. Neither the New Yorker investing in a California bond nor the Californian with the New York bond will owe federal tax on the interest, but he or she will owe state income tax. In states with low income tax rates, that may not matter. But in high tax states like California and New York, the extra tax can cut into your returns.

So the mutual fund folks have come up with an antidote for that, too—single-state municipal bond funds. By restricting investment to the investor's home state, these funds generate income that's exempt not only from federal taxes but from state and city income taxes as well. For the tax-weary folks of New York City, a New York bond fund is said to be "triple-tax-exempt." The largest municipal fund of all, in fact, is the Franklin California Tax-Free Income Fund. It's also one of the oldest, dating back to 1977.

No longer do you have to live in a big, heavily populated state to have a single-state fund to call your own. Single-state funds abound in 42 states and Puerto Rico, though New Yorkers and Californians have the most funds to choose from (Table 2-46). If a state isn't represented, it may be because the tax laws are not amenable to it. If there's no state income or personal property assessment that taxes financial holdings, there's no need for a single-state muni fund—though Texas has 24 of them anyway. Illinois, for instance, does have a state income tax, but does not exempt interest earned from most Illinois municipal bonds. So there's no particular advantage for an Illinois taxpayer to invest in most Illinois bonds.

The big drawback of single-state funds is just that: All the bonds come from a single state and rise and fall on the financial condition of the state, its local governments, and bond-issuing authorities. In December 1994, the muni market in general and the California market in particular were rocked when Orange County disclosed it had

TABLE 2-46

STATES WITH SINGLE-STATE BOND FUNDS

State	Funds	State	Funds	State	Funds
ALABAMA	8	MARYLAND	44	OREGON	21
ARIZONA	40	MASSACHUSETTS	59	PENNSYLVANIA	71
ARKANSAS	9	MICHIGAN	59	PUERTO RICO	2
CALIFORNIA	152	MINNESOTA	49	RHODE ISLAND	3
COLORADO	26	MISSISSIPPI	4	SOUTH CAROLINA	20
CONNECTICUT	26	MISSOURI	20	SOUTH DAKOTA	1
FLORIDA	93	MONTANA	1	TENNESSEE	25
GEORGIA	35	NEBRASKA	2	TEXAS	24
HAWAII	10	NEW HAMPSHIRE	1	UTAH	5
IDAHO	6	NEW JERSEY	56	VERMONT	2
INDIANA	1	NEW MEXICO	11	VIRGINIA	42
IOWA	3	NEW YORK	121	WASHINGTON	6
KANSAS	9	NORTH CAROLINA	43	WEST VIRGINIA	10
KENTUCKY	15	NORTH DAKOTA	3	WISCONSIN	6
LOUISIANA	13	OHIO	57		

DATA: MORNINGSTAR INC.

what was eventually determined to be about $2 billion in losses in its investment portfolio, a fund (not a mutual fund) in which Orange County and many smaller jurisdictions had money that was needed to service their debt.

Within days, the county filed for bankruptcy, which put all debt service in doubt and sent bond prices into a skid. The NAV of the Franklin California Tax-Free Fund, the largest California muni fund, dropped 1.32 percent. Franklin California Insured Tax-Free Income Fund took the same percentage hit, even though bond insurers would step in to make up any payments Orange County borrowers missed. In contrast, the nationally diversified Franklin Federal Tax-Free Income Fund fell, too, but only 0.8 percent.

Insured funds are popular with New York investors as well, since the Empire State also seems to undergo a fiscal crisis every few years. Ironically, in New York as in many other states, high-quality bonds of well-known issuers aren't always a safe harbor. When the muni market gets the shakes, the first bonds to get dumped are those of the highest quality. They're the most liquid. Provided they don't default, the lesser credits and lesser-known names seem to hold up relatively well. They don't go on the auction block. Many muni funds that have "high-yield" in their names achieve that objective just by seeking out the higher interest rates of the little-known issuers.

If you've decided to invest in tax-exempt funds, you still have to make the same kinds of decisions you make with taxable funds. Do you want a fund with short-, intermediate-, or long-term bonds? Is there a single-state fund for your home state, and is the yield competitive? The muni fund classifications are organized along maturity and geographic lines. They are municipal national long-term, municipal national intermediate-term, municipal single-state long-term, municipal single-state intermediate-term, and municipal short-term, which takes in both national and single-state funds. Funds that invest in insured bonds usually say so in their names. Those that invest in junk-rated or unrated municipal bonds generally use "high-yield" in their names.

The menu of muni offerings is broad, so a good fund can make use of it to diversify a portfolio, both geographically and by the type of project the bonds finance. General obligation (GO) bonds—those backed by the credit and taxing power of the issuer—are only a small part of the muni bond line-up. Far more numerous are revenue bonds, which are paid off by rentals, fees, tolls, and the like from roads, bridges, tunnels, arenas, ballparks, water works, sewage treatment plants, power plants, parking structures, housing, and hospitals.

Revenue bonds are riskier than GOs—after all, the project's revenue can easily fall short of projections. That's a risk with nonessential public projects like arenas and stadiums. Suppose a project runs far over budget or is never completed? That's what happened with the Washington Public Power Supply System in the early 1980s, which failed to complete or build several nuclear power plants that it financed with revenue bonds.

If your fund manager has done some savvy bond trading and racked up some capital gains, the fund will have to make a capital gains distribution too. Sorry, capital gains from tax-free bonds are taxable. But such distributions are infrequent. Still, investors who don't want capital gains should stick to yield-oriented funds that emphasize bonds selling at a premium, or above par. Such funds don't climb as much in a falling rate environment, nor do they melt as quickly if interest rates climb.

Like their taxable counterparts, muni funds are creatures of interest rates. But munis don't move in lock-step with Treasuries either. At times they can be more volatile. In the spring of 1987, when interest rates rose swiftly in the government bond market, investors swamped the muni fund managers with demands for redemptions. With insufficient cash on hand to meet them, muni funds had to sell bonds into a falling market in order to meet redemptions. Since the municipal bond market is far less liquid than the Treasury bond market, even big institutional investors must take huge discounts in price in order to sell bonds quickly. Between mid-March and mid-April 1987, the T. Rowe Price Tax-Free Fund lost 9.22 percent of its net asset value.

On the other hand, sometimes the muni market will outperform taxables. In 1988, for instance, government bonds finished the year about where they started. The muni bonds, in contrast, gained about 6 points, or $60 per $1000 bond. Why? A shortage in supply combined with a pickup in demand from shell-shocked equity investors. Supply and demand of muni bonds does have an effect on prices and, in turn, on yields. In 1992 and 1993, muni funds outdistanced the taxables, even though the muni market was flooded with record new issuance. That's because demand was so strong. In 1994, the supply of new bonds dropped to nearly half. But with rising interest rates and tax-law changes affecting the treatment of market discount bonds, demand—thus prices—dropped even more. As a result, on a total return basis, muni funds did far worse than taxables.

Money-Market Funds

Money-market mutual funds are a breed apart from stock and bond funds. Their principal difference is that they keep their share prices at a constant $1 per share. They're able to do this because they invest in very short-term debt instruments. Usually, price fluctuations in those investments are so small that funds can maintain their constant dollar price. Thus, a money-market mutual fund account will look a lot like a bank account.

As with bond funds, there are taxable and tax-free money-market funds. The taxable funds come in several categories, depending on the kind of investments they make (Table 2-47). U.S. Treasury-only funds invest in just Treasury securities. They have the lowest yield but are considered the safest. Then comes those that invest in Treasuries and repurchase agreements, a sort of loan that's backed by Treasuries. The next category invests in U.S. Government agency securities, such as those issued by Fannie Mae and Freddie Mac. The general purpose funds may invest in all of the above, but also seek higher

Muni funds may generate taxable gain.

yields from bank-issued instruments and short-term corporate debt. Tax-exempt funds invest in the short-term instruments issued by state and local governments.

TAXABLE FUNDS

In 1981, when short-term interest rates were in the high teens, money-market funds looked like the dream investment. Interest rates on bank deposits were regulated, and passbook accounts—the province of the small investor—paid about 5.5 percent. The average money-market fund paid nearly 17 percent! That's when Americans who never heard of mutual funds got their introduction to them. And it was because of the high yields of the money funds. During the 1980s and into the 1990s, as interest rates headed south, so did the returns from money-market funds (Figure 2-2). And as returns continued to drop, so did investor interest and media attention.

Well, money-market funds are back on investors' radar screens. True, the dramatic rise in short-term interest rates and the consequent volatility in bond funds made money funds look a lot more attractive in 1994 than they had looked in years. But what drew the public attention to money funds again were shocking revelations that some 15 sponsors of 35 money-market funds put up $769 million to avoid "breaking the buck," that is, having to reprice the money-fund shares (kept constant at $1 NAV) because of investments gone bad. Among those bailing out their own funds were Bank of America, Kidder Peabody, United Services, and Value Line. No one came to the rescue of the tiny Community Bankers U.S. Government Money Market Fund, and the fund broke the buck and liquidated for 94 cents on the dollar.

Tax-exempt money-market funds hit the news, too, after Orange County, California, declared bankruptcy. *Money Market Insight*, an industry publication, estimated that sponsors of at least "25 major funds" sought regulators' permission to buy Orange County securities from their funds, lest the securities stop making interest payments. Some sponsors like Franklin and Putnam bought the securities from the funds, while Alliance Capital backed them up with a letter of credit (which would pay off if the securities didn't). Benham and Calvert funds also provided guarantees. In all cases, the fund managers were trying to avoid breaking the buck.

Breaking the buck is the money-fund managers' and the regulators' worst nightmare. In-

TABLE 2-47

MONEY-MARKET MUTUAL FUNDS: THEY'RE NOT ALL THE SAME

Money-Market Fund	Comments	Yield*
100% U.S. TREASURY	Highest safety, but lowest yields. Interest is subject to federal tax, but is exempt from state and local income taxes in most states.	4.79 %
U.S. TREASURY AND REPO'S	Invests in repurchase agreements, in which a bond dealer sells securities, agreeing to buy them back on a certain date at a higher price. Difference between two prices is the interest.	4.90
U.S. GOVERNMENT & AGENCIES	May also invest in securities issued by U.S.-backed agencies such as Federal National Mortgage Assn. Agency paper is highly-rated and has nearly the same as credit quality as U.S. Treasuries.	4.95
GENERAL PURPOSE	Can also buy high-quality commercial paper of corporations and non-insured bank-related investments, which adds some credit risk. A few "second tier" funds purchase lower-quality paper for a higher yield (5.07%).	5.03
TAX-FREE	Invests in short-term municipal securities, such as tax anticipation notes. Exempt from federal taxes, but not state and local taxes. State-specific funds avoids taxes for taxpayers of those states (3.04%).	3.10

DATA: IBC MONEY FUND REPORT, BUSINESS WEEK   *1997

vestors recognize that stock and bond funds can fluctuate in NAV, but money funds are not supposed to do so. Usually, the funds invest in instruments that are so short in maturity that the portfolio fluctuations are minute, and thus, the fund can maintain its net asset value at $1 per share. The small profits and losses in the portfolio can be accounted for by varying the payout. If there's a small capital gain, the fund can just pass it along as a little extra yield. By the same token, small losses in principal can be absorbed by the income stream, resulting in a slightly lowered payout. Many funds use an accounting method that allows them to carry the securities on their books at cost. Under those rules, assets don't fluctuate in value at all.

What went wrong in 1994 was that some funds had invested in derivatives such as inverse floaters or "structured notes" which were engineered to pay higher yields in a falling interest-rate environment. When interest rates spiked, these derivatives plunged in price and could no longer be valued at 100 cents on the dollar. These derivatives worked fine for the funds as interest rates fell, since they allowed the funds to pay higher yields than they otherwise would. But

FIGURE 2-2

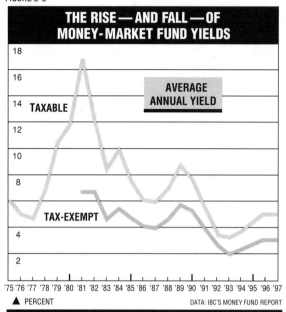

THE RISE — AND FALL — OF MONEY-MARKET FUND YIELDS

AVERAGE ANNUAL YIELD

TAXABLE

TAX-EXEMPT

▲ PERCENT   DATA: IBC'S MONEY FUND REPORT

money funds, a money-market fund statement ends up looking a lot like that of a bank account. If you have 15,271 shares, you also have $15,271. Interest earned each day is usually credited daily. The payments are technically "dividends," but they are the functional equivalent of interest. And since the funds behave an awful lot like bank accounts, it's not surprising that many people use them in just that way. There's one big difference, though, and that's the reason for the emphasis on safety—money-market mutual funds are not government-insured.

In general, money-market fund yields have been higher—on average about 1 percentage point more—than bank money-market deposit accounts. As short-term rates shot up in 1994, the yield advantage over bank money-market deposit accounts increased to the point where money funds were paying more than double bank money-market account rates and even more than six-month certificates of deposit. That's because money-market funds pass along to their investors all they earn—less expenses, of course. A bank money-market deposit account is an administered rate. The bank decides what it will pay on deposits. Though they are somewhat linked to the general level and direction of interest rates, banks tend to pay only what they must to maintain the deposits. That is, if they even want or need to maintain them. If loan demand is weak, as it was for most of 1991 and 1992, banks can always lower their interest rates enough to encourage depositors to take their money elsewhere.

Most money-market funds offer some kind of checking privileges too. However, since they usually require a minimum check amount of several hundred dollars, you'll need a conventional checking account as well. If you want check-writing privileges, be sure to read the portion in the prospectus that describes the program. Not only can there be restrictions on the minimum amount of the check, but also on the number of checks written each month.

But as an investor, you're probably not very concerned with check-writing—though it's handy to have, even if you don't make much use of it. To make your life easier, you'll probably want to have money-market fund accounts with fund groups in which you have other mutual funds.

So, if you have several Franklin, Putnam, or Scudder funds, you might find it convenient to keep a money-market fund there. Suppose you wanted to invest $10,000 in an equity fund, but spread it over a year's time. You might start with

when rates started climbing, these derivatives' yields fell and the funds could not sell the derivatives without taking a large loss that would break the buck. The SEC later issued rules about what money funds could not invest in, which included the same sort of securities that had caused the problems.

It was not the first time that investments gone sour threatened to break the buck. That happened when a few funds, in stretching for yield, bought "junk" commercial paper that went into default. In both cases, the two sponsors, T. Rowe Price Associates and Value Line, Inc., bought the commercial paper from the funds at the funds' cost, and the parent company, not the money fund, took the loss. In response, the SEC tightened regulations on credit quality of fund investments. Still, credit problems do pop up. In early 1997, Mercury Finance Co., which makes used car loans, had serious financial problems that had not been properly disclosed. One rating agency had rated Mercury's commercial paper (very short-term notes) investment-grade, while nearly all others considered it in the second tier. While many money-market funds won't invest in such "split-rated" securities, Strong Heritage Money Market Fund did. When the depths of Mercury's problems came out, Strong Capital Management stepped in and bought the commercial paper from the fund. Had it not done so, the fund would have "broken the buck."

Since the mutual fund industry and the SEC have long adopted the $1 per share practice for

$1000 in the equity fund and put the balance in one of the money-market funds. If you set it up with telephone switching privileges, you can gradually shift from the money fund into the stock fund with a series of phone calls.

In the same way, the money-market fund is a good parking place for your money. If you're switching out of a stock or bond fund, you can park the cash in the fund group's money fund while you're deciding what to do next with your money. If you like the fund's yield better than the prospects for stock or bond funds, you may decide to let the money sit. With a money-market fund, your assets are not idle. They earn interest every day.

Since there's a great deal of similarity in investment policy and services, investors who spend considerable time shopping for stock or bond funds pay little attention to their money-market funds. Though there are differences in the quality of the money-market instruments in which money funds invest, by and large those differences are not great. If you're otherwise weighing the risks of a growth fund versus a balanced fund, the difference between money funds is trivial.

If you look at money-market-fund yields that are published in the newspaper financial sections every week, it looks like there can be as much as two percentage points of difference in yields. But that can be deceptive. In the very short term, yields are volatile and any week's yield will depend on the various maturities of the fund.

The shorter the maturity, the faster the yield will respond to changes in interest rates. Suppose one fund has an average maturity of 30 days and another has 15 days. If interest rates rise in the next two weeks, the yield on the 15-day fund is going to go up faster. That's because the fund has more investments maturing sooner and will be able to roll them over at higher interest rates. But if interest rates fall during the period, the longer maturity fund fares better, because it will hold onto its higher-yielding investments much longer.

As a result of the fluctuations in rates and portfolio maturities, week to week the differentials look big. But over a year's time those differences smooth out. In fact, *Income & Safety*, a newsletter that tracks money-market funds, says that the difference between the highest- and lowest-yielding fund in any year is about 0.9 percentage point. That means that, if you had a $10,000 average balance, and you had the worst-yielding fund, you would receive only $90 less income than from the very highest-yielding fund. Of course, the larger the average balance in your money-market fund, the more you want to focus on the yield. That 0.9 percentage point spread on a $100,000 account is $900—and that's not insignificant.

Still, the search for yield has its limitations. Returns are far more homogeneous in money-market funds than in stock or bond funds. That's because money-market funds must live within fairly narrow strictures set down by industry practice and the Securities & Exchange Commission. Funds mainly invest in U.S. Treasury bills, repurchase agreements, certificates of deposit, bankers acceptances, and commercial paper. But it's also obvious from the events of the last year that perhaps not all funds—at least not the ones that got into trouble—were investing solely in these tried-and-true instruments. Following is a brief description of each.

U.S. Treasury bills. These are short-term obligations of the U.S. government, which come in three-month, six-month, and one-year maturities. Individual investors can buy these on their own, but there's a $10,000 minimum. Other U.S. government agencies also raise short-term funds in the money-markets from time to time. Their securities are also permissible in many funds. Those include the Farm Credit Bank, Fannie Mae, Freddie Mac, and the Student Loan Marketing Association.

Repurchase agreements. "Repo's," as they're commonly known, are short-term borrowings using U.S. government securities as collateral. They work like this. A bank or securities dealer has an inventory of Treasury bonds it needs to finance for, say, 20 days. Sometimes the term of the loan is merely overnight. The dealer borrows from a money-market fund and gives the fund securities as collateral for the loan. The arrangement is called a repurchase agreement because the borrower agrees to "repurchase" the collateral by paying back the loan. The credit on the line is the bank's or dealer's, but as long as the fund can claim the securities in case of default, the credit quality is considered high.

Bank certificates of deposit. Most people are familiar with CDs, but the funds invest in "jumbos"—CDs over $100,000 that are not insured by the FDIC. The creditworthiness of the bank is the only thing that backs them up. Sometimes money-market funds invest in Eurodollar CDs,

Money funds have strict investment guidelines.

which are dollar-based CDs issued by European, usually London, branches of U.S. banks. The interest rates are usually a little higher than those of domestic CDs. Yankee CDs are issued in the United States by branches of foreign banks.

Banker's acceptances. These instruments are irrevocable obligations of the banks that issue them, so their quality is similar to that of a bank's certificate of deposit. Acceptances are created as a financing tool for international trade, but holders of the acceptances can raise cash immediately by selling them into the money market. Money-market funds often buy them.

Commercial paper. As a less costly alternative to bank borrowings, many large corporations raise funds through commercial paper, or short-term IOUs. There is no collateral behind commercial paper. The only backing is the creditworthiness of the issuer.

If you look behind the yields available on these sorts of instruments, you can see why all money-fund yields lie within a tight range. In early 1998, for instance, three-month T-bills yielded 5.07 percent; high-grade commercial paper, 5.44 percent; and CDs, about 5.23 percent. In that interest rate environment, the average taxable money fund yielded 5.05 percent. There's no way a money fund could earn even 7 percent, especially since money funds have management fees and other expenses as well.

With yields in a narrow range, there's little value a portfolio manager can add by actively trading assets. So the major determinant in performance is overhead. All money funds are sold without sales fees, but in choosing a fund be sure there are no hidden sales fees, known in the mutual fund trade as "12(b)-1" fees, coming out of the portfolio. In selecting a fund also be sure to choose one where the total expenses—management fees and other costs such as printing, mailing, and auditing—come to less than 0.50 percent. That's important because what you earn from the fund is the gross yield less expenses. And when yields are low, expenses play an even greater role. Remember, 0.50 percent on a 5 percent yield is 10 percent of the income. Sometimes fund companies waive all or part of their fund expenses in order to boost the yield. And then they advertise that higher yield as a draw for the fund. If someone's willing to subsidize your investments, why not? Just be sure to ask how long the waiver is expected to continue. Most funds will guarantee a

fee waiver through a certain date, but they often extend them. And even when fund sponsors start to implement the fees, they usually don't take them all at once but phase them in over time. Flex-Fund Money Market Fund, part of the Flex Funds Group, takes yet another approach. The fund's goal is to deliver a yield that's in the top 10 percent of all money-market funds, and the fund sponsor will waive all or part of the expenses to assure the fund's place at the top.

All this begs the question, "Should you invest in a money-market fund based on yield and expenses?" Historically, this has been the best way to go, though in the last few years credit and maturity risks have emerged as major concerns as well.

To ward off potential problems in the money funds, the Securities & Exchange Commission has pulled in its reins in recent years. First of all, the regulators lowered the ceiling on the maximum average maturity of a money-market fund portfolio to 90 days from 120 days. In general, the shorter the maturity of a security or a portfolio, the lower the risk of owning it.

Then, the SEC also came down hard on credit quality. Funds can no longer invest in below-investment-grade commercial paper. And no more than 5 percent of the fund can be invested in the lower tier of investment-grade paper, that which is rated A-2 by Standard & Poor's and P-2 by Moody's.

Finally, in the wake of the 1994 derivatives crises, the SEC banned several sorts of derivatives from money-market funds, mainly because their values can change drastically given a change in interest rates. Those off limits to money funds are inverse floaters, leveraged floaters, CMT (Constant Maturity Treasury) floaters, floaters whose interest rates are capped, and floaters whose resets lag changes in short-term interest rates. All of these instruments gained popularity as interest rates came down. That's because with these instruments, payouts actually increased or decreased at a slower rate. Of course, when interest rates started moving up, these floaters' payouts shrank—and so did their values.

With the banning of the most dangerous derivatives, the most cautious investors can probably sleep comfortably using a U.S. government money-market fund. The securities are free of credit risk but have lower yields than the general purpose funds. Still, in times of economic uncertainty, many fund analysts say going for the governments is advisable, even if you have to settle for a lesser return.

High costs can decimate money fund returns.

It's not even a certainty that one has to give up any yield. By careful fund shopping it's possible to find some government funds with better yields than those which also include bank CDs and commercial paper. Moreover, even if you switch from a general purpose to a government money-market fund in the same fund family, the difference in yields may not be more than 0.30 or 0.40 percentage point. That's a small price to pay if you're worried about credit quality.

U.S. government funds have another virtue that's sometimes overlooked. Just as the federal government doesn't tax interest earned by investing in state and local government debt, most state and local governments don't tax interest earned on federal government debt. If you are in a high-tax state like New York or California, that exemption can effectively add as much as 1 percentage point to the yield.

Not all government funds qualify for this tax treatment. Interest from repurchase agreements doesn't count because the income is coming not from the government securities but from the borrower who is posting the securities as collateral for a loan. If this is the case, you might consider a money-market fund that holds only U.S. Treasury securities.

TAX-EXEMPT FUNDS

Tax-exempt money-market funds have many of the same characteristics and features as taxable money funds: short-maturity securities, liquidity, and check-writing privileges. But what makes these different—and so alluring to many investors—is that the income is out of the Internal Revenue Service's reach.

These funds escape taxes by investing in a variety of short-term instruments that are issued by state, county, and municipal governments and public authorities. For instance, most communities collect taxes several times a year, but their need for cash doesn't totally conform to that tax collection schedule. So they may issue tax anticipation notes, which are short-term borrowings meant to carry the municipality or agency over until the tax receipts roll in. In a like fashion, there are bond anticipation notes—issued as temporary financing until long-term bonds can be sold—and revenue anticipation notes, which may keep a government unit in operation until other revenue such as a federal grant is collected.

The tax-free money funds also rely heavily on "put bonds" and variable-rate demand notes. In either security the interest rate is reset frequently, sometimes in as short a period as seven days. If the fund manager doesn't like the new interest rate, he or she can always give them back or "put" the bonds back to the issuer for redemption.

Such bonds are rarely put back. The rates are set so that they are competitive with the current rates in the tax-exempt market. Such bonds, which are often backed with a bank letter of credit to assure investors the money will be there to redeem them, almost always trade at par. That makes them especially good investments for money-market type funds that strive to hold their net asset values constant at $1. In fact, investment bankers devised these floating-rate securities largely to meet the needs of tax-exempt money-market funds.

When looking at tax-free funds, remember that the income is not necessarily out of the reach of state and local tax officials. States usually exempt income from municipal securities issued in their state, but don't give a hoot about those issued by others. So a general purpose tax-exempt money-market fund may not be totally tax-free. The only part of the income that your state income tax authorities will waive is that which is from your own state. If you're a Michigan resident and 5 percent of the income generated by your tax-free fund came from Michigan securities, the Michigan tax folks will still take a bite of the other 95 percent of your supposed tax-free income.

For many people, that may not be much of a bother. If the local tax is minimal, the tax-free fund may still be a great deal. But if you live in California, Connecticut, Massachusetts, Michigan, Missouri, New Jersey, New York, Ohio, or Pennsylvania, you can find tax-free money-market funds that invest in short-term securities of governments and public authorities in those states. All the income passes to the shareholders untaxed by any governmental authority.

In the early 1990s, rates on conventional money funds had dropped so low that they were almost the same as tax-free funds. But in 1997, that was not the case. The average taxable money fund yield was 5.10 percent; for tax-free funds the figure was 3.14 percent. For all but the investors in the very highest tax bracket, the aftertax return on the taxable fund was higher than the tax-exempt returns. But this is not always true. Investors need to regularly monitor the two rates. In general, the closer they are to one another the more attractive the tax-free fund becomes.

> Single-state funds offer high aftertax yields.

The most important consideration when looking at tax-free money funds is your overall tax bracket. The bigger the bite from the federal, state, and local taxing authorities, the better a tax-free fund is going to feel. A New York City resident paying the top marginal tax rate is going to find the yield on a "triple-tax-exempt" money-market fund (the "triple" comes from the fact that it's free from federal, state, and city income taxes) attractive. In early 1997, some New York tax-exempt money funds were as high as 3.43 percent. That's the equivalent of 6.35 percent for a New York City resident in the highest federal, state, and city income tax brackets.

Single-state tax-free funds suffer some drawbacks, mainly lack of diversification. If the state you live in is undergoing fiscal woes, that will reflect back in the marketplace for all municipal securities issued in that state. Remember the Orange County bankruptcy and the effect on California muni bond funds? Though the NAVs did not fluctuate, many California tax-exempt money funds also had Orange County securities. Franklin Resources, for instance, the parent company of Franklin Funds, didn't wait for bad news. It bought $7.1 million in unsecured Orange County debt from two of its California tax-free money-market funds, just in case the securities failed to pay off.

Another problem with single-state funds is a potential shortage of investments. What if money pours in faster than the portfolio managers can find creditworthy investments? Fund managers sometimes have to venture over the border to other states to fill up their funds with quality investments. That means a small portion of the funds' earnings will wind up subject to state income tax.

Closed-End Funds

One of the hottest stocks on the New York Stock Exchange a few years back was not even an operating company. The stock was the Turkish Investment Fund, which shot up 171.3 percent in 1993. The Turkish Investment Fund is one of several hundred closed-end funds. These funds, whose format actually predates mutual funds by more than 100 years, are similar to mutual funds in that they are professionally man-

TABLE 2-48

CLOSED-END EQUITY FUNDS		
BEST RETURNS		
Period	Fund	Total return*
1997	TURKISH INVESTMENT	65.8%
1995-97	EUROPEAN WARRANT	46.4
1993-97	FIRST FINANCIAL	37.2
1988-97	FIRST FINANCIAL	29.5

*Average annual net asset value, pretax   DATA: MORNINGSTAR INC.

aged portfolios of securities and are regulated by the same laws.

Many mutual fund management companies run closed-end funds too, and for many of those funds the portfolios look a lot like their mutual fund counterparts. The returns from the best closed-end funds are much like the returns from regular mutual funds (Tables 2-48 and 2-49).

Long overshadowed by mutual funds, closed-end funds had a resurgence over the last 10 years. After the 1987 stock market crash, stockbrokers could not interest their clients in anything much except closed-end bond funds. In 1988, for instance, more than $21 billion went into those funds. And in 1989, as investors became caught up in the sweeping changes in Europe and Asia, they scrambled to buy closed-end equity funds, like the Spain Fund, that were dedicated to investing in single foreign markets. In fact, in 1989 closed-end "single country" funds were 3 of the top 10 performers on the New York Stock Exchange. (The Asia Pacific Fund was No. 4; the Thai Fund, No. 5; the Germany Fund, No. 10.) In 1993, about $17.3 billion was raised for 123 closed-end funds: $15.3 billion for 99 bond funds and $2 billion for 24 equity funds.

In the last few years, however, closed-end funds have all been ignored by investors. Unlike regular mutual funds, mutual fund managers don't usually spend money to promote them. With investors going wild for regular funds, the closed-end funds get no attention. Brokers tend only to recommend them to customers when they're new and pay a higher commission. Once established, the commission drops, so the brokers turn their attention elsewhere. Even when performance is relatively good, these funds are often starved for investor attention.

The big difference between closed-end funds and mutual funds lies in how investors get their money into and out of them. Mutual funds are "open-ended." When investors want to buy into a fund, the fund management company issues new shares at the fund's net asset value plus a sales charge if the fund is a "load" fund. So if the net asset value is $10 a share, and you invest $10,000, the fund management company will credit you with 1000 shares. When you want to sell your 1000 shares, the fund management buys them back from you at the prevailing net asset value.

Closed-end funds raise capital differently. Suppose a fund management company wants to start a new venture, the Closed-End Fund. The management company hires an investment bank, which organizes the underwriting and finds buyers for the soon-to-be-issued shares. The investment bank gets commitments from investors for $100 million. So the fund goes public, selling new shares at $10 each (that's the typical starting price), and the fund issues 10 million shares— and that's all. If someone wants to buy or sell shares in the Closed-End Fund after the initial underwriting is completed, he or she has to do it as with any stock: on the stock exchange where it trades.

Is that a big deal? It can be. Suppose the Closed-End Fund portfolio managers are very savvy and the net asset value of the fund goes to $15. An investor decides to take profits and asks her broker to sell the shares. But the broker reports back that he can only get 13½, or $13.50 a share.

True, the portfolio's worth $15, and $13.50 is 10 percent less than what the stock is worth. But the fund company isn't going to redeem the shares, and the only way to liquidate them is to find a buyer. And there's no law that a seller has to receive NAV. The seller can get only what a buyer will pay.

That's not an unusual case. Closed-end equity funds typically sell at a discount to their underlying net asset value, a discount that in the past has been as large as 40 percent. With closed-end bond funds, the discounts are smaller, but they can still move into the double digits. Right after their initial offerings, closed-end funds tend to trade at modest premiums to their net asset values. But often within four to six months they're trading at discounts to their NAVs. That's why most investment managers counsel investors never to buy initial offerings of closed-end funds.

A close look at the mechanics of the closed-end fund shows why they tend to trade at discounts to their NAVs. Go back to the initial public offering. Suppose Closed-End Fund goes public at $10 a share. Out of each $10, about 75 cents goes for

TABLE 2-49

CLOSED-END BOND FUNDS		
BEST RETURNS		
Period ▼	**Fund** ▼	**Total return*** ▼
1997	ELLSWORTH CONVERT. GROWTH & INCOME	24.3%
1995-97	SCUDDER GLOBAL HIGH INCOME	24.9
1993-97	EMERGING MARKETS INCOME	24.3
1988-97	LINCOLN NATIONAL CONVERTIBLES	16.6

*Average annual net asset value, pretax   DATA: MORNINGSTAR INC.

underwriting fees and other selling expenses, leaving only $9.25 of the net asset value. Or, turn it around this way: At $10 a share, the fund is selling at an 8 percent premium to its net asset value. That makes it an overpriced stock from the start. Fees and expenses for bond funds usually eat up about 4 to 5 percent of the initial offering price.

There are two ways for the fund's share price to go up. The obvious way, of course, is through superior management. A winning portfolio will boost the net asset value, and that will more or less carry the fund shares upward (though not necessarily dollar for dollar). The other way is for investors who missed the initial offering to bid up the shares on the market.

But there won't be that many investors to bid up the shares. With most closed-end funds, the size of the offering is a function of how much the brokers can sell. Sure, the underwriters might plan a $100 million offering, but if the sales force brings in $300 million in orders, they'll boost the issue to $300 million. That means nearly all the initial demand for a closed-end fund is met on the offering. After the fact, there are few investors who want to buy shares who haven't already done so.

Then, for a few months, the investment bank that underwrote the fund usually buys shares to keep the price up. But sooner or later, the investment bank goes on to underwrite Closed-End Fund II. The brokers start calling clients to talk up the new fund, not to solicit orders for the Closed-End Fund. They can earn a much larger commission on a new fund than they can earn from taking an order for the existing one.

Meanwhile, some of the original investors in the Closed-End Fund start to sell, and there aren't many buyers for the shares. Prices begin to fall and eventually slip below net asset value. Studies show that after four months the average discount for a domestic equity fund is 10.3 percent, and for a single-country equity fund, 11.4

percent. Bond funds seem to hold up better. They trade at an average discount of only 0.12 percent.

Fund managers don't spend money to promote existing closed-end funds as they do with the open-end mutual funds. If they advertise an open-end fund, the new dollars brought into the portfolio will generate additional management fees. Since closed-end funds can't add new dollars to their portfolios, managers have no incentive to advertise.

Closed-end funds can raise additional capital through "rights" offerings, and many did in 1993. In such offerings, existing shareholders are issued rights to buy new shares at a set price, usually a small discount to net asset value. If shareholders choose not to buy, they can sell the rights to other investors who may want them.

Many fund analysts and investors have been critical of rights offerings for several reasons. First, fund managers usually launch the rights offerings at the wrong time. The closed-end bond funds that did so well in 1993 used the proceeds to buy bonds while interest rates were nearing a low point—thus making bonds "expensive." By adding a lot of newly purchased lower-yielding bonds to a portfolio with a lot of higher-yielding bonds, rights offerings dilute the funds' earnings and thus work to the disadvantage of the shareholder. The best time to be loading up on bonds is when yields are high, not low. But you rarely see rights offerings in the throes of a bear market, such as the one bond funds were in in 1994.

But shareholders are not the primary concern in a rights offering. The principal beneficiaries of these deals are the investment bankers, who underwrite them, and fund management companies, whose income is based on assets under management. The more money they can lure into the fund, the more money they will make. The other complaint is that the rights offerings are often "coercive." That means that if investors want to maintain their same proportion of ownership in the fund and their share of the income, they have no choice but to invest.

Investor-friendly fund managers are those that take steps to bolster fund share prices if they drop to a large discount to their net asset value. Some funds now have provisions that allow them to buy back their own shares on the market if the discount widens to 10 percent or more. And often the ploy works. For instance, the Franklin Multi-Income Trust, which invests mainly in junk bonds and utility stocks and uses borrowed money to do it, was trading at a 31 percent discount to its NAV near the end of the third quarter of 1990. Then Franklin Resources, the fund's adviser, announced a share buyback. Two weeks later, the shares traded at a slight premium.

And, should the discounts prevail for too long, many funds have new provisions that allow the shareholders to vote to convert to an open-end fund. Once that happens, the discount disappears because investors can then take their money out at net asset value. Just look at the T. Rowe Price New Age Media Fund. The fund sold at around a 20 percent discount to net asset value for over two years. Some investors lobbied to convert the fund into a mutual fund. In February 1997, the directors agreed to do it. The stock price jumped immediately, narrowing an 18 percent discount to 5 percent.

At times, some closed-end funds have traded at enormous premiums, too. Stockbrokers will remind you of that if you rebut their closed-end fund sales pitch. After all, remember the Spain Fund, which at one point in time traded at a premium of 144.5 percent of net asset value. What this means is that investors were willing to pay more than $24 a share for every $10 in assets. Such misvaluations don't last for long. Less than a year later, Spain Fund was trading at a discount of 10 percent to net asset value.

Shares of some single-country funds used to command premiums in the marketplace because they had a "franchise" that couldn't be duplicated. Sometimes closed-end funds trade at a premium because the underwriters could not satisfy all the demand for an issue. But most franchises have disappeared as competitive funds start up and many emerging markets open their doors to foreign investors.

Watch out when buying closed-end funds during "crisis" situations. Suppose you thought the collapse of stock prices in Southeast Asia was way overdone, and you wanted to do some smart contrarian investing. Naturally, a closed-end Asian equity fund selling at a 10 percent discount to NAV might seem better than a similar open-end fund selling at NAV. But individuals, not institutions, dominate the trading in closed-end funds, and they are slow to react. The market price of the country fund shares will sell off, but often they decline at a much slower pace than the underlying portfolios. That might cushion the losses for the investors already in the fund, but the net result is that these funds end up trading at a large premium to their NAVs. Months after Thailand's stock market and currency plunged, the two closed-end Thai funds were selling at premiums of nearly 50 percent. And in early 1998, the closed-end Indonesia funds traded at prices that were more than twice the value of their rapidly depreciating portfolio. So the best bet is to wait until the market stabilizes, or just stops falling, and let the discount settle down.

For all the caveats about closed-end funds, they can be smart buys, especially when you might otherwise invest in the open-end fund with a similar investment style (sometimes even the same fund manager). As portfolios, view them much like conventional funds and judge their investment savvy by the same criteria.

Like the open-end mutual funds, the closed-end funds break down into the same categories as do equity and bond funds. That allows investors to make better comparisons to see if some closed-end fund might better fulfill a role in a portfolio than an equivalent mutual fund.

Since there are so many open-end analogs of closed-end funds, why bother with the closed-ends? If the closed-end is selling at a large discount to the open-ends, it may offer a better opportunity. Suppose you're interested in a growth fund in health-care so you zero in on H&Q Health Care Investors. The portfolio looks good, as does the track record. In addition, the shares sell, for argument's sake, at a discount of 17 percent from net asset value.

To know if a closed-end fund's discount makes it a buy, the discount has to be compared to its historic range. A 17 percent discount may look good, but perhaps the shares have sold at a 35 percent discount as well. As it turns out, H&Q Health Care Investors traded in a range between net asset value and a 19 percent discount to NAV. That fact says the fund is trading relatively cheaply, and it may be a good time to buy.

In fact, an investor who is bullish on health-care stocks may do much better in the specialized closed-end fund than in an open-end portfolio. The closed-end fund gives you more upside potential. And here's how. Suppose you buy H&Q, with an NAV of $12, for $10 a share. (In that case, the fund is selling at nearly a 17 percent discount.) Then the stock market starts to rally, health-care stocks do well, and the health-care portfolio climbs 20 percent. So now the net asset value of the fund is $14.40 ($12 plus 20 percent). If the fund still had a 17 percent discount, H&Q Health Care Investors would trade at $12.45. But if health-care stocks were especially strong, investors would become more willing to bid up for the closed-end fund and the discount on the fund would narrow and perhaps disappear. Suppose that at the end of a year, the discount on

H&Q narrows to 5 percent. There's already an appreciation of 20 percent in the portfolio, which brings the NAV to $14.45. Discount that by 5 percent, and the selling price is $13.68. (Since shares trade in eighths of a dollar, round that out to $13.63, or 13⅝.) The original investment was $10 a share and selling at $13.63 represents a 36 percent return (before commissions). An open-end health-care fund might have had only a 20 percent gain. In a bull market the narrowing of a discount on a closed-end fund can give an investor an extra edge.

Of course, if the market turns down, that premium/discount works just the other way. What if the portfolio lost 20 percent of its value and the discount widened to 25 percent? The $12 NAV would then be worth only $9.60—and a 25 percent discount from that is $7.20. The portfolio declined 20 percent, but because of the widening discount the fund price is off 28 percent. In a bear market investors in closed-end funds may be hit harder than regular mutual fund investors.

So much for funds bought at discounts. Let's look at what happens when funds are purchased at a premium. Suppose you buy a fund on the initial offering for $10 a share. After underwriting fees and such, only $9.25 is left for NAV. So, in effect, you pay an 8 percent premium. Let's say the portfolio managers do a good job and the portfolio climbs 20 percent to $11.10. But instead of a premium the fund now sells at a 2 percent discount. If you sell, all you can get is $10.87. So the portfolio went up 20 percent, but the investor could realize less than 9 percent. You're taking an extra risk if you buy closed-end funds selling at a premium to net asset value.

All told, because of differences between share price and NAV in closed-end funds, many fund investors may choose to avoid them altogether and stick with the more familiar and somewhat simpler open-end variety. But there are times when closed-end funds can be the better buy. Mario Gabelli, Charles Royce, and Martin Zweig are just a few investment managers who run both closed- and open-end funds. If you would consider investing in one of their open-end funds, perhaps you should consider a closed-end fund that's selling at a discount.

Look, for instance, at the open-end Royce Value Fund and the closed-end Royce Value Trust. The two have the same portfolio managers and many of the same stocks since they both specialize in value investing in small-to-medium-sized companies. The difference is that the closed-end fund usually sells at a discount. That

> Avoid buying closed-end funds at a premium.

means that with the closed-end fund you get $1 worth of stock for perhaps 90 or 95 cents. With the open-end fund you get $1 worth of stocks for $1.

If you own closed-end funds, you should also keep your eye on any open-end clones. Sometimes there's money to be made by trading a closed-end fund at a premium for a similar mutual fund. Templeton Emerging Markets, a closed-end fund, has the same portfolio manager and investment policy as the open-end Templeton Developing Markets Fund. But Templeton Emerging Markets spent most of 1992 trading at an average premium to net asset value of 25 percent. The open-end fund would have been the better buy—even after paying the load. In 1993, in fact, John Templeton himself unloaded his shares of the closed-end Templeton Emerging Markets Fund at a premium of 25 percent over net asset value, and reinvested the proceeds in the open-end fund.

Fund companies such as Franklin, Massachusetts Financial Services, Oppenheimer, and Putnam also operate closed-end bond funds with investment goals similar to their open-end bond portfolios. Bond funds can trade at discounts to NAV, but usually not to the extent of equity funds.

Investing in a closed-end bond fund that's selling at a discount to NAV may result in a higher yield than in a comparable open-end bond fund. Suppose there are open-end and closed-end bond funds with the same manager and similar portfolios. Both have NAVs of $10 per share and a 20 cents per quarter payout, or 80 cents a year. The open-end fund has a yield of 8 percent. But the closed-end fund trades at $9.50, a 5 percent discount to NAV. Buy the closed-end fund, and the same 80-cent payout becomes an 8.4 percent yield. Less money for the same payout results in a higher yield.

The other time to consider closed-end bond funds is when interest rates are falling. When short-term interest rates drop, investors seek to maintain their yields by pulling money out of money-market funds or CDs and buying long-term bond mutual funds. But such a strategy is often self-defeating. What money comes pouring into open-end funds during a time of falling interest rates will be invested at a lower interest rate than the "older" money. That lowers the average yield of the fund and dilutes returns for all shareholders. Closed-end bond funds, because they don't take new money into the portfolio, don't suffer from this sort of dilution problem (unless,

Closed-end bond funds borrow to boost yields.

of course, the management launches a rights offering).

Buying closed-end bond funds in a period of falling interest rates has some pitfalls, too. After all, a falling-rate environment is a bull market for bonds, so the market prices for closed-end bond funds may trade up to a premium to net asset value. In 1993, for instance, the ACM Government Income Fund sold at a premium as high as 10.9 percent to the value of its portfolio. In that case, the buyer paid $1.09 for every $1 worth of bonds. Moreover, the fund is only earning interest on $1 worth of bonds. So the investor, in effect, is buying a bond at a premium.

But there's a big difference between buying a bond at a premium and a bond fund at a premium. With the bond fund, the investor has all the interest rate risk of a bond, but something more. An investor in a U.S. Treasury or investment-grade bond knows what the interest payment is going to be. On the other hand, bond fund "dividends"—they're technically dividends even though the payout is earned from interest—can be cut, and often are, in a period of declining interest rates. Funds that don't cut—and aren't earning the dividend—could end up making a nontaxable distribution. That's not a freebie, like interest on municipal bonds. A nontaxable distribution means the fund never really earned the money it distributed, so the distribution is considered a return of the investor's own capital. That can be especially annoying to investors who paid a premium for their bond funds. The money comes back at net asset value.

Investors in many closed-end bond funds might be lured by high yields that are produced with leverage. Here's how the funds work. Suppose the funds raise $200 million from investors for regular closed-end bond fund shares. The bond fund then sells perhaps $100 million in preferred stocks—typically to corporations or other institutional investors. The preferred shares pay a dividend that can be either a fixed or a variable interest rate.

So now, the leveraged bond fund can invest $300 million instead of $200 million. Suppose the fund can invest the money to produce an 8 percent interest rate, while paying an average 5 percent rate on the preferred shares. The $200 million earns $16 million a year. The $100 million earns $8 million, less $5 million paid to the preferred stockholders. So the $100 million nets an extra $3 million for the common stockholders. Instead of $16 million in income, the fund earns $19 million. So far, so good.

But what happens if the interest rates climb and bond prices tumble? The portfolio losses to the leveraged fund will be magnified. In the junk bond debacle of 1989 and 1990, among the most battered junk bond funds were those that had leveraged the portfolio. In addition, if the rate on the preferred shares moves up higher than the interest payments on the bonds in the portfolio, the bond fund could be in the position of having to pay the preferred shareholders out of the common shareholders' capital.

The moral of the story: If a closed-end bond fund seems to promise a return that's higher than what the market bears, you have to ask how the fund produced it.

Buying and Selling: The Essentials

Until not too many years ago, investing in mutual funds was an "either or" business. You either bought them through a salesperson—a stockbroker, a financial planner, or, sometimes, a dually-licensed life insurance agent—or you bought them direct from the mutual fund company. If you bought through a salesperson, you paid a sales charge or "load," a fee that compensates the salesperson for selling you the fund. If you bought directly from the fund company, there was no salesperson, so the fund was purchased "no load," without that fee.

In essence, the load and no-load arrangements represented two ways to distribute funds, and most fund companies followed one or the other. Companies such as Alliance Capital, Franklin, Putnam, and Templeton are load-fund groups and sell through brokers. The funds are sometimes called "broker-dealer" funds. (These funds also include the brokers' in-house proprietary products, such as Merrill Lynch's mutual funds.) Janus, T. Rowe Price, Scudder, and Vanguard are no-load groups. They sell without the presence of an intermediary. Instead, they sell through the mail, toll-free telephone lines, and, in some cases, walk-in investor centers. A few, like Fidelity and Dreyfus, though mainly no-load, develop and sell load funds as well.

Now, new ways to invest in mutual funds which are neither load nor no-load are emerging. One model is the mutual fund network, the oldest, biggest, and best-known of which is Charles Schwab & Co.'s Mutual Fund Marketplace. The network addresses one of the drawbacks of investing in multiple funds of several no-load companies: You must maintain relationships with numerous fund companies and keep track of paperwork for every company with which you deal. Plus, the network makes moving money from, say, a Janus to a Scudder fund as easy as moving from one Janus fund to another. Of course, those who run these networks are in it for the money, and with no-load funds, who's going to pay the firm that runs the network? Some fund groups, such as Invesco, Janus, Strong, and American Century, find this distribution arm so compelling that they pay the networks an annual fee, about 0.25 to 0.35 percent of assets under management, for bringing them customers.

The networks make simple what was previously difficult—managing diverse portfolios of no-load funds. The networks also make it possible for many salespersons to leave their firms and set up shops on their own. Instead of selling Franklin and Putnam funds with loads attached, they use the no-load networks. Instead of collecting a commission for selling a particular fund, they manage a portfolio of commissionless funds, assessing an annual "management fee." Many load-fund companies, not wanting to miss out on this business, now make their funds available no-load to investors who buy through advisers who charge fees. And the big brokerage firms, seeing the popularity of fee-based mutual fund investing, are changing their ways as well. Now major brokerage firms like Merrill Lynch, Smith Barney, and Prudential Securities are offering large numbers of funds, load and no-load, on a fee-only basis. And even fund companies like Fidelity, Vanguard, American Express, and Strong have networks that can plug in others' funds besides their own.

A little confusing? First, let's take a few steps back.

What You Need to Know About Loads

For most of their history, mutual funds were sold by salespeople working for the fund companies, brokerage firms, and insurance companies. And for most of that time, the funds came with a stiff "load," or commission. Today, most funds sold by brokers are commonly known as "load" funds.

Until the mid-1980s, the load was an 8.5 percent up-front sales charge that swallowed a big chunk of money right off the top of an investment. That meant that out of a $1000 investment, $85 would go toward commissions and only $915 into investments. The 8.5 percent charge usually applied to investments of less than $10,000. For large amounts, the sales charge would start to scale back and might even disappear after, say, $1 million. A few fund groups even levied a load on the reinvested dividends and capital gains, though the regulators kept it a tad lower than the initial front-end load. True, the commission seemed high, but salespeople would remind investors that, unlike stocks and bonds, it was only paid on purchase—not again when the fund was sold.

There are many more load than no-load funds. That's because many funds need brokers to bring them investors. Some no-loads with excellent track records never really attracted investors until they added loads. That allowed them to pay brokers to sell their funds. The first year AIM Weingarten was a load fund, assets under management increased by about $98 million, or 58 percent. For instance, the Pasadena Growth Fund switched from no-load to a 3 percent load to encourage brokers to sell the fund. But, says Roger Engemann, the portfolio manager, the 3 percent load proved too small to get the brokers excited about the fund. Then, on the advice of a major brokerage firm, the fund boosted the load to 5.5 percent—and sales took off. The fund more than doubled its assets in less than a year.

In 1992, mutual fund regulators on the U.S. Securities & Exchange Commission staff proposed negotiated loads—allowing fund companies, brokers, and investors to dicker over price. After all, stock commissions have been negotiable since 1975—why not funds? The fund industry howled, and the SEC commissioners didn't press it. The matter died.

NO-LOAD FUNDS

In the early 1970s, the stock market plummeted and so did mutual fund sales. To shake off the slump, some companies started to sell their funds direct to investors without a sales charge, or "no load." No-load funds weren't brand new then, either. But the early no-loads were started by investment counseling firms like T. Rowe Price

for accounts deemed too small for individual management and were not widely marketed.

But along with the no-loads came liberalized rules on mutual fund advertising. Then fund management companies like Dreyfus and Fidelity began dropping the loads from some funds, and when new funds were launched they came without loads. Money-market funds, which drew millions of new investors into mutual funds in the 1970s, were also sold no-load. Their popularity worked to the advantage of the no-load fund families.

Until the mid-1980s the mutual fund universe was split between the "loads," which stuck with their 8.5 percent sales charges, and the no-loads. Then the load funds, feeling investor resistance to the stiff fees, started lowering their sales charges. Now, there are only a handful of funds with 8.5 percent loads. Most of the load funds have dropped their fees to the 4 to 6 percent range. Increasingly, they have also offered funds with different methods to pay the sales charge, the "back-end load" and the "level load."

BACK-END LOADS

They call it a back-end load, "redemption fee," "exit fee," or, technically, the "contingent deferred sales charge." The fee starts at 4 or 5 percent of the value of the fund you're selling, depending on the fund. If you sell your shares in the first year, you pay the full charge. In the second year, your exit fee drops by 1 percentage point, and so on. By the fifth or sixth year the redemption fees are usually gone, so if you're truly a long-term investor, you may never pay that fee.

Back-end loads were first introduced in the mid-1980s. But this alternative didn't really take off until the late 1980s, when Merrill Lynch introduced "dual pricing." Dual pricing creates two classes of shares for each fund: "A" shares, which carry a one-time up-front load, and "B" shares, which carry the back-end load. Now dual pricing is widespread among brokerage house proprietary funds, and even among the independent fund managers that sell through brokers. While many use the A and B share method, a few, such as Eaton Vance, offer a separate line-up of funds with back-end loads.

During the 1980s, as the load funds lowered up-front sales charges and introduced back-end loads, some no-load companies were going the opposite way. Fidelity Investments, for instance, slapped "low-loads"—2 or 3 percent sales charges—on funds that were previously sold no-load. Fidelity

A no-load fund may have hidden sales fees.

used the load not to pay brokers, but to pay for its extensive advertising.

By the 1990s, even though the mutual fund industry enjoyed record sales, investors were resisting loads. Strong Funds, which had low-loads on its equity funds, dropped them altogether in late 1992. Fidelity now waives its low-loads on most funds purchased in retirement accounts. (Select Portfolios and a few others are excluded.) In recent years, some load funds with hot performance, such as Oberweis Emerging Growth, switched to no-load. And Heartland Value Fund dropped its front-end load in favor of a back-end load and eventually went no-load. (There are still a few funds going in the opposite direction. Evergreen Funds switched to loads after the fund management company was acquired by a bank.)

Just because a fund is no-load does not mean there are no fees. For instance, the Vanguard Group levies "transaction fees" on its index funds ranging from 0.5 percent to 1.5 percent, depending on the fund. The difference between this fee and most loads is that the proceeds go to the fund, not to the fund sponsor. The fee is to offset the transaction costs of investing the money. (In most funds, that cost is not explicit but indirect and it is reflected in the price that a fund pays for securities.) At the same time, the Vanguard index funds levy a $2.50 per quarter "maintenance fee" on accounts with less than $10,000 in them. That takes care of reports, statements, and the like. In most funds, that cost ends up on the line itemized as "other expenses."

Some no-loads charge redemption fees, too, but they're usually meant to discourage short-term trading. Vanguard has a 1 percent redemption charge on three of its Specialized Portfolio series for shares held for less than one year. On the Vanguard Horizon funds, that 1 percent contingent fee extends to shares held less than five years. The Pennsylvania Mutual Fund and most of the others in the Royce Fund family levy a 1 percent exit fee on shares redeemed within a year of purchase.

Since the wide variation in loads has so muddled the distinction between load funds and no-loads, the terms don't mean so much anymore. In fact, the Investment Company Institute, the fund industry's trade association, looks at funds by the method used to distribute them, not by the sales charges. There are "sales force" funds—those sold to investors through sales folks—and "direct marketing" funds—those sold by the management companies directly to investors (Table 3-1).

TABLE 3-1

THE BIGGEST FUND MANAGERS

Fund management company	Assets Billions*	Direct marketing No-load, low-load, and institutional	Sales force Load and deferred
FIDELITY	$521.4	●	●
VANGUARD	321.4	●	
AMERICAN FUNDS	224.4		●
MERRILL LYNCH	197.6		●
FRANKLIN/TEMPLETON	168.6		●
PUTNAM	159.1		●
SMITH BARNEY	95.2		●
DEAN WITTER	90.6		●
FEDERATED	88.4	●	●
DREYFUS	87.9	●	●
T. ROWE PRICE	81.1	●	
AIM MANAGEMENT	78.6		●
OPPENHEIMER FUNDS	73.3		●
AMERICAN EXPRESS (IDS)	71.4		●
AMERICAN CENTURY	60.0	●	
SCHWAB	55.4	●	
PRUDENTIAL	53.3		●
JANUS	51.3	●	
MFS	48.5		●
ALLIANCE CAPITAL	48.4		●

*As of Dec. 31, 1997. Excludes all variable annuities and off-shore funds.

DATA: STRATEGIC INSIGHT, BUSINESS WEEK

"HIDDEN LOADS"

If the loads, low-loads, and no-loads aren't confusing enough, consider the "12(b)-1" fee, or what some commentators call the "hidden load." The 12(b)-1 charge, named for the U.S. Securities & Exchange Commission rule which enabled funds to levy it, is, like loads, meant to help defray marketing and distribution costs. Sales force fund companies can use the 12(b)-1 revenues to compensate brokers for their selling efforts. Direct marketing companies, on the other hand, use the money to pay for advertising. At least half of all funds levy some sort of 12(b)-1 fee.

What's very different about this charge is how it is collected from the shareholders. Instead of paying the charge once when investors buy the fund (front-end load), or when they sell it (back-end load), investors pay this fee from the fund's assets. In that sense, the 12(b)-1 charges are treated just like the fees shareholders pay for portfolio management, administration, auditing, printing, postage, and other expenses.

There are limits on 12(b)-1 fees. The fee—which must be disclosed in the prospectus—has a maximum of 0.75 percent of assets per year, or 75 cents per $100 of assets, plus a 0.25 percent "service fee," for a total of 1 percent. Many funds, in fact, charge less. Many sales-force companies with front-end loads also offer funds with back-end loads and 12(b)-1 fees. Many no-load funds have 12(b)-1 fees, too, but the charge is usually much smaller than with a sales-force fund. The rules say that a fund that calls itself "no-load" can have a 12(b)-1 fee of no more than 0.25 percent. Funds with 12(b)-1 charges are noted in the BUSINESS WEEK Mutual Fund Scoreboard.

One percent may not sound like much, but think about it this way. On a $10,000 investment, that's $100 in the first year. But you have to pay 1 percent every year you're in the fund. And, providing that the fund is increasing in value, that 1 percent represents more money each year. Rules enacted in 1992 are designed to put a cap on 12(b)-1 fees so that investors don't pay more in such fees than they would have had they paid an 8.5 percent load. But that cap pertains to the entire fund and not to any individual investor. According to experts, the 12(b)-1 fee on a fund that is not growing would eventually hit the cap. But a fund that's taking in new money may never hit its cap. So investors in those funds may end up paying the 12(b)-1 fee indefinitely.

Confusing enough? It's getting worse. Alliance Capital is one of a number of fund companies that have A, B, and C classes of shares for all its stock and bond funds. (A few companies have more classes than that, but three is usually the largest number of classes offered to the individual investor.) The A shares carry a 4.5 percent up-front load. The B shares have an ongoing 1 percent annual 12(b)-1 charge and a declining back-end load. For equity funds, the back-end load is 4 percent in the first year, declining 1 percentage point a year, and disappearing in the fifth year. For fixed-income funds, the back-end load starts at 3 percent and disappears in the fourth year.

The C shares charge neither front- nor back-end loads—they just levy a 1 percent a year fee. That's perhaps why it's called the "level-load" fund. Like the 12(b)-1 fee, this level-load comes out of the fund's assets every year. You might call it the "forever load." Introduced just a few years ago, some fund executives thought they would quickly outpace both front- and back-end shares in new sales, but that hasn't been the case. According to Morningstar, Inc., 60 percent of the level-load funds have less than $5 million in assets, and 25 percent less than $500,000. Perhaps it's because the shares probably are neither the best deal for investors, nor for the commissioned salespeople who sell them.

> A 12(b)-1 fee can erode your profits.

Although most fund companies call their front-end load shares "A," back-end load shares "B," and level-load shares "C," don't assume all A's, B's, or C's are alike. In some fund groups, for instance, the C shares are for institutional investors, or reserved for investors who come to the fund via an employer-sponsored retirement plan.

Some companies, like Neuberger & Berman and Oppenheimer Management, use the "Y" designation for institutional shares. But not all use "Y" that way. Evergreen Funds, for instance, uses Y to designate shares purchased when the fund was still a no-load fund company. New shares are in A, B, and C classes. Some fund managers create multiple classes of shares and call them institutional or "trust" shares. In most cases, those are shares that are distributed through bank trust departments. "Retail" shares are for individual investors.

And what about "Class II" shares? Franklin Funds launched that plan a few years ago. These shares are an alternative to front-end loads, but have a totally different payment structure: Investors would pay a 1 percent load at time of purchase, and another 1 percent of assets if they sell the fund within two years. Class II shareholders also pay higher 12(b)-1 fees of 0.65 percent for bond funds and 1 percent for equity funds.

And mutual fund companies are always coming up with new ways to sell mutual funds, too. One method that's catching on is the "hub and spoke" or "master and feeder" fund arrangement. It works like this: A fund company sets up and manages, for example, a government bond fund. That's the hub. Since this company distributes directly to individual investors, it opens a no-load government bond fund. But instead of owning government bonds, the fund owns shares in the hub, which is a government bond fund. Next, the fund company thinks banks might want to sell this government bond fund to their customers. So it creates another spoke, perhaps with the bank's name on it, sold with a 4 percent load.

The process can go on and on, creating spokes for sales through different distribution channels—institutional investors, retirement plans, and offshore investors—all feeding into the same hub. The advantage of this arrangement is that it's cheaper to run one large, centralized hub portfolio than several smaller funds. That savings should be passed on to the investors in the form of lower expenses.

Investors, for the most part, may not even realize their fund is the spoke of a hub. And, if they're satisfied with results, they may not care. But suppose you paid a load for a spoke fund, while others bought the same hub for a lesser load, or even no load. Right now, a broker selling you a spoke has no obligation to tell you there's another spoke for the same hub with a different pricing scheme. So you may well ask.

Loads, low-loads, hidden loads. Does this mean you forgo all of them and just concentrate on no-load funds? Not necessarily. What is important is that those who invest in mutual funds understand the sales charges, exit fees, and ongoing distribution fees and how they affect the total return from their investments. The U.S. Securities & Exchange Commission, for the most part, has been fairly vigilant on fee disclosure. Their philosophy has been to provide investors with all the information and let the buyer decide. But that puts the burden of fathoming the fee structure back on the fund buyer.

To Load or Not to Load?

Why would anyone buy a load fund? In most cases you can find a no-load analog of most any load fund. True, there are some excellent load funds, but there are also great no-loads. And portfolio performance has nothing to do with whether you paid a broker to sell you the fund. So if you're going to go to the trouble of researching mutual funds at all, you might as well buy no-loads, right?

Perhaps. That's a question only you can answer for yourself. If you're reading this book, it may be because you want to take these decisions into your own hands. You don't want to use a broker, financial planner, or investment adviser. But it's a mistake to dismiss load funds out of hand. If you do, you're cutting yourself off from a large part of the mutual fund universe and many excellent investment opportunities.

When the only alternative to the no-load was an 8.5 percent load, the scales tipped heavily toward the no-load. But today there are former no-load funds that sell with 2 and 3 percent low-loads, and former full-load funds with 4 percent loads. And then there's the back-end load, which many investors never have to pay.

In determining whether to pay a load you have to consider how long you anticipate staying with the fund. Everyone's financial plans are subject

to change, of course. And if yours do change, most load fund families have a wide range of portfolios to choose from, just like no-loads. And intrafamily switches, such as moving from a Putnam international bond fund to a Putnam government bond fund, can usually be done without paying another load. Increasingly, some load-fund groups, like Fortis and Prudential, will let investors switch funds out of other load funds and into theirs without paying a new load. Of course, that's not going to help you if you will end up owing the fund a redemption fee. So if you want to retain the flexibility of moving to other funds of other managers, consider taking the charge up front.

If your investment is for your retirement nest egg or your toddler's college education, a load should not stand between you and the best possible fund. After all, even an 8.5 percent load—and there are very few of them left—over a 10-year holding period works out to less than 1 percent per year. That kind of sales burden can be easily overcome in the performance of an exceptional load fund versus a mediocre no-load.

But most investors are not faced with a choice of 8.5 percent versus no charge. What about choosing between A and B shares? Suppose you're interested in the MFS Emerging Growth Fund. The A shares have an up-front 5.75 percent load, which is fairly stiff in today's market. The B shares, on the other hand, have no up-front load. But there are 12(b)-1 fees amounting to 1 percent a year, and a back-end load that's 4 percent in the first and second year, but then declines 1 percentage point a year until it disappears in the seventh year. What's the best buy?

Depends on your assumptions for your holding period and the rate of return on your investment. If you assume a $10,000 investment and an average annual return of 10 percent a year, the B shares provide better returns up until year 8, even if you redeem and trigger the back-end load. According to Multiple Class Calculator, a software program developed by Money Marketing Inc., the B shares earn more money until year 8, when the A shares nudge them out by $9. After that, the advantage goes to the A shares, but not by much. In year 10, the A shares only beat the B shares by $14. And the higher the assumed return, the longer the B shares retain their edge.

What if you have three choices, as is the case with MFS Emerging Growth's sister fund, MFS OTC Fund (Table 3-2). That fund has A, B, and C shares. The C share has neither an up-front nor back-end charge, but levies 1 percent a year for-

Differences between load and no-load funds are blurring.

TABLE 3-2

PAY THE LOAD NOW, LATER, OR FOREVER?

MFS OTC Fund has three classes of shares. "A" shares have a traditional front-end load of 5.75%, and a 1.36% expense ratio. "B" and "C" shares have expense ratios, 2.43% and 2.36% respectively, because of the higher 12(b)-1 fees. "B" shares have a 4% redemption fee if you cash out in the first or second year, 3% in the third and fourth, 2% in the fifth, and 1% in the sixth year. Assuming a $10,000 initial investment and a 10% average annual return, which shares make most sense?

Year-End	A shares	B shares	B, if redeemed	C shares
1	$10,239	$10,757	$10,357	$10,764
2	11,124	11,571	11,171	11,586
3	12,085	12,447	12,147	12,472
4	13,129	13,389	13,090	13,424
5	14,264	14,403	14,203	14,450
6	15,496	15,493	15,393	15,554
7	16,835	16,666	16,666	16,742
8	18,289	17,928	17,928	18,021
9	19,870	19,477	19,477	19,398
10	21,586	21,160	21,160	20,880

DATA: MONEY MARKETING INC.

ever. Suppose you go with the same $10,000 investment and assume a 10 percent average annual return. In the early years, the C shares work out best. That's because there is neither a big bite up front, nor one on the back end. For instance, in year 2, the C shares are worth $11,586 versus $11,124 for the A shares and $11,571 for the B shares before redemption, $11,171 after.

But the A shares have a much lower expense ratio than the B or C shares. And over time, that gives the advantage to A-share investors. In year 7 and beyond, the advantage swings to the A-share owners; they have a $169 advantage over B-share holders, and a $93 advantage over C-share holders. By year 10, the A-share holders are $427 ahead of the B-share holders, and $706 over the C-share holders. Obviously, the C shares, which are the cheapest in the earlier years, could end up costing the most if the investment is truly a long-term one. Perhaps the C shares are appropriate if, at the start, you believe the investment will be redeemed in the first few years. Still, many people have a hard time swallowing that chunky up-front sales load. If that's the case, B shares may make the best choice under certain conditions. MFS, for instance, will automatically convert B shares into A shares after the customer has passed the period in which a back-end charge might be levied, usually six years. That way, the investor is also relieved of the heavier 12(b)-1 burden that's in the B shares.

In weighing a load versus a no-load fund, you should also consider the fund's investment parameters. For instance, equity funds generally have broad charters and often disparate results. So even if both funds are growth funds, the differences in returns of growth funds are great and having the "right" fund is important. Paying a modest load for an equity fund that's demonstrated superior results may be better than buying just any no-load.

At the other extreme, short-term bond funds all maintain a fairly similar portfolio, and the differences in returns from one fund to the next are small. So it doesn't make sense to pay a load for a short-term bond fund when there's little likelihood that it will show any better performance than a no-load fund.

There is at least one reason to pay a load—to compensate a broker or financial planner for the time he or she spends meeting with you and monitoring your investments. Perhaps a recommendation for one equity fund does not merit paying a 5.75 percent load. But if a financial planner takes the time to tailor a portfolio of funds for you, he or she has to be paid. The load is one way to do it.

There are other ways as well. Many financial planners, for instance, put their clients' money into no-load funds and then charge an annual fee for the entire portfolio, perhaps 1 or 2 percent. That's not necessarily a better deal for investors, either. You might be better off paying your planner by investing in load funds—providing the planner still delivers good service long after being paid. Six percent off the top of the initial investment may sound steep, but if the fund managers have sliced off 1 percent a year for 10 years, you've paid a whole lot more.

Keep in mind, too, that while it's common practice to refer to a fund as a "4 percent load" or a "6 percent load," not everyone pays the full freight. If the fund carries a sales charge, there are ways to minimize the costs. Most load-fund groups have fee schedules that slide downward for progressively larger investments. Typically, purchases up to $10,000 carry the maximum load. Before making a large investment in a load fund, ask the broker about the next "breakpoint," the dollar amount necessary to qualify for a lower load. In some cases, it might be worth making an extra $1000 or $2000 investment to qualify for the lower sales charge. At the high end, the sales fee often drops to 1 percent—or even totally disappears on major investments of $1 million or more.

Suppose you plan to invest $15,000, but you

won't be able to put the money in all at once. Check with your broker to see if the fund management company will let you sign a letter of intent. In such an agreement you pledge to invest over a 13-month period a specified amount which, if invested at one time, would qualify for a reduced sales charge. If you fail to fulfill the letter of intent, you'll owe the fund the difference between the sales charges you've paid and what you should have paid. The company can take the money from your account.

If you're spreading your investments over several funds in the same load-fund group, many funds will give you the same break as if the investment were made in one fund. And all the funds don't have to be for the same account. If you're investing for your personal funds, your IRA, a spousal IRA, and some custodial accounts for the kids, you can probably get a discount that takes in the total investment. But you have to ask.

Mutual Fund Networks

If you opened a stock brokerage account and invested in, say, 10 stocks, you could buy, sell, and keep track of them through one account. It used to be nearly impossible to do the same with mutual funds, except if you kept your investments to one fund family. You could mix and match multiple funds in one account using a commissioned broker or financial planner, but you would still be limiting yourself to a little more than half the fund universe. You would not be able to include, say, T. Rowe Price or Vanguard offerings, since they don't pay commissions to brokers.

Mutual funds are not as interchangeable as stocks, but thanks to the mutual fund networks, they're heading that way. You can think of the networks as sort of a family of fund families. The discount brokerage firm of Charles Schwab & Company originated the network concept more than a decade ago in a program called Mutual Fund Marketplace (MFM) (Table 3-3), and it now has more than $100 billion. MFM has over 1343 funds available to the individual investor and nearly all of them you would recognize as no-load funds. Within the MFM is the OneSource program, with 818 funds which can be purchased with no fee. With OneSource funds, the fund com-

pany pays the broker, often through a 12(b)-1 charge. For the others, there is a small transaction charge.

For the other no-load funds, you pay a transaction fee to Schwab. For trades up to $15,000 in size, the fee is 0.7 percent of the investment. The fee is 0.2 percent on the next $15,001 to $100,000, and 0.08 percent on everything over $100,000. A $10,000 trade costs $70 and a $25,000 trade, $125. Schwab officials say that, on average, clients in the Mutual Fund Marketplace program end up paying commissions of about 0.3 percent of the amount invested. Investors can get a 10 percent discount by conducting their trades by an automated phone line or by computer link.

So why would anyone pay Schwab to invest in a fund that doesn't charge commissions? If all you ever planned to do was to buy that one fund, there's no good reason. And the commission structure makes the purchasing of no-load funds uneconomical for small trades or monthly investing programs. The transaction fee is 0.7 percent for $5000 which is $35. But it will cost you $39 anyway. That's because Schwab, like most stockbrokers, has a minimum transaction charge—and in Schwab's case, it's $39. If you're stashing away a couple of hundred dollars a month in a fund, you would do better to deal directly with the fund. You don't want to spend $39 to invest $200.

Many investors like the convenience of the Schwab program even if they have to pay the fees. Rather than a statement and an account with every fund, Schwab delivers a consolidated statement. At tax time there's one Form 1099. If you want to sell one fund and redistribute the proceeds into three other funds, you can effect

TABLE 3-3

FUND-SHOPPING THROUGH DISCOUNT BROKERS

	Toll-free phone
ACCUTRADE	800-882-4887
AMERICAN EXPRESS FINANCIAL DIRECT	800-658-4677
K. AUFHAUSER & CO.	800-368-3669
BARRY MURPHY & CO.	800-221-2111
FIDELITY BROKERAGE SERVICES	800-544-0214
NATIONAL DISCOUNT BROKERS	800-888-3999
NATIONSBANC INVESTMENTS	800-926-1111
QUICK & REILLY	800-221-5220
SEAPORT SECURITIES	800-221-9894
CHARLES SCHWAB & CO.	800-435-4000
VANGUARD BROKERAGE SERVICES	800-992-8327
WATERHOUSE SECURITIES	800-934-4443
JACK WHITE & CO.	800-323-3263

DATA: BUSINESS WEEK

the change with one phone call instead of several. If you're switching funds, there's a $15 fee for the fund you're switching out of and the regular commission for the one you're going into. In One-Source, investors are permitted 15 free trades a year, as long as the funds have been held more than 90 days.

There's another advantage, too. There are some excellent funds with high minimum investments. Two highly regarded bond funds, PIMCO Low Duration and PIMCO Total Return, require minimum investments of at least $500,000 to open an account. But invest through Schwab and you can buy in for as little as $1000. Schwab lowers thresholds because it maintains an "omnibus" account with each no-load fund. That means that PIMCO treats all Schwab customers as one account. Schwab, in turn, keeps track of how many shares of that account belong to each customer. So Schwab can offer lower minimum investments because it is pooling funds from a large number of clients.

Schwab has even extended the Mutual Fund Marketplace program to load funds like American, Colonial, Franklin, Pioneer, Putnam, and Templeton. But the regulations bar brokers from discounting the loads. Still, buying load funds through Schwab or one of its competitors may appeal to investors who want the funds but do not want to deal with the full-service brokers who usually sell them.

Fidelity Investments' FundsNetwork program is similar to Schwab's, offering 3300 no-load and load funds, 800 of them without a transaction fee. Transaction charges are two-part, a base fee plus a variable fee depending on the size of the transaction. For investments of up to $5000, the fee is a flat $35; for investments over $5000, it's $35 plus 0.2 percent of the amount in excess of $5000. A $10,000 investment works out to $35 plus $10 (0.2 percent of $5000) or $45. Fidelity caps the maximum transaction charge at $150. Those rates are for placing orders through a Fidelity representative. For touch-tone phone service, the minimum drops to $30, the maximum, $120. The biggest bargains are for on-line trading. The fee is a flat $28.95, regardless of the size of the investment.

Several other discount brokers run broad-based mutual fund programs like Schwab's. Jack White & Company has some 4500 no-load and low-load funds. The minimum charge is $27 per trade on trades of up to $5000, $35 for trades of $5001 to $25,000, and $50 for trades in excess of $25,000. Jack White also has a no-fee service with, at last count, 1200 funds.

Load-fund investors may also check out Jack White's CONNECT System. It allows investors to buy load funds without paying loads. Instead, there's a flat $200 fee, no matter how large the purchase.

Suppose an investor would like to place $25,000 in a fund with a 4.5 percent front-end load. That would take $1125 off the top of the investment. The CONNECT charge for the sale would be a flat $200. CONNECT places the buyer's offer on an electronic bulletin board and looks for a seller. CONNECT pays half the fee, or $100, to the seller as an incentive to sell through the Jack White system instead of cashing out through the fund company. And CONNECT can't guarantee that it can match up willing buyers and sellers on the spot, or even on the day that the order is placed. But the system is expected to become part of every security broker's electronic bulletin board, which will enable Jack White to attract fund buyers and fund sellers.

Advisers and "Wraps"

The emerging mutual fund networks are doing more than changing the way many individuals buy and sell funds. They're changing the way brokers and investment advisers conduct their businesses as well. Over the last few years, thousands of brokers have left brokerage firms, where they got paid for their advice through commissions, and have opened up their own firms where, instead of charging commissions, they levy a fee based on the client's assets under management.

Instead of selling traditional load funds from companies like Alliance Capital, Franklin, and Putnam, they channel their clients' money into no-load funds through the networks. They're putting so much in, in fact, that some load-fund groups—not wanting to miss this burgeoning market—make their funds available no-load through the networks to the advisers' clients. Total assets under the control of fee-based advisers amount to about $370 billion. The portion of those assets in mutual funds is an estimated $75 billion, according to Cerulli Associates, Inc.

Fee-based advisers don't get paid for selling any particular fund—only for their advice. Of course, in theory, a traditional load fund performs the same function. The difference is that instead of paying the salesperson at the time of sale, the client pays the salesperson over time. Perhaps more important, in a traditional load fund, the salesperson is paid the same no matter how the investment performs, and you may never hear from him or her again.

With an asset-based fee arrangement, the salesperson is, in effect, on the "same side of the table" and you're in a long-term relationship. If the advice is good, the assets under management grow, and so does the adviser's annual fee. Conversely, if the client loses money, so does the adviser. Paying an adviser through asset-based fees is not necessarily cheaper than traditional loads, and, indeed, could wind up being more expensive. But it should only be more if the fund performs well. Most people don't mind paying for good advice and good service.

Keep in mind, too, that fee-based arrangements only work out well if the fee is reasonable. Many independent advisers charge in the range of 1 to 1.5 percent of assets and the larger the account, the lower the percentage. Most major brokerage firms have a similar arrangement, called the "wrap" account—so-called because it wraps all costs into one price. But the fees may be as high as 3 percent. For a portfolio of mutual funds, that's much too high since the fee mainly covers fund selection and monitoring. The actual stockpicking—which is far more complex—takes place within the mutual funds themselves, and that's paid for through the funds' operating expenses.

The fee-based arrangement isn't for everyone. For starters, do you need or want the help? If you feel comfortable and have the time to do it yourself, you don't need an adviser. If you'd like one—but don't have a minimum of six figures to invest, it may be hard to find an independent adviser to take your account. Some advisory firms, in fact, want a $200,000 minimum investment. If you can't meet the minimum, and want an adviser, you will have to pay steep hourly rates or go for traditional load-fund products. If you're successful, you may eventually accumulate enough money to switch to an asset-based arrangement.

Considering hiring an adviser to manage a portfolio of mutual funds? Lots of people are doing it, even those who have the savvy to invest the money themselves. Many of those who have the ability just don't have the time. Many people find investment advisers the same way you find other professionals—through referrals and recommendations from friends, relatives, and co-workers. But don't hand over your money to anyone without a thorough investigation—sometimes known as "due diligence" in the investment world—of your own.

Many people who give investment advice, sell securities, and manage money are registered with the U.S. Securities & Exchange Commission. That may sound august, but it means little and assures nothing. All it takes to become an SEC-registered adviser is to complete a lengthy form and pay the $150 fee. No examinations are required, and there is no requirement for education in investment theory and practice. The SEC's Form ADV, which advisers must complete, asks about education, professional credentials, work experience, and the like, but having none of that is no bar to getting the registration. That's why it's imperative to ask an adviser for a copy of his or her ADV. The law requires that he or she provide you with Part II, which describes the investment program, fees, and charges. But ask for Part I as well. The SEC can investigate investor complaints against registered advisers, but as far as regular audits, they are few and far between—on average, once every four decades.

All but a handful of states require investment advisers to register, and many also require they pass some national examinations. But the tests usually deal with the rules and regulations of dealing with clients. They don't test for the adviser's knowledge and understanding of the investments. There are private organizations and professional associations that do that, such as the Association for Investment Management and Research, which awards the Chartered Financial Analyst designation, and the College of Financial Planning, which grants the Certified Financial Planner certificate. If the adviser has one or more such designation, it's definitely a plus. And don't take the adviser's word for it. You may want to call the professional group yourself to verify the credentials.

Most advisers have a track record they can show you. But it's not necessarily going to be useful information. Putting on the best show, the adviser might show you a sample portfolio with what seems to be a high return. But that portfolio might have been devised for a client with far more risk-taking ability or tolerance than you have. So if you are a conservative investor, ask to see what the adviser has done for someone more like yourself. And a really good adviser won't take your word for it that you're a conservative investor. He or she should ask probing questions and perhaps give you a little written quiz to get a better sense of your risk-taking ability. Most people can take more risk than they think they can, and as a result short-change themselves in the long run. A good adviser will spot that and encourage you to correct it.

Hiring an adviser? Check references carefully.

Once you have decided on an adviser, make sure you understand what services—such as regular consultations and monthly or quarterly reports—the adviser is going to provide, what it's going to cost, and how payment will be collected. Then, the adviser will open up an account for you, probably with a brokerage firm that has a mutual funds network. The account must be in your name, not the adviser's. You should give the adviser the power to make buy and sell decisions for the portfolio. After all, that's the point of having an adviser. But make sure you receive the confirmation slips and brokerage statements that show the activity in the account. Do not give the adviser the power to take money out of the account. Only you should be able to do that.

> Don't let the prospectus scare you.

Buying on Margin

The convenience and simplicity of the mutual fund networks have also made them popular with mutual fund "market-timers," investors who move assets around, following rigorous technical formulas, trying to capture upside moves in the stock market while steering clear of downdrafts. For more aggressive investors, the program allows the purchase of mutual funds on "margin."

Margin buying works this way. Suppose a fund investor believes stocks are about to stage a big rally and thinks highly of the Janus Special Situations Fund. She decides to invest $10,000 in that fund. If the fund goes up 25 percent in the next six months, the investment is worth $12,500, and the investor can cash out at a profit of $2500. But if the investor buys on margin, she could invest $20,000 in the fund: $10,000 is her money and $10,000 is a loan from the brokerage firm. The interest rate on the loan is usually the broker's loan rate (a figure similar to a bank's prime rate) plus anywhere from 0.5 to 1.5 percent, depending on the size of the loan.

If the fund goes up 25 percent, the leveraged investor's holding climbs to $25,000, and if she sells it, there is a 50 percent return on the original $10,000 investment—a $5000 profit. Well, not quite. Remember, the investor took a loan from the broker to buy the shares. Suppose she borrowed $10,000 for six months at 10 percent interest. That comes out to $500. All told, the investor nets (before commissions) $4500 on her original $10,000. In a cash account that does not use margin, the net profit would be $2500.

But not all margin plays work out so well. What if the value of the investment remained unchanged for six months? Then the margin investor is out the interest. Worse yet, the fund headed south instead of north and declined by 25 percent. So the $20,000 investment is now worth $15,000. What if the margin investor sells at that point? She owes the broker the $10,000 originally borrowed and $500 interest to boot, leaving her with $4500 out of an initial $10,000 investment. Don't use margin buying unless you know exactly what you're doing and can stand the loss.

Prospecting the Prospectus

Nobody wants to read a prospectus. It's a legal document that describes a mutual fund, often in legal and financial terms that may sound awfully technical. But the language is precise for a reason. The SEC has strict guidelines about what the fund can say about itself and how it must present information on past performance, expenses, and fees. Remember, the SEC's approval of a prospectus is only that. It is not an endorsement of any particular investment.

Read it. Okay, scan it and save it, and refer to it if you are going to try something new. There are Fidelity customers who lost money in October 1997 and would not have if they had read the rules in the prospectus. Here's what happened: The markets in Asia had already closed for the day on October 28, after another day of plunging prices. But the U.S. stock market, after some initial selling, recovered that day. These Fidelity investors, betting that it was highly likely that the Hong Kong market would rally the next day, put in orders for the Fidelity Hong Kong & China Fund. If they bought it at October 28th's depressed price, they could likely sell it much higher on the 29th.

But Fidelity had exercised a right that's clearly stated in the prospectus. Instead of calculating the fund's October 28 net asset value based on the closing prices in Hong Kong, they opted for "fair value pricing"—a valuation based on what these Hong Kong stocks were worth given the new stronger market on the 28th in the United States. Those traders trying to exploit this timing discrepancy cried foul, since they had ended up buying the shares at prices much higher than they thought they were going to pay.

But Fidelity was well within its rights, as spelled out in the prospectus.

If the prospectus looks daunting today, it's only a shadow of what it was just a few years ago. It's easier to read; its figures are easier to compare; and there's a lot less bulk. Most of the objective information you need is in there: sales charges and fees, investment policy, and administrative matters like the procedure for redeeming shares or switching into other funds. If the fund has an operating history, the prospectus will provide historical data too. What the prospectus won't have is a glowing recommendation from a sales rep or a complimentary article from a financial publication. That may be included in sales literature that's stuffed into the same envelope.

Believe it or not, prospectuses are improving. Direct marketers like Fidelity, who don't have salespeople to explain their funds to investors, are making efforts to both simplify the prospectus and, as much as the lawyers allow, explain things in "plain English." In fact, with the blessings of the SEC, some fund companies are currently providing vastly simplified "plain English" prospectuses that fit neatly on two sides of an 8½- by 11-inch piece of paper—with room to spare.

Simplifying a prospectus is never easy because it's a document that's trying to serve two purposes. Its stated objective is disclosure: informing investors how a fund invests and operates. But it's also a document that mutual fund company lawyers design as a litigation shield, making sure the fund managers will be able to run the fund without inviting lawsuits.

STATEMENT OF ADDITIONAL INFORMATION

There's plenty of detail in the prospectus, but the investor can also ask the fund to send the Statement of Additional Information (SAI). This bulkier presentation is more of what prospectuses used to be. It covers the same ground as the prospectus, but in far more detail. For instance, the prospectus for the Fidelity Growth & Income Portfolio (dated September 25, 1997) is 30 pages, set in double columns, double-spaced, with charts and tables, and ample white space. Each page is 8¾ by 5⅜ inches in size. That's a fairly slim mutual fund prospectus. The SAI for the same fund is twenty-seven 8½- by 11-inch pages—single-spaced, largely unbroken by charts and tables. How do they differ? The prospectus, for instance, has a heading worded "Adjusting Investment Exposure," followed by two paragraphs outlining in summary form that the fund can use "various techniques" to increase or decrease its exposure to changes in security prices, interest rates, foreign exchange, and other factors that affect security prices. In contrast, Fidelity Growth & Income's SAI details those techniques in two single-spaced, 8½- by 11-inch pages.

For most investors, the prospectus should suffice. But you should be aware of the SAI. In a 1991 case decided in a federal appellate court in New York, the judges ruled investors are responsible for knowing what's in the Statement of Additional Information. An investor challenged a fee that he said wasn't in the prospectus. The court said it was—but in the SAI. And since the existence of the SAI was noted in the prospectus and is legally part of the prospectus, he could not claim he was unaware of the charge. In Growth & Income's case, the mention of the SAI is right on the cover of the prospectus, along with a toll-free telephone number which a prospective investor can call to obtain it.

State securities administrators (who oversee the activities of securities firms at the state level) have been urging fund investors to request SAIs and urging the SEC to require more detailed information in the prospectuses so investors don't have to read both documents. The SEC's Division of Investment Management, which regulates mutual funds, has resisted any moves that might fatten up the prospectuses. If the prospectus is a little-read document now, it will be even less so if it is a thicker and more detailed document.

TAKING A CLOSER LOOK

Don't let the prospectus unnerve you. The financial matters and investment policies may be unique. But much of the other material is boilerplate and doesn't vary much from fund to fund. And not all of it is pertinent to every investor. As long as your planned investment isn't for your Individual Retirement Account or other tax-deferred program, you don't need to read the IRA section in the prospectus.

When thumbing through the prospectus, look for important statistical nuggets like the fund's results and expenses. The documents plainly outline all sales charges, deferred sales charges, redemption fees, exchange fees, management fees, 12(b)-1 fees, and other pertinent expenses. There will also be a condensed financial history of the fund. (Most of these data are also available in the BUSINESS WEEK Mutual Fund Scoreboard.)

Want to take a closer look? Go to Figures 3-1 and 3-2, which are pages five and six from the

Financial statements give a sense of the fund.

FIGURE 3-1

Expenses

Shareholder transaction expenses

are charges you may pay when you buy or sell shares of a fund. In addition, you may be charged an annual account maintenance fee if your account balance falls below $2,500. See "Transaction Details," page 27, for an explanation of how and when these charges apply.

Maximum sales charge on purchases and reinvested distributions	None
Deferred sales charge on redemptions	None
Exchange fee	None
Annual account maintenance fee (for accounts under $2,500)	$12.00

Annual fund operating expenses

are paid out of the fund's assets. The fund pays a management fee to FMR. It also incurs other expenses for services such as maintaining shareholder records and furnishing shareholder statements and financial reports. The fund's expenses are factored into its share price or dividends and are not charged directly to shareholder accounts (see "Breakdown of Expenses" page 16).

The following figures are based on historical expenses of the fund and are calculated as a percentage of average net assets of the fund. A portion of the brokerage commissions that the fund pays is used to reduce the fund's expenses. In addition, the fund has entered into arrangements with its custodian and transfer agent whereby credits realized as a result of uninvested cash balances are used to reduce custodian and transfer agent expenses. Including this reduction, the total fund operating

expenses presented in the table would have been 0.71%.

Management fee	0.50%
12b-1 fee	None
Other expenses	0.23%
Total fund operating expenses	0.73%

Examples: Let's say, hypothetically, that the fund's annual return is 5% and that its operating expenses are exactly as just described. For every $1,000 you invested, here's how much you would pay in total expenses if you close your account after the number of years indicated:

After 1 year	$ 7
After 3 years	$ 23
After 5 years	$ 41
After 10 years	$ 91

These examples illustrate the effect of expenses, but are not meant to suggest actual or expected costs or returns, all of which may vary.

 **Understanding Expenses**

Operating a mutual fund involves a variety of expenses for portfolio management, shareholder statements, tax reporting, and other services. These costs are paid from the fund's assets; their effect is already factored into any quoted share price or return.

Fidelity Growth & Income Portfolio (the prospectus is dated September 25, 1997). Look at the expense summary. You can see there is no sales charge on purchases or reinvested distributions, no deferred sales charge on redemption, and no exchange fees. There is a $12 annual account maintenance fee for accounts with less than $2500—and it applies across the Fidelity universe.

Then come the operating expenses. The introductory note explains what goes into the charges. The management fee, which can vary depending on the fund's performance, is estimated to be 0.50 percent, or 50 cents per $100. "Other" expenses, which include such administrative costs as maintaining shareholder records and furnishing reports and financial statements, amount to another 0.23 percent.

If you add up all the fund operating expenses, they amount to 0.73 percent, or slightly less than three-quarters of 1 percent of the fund's net assets. So what does that mean to your bottom line? You can find that right below, which shows the cumulative impact of sales charges and expenses. If you invest $1000 and earn 5 percent a year, you've spent $7 on sales and operating expenses in the first year, $23 after 3 years, and up to $91 after 10 years. Actually, a 5 percent assumed rate of return for this fund is absurd, and if that's all you thought you could earn, you certainly would not invest in it. However, that's not the point. The SEC requires funds to use that reporting format account to make it easier for investors to compare fees and expenses.

If the fund is brand new, be sure to check whether the fund management company is subsidizing the fund's overhead or waiving management fees. Don't snub these funds—if someone's

FIGURE 3-2

Financial Highlights

The financial highlights table that follows has been audited by Coopers & Lybrand L.L.P., independent accountants. The fund's financial highlights, financial statements, and report of the auditor are included in the fund's Annual Report, and are incorporated by reference into (are legally a part of) the fund's SAI. Contact Fidelity for a free copy of the Annual Report or the SAI.

Selected Per-Share Data

Years ended July 31	1997	1996	1995	1994[F]	1993	1992	1991	1990	1989	1988
Net asset value, beginning of period	$ 28.20	$ 25.10	$ 22.17	$ 21.90	$ 21.34	$ 19.92	$ 17.10	$ 18.56	$ 14.56	$ 17.44
Income from Investment Operations										
Net investment income	.46[C]	.49	.43	.45	.53	.50	.46	.58	.76[D]	.55
Net realized and unrealized gain (loss)	11.44	3.99	4.14	1.07	3.02	1.94	3.10	(.02)	3.86	(1.58)
Total from investment operations	11.90	4.48	4.57	1.52	3.55	2.44	3.56	.56	4.62	(1.03)
Less Distributions										
From net investment income	(.48)	(.48)	(.40)	(.48)	(.59)	(.38)	(.52)	(.75)	(.62)	(.50)
From net realized gain	(1.12)	(.90)	(1.24)	(.77)	(2.40)	(.64)	(.22)	(1.27)	—	(1.35)
Total distributions	(1.60)	(1.38)	(1.64)	(1.25)	(2.99)	(1.02)	(.74)	(2.02)	(.62)	(1.85)
Net asset value, end of period	$ 38.50	$ 28.20	$ 25.10	$ 22.17	$ 21.90	$ 21.34	$ 19.92	$ 17.10	$ 18.56	$ 14.56
Total return[A,B]	44.16%	18.39%	21.95%	7.08%	19.10%	12.75%	21.89%	3.22%	32.66%	(6.04)%

Ratios and Supplemental Data

	1997	1996	1995	1994	1993	1992	1991	1990	1989	1988
Net assets, end of period (In millions)	$ 34,284	$ 19,206	$ 12,106	$ 8,757	$ 6,646	$ 4,199	$ 2,686	$ 1,910	$ 1,428	$ 1,188
Ratio of expenses to average net assets	.73%	.75%	.78%	.83%	.83%	.86%	.87%	.87%	.89%	1.02%
Ratio of expenses to average net assets after expense reductions	.71%[E]	.74%[E]	.77%[E]	.82%[E]	.83%	.86%	.87%	.87%	.89%	1.02%
Ratio of net investment income to average net assets	1.43%	1.82%	2.21%	2.09%	2.67%	2.49%	2.62%	3.43%	4.76%	3.69%
Portfolio turnover rate	38%	41%	67%	92%	87%	221%	215%	108%	97%	135%
Average commission rate[G]	$ .0433									

[A] Total returns do not include the former one time sales charge.
[B] The total returns would have been lower had certain expenses not been reduced during the periods shown.
[C] Net investment income per share has been calculated based on average shares outstanding during the period.
[D] Net investment income per share contains a special dividend of $.09 per share.
[E] FMR or the fund has entered into varying arrangements with third parties who either paid or reduced a portion of the fund's expenses.
[F] Effective August 1, 1993, the fund adopted Statement of Position 93-2, "Determination, Disclosure, and Financial Statement Presentation of Income, Capital Gain, and Return of Capital Distributions by Investment Companies." As a result, net investment income per share may reflect certain reclassifications related to book to tax differences.
[G] For fiscal years beginning on or after September 1, 1995, a fund is required to disclose its average commission rate per share for security trades on which commissions are charged. This amount may vary from period to period and fund to fund depending on the mix of trades executed in various markets where trading practices and commission rate structures may differ.

going to give you a free lunch, take it. But free lunches don't last forever. It's common for fund management companies to subsidize money-market and bond funds when they're trying to build assets, and they'll often do it for equity funds as well. If the fund company absorbs 0.50 percentage point in expenses, it can really make a money-market or bond fund stand out. And, of course, that's the point. The yield looks alluring, and the money flows in.

But watch out. The prospectus must disclose the full fee structure even if shareholders are not paying it. The point is, you should be aware of what the fees are and what they would be if they were paid. Without the waiver, some of these funds may not look as attractive as others with no waiver, but lower expenses. You can put the money in and take the free lunch. But be ready to leave if and when full rates are levied.

The financial statements also give you some feeling for the fund. The numbers may look scary, but they're really pretty simple. Go to Figure 3-2. Start with the first column, which is for the fiscal year ending July 31, 1997. The top line, net asset value (NAV), beginning of the period, tells you just that—what a fund share was worth on August 1, 1996, the start of the fiscal year. Seven lines down, you come up with net asset value at the end of the period, $38.50. The steps in between explain how the fund got from the beginning NAV to the end-of-period NAV.

Start with "net investment income." That's 46 cents a share. It's what's left from stock dividends and interest from fixed-income or money-market holdings after paying for fund expenses. Such expenses include fund managers, record-keeping, postage, auditing, and legal fees. That 46 cents is available for distribution to Fidelity Growth & Income shareholders. That's only a 1.43 percent yield (you can see that near the bottom of the table on the line "ratio of net investment income to average net assets"). A low yield, for sure, but remember that dividend yields have been low for years. Investors, in general, have not rewarded companies for paying higher dividends, so companies nowadays tend to buy back shares with their extra cash. That tends to increase earnings per share.

The big money in equity funds now comes from capital gains. Look at the line "net realized & unrealized gain (loss) on investments." When a mutual fund sells a security at a profit, it has a "realized" gain; when it sells at a loss, it's a realized loss. If a fund continues to hold stocks that are worth more than the fund paid for them, the

stocks represent unrealized gains. Likewise, stocks in a portfolio that are valued at less than their cost are unrealized losses. To get "net" gains, the fund tallies the gains and losses, both realized and unrealized. If the number is positive, as it is here, the fund had net gains. If negative, net losses. In fiscal 1997, the Fidelity Growth & Income Portfolio had net gains of $11.44 per share. That, plus net investment income, gives you the next line, "total from investment operations" of $11.90 per share.

Mutual funds must make distributions of income and realized capital gains in order to preserve their unique tax status (see more on that in Chapter 6). So go to the next section, "less distributions." The next line tells you there was 48 cents a share in income distributions. But wait! The fund earned 46 cents in net investment income. Well, fund distributions for tax purposes are made on a calendar year basis, and for book purposes, on a fiscal year basis. So since Fidelity Growth & Income keeps a different fiscal year, the distributions aren't usually the same. Nonetheless, that 48 cents came out of each fund share in fiscal 1997, so it's recorded here. Then there was a distribution of $1.12 a share in net realized gains, for a total of $1.60.

The next group of figures, "ratios and supplemental data," should help compare this fund to others. The ratio of expenses to average net assets is 0.73 percent for fiscal year 1997. But the next line, "ratio of expenses to average net assets after expense reductions" is what the shareholders actually pay. The footnote indicates that the fund management company has recaptured part of the brokerage commission rebates (known in the investment business as "soft dollars") to pay for some fund expenses. In this case, it's 0.02 percent. That may not sound like much, but it's over $5 million on this $34.3 billion fund. So the expense ratio, after these cost reductions, is 0.71 percent, which is about 40 percent below the all-equity fund average.

Before moving on, look at the expense ratio and how it changes from year to year. The number is trending downward. That's to be expected, since the Fidelity Growth & Income Portfolio is the fifth-largest equity mutual fund and second only to Magellan in the Fidelity fund family. It should have some economies of scale in its operations that benefit its shareholders. Be wary of funds in which this ratio is moving up.

The last line, "portfolio turnover rate," 38 percent, means that securities amounting to 38 percent of the total assets of the fund changed hands during the year. That means if a fund had $100 million in assets, the value of the securities that "turned over" during the year amounted to $32 million. Fidelity Growth & Income, whose average assets were $26.7 billion during this fiscal year, had securities trades worth about $10 billion. Thirty-eight percent turnover is low. The average equity fund has a turnover of 80 percent. (There's more about portfolio turnover in Chapter 7.)

Following the financial highlights, there's a short section on fund performance, showing the average annual total returns and cumulative total returns for the fund over various fiscal-year periods. The fund performance is also compared to the S&P 500 and to the Lipper Growth & Income Funds Average. Perhaps more meaningful to investors is another table that shows the fund's returns year by year on a calendar year basis. This table also compares each year's returns to that of the S&P 500, the Lipper Growth and Income Funds Average, and the U.S. Consumer Price Index.

INVESTMENT POLICY

After the financials, the prospectus turns to the investment objective. In the Growth & Income prospectus, for instance, the section is called "Investment Principles and Risks." The investment policy section will outline the overall strategy, the permitted investments in the broadest of terms (i.e., stocks or U.S. government or government-guaranteed securities), and restrictions, if there are any.

For a fund with a descriptive name (i.e., a fund that says small company or health care or North America in its name), pay particular attention to what else the fund can do. For instance, in early 1995, a group of shareholders filed a lawsuit against the Alliance North American Government Income Fund, which suffered severe losses during the Mexican currency crisis. The lawyers' complaint? The fund name said it was North American, but the fund had invested in Argentina, which, of course, is in South America. But the prospectus noted that only 65 percent of the fund had to be in North American debt obligations— and the fund met that condition. (In addition, in reports to shareholders, the fund had advised them of the Argentine holdings—yet another reason to read those shareholder reports.)

Pay careful attention to the investment objective and how the fund managers plan to achieve it, especially the kind of risk they might undertake (with your money). Be forewarned. Most fund prospectuses are written in a way that gives fund managers the widest latitude and discretion.

Some funds try to boost returns by trading futures and options contracts or other derivatives. That must be spelled out. Is preservation of capital the utmost priority? Don't assume it is, even if the investment is a government bond fund. Some sacrifice net asset value in order to deliver a high payout, and it says so—though not in such blunt language.

The information in this section helps to describe the fund's character. First Eagle Fund of America, for instance, says it will pursue capital appreciation with a flexible investment strategy that may include junk bonds, foreign securities, restricted securities (illiquid securities that are not publicly traded), and "special situations"—opportunities that may arise from liquidations, reorganizations, mergers, material litigation, technological breakthroughs, or new management and management policies. Moreover, First Eagle may buy and sell options and futures contracts and even "leverage its assets for securities purchases"—that's another way to say the fund buys on margin. If you'd sleep better with a fund that invests solely in well-known blue-chips, First Eagle is probably not for you.

SHAREHOLDER SERVICES

Look for services and conveniences. The standard ones are automatic investment and reinvestment of dividends and capital gains distributions. They'll be described in the prospectus. Most money-market funds and many bond funds also offer check-writing privileges. But those that do will often require that you write a check of $500 or $1000 at the least, so don't plan on using these funds to pay at the supermarket. Convenient as they are, such privileges are no substitute for a conventional checking account. (U.S. Global Investors Treasury Securities Cash Fund is a U.S. money-market fund with no minimum check size, and no limit on the number of checks written.)

Automatic investing is an arrangement you set up between the fund company and your bank. You can make periodic investments from your checking account to a designated mutual fund. It's an excellent way to accumulate capital, and unlike a contractual arrangement that some funds still market, you can stop or alter the program at your discretion without any penalty.

Most fund groups ordinarily roll over the dividends and capital gains into new shares. That's

The fund's investment goals should match yours.

one of the major benefits of investing in mutual funds. By reinvesting your earnings you have the opportunity to compound the growth rate of the fund. It's the same idea as earning interest on your interest.

Be sure to indicate on your application what you want done with the dividends and distributions. Those using funds for income sometimes take the dividends in cash or have them deposited into their money-market funds and reinvest the capital gains. If you give no indication at all, the funds will reinvest all the proceeds. If you're a long-term investor, reinvest.

Redemptions

Putting money into a mutual fund is simple. Fidelity Investments' walk-in centers, for instance, make investing easy by having personnel on hand to field questions, take applications, and accept checks. But though you can invest at one of these locations as though you were making a deposit at a local bank, you can't make a "withdrawal" on the spot. The money must come through regular channels, either a check by mail or by bank wire.

Getting money out isn't quite as simple as putting it in. But there's a whole lot less bother to taking money out if you plan for it on the way in. Some investors are surprised to find a $5 exchange or redemption fee taken out of their proceeds when they get their account statement. But if you've read about the fund's redemption procedures in the prospectus ahead of time, it should not be a shock. It has to be in the fee table, along with information about sales charges, 12(b)-1 fees, and the like.

Most funds offer telephone redemption privileges. But that's not something to request on the day you want the money. It's best to do it when setting up the account. If you have an existing account that doesn't have telephone switching privileges, request the form that permits it. And don't assume that if some funds in a family of funds offer telephone redemption, all the funds in the group do. Several of the Vanguard equity funds, for instance, are off-limits to telephone switches.

Even when a fund offers telephone redemption there may be limits on the amount of money

that can be withdrawn or the number of switches within a given period. Plan on following the advice of a mutual fund timing service? Ask if the fund group has any qualms about letting frequent switchers into their funds. (That's something you won't find in the prospectus but will have to ask a fund representative yourself.) Sometimes fund groups permit intrafamily telephone switches from an equity fund to a bond fund or money-market fund, but may restrict telephone withdrawal from the fund group. Depending on the amount of money involved (sometimes it's anything over $5000), the fund company may want written instructions.

Obtaining quick access to your funds is especially important with money-market funds since they're most often used as liquid assets or "rainy day" emergency money. All money-fund accounts should be set up with telephone redemption privileges.

Ask for check-writing privileges too. Even if you don't use the checks for regular bill-paying, the checks provide quick access to your account. Most funds can transmit funds by wire to your bank, but again that's not something to negotiate over the phone on the day you need the money. If you want this service, the fund will ask for the appropriate banking information on the application. There's usually a charge for the service as well as a minimum amount of money that must be wired.

Pay particular attention to a fund group's rules on withdrawals. They're not all the same. For many funds a signature on a redemption letter may not be enough. The company may require that the signature (and that of any other person whose name is on the account) be "guaranteed." A signature guarantee is an endorsement that verifies that the signature is genuine. The guarantor will compare the authenticity of the signature to one already on file. You're supposed to sign the letter in the presence of the guarantor.

Many funds accept guarantees from commercial banks or savings institutions that are members of the Federal Deposit Insurance Corporation or brokerage firms that are members of the New York Stock Exchange. Some may accept others like state-insured thrifts and federally insured credit unions, but ask the fund service personnel first. A notary public's seal is usually unacceptable.

Building an Investment Portfolio

You've been reading about some of the new wonder drugs on the market, and you give your doctor a call. "Doc, these new drugs sound great. How about writing me some prescriptions for the two or three that you think are best?" Sounds absurd, doesn't it? First you have to know what ails you before you get a prescription.

Yet many investors choose their investments the same way. They hear about a hot-performing fund, or a fund with a novel investment twist, and jump in. What they need to do first is examine their financial goals and decide what exactly they are trying to achieve through their investments (Table 4-1). Only then can they make a sensible choice from the multitude of investment opportunities. There are hundreds of excellent mutual funds out there, but not every one of them—even those with the highest BUSINESS WEEK ratings—is appropriate for every investor.

Determining Your Financial Goals

The 35-year-old physician with two preschool-aged children needs to build capital—and has time on her side. She would probably benefit from an all-equity portfolio, with the number of funds depending on how much money she was starting with. With $10,000 or so, she might go for five funds: a large-cap blend fund such as the Vanguard Index 500, which tracks the S&P 500; a mid-cap blend fund such as Mairs & Power Growth Fund or a mid-cap value fund like Strong Schafer Value Fund; a small-cap value fund such

as Royce Micro-Cap; a small-cap growth fund such as Baron Asset Fund or Acorn Fund; and a foreign fund such as Janus Overseas, T. Rowe Price International, or Templeton Foreign. With, say, $40,000 to $50,000 in assets, she might add large-cap growth and large-cap value funds to supplement or supplant the index fund and a diversified emerging markets fund to supplement the international component.

The 45-year-old computer programmer, having built some savings through aggressive investing, may have to settle for a lower return to steady his investment portfolio. He's about to embark on years of college tuition payments for his children and he wants to be sure the money will be there when he needs it. So he's keeping at least one year's worth of tuition and room and board payments in an ultrashort bond fund like the Strong Advantage Fund. He's lightened up a bit on the more aggressive small-cap and mid-cap growth funds. Now, less volatile funds like Vanguard/Windsor II Fund, Fidelity Equity-Income, and Third Avenue Value Fund have more appeal

TABLE 4-1

BEFORE INVESTING, CONSIDER...

▶ Do you need current income from your investments?

▶ How soon will you need the proceeds of your investments?

▶ How will inflation affect you?

▶ How much risk are you willing to take?

▶ How will taxes affect your investments?

▶ What kind of temperament do you have for investing?

to him. He still owns international funds, which make up 25 percent of his portfolio. And, except for the college money that's tucked away in the ultrashort bond fund, it's still an all-equity portfolio.

The 55-year-old lawyer is finished with his children's education and is now socking it away for retirement about 10 years hence. He still has 80 percent of his portfolio in equities, but only about 10 percent is in the volatile small-cap growth funds. As his tolerance for risk has lessened, he's tilting more of his equity investments to the value categories—small-cap value, mid-cap value, and large-cap value. On the international side, he also has value-oriented funds, such as Tweedy Browne Global Value.

His friend, also 55, is a corporate executive who fears that cutbacks might cost him his job and force him into early retirement. He too is moving from more aggressive equity funds to tamer funds such as T. Rowe Price Equity-Income. For the fixed-income portion of the portfolio, he chooses less volatile intermediate-term bond funds like American Century-Benham GNMA Income and Harbor Bond.

Mutual funds, like all investments, are only means to an end, not an end in themselves. They're used to accumulate a down payment for your first home, as an educational fund for your children, or as a nest egg for your retirement. So before you choose the investment vehicle, you need to assess what goal you want to achieve through your investments. If you go to a travel agent, the first question is, "Where do you want to go?" not "Which airline do you want to fly?"

The conventional wisdom says younger people should take on the most risky investments and gradually shift over to less risky investments as they age. By the time they're retired they should be into income-producing vehicles almost entirely. But the conventional wisdom is too general to serve everybody's needs. If you're in your late twenties, and saving to buy a home, you don't have decades to wait. You'll need money-market funds and short-term bond funds to help you achieve that objective. You may have a two-track investment plan. Keep taxable assets in the shorter-term investments and keep the long-term investments, like growth-oriented equity funds, in your IRA.

Likewise, many retirees shift too quickly into income-producing investments, whether they need them or not. Younger retirees, in particular, might do best if they stick with equities when their various pensions and other sources of retirement income suffice. Life expectancy is going up, and retirees in their early sixties may live well into their eighties. That means they need to increase their capital faster than the rate of inflation. They're going to need equity investments to do that.

To help choose the most appropriate funds for an investment program, you should first answer the following series of questions.

DO YOU NEED CURRENT INCOME FROM YOUR INVESTMENTS?

If you're the kind of person who needs to spend the interest from your certificates of deposit, you need current income. Most investors for whom current income is a priority are retirees, but not exclusively. Sometimes families may have some investment capital, obtained perhaps through an inheritance, but need to use it to generate income to meet expenses. A single parent, for instance, may need income from investments to supplement other sources.

Figure how much income you need from your investments. Start with an estimate of how much regular income you need in total, and then subtract all other sources, such as salaries, pension payments, Social Security payments, and the like. Suppose you need $60,000 a year, and all other sources produce $50,000. Your portfolio will have to produce $10,000. Long-term interest rates are around 6 percent, and yields on stocks are, on average, only 1.6 percent. You'll need at least $167,000 invested in long-term bonds (or bond funds) to produce $10,000. But if you have $300,000 you can count on, the other $133,000 could be invested for capital appreciation. That will enable you to build a larger portfolio for the day when $10,000 won't be enough.

If you have a regular income from your job that meets your needs, current income should not even be a consideration. You should emphasize investments that shoot for capital gains, not income. Sure, you balance the two. But remember, investments that maximize current income, like money-market mutual funds, provide no capital gains. And many bond funds that maximize current income will, at times, suffer capital losses.

These guidelines are not inviolable absolutes. When short-term interest rates are high, say 12 percent, a money-market mutual fund is going to be a hard investment to beat. The return would be so large and the risks so minimal that no other investment would look competitive.

HOW SOON WILL YOU NEED THE PROCEEDS OF YOUR INVESTMENTS?

Identifying the right time horizon goes a long way toward finding the right funds. If you're saving for a goal 15 years distant—like college tuition for a preschooler—you can rely on equity funds to carry the weight of reaching your goals. Over long periods of time they outperform bond and money-market funds. For periods of less than 10 years, short- and intermediate-term bond funds have to play a greater role in the portfolio. Cash that's going to be tapped in a year or less should be invested in a money-market fund.

Some people fail to grasp the importance of the time horizon. What is the long term, they say, but a series of short terms back to back? So why not just invest short term and continue to reinvest over and over again?

Here's why. In the 70 years for which good records exist, U.S. Treasury bills—the safest short-term investment around—have delivered an average annual return of 3.8 percent, and long-term government bonds, 5.2 percent. During the same period, the total return on common stocks—capital appreciation plus reinvestment of dividends—averaged 11 percent per year. The story is much the same if you look at only 30 years. Fixed-income returns are higher, but they still lag well behind equities.

The time horizon is easy to quantify. If it's 1998 and your child starts college in 2008, his or her education fund has a time horizon of 10 to 14 years. If you're 40 now and have a 401(k) retirement plan at work, the 401(k)'s time horizon is at least 19 years (you can start withdrawing funds at age 59½), but it's more likely to be 27 or 30. Think of the time horizon as a balance sheet: The assets are your investments, the liabilities are the expenses to be funded in future years.

HOW WILL INFLATION AFFECT YOU?

Since your investment dollars will ultimately be used to "purchase" goods or services some time in the future, then inflation, the erosion of purchasing power, is an important matter that must be considered in your investment portfolio. If you don't take the impact of inflation into account in your investment planning, you risk being ravaged by its effects.

Think of it this way. You invest $1000 in a 30-year U.S. government bond paying 6 percent interest. You collect $60 a year (actually, $30 every six months), and in 30 years you get back your $1000. Suppose that for now the $33 semi-annual payment buys you and your spouse dinner at a modestly priced restaurant (and you don't order alcoholic beverages and you skip dessert).

What will it buy in 10 years? If inflation is modest, say only 3 percent, that $33 will be $24.50 in today's money. So, in 10 years, what bought dinner for two now may buy lunch for one—maybe. What about the principal? If inflation averages only 3 percent a year for the next three decades, the $1000 will have only about $412 worth of purchasing power. Maybe dinner for one, if you're lucky.

To get a jump on inflation, you have to buy equity funds. Common stocks and small company stocks have shown over the long haul that they beat the Consumer Price Index hands down. True there are times—like the 1970s—when inflation ravaged the stock market. Stocks in general don't usually beat inflation in periods when inflation is accelerating. But small company stocks can do well in inflationary periods if the companies' growth rates outpace inflation.

International stock and international bond mutual funds should also help guard a portfolio from inflation. In periods of inflation in the United States, the dollar tends to drop in value against foreign currencies. This in itself feeds inflation because U.S. consumers must pay more dollars for imported goods. But when the dollar goes down in value, assets denominated in foreign currencies go up. So to the extent you have money in foreign assets, you have a hedge against the declining value of your dollars.

HOW MUCH RISK ARE YOU WILLING TO TAKE?

As the jocks will tell you, "No pain, no gain." Well, in the investment world the pain is the risk and volatility. We don't seem to mind when the Dow Jones industrial average shoots up 100 points in a day, but we're unhappy when it's down that much. People say they don't like volatility and risk, but what they're really telling you is that they don't want their investments to go down. Nobody ever complained when their investments went up.

Most investors are so risk averse that they fail to make objective judgments. Taking risks isn't easy. Psychologists studying how people make financial decisions have found that most will shy away from risks, even when the odds dictate otherwise. Many people pay a premium in the form of a lower return on their investment for the greater certainty of preserving that capital.

To best fight inflation, invest in equity funds.

That's because most people are more influenced by their fear of losses than by the prospect of gains. Behavioral psychologists, in fact, find that the pain of a loss looms twice as large as the pleasure of an equivalent gain. Even if the odds are 50-50, the average person will take a risk only if he or she can win twice as much as he or she can lose.

Investors often avoid risks because they're more influenced by recent history than by a long run of events. For most of 1987, investors couldn't get enough of the stock market. From January through August, the Dow industrials gained over 800 points. The fact was, as the Dow climbed, it became very risky. Stocks entered the overvalued zone in terms of corporate earnings, book value, and dividend yields. But as the market went up, people paid little attention to those risks.

Then the market crashed, losing 508 points on October 19, 1987. More than one-fifth of the market value of Corporate America was washed away in six and a half hours. In the following weeks stocks were marked down by more than a third from the summer's high, yet no one wanted the merchandise. They were afraid, or waiting for the 50-percent-off sale. Of course, the weeks after the crash, in retrospect, were the time to buy. Yet investors were far too scared to do so.

If you're like most investors, you've erred on the side of caution. You have probably underestimated the amount of risk you can take (like having too much in money-market funds relative to your investment goals) and are paying for it dearly in lost opportunities. It's a serious matter when it comes to pension savings. When companies give employees the option of directing how their pension funds are to be invested—the nub of the increasingly popular 401(k) plans—they have tended to choose fixed-income investments. Only in the last few years have participants opted for equity investments. Still, the existing base of 401(k) money is still overweighted with interest-bearing investments. Younger employees, in particular, need stocks if they are to have enough on which to retire. When companies direct the pension plan investments, they place 60 to 70 percent of the assets in stocks.

If you have a long time horizon, your ability to take risks is greatly enhanced. Here's why. The long-term return from owning stocks is 11 percent, more than twice as much as from bonds. But, of course, stocks don't achieve that return year-in and year-out. In 1995, 1996, and 1997, for instance, the stocks in the Standard & Poor's 500 stock index racked up total returns (price appreciation plus dividends) of 37.5, 22.9, and 33.4 percent, respectively. And 1991 was a banner year as well, with a 30.4 percent gain. In 1992, the return was a more modest 7.6 percent; in 1993, the return was 10.1 percent; and in 1994, only 1.3 percent. Over the last six decades the best year was 1933—in the depths of the depression. Stocks gained 54 percent. The worst year was two years earlier, in 1931, when stocks lost more than 43 percent of their value. Since World War II the best year was 1954, up 52.6 percent; the worst, 1974, down 26.5 percent.

Though any one year's results can be a stunner, over time the law of averages takes over. In any one year, statisticians estimate, the probable return from common stocks is between –10 percent and +30 percent. But over a five-year period, that expected range of returns narrows considerably—from +1 percent to +19 percent. And over 20 years, the range of expected returns is +5.5 to +14.5 percent. Simply put, the more years in your average, the more likely your results will look like the long-term average.

HOW WILL TAXES AFFECT YOUR INVESTMENTS?

Most investment advisers would caution you against making an investment solely because it shelters you from taxes. For many years lots of buildings were built because investors coveted the tax-sheltering attributes of commercial real estate. That they had tenants for the buildings was only a secondary consideration. The best investments are those that make sound economic sense.

But once you've identified a good investment idea, you should see how it stands up to the tax system. To do that, you have to know—or have a pretty good approximation of—what your marginal tax bracket is. And don't forget to include state and local income taxes when you make that calculation.

Suppose your combined federal and state marginal tax bracket is 35 percent. What that means is that for every additional $1 in income, the tax folks siphon off 35 cents. So you have to start asking yourself, "How much do I want to bring in, and how much can I defer?"

When it comes to the taxes, mutual funds don't have a whole lot of leeway. The tax laws say a fund must pay out 98 percent of its net income and realized capital gains each year (that's net after deducting the expenses of running the fund). A fund that yields 5 percent may leave shareholders with only 3.25 percent after they've paid taxes.

If you want to minimize taxes, concentrate on small-cap and mid-cap growth funds. For one, the sorts of stocks these funds buy pay few or no dividends. And if the portfolio manager has a policy of holding stocks for the long term, he or she is not going to do a lot of trading. Trading and, more importantly, profits from trading produce gains that must be passed on to shareholders. Some fund advisers recommend index funds because of their ultra-low turnover. The only time they sell a stock is when it is removed from the index, an infrequent occasion.

In the matter of bond and money-market funds, it's always wise to examine whether a lower-yielding tax-free fund will provide a greater aftertax return than a taxable one. Table 4-2 walks you through the calculation of how to know whether a tax-free investment will provide a better return than a taxable one.

Of course, if you're investing within the confines of a tax-deferred account, like an IRA, you don't give a hoot about taxation. There's no tax until you start withdrawing from a conventional IRA or a 401(k), and in the case of a Roth IRA, there's no tax on withdrawal. About the only thing you need to remember is: Tax-free municipal bonds or bond funds don't belong in a tax-deferred plan.

WHAT KIND OF TEMPERAMENT DO YOU HAVE FOR INVESTING?

Looking at income needs, taxes, time horizons, and the like, it's easy to come up with an objective conclusion such as: I should put 70 percent of my money in small-cap and mid-cap growth funds. All well and good. You understand the rationale and fully accept the notion that, with your time horizon, the riskier, higher-return vehicles should deliver the best results.

But if you're the sort of person who shudders at the thought of losing a piece of your principal, who worries about every twist and turn of the stock market, who would become stressed out if your investment went south for a while, this investment program is not for you. If you like the plan, but your spouse doesn't, it's not worth straining a marriage. If 70 percent is too heavy a concentration in equities, see if you can start with 25 percent in a stock mutual fund. If you (or your spouse) can get comfortable with that, then you can always increase the percentage of your assets in equities. Don't be ashamed to move cau-

tiously. Advice comes from others, but the money that's invested on that advice is yours.

Research on how people make investment decisions has turned up some interesting observations that may help you examine your ability to take investment risks. In her work on the psychological characteristics of individual investors, Marilyn MacGruder Barnewall, a financial consultant, describes the "passive investor" and the "active investor."

Passive investors—and most people fall into this category—have a greater need for security than tolerance for risk. In fact, they usually per-

TABLE 4-2

WHAT'S A SINGLE-STATE MUNI BOND FUND WORTH TO YOU?

State	FEDERAL MARGINAL TAX RATE				State	FEDERAL MARGINAL TAX RATE			
	28%	31%	36%	39.6%		28%	31%	36%	39.6%
ALABAMA	31.6	34.5	39.2	42.6	MISSOURI	32.3	35.1	39.8	43.2
ARIZONA	31.5	34.3	39.1	42.5	MONTANA	35.9	38.6	43.0	46.2
ARKANSAS	33.0	35.8	40.5	43.8	NEBRASKA	33.0	35.8	40.5	43.8
CALIFORNIA	34.7	37.4	42.0	45.2	N. HAMPSHIRE	31.6	34.5	39.2	42.6
COLORADO	31.6	34.5	39.2	42.6	NEW JERSEY	30.5	35.4	40.1	43.4
CONNECTICUT	31.2	34.1	38.9	42.3	NEW MEXICO	33.7	36.9	41.4	44.7
DELAWARE	33.0	35.8	40.4	43.8	NEW YORK	32.9	35.7	40.4	43.7
DIST. OF COL.	34.8	37.6	42.1	45.3	N. Y. CITY	35.3	38.1	42.6	45.8
GEORGIA	32.3	35.1	39.8	43.2	N. CAROLINA	33.0	36.3	41.0	44.3
HAWAII	35.2	37.9	42.4	45.6	N. DAKOTA	36.6	39.3	43.7	46.8
IDAHO	33.9	36.7	41.2	44.6	OHIO	32.8	35.6	40.6	43.9
INDIANA	31.2	34.0	38.8	42.3	OKLAHOMA	35.2	37.9	42.4	45.6
IOWA	35.2	37.9	42.4	45.6	OREGON	34.5	37.2	41.8	45.0
KANSAS	33.6	36.3	41.0	44.3	PENNSYLVANIA	30.0	32.9	37.8	41.3
KENTUCKY	32.3	35.1	39.8	43.2	RHODE ISLAND	33.5	36.9	42.3	46.2
LOUISIANA	30.9	35.1	39.8	43.2	S. CAROLINA	33.0	35.8	40.5	43.8
MAINE	33.4	36.9	41.4	44.7	TENNESSEE	32.3	35.1	39.8	43.2
MARYLAND	33.4	36.2	40.8	44.1	UTAH	33.2	35.8	40.5	43.8
MASS.	36.6	39.3	43.7	46.8	VERMONT	33.0	36.3	41.8	45.6
MICHIGAN	31.2	34.0	38.8	42.3	VIRGINIA	32.1	35.0	39.7	43.1
MINNESOTA	33.8	36.9	41.4	44.7	WEST VIRGINIA	32.7	35.5	40.2	43.5
MISSISSIPPI	31.6	34.5	39.2	42.6	WISCONSIN	33.0	35.8	40.4	43.8

Suppose you are a Californian with a combined federal and state marginal tax bracket of 42%. What's the tax-equivalent yield for a California municipal bond fund yielding 5%? Here's the calculation:

$$\frac{\text{Tax-free yield}}{1 - \text{Combined marginal tax rate}} = \text{Tax-equivalent yield}$$

$$\frac{5}{1 - (0.42)} = \frac{5}{0.58} = 0.0862 \text{ or } 8.62\%$$

The 5% yield would be the equivalent of an 8.62% taxable yield.

DATA: FRANKLIN RESOURCES, BUSINESS WEEK

Make sure
you have a
cash stash.

ceive risks to be greater than they are. These people typically have come by their wealth "passively"—by inheritance or by risking others' capital to achieve their wealth. Included in this group are most corporate executives and most people who are employed by others. This is not to suggest that those who work for salaries do nothing for them, but the investment capital at stake in their enterprise is not theirs—and that's a critical factor. Passive investors are more likely to use brokers, investment advisers, or financial planners.

Active investors, on the other hand, are individuals who have earned their own wealth in their lifetimes. Barnewall says these people understand how to take risks and have a higher tolerance for risk than a need for security. In fact, they often underestimate their risks. Their tolerance for risk is high, she says, because of a strong belief in themselves. They usually feel most comfortable with investments which they "control." So, for some active investors, mutual funds may be unappealing since the funds' portfolio managers are the ones calling the shots on what stocks to buy and sell. On the other hand, the mutual fund universe is diverse enough to offer many choices and timing decisions, so an active investor can still achieve a lot of control. Nonetheless, direct sales funds would probably be more appealing to active investors than those sold through brokers or other intermediaries.

Of course, no one is totally one thing or the other. Passive investors may maintain, say, 70 percent of their investments in relatively secure products like certificates of deposit, money-market funds, and bond funds, with the other 30 percent in more risky ventures like growth funds. Active investors may do just the opposite.

The investment counseling firm of Bailard Biehl & Kaiser takes a different approach to sizing up investors' ability to take risk. Their work identifies four sorts of investor profiles: "adventurer," "celebrity," "individualist," and "guardian." Adventurers are just that. They like risk and they often make intuitive judgments. Celebrities are the trendies—fashion followers wanting to do what's hot rather than what's best. Individualists are the entrepreneurial sort and take a rational, methodical approach to most everything they do. Then there's the guardians, who are nervous about preserving their wealth and seek guidance in doing so.

Do you recognize yourself in one of these categories? Are you an adventurer? If so, you may need to practice a little self-restraint. Before embarking on a financial adventure, be sure you have enough of your assets under a fairly conservative investment program. Celebrity? You need restraint too. Your history is probably one in which you've made a lot of investments, but have not earned much to show for it. Individualists, as it turns out, often make the best investors.

Putting It All Together

Okay, you now know what you want from your investments and have a good idea of what kind of investor you are. You still need to choose a mutual fund portfolio. And with over 6000 funds (including money-market funds) available, the job is not easy. But don't be overwhelmed by it. Think about your favorite supermarket. There are thousands of items on its shelves and in the refrigerated and freezer cases, but does that fact prevent you from shopping? You choose what you need and virtually ignore the thousands of items you don't need. True, the supermarket is familiar ground, while the mutual fund market is not. Yet with a good shopping list and smart shopping skills, it's possible to assemble an ideal portfolio of funds.

What you need is an idea of the categories of funds you want and in what proportions. In theory, the higher-risk funds should provide the higher rewards, though that's over a multiyear period. You certainly can't make that generalization for short-term results. To get an idea of how the various categories of funds stack up on risk, look at Figure 4-1. Keep this chart of relative risk in mind as you design and assemble a portfolio of funds.

The risk spectrum here goes from 0 to 10. Money-market funds, for purposes of this exercise, will be assumed to have zero risk. The riskiest funds here are precious metals funds, which are well ahead of the next two risky funds, Latin America and Pacific ex-Japan. (These calculations are based on the last five years of performance.) The most volatile of the diversified funds, emerging markets, is still far less risky than precious metals and Latin America. The equity funds that mix in bonds and cash, the hybrid funds, have a much lower risk profile, between 2.4 and 3.1. Among the specialty funds, utilities funds have similar risk characteristics. They're all a little riskier than any of the bond funds, which pretty much cluster between 1 and 2.

FIGURE 4-1

MUTUAL FUNDS RISK SPECTRUM

Are specialized funds riskier than diversified equity funds? How much risk is there in bond funds compared to equity funds? Here's a chart that can help investors understand the relative risk of various types of mutual funds. The risk scale goes from 0 to 10, with 0 defined as no risk. Money-market funds are not on the chart, since there are no fluctuations in their net asset value (NAV). Some specialized funds, like technology and precious metals, are at the high end of the risk spectrum. The NAVs of these funds can fluctuate sharply.

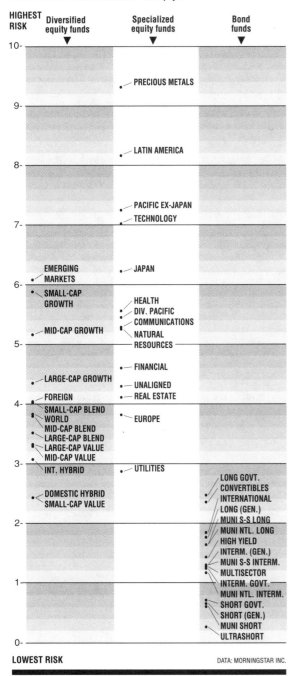

HIGHEST RISK

Diversified equity funds | Specialized equity funds | Bond funds

PRECIOUS METALS

LATIN AMERICA

PACIFIC EX-JAPAN
TECHNOLOGY

EMERGING MARKETS
JAPAN

SMALL-CAP GROWTH
HEALTH
DIV. PACIFIC
COMMUNICATIONS
MID-CAP GROWTH
NATURAL RESOURCES

FINANCIAL
LARGE-CAP GROWTH
UNALIGNED
FOREIGN
REAL ESTATE
SMALL-CAP BLEND
WORLD
MID-CAP BLEND
EUROPE
LARGE-CAP BLEND
LARGE-CAP VALUE
MID-CAP VALUE
INT. HYBRID
UTILITIES

DOMESTIC HYBRID
SMALL-CAP VALUE

LONG GOVT.
CONVERTIBLES
INTERNATIONAL
LONG (GEN.)
MUNI S-S LONG
MUNI NTL. LONG
HIGH YIELD
INTERM. (GEN.)
MUNI S-S INTERM.
MULTISECTOR
INTERM. GOVT.
MUNI NTL. INTERM.
SHORT GOVT.
SHORT (GEN.)
MUNI SHORT
ULTRASHORT

LOWEST RISK

DATA: MORNINGSTAR INC.

First, before making an investment, be sure you have a cash reserve that totals a minimum of six months' living expenses. Set it aside in a money-market mutual fund. That's not part of the long-term investment program. It's a rainy-day account, and if you tap into it, be sure to replenish it. If you're in a high tax bracket, you might consider using a tax-free money-market fund instead of a taxable one.

YOUR ASSET ALLOCATION PLAN

When you're ready to invest, you need an "asset allocation" plan. That's just a strategy on how to divvy up your money. A sample asset allocation plan may recommend placing 50 percent of the portfolio in U.S. equities, 30 percent in bonds, 10 percent in foreign stocks, and 10 percent in foreign bonds.

Many money managers devise allocations with elaborate computer models that make the whole process look about as simple as performing the calculations to guide a spacecraft to Mars. Most of the popular personal finance software programs also perform this function. Many mutual fund companies will also give you software that will do the same, usually putting you through a quiz, adding up points, and recommending an asset allocation plan based on your score. Some of the more sophisticated programs will allow you to set minimum or maximum allocations, such as no less than 10 percent or more than 50 percent, for various sorts of asset classes (for our purposes, large company mutual funds, small company funds, international funds, etc.). It then crunches the numbers, spitting out a range of asset mixes that go from the safest to the riskiest.

Some of the programs describe the probability of achieving or exceeding your goal over several time periods. One hint: Don't take the first allocation that pops up. If the program allows it, tinker with the choices and the parameters until you get something that "feels" right. What happens if I add more stocks? Change my time horizon? Once you have a plan, it's easy to implement it through mutual funds. Large-cap funds fit big stocks; small- and mid-cap funds fit little stocks; international funds fit foreign stocks; money-market funds fit Treasury bills, etc.

There are other ways to get help in devising your plan. If you are working with a broker, financial planner, or investment adviser, that's part of his or her job. Even the direct marketing fund companies are now helping investors with asset allocation. Firms like Dreyfus, Fidelity,

T. Rowe Price, Scudder, and Vanguard, to name a few, all offer various worksheets, computer software, consultations, and seminars.

ACHIEVING YOUR FINANCIAL GOALS

The right asset allocation plan starts with the financial goal. Are you trying to accumulate a specific amount of money? Perhaps you want to be able to send your four-year-old to a top-drawer private college, which, in today's dollars, costs about $33,000 a year for tuition, books, and living expenses. How much will you need?

Hold on to your hat. Assume that costs will rise at 8 percent a year, since educational expenses have continued to run far in excess of the Consumer Price Index. Today's $33,000-a-year college costs will be nearly $100,000 a year 14 years hence, when your preschooler starts college.

How are you going to get that money? To fund a $100,000 expense, you'll need 100 zero-coupon Treasury bonds that mature in 2012. In early 1998 such bonds had a yield of 5.99 percent, and would cost $421.56 each, a little more than $42,156 for the lot. (Zeros are sold at a discount to face value and mature at par.) And that would only take care of one year's education. What about the other three? Graduate school? And other children?

But if you could earn a higher rate of return on your investments, you wouldn't need to put as much up front. True, the long-term return from stocks is only 11 percent, but suppose that through savvy mutual fund investments you could earn 2 percentage points more? Then you would only have to put up a little less than $20,000 to get $100,000.

If you don't happen to have a spare $20,000 either, you're going to have to start a regular savings and investment program. The college fund planning kits available from many fund companies and brokerage firms will help you determine how much you'll need and how much you have to save per month or per year to achieve that goal. For instance, if you can earn an average 10 percent return, saving about $250 a month—for the next 14 years—will get you $90,000. But if, through more aggressive and riskier investments, you get an average 12 percent return, your $250 a month should come out to around $107,000. Of course, that only covers one year of college. But look at it this way: As you and your child or children get older, you should be putting more money away each month. The more you put away, the more you'll earn.

SAVINGS FOR RETIREMENT

And what about savings for retirement? Projecting how much you're going to need in 25 years to carry you through another 20 or so after that may seem pointless. But many mutual fund companies, brokerage firms, and financial planners have worksheets or software that can walk you through the exercise. You don't have to be an actuary, nor do you have to know what your grocery bill will be in the year 2020. Expenses are calculated in today's dollars, and they are later multiplied by an inflation factor. Based on your current nest egg and how much you can expect it to grow, the worksheet will tell you how much a year you have to save in addition to reach your retirement goal.

But let's face it. The longer your time horizon, the less accurate specific targets are going to be. You might just approach the investment in a way that would let you earn a rate of return in excess of the inflation rate. That should preserve purchasing power and build some extra capital too.

TABLE 4-3

THE LONG, LONG HAUL

What would have happened to $1000 invested in each of these funds for the 57-year period, Jan. 1, 1940–Dec. 31, 1997?

	Total value ▼	Average annual total return* ▼
EQUITY FUNDS		
INVESTMENT CO. OF AMERICA	$1,202,098	13.3%
FIDELITY FUND	1,138,233	13.1
KEYSTONE STRATEGIC GROWTH (K-2)	1,046,246	13.0
LORD ABBETT AFFILIATED FUND	884,727	12.6
SELIGMAN GROWTH	838,244	12.5
SELIGMAN COMMON STOCK	797,698	12.4
BALANCED FUNDS		
DELAWARE FUND	$501,850	11.5%
AMERICAN BALANCED	281,378	10.4
GEORGE PUTNAM FUND OF BOSTON	256,536	10.2
CGM MUTUAL	241,138	10.1
ALLIANCE BALANCED	189,892	9.6
BOND FUNDS		
KEYSTONE HIGH INCOME (B-4)	$179,599	9.5%
LORD ABBETT U.S. GOVERNMENT SECS.	103,154	8.5
SCUDDER INCOME	67,486	7.7

*Pretax return, includes reinvestment of dividends and capital gains

DATA: CDA/WIESENBERGER, MORNINGSTAR INC.

Over the past 70 years, stocks have beaten the inflation rate handily, with an average return that is 7 percentage points higher than the Consumer Price Index. Small company stocks, the sort you find in small-cap funds and some mid-cap mutual funds, did even better, 9 percentage points higher. Over a 57-year period starting in 1940, Investment Company of America achieved an average annual return of 13.3 percent (Table 4-3). The comparable inflation figure during that time was about 4 percent. According to Wiesenberger Investment Companies Service, five other funds also earned 12 percent or more per year.

Bonds, on the other hand, have only topped the inflation rate by a little more than 1 percentage point. But some bond funds that have been around for 57 years have fared far better: For the period 1940 through 1997, Keystone High-Income B-4 averaged 9.5 percent and Lord Abbett U.S. Government Securities, 8.5 percent.

True, bonds in general have not given much inflation protection, but it's quite possible that bonds will provide better returns in the future. That's because a fundamental shift has taken place in the capital markets and the way that interest rates are determined. Prior to 1979 the Federal Reserve—the U.S. central bank and traffic cop for the money that flows through the economy—would look at the economy, decide what the interest rate should be, and then try to manage the money supply in such a way as to achieve that rate.

That approach often fueled inflation since the Fed, though independent, was always under political pressure to keep interest rates down. The central bank often erred by keeping interest rates too low, which, in itself, is a contributing factor to inflation. But in the 1980s the Fed—and the rest of the world's major central banks—changed course, concentrating on the appropriate supply of money for the state of the economy. With tighter controls on the creation of money, the central bankers now let market forces determine interest rates.

The bright side of this more volatile world of bonds is that the "real" rates of return—what you're left with after counting the effects of inflation—have been high for the past decade and are likely to remain so. During the 1980s, for instance, the real rate of return on long-term government bonds was as high as 6 percentage points. While that abnormally high number did not last, it's a good bet the real rates will stay

well in excess of the 1.4 percent rate experienced over the last six decades.

One new development that bears watching is the Treasury's new inflation-indexed bonds. These long-term bonds, first issued in 1997, pay a low interest rate, around 3 percent, which remains the same for the life of the bond. The inflation adjustment is made to the principal. Several mutual fund companies have launched funds to invest in them, but it's too soon to tell if these bonds are a good investment or not. One thing is certain. The upward adjustments in the value of principal will be taxed as income, even though there is no payout. Thus, these sorts of bonds and bond funds should be held in a tax-deferred account only. Otherwise, you end up paying taxes on what some people call "phantom" income.

LOOK TO YOUR HORIZON

Since stocks remain the best long-term investments, mutual fund investors with long time horizons should invest heavily in equity funds. So start with the premise that investors in their twenties and thirties, and perhaps even through their forties, should invest in equity mutual funds. Their investment horizons are 20 years or more.

Those whose horizons are between 10 and 20 years—say the 40- to 50-year-olds—might begin to lower their risks by moving some of their assets into more conservative equity funds and some bond funds. Even at retirement, investors shouldn't shy away from equities. With improved medical care, many persons in their mid-sixties might well live another 20 years. These people are still going to need to keep some equities. If they convert everything to fixed-income investments early in their retirement, they may produce more income now but risk not having enough capital later.

Figure 4-2 lays out five different portfolio mixes for five different decades of life. Suppose you're in your early thirties. Your investment horizon is at least 30 years or so, you can tolerate a good deal of risk, and you need inflation protection. So you split your money into four pieces, putting equal amounts into large-cap, mid-cap, small-cap, and foreign funds. Within those groupings, choose both growth and value funds.

By your forties you may want to come down a notch in the riskiness of your equity funds. Perhaps now you would trim back the equity funds and use that portion of the allocation for high-yield bond funds. These funds bridge the stock and

Your fifties are peak years for investment.

FIGURE 4-2

BUILDING A MUTUAL FUND PORTFOLIO FOR YOUR NEEDS

THE 20s Single or married, the investment horizon calls for growth-oriented funds. Still, if you are yet to purchase a home, you will need some of your assets in a low-risk fund like a short-term bond fund. If you already have a home, consider the sample portfolio for the 30s.

20% LARGE-CAP
40% MONEY-MARKET OR SHORT-TERM BONDS
20% SMALL-CAP OR MID-CAP
20% FOREIGN

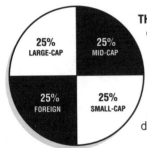

25% LARGE-CAP
25% MID-CAP
25% FOREIGN
25% SMALL-CAP

THE 30s Married, with small children, and you already have purchased a home. You're starting on a long-term investment program. College bills are a dozen or more years ahead of you, and retirement is decades away.

THE 40s You're more secure financially, but you have a more cautious investment program now. College may be a near-term expense. Retirement is still 20 or so years away. So the asset mix changes, and you introduce more conservative vehicles like high-yield bond funds, and short- or intermediate-term bond funds. That lowers the portfolio risk, but still provides long-term growth.

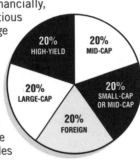

20% HIGH-YIELD
20% MID-CAP
20% LARGE-CAP
20% SMALL-CAP OR MID-CAP
20% FOREIGN

20% HIGH-YIELD
20% SHORT- OR INTERMEDIATE-TERM BOND
15% FOREIGN
20% SMALL-CAP OR MID-CAP
25% LARGE-CAP

The 50s You're still married, but you're empty nesters now. The children are grown, and finished or nearly finished with their educations. You are in your peak earning years, and should take advantage of that to sock it away for retirement.

THE 60s You're retired, but don't run from the equity funds. Hopefully, you have many, many years ahead of you, and will need to grow your capital. Only equities can do that.

DATA: BUSINESS WEEK

20% SHORT-TERM BOND
15% HIGH-YIELD
FOREIGN 10%
25% MID-CAP
30% LARGE-CAP

bond world, and exhibit characteristics of each (see Chapter 2). They can generate a return close to the long-term return from stocks, but with more income and less volatility. Since these funds' relatively large payouts are subject to ordinary income tax, these funds are best used in the confines of a tax-deferred retirement-type account.

For most people, the fifties are peak years for saving. Your earnings growth may have flattened out at this point, but often children are grown and educated, so your expenses have gone down. Disposable income grows and so does your ability to invest. At this point many people are more interested in socking it away than rolling the dice, so they come to depend more on fixed-income investments. You may keep your equity investments intact, but start to put new investment dollars into tax-free municipal bond funds.

For new retirees, the best investment advice is: Don't shorten your time horizon very much. If you put too much money into current income producers like money-market funds or short-term bond funds, you risk depleting your capital when it should be growing. And remember, too, that although $1 per share net asset value of money-market funds appears solid, the income produced by those $1 shares is quite volatile.

Suppose you've decided to put 40 percent into large-cap funds, 40 percent into mid-cap and small-cap funds, and 20 percent into international funds. How many funds do you need? One from each category? Two? You may decide that no fund should have more than 20 percent of your assets, so you choose two funds each for the growth and maximum growth portions of the portfolio and one international fund. If your entire stake were, say, $10,000, you might put $2000 each into two growth funds, $2000 in each of two more aggressive funds, and $2000 in one international fund—for five funds in all. If you have $50,000, you might want to introduce a few more funds into your portfolio.

Once you get started in mutual funds there are so many good opportunities that you may be tempted to invest in a lot of different funds. There's no sin in that by itself, but keep in mind that if you own a dozen funds when half a dozen would do, you're also burdening yourself with more paperwork. If you're using load funds, concentrating your investment dollars will allow you to qualify for discounts on the sales charge that aren't available to you if you're always investing small amounts. Finally, except for some specialty funds, most mutual funds are diversified to start with, so piling fund upon fund gives you little added benefit.

If the whole notion of a personalized asset allocation plan seems like overkill, there are alternatives. For instance, there's the "fund of funds" approach to asset allocation. T. Rowe Price has two Spectrum funds. Spectrum Growth divvies up your money among other Price equity funds and Spectrum Income does the same for fixed-income funds. The Vanguard STAR Fund tries to strike a balanced portfolio through investment in other Vanguard stock and bond funds. Fidelity Investments has a worksheet that helps you decide how much risk you can tolerate. The exercise leads you toward one of three asset allocation funds: Fidelity Asset Manager or Fidelity Asset Manager: Income, a slightly more conservative choice; or Fidelity Asset Manager: Growth, the most aggressive of the trio (see Chapter 2).

Several funds companies, such as Fidelity and Stagecoach, offer "life cycle" funds. Rather than your having to make the moves from the more aggressive to the more conservative funds as you age, these funds have a target "maturity." You choose the fund whose target maturity is around the time you want to retire. That way the fund's style of management mellows out with age, and you, in theory, don't have to worry about changing funds as you get older. It's an interesting concept, but there is no long-term record yet with these sorts of funds.

Using the Scoreboard Ratings

The BUSINESS WEEK Mutual Fund Scoreboard will help you to find the funds you need. We've made some changes in the ratings this year, but only in the symbols. In the past, we've rated funds using upward and downward-pointing arrows in seven categories, from three up arrows the best, followed by two-up, one-up, average, one-down, two-down, and three-down, the worst. Now, we've abolished the arrows, using letter grades with plusses and minuses instead. But we still have seven ratings categories, and the methodology for calculating those ratings has not changed. Now, A is superior, B+ is very good, B is above average, C is average, C– is below average, D is poor, and F is very poor. (Read more about the ratings in Chapter 7.)

You'll notice that lots of funds have no ratings. These funds are too new to be rated. That is, they don't have the five-year track record to qualify for a rating (three years for closed-end funds). Should you invest in them anyway? Many investment pros advise against it. There are enough long-lived funds in most fund categories that you don't need to use a fledgling fund.

If you buy funds through a broker or financial planner, no doubt you'll get a call to invest in a "hot" new mutual fund. There's no hurry. Remember, mutual funds are open-ended, and funds constantly take in new investments and create new shares. (If the broker is soliciting for a new closed-end fund, hang up the phone. Chances are, you'll be able to buy it cheaper six months to a year later. For further information, refer to Chapter 2's section on closed-end funds.)

Suppose you're getting a pitch for a technology fund and the time seems right to invest in technology. But there are already plenty of existing funds to choose from—and these funds have track records. If the fund is so unique that no alternative exists, you should be even more wary of putting your money down. The garbage dump of the investment business is strewn with great concepts that worked in theory—but not in practice.

Fund management companies often start new funds after an investment idea becomes hot. High-tech stocks, for instance, dazzled investors when the 1980s bull market took off in mid-1982. But technology funds that raised large sums during that period stumbled badly in subsequent years. It took until the early 1990s for these funds to really shine again. In the late 1980s, many short-term world income funds opened, seeking to capture the high short-term yields from abroad. The funds' high payouts were like manna to yield-starved U.S. investors until the European currency system came unglued in 1992—and chewed up the net asset values of these funds. The same thing happened with emerging markets debt funds in 1994.

One way to avoid problems is to adhere to an old rule of thumb in the fund business: Don't invest in a mutual fund until it has a five-year track record. Paying heed to this dictum would have saved investors from some of the newer "concept" funds—like short-term world income funds—which no doubt came to market when the concept was hot. True, it's near impossible for the average investor to look at the prospectus for such a fund and say it won't work. But time is a good test. The concept came undone within three years.

There are times to consider a new fund and waive the rule. Suppose the portfolio manager of

Beware of funds run by market "gurus."

a fund you already own and like starts a new fund. You may well follow him or her. A mutual fund is only a shell, an investment vehicle, and has no life of its own other than what its manager gives it. So following a respected manager can make sense. For instance, Thomas Marsico, the highly-regarded portfolio manager of the Janus Twenty and Janus Growth and Income Funds, left Janus in 1997 to start his own funds. In that sort of situation, following the manager to his new venue makes good sense.

On the other hand, beware of funds run by market "gurus." Some popular market soothsayers have learned the hard way that prognostication and portfolio management are very different skills, and that if you have one skill, you don't necessarily have the other. In mid-1987, for instance, Shearson Lehman Brothers launched a fund managed by its superstar stock market strategist, Elaine Garzarelli. In the first few months, Garzarelli made a brilliant call. She left the market in September and largely steered clear of the October 19, 1987 crash.

That well-publicized fact drew in even more investors. At the end of 1987 the fund totaled $685.5 million. But in 1988 Garzarelli missed the stock market's rebound. In fact, the fund lost 13 percent in net asset value while the S&P was up about 16.5 percent. The fund continued to trail the stock market and investors left in droves. Finally, in June 1994, the fund's sponsor, Smith Barney, Inc. (which had acquired the fund in 1993), proposed to merge it into another fund, without Garzarelli at the helm. The remaining shareholders approved the proposal and the remaining $129 million in assets were folded into another Smith Barney fund.

Even if you limit your shopping list to top-rated funds, you may have a hard time finding B+ and B-rated funds in every category. That's why the BW Scoreboard carries a category rating, one based on risk-adjusted performance of funds in the same fund category. With these category ratings, it's possible to identify the best funds in sectors of the market that are performing poorly relative to other sorts of funds. For instance, most precious metals funds have terrible ratings when compared to all funds. But if you are interested in a precious metal fund, these category ratings allow you to identify the best of the lot.

LOAD OR NO-LOAD?

If you want to work with a broker or a financial planner who's also a broker, you may be restricted to the funds that they sell. You pay the salesperson either through the front-end load, or through higher 12(b)-fees. (See Chapter 3.) A fast-growing alternative to the traditional brokerage arrangement is the fee-only adviser. Even some large brokerage firms are offering this option today. Under these arrangements, you purchase load funds at net asset value. You compensate the adviser through an annual fee based on the amount of assets under management.

If you want to run your account yourself, choose no-loads. Why pay for advice you don't want? You can invest by contacting the fund companies directly. That's fine if you want to invest all in one family, but it's cumbersome if you want to mix and match funds from different families. That's where the mutual fund networks really make sense. You can open an account with Schwab or Fidelity, buy funds from a large number of fund companies, and do it all through the brokerage firm—one account number, one phone number, one statement.

A MINIMUM INVESTMENT?

Suppose you have $2000 to invest in each of five funds. You call the toll-free telephone number for the funds to get a prospectus and sales material. But remember to ask about the initial investment. Direct-sales funds, in particular, usually have higher minimum investments than broker-sold funds. Many direct-sales funds carry minimum initial purchases of $1000 to $3000 for equity funds and often a little higher for bond funds. Broker-sold funds usually have minimum buy-ins in the $250-to-$500 range. Both types of funds usually lower the threshold significantly for IRA or other retirement accounts, or for investors who enroll in a monthly investment plan.

TAXABLE OR
TAX-DEFERRED ACCOUNT?

When assembling a portfolio of mutual funds, it's hard enough to come up with the right mix of funds. To maximize your returns, you have to be selective about which investments you put in the confines of the IRA or 401(k) and which you hold in taxable accounts. "Asset placement picks up where asset allocation ends," says Joel M. Dickson, an investment strategist for the Vanguard Group. "The idea is to put your money in the place where it will work best for you on an after-tax basis."

Asset placement, or what's also known as "preferred domain," has always been important, especially to high-income investors. But the new

Do-it-yourself investors buy no-load funds.

tax law, which widens the gap between the tax rates on capital gains and on ordinary income and expands the availability of Individual Retirement Accounts, makes asset placement that much more important.

The basic strategy is to put investments that produce interest and dividend income into tax-deferred accounts like IRAs, 401(k)s, and variable annuities; those that produce capital gains should reside in your taxable accounts. This, of course, presumes that you have investments outside your tax-deferred accounts. If you have nothing beyond your 401(k) and don't expect to for some time, asset placement is not yet a concern. Just stick to your optimal asset allocation plan.

If you're an investor nearing retirement, the changes in the tax law might dictate a new look at asset placement as well. William S. Young, a financial adviser with the First Financial Group in Towson, Maryland, says new retirees in higher tax brackets should benefit by keeping income-producing investments in their tax-deferred retirement accounts as long as possible, and instead draw down their taxable equity investments to supplement their pension payments. Some of the money they take from equity funds, for instance, will be taxable, but at the new low capital gains rate. Any money they take in income from IRAs and the like will be fully taxable at ordinary income rates.

To review your asset placement, first look at your holdings by their asset classes. Take government or corporate bond funds. Their chief attribute is that they generate interest income, taxable at ordinary tax rates. If you're in the 31 percent federal tax bracket—for a couple filing jointly, taxable income between $102,300 and $155,290—nearly a third (more if you are also subject to state and local income tax) is lost to taxes.

If you hold taxable bond funds for long-term investment, it's best to do so within the confines of an IRA or 401(k). In a traditional IRA or 401(k), the tax on the interest income is deferred until you withdraw the money in your golden years. In the new Roth IRA, which totally flips the retirement account in that contributions are not deductible but earnings are, those dollars will never be taxed.

High-yield bond funds seem especially well-suited for all tax-favored accounts, since they generally throw off the highest payouts. Consider the high-yielding Dreyfus High-Yield Securities Fund. Its 1997 distribution yield was 11.2 percent. Held in a taxable account, the net return to the 31 percent bracket tax-payer is only 7.8 percent. In a tax-deferred account, that high yield keeps compounding until it's withdrawn. In a Roth IRA, it's never taxed.

If you have exhausted all your tax-deferred avenues and you have money in taxable accounts, seek funds with a track record of paying out only minimal taxable distributions. One way to identify them is by combing the financial statements in fund prospectuses, looking for those with the smallest distributions relative to the net asset value in the fund. An easier way is to compare pretax and aftertax returns. (Both are in the BUSINESS WEEK Mutual Fund Scoreboard.) Divide the aftertax by the pretax return, and the higher the number, the more tax efficient the fund.

For the 1995–1997 period, one with relatively high fund returns, we had 200 funds with at least 95 percent tax efficiency. Among them: Baron Asset, Founders Passport, MFS Emerging Growth B, Putnam New Opportunities, Rydex OTC, and Vista Small Cap Equity A. As you can tell from the names of the funds, most of these tax-efficient funds invest in smaller, emerging growth companies. Such companies usually pay little or no dividends, so there's no taxable dividend income that the fund has to pay out.

But don't equate all emerging growth funds with high tax efficiency. The aftertax returns of IDS Discovery, Safeco Growth No Load, and Strong Discovery were all about one-third less than that of the pretax returns. It doesn't all come from dividend or interest income. Profits on stocks held less than a year (18 months in the new bill) are taxed at the ordinary income rate, and so a fund with a rapid-fire trading strategy might also generate a lot of unwanted ordinary income.

If your asset allocation plan calls for more conservative equity funds, ones that invest in larger dividend-paying stocks, you may want to put those in tax-favored accounts. Many funds with "growth and income," "equity-income," and "balanced" in their names do well in a retirement account. So do specialty funds that invest in utilities or real estate investment trusts, which deliver much of their return through dividend income.

If you decide you need some placement related restructuring in your portfolio, remember to do it carefully. Shifting funds within an IRA or 401(k) is easy and does not carry any tax consequences. But if you make any changes in your taxable accounts, you are creating a "taxable event." If

Look at a fund's "tax efficiency."

you have a taxable investment with a large unrealized gain, you might move the money out over several years and spread the tax bite rather than move the money all at once. If your investment program is long-term, you have time to get your assets in place.

Building and Rebuilding Fund Portfolios

Retirees need equity funds too.

In assembling your own portfolio, it's worthwhile to examine others' portfolios. The point is not necessarily to use the same funds in the same way, but to see the kinds of funds professionals use for particular purposes and in what proportions. You can also try to understand some of the logic that goes into these decisions. For example, what about a portfolio for a college-bound toddler? Table 4-4 presents one from Debra B. Silversmith of Sterling Partners in Denver, Colorado. It's for a 3-year-old whose grandparents invest $10,000 in her name. Silversmith recommends a portfolio weighted toward funds that emphasize small and midsize companies whose growth prospects are higher than those of the companies in the S&P 500. "Over time, the higher growth rates should lead to greater fund performance," she says.

That's true, as long as you select funds whose managers are skilled at playing the growth-stock game. As the table shows, for the 40 percent of the portfolio dedicated to smaller company stocks, she chooses Baron Asset Fund and the Kaufmann Fund. Baron, which has outperformed its competitors for nearly 10 years, is light on technology stocks. Kaufmann Fund, on the other hand, carries a heavy complement of tech stocks. Both are run by veteran portfolio managers, not rookies. For mid-cap companies, Silversmith selects the Oakmark and Strong Opportunity funds. Oakmark, a top-rated fund, is a mid-cap value fund, a good offset to the more growth-oriented Baron and Kaufmann.

Looking abroad, she chooses Janus Worldwide Fund. She used to use Warburg Pincus International Equity, but dropped it because of manager turnover and more Japanese exposure than she liked. Janus Worldwide has a value orientation, and it does have some U.S. exposure as well.

Silversmith thinks this portfolio could earn an average annual return of 14 percent a year. If she's right—and that's an ambitious goal—the $10,000 will grow to more than $70,000 when this preschooler turns college freshman. Private college already costs nearly $30,000 a year, so good fund choices are not enough. Her parents will need to add money over the years. For additional investments, Silversmith would allocate the money in the same proportions.

FUNDS FOR A 401(K)

Employees often freeze when they're asked to choose from five or six investment options in their companies' 401(k) plans. So consider the plight of the General Motors Corp. employees, who can select from among 50 Fidelity mutual funds. That's where adviser James B. Kruzan of Investment Management & Research Inc. in Clarkston, Michigan, spotted a business opportunity. He advises GM employees on fund selection for their 401(k)s.

Take, for instance, a 43-year-old executive who has amassed $50,000 in his 401(k), but has it invested in a haphazard mix of stock and bond funds. He'd like to have a well constructed equity portfolio but hasn't a clue which funds to choose and in what proportions.

Since the employee is 25 years from retirement, Kruzan recommends a fairly aggressive mix that he believes will beat the S&P 500 by an average 2 percentage points a year: 40 percent for funds that buy small-cap stocks, 20 percent for mid-cap, 10 percent for large-cap, and 30 percent for foreign stocks. That's the outline, and it's a plan that could be fulfilled by scores of funds, not just Fidelity's. But for the GM clients, Kruzan selects from the Fidelity menu. For the most aggressive funds, he chooses Fidelity Low-Priced Stock, Fidelity Emerging Growth, and Fidelity OTC. For the mid-cap slot, he picks Fidelity Mid-Cap Stock. The big-stock slice splits between Fidelity Growth & Income and Fidelity Dividend Growth.

Kruzan then divides the international portion into four parts, allocating 9 percent each to Fidelity Diversified International and Fidelity Emerging Markets. Two regional funds, Fidelity Canada and Fidelity Europe, get 6 percent each. Kruzan says the Canadian fund is as much a natural resource fund as a country fund, since natural resources make up a large part of Canada's economy. He likes the Canadian fund and thinks U.S. investors often overlook their northern neighbor. "The slow growth, low interest rate environment that is so good for our market should benefit our biggest trading partner as well," he says.

For ongoing contributions, Kruzan suggests 25 percent each in the following four funds: Fidelity Low-Priced Stock, Fidelity OTC Fund, Fidelity Mid-Cap Stock, and Fidelity Emerging Markets. "That allows you to use these funds' higher volatilities to your advantage by buying more shares at bottoms and fewer at tops," says Kruzan.

THE ROLLOVER IRA

With companies shrinking their payrolls, long-time employees often walk away with six-figure pension distributions and no idea of how to invest them. "That's the kind of help many of our new clients need," says William S. Young of First Financial Group in Towson, Maryland.

Look at the example of a 50-year-old single woman with $100,000. She's not a gambler, but she is willing to take as much risk as her adviser thinks is appropriate. So Young devised an all-equity portfolio with moderate risk. "With at least 10 years to go before retirement, you can go with an all-stock portfolio," says Young. "In all the 10-year periods since World War II, bonds have beaten stocks less than 10 percent of the time."

Unlike Silversmith, who is paid a percentage of assets under management, Young earns his pay from commissions—and so chooses from the load funds. And when a fund has front-end or back-end shares, he recommends the up-front "A" shares, because they're most cost-effective for long-term investors.

Young's prescription is simple: He eschews the latest highflier funds for those that he believes show "consistency of results." The first two holdings, Putnam Growth & Income A (15 percent) and Guardian Park Avenue (25 percent) are "core" funds, with Putnam having a "value" (higher dividend, low price-earnings ratio) approach, while Guardian is more growth-oriented. He also likes Guardian's quantitatively driven stock selection system. "It's proven and disciplined," he says.

Young's also taken an unusual step for a relatively small portfolio: adding a 10 percent holding in Seligman Communications & Information Fund. "I have come to the conclusion that technology is so important it has to be here, even if it brings more volatility to the portfolio." To offset some of that additional volatility, Young picks up most of his foreign exposure through two Ameri-

TABLE 4-4

FOUR FUND EXPERTS GO SHOPPING FOR YOU

HEAD START ON A COLLEGE FUND

Investment adviser Debra Silversmith suggests this portfolio for a 3-year-old whose grandparents put $10,000 in her name to launch a college fund. They're all no-load funds, available through the big discount brokers or directly from the fund companies.

FUND	ALLOCATION
OAKMARK	20%
STRONG OPPORTUNITY	15
KAUFMANN	20
BARON ASSET	20
JANUS WORLDWIDE	25

AN ALL-FIDELITY 401(k) PORTFOLIO

Adviser James Kruzan counts many General Motors managers among his clients, and many of them look to him for help in choosing among the 50 Fidelity mutual funds in GM's 401(k) plan. This allocation plan is for a 43-year-old with $50,000 in his 401(k), but could as easily be used by anyone wanting an all-Fidelity line-up.

FUND	ALLOCATION
FIDELITY LOW-PRICED STOCK	16.0%
FIDELITY EMERGING GROWTH	12.0
FIDELITY OTC	12.0
FIDELITY MID-CAP STOCK	20.0
FIDELITY DIVIDEND GROWTH	5.0
FIDELITY GROWTH & INCOME	5.0
FIDELITY DIVERSIFIED INT'L.	9.0
FIDELITY EMERGING MARKETS	9.0
FIDELITY CANADA	6.0
FIDELITY EUROPE	6.0

GAME PLAN FOR A ROLLOVER IRA

Financial planner William Young suggested this portfolio for a 50-year-old single woman who is leaving a job with a $100,000 lump-sum payment that will be rolled over into an IRA. As a commission-based adviser, Young sells load funds. He recommends shares with up-front loads, since they are cheapest in the long run.

FUND	ALLOCATION
PUTNAM GROWTH & INCOME A	15%
GUARDIAN PARK AVENUE A	25
SELIGMAN COMM. & INFO. A	10
SMALLCAP WORLD	20
CAPITAL WORLD GROWTH & INCOME	30

FOR THE GOLDEN YEARS

Madeline I. Noveck recommends this portfolio for a 62-year-old with a $500,000 lump-sum pension payment. This retiree has other income sources, and needs to generate $7500 a year from this nest egg. Noveck uses both load and no-load funds.

FUND	ALLOCATION
TORRAY	16%
T. ROWE PRICE MID-CAP GROWTH	10
NEUBERGER & BERMAN GENESIS	5
UAM FPA CRESCENT	4
BT INVESTMENT INTL. EQUITY	15
CGM REALTY	8
T. ROWE PRICE NEW ERA OR VAN ECK HARD ASSETS	6
HARBOR BOND	18
VANGUARD F/I SHORT-TERM CORP. BOND	6
WARBURG PINCUS GLOB. FIXED-INC. OR PIMCO FOREIGN	7
MONEY-MARKET FUND (YOUR CHOICE)	5

DATA: BUSINESS WEEK

can Funds offerings: Capital World Growth & Income and Small Cap World. He had previously used Templeton Foreign Class I in this slot, and that's still a good choice. But using two funds from the American Funds group reduces the sales charges his client would have to pay.

EQUITY FUNDS FOR RETIREMENT

Retirement is no reason to drop equity investments. In fact, the longer you hope to live, the more you're going to need them. That's the approach adviser Madeline I. Noveck of Novos Planning Associates Inc. in New York takes in constructing a $500,000 portfolio for a 62-year-old recent retiree.

Noveck works with a large palette of funds, both no-load and load, since that affords more and better investment options. If she uses a load fund, the portion of the commission paid her is credited against her regular asset-based fees. Noveck's list is long, with 11 funds. But she's working with more money, which usually requires more funds. And the client has two needs: the generation of about $7500 a year to supplement his current retirement income and capital appreciation so there will be enough to fund the next 20 years or so in retirement. She believes her portfolio can beat the S&P 500 return but with less volatility.

Like our other advisers, Noveck covers every segment of the stock market. For large- to mid-cap stocks, she chooses the Torray and the T. Rowe Price Mid-Cap Growth Funds. Torray is a large-cap value fund, and T. Rowe Price, more mid-cap growth. They complement rather than duplicate each other. For smaller companies, she chooses Neuberger & Berman Genesis and UAM FPA Crescent Funds (it's an institutional fund, not in the BW Scoreboard). She has no recommendation for a small-cap growth fund. She's not comfortable with the level of risk in any small-cap growth funds.

For foreign investments, Noveck suggests BT Investment International Equity, which invests both in major and emerging markets, is currently overweighted in Europe and manages even to make a little money in Japan. Better yet, she says, the fund is still relatively small and is growing more slowly than some other high-performance international funds.

Noveck also places money in funds that don't correlate to the market in general and thus diversify the portfolio. For instance, she allocates 6 percent to either Van Eck Hard Assets for load investors or T. Rowe Price New Era for no-load

investors. Both are natural resources funds and would serve as bulwarks against inflation—though at the moment, of course, it seems unnecessary. For real estate, another low-correlation category, Noveck suggest CGM Realty, a mix of both REITs for income and real estate companies for growth.

For income and diversification, Noveck uses Harbor Bond, a well-managed intermediate-term fund, and Vanguard Fixed-Income Short-Term Corporate Bond, a lower risk, low-expense offering. For foreign bonds, she suggests PIMCO Foreign Bond for load investors, or Warburg Pincus Global Fixed-Income as a no-load alternative. Five percent goes to a money-market fund ("choose one with a high yield") both for diversification and liquidity.

RESTRUCTURING A PORTFOLIO

So you have a few funds tucked away in an IRA to which you haven't contributed for years. Several funds are still sitting in a 401(k) at a former employer. Then there's a sheaf of funds you've bought yourself over the last few years, listening to tips from fund fanciers at work and from your own perusings of the covers of the personal finance magazines. Does this describe you or someone you know?

Many people have mutual fund portfolios, but they were never planned out or chosen in a way to cover a particular range of investment styles or asset classes. That doesn't mean they haven't made money. In a bull market, most anything can do well.

Still, even if you have a collection of funds that have done well, it may not be the optimal mix for you. The best portfolio for you depends on your tolerance for risk in the value of your portfolio. Look at the "Cranes," a couple in their early 40s who sought the assistance of Lou Stanasolovich of Legend Financial Advisors Inc. in Pittsburgh for restructuring their portfolio (Figure 4-3). Through IRAs, Keogh plans, and other mutual fund investments, they had over $500,000 in a portfolio that was 80 percent in equities.

Like many investors who came to funds during the 1990s, the Cranes had never seen their investments mauled in a bear market. When Stanasolovich showed them what happened to their funds during the 20 percent market decline in 1990, they decided to slice their equity allocation. So Stanasolovich reviewed the portfolio, came up with a new asset allocation plan, and chose the best funds to implement it. He was able to work with some of the funds they already had.

Good fund portfolios come from good plans.

FIGURE 4-3

RESTRUCTURING A PORTFOLIO OF FUNDS

BEFORE

The "Cranes," a couple in their early 40s, held $544,051 in taxable and tax-deferred retirement accounts—more than 80% of it in 15 equity mutual funds. Working with Lou Stanasolovich of Legend Financial Advisors, they decided to scale back their equity holdings about 60%. Stanasolovich analyzed the funds for investment style and performance and developed a new investment plan.

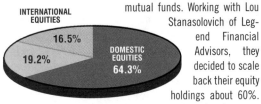

	Allocation (%)	Investment Category
DOMESTIC EQUITIES†		
BERGER 100	2.9	MID-CAP GROWTH
NEUBERGER & BERMAN MANHATTAN	1.0*	MID-CAP BLEND
T. ROWE PRICE CAP. APPREC.	4.4*	MID-CAP VALUE
JANUS TWENTY	2.9	LARGE-CAP GROWTH
AMER. CENT.-20th CENT. ULTRA INV.	8.2	LARGE-CAP GROWTH
GROWTH FUND OF AMERICA	10.0*	LARGE-CAP GROWTH
CGM MUTUAL	6.0	LARGE-CAP VALUE
AMERICAN MUTUAL	11.3*	LARGE-CAP VALUE
WASHINGTON MUTUAL INVESTORS	8.1*	LARGE-CAP VALUE
T. ROWE PRICE EQUITY-INCOME	5.5*	LARGE-CAP VALUE
INVESCO INDUSTRIAL INCOME	3.6	DOMESTIC HYBRID
INTERNATIONAL EQUITIES		
SMALLCAP WORLD	8.8*	SMALL-CAP GROWTH**
MONTGOMERY EMERGING MARKETS	0.7	DIV. EMRG. MKTS.
OAKMARK INTERNATIONAL	0.8	FOREIGN
EUROPACIFIC GROWTH	6.2*	FOREIGN

†Includes 0.4% in stocks *Funds in tax-deferred retirement accounts **Advisors considers this an international fund, while Morningstar puts it with domestic funds.

AFTER

Stanasolovich slashed domestic equities to 23%, mainly by cutting large-cap and mid-cap funds. He added small-cap growth and small-cap value funds, and substituted Davis New York Venture for large-cap value. He unloaded all the international equity funds except Oakmark International, and added a foreign fund and an emerging market fund. Eight percent went to short-term bond funds, 21% to long-term bond funds, and 6% for international bonds. For further diversification, he added a 15% holding in real estate, and 11% in a risk-arbitrage and other equity funds which have a low correlation with the market.

	Allocation (%)	Investment Category
SHORT-TERM DOMESTIC BONDS*		
PIMCO LOW DURATION	2%	SHORT-TERM
BLACKROCK 2001**	6	SHORT-TERM
LONG-TERM DOMESTIC BONDS*		
LOOMIS SAYLES BOND	8	LONG-TERM
NORTHEAST INVESTORS	8	HIGH-YIELD
PIMCO COMMERCIAL MORTGAGE**	5	INTERM.-TERM
INTERNATIONAL BONDS*		
PIMCO FOREIGN	6	INTERNATIONAL BOND
DOMESTIC EQUITIES		
BERGER SMALL COMPANY GROWTH	6	SMALL-CAP GROWTH
SKYLINE SPECIAL EQUITIES	6	SMALL-CAP VALUE
DAVIS NEW YORK VENTURE A	11	LARGE-CAP VALUE
INTERNATIONAL EQUITIES		
OAKMARK INTERNATIONAL	5	FOREIGN
HARBOR INTERNATIONAL GROWTH	5	FOREIGN
TEMPLETON DEVELOPING MARKETS I	6	DIV. EMRG. MKTS.
REAL ESTATE		
HEITMAN REAL ESTATE-INSTL.	7	REAL ESTATE
COHEN & STEERS SPECIAL EQUITY	8	REAL ESTATE
OTHER		
MERGER	4%	MID-CAP BLEND
CALDWELL & ORKIN MARKET OPP.	3	DOMESTIC HYBRID
BARR ROSENBERG MARKET NEUTRAL	4	N/A

*Funds in tax-deferred retirement accounts
**Closed-end fund

DATA: LEGEND FINANCIAL ADVISORS INC., MORNINGSTAR INC.

But he sold many of the equity holdings to make room for bond and real estate funds he thought were necessary to balance out the portfolio. He also placed most of the bond and real estate funds inside the tax-deferred retirement accounts. That way, he minimized the taxes on the income they produce. In a like manner, he tried to do much of the selling that needed to be done in the retirement accounts, thereby dodging capital gains taxes. Keep that in mind if you have restructuring of your own to do.

What Stanasolovich did was to drastically reduce the domestic equity allocation, the part of the Cranes' holdings that was most vulnerable to a decline in the U.S. stock market. He took the allocation down from 64.3 percent to 23 percent. He also reduced the number of domestic equity funds from 11 to 3 and changed them all. He uses

Davis New York Venture A, a large-cap value fund, and 6 percent each in Skyline Special Equities and Berger Small Company Growth. Skyline covers the value side, Berger the growth. The old portfolio was overweighted in large-cap stocks. In restructuring, Stanasolovich introduced small-cap and mid-cap holdings as well.

In the makeover, Stanasolovich also increased the international equity exposure and introduced international bonds. He chose PIMCO Foreign, an institutional fund that's open to clients of investment advisers. That fund buys mainly investment-grade bonds.

The new portfolio got a domestic junk bond fund, Northeast Investors, and Loomis Sayles Bond, a long-term fund, and PIMCO Commercial Mortgage, an intermediate portfolio. For short-term bonds, he uses PIMCO Low Duration Fund and BlackRock 2001, a closed-end fund which matures in four years.

To further diversify the portfolio's asset mix, Stanasolovich introduced two real estate funds: Cohen & Steers Special Shares and Heitman Real Estate, an institutional fund. He also put a small amount of money into unique funds with low market correlations: the Merger Fund, the only mutual fund built exclusively on risk-arbitrage; Caldwell & Orkin Market Opportunity Fund, a value fund that also short-sells stocks; and Barr Rosenberg Market Neutral Fund, which buys undervalued stocks and short-sells what it considers to be overvalued stock. The Rosenberg fund is brand new, but the underlying investment strategy has long been used by Rosenberg in institutional portfolios.

Making Your First Investment

You've got your investment goals, you know which funds you want to buy, and you're rarin' to go. But then you hesitate and freeze. Fear and doubt set in. You wait; you do nothing; you miss many opportunities.

Here's how to get off the mark. If you're a long-term investor, buying today, next week, or next month may not make much difference to your results. If you could perfectly predict stock market tops and bottoms, it would make a difference. But let's face it, if you could do that, you wouldn't be dabbling in mutual funds. You'd be playing the futures or options markets and making a bundle.

When you choose to plunk down your money can matter. But it's not because you have a hunch about the direction of the market. If you are deal-ing with a taxable investment, you should avoid a mutual fund or closed-end fund just before a dividend or capital gains distribution. Here's why. Funds are required to distribute nearly all of their income and realized capital gains (more about that in Chapter 6). The funds' distribution policies vary. Some equity funds pay out income dividends quarterly (bond funds often pay monthly) if they earn dividends or interest. Capital gains, if there are any, are usually declared once a year, mostly in December. You can find out distribution dates by calling the fund's toll-free line.

Suppose you invest $10,000 in a fund with an NAV of $10 per share and you get 1000 shares. Then, a few days after your investment, the fund declares a capital gains distribution of $1 per share. What happens is this: Each share pays out $1, so the NAV drops to $9 per share. Your 1000 shares are now worth $9000 (assuming there has been no other change in NAV). You reinvest the distribution and that $1000 gets you another 100 shares. So you still have an investment worth $10,000.

But you also have a tax liability. The $1000 distribution is taxable to you, but did you really earn it? Was your capital invested long enough for the managers to earn that kind of money? The gains were earned on money invested long before your money ever found its way to the fund. By investing in advance of the distribution, you wind up being taxed on something you didn't earn. You would have been better off waiting until after the distribution. Before you make a sizable investment in a fund, it's always smart to call to find out if any dividends or distributions are forthcoming.

So, for tax reasons, it does matter when you invest. For pure investment purposes, the advantages of timing are not so obvious. The question seemed particularly compelling in August 1989, when the Dow Jones industrial average raced past the 2722 point—the highwater mark that had been reached on August 25, 1987. Between August 1987 and August 1989 there was a 1000-point decline—508 of it on October 19, 1987—and a remarkable recovery. (On October 27, 1997, the Dow Jones industrials fell 554 points, though because the market was so much higher, the percentage loss was far less.) Had the investors who bought equity mutual funds on August 27, 1987, bounced back, too?

BUSINESS WEEK asked Morningstar, Inc., which provides the data for the Mutual Fund Scoreboard, to measure equity fund performance

For tax reasons, it matters when you invest.

between August 25, 1987, and September 1, 1989, when the Dow had closed at 2752. The survey covered 727 funds and looked at the total returns generated during a two-year period.

The mutual funds, for the most part, did an admirable job for their shareholders—even those who, in retrospect, had invested on perhaps the worst day of the year, if not the decade. Approximately 80 percent of the funds broke even or better. More than 400 funds, or 56 percent, beat the 9 percent return that could have been earned by investing in the Dow stocks during that time. About 300 funds, more than 40 percent, beat the 13 percent total return of the Standard & Poor's 500 stock index during that period. The average U.S. diversified equity fund returned 11 percent. Counting all equity funds—including international and specialty portfolios—total returns averaged 9.6 percent, slightly above the return on the Dow.

The folks at T. Rowe Price mutual fund group conducted a test to measure the impact of timing. Suppose you were a diligent investor and every year you put $2000 into the stocks of the S&P 500. But you were also the world's worst market timer. It seems that every year you managed to invest your $2000 in the stock market at the high for the calendar year.

Well, even if your timing is lousy, there's still a payoff to your discipline. Between 1969 and 1989, the period of the study, the investor who picked the worst day of each year to invest still did well. From his or her $40,000 in contributions ($2000 a year for 20 years), the hapless market-timer amassed a stake of $175,422, an 11.4 percent average annual return. Of course, the perfect timer—the person who invested two grand at the lowest point of each year—did much better. The perfect investor wound up with $226,365, a 13.5 percent average annual return. Granted, there's a $50,000 difference between the best and the worst timer, but as a practical matter most investors' results would be at neither extreme.

There are other ways to ease yourself into mutual funds. Suppose you have a lump sum of $25,000 to invest, but you're leery of doing it all at once. Why not break the total pie into smaller slices, say, $5000 each, and feed them into your mutual funds gradually over the next year? You put $5000 into the funds at first, and the other $20,000 into a money-market fund. You have four more "payments" to make before you're totally invested. Put the next $5000 slice in three months from now, and another $5000 each at six months, nine months, and one year. That way, if the market is lower at some time in the next 12 months, you have an opportunity to get in at lower prices.

Though most investors fear a plunging equity market, the bond market can also give them a jolt. Fixed-income investors usually stampede into bond funds when interest rates are falling, anxious to hold onto yields that are slipping away. But at the same time, as a portfolio's yield is going down, the prices of its bonds are going up. That means investors chasing yields are also buying heavily into a rising market.

It may not be necessary to chase intermediate- and long-term bonds. Odds are you'll see today's prices and yields again in the next few years. Between 1987 and 1997, for instance, the long-term rate on U.S. government bonds has fluctuated between 5.7 and 10.2 percent. At the low end, bond prices were said to be "high"; with the higher yield, bond prices were said to be "low." Stock prices, in theory, have no upside boundary. Stocks have infinite lives and their potential is tied to the success of the company.

But bonds have finite lives and what they can pay investors is fixed. So bond prices are constrained by the level of interest rates. Over time, the range of interest rates will vary, but you can bet there will be a trading range. When the economy is booming, rates go up; when the economy is slumping, rates come down. As long as there is a business cycle, there are going to be fluctuations in interest rates.

> Dollar-cost averaging is a contrarian strategy.

Dollar-Cost Averaging

If you're feeding a bankroll into mutual funds over time, what you're really engaging in is a time-honored practice called "dollar-cost averaging." This investment strategy is simple. You invest a fixed number of dollars at periodic intervals, usually monthly or quarterly. When the price of the investment is low, your fixed dollar investment buys more. When prices are high, the same amount of dollars buys less. But so long as the total return of your investment is in a generally rising trend, dollar-cost averaging will almost ensure that your average cost per share will be less than the current price. If you're part of a 401(k) plan or some other savings incentive plan, you're already practicing dollar-cost averaging.

Let's look at this a little more closely. Suppose you want to invest $200 a month in an equity mutual fund. You've arranged with your bank for an electronic transfer of the money from your checking account once a month on the day of your choice.

To see how this works, let's look back at how a monthly investment program would have fared (Table 4-5). Suppose an investor put $200 a month

TABLE 4-5

HOW DOLLAR-COST AVERAGING WORKS FOR FUND INVESTORS

In January 1994, an investor decided to start a program of dollar-cost averaging. He selected American Century–20th Century Ultra Investors, and decided to invest $200 on the first business day of every month, and reinvest any dividends or capital gains if and when they're paid.

1994 SUMMARY Invested $2400, purchased 115.921 shares at an average cost of $20.66 per share

Date	Price/Share	Shares purchased	Total shares
January	$21.18	9.443	9.443
February	22.66	8.826	18.269
March	22.18	9.017	27.286
April	20.71	9.657	36.943
May	21.25	9.412	46.355
June	20.46	9.775	56.130
July	19.24	10.395	66.525
August	19.60	10.204	76.729
September	20.41	9.799	86.528
October	20.16	9.921	96.449
November	21.07	9.492	105.941
December	20.04	9.980	115.921

Dec. 17, paid a capital gains distribution of $0.6452 per share, or $74.79   19.32   3.871   119.793

1995 SUMMARY Invested $2400, purchased 103.391 shares at an average cost of $23.21 per share

Date	Price/Share	Shares purchased	Total shares
January	$19.61	10.199	129.991
February	19.49	10.262	140.253
March	20.26	9.872	150.125
April	20.95	9.547	159.671
May	21.28	9.398	169.070
June	22.19	9.013	179.083
July	24.14	8.285	186.368
August	26.10	7.663	194.031
September	26.55	7.553	201.564
October	27.25	7.339	208.903
November	28.16	7.102	216.005
December	27.86	7.179	223.184

Dec. 16, paid a capital gains distribution of $1.2991 per share, or $289.94   25.00   11.598   234.782

1996 SUMMARY Invested $2941.62, purchased 104.866 shares at an average cost of $28.05 per share

Date	Price/Share	Shares purchased	Total shares
January	$26.20	7.634	242.415
February	26.44	7.564	249.980
March	26.83	7.454	257.434
April	26.73	7.482	264.916
May	27.98	7.148	272.064
June	29.05	6.885	278.949
July	28.68	6.974	285.922
August	26.46	7.559	293.481
September	26.60	7.519	301.000
October	29.20	6.849	307.849
November	29.41	6.800	314.649
December	31.70	6.309	320.959

Dec. 19, paid a capital gains distribution of $1.6875 per share, or $541.62   28.98   18.689   339.648

1997 SUMMARY Invested $5341.23, purchased 186.357 shares at an average cost of $28.66 per share

Date	Price/Share	Shares purchased	Total shares
January	$27.84	7.184	346.832
February	30.50	6.557	353.389
March	29.30	6.826	360.215
April	27.57	7.254	367.469
May	29.09	6.875	374.345
June	32.23	6.404	380.749
July	33.00	6.061	386.809
August	36.18	5.528	392.337
September	35.00	5.714	398.051
October	35.76	5.593	403.644
November	34.50	5.797	409.441
December	34.84	5.741	415.182

Dec. 19, paid an income dividend of $0.0133 per share, or $5.52 and a capital gains distribution of $7.0709 per share, or $2935.71   26.54   110.823   526.005

After four years, the investor has invested $9600 out of his pocket, plus another $3842.06 from reinvestment of dividends and capital gains distributions. He owns 526.005 shares at an average cost of $19.62 per share. On Dec. 31, 1997, the price per share is $25.52. The total investment is worth $13,960.

DATA: AMERICAN CENTURY INVESTORS, BUSINESS WEEK

into American Century–20th Century Ultra Investors starting in January 1994.

At the start of the program, the price per share was $21.18. So in the first month the investor bought 9.443 shares (that's 200 divided by 21.18). By the beginning of February, the NAV had climbed to $22.66. That means he already has a small paper profit in his first shares, but he gets slightly fewer shares for his next $200—this time, only 8.826. The relationship between share price and shares purchased is simple: the higher the price, the fewer shares purchased; the lower the price, the more shares purchased.

As you can tell from the share price, this fund rocketed from the time of the first purchase in 1994 and peaked in August 1997, at $36.18 a share. Of course, the net asset value did not go up in a straight line. In fact, in 1994, a few months after beginning the investment program, the price went as low as $19.24. But with the discipline of monthly investing and a long-term investment horizon, that worked to the investor's advantage. When the price was $19.24, his $200 bought more shares. When the price finally rebounded, he owned more shares on which to profit. All told, the investor had accumulated 526.005 shares from the monthly investments and distributions. At the end of four years, the investor had an unrealized average profit of $1.02 per share, or $535.53 in an account worth $13,960.

If you think about it, dollar-cost averaging is a contrarian investment strategy. When the prices are low—indicating that investors are not buying stocks—dollar-cost investors are buying stocks, and they're getting more shares. When the bulls are running, these investors are still buying. But the fixed-investment plan restrains them from any wild excesses, such as stepping up investments when the market is roaring or dropping out entirely when stocks are sagging. Bull market or bear market, they're investing the same amount. As long as you hold on for the long term (the average annual return for stocks is over 10 percent) and you choose a well-managed fund, dollar-cost averaging should pay off handsomely.

For sure, the investor who put in a lump sum of $9600 (the total out-of-pocket cost) back in January, 1994 would have far surpassed the investor who put in $200 a month. But that misses the point. Not everyone has a big lump sum to invest, but most people can come up with some monthly contribution.

Switch Funds! The Timing Game

Mutual fund purveyors have always cultivated the image that their wares are long-term investments. Of course, long-term doesn't mean the same thing to all people, but most of us would agree that long-term is at least more than a year, and probably a few beyond that.

However, during the last decade or so, the fund management companies have also made it quick and simple to purchase and redeem funds. It's become so easy to move large sums of money by telephone that some now use mutual funds for trading, which has a much shorter time horizon than investing. What most of these traders are trying to do is to employ a strategy called "market-timing."

The object of the game is to get your money invested early in a market upswing and to get your profits out before the downturn. Traders have long done this with individual stocks and, more recently, with options, futures, and no-load mutual funds. No-load equity funds seem to be made for market-timing. They already are, like the market, a diversified basket of stocks. And getting in and out is cheap and easy.

The idea of market-timing is appealing. Everyone wants to participate in rallies and dodge the declines. Many newsletter advisers and telephone hotline tipsters run market-timing advisory services, but you have to be skeptical about whether they're worthwhile or if the principle is even sound.

Take a look at the records of the market-timers. One timing system used by the newsletter *Systems and Forecasts* racked up a 16.9 percent average annual total return in the 10-year period ending December 31, 1997, according to the *Hulbert Financial Digest* (Table 4-6). That may sound good, but it's not even as good as the return of the S&P 500 or the broader Wilshire 5000 Value-Weighted Total Return Index. More important, about 170 mutual funds did better, among them Baron Asset, Fidelity Contrafund, FPA Capital, Janus Twenty, Kaufmann, and PBHG Growth.

The record shows that market-timing is no sure thing. What's perhaps even more surprising is how poorly some of the newsletters—which charge subscribers several hundred dollars a year for "advice"—actually performed. Following the advice of *The Elliot Wave Theorist*, a

> Few timers ever beat the market.

TABLE 4-6

THE MARKET-TIMING GAME

Newsletter	Portfolio/ timing system	Average annual total return*
SYSTEMS AND FORECASTS	"Time Trend"	16.90%
BOB BRINKER'S MARKETIMER	Aggressive Growth Fund Portfolio	15.81
MARKET LOGIC	Seasonality Timing System	15.73
THE BIG PICTURE	Master Key	14.99
TIMER DIGEST	"5 & 10" Consensus	14.92
FUND EXCHANGE	U.S. Margined Timing Model	13.62
INVESTORS INTELLIGENCE	Fidelity Switch Fund (Equity)	13.42
FABIAN PREMIUM INVST. RESOURCE	Domestic Fund Composite	13.41
PROFESSIONAL TIMING SERVICE	"Supply/Demand" Formula	13.05
MARKET FUND FORECASTER	Trader's Corner Portfolio	12.62
THE DINES LETTER	Long-Term	12.39
DOW THEORY LETTERS	Primary Trend	11.05
THE MARKETARIAN LETTER	Mutual Fund Portfolio for Traders	10.75
THE MUTUAL FUND STRATEGIST	MIRAT—Rydex Growth Portfolio	10.51
THE DINES LETTER	Intermediate-Term	9.96
FUND EXCHANGE	U.S. Market Timing Model	9.86
THE MARKETARIAN LETTER	Mutual Fund Portfolio for Investors	9.72
GROWTH FUND GUIDE	Timing Only: Mutual Fund Allocation	9.68
PERSONAL FINANCE	Fund Portfolio for Short-Term Traders	9.46
THE PROFESSIONAL TAPE READER	Intermediate-Term	8.95
THE PROFESSIONAL TAPE READER	Short-Term	8.34
INVESTECH RES. MARKET ANALYST		7.85
INVESTECH RES. MF ADVISOR		7.70
THE PROFESSIONAL TAPE READER	Long-Term	7.18
STOCK MARKET CYCLES	Fidelity Select Switchers	6.65
FUTURES HOTLINE MUTUAL FUND TIMER	Stock Fund Model	6.38
THE ELLIOT WAVE THEORIST	Investors	5.84

BENCHMARKS

STANDARD & POOR'S 500	18.04%
WILSHIRE 5000 VALUE-WEIGHTED TOTAL RETURN	17.57
U.S. DIVERSIFIED EQUITY FUNDS	15.74
ALL EQUITY FUNDS	14.24

*Jan. 1, 1988-Dec. 31, 1997   DATA: *HULBERT FINANCIAL DIGEST*, MORNINGSTAR INC.

with taxable funds—that is, anything outside an individual retirement account or other such tax-deferred retirement plan—would hardly be worth the trouble. Every switch is what the accountants call a "taxable event." Assuming that you were making profitable trades over the last 10 years, you might have paid as much as a 50 percent tax on the gains (prior to 1987). And that's before state and local income taxes, too.

Academic studies of market-timing cast doubt on its efficacy. In the mid-1980s, two University of Calgary professors determined that an investor who accurately predicted every bull and bear market from 1926 to 1983—buying stocks at the beginning of bull markets and switching to Treasury bills at the onset of bear markets—earned an 18.2 percent average annual return, even assuming a 1 percent commission was paid on each trade.

By comparison, the buy-and-hold investors only earned an 11.8 percent average annual return during the same period. But no market-timer has a perfect record. What if your market-timing was right about 50 percent of the time? Too bad. If so, your average annual return would have dwindled to 8.1 percent. To beat the buy-and-hold investor, the professors concluded, the timer would have had to be right 70 percent of the time.

One of the problems with market-timing is that the stock market typically makes large gains in relatively short periods, followed by longer periods when not much seems to happen at all. Rushmore Funds, for instance, looks back at the performance of the S&P 500 index during the 1980s. For the entire decade, the average annual return was 17.6 percent. But if you take out the 10 days when stocks made their largest gains, the average annual return drops to 12.6 percent. Take out the 20 best days for stocks, and the return is only 9.3 percent. The point is, if you're not invested during those short bursts of activity, you can miss a lot of the potential rewards.

Or look at the T. Rowe Price New Horizons Fund, one of the oldest and largest of the funds specializing in small companies. In 1990, the fund's sponsors calculated that 80 percent of the gains over the prior 30 years, or 120 quarters, actually occurred in 12 of the quarters. So to time that kind of fund successfully, you would have had to have been invested in the fund during only 12 of 120 quarters. Unless you can tell with absolute certainty which quarters are the critical ones, buy-and-hold would be a better strategy.

market-timer would have ended up with less than a 6 percent average annual return. He or she could have done almost as well in a money-market fund with a lot less trouble.

More importantly, market-timing results represent gross returns before taxes. Market-timing

There's no better example of this than the first quarter of 1991. The New Horizons Fund rocketed up 28 percent in just three months. Yet at the end of December 1990, the economy was in recession and war was about to erupt in the Persian Gulf. If your assets had been in a money-market fund then, would you have shifted them into stocks, given the gloomy atmosphere?

Though the numbers suggest the odds are against them, market-timers keep trying. But sometimes market-timing can be downright disruptive and harmful to long-term investors. Suppose you're a portfolio manager running a $100 million fund. You normally keep about 5 percent of your assets in cash to meet redemptions and seize upon new investment opportunities.

Then some market-timers start pumping money into your fund. If the timers are following a variety of trading systems, that might not be so bad since they would not all trade at the same time. But suppose a market-timing adviser who had a wide following among both institutions and individuals moves to a particular mutual fund, bringing along about $10 million in assets. At first you are delighted, as it's a vote of confidence in your abilities. (It also pleases the bosses, since the greater the number of dollars in the fund, the more management fees it generates.) Everything goes along swimmingly, and in six months or so the fund goes up 20 percent. The market-timer's followers see their collective $10 million increase to $12 million.

But one day the market-timer says switch— and all of a sudden his or her followers want their money out. The fund has $6 million in U.S. Treasury bills that can be sold to raise cash, and another $1 million in new money came in that day. But to redeem $12 million, you have to sell $5 million worth of stocks. That may not be all bad, since it never hurts to take a profit. But what if your game plan—successful thus far—had called for buying, not selling? Or what if it isn't a particularly good time to sell? Trading has a cost, too, that comes out of the fund's assets. If timers make excessive switches in and out of a fund, it could hurt the returns left for the other shareholders.

As much as management companies love to "gather assets," from time to time they have quietly invited market-timers or suspected market-timers to take their business elsewhere. For instance, the Kaufmann Fund, which invests in many small, emerging growth companies, once returned a $25 million check to a wealthy investor. Lawrence Auriana, one of the portfolio managers, said he feared what would happen when this investor asked for his money back all at once. Auriana said the fund might have to dump stocks just to redeem that big shareholder's account, which could be detrimental to the other shareholders. Auriana says there are market-timers in the fund, but they don't have enough fund shares to be disruptive.

So many fund sponsors now discourage market-timers from investing in their funds that one relatively new fund family, Rydex, decided to tailor its funds for timers and welcome the fundswitchers. Rydex Nova Fund is the bullish fund that timers buy when they think stocks will go up. It's a souped up index fund, which buys mainly in stock-index futures and options to keep liquidity high and transaction costs down. Nova also has an extra weighting of call options that makes it more volatile than the S&P index itself—so anyone buying this fund had better be right.

Rydex Ursa is the bears' fund, designed to rise in NAV as stock prices head south. That's because this fund sells index futures and buys put options, both of which yield gains as stocks stumble. (In that sense, it can be used not only by timers but by anyone looking to hedge against a decline in the market.) To keep out the small fry, Rydex requires a minimum $25,000 investment.

Market-timing pays only if you're very, very good at it—and then, only if you don't have to pay taxes on the gains. Mutual funds work best when used as long-term investments. No matter what kind of calendar you use, two days is not the long term.

> Some funds may spurn frequent switchers.

Monitoring Your Mutual Funds

So now you have a portfolio of mutual funds—which, in effect, gives you a group of top-drawer professional money managers to work for you. And those managers are backed up by scores of staff members who can turn up information and analysis that you could never hope to assemble on your own.

Ah, it would be nice if you could leave your mutual funds on autopilot and watch your fortune just mount up. But nothing is that perfect. Many mutual funds can be buy-and-hold investments, but none of them are buy-and-forget. To keep on top of your mutual fund portfolio takes some of your time. Fortunately, it's not a lot of time. An hour or two a month would probably take care of most investors' needs.

Most people keep tabs on their funds by following them in the financial pages of their daily newspapers. But there are other ways as well. With a computer and modem, you can access mutual fund prices through many on-line services or on the Internet, including BUSINESS WEEK Online (www.businessweek.com). Many popular money-management programs download the data directly into your computer. Nearly all fund companies maintain toll-free phone numbers that allow you to check on prices and your account status.

Tracking Funds in the Financial Pages

Mutual fund prices are quoted daily in *The Wall Street Journal*, *Investors Business Daily*, and just about any newspaper that carries daily financial tables. In addition, Sunday newspapers usually have the mutual fund tables that summarize the high, low, and last price for the week. Not every fund makes it into the newspapers. To qualify, the fund needs a minimum of 1000 shareholders or $30 million in assets.

In the newspaper, fund tables are organized alphabetically by fund family (from AAL Mutual to Zweig Funds), and then alphabetically within families. Many large fund families are broken into subgroups to make it easier to find funds. For example, Fidelity is so large that its funds are broken into several groups, such as Fidelity Investments (where you'll find Magellan, Puritan, and the best-known Fidelity products), Fidelity Selects (the specialty portfolios), and Fidelity Spartan (a line of low-overhead funds). Load-fund families that have several share classes break their funds into smaller groups, such as Alliance Capital A, Alliance Capital B, and Alliance Capital C. Not all funds are parts of families, but they're still integrated into the tables in alphabetical order.

Each fund's name is followed by several columns of fund prices, all represented in dollars and cents. There's net asset value, followed by the offer price, which is the NAV plus the load for funds sold with front-end loads. The last column is the daily price change, which, for most mutual funds, usually amounts to pennies per day. In addition, there are letters that serve to footnote such features as 12(b)-1 plans, redemption fees, or an income or capital gains distribution. Over 600 newspapers still carry this basic table, which is distributed by the Associated Press.

But now, some newspapers are starting to vary their mutual fund tables. From Monday through Thursday, *The Wall Street Journal*, for instance, shows three basic features—NAV, NAV net change from previous day, and year-to-date return. On Fridays, the tables are expanded to show the last four-week, and one-, three-, and five-year periods. In addition, the funds get a letter grade for their one-, three-, and five-year showings. An "A" puts their performance in the top 20 percent of funds with the same investment objective. An "E" puts them in the bottom 20 percent. In addition, the *Journal*'s Friday tables include data which change little from week to week—investment objective, maximum initial sales charge, and expense ratio. The *Journal*'s data come from Lipper Analytical Services, Inc.

Some major newspapers, including *The New York Times* and *Chicago Tribune*, carry a somewhat different presentation developed by Morningstar, Inc. *The New York Times* version, for instance, carries the previous day's NAV only, along with a percentage price change, not the price change in dollars and cents. Otherwise, the remaining data also change daily. On Tuesday, it's maximum sales charge; Wednesday, one-year total return; Thursday, three-month return; and Friday, year-to-date return. On Saturdays, funds with at least three years of performance history get a return/risk rating. The return rating goes from 1 to 5, 1 being the lowest relative return among funds with the same investment objective. The risk rating also goes from 1 to 5, 5 being the lowest risk and 1 the highest risk. Thus, a fund with a 5/1 rating would have terrific returns achieved with very high risk.

If you're familiar with stock tables, you'll notice that mutual fund tables are different. Mutual fund pricing, for instance, goes down to the penny—$8.71, or $15.46, or $65.03, or whatever. Most stocks are now priced in sixteenths—a unit of 6.25 cents.

Day to day, the movement of mutual funds seems almost glacial. Pick up one of the daily tables and scan the right-hand column, headed by "NAV chg" or "Change in net asset value." The changes are usually small: "−.02, +.03, −.07, +.11." If the stock market has made a big move up or down that day, those numbers will usually show greater changes, but by and large the movements are small.

There are several reasons for this. First, mutual funds are highly diversified pools of assets and not all the securities move in the same direction at the same time. For example, if there are 100 stocks in a fund, the change in net asset value is the difference between the 50 that went up that day, the 40 that went down, and the 10 that had no change at all.

Whatever the market's move, the mutual fund tables appear to mute the effect. Take a look at the stock market's activity on December 29, 1997. The Dow Jones industrial average went up to 7679.31 from 7792.41, a 1.47 percent move. Suppose your mutual fund behaves much like the

Dow, and has a net asset value of $15. A 1.47 percent gain on $15 is just 22 cents.

Look at the mutual fund table that appeared in *USA Today* on December 30, 1997—which reported results of December 29 (Figure 5-1). The NAV of the Fidelity Blue Chip Growth Fund ("BluCh" in the table under the boldface heading "Fidelity Invest") closed at $38.50, a 68-cents-per-share gain. That's a 1.8 percent gain, which is better than the Dow.

If you scan down a few more lines to check out Fidelity Fifty Fund, you see a 32-cent gain. But Fidelity Fifty did better than Blue Chip because its gain was 32 cents on top of a lower NAV of $14.69. So the Fidelity Fifty gain was 2.2 percent. Don't let those cents fool you. What counts is the level of the NAV before you measure the change. To get the previous day's NAV, add back the losses or subtract the gains from the current day's NAV. Some newspapers even report the day's percentage gain.

Watching your bond funds rise and fall can be like watching the grass grow. The 30-year U.S. Treasury bond—the benchmark by which the bond market is most commonly measured—was 5.92 percent, up 0.02 percent for the day. So there was very little change in the bond funds. The Vanguard Fixed-Income Long-Term U.S. Treasury Fund, which is most sensitive to changes in bond prices, dropped 2 cents in NAV.

INTERPRETING THE FUND TABLES

Many newspapers use the abbreviated presentation shown in Figure 5-1. The first column is the NAV, based on December 29 closing prices. The second column is the change in the NAV from December 26, expressed in dollars and cents. The third column, "YTD%," is the year-to-date performance, which is change in net asset value plus reinvestment of dividends and capital gains distributions.

Note how the fund tables are organized. Most funds are listed within families such as AAL Mutual, AARP Investment, and so on. Then they're alphabetical within those families. The tables include both stock and bond but not money-market mutual funds. Funds not part of large fund groups are listed alphabetically along with the fund families, but they will be listed in regular type while the fund families are in boldface.

Look at the listings and you'll see some single letters after the fund names. A capital letter, usually A or B, attached at the end of the fund name usually denotes a class of share. Under Fidelity Advisory, for instance, you will find A, B, and I shares. A shares have a front-end load, B shares

FIGURE 5-1

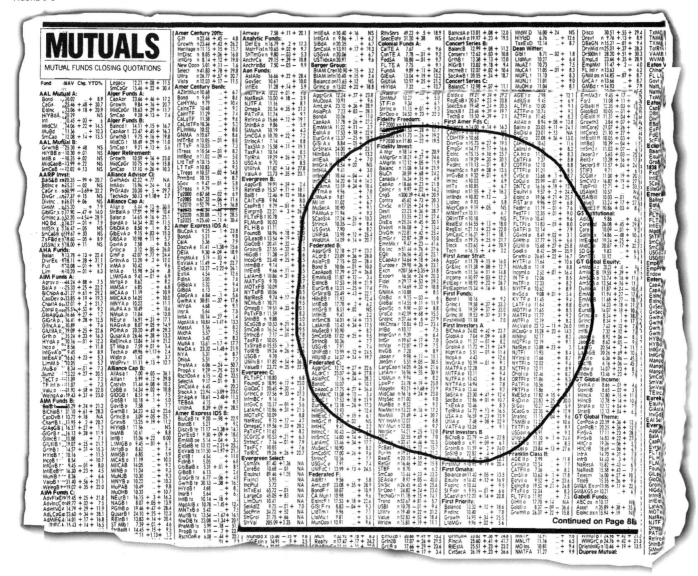

a back-end load with redemption, and I shares are for institutional investors. Or look at Galaxy Funds Retail and Galaxy Funds Trust. Retail shares are for individual investors, trust shares for bank trust customers. Whether the fund family uses a letter, or "retail" and "trust," the underlying portfolios are the same. What's different is how the fund shareholder pays for the fund. When the returns of two classes differ, it's because differing amounts of fees are taken out of the fund. (See Chapter 3 for a discussion of multiple classes of shares.)

Then there are various lowercase letters used throughout the table. The "n" means the fund is no-load. The "p" indicates that the fund levies a 12(b)-1 fee for distribution expenses. (Need an explanation? See Chapter 3.) Some funds have an "r." That indicates a redemption fee. How much? That's not in the table, but it's an indication that if

you sell your fund for the NAV listed in the table, you may not collect the full amount. You'll also see many funds with "t" accompanying them. That footnote tells you that both "p" and "r" apply to this fund.

The footnotes "p," "r," and "t" are there all the time. They describe an ongoing characteristic or policy of the fund. But on occasion you may see an "x," "e," or "s." The "x" may be familiar from the stock tables. It means the fund just paid a dividend. Investors buying after the fund has "gone ex-dividend" do not collect that dividend. Often the fund appears to decline in net asset value. But the decline may only reflect that money was paid out of the fund. If a fund pays a 10-cents-a-share dividend, and goes down 5 cents a share on the ex-dividend date, that means the fund would have risen a nickel a share had the dividend not been paid.

When a fund pays a capital gains distribution, the symbol is an "e" instead of an "x." No matter, the effect on the fund pricing is the same. The "s" works the same way as an "x," except that it means the dividend is paid in stock instead of cash.

There may be some funds with no NAVs after their names. This usually means the fund company didn't yet have the price available when the National Association of Securities Dealers came to collect it. The day after the October 1987 stock market crash, the fund table was strewn with blanks. That frightened many people, who thought their funds had been wiped out.

Money-market fund quotes are not usually in daily newspapers. They can be found on Thursdays (they're released on Wednesday) and sometimes in Sunday newspapers, too. Net asset value for money funds is assumed to be held constant at $1 a share, thus there's no point in reporting it. What is reported in the money-market fund table is the annualized yield for the last 7-day period. If it's 4.88 percent, that doesn't mean the fund paid 4.88 percent over the last 7 days, but that the rate paid, held constant over a year, would be 4.88 percent. If the newspaper also includes 30-day yield, compare the two. If the 7-day is higher than the 30-day yield, it's because interest rates have gone up. If the 7-day yield is less than the 30-day yield, rates have come down.

Another useful figure in the money-market fund table is the average maturity. That figure is quoted in days. Consider the $45 billion Merrill Lynch CMA Money Fund. In late 1997, the fund had a 71-day average maturity. Of course, the money-market funds have billions in securities maturing every day. But a 71-day average maturity means that the average of all the maturities in the fund is 10 weeks. Zurich YieldWise Money Fund had an average maturity of 20 days, or a day short of three weeks. The industry average for taxable money funds was 56 days.

Okay, so now short-term interest rates rise. Which fund will deliver more yield to its shareholders? The Zurich fund, for sure, because it will take just several weeks before all the money rolls over and is reinvested at higher rates. In contrast, it will take 2½ months for the Merrill fund to gain full advantage of the higher rates. The Merrill fund's yield will go up more slowly.

Now suppose interest rates come down. The investors in the Merrill fund will hold on to the higher yields longer. The yield from the Zurich portfolio will come down much faster. In fact, the Merrill fund, with what is a long maturity for a money-market mutual fund, was fully expecting a drop in short-term rates.

The maturities of money-market funds are not static either. When portfolio managers anticipate that interest rates will fall, they buy longer-maturity securities for the portfolio, hoping to hold on to the higher rates longer. In like manner, they shorten maturities in anticipation of rising interest rates. Some investors track the ups and downs of portfolio maturities as market indicators. If the average maturity lengthens, that represents the collective opinion of hundreds of fund managers that rates are heading down. It may not be right, but it tells you what the conventional wisdom is.

Keeping track of closed-end funds is a little trickier. You can find the share prices every day under the appropriate stock market listing—New York Stock Exchange, American Stock Exchange, or the NASDAQ National Market System (over-the-counter market). But what you see is the per-share price, which, as you know, is usually different from net asset value.

The NAVs of closed-end funds are generally reported in the financial pages once a week. Closed-end funds usually report NAVs on Friday and you can find them in the newspapers over the weekend (Mondays in *The Wall Street Journal* and *Investors Business Daily*).

Keeping Score

The whole point of watching your funds' performance is to make sure that they are doing what's expected of them. Fund managers might have all the best intentions, but they're human, too.

The first thing investors want to know about a fund is the total return—for the quarter, for the year, or for any other period. The total return—appreciation plus reinvestment of dividends and capital gains—allows investors to compare a fund's performance to that of a benchmark index like the S&P 500, and also to other funds.

Computing the total return is simple. Let's look at the case of American Century–20th Century Heritage Investors (Table 5-1). Suppose you invested your money on the first business day of 1993. Heritage had a net asset value of $9.31 per share. On the last day of the year, the NAV was $10.61. And during the year, the fund paid dividends and capital gains distributions amounting to $0.5738 per share.

redemption fee that applies to you, and you're considering selling the account, you should subtract that from the current value of the shares.

Next, subtract your initial investment. If you paid a load, that's already figured into the initial investment. If you reinvest dividends and capital gains, there's no need to add them back. They're counted in the current value of your shares. If you don't reinvest and you take distributions in cash, you have to add them back to the current value figure. Then take the difference, $415, and divide that by the initial investment, $2000. That yields 0.208, so multiply that by 100 to come up with 20.8 percent.

Suppose you are investing in a mutual fund on a monthly schedule. Then the calculation starts to get a little stickier. To get an exact return, you need to use a complex method called the internal rate of return, which accounts for the timing of the investments into the fund. Leave that to the professionals, or to a computer program that can provide it. You can get a rough approximation of your return by calculating your average cost per share (see "Dollar-Cost Averaging" in Chapter 4). Do all the numbers have you breaking out in a cold sweat? Calm yourself. With a pocket calculator, a pencil, and paper, you can do it yourself just fine.

Let the Computer Do It

You certainly don't need a computer to keep track of your mutual funds. But if you do have a personal computer and are willing to take the time to master new software, there are a number of money and investment management programs that simplify the "keeping up" process. Some of the better-known commercial software in this category is Quicken, Managing Your Money, and Simply Money. If you're adept at using the spreadsheet programs like Microsoft Excel or Lotus 1-2-3, you can create your own portfolio record-keeping systems.

The programs allow an investor to set up multiple portfolios: yours, your spouse's, the IRA, the kids', each with an unlimited number of investments. You could also treat each mutual fund as a portfolio. Fund investors might find it convenient to organize portfolios by the fund family—like Fidelity or Franklin—or by the broker who handles the account—like Dean Witter or PaineWebber.

Next, subtract the initial NAV, or $9.31. That amounts to $1.8738 per share, which is the fund's "profit" for the year. Next, divide the $1.8738 profit by the starting NAV, $9.31, which comes to 0.2013. To turn that into a percentage, just multiply by 100. The total return is 20.13 percent.

Though this calculation covered a one-year period, the method works for any time period. The key to taking an accurate measurement is to remember to include all the dividends and distributions.

But the total return is a measure of how well the portfolio managers performed. That doesn't necessarily tell you how well your own investment is doing. For instance, if you paid a load or sales charge, that won't be reflected in the total return calculation that uses NAV. So here's a way to calculate your own return.

Suppose you invested $2000 in a mutual fund and reinvested dividends and capital gains distributions of $325. At the end of the year, your account is worth $2415. To figure your return, take the value of your shares at the end of the period—$2415. If the fund has a back-end load or

Computer power is particularly handy for investors who make frequent purchases and regular reinvestment of dividends and capital gains. If you invest monthly and reinvest the income and distributions, you will be making 12 to 16 transactions a year. By entering each one into the computer program, the investor knows exactly how many shares of each investment he or she has, what it's worth, and what the average cost is.

More important, the programs show each transaction individually as well as what the profit or loss is on that particular investment. Suppose the overall investment is in the black, but several purchases of funds were made at higher prices and are in the red. These programs will flag those transactions—which is awfully helpful for tax-planning purposes.

Among the tax-oriented programs, CompuVest is an excellent choice. It can calculate your "cost basis" the three different ways that are accepted by the IRS (more on that in Chapter 6), allowing you to select the one that's most advantageous. (CompuVest sells for $34.95, including shipping, and can be returned within 30 days. Call 1-800-532-2392.) Another excellent new entry in this category of software is TaxTracker for Windows (available for $49 from the No-Load Fund Shareholders Assn., Inc., 1-800-966-5623). Though designed for the fund investor, TaxTracker is easily adaptable for stocks and bonds as well. Another feature here that's not in most financial software is an internal rate of return calculator. That will allow you to make a more sophisticated measure of your investment performance. You can also order the program at the Internet address (http://www.manhattanlink.com).

> Computers can simplify investing.

Mutual Funds Online

If you have a computer and a modem, you probably already subscribe to one of the online services, such as America Online or to an Internet access service (Table 5-2). The online world is emerging as a valuable tool for tracking, researching, and keeping up with mutual funds. We hope BUSINESS WEEK Online (www.businessweek.com) will be the place to go in cyberspace for the lowdown on mutual funds.

That's because our website now carries an interactive version of the BW Mutual Fund Scoreboard, one that allows you to search for funds in many ways. Trying to find data on specific funds? You can find them alphabetically. Thinking about adding a foreign or a technology fund to your portfolio. You can ask the Scoreboard to give you a list of either. Just want A-rated bond funds? You can do that as well. Want even more info on a fund than we provide? We've included links to Morningstar pages as well. There are also links to Personal Wealth, a new and exciting web service from Standard & Poor's Corp. (Both BUSINESS WEEK and S&P are owned by the McGraw-Hill Cos.)

What's also great about the online Scoreboard is that we're no longer confined by the printed page. We'll be including data on around 4000 equity and bond funds and will be able to include more as more data becomes available. Best yet, the online version of the Scoreboard will be updated monthly—ratings and all—instead of the annual update that appears in print. This will allow you to better track your funds and hone in on the BUSINESS WEEK ratings throughout the year. BW Online already has a Mutual Fund Corner, which collects all the magazine and BW Online stories of interest to fund investors.

The World Wide Web opens up vast new resources—and a lot of worthless information as well. We've already screened some of the offerings, and there are excellent home pages worth checking out. Start with NetWorth, a centralized starting point. To get beyond the first pages, you have to register, but it's free. You'll get a password. You can keep a portfolio online, download shareholder reports, interviews with fund managers, and even fund prospectuses. (Stuff a prospectus in a computer file and save a tree.) NetWorth also allows you to download data to Quicken and other personal finance software. Other good fund-stops include Mutual Funds Magazine, Schwab, Fidelity, and Vanguard. For fans of closed-end funds, the Internet Closed-End Fund Investor offers some great information and tools that are not readily available elsewhere online.

Fund investors who venture online should also join the newsgroup, "misc.invest.funds." That's a message board where fund folks meet to ask questions, exchange opinions, and gather insight into mutual funds. Want to know why your hot fund was down 2 percent last week when the market fell less than 1? Post the question. Someone might have the answer—and that person may even be from the mutual fund company.

TABLE 5-2

FUND "SURFING" ONLINE

The Internet

BUSINESS WEEK Online
Top-drawer news, analysis, commentary from a world-class business magazine. New feature is BW Mutual Fund Scoreboard in an interactive version that is updated monthly. Mutual Fund Corner at site collects articles of interest to fund investors.

http://www.businessweek.com

NetWorth
Fund information for more than 30 companies, with links to many home pages. Can also download data to Quicken and other personal finance programs. Service is free, but requires registration.

http://networth.galt.com

Mutual Funds Interactive
Good commentary, profiles and chat, plus market news, fund quotes, and portfolio tracking. Be sure to bookmark this site.

http://www.fundsinteractive.com/

Morningstar
Snappy new site, with loads of fund research to help you plan a portfolio. Links with brokerage firms let you invest as well. Service is free, but requires registration.

http://www.morningstar.net

Mutual Fund Investor's Corner
Sponsored by the Mutual Fund Education Alliance, a trade association of the direct-marketed (mainly no-load) funds. Fund info limited to that of members companies, but that's mainly what the do-it-yourself investor would want anyway.

http://www.mfea.com

FundAlarm
Maintains data on 500 funds (mainly those over $500 million), and tracks the funds vs. various benchmarks. Is one of yours a "three alarm" fund, and therefore should be dumped?

http://www.FundAlarm.com

Mutual Funds Magazine
Includes current and past stories from the magazine, and a screenable database of funds.

http://www.mfmag.com

SEC EDGAR Database
The U.S. Securities & Exchange Commission's electronic database, for those who want to read the official mutual fund filings.

http://www.sec.gov/edgarhp.htm

Schwab Online
The cyberdoor to the nation's largest discount brokers, which includes information on Schwab's popular Mutual Fund Marketplace and OneSource programs.

http://www.Schwab.com

Fidelity Investments
The home page for the nation's largest fund company and for its brokerage firm. Plenty of performance info, and prospectuses as well.

http://www.fid-inv.com

Jack White & Co.
Discount broker with the most number of funds, 4200 at last count. Website is not as slick as some, but if you want fund selection, no one offers more.

http://pawws.com/jwc/jwms.html

Vanguard Mutual Funds
Quiz yourself on your mutual fund knowledge, but don't worry if you don't do too well. You can enroll in the Vanguard University where you can learn how to build portfolios of funds, guided by the works of John C. Bogle's, founder and chairman.

http://www.vanguard.com

IBC Money Fund Monitor
The place to go for the latest information on money-market mutual funds. The site also includes news and commentary on the money-market activity, interest-rate developments, regulatory issues, and fund strategies. Carries data on more than 1200 taxable and tax-free money-market.

http://www.ibcdata.com

Internet Closed-End Investor
A great online service for an often-overlooked investment vehicle—the closed-end fund. Fund data, charts, screening capability, and more. Some services free, some require subscription.

http://www.icefi.com/

Online Services

America Online
Mutual Fund Center is a great jumping off point, collecting info on funds from around AOL and the Internet. Other funds-stops include Morningstar, American Association of Individual Investors, and BUSINESS WEEK Online's Mutual Fund Corner. Sage, a site whose motto is "Making Sense of Mutual Funds," is a winner—and an AOL exclusive. Call 1-800-641-4848.

CompuServe
FundWatch by *Money Magazine* includes reports from CDA/Wiesenberger, has ability to screen database. Morningstar and Value Line reports also available. Call 1-800-848-8990.

Prodigy
Comprehensive mutual-fund data provided by Micropal, with weekly updates. Another service, charts fund NAVs. Mutual Fund Center has daily price quotes and news about mutual funds and fund companies, provided by Dow Jones. Call 1-800-PRODIGY.

DATA: BUSINESS WEEK

When Your Fund Is Ailing

You're tracking your funds, diligently keeping records of weekly prices, remembering to count distributions in your returns. Then you start to notice that one of your funds is slipping. The stock market is moving up modestly but this fund is heading south.

The long-term record is still exceptional, and you're a long-term investor. So you stick with the fund—and watch it slip away. Now you're not only lagging the market, but you're losing real money. What do you do?

You're facing the most difficult question in all of investing: When do you jettison a fund that's in a funk? Suppose you sell and it turns out to be the bottom of the decline. You might regret it later. Maybe you paid a load to get into the fund, and so are reluctant to leave now. Sometimes people just refuse to admit they made a bad investment—there's too much ego involved. So they're slow to sell when perhaps they should.

Before pushing the "sell" button on a poorly performing fund, ask some questions about it. The most important: How is the fund doing relative to its market sector and peer group? Suppose the S&P 500 delivered a total return of 10 percent over the previous period and your small-cap growth fund gained only half that much. The question is: How much better did the other small-cap growth funds perform? Perhaps your fund, while dragging behind the market, did well among its peers. So besides comparing your fund to the market, compare your fund to similar funds.

If you had owned a high-yield bond fund in the latter half of 1989 and 1990, you may have been dismayed by plunging net asset values. At that time, no junk fund was going to look good. And the question wasn't, "Do you want to own this junk fund or another junk fund?" but "Do you want to invest in a junk bond fund at all?" You may have invested in one of the better junk bond funds. But you have to compare yours to others to know that.

Sometimes you make a bet without realizing it, and the failure of the investment is not entirely the manager's. If you buy a long-term government bond fund, the investment won't succeed unless long-term interest rates come down—or at least stay flat. If they go up, your fund is going to falter. You may choose to sell out,

but don't replace your fund with another long-term bond fund at the same time. If you're attracted by the long-term results of these sorts of funds, then you just stick with them, through good times and bad.

An investment in narrowly defined funds such as technology or health care or Latin American equities or emerging markets debt is a good bit riskier than in a broad-based fund with a wide menu of portfolio options. If you owned a Southeast Asian equity fund in late 1997, you can't blame the portfolio manager for not beating the S&P 500. You might expect him to beat his peers, but certainly an Asian fund could not be expected to dodge a macroeconomic event.

What was your motivation in choosing this investment? If you were trying to seize upon a trading opportunity, like a big rally in Asian stocks, you might as well sell, since the opportunity didn't materialize. If you bought to diversify your portfolio and to take advantage of a long-term growth opportunity, you should hold on nonetheless—and perhaps even increase your investment. If you bought the fund to diversify your holdings, don't fret. Chances are some of your other funds are doing quite well.

Before you jettison a mutual fund, you have to remember that few funds do well under all market conditions. What you should expect is that gains in up periods outweigh the losses in the down periods. The Vanguard/Windsor Fund is a case in point. The fund, then managed by John B. Neff, fared only about half as well as the S&P 500 in 1989 and fell more than twice as much as the market during 1990. Neff's "value" style of investing, which has proved successful for years, leads him to buy out of favor, high-dividend-paying stocks like autos, banks, and insurers. Those were among the worst-performing stock groups of the year. But the history of Neff's style of investing is that when the tide turns his way, he more than makes up for downswings. That's starting to happen. In 1992, Windsor more than doubled the returns of the S&P 500; in 1993, it nearly doubled the market index. And even in the difficult year of 1994, the fund finished slightly behind the total return of the S&P 500, but ahead of most mutual funds.

What if large-cap value funds performed well—but Windsor didn't. Then you may have good reason to fire the fund. Indeed, it's because the best fund managers run into downdrafts that you diversify your mutual fund investments. That's why you might offset Windsor with, say, the Janus Fund or T. Rowe Price Blue Chip

Growth, which choose companies for their earnings growth rather than value characteristics. If Windsor tried to boost its returns by loading up on small stocks of fast-growing high-tech companies, that too would be reason enough to dump the fund. Ask the professionals who advise pension funds on selection of investment managers: The only sin worse than underperforming the market is not following your stated investment program.

In short, don't dump a fund just on performance alone. Compare your fund to an appropriate market index, like the S&P 500; the S&P MidCap 400; or for small-cap stocks, the Russell 2000. Foreign funds can be compared to the foreign market indexes, such as those published by Morgan Stanley or Goldman Sachs. Bond funds should be compared to an appropriate bond index, depending on the maturity of the fund. Lehman Bros., Merrill Lynch, and Salomon Bros. all have numerous bond indexes for every segment of the bond market—corporates, Treasuries, global, mortgage-backed—and by maturity, too—short-, intermediate-, and long-term.

Keep in Touch with Your Fund

When you buy a mutual fund you are, in effect, "hiring" an investment manager to do a job for you, such as investing in small- to medium-sized companies. So to oversee your fund portfolio, you have to make sure your managers are doing what they told you they would do. If you invest in a small-cap fund, you don't want the manager spending your money on IBM, AT&T, and GE.

Funds do change gears, but they're supposed to notify you. As a shareholder, you're entitled to get periodic reports—at least semiannually, though many report quarterly as well. But the information in a report may be quite dated by the time you see it. Funds have 90 days after the close of their fiscal half and full fiscal year to deliver shareholder reports. Still, even a somewhat dated report can be informative.

Shareholder reports vary in their content and presentation. The Gintel Fund, for instance, has a very simple report, but it's quite informative nonetheless (Figure 5-2). All fund reports will show the market value of a security on the day of the report. But Gintel's also discloses the purchase price of the investment. That's a line-by-line report card on how the fund manager is doing.

The Gintel Fund lists its stocks by their value of the holding in the portfolio. Federal National Mortgage Association (which has since changed its legal name to its nickname, "Fannie Mae") is by far the largest holding, with 150,000 shares. What makes it the largest is not the number of shares, but the market value of those shares (price times the number of shares) which, the statement shows, is $15,525,000. Now compare that to the purchase cost of $8,108,946, and you can also see that the fund has a tidy profit, a near double, in the stock. If thinking in millions is a little unwieldy, Gintel reports per-share cost and market value, too. By disclosing cost, this fund also shows its losing positions—stocks whose market value is now below the fund's cost. By comparing cost and market value, you can see

FIGURE 5-2

GINTEL FUND
Status of Investments
September 30, 1995
(Unaudited)

Common Stocks		Purchase Cost	Market Value	Per Share Cost	Per Share Market	% of Net Assets
150,000	Federal National Mortgage	$8,108,946	$15,525,000	54.06	103.50	15.9
355,000	Checkpoint Systems	2,846,216	9,363,125	8.02	26.38	9.6
150,000	Union Camp	6,750,336	8,643,750	45.00	57.63	8.9
700,000	Chart Industries	3,321,550	6,125,000	4.75	8.75	6.3
665,000	Oneita Industries, Inc.	8,414,133	5,652,500	12.65	8.50	5.8
150,000	Capstead Mortgage	2,932,501	4,781,250	19.55	31.88	4.9
90,000	Schering-Plough Corp.	2,147,611	4,635,000	23.86	51.50	4.8
100,000	FirstFed Michigan	868,021	3,512,500	8.68	35.13	3.6
50,000	DuPont	2,798,852	3,437,500	55.98	68.75	3.5
50,000	Phelps Dodge	2,992,527	3,131,250	59.85	62.63	3.2
48,000	Fluor	2,223,496	2,688,000	46.32	56.00	2.8
100,000	Singer Co.	2,497,273	2,662,500	24.97	26.63	2.7
52,500	Weyerhaeuser	2,101,374	2,395,313	40.03	45.63	2.4
100,000	New Park Resources	1,946,258	1,750,000	19.46	17.50	1.8
100,000	Vertex, Inc.	1,550,000	1,725,000	15.50	17.25	1.8
25,000	Johnson Controls	1,195,851	1,581,250	47.83	63.25	1.6
25,000	Tyco International	1,278,937	1,575,000	51.16	63.00	1.6
75,000	Price/Costco	1,011,188	1,284,375	13.48	17.13	1.3
30,000	Black & Decker	750,260	1,023,750	25.01	34.13	1.0
20,000	Pepsico Inc.	696,562	1,020,000	34.83	51.00	1.0
100,000	OHM Corp.	693,749	900,000	6.94	9.00	0.9
25,000	WorldCom	608,749	803,125	24.35	32.13	0.8
25,000	OrNda Healthcare	433,750	531,250	17.35	21.25	0.5
	Miscellaneous Securities	4,355,479	4,447,601			4.6
	Total Investments	$62,523,619	89,194,038			91.3
	Cash and Short-Term Investments		8,482,994			8.7
	NET ASSETS		**$97,677,032**			**100.0**
	NET ASSET VALUE PER SHARE		$15.77			
	INCREASE IN NET ASSET VALUE PER SHARE YEAR-TO-DATE		26.6%			

that just two (Oneita Industries, Inc. and New Park Resources) of the 23 holdings are in the red.

But that cost information isn't always in the reports. Typically, the reports show the security and its market value on the date of the report. The American Funds group, for instance, doesn't provide the shareholder's costs, but does a good job in portfolio reporting. Look at Figure 5-3, from the 1997 Annual Report of Growth Fund of America. At the top, there's summary information on major industries in which the fund is invested and the 10 largest holdings. Without reading any further, the shareholder can see how his or her money is deployed. For instance, broadcasting and publishing is the largest indus-

FIGURE 5-3

Investment Portfolio
August 31, 1997

Largest Industry Holdings

Broadcasting & Publishing 13.95%
Electronic Components 12.19%
Data Processing & Reproduction 11.03%
Business & Public Services 8.50%
Health & Personal Care 5.07%
Cash & Equivalents 14.54%
Other Industries 34.72%

Largest Individual Holdings	Percent of Net Assets
Time Warner	4.09%
Federal National Mortgage Assn.	3.06
Philip Morris	2.67
America Online	2.55
Walt Disney	2.04
Intel	1.80
Texas Instruments	1.76
Tele-Communications, TCI Group	1.62
Comcast	1.61
Tele-Communications, Liberty Media Group	1.53

Equity Securities (Common & Preferred Stocks)	Shares	Market Value (000)	Percent of Net Assets
Broadcasting & Publishing — 13.95%			
Time Warner Inc. A leading media and entertainment company. Operations include publishing, film and TV production, recorded music and cable TV. Has acquired Turner Broadcasting System, Inc.	9,250,750	$476,414	4.09%
Tele-Communications, Inc., Series A, TCI Group[1] One of the largest cable operators in the U.S.	10,789,300	188,813	1.62
Comcast Corp., Class A special stock	6,339,762	148,588	1.61
Comcast Corp., Class A One of the country's fastest growing cable TV operators. Also owns cellular telephone franchises and QVC, a cable shopping network.	1,680,000	39,060	
Tele-Communications, Inc., Series A, Liberty Media Group[1] Owns a controlling stake in Turner Broadcasting System, Inc. and a 50% interest in The Discovery Channel.	6,752,237	178,090	1.53
Viacom Inc., Class B[1] Produces feature films and TV shows, operates TV and radio stations and owns several cable channels, the country's largest book publisher, Simon & Schuster, and Blockbuster Entertainment.	6,000,000	177,750	1.53
News Corp. Ltd. (American Depositary Receipts) (Australia)	5,400,000	97,537	1.27
News Corp. Ltd., preferred (American Depositary Receipts) Owns broadcasting, newspaper, publishing and entertainment assets in North America, Europe, Australia and Asia.	3,363,750	50,876	
E.W. Scripps Co., Class A Owns newspapers, television and radio stations, and cable television systems across the U.S.	1,660,000	65,259	.56
Cox Communications, Inc., Class A[1] One of the largest cable TV operators in the U.S. and a fully diversified media company.	2,000,000	54,125	.46
Chris-Craft Industries, Inc.[1] A television broadcasting company.	1,050,085	51,520	.44

try sector in the portfolio, commanding 13.95 percent of the assets, and the second largest is electronic components, with 12.19 percent.

Then look at "Largest Individual Holdings." The single largest holding in the portfolio is Time Warner, one of the the world's major media companies, which alone accounts for 4.09 percent of the fund assets. Four other top 10 holdings come from the broadcasting and publishing, or media, sector—Walt Disney, Tele-Communications/TCI Group, Comcast, and Tele-Communications/Liberty Media Group. Intel and Texas Instruments, the No. 6 and No. 7 holdings, belong to the electronic components group.

If you want more information, there's plenty to follow. Look down the page. The first broad category listed is "Broadcasting & Publishing." And under that heading, the companies are listed according to the market value of the investment. Time Warner Inc., worth $476,414,000 at the time of the report, is first. What's informative about this report and others produced by American Funds is the description of the individual companies, something that is not often provided in mutual fund literature.

Most reports include a letter to shareholders from the president of the fund management company or from the portfolio manager. The letter typically discusses market conditions, though by the time you get the report the quarter will be long past. Twice a year, the fund is supposed to provide you with a copy of the portfolio. You don't have to second-guess the portfolio manager, but a quick scan might tell you a few things. If the fund is supposed to invest in small, fast-growing companies—and you don't recognize many of the companies' names—then the fund manager is probably pursuing what he or she promised to pursue. If you have a high-quality bond fund and you find it's peppered with junk bonds, you ought to ask a few questions. Don't be bashful. Call the fund management company and ask for an explanation.

The quality of shareholder reports varies widely. Some fund managers are brutally frank when they have had a period of bad performance; others are elliptical or evasive, and never admit head-on when their results are poor. Charles T. Freeman, portfolio manager of the Vanguard/Windsor Fund, includes a report card on his performance by comparing the performance of major fund holdings with their industry group. It's a practice he carried on from his predecessor, John B. Neff. For instance, in the October 31, 1997 annual report, Freeman gave himself A's for his investments in airline, finance, and telecommunications stocks. But he awarded himself a D+ for his 15 percent position—the second largest after finance—in basic materials stocks like aluminum, chemicals, paper, and steel companies. That's the second year in a row that sector disappointed. He gave himself a D for his investment in agriculture-related stocks, but the entire position was only 6 percent of the fund. Few funds are as informative and frank as Windsor, though Vanguard, in general, provides fairly complete reports.

Morningstar's analysts also rate funds' reports to shareholders. They look at the amount of financial information—above and beyond what's required by law—and the presentation. Is it organized in a reader-friendly manner? Can the shareholder learn something about the investment from the reports?

At one time, Morningstar discovered some correlation between shareholder reports and good returns. In a 1993 study, analysts found that 45 funds with A ratings on their shareholder reports had five-year average annual returns of 20.8 percent. Funds with B-rated reports had an 18.1 percent average annual return for the five-year period. The funds with reports rated B through D all had average annual returns around 15.5 percent. There were only six funds that flunked. But these funds with F-rated reports had nothing much to say for themselves. Their five-year average annual return was a skimpy 4.7 percent. In 1998, we asked Morningstar to revisit the study. This time, there was a similar correlation between quality of reports and the strength of returns. Interestingly enough, though, shareholders don't have to pay a whole lot more to get a good report. Morningstar found that funds with better-rated reports had lower expense ratios.

There are other times that you hear from a fund. Every time the prospectus is updated, you should get a new copy. That's to keep in your files. If there has been some major change in policy, such as imposition of a load or 12(b)-1 fee, or a change in redemption procedures, it should be highlighted or noted to investors in a separate letter.

Finally, most mutual funds are corporations, registered in various states and governed by the laws of that state. If the state requires annual meetings, your fund will send you a proxy statement, a proxy card, and an invitation to the meeting. At the least, the proxy will have a ballot for election of the fund directors and the hiring of the auditors.

Shareholder reports vary widely in quality.

FIGURE 5-4

T.Rowe Price
T. Rowe Price Associates, Inc., 100 East Pratt Street, Baltimore, MD 21202

James S. Riepe
Managing Director

Dear Shareholder:

All of the T. Rowe Price mutual funds will hold shareholder meetings in 1994 to elect directors, ratify the selection of independent accountants, and approve amendments to a number of investment policies.

The T. Rowe Price funds are not required to hold annual meetings each year if the only items of business are to elect directors or ratify accountants. In order to save fund expenses, most of the funds have not held annual meetings for a number of years. There are, however, conditions under which the funds must ask shareholders to elect directors, and one is to comply with a requirement that a minimum number have been elected by shareholders, not appointed by the funds' boards. Since the last annual meetings of the T. Rowe Price funds, several directors have retired and new directors have been added. In addition, a number of directors will be retiring in the near future.

Given this situation, we believed it appropriate to hold annual meetings for all the T. Rowe Price funds in 1994. At the same time, we reviewed the investment policies of all of the funds for consistency and to assure the portfolio managers have the flexibility they need to manage your money in today's fast changing financial markets. The changes being recommended, which are explained in detail in the enclosed proxy material, **do not alter the funds' investment objectives or basic investment programs.**

In many cases the proposals are common to several funds, so we have combined certain proxy statements to save on fund expenses. For those of you who own more than one of these funds, the combined proxy may also save you the time of reading more than one document before you vote and mail your ballots. The proposals which are specific to an individual fund are easily identifiable on the Notice and in the proxy statement discussion. If you own more than one fund, please note that **each fund has a separate card. You should vote and sign each one,** then return all of them to us in the enclosed postage-paid envelope.

Your early response will be appreciated and could save your fund the substantial costs associated with a follow-up mailing. We know we are asking you to review a rather formidable proxy statement, but this approach represents the most efficient one for your fund as well as for the other funds. Thank you for your cooperation. If you have any questions, please call us at 1-800-225-5132.

Sincerely,

James S. Riepe
Director, Mutual Funds Division

CUSIP#779572106/fund#065

If the fund management contract is up for renewal as well, you'll be asked to approve that, along with any changes in fees or sales charges. Late in 1997, for instance, the shareholders of the Acorn Fund overwhelmingly approved the management company's request for a hike in the management fee schedule that added about 0.25 percentage points to the fund's expenses. Management argued that the costs of hiring top investment talent were going up, and the fund needed to pay more to stay competitive. The fund has an excellent long-term record, paid management, and added that even with the increase, the expense ratio, about 0.87 percent, would be well below the industry average.

Shareholders also may be asked to okay mergers and changes in investment management firms and do such routine things as elect directors (from a list of nominees) and ratify the board's choice of auditors. If there is any change in investment policy, it should also be a ballot question. For instance, many domestic equity funds have changed policy to allow investment in foreign securities, usually with a limit on the percentage of fund assets that can be invested abroad. If you're against that in principle, then vote no. But the overwhelming chances are that you'll be outvoted.

Other than the serious business, such as approving fees, it's easy to dismiss the proxies as not even being worth your time to read and consider. But don't toss them out—not even seemingly innocuous proxies from money-market funds (Figures 5-4 and 5-5). Vote, sign, and return them in the postage-prepaid envelope. You don't have to vote yes, and you can abstain. But it's critical to return the proxy because the funds need a quorum to hold a meeting. (In signing the proxy, you give persons named on the statement the ability to vote your shares as you direct.) You have as many votes as you have shares. If a fund fails to obtain enough proxies for a quorum, it will have to conduct another mailing. And shareholders bear the cost of proxy solicitation.

Few funds have meetings anymore. Many conduct votes by proxy without convening a meeting. The meeting is an opportunity to ask questions of fund managers, but there probably isn't anything you're going to learn in person that you couldn't find out from a phone call or letter to the shareholder services department.

When the Fund Manager Changes

One of the toughest questions in mutual fund investing is what to do when the portfolio manager changes, especially "star" managers like Peter Lynch, who piloted the Fidelity Magellan Fund to tremendous successes and took an early retirement from fund management in 1990. Of course, Lynch's departure was big news. But how do you know if there's been a change in portfolio managers?

For starters, the management company has to tell you in the fund documents. That's a new development in fund regulation. Until a few years ago, funds were under no obligation to tell and many preferred not to. And, in case you haven't picked up on it before, BUSINESS WEEK Mutual Fund Scoreboard also notes when the portfolio manager of an equity fund has changed.

FIGURE 5-5

T. Rowe Price — We Need Your Proxy Vote Before April 20, 1994

Please refer to the Proxy Statement discussion of each of these matters.

THIS PROXY WHEN PROPERLY EXECUTED WILL BE VOTED IN THE MANNER DIRECTED HEREIN BY THE SHAREHOLDER. IF NO DIRECTION IS MADE, THIS PROXY WILL BE VOTED FOR ALL PROPOSALS.

Please fold and detach card at perforation before mailing.

1. Election of directors. FOR all nominees listed below ☐ (except as marked to the contrary) WITHHOLD AUTHORITY to vote ☐ 1. for all nominees listed below

(INSTRUCTION: TO WITHHOLD AUTHORITY TO VOTE FOR AN INDIVIDUAL NOMINEE STRIKE A LINE THROUGH THE NOMINEE'S NAME IN THE LIST BELOW.)

Leo C. Bailey   Donald W. Dick, Jr.   David K. Fagin   Addison Lanier   John H. Laporte   John K. Major
Hanne M. Merriman   James S. Riepe   Hubert D. Vos   Paul M. Wythes

2. Approve changes to the Fund's fundamental policies. FOR each policy listed below (except ☐ as marked to the contrary) ABSTAIN ☐ 2.

If you do **NOT** wish to approve a policy change, please check the appropriate box below:

☐ (A) Borrowing   ☐ (E) Purchasing Securities   ☐ (I) Investment Companies   ☐ (M) Ownership of Securities
☐ (B) Commodities & Futures   ☐ (F) Real Estate   ☐ (J) Purchasing on Margin   ☐ (N) Illiquid Securities
☐ (C) Lending   ☐ (G) Senior Securities   ☐ (K) Oil & Gas   ☐ (O) Short Sales
☐ (D) Single Issuer   ☐ (H) Control   ☐ (L) Options   ☐ (P) Unseasoned Issuers

3. Ratify the selection of Coopers & Lybrand as independent accountants. FOR ☐ AGAINST ☐ ABSTAIN ☐ 3.

4. I authorize the Proxies, in their discretion, to vote upon such other business as may properly come before the meeting.

CUSIP#779572106/fund#065

T. ROWE PRICE OTC FUND, INC.   MEETING: 8:00 A.M. EASTERN TIME

THIS PROXY IS SOLICITED ON BEHALF OF THE BOARD OF DIRECTORS

The undersigned hereby appoints John H. Laporte and James S. Riepe, as proxies, each with the power to appoint his substitute, and hereby authorizes them to represent and to vote, as designated below, all shares of stock of the Fund, which the undersigned is entitled to vote at the Annual Meeting of Shareholders to be held on Wednesday, April 20, 1994, at the time indicated above, at the offices of the Fund, 100 East Pratt Street, Baltimore, Maryland 21202, and at any and all adjournments thereof, with respect to the matters set forth below and described in the Notice of Annual Meeting and Proxy Statement dated March 9, 1994, receipt of which is hereby acknowledged.

Please sign exactly as name appears. Only authorized officers should sign for corporations. For information as to the voting of stock registered in more than one name, see page 3 of the Notice of Annual Meeting and Proxy Statement.

Dated: _____ , 1994

_____

Signature(s)
CUSIP#779572106/fund#065

Does a change in leadership matter? It depends on the sort of fund. With a money-market fund and even many bond funds, the manager may not matter much at all. And some fund management companies, such as the American Funds and American Century Investors, take a team approach to investment management, so one portfolio manager may hardly be missed. Vanguard/Windsor's Neff stepped down at the end of 1995, but was succeeded by Charles T. Freeman, a deputy who spent 25 years at his side. That fund's investors should be fairly confident of a continuity in investment style.

But that's not always the case. With many equity funds the manager has a lot of latitude. When Peter Lynch retired from the Fidelity Magellan Fund, mutual fund analysts were split over whether to sell. Six months after Lynch's departure, those who sold looked smart. It wasn't that Morris Smith, Lynch's successor, fumbled. Just weeks after he took over the reins, the stock market went into a swoon. True, Magellan under-performed a poorly performing market. But the fund is so large, and owns so many stocks, that it's quite possible that the performance in the second half of 1990 may not have been much different had Lynch remained at the helm.

In 1991, when the stock market rallied, so did Magellan, up 41 percent for the year. But early in 1992, Smith, citing a need for a break, left the fund, too. Jeffrey Vinik, Smith's successor, trailed the market, too, early in his tenure, and some analysts wondered whether it was time to leave the fund. But Vinik also had an excellent track record (he formerly ran Fidelity Contrafund and Fidelity Growth & Income Fund). In 1993, in fact, Magellan posted a 24.7 percent total return, more than doubling the return of the S&P 500—one of the best relative performances since the early 1980s, when the $31.7 billion fund was less than $1 billion in size. In 1996, Vinik invested 20 percent of the fund in Treasury bonds—and the bond market sank. He left the fund at the end of May. He was succeeded by Robert E. Stansky, another top manager.

Neither Lynch's, Smith's, nor Vinik's departure was fatal for Magellan because Fidelity has an exceptional pool of managerial talent and an army of talented research analysts. In fact, the company changes fund managers frequently. In 1996, however, the company made a slew of changes in the spring to try to improve sagging performance. Later in the year, manager departures resulted in further shifts. More than half the equity funds got a new manager during 1996. The short-term impact, at least, was not good. Most of Fidelity's diversified U.S. equity funds trailed the market through 1997.

Perhaps to protect against the investors' following a star manager out the door, many fund companies have been naming co-managers to funds. The idea, at least, is that if one manager leaves, the second provides continuity and the fund company can say the same management is in place. So when Carlene Murphy Ziegler, co-manager of the Strong Opportunity and Strong Common Stock, resigned in 1994, co-manager Dick Weiss was still in place, along with Marina Carlson, who had been named as an additional co-manager earlier in the year.

Even so, many investment managers and financial planners switch funds when a well-regarded fund manager leaves. There have been no definitive studies yet, but Morningstar, for example, uncovered some interesting anecdotal evidence in late 1990. It looked at five managers who switched funds and measured how the old funds had done since the switch versus how the new funds performed under the star managers. In all five cases, investors following the manager to the new fund would have done better.

But there's anecdotal evidence to the contrary as well. Donald Yacktman built an enviable record with Selected American Fund, but left Selected in early 1992 to set up the Yacktman Fund. The results, so far, have been mixed. Yacktman's reputation was enough to draw in $70 mil-

lion or so in the first six months, a decent start considering that Yacktman did not have a large fund company or marketing muscle behind him. But the investment returns were a different story. In 1993, his first full year in operation, Yacktman Fund was down 6.6 percent. In 1994, the growth stocks he favored rebounded and his fund was up 8.8 percent, and he logged a 29 percent return in 1995. In 1996, he beat the S&P 500, earning a 26 percent return, but in 1997, like most managers, he earned a decent return but failed to beat the S&P.

Yacktman's departure from Selected American also spurred an unusual chain of management. Selected Financial Services, the management company, replaced Yacktman with another manager. Unhappy with the performance, the independent directors of the fund—members of the board of directors who were not Selected employees—voted to dismiss Selected as the management company and hired Shelby Davis, the highly regarded manager of the Davis New York Venture Fund, to run the fund. (Davis retired in 1997, but his son runs the fund.)

Sometimes there's a change when the ownership of a fund management company is taken over. In 1992, for instance, Franklin Resources, which owns Franklin Funds, took over the Templeton fund company but left the Templeton fund managers in place, since Franklin bought Templeton in part for its investment expertise. No need to change. When T. Rowe Price Associates took over the USF&G funds, it folded most of them into already existing T. Rowe Price funds. So those fund investors got new managers. In cases like that, investors may want to review the record of the new managers. In late 1993, Pioneering Management, the company that manages the Pioneer family of funds, took over five Mutual of Omaha funds, but did not merge them into its own funds. Instead, in all but one municipal bond fund, Pioneer installed its own portfolio managers. In such a case, find out which other funds your new manager has run and check out his or her records.

Or look at the situation when the management company brings in a new manager to revamp a laggard fund. That's what happened in early 1997 when Warburg Pincus lured Brian Posner away from Fidelity to run its once-golden but then lagging Warburg Pincus Growth & Income Fund. Berger Funds did the same a month later, when it hired Patrick Adams, formerly of Founders and Kemper Funds, to revamp the laggard Berger 100. At the end of 1996 these funds' shareholders

Mutual fund companies are merging.

were hurting: their trailing three-year records were only half that of the average U.S. diversified funds.

Long-time shareholders applauded both moves, and by the end of the year, the results were mixed. Posner succeeded in repositioning his fund and managed a hefty 30.3 percent total return. Adams overhauled his portfolio as well, but the results were nowhere as good—a 13 percent total return, about the same as the last year under the previous manager. Worse yet, both new managers traded away much of the portfolios and created large capital gains distributions. Posner's results were strong enough that the aftertax return was still about 23 percent. Under Adams, Berger 100's wan 13 percent pretax shrunk to 4.5 percent aftertax.

What created the large taxable distributions was exactly what the two managers had been brought in to do—overhaul and, hopefully, reinvigorate the funds. To those who had held the fund in tax-deferred accounts, the distributions were nonevents. And to taxable investors who had been in the funds a long time, the tax on the distributions was probably a small price to pay to get their investments back on track—at least Warburg fund seems like it is.

But any taxable investor who rushed to buy these funds after the new managers were appointed did not get any great deals. Moral of the story: if a lagging fund gets a hot new manager, wait until the portfolio has been overhauled—and the resultant gains distributed. Otherwise, you can end up paying taxes on profits you never made.

Mutual Fund Mergers

For the most part, if a fund does a reasonable job of meeting its investment objectives, the management company isn't going to tinker with success. Most of the time it's poorly performing funds or funds in poorly performing sectors of the stock market that get a makeover. Often, the makeover is simply merging the weaker fund into a stronger one.

A mutual fund merger can take place in one of several ways. For instance, several funds within the same family may be combined. That's what is usually done with small, poorly performing funds. Such funds are in a Catch-22 situation. Since

they're very small, they tend to have higher overhead and expense ratios, which cut into their total returns. And without strong returns, they are unable to attract new investments—and so they remain small.

For instance, in 1994, Oppenheimer Funds (with shareholder approval, of course) renamed the Oppenheimer Global Bio-Tech Fund—the top-performing fund of 1991—the Global Emerging Growth Fund, giving the fund a much broader investment mandate. Then it merged the smaller Oppenheimer Global Environmental Fund into the Emerging Growth Fund. Oppenheimer officials said the company made the switches to get out of the sector fund business. Because of bear markets in both sectors, neither fund was flourishing—or attracting new money. As an emerging growth fund, of course, the fund could invest in biotech and environmental companies, as well as a whole lot more.

Another sort of merger is when a small fund family leaves the business entirely and turns over the funds' management to a major management company. Some of the companies that gave up fund management over the last several years had funds with combined assets of less than $100 million.

Then there's the "rationalization" merger, when two companies combine and try to streamline the fund offerings by merging like funds. That's what happened in 1994, when Smith Barney Inc. merged 12 funds—including five money-market mutual funds—it had picked up in the Shearson acquisition. Among those merged was the underperforming Smith Barney Shearson Sector Analysis Portfolio, run by Wall Street guru Elaine M. Garzarelli, folded into what is now Smith Barney Strategic Investors.

The best bet is that you will see more fund company mergers in the next few years as industry growth slows and companies combine to achieve more economies of scale. Fund companies are also combining to broaden their product lines. That's some of the motive behind the 1994 merger of Van Kampen Merritt, a fixed-income group, with American Capital, which is more of an equity-fund manager. In 1996, the combined company was purchased by Morgan Stanley, which managed mainly international funds. But in 1997, Morgan Stanley agreed to merge with Dean Witter Discover & Co., and Dean Witter has a wide range of funds.

What does it mean for fund shareholders when the management companies merge? Depends on the merger. After Franklin Resources bought

Investors may benefit in a fund merger.

Templeton (1992) and Mutual Series (1996), fees rose somewhat. That's not surprising. Franklin paid handsomely for both and wanted to recoup its investment. Still, investors who owned any of the Mutual Series Funds prior to the merger got "Z" class shares, which gave them the right to continue to invest in their fund and any other Mutual Series Fund on a no-load basis. New shareholders pay a load. The Zurich Group bought Kemper Funds in 1995 and Scudder Stevens & Clark in 1997, but the results of that merger are not yet all that apparent. There have been marginal performance gains at Kemper, and it's too soon to see any changes at Scudder. And United Asset Management acquired PBHG Funds in 1995 and Pacific Financial (Clipper Fund) in 1997, and there's been no visible changes at all.

Some of these fund-company linkups will no doubt result in mergers at the fund level. It would be unlikely for a Kemper load fund to merge with a Scudder no-load, but you might find a successful fund on either side cloned for the other one. That's potentially a plus for shareholders.

If the merger is of, say, two no-load companies or two load companies, then you're more likely to see poorly performing funds merged into larger, stronger funds. This can be a blessing. You get new fund shares for the old in a tax-free exchange. The new management company usually folds the acquired funds into its own, trying to match up funds with similar objectives.

Change Objectives, Change Funds

Investors' objectives, their ability to assume risks, and their income needs change over time—usually in a gradual and predictable way. But sometimes the changes are abrupt, such as the loss of a job or the death of a spouse. Should objectives change, investors might find that, while their small-cap growth fund has done a good job, it is no longer an appropriate investment for them.

Likewise, changes in tax status may also dictate a shift in funds. As income increases, so should the relative attractiveness of tax-exempt bond and money-market funds. Once in retirement, an investor might find that taxable bond funds offer more return even after paying taxes. These sorts of shifts don't need to happen all at once, and in fact might best be accomplished in stages. If moving funds results in a capital gains tax liability, the investor might want to spread the move out over several tax years.

Taxes and Record-Keeping

By now, you're gung ho on mutual funds. Strong returns, smart management, diversification, low costs, and ease of investing make them wonderful investments. What's the catch? For all the conveniences of investing in mutual funds, there is one big drawback. Depending on the funds you choose, you just may generate a blizzard of paper. Tempted as you may be to ignore or throw away those confirmation statements, don't. At some time you may sell shares of a fund or liquidate all your holdings in the fund. Then you're going to need those records.

Each time you make an investment in a fund, you'll get a statement from the fund management company (Figure 6-1). It will show the date and amount of the investment, the dollar price per share, the number of shares purchased, and the total number of shares in the fund. Redemptions trigger more paper. Switch dollars from, say, a long-term bond fund to a money-market fund, and you may get three statements: one from the bond fund showing the redemption of shares, one from the money-market fund showing a new investment, and another statement indicating an exchange has taken place.

Suppose you are making monthly investments as part of your own dollar-cost averaging program. That's 12 statements a year. And every year the statements should be cumulative. That is, the year's first statement shows a balance forward and the number of shares carried over from the previous year. Then, after the January purchase, you'll get a statement showing the January account activity. In February, it will show February and January. In March, you get all three months, and so forth. By December you should have the entire year's transactions on one statement. So one way to cut down on the file space is to toss out the previous 11 months' statements, as long as you have an up-to-date record of the account activity.

Remember, too, that your investments and redemptions are not the only transactions that generate paper. Every time the fund pays a dividend or capital gains distribution, another statement goes into the mail. Many funds make distributions monthly or quarterly. That can trigger more paper, too. It's enough to make you want to buy growth-oriented equity funds, since most of them make distributions only once a year.

Now, imagine a fund that you bought on several occasions and at various prices, whose shares you sold a few times, also at various prices, and whose earned distributions were reinvested in the funds, also at various prices. You have tons of paper to start with. But your biggest headache isn't paper—it's taxes.

No, even the computer won't stop the blizzard. Good software will help you keep track of the information and make it easier to manage. But the postal service is going to keep on delivering the statements. And the information on each of them has to be entered properly into the program.

Mutual Funds' Special Tax Status

Understanding mutual funds and taxes takes a little extra effort. There's a set of rules that governs how the mutual fund must behave to keep its special tax status. (The rules apply to closed-end funds, too.) And then, once the fund has paid out its earnings, it's up to the shareholders to keep track of them properly. If you miss reporting a dividend or capital gains distribution (the fund sends out 1099-DIVs telling you exactly how much), you're likely to get a letter from the IRS and a bill for the taxes due—plus interest and a penalty.

FIGURE 6-1

THE**Vanguard**GROUP.

December 31, 1997, year-to-date   Page 1 of 2

Vanguard Index Trust-
Total Stock Market Portfolio

SAMPLE SHAREHOLDER
123 ANYROAD ST
ANYTOWN PA 19191-1919

For prompt service when calling please provide your
Statement number: 001234567
(800) 284-7245   -   Voyager Service
(800) 662-6273   -   Tele-Account
Fund number: 85
Account number: 987654321

ACCOUNT VALUE	On 12/31/1996	On 12/31/1997
	$ 44,007.19	$ 66,617.84

Trade date	Transaction		Dollar amount	Share price	Shares transacted	Total shares owned
	Balance on 12/31/1996			$ 17.77		2,476.488
3/25	Income dividend	.06	$ 148.59	18.50	8.032	2,484.520
3/25	ST cap gain	.01	24.76	18.50	1.338	2,485.858
3/25	LT cap gain	.03	74.29	18.50	4.016	2,489.874
6/25	Income dividend	.06	149.39	20.76	7.196	2,497.070
9/24	Income dividend	.06	149.82	22.58	6.635	2,503.705
12/03	Check purchase		9,000.00	23.10	389.610	2,893.315
12/23	Income dividend	.142	410.85	21.89	18.769	2,912.084
12/23	ST cap gain	.08	231.47	21.89	10.574	2,922.658
12/23	LT cap gain	.15	434.00	21.89	19.826	2,942.484
	Balance on 12/31/1997			$ 22.64		2,942.484

Income dividends	$ 858.65	Total cost basis on 12/31/1997	$ 39,467.79
Short-term gains	256.23	Average cost per share	13.41
Long-term gains	508.29		
Total income year-to-date	$ 1,623.17		

The current Fund distribution was payable on
January 2, 1998.

Purchases year-to-date	$ 9,000.00

Remember, if you sell shares of a fund, the fund company also has to report the proceeds of the sale to the IRS. That means you will have to account for that transaction as well. You won't forget to do it, since the fund will remind you with Form 1099-B. (Like the 1099-DIV, you get one copy, the IRS gets the other.) There may be taxes due, or you may actually have a loss that can be applied as a deduction against them. Without good records, you could end up paying too little in taxes and get caught, or, worse yet, paying more tax than necessary.

Let's start with the tax status of the mutual fund itself. Remember, most mutual funds are also corporations, and shareholders of corporations, in effect, pay tax twice. The corporation pays taxes on its earnings and, if any of the earn-

ings are paid to shareholders as dividends, they're taxed again as part of shareholders' income. But mutual funds escape this double taxation. The fund is treated as a "conduit"—all the income and responsibility for paying the tax on that income pass through the fund to its shareholders.

To keep their special tax status, mutual funds have to live within rigorous rules. There are requirements about diversification. For instance, a fund can't hold more than 10 percent of the outstanding voting stock in a particular company.

Mutual funds must distribute 98 percent of their income and dividends—and do it in the calendar year in which they are earned. In addition, the funds must distribute 98 percent of their net realized capital gains—both short- and long-term capital gains. (Tax-exempt funds must distribute 90 percent of their tax-exempt income.) A fund that fails to meet this distribution test can be hit with a 4 percent excise tax on the undistributed income.

How much a fund distributes in income and capital gains has direct bearing on its aftertax return. (More on aftertax returns in Chapter 7.) Suppose two mutual funds have the same pretax total return. One made no income or capital gains distributions because it did not buy dividend-bearing stocks and tended to hold rather than trade the stocks in the portfolio. The second fund had the same total return, but about half of it came in the form of distributions. The one that made no distributions would have the higher aftertax return. Of course, if the fund is held in an IRA or other tax-deferred plan, the distributions don't matter. But if the account is taxable, a fund's history and policy of making distributions is a real concern in deciding whether to invest in a particular fund.

When looking at the distributions, remember that not all are taxed equally. Distributions of dividends, interest income, and short-term capital gains are taxed at the same rate at which the shareholder's earned income is taxed—and that can be as high as 39.6 percent. Long-term capital gains—and they're long-term if they were generated by investments held for more than 18 months—get the most favorable tax treatment: The maximum rate is 20 percent, no matter how high the shareholder's regular tax rate is. Investments held more than 12 months but less than 18 months are subject to a 28 percent maximum capital gains rate.

Many funds, especially those that practice a buy-and-hold investment strategy, often have huge unrealized and undistributed capital gains in their portfolios. Morningstar, Inc. measures these gains and expresses the magnitude as a percentage of the fund's total holdings. BUSINESS WEEK now includes this number in the Scoreboard under the heading "Untaxed Gains" (see Chapter 7).

Suppose a fund has an untaxed gain of 30 percent. That means 30 percent of the portfolio is unrealized capital gains. If the fund were liquidated tomorrow at $10 a share, the locked-in profits would be unlocked or "realized" in tax terms, and $3 would come back to shareholders as a capital gain. Some investors are wary of funds with high untaxed gains because they think they may be stuck paying tax on the capital gains earned long before they went into the fund.

Sometimes mutual funds have realized net losses, rather than realized gains. But tax rules do not allow mutual funds to distribute their losses to their shareholders. However, the funds can carry the losses forward for eight years and use them to offset future taxable gains. Some bond funds are in that position right now. As those markets recover, the funds are able to offset their gains with these losses.

That may not assuage those who watched their funds undergo partial meltdowns, but it does suggest an investment strategy. Provided a fund meets all your other criteria, investing in a fund with tax losses makes sense. Some other investors realized the loss, but as a new investor to the fund you can get the benefit of the gains they shelter.

Though fund directors can vote to make the distributions at any time, tax considerations result in distributions piling up toward the end of the year. Some funds have a policy of making quarterly income distributions and some may make capital gains distributions at least once during the year. But if a fund has any income or gains to distribute, you can count on most funds making payouts in December. Sometimes the distribution may even be declared on December 31 and not paid until January. That doesn't get shareholders out of paying taxes on it for the year that ended in December.

Mutual fund companies usually mail Form 1099-DIVs to shareholders by the end of January. This form reports dividend distributions, capital gains distributions—broken out to show those that are short-term and those that are long-term—and, if applicable, taxes paid to foreign governments. (That may come into play in international funds.) Nontaxable distributions should be noted here, too. Check the figures against your own records and make sure they're correct. The numbers you see on the form are the same numbers that the IRS is going to see.

> Mutual fund distributions bunch up at year-end.

Ducking the Distribution

It's a good idea to start checking with funds around Thanksgiving to ask about upcoming distributions. A customer service representative will usually know if a distribution is planned. Sometimes the fund management company will announce the exact date and the per-share distribution rate. Some will give shareholders who ask an estimate of the time and the amount to be paid. You may have to keep calling until you get the information. The funds themselves often don't know the date and size of the distribution until late into the year.

You may recall some brouhaha surrounding the Fidelity Magellan Fund in late 1994. What had happened was that Fidelity, as is common practice, told investors in November that Magellan would make a $4.32 per-share capital gains distribution in December. No doubt some Magellan investors may have made tax-related moves, such as selling Magellan or taking losses in other funds to shelter the Magellan gain. Three weeks later, Fidelity said oops, we made a mistake. There isn't going to be a distribution.

The incident was a stunner, not because anybody lost any real money, but because the large estimation error—in excess of $2 billion—was in the largest equity fund and was made by the largest mutual fund management company. But fortunately, such errors about distributions are rare and, needless to say, Fidelity and others are going to be double, triple, and quadruple checking those estimates in the future.

There are several good reasons to obtain the distribution information near the end of the year. First, if you are planning any new fund investments, you have to be careful about purchasing shares right before the distribution dates. You could end up getting a distribution of profits earned long before you ever invested in the fund (see Chapter 4).

You may also want to get out of a fund ahead of the distribution date, for much the same reason. For instance, just look back at 1997. Suppose you had invested in a small-cap growth fund in the spring. Pretend for a moment you paid $10 a share.

Then move ahead to early December when the fund has lost 20 percent of what you paid for it. But remember that early in the year the market rallied. What if the fund manager had used the rally to take some profits amounting to $1 per share? The fund would have to distribute those profits before the end of the year. If you still owned the fund, you would be hit with a taxable distribution of capital gains. You would be stuck paying taxes on gains, but your investment, so far, is actually showing a loss.

That's why you should consider selling the fund before the distribution. If you do so, you can realize a tax-deductible loss. Then you have one

of two alternatives. If you want to remain fully invested, you can switch to a fund with a similar investment policy—but after that fund has made its distributions for the year. Or, you can stay on the sidelines for 31 days and then return to your fund. The risk in that ploy is that the fund will go up in price a bit before you can get back in. The IRS says you have to wait 31 days before buying back a fund sold for a tax loss—otherwise the loss will be disallowed as a deduction.

Tax Swapping

As the year rolls to a close, some investors like to do "tax swapping." The term comes from the bond market, but can apply to any investment. The idea is to look for a fund in which you may have an unrealized loss and then sell the fund to take the loss and generate a tax deduction. At the same time, you move a like amount of money into a mutual fund with characteristics similar to the one just sold (Table 6-1). The idea is to take advantage of your losses—make the best of a bad situation—while keeping your investment program in place.

Swapping within the same fund family is easiest. In large fund families there is often more than one fund with similar objectives. You may want to switch the Fidelity Contrafund for the Fidelity Dividend Growth Fund. They're both midcap blend funds. Fidelity Equity–Income and Equity–Income II, as their names might suggest, are also interchangeable.

Load fund investors should find it most practical to remain within their fund groups. Investors are usually able to switch load funds without paying another load, as long as the load of the new fund is less than or equal to the old one. For instance, if an investor moves her money from a fund on which she paid a 4 percent load into another fund in the same family that has a 5.5 percent load, she will probably have to pay only a 1.5 percent load to make up the difference.

Some advisers discourage investors from swapping funds purely for tax purposes. If a swap triggers redemption fees or new sales charges, that has to be figured in to determine whether there would be any benefit from the trade. If, on the other hand, you can justify selling one fund and buying another as a good investment decision, then the ability to save some money on taxes takes a little of the bite out of the loss.

Avoid the distribution if you can.

TABLE 6-1

SAVING ON TAXES BY SWAPPING FUNDS

If you have a loss in a mutual fund, you may want to sell it for a tax loss. If so, you may want to shift the money into a similar fund so as not to change your investment goals. The funds within each grouping have similar investment policies and risk profiles. They can make suitable swaps.

FUNDS	COMMENTS
FIDELITY CONTRAFUND FIDELITY DIVIDEND GROWTH JANUS MERCURY JANUS OLYMPUS	Contrafund and Dividend Growth make good switch candidates under the Fidelity umbrella. Likewise, these Janus funds are similar enough to make good switch candidates as well.
FIDELITY EQUITY-INCOME FIDELITY EQUITY-INCOME II VANGUARD/WELLESLEY INCOME VANGUARD/WELLINGTON	Clone funds can make good swap candidates. These Fidelity equity–income funds are fairly similar. Likewise, the two Vanguard funds don't share the same name, but they're close in investment style and practice.
FIDELITY EMERGING MARKETS LEXINGTON WORLDWIDE EMERGING MARKETS T. ROWE PRICE INTERNATIONAL SCUDDER INTERNATIONAL	The two emerging markets funds, though offered by different companies, should be similar enough for tax-swapping. The T. Rowe Price and Scudder international funds have similar portfolio characteristics.
TEMPLETON GROWTH TEMPLETON VALUE TEMPLETON WORLD	Many Templeton equity funds are interchangeable. The Developing Markets, Foreign, Real Estate, and Small Companies funds are unique, and are not interchangeable with each other nor other Templeton funds.
BABSON ENTERPRISE II FIDELITY LOW-PRICED STOCK HEARTLAND SMALL-CAP CONTRARIAN ROYCE VALUE	These funds are all from the small-cap value category. Their companies are usually prosaic rather than cutting edge, but that doesn't mean they can't make money for mutual fund shareholders.
AIM CONSTELLATION AIM GROWTH AMER. CENT.–20TH CENT. VISTA INVESTORS PBHG GROWTH	These funds comb the market for companies with earnings momentum, and they try to hang on to them as long as earnings growth is accelerating. The AIM funds are load, American Century and PBHG, no-load.
BABSON BOND FIDELITY INTERMEDIATE BOND VANGUARD BOND INDEX TOTAL MARKET	Swapping bond funds is easier than equity, since these funds usually have easily identifiable investment characteristics such as maturity, credit quality, and tax status.
INVESCO HIGH-YIELD T. ROWE PRICE HIGH-YIELD VANGUARD FIXED-INCOME HIGH-YIELD	All high-yield, or junk bond funds, are not alike. These all have the reputation for investing in "better quality" junk bonds.

DATA: MORNINGSTAR INC., BUSINESS WEEK

What's My "Cost Basis"?

Mention the term "cost basis," and eyes glaze over. But it's not a big deal. It's just a measure of how much money you put into an investment. If you bought 100 shares of General Motors at $50 per share and paid the broker a $50 commission, your cost basis is $50.50 per share, or $5050.

In just the same way, loads and redemption fees work their way into the cost basis for funds.

If you paid a 5 percent load when you bought the fund, that was already figured into your purchase price. So you don't need to adjust for that. Suppose you sell shares and there's a 1 percent redemption fee. If your shares were sold for $5000, a 1 percent exit charge would take $50 out of your proceeds. So your net is $4950, not $5000.

What's complicated about mutual fund record-keeping is that most people don't buy nice round lots, like 100 shares. Many invest a nice round amount, like $1000 or $10,000. Odds are that most shareholders end up with some odd number of shares, with fractional shares rounded off to three decimal places.

Those who reinvest dividends and capital gains must count them when computing their cost basis. Reinvesting a taxable distribution is the same as putting new money into the fund. Forget to include those distributions in the cost basis, and you can wind up paying too much tax. For the most part, investors or their tax advisers are usually on their own when calculating their cost basis. Many companies are providing average cost data—and that's a big help. But hold on to your records, you may need to do it yourself.

What if you don't have good records? Most fund companies will help to reconstruct transaction history records by providing copies of past statements. Depending on the fund, and how many years' worth of data you need, you may be charged a nominal fee for the service.

Suppose you sell all the shares in a mutual fund account. It's easy to compute your cost basis. Add up all the money you invested directly and through dividend reinvestment. That's the total cost. Then, divide that sum by the number of shares you have. That's the average cost per share. To figure your gain or loss, subtract the cost from proceeds of the sale. If you have shares in the account that are both long-term (held for more than 18 months) and short-term (less than 12 months) and medium-term (more than 12 months but less than 18), be sure to note that, even if you use the same cost basis for holdings of various duration. This information is reported on Schedule D of the 1040, the individual's tax return. (This method of computation is also known as the "average-cost" or "single-category" method, and we'll come back to it later.)

You can take this average cost approach a step further, to the "double-category" method. Under this tax treatment, you calculate separate cost bases for the long-term shares and for the short-term shares. This method demands extra work, but may be worthwhile for investors who are in tax brackets of 31 percent or higher. (For single taxpayers, that's taxable income of $61,400 or more; for married persons filing jointly, $102,300 or more.) That's because while the tax rate on short-term gains is the same as on your salary and investment earnings like dividends and interest, the rate on medium-term capital gains is capped at 28 percent and long-term, 20 percent. If you have gains, most likely the biggest gains are in the shares held long-term, so you should allocate most of the gains to these shares. If you use the average-cost method, you'll end up putting more of the gain on the short-term shares, and that will result in a bigger tax bite.

The tax situation gets stickier if some but not all the shares are sold. Look at Table 6-2. Suppose that on November 12, 1997, the fund's NAV is $10.50, your average cost is $10.87 per share, and you're considering selling some shares. You think you have a taxable loss of $0.37 per share. But that's only if you liquidate the entire account.

If you make a partial redemption and don't specify any specific method you wish to use to calculate your gains and losses, the IRS will assume the first shares in are the first shares out. Suppose you ask the fund for a $3000 redemption. That would result in the sale of 285.714 shares ($3000 divided by $10.50). The IRS would assume those shares were from the first 300 shares bought on February 15, 1996, at $10 per share. Even though you have a loss on the entire investment, selling those shares even at November 12's depressed price would result in a small taxable gain.

But there are alternatives. You could sell shares in a way that would generate a tax-deductible loss. Go back to your average cost per share, $10.87. You can use the single- or double-category methods to calculate the tax liability on partial redemptions. (Remember that you have to note which method you're using on your tax return.) Sell $3000 worth of shares by the single-category method and, instead of a gain, you get a tax loss of $105.71.

Finally, there's the "specific shares" method, which is perhaps the best approach. But it takes some planning. You must designate in writing which shares are to be sold, and do so in advance of the transaction. The advantage of this method is you can pinpoint the highest-cost shares, those purchased on June 2 and September 28, 1996, and July 6, 1997. The share prices paid on all three dates are higher than today's NAV. By selling these shares, you can redeem $2675.84, with a tax deductible loss of $324.17.

Don't forget that with the specific shares method—as with all the options—once you choose to redeem shares in a fund under this method, all future redemptions must use the same method. You can't use specific shares this year and the single-category method next year. Investors using the single-category or double-category methods to compute taxes should attach a note to their tax returns saying so. Those using first-in, first-out or the specific shares methods need not do so, but should maintain their records in case of an audit.

Keep in mind that there are rule changes from time to time, so it's best to consult with your

TABLE 6-2

CALCULATING TAXABLE GAINS AND LOSSES

On Nov. 12, 1997, the net asset value, or per-share price, of a fund is $10.50. The total value of your holdings is $7305.51. You are thinking about selling all or part of your shares in the fund. There are several ways to compute tax liabilities. Your goal should be to minimize the tax bite.

Investment Date	Amount Invested	Price/ Share	Shares Purchased	Total Shares
Feb. 15, 1996	$3000.00	$10.00	300.000	300.000
June 2	1000.00	11.75	85.106	385.106
Sept. 28	1000.00	12.25	81.630	466.740
Dec. 15 Distributions of $0.20 per share income, $1 per share capital gains				
Reinvest income	93.35	11.20	8.385	475.075
Reinvest capital gains	466.74	11.20	41.673	516.748
May 10, 1997	1000.00	11.00	90.909	607.657
July 6	1000.00	11.35	88.106	695.763
Total investment	$7,560.09	**Average price/share** $10.87		

If you are selling all the shares, you can choose from these methods:

SINGLE-CATEGORY Take the average cost of your shares, $10.87, and deduct the $10.50 your shares are worth now. That's a loss of $0.37 per share. With this fund, you have 300 shares held more than 18 months for a $111 long-term capital loss; 166.736 shares held between 12 and 18 months for a $61.69 medium-term loss; and 229.023 held less than 12 months for an $84.74 short-term loss.

DOUBLE-CATEGORY In the prior method, you calculate the average cost and apply it to all shares in all three holding periods. In the double-category method, you calculate three average costs—for the long-term, medium-term, and short-term shares—and then deduct that cost from the current net asset value. There are 300 long-term shares with an average cost of $10 per share. Since the shares are now at $10.50, the long-term shares have a $0.50 a share long-term capital gain. You also have 166.736 medium-term shares with an average cost of $12.00, for a $250.10 loss. You have owned 229.023 shares with an average cost of $11.18, for a $155.74 short-term loss.

If you are selling some but not all of your shares, you can choose from these three methods:

AVERAGE COST Using the single-category method to redeem $3000, you end up selling 285.714 shares at a loss of $0.37 per share (the average loss per share), for $105.70 long-term capital loss on the lot. It's considered a long-term loss because unless specifically noted (see below), the IRS assumes that the oldest shares are sold first.

SPECIFIC SHARES Direct the fund company to sell the highest-cost shares, those bought on June 2 and Sept. 28 of 1996 and July 6, 1997. The June 2 shares are now worth $803.61, for a $109.39 loss; the Sept. 28 shares are worth $857.12, for $142.89 loss. Both are medium-term losses. The July 6 shares are worth $925.11, for a short-term loss of $74.89. Specified redemption yield is $2675.84, with $324.17 in tax-deductible losses.

FIRST-IN, FIRST-OUT If you don't tell your mutual fund company which shares to sell, the IRS assumes the oldest shares are sold first. In the above example, the first 300 shares have a cost basis of $10 each. If you sell these shares at $10.50, you have a taxable gain of $150 even though the total investment is in the red. Under the circumstances, this is the least desirable method to use.

DATA: BUSINESS WEEK

accountant or tax adviser. It's also a good idea to call the Internal Revenue Service to get a free copy of Publication No. 564, "Mutual Fund Distributions," for the official treatment of the subject.

Tax-Deferred Investing

IRAs

Mutual fund companies make great places to open up individual retirement accounts (IRAs) and other retirement programs. The companies offer professional management, diversification, and a bent for long-term investing. Mutual fund executives love to rake in retirement dollars, since the money tends to stay in place and generate fees for years. Most fund management companies will shower you with plenty of literature on IRAs and the like, and they also have specialists on hand to explain some of the finer, more technical aspects of the programs. Fidelity Investments will even waive sales charges on many of its equity funds for IRA accounts.

Mutual fund companies manage a little more than 47 percent of all IRA assets, according to

Pay IRA fees out of your checkbook.

the Investment Company Institute. That's up from only 33 percent just a few years ago, and it dwarfs the IRA assets held by other financial intermediaries, like banks, savings and loans, and insurance companies. What the IRA holder gets from a mutual fund that he or she doesn't get from a depository institution is an enormous variety of investment options. (Remember, though, that mutual funds are not insured.) The only mutual funds that don't make good IRA investments are tax-exempt funds. If the interest is already free from taxation, what's the point of sheltering it?

IRAs now come in several varieties: the traditional tax-deductible IRA, the nondeductible IRA, and the Roth IRA. In the original IRA, the contribution is tax deductible in the year it's made, all the earnings of the investment are tax-deferred, and the entire proceeds of the IRA become fully taxable when it's withdrawn. In the nondeductible IRA, investors are able to make aftertax contributions to an IRA, enjoy the tax-sheltered buildup of the investment returns, and pay taxes on only the earnings when they start withdrawing from the account at retirement. With the Roth IRA, the contribution is not tax deductible, but all the earnings build up tax free and are not taxed at withdrawal.

One significant difference between the Roth plan and the others is that there is no requirement to start withdrawing the funds at any age, and taxpayers can continue to contribute to them as long as they wish. With traditional tax-deductible and nondeductible IRAs, taxpayers must start withdrawals by age 70½ and are barred from making further contributions beyond that age.

The traditional IRA makes more sense if you expect that your tax bracket in retirement will be lower than your tax bracket is now. The Roth IRA might appeal to investors who already have good pension plans and substantial assets and expect to remain in a high tax bracket when they retire. Of course, Congress seems to revise tax law every few years, so who really knows what your tax bracket will be 20 years hence?

In enacting the Roth IRA, Congress also allowed taxpayers with adjusted gross incomes (AGI) under $100,000 to convert all or part of their traditional IRA assets to the Roth IRA. There is a catch, though. Investors will have to pay tax at the time of conversion because no tax has been paid on those assets yet and none will be in the future. However, the tax on the conversion is spread over four years. For instance, if you were converting a $100,000 traditional IRA to a

Roth IRA, you would have to add $25,000 a year to your taxable income for the next four years. Should you switch your IRA to the Roth plan? That's a complex question. Many mutual fund companies can provide you with information and even software to walk you through the decision. If you have a tax adviser, you might discuss the question with him or her.

The traditional IRA is always fully deductible for those who are not covered by employer pension plans. But in 1998, it will also be fully deductible for singles with less than $30,000 in AGI and couples with less than $50,000, even if they are covered by an employer's plan. It will be partially deductible up to $40,000 in AGI for individuals and $60,000 for couples. In addition, recent revisions to the tax law raises those limits gradually each year through 2005 for individuals and 2007 for married couples.

The Roth IRA generally allows most taxpayers to participate even if they are in employer-sponsored plans. Starting in 1998, single individuals with AGIs of up to $95,000 and married couples with AGIs to $150,000 can make full contributions of $2000 and $4000, respectively. A partial contribution can be made by singles with AGIs of $95,000 to $110,000 and by married couples with AGIs of $150,000 to $160,000. Those with incomes above these limits can contribute to nondeductible IRAs. In any case, the maximum annual contribution to any sort of IRA is $2000 for individuals and $4000 for married couples.

Education IRA. An IRA for a child? Yup. And junior doesn't have to wait until he's a senior citizen to use the money. Tax law now allows families to establish nondeductible IRAs for their children that can be used to pay for college expenses. Let's face it. Even if you start at birth and invest in the best-performing funds, it's never going to put the little tyke through Harvard. The maximum contribution is $500 per year per child.

But remember there are other ways to save for your child's education. If you establish a custodial account in your child's name, the first $650 in earnings is tax-free. (That's the limit for the 1997 tax year, and it is adjusted annually for inflation.) The income between $651 and $1300 is taxed at the child's rate, and income above $1300 is taxed at the parent's rate. All of this applies to children under 14. Those over 14 pay tax at their own rates.

Transfers. Perhaps you have an IRA at a local bank earning a measly rate of interest. You can move the account to a mutual fund or group of funds. Ask the mutual fund company to send you the applications and the transfer documents and give them to the institution from which you wish to withdraw your IRA. (If you withdraw a certificate of deposit before maturity, you may owe a penalty to the bank.)

The bank will send you the funds, or you can instruct the institution to transfer the funds directly to the new mutual fund company. Make sure the money is reinvested in another IRA within 60 days, or the government will assume you made a premature withdrawal and hit you for tax and a penalty. Moving an IRA from one institution to another is called a "rollover."

Persons who will be receiving their pension benefit in a lump sum distribution because they're either retiring or changing jobs are especially in need of some advance planning. Unless the money is transferred directly from the employer into an IRA or other qualified pension plan, the distribution will be subject to a 20 percent withholding tax. Those hit with the special tax then have 60 days to put the money into an IRA rollover or face additional taxes, including a 10 percent penalty for persons less than 59½ years old. If you need help with a rollover, most any mutual fund company will walk you through it.

Whatever sort of tax-deferred retirement account you have with a mutual fund company, you may have to pay an annual IRA "custodial" or "maintenance" fee. The fee, which takes care of the additional paperwork of an IRA, is typically $10 a year per fund (or much higher at a full-service brokerage firm), but competition for the retirement accounts is so keen that many companies are starting to waive the custodial fee for all accounts over a certain size, say $5000 or $10,000.

Many mutual fund companies send a bill for the annual fee. If the bill's not paid by the due date, the management company will deduct it from the account. If you don't get a bill, ask the fund company when the fee is due. Make plans to pay the fee out of your checkbook and not out of the retirement account. Since contributions to IRAs are limited, you don't want to take anything out of the account if you can avoid it.

KEOGH PLANS

The IRA isn't the only kind of retirement program offered by mutual fund companies. Funds also hold about one-third of the money invested in retirement plans by the self-employed. Commonly known as Keogh plans, these plans are far more generous, allowing the self-employed to stash away as much as 20 percent of their income,

up to $30,000, and deduct it from the current year's taxes. These are far more complicated than the simple IRA, and get even trickier when the self-employed person has employees, too. Consult an accountant or tax adviser before starting one of these programs.

There are several varieties of Keogh. The program that allows the largest contribution (and highest deduction) is least flexible, and the contribution must be made every year. Other programs are less demanding, but the maximum contribution is less, too. There's also the Simplified Employee Pension—Individual Retirement Account, otherwise known as SEP or SEP-IRA. The employer can contribute up to $30,000 or 15 percent of the employee's compensation, whichever is less.

401(K) PLANS

Most mutual fund companies offer their funds in 401(k) plans. Unfortunately, as an employee, you cannot start a 401(k) program for yourself; your employer has to do it. You can ask the company to offer a plan with the investment options coming from a mutual fund family. One of the features that makes 401(k)s different from conventional corporate pension plans is that the employee gets to choose how the money is invested. That's why mutual funds make excellent homes for 401(k) plans. Look at the array of choices (though not every fund in every group of funds may be eligible for the program). Mutual funds can also service 403(b) plans, which are similar to the 401(k), except they are exclusively for the employees of certain charitable organizations or public school systems.

In such plans, an employee can choose to place up to a certain percentage of his or her pretax income in the 401(k). How much depends on how a company's plan is structured. The maximum is commonly around 10 percent, but some go as high as 15 percent. Then, too, the law puts a cap on the amount of money you can contribute on a pretax basis, which in 1998 will be $10,000. The amount is subject to inflation adjustments. In addition, employers often "match" employee contributions in part or in full. The earnings of the 401(k) account are also tax-deferred until the money is withdrawn at retirement.

VARIABLE ANNUITIES

Imagine owning a mutual fund that pays interest, dividends, and capital gains and not having to pay any tax year to year. You can't take the money out until you're at least 59½ or you pay a tax penalty—and perhaps a penalty to the fund com-

> Mutual funds work well in 401(k) plans.

pany, too. Isn't this a mutual fund IRA? No, but you're close.

It's a variable annuity, and it's growing in popularity. Sales have grown from about $30 billion in 1993 to $85 billion in 1997, according to Cerulli Associates, Inc. During the same period, assets have more than doubled to $572.2 billion from $246.4 billion.

Most major mutual fund companies offer variable annuities or manage variable annuity investments for insurance companies. The prime customers for variable annuities are mutual fund investors within 20 years of retirement who have assets they can sock away until then and who can benefit from the tax deferral on investment income. Many babyboomers already fit that category, and more will in coming years.

The variable annuity probably sounds a lot like an IRA or a 401(k) plan, but with several critical differences. For starters, the contributions are not tax deductible. But, unlike any IRA or 401(k), there is no limit to what an investor can put into the annuity.

It's important to know that the costs of investing in a variable annuity can be significantly higher than investing in comparable mutual funds. Depending on the annuity plan, the investor who cashes out before retirement may still pay a load, or a redemption or surrender charge. The redemption charge for some annuity products can be as high as 10 percent—and that's before any tax consequences. Don't invest in these annuities unless you're 99 percent sure you're not going to need the money for at least a decade. In addition, the portfolio management expenses may be higher for annuity funds than they are for comparable mutual funds, since the annuity funds are usually smaller in size and don't enjoy the same economies of scale.

There's an annuity charge or "wrapper," which pays for a guarantee provided by an insurance company. The guarantee, which on average costs 1.27 percent per year, merely assures the investor's heirs that in case he or she dies while the annuity is in force, the annuity will be worth at least as much as what was put in. (That's why variable annuities have to be offered by a life insurance company.)

This feature would have come in handy for the heirs of someone who had invested in a variable annuity with equity funds in January 1994, and died in April, when the investment might have been worth 20 percent less. As a practical matter, this insurance is only worthwhile in the first few years of the investment.

After all, if the annuity is worth less than the investment after 10 or 20 years, you chose the wrong annuity. Annuity buyers can't elect to waive this guarantee. It's the distinguishing feature that makes it an annuity—a life insurance product that allows the earnings to build up on a tax-deferred basis. Some annuities now have a "step-up" provision that keeps raising the guaranteed death benefit. But that isn't free. Such annuities have higher fees.

The variable annuities may look—and behave—much like mutual funds, but the terminology is different. A mutual fund that's connected to a variable annuity is a "subaccount." There are no fund shares in a variable annuity; instead, the worth of the investment is tracked in "accumulation unit value," which, for practical purposes, is the same thing. The average variable annuity has seven subaccount options.

Because of the higher fees and surrender charges, the variable annuity only makes sense as a truly long-term investment. It is often sold as a tax shelter (remember the earnings of the investment are not taxed until withdrawal), but it's really best used as a long-term savings vehicle.

Morningstar classifies the variable annuity subaccounts as it does equity and bond mutual funds. But there are a few exceptions. All the domestic equity categories are the same, except for specialty subaccounts. There are only enough subaccounts to justify natural resources, real estate, and utilities categories. All other specialized funds are lumped into an "unaligned" grouping. For international equity, Morningstar uses the broader foreign, world, diversified emerging markets categories and international hybrid categories and forgoes the regional funds. Among the bond subaccounts, there's long-, intermediate-, and short-term general bond and government bond categories, plus high-yield, international, and money-market. For yield-oriented investors, most variable annuities also have a "fixed" account option, which works much like a bank CD.

Selecting a variable annuity takes all the same savvy as choosing a mutual fund—and then some. You are not only buying an investment vehicle, but an insurance wrapper as well. And you can often get many of the same investment funds inside different wrappers. For instance, Fidelity Retirement Reserves is a series of variable annuity portfolios that are managed much like their Fidelity mutual fund counterparts. You can call a Fidelity 800 number or drop in at a Fidelity

Variable annuities behave much like funds.

investor center and obtain the prospectus and the application for the Fidelity variable annuity with the insurance wrapper coming from Fidelity's own insurance company. Fidelity recently began offering access to several other fund company subaccounts under the umbrella of the Fidelity annuity.

It's a radical departure for Fidelity to offer its customers other managers' wares, but it's fairly common practice in the variable annuity world. Nearly all the Fidelity-managed subaccounts in Fidelity Retirement Reserves are also available in other insurors' products. The popular Fidelity VIP Fund Equity-Income subaccount is available in 121 different variable annuity products offered by Aetna Life & Casualty, Life of Virginia Commonwealth, Nationwide Life Insurance, and dozens of other companies. What's different? For one, the service. If you buy the annuity direct from Fidelity, you're pretty much on your own. On the other hand, if you buy the fund through an annuity sold by a life insurance agent, you get the agent to help you choose the fund and monitor performance.

What else is different? The cost. Most annuities are sold without a front-end load. But the redemption fees and insurance costs can vary greatly. (Portfolio expense, the cost of running the investment itself, is the same no matter which insurance company offers the fund.) If you invest in the Fidelity Equity-Income annuity subaccount through Fidelity's Retirement Reserves variable annuity, the insurance expense is 1 percent a year, contract fee $30 a year, and there's a 5 percent declining surrender charge in the first year, declining 1 percent a year for five years. Purchased through Nationwide's Best of America annuity, the contract fee is $30. But the other charges are much higher: 1.30 percent a year for insurance expense and a surrender charge that starts at 7 percent and declines 1 percent a year for seven years.

If you're seriously considering an annuity and don't need a salesperson to help you, look into the low-cost annuity products from Vanguard, Scudder, T. Rowe Price, and Charles Schwab. There are no loads or surrender charges on the policies. Insurance expenses are low, too—0.85 percent in the Schwab plan, 0.70 percent in Scudder, 0.55 percent in T. Rowe Price, and 0.48 percent at Vanguard. Vanguard and Schwab charge a $25 a year contract fee, while Scudder and T. Rowe Price don't charge at all. Minimum investments are $2500 at Scudder, $5000 at Schwab and Vanguard, and $10,000 for T. Rowe Price.

Before investing in any variable annuity, compare the annuity's investment options to a similar, taxable mutual fund. You may find the higher charges and loss of financial flexibility may weigh heavier in your decisions than the opportunity to defer taxes on the fund's earnings. If you would choose a small-cap or mid-cap growth fund for the annuity, the deferral may not be worth it. Those sorts of funds don't earn enough dividend income to distribute, and capital gains distributions are not that frequent. Want a government bond fund for your variable annuity? In that case, don't even bother. Buy municipal bond funds. The income is tax-exempt, there are no annuity charges to pay, and you can get your money out when you want it, without paying a tax penalty.

Variable annuities make most sense for investment options that would generate a lot of income in a taxable account—like high-yield bond and equity-income funds. They're also practical if you are an investor who likes to make frequent shifts between investments—moves that become taxable events when done outside the tax shelter of an annuity or qualified retirement program.

In pitching a costly annuity, some salespersons will play up the annuitizing feature. They'll say that when it's time to swap the nest egg for an annuity—guaranteed stream of payments—their company is the most generous. That may be so, but you don't have to buy their variable annuity. When you're investing for retirement, buy the variable annuity that makes the most investment sense. When it comes time to annuitize, you can always switch the money to another company. And most annuities are never annuitized—people take a lump sum, make periodic withdrawals, or leave the money to their estate.

Because of the higher costs, variable annuities are for most people not the retirement vehicle of first choice. First, if you qualify to make investments in either a conventional or Roth IRA, do that first. And if your company has a 401(k) or other defined contribution plan, be sure you are taking full advantage of that as well, making the full tax-deductible contribution and perhaps maxing out your aftertax contribution option if you have one. If you are self-employed, a Keogh or SEP-IRA should take preference over a variable annuity. Only after you've taken full advantage of more cost-effective retirement investment programs should you embark on the variable annuity.

Watch out for high fees on variable annuities.

Using the BW Scoreboard

The BUSINESS WEEK Mutual Fund Scoreboard works like a road map of the mutual fund world. It provides tons of information about returns, fees, sales charges, and risk that should help you avoid hazards and dead ends on your financial journey. But even with the best of road maps, you still need to have some map-reading skills. That's the point of this chapter.

The equity Scoreboard that appears in the back of the book covers 885 equity funds. That's not every one, not by a long shot. But we have all the major funds with assets greater than $160 million. At BUSINESS WEEK Online (www.businessweek.com), we're not confined by paper. We have nearly 2300 equity mutual funds. Even that's not the whole universe, but certainly with that many funds, there are enough choices.

To keep the numbers a little more manageable, we don't include funds that are only open to institutional investors. (One way to spot them is their $1 million minimum investments.) Nor do we include more than one class of shares of funds with multiple share classes. The variation between share classes of the same fund is a function of fees, not portfolio performance. The underlying investments are the same. We also exclude funds with less than 12 months of performance data.

The bond fund Scoreboard in this book has 653 funds, selected by the same process as with equity funds, with some modifications. And we have 1700 bond funds in the expanse of the online world. The closed-end fund Scoreboard has 120 equity funds and 350 bond funds.

At the start of each Scoreboard, there's a summary description of the sort of data that are under each column heading. In this chapter we'll take a more in-depth look at some of the headings. For a thorough discussion of the investment categories, please refer to Chapter 2.

Ratings

The first column after the fund's name is the overall rating. The best grade is an A, signifying superior performance. B+ is very good, and B, above average. Then comes C, or average, and then the subpar categories: C– for below-average performance, D for poor performance, and F for very poor performance (Figure 7-1).

There are many funds with returns that look very good, yet their ratings are average at best. At the same time, there are highly rated funds with seemingly so-so returns. The reason for this is simple. BUSINESS WEEK ratings don't merely reward funds for winning the year's best-performance contest. You don't need a ratings system for that because the returns tell all. What the BW ratings system asks is not only how much money a fund made for its shareholders, but also how much risk the fund took in the process.

In rating fund performance we define risk as the potential for losing money. In the strict sense, risk goes both ways. A fund can be said to have high risk if it is volatile—net asset values swing wildly to the upside as well as the down. But as a practical matter, an investor would not complain if a fund appreciated twice as fast as the S&P 500. He or she may accept—but won't like—the fact that the fund has fallen twice as much as the S&P 500. So the ratings, which are calculated by Morningstar, Inc., don't penalize a fund for upside volatility.

To come up with fund ratings, we measure a fund's last five years of returns. (For closed-end funds, we measure the last three years.) For the overall BW rating, the returns are calculated assuming that you paid the maximum sales charge, or load, if applicable. Obviously this gives the no-load funds a head start on the load funds, since an investor who pays a 5 percent up-front

FIGURE 7-1

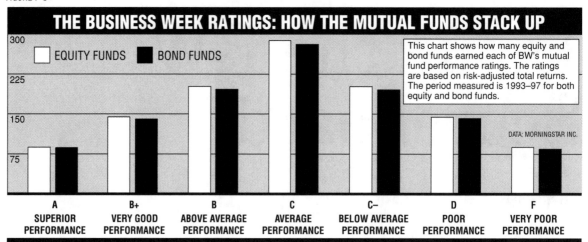

THE BUSINESS WEEK RATINGS: HOW THE MUTUAL FUNDS STACK UP

☐ EQUITY FUNDS ■ BOND FUNDS

This chart shows how many equity and bond funds earned each of BW's mutual fund performance ratings. The ratings are based on risk-adjusted total returns. The period measured is 1993–97 for both equity and bond funds.

DATA: MORNINGSTAR INC.

| A | B+ | B | C | C– | D | F |
| SUPERIOR PERFORMANCE | VERY GOOD PERFORMANCE | ABOVE AVERAGE PERFORMANCE | AVERAGE PERFORMANCE | BELOW AVERAGE PERFORMANCE | POOR PERFORMANCE | VERY POOR PERFORMANCE |

sales charge has to earn 5.26 percent just to break even. (That's right, 5.26 percent. A 6 percent load would reduce a $1000 investment to $950. To get back to $1000, the investor would have to earn 5.26 percent.)

If a fund has been in operation for more than a year but less than five, we still report on it. We insist on a minimum track record before we rate a fund so we can track the fund's behavior under varying economic conditions. For instance, the 1998 equity fund ratings cover the period 1993 through 1997. We see fund performance under a variety of conditions: a drawn-out economic recovery, a robust expansion, and slower but steady growth; a bout of falling interest rates and rising ones; and disinflation and fears of an acceleration of inflation.

To derive the BW rating, we start with the fund's five-year total return. (These numbers are under the column heading "Average Annual Total Returns (%)." We then adjust the pure performance number by subtracting the "risk-of-loss" factor. (See the section, "Risk," later in this chapter.)

The funds are then rated based on a statistical distribution. The top 7.5 percent of the funds get A's. The next 12.5 percent of the funds get B+'s, and the following 17.5 percent, B's. Then there's the group in the middle—the C-rated funds. This is the largest group, with 25 percent of all rated funds. The ratings are symmetrical on the negative side: There are as many funds with F's as with A's. There is an exception. To get a B or better rating, an equity fund must also beat the S&P 500 on a risk-adjusted basis.

The risk adjustment can change a fund's place in the line-up considerably. Adjusting high-

return funds for their high risks might bring them down to the middle of the pack. Likewise, more modest performers with very low risk profiles often end up a lot higher in the relative standings after the adjustment is made.

The bond fund Scoreboard rates municipal bond funds against other muni funds rather than comparing them to all the other bond funds, which are taxable. If not for the separation, muni funds would always be at a disadvantage since, as tax-exempts, their yields are lower than those of comparable taxable bonds.

For most of the Scoreboard's history, the highest rated equity funds have tended to have low or very low levels of risk. But in the late 1980s, the Japan Fund and Merrill Lynch Pacific Fund, for instance, captured top honors for several years even with their high risk levels. The same thing happened with some technology and health funds in the 1990s. Their performances were so strong that even the fairly stiff risk-of-loss factor wasn't enough to knock them out of the top ratings group.

Should you invest in only the top-rated funds? It's a good place to start your search. But don't end it there. Suppose your investment plan shows you have a long time horizon and a good tolerance for risk. Then you would want to have some small-cap growth, mid-cap growth, and foreign funds as well. But right now, there are no small-cap growth or foreign funds with A ratings for overall performance. (There's one mid-cap growth fund.) That will not always be the case, but it is now, owing to the market conditions of the last several years.

That's why we have developed category ratings as well. We approach category ratings the same way as overall BW ratings. The only difference is that the funds are rated against one another within a single category instead of against all other Scoreboard funds. This second layer of ratings makes it easier to identify funds with good risk-adjusted returns compared to their peers, even if they are not particularly good compared to all funds.

The most extreme case of this is, of course, the precious metals funds. Every one of the 25 funds that is rated (including those online) gets an F. But comparing these funds only to one another, we find that one, Lexington Strategic Silver, earned an A, and two, Oppenheimer Gold & Special Minerals A and Franklin Gold I, got B+'s.

Not everyone wants to invest in a precious metals fund. But these category ratings also have more mainstream applications. For instance, in the 1993–1997 period, only one fund from one of the three growth categories (large-, mid-, and small-cap) earned an A for an overall rating. But investors still want to own these sorts of funds, and the category rating helps to identify the best of them. There are five large-cap growth, five mid-cap growth, and three small-cap growth funds with A category ratings. And with the category ratings, we have also identified five foreign and three world funds with superior returns. We've done category ratings with bond funds as well.

There is a caveat with category ratings. There aren't ratings for every category. To calculate category ratings, a category needs to have at least seven funds (we have seven levels in the ratings system) with five years of performance data (the number of years we require for ratings). In the 1998 Scoreboard, we had 42 diversified emerging markets funds, but only five with five years of performance history. As a result, we could not perform a category rating on these funds. But we should be able to do so in 1999, when we rate returns for the 1994–1998 period.

What if the overall BW rating of one of your funds declines? That's not a sign to dump the fund. Sometimes funds will decline in rating not so much from their own performance, but from the relatively stronger returns of others. What you should check is whether the fund is underperforming the other funds in its category. Then, you have to do a little investigation as to why the fund underperformed, and you may determine you want to sell.

The one problem with this ratings system is endemic in all performance measurements. They are based on past performance, which is not necessarily the best predictor of the future. But we do know that there is a tendency for winners to repeat and for funds' risk characteristics to stay fairly constant. Depending on the funds, the investment style can be constant as well. In that sense, a thorough assessment of past performance can be useful in investing for the future. The past may not be perfect, but it's the only data we have. What counts is how you use it.

Size

For many years the conventional wisdom held that great mutual funds grew into mediocre ones. Here's why. Suppose a fund manager builds an enviable track record with a small fund. The fund gets bigger through appreciation of the assets. But, more important, investors begin to notice it or the fund manager buys big ads to herald his or her success. Money pours in and the fund manager who was a whiz with a $50 million portfolio now has to find enough attractive stocks to fill a $500 million portfolio.

TABLE 7-1

THE LARGEST EQUITY FUNDS

Fund	Assets (Millions)*
FIDELITY MAGELLAN	$63,035.4
VANGUARD INDEX 500	48,264.6
INVESTMENT COMPANY OF AMERICA	39,717.7
WASHINGTON MUTUAL INVESTORS	38,246.0
FIDELITY GROWTH & INCOME	35,785.6
FIDELITY CONTRAFUND	30,263.0
VANGUARD/WINDSOR II	23,545.0
FIDELITY PURITAN	22,821.8
AMERICAN CENTURY—20TH CENT. ULTRA INV.	22,204.5
VANGUARD/WELLINGTON	21,340.3
FIDELITY EQUITY-INCOME	21,177.7
VANGUARD/WINDSOR	20,836.6
FIDELITY ADVISOR GROWTH OPPORTUNITIES T	20,408.6
INCOME FUND OF AMERICA	20,220.8
JANUS	19,280.2
EUROPACIFIC GROWTH	18,853.5
PUTNAM FUND FOR GROWTH & INCOME A	17,297.8
FIDELITY EQUITY-INCOME II	16,977.5
NEW PERSPECTIVE	16,202.7
DEAN WITTER DIVIDEND GROWTH B	15,422.9

*As of Dec. 31, 1997   DATA: MORNINGSTAR INC.

Rapid growth of assets can sometimes undermine the very success that generated the growth. Perhaps a portfolio manager can keep performing nearly as well at $100 million, but can he or she sustain the pace at $700 million or $1 billion? That depends on the manager and the nature of the stocks invested in. If his or her success has been built on finding little gems and buying them before they're "discovered" by Wall Street, it's going to be difficult. The manager might find enough of them to make an impact on a $100 million or even a $500 million portfolio. But the available supply of great little stocks is not going to expand. If anything, the supply could diminish, as others, seeing the success, rush to buy the same sorts of stocks.

The portfolio manager will usually have to start making investments in companies larger than those on which he or she built this reputation. That isn't necessarily bad, but it does change the nature of the portfolio. Or, to get enough small stocks into the portfolio, it might be necessary to lower the standards for the kinds of stocks bought. That isn't good.

If the fund primarily invests in blue-chip and large-capitalization stocks, a fund's size is less of a problem. A $1 billion blue-chip fund may not be any less nimble than a $100 million one. And for bond funds, in which the fund's expenses often make the difference between superior or mediocre results, size can be a help rather than a hindrance.

Of course, the legendary Peter Lynch challenged that wisdom with Fidelity Magellan Fund. Mutual fund analysts and the financial press had predicted the fund's stellar performance would poop out when the fund reached $1 billion in assets. Before Lynch retired in 1990, the fund was nearly $14 billion. In 1993, for instance, Fidelity Magellan had more than doubled the return of the S&P 500—and it started the year with $22.3 billion. By year-end, the fund was at $31.7 billion. True, Magellan's best days came before it was a billion-dollar fund. But since then its record has been far better than funds a fraction of its size. By the end of 1997, Magellan was $63 billion.

While Fidelity Magellan is still the largest fund by far, there are some other fast-growing megafunds. The assets of Vanguard Index 500, the second-largest fund at $48.3 billion (Table 7-1) grew by 29 percent in 1997. Bond funds are, on average, smaller than equity funds. Even the largest, Franklin California Tax-Free Income I,

TABLE 7-2

THE LARGEST BOND FUNDS

Fund	Assets (Millions)*
FRANKLIN CA TAX-FREE INCOME I	$14,681.1
FRANKLIN U.S. GOVERNMENT SECURITIES	9,287.8
VANGUARD F/I GNMA	8,725.2
BOND FUND OF AMERICA	8,176.1
FRANKLIN FEDERAL TAX-FREE I	7,096.2
VANGUARD MUNI INTERMEDIATE	6,849.4
IDS HIGH-YIELD TAX-EXEMPT	5,773.1
MERRILL LYNCH CORPORATE HIGH-INCOME	5,526.8
DEAN WITTER U.S. GOVERNMENT SECURITIES	5,414.6
FRANKLIN HIGH YIELD TAX-FREE I	5,226.5
VANGUARD BOND INDEX TOTAL	5,010.0
FRANKLIN NY TAX-FREE INCOME	4,826.6
VANGUARD F/I SHORT-TERM CORPORATE	4,595.5
AARP GNMA & U.S. TREASURY	4,565.5
VANGUARD F/I HIGH-YIELD	4,543.9
AARP HIGH-QUALITY BOND	4,513.7
OPPENHEIMER STRATEGIC INCOME A	4,013.0
KEMPER HIGH-YIELD A	3,662.4
VANGUARD F/I LONG-TERM CORPORATE B	3,599.2
KEMPER U.S. GOVERNMENT SECURITIES A	3,484.8

*As of Dec. 31, 1997   DATA: MORNINGSTAR INC.

is smaller than any of the 20 largest equity funds (Table 7-2).

There are some drawbacks to being a small equity fund. Expense ratios for small funds are almost invariably higher. That's because every fund has certain fixed costs like legal, audit, and registration fees that don't vary much with the size of the fund. Since small funds have fewer assets over which to spread these fixed costs, shareholders in the small funds usually bear higher expenses than those in larger funds.

One other note about asset size. Along with the one-year total return figure, asset size can be used to ascertain how much new money has been added to the fund over the last year. Suppose the fund assets grew 50 percent over the last year. If the fund had a 30 percent total return, figure that 30 percent of the growth came from appreciation and 20 percent from new investments.

If the fund had grown only 20 percent, that's an indication that more dollars went out than came in. This rough calculation works pretty well for equity funds, in which income and capital gains distributions are left to be reinvested. However, it may not work so well for bond funds, since investors who use them to supplement their incomes take the distributions in cash.

Fees

The sales charge is a critical matter for fund investors. Load, no-load, or low-load, it's all here. Some funds have a redemption charge instead of an up-front load. If so, the maximum redemption fee will be under this heading, along with an asterisk noting that it's a redemption fee rather than front-end load. All you need to know about sales charges is in Chapter 3.

Expense ratios are different from sales charges. Whether or not a fund has a sales charge, it still costs to keep it going. Out of the fund's assets come ongoing costs for management, administration, printing, postage, lawyers, auditors, and the like. These costs are totaled and divided by the net assets in the fund. In the case of the Steadman funds, which have been closed to new investors for years, the expenses are extraordinarily high because the funds are so small. Most responsible fund companies would not have allowed that to continue; they would at least have merged the funds to reduce the overhead (Table 7-3). Funds that leverage their portfolios with borrowed money to buy stocks on margin also have high expenses. They end up reporting the interest expense in the expense ratio. International funds also run higher expenses than domestic, just because operating in foreign markets is costlier.

Remember the hidden loads—the 12(b)-1 charges—discussed in Chapter 3? Just to recap, the 12(b)-1 fee—named for the SEC ruling that permitted it—allows fund companies to dip into shareholder assets to pay "distribution" costs. Funds can be used for advertising or marketing expenses, and often they're used to compensate brokers for selling the fund. These charges do find their way into the expense ratio. Chances are, if the fund has an expense ratio of over 2 percent, it's either a very small fund or it levies a 12(b)-1 fee. Those who take such fees are noted in the Scoreboard.

Some funds may show up with 0.00 percent expenses. That could mean the fund is new, and the management company is waiving fees and absorbing expenses to help the fund get started. The Vanguard STAR and LifeStrategies funds

TABLE 7-3

EXPENSE RATIOS: EQUITY FUNDS

Fund HIGHEST	Expense ratio*	Fund LOWEST	Expense ratio*
STEADMAN AMERICAN INDUSTRY	17.69%	VANGUARD STAR TOTAL INTL.	0.00%
STEADMAN TECHNOLOGY GROWTH	11.94	CAPITAL MANAGEMENT MIDCAP INV.	0.00
STEADMAN ASSOCIATED	7.34	VANGUARD LIFESTRAT. CONS. GROWTH	0.00
FRONTIER EQUITY	7.29	PAYDEN & RYGEL MARKET RET. A	0.00
STEADMAN INVESTMENT	6.48	PRINCIPAL PRES. PSE TECH 100	0.00
AMERICAN HERITAGE	6.42	VANGUARD LIFESTRAT. GROWTH	0.00
APEX MID CAP GROWTH	5.25	FREMONT EMERGING MARKETS	0.00
GAMERICA CAPITAL A	5.16	VANGUARD STAR	0.00
EAST END CAP. APPRECIATION	4.84	VANGUARD LIFESTRAT. MODERATE GROWTH	0.00
MERGER	4.29	KEY STOCK INDEX	0.00
ALLIANCE ALL-ASIA INVESTMENT B	4.07	VANGUARD LIFESTRAT. INCOME	0.00
MATTERHORN GROWTH	4.00	WILLIAM BLAIR VALUE DISCOVERY	0.00
MAXUS LAUREATE	3.92	VISION GROWTH & INCOME	0.00
MERRIMAN LEVERAGED GROWTH	3.70	EMERALD EQUITY VALUE RET.	0.00
RAINBOW	3.67	EMERALD INTL. EQUITY RET.	0.00
CENTURIAN T.A.A. C	3.54	T. ROWE PRICE SPECTRUM GROWTH	0.00
PRUDENTIAL DISTRESSED SECS. B	3.51	FIDELITY FREEDOM 2030	0.08
MERRILL LYNCH ASSET GROWTH B	3.50	FIDELITY FREEDOM 2000	0.08
BENDER GROWTH C	3.50	FIDELITY FREEDOM 2020	0.08
SMITH BARNEY PACIFIC B	3.47	FIDELITY FREEDOM 2010	0.08

*1997, funds with little or no expenses may be funds of funds or subsidized by the fund companies   DATA: MORNINGSTAR INC.

are funds of funds, investing in other Vanguard portfolios. As such, Vanguard does not charge any fees for these two funds, but collects the fees on the funds these funds invest in. The T. Rowe Price Spectrum funds have the same arrangement with their parent company.

In general, the equity funds with the lowest overhead are index funds. That's because index funds have virtually no management cost. The fund manager merely buys the stocks that are in the index, and sells them if they are dropped from the index. A computer can monitor the portfolio to make sure it's behaving like the underlying index.

The average expense ratio for the funds in the equity Scoreboard varies slightly year to year. (In 1997 it was 1.21 percent.) What this means to you is simple. About $1.21 out of every $100 goes toward expenses. Bond fund expenses, on average, run about 1.01 percent for taxable funds, 0.85 percent for tax-free funds.

All things being equal, a lower expense ratio is better than a higher one. But if an equity fund has built up a strong track record, even with a high-end expense ratio, that's no reason to shun it. Fund performance is reported net of expenses.

Thus, if the fund runs up high costs and still turns out impressive results, so be it. The only caveat is that when the fund hits a downdraft—and all do—a high overhead is going to make it even more painful.

Bond fund investors should be especially sensitive to expense ratios, looking first to funds with the lowest ones and steering clear of those with the highest (Table 7-4). That's because bond fund returns are typically in the single-digits. If the fund earns 7 percent and eats up 1 percent in operating expenses, it will only deliver 6 percent to shareholders. That may not sound like much overhead, but one out of every seven dollars earned by the fund—14 percent of the earnings— was chewed up in overhead. On the other hand, if an equity fund earns 50 percent, few investors are going to care if the expense ratio was 1 or even 2 percent.

If the fund manager is subsidizing the fund's overhead in any way, it's useful to know what the expense ratio would be if the fund were paying its way entirely. Such subsidies don't last forever, and one day shareholders will have to pay the full freight. For several years Dreyfus Corp. and Fidelity Investments waged a fierce battle

TABLE 7-4

EXPENSE RATIOS: BOND FUNDS

Fund **HIGHEST** ▼	Expense ratio* ▼	Fund **LOWEST** ▼	Expense ratio* ▼
ERNST GLOBAL ASSET ALLOCATION	4.99%	GE TAX-EXEMPT B	0.00%
NEW YORK MUNI	3.77	STRONG INTERNATIONAL BOND	0.00
COMPASS GOVERNMENT INCOME INVST. B	3.69	LANDMARK NATL. TAX-FREE INCOME A	0.00
FUNDAMENTAL U.S. GOVT. STRAT. INC.	3.53	STRONG MUNICIPAL ADVANTAGE	0.00
CALIFORNIA MUNI	3.26	AMERICAN NATIONAL TAX-FREE	0.00
ALLIANCE NORTH AMER. GOVT. INCOME B	3.05	STRONG SHORT-TERM GLOBAL BOND	0.00
ALLIANCE LIMITED MAT. GOVT. B	2.94	CGM AMERICAN TAX-FREE	0.00
MERRILL LYNCH GLOBAL CONV. B	2.64	FRANKLIN STRATEGIC MORTGAGE	0.00
PAINEWEBBER STRATEGIC INCOME B	2.63	LORD ABBETT TAX-FREE INCOME MN	0.00
ALLIANCE GLOBAL STRATEGIC INCOME B	2.60	VISION U.S. GOVERNMENT SECURITIES	0.00
VAN KAMPEN AMER. CAP. STRATEGIC INCOME B	2.57	VISION NY MUNICIPAL INCOME	0.00
FUNDAMENTAL F/I HI-YIELD MUNI	2.49	ECLIPSE ULTRA SHORT-TERM INCOME	0.00
BJB GLOBAL INCOME A	2.43	T. ROWE PRICE SPECTRUM INCOME	0.00
LEXINGTON CONVERTIBLE SECS.	2.39	PAYDEN & RYGEL INVST. QUALITY BOND A	0.00
GABELLI GLOBAL CONVERTIBLE SECS.	2.35	DREYFUS INTERM.-TERM INCOME	0.00
GT GLOBAL HIGH-INCOME B	2.34	LORD ABBETT TAX-FREE INCOME GA	0.03
VAN KAMPEN AMER. CAP. GLOBAL GOVERNMENT B	2.33	FRANKLIN WA MUNICIPAL BOND	0.10
VAN KAMPEN AMER. CAP. INTERM. MUNI B	2.32	FRANKLIN AR MUNICIPAL BOND	0.10
ALLIANCE GLOBAL DOLLAR GOVERNMENT B	2.26	PACIFIC HORIZON SHORT-TERM GOVT.	0.11
NICHOLAS-APPLEGATE INCOME & GROWTH C	2.25	AMERICAN CENTURY–BENHAM FL MUNI. INTERM.	0.13

*1997, funds with little or no expenses may be funds of funds or subsidized by the fund companies

DATA: MORNINGSTAR INC.

between two big money-market funds, using waivers of management fees to boost yield and make their funds more attractive. If that's the case, the fund prospectus should spell out how much the fees would be without the subsidy. That might give a more realistic picture of the fund.

Total Return: Pretax and Aftertax

Total return is the fund's appreciation, including reinvestment of dividends and capital gains. The equity fund Scoreboard shows pretax and aftertax returns for 1997 and, if applicable, the average annual pretax and aftertax returns for the 3-, 5-, and 10-year periods. In the bond fund Scoreboard, the total returns are reported under the "Performance" heading. If your money was invested for the entire year and you added no new money, only reinvesting the dividends and capital gains, this reported total return should be your actual return too. If the money came in at any other point during the year, or if you made multiple investments in the fund, your own results will be different.

Yield is the fund's dividend payout as a percentage of its assets. It does not include capital gains distributions. This figure will be high in bond funds (it's under the "Portfolio Data" heading) and relatively low for equity funds. Most small-cap growth and mid-cap growth funds often have no yield at all, since the funds invest in companies that reinvest their profits for expansion rather than pay them out as dividends.

Sometimes a bond fund's total return will be less than the payout. That means that the NAV declined during the prior year. If a bond fund is paying out a yield higher than its total return, the fund's income distributions may be a return of your principal. Such payouts, also known as return of capital, are tax-free. Don't cheer about it. It's not a freebie. In effect, you're getting your own money back because the fund couldn't earn a real return on it. Of course, the income distribution just may be a lot higher than the total return because of a loss in principal—not uncommon in years in which interest rates rise and bond prices sag.

In the equity Scoreboard, you will also find aftertax returns. These figures are the same as

the total return, less federal income taxes. Of course, not every fund shareholder pays the same tax rate. So for purposes of calculating aftertax returns, we've used the highest tax rate on income and capital gains that was in effect during the period. Since 1991, we have kept the top rate at 31 percent even though rates have gone higher for some shareholders. So few taxpayers pay the higher rate that it doesn't make much sense to use it for calculations that a large number of mutual fund investors will have to use.

If taxes affected all equity funds equally, there would not be much point to showing these numbers. But exactly how taxes affect funds depends on how the fund earned its returns. As you remember from Chapter 6, mutual funds have to pass along essentially all of their net dividend, interest, and realized capital gains during the year in which they are earned. (There is no tax due on income and capital gains generated by funds in qualified retirement programs like IRAs, Keoghs, and 401(k) plans.)

Take a fund that invests in a lot of high-dividend stocks. Those dividends are part of the fund's return, and will be passed along to investors every year. That means those dividends will be part of a taxable distribution even if, like most fund shareholders, you choose to reinvest the dividends in new fund shares. Suppose a fund earns a dividend yield of 6 percent and appreciates 6 percent, for a total return of 12 percent. Assuming the fund makes no capital gains distributions (it wouldn't have to unless it sold stocks at a profit), you could say that half the fund's return was taxable to you. If you are in the 31 percent bracket (and for simplicity, set aside state and local income taxes), the aftertax return would be 10.14 percent. How so? After taxes, the 6 percent yield is 4.14 percent. Add that to the 6 percent appreciation, and the return comes to 10.14 percent.

Next, suppose a fund is up 12 percent from capital appreciation, and there is no dividend or income distribution. If half of that return were a capital gains distribution, then, assuming the gains were long-term (held by the fund for more than 18 months), that 6 percent would be taxable at the maximum capital gains rate of 20 percent. That distribution comes out to 4.8 percent after taxes, dropping the aftertax return to 10.8 percent.

Now suppose the fund earned a 12 percent total return, but paid out no taxable dividend or capital gains distributions. In that case, the after-tax return is the same as the pretax return but that doesn't mean you don't pay taxes on your

The tax bite may affect your fund choices.

gains. You pay taxes when you or the fund earns income or realizes capital gains. If your fund is able to increase its net asset value without making distributions, that's fine as long as you own the fund. But should you sell the fund, you'll be hit with a taxable gain at that time. Equity mutual funds can help you defer taxes, but not avoid them.

How much attention you have to pay to after-tax returns depends on your tax bracket and investment needs. If you're in the 28 percent bracket, these figures will overstate the tax bite. If you're in the 36 percent or 39.6 percent brackets, the tax impact will be understated. If you're trying to minimize taxes, seek funds whose after-tax returns are fairly close to the pretax results. That means there was little tax impact. You might also steer clear of funds that rely heavily on bonds and dividend-paying stocks. But keep in mind when choosing funds that minimize taxable income that you may be taking on more risk. Funds with higher payouts tend to be more conservative and more stable funds.

> "History" measures relative performance.

History

This section, formerly known as "Trend," looks at how a fund performed relative to other funds. For equity funds, there are a total of four boxes, each representing a prior 2½-year period. For bond funds, each box is a 1-year period.

The boxes read from left to right, so, in the equity tables, the box farthest to the left represents the period that runs from 7½ to 10 years past. (For the 10 years ending December 31, 1997, that box covers the period running from January 1988 through June 1990.) The box on the right is the most recent 2½-year period, July 1995 through December 1997. Each box has a number—1, 2, 3, or 4—which indicates which quartile the fund was in during each period.

Suppose the fund's boxes look like this: 3-4-2-1. This means that in the first two periods the fund's performance put it in the bottom half of all funds—in fact, it was in the bottom quartile in the second period. But the fortunes then switched around five years ago. For the third period, the fund jumps to the second quartile, and to the first quartile for the most recent period.

Remember, the "History" figure measures performance relative to all other funds, not the absolute performance discussed under total returns. If the market goes through a few bad years, even the top-quartile funds may have had absolute returns that looked pale. Conservative equity funds are more likely to show up near the top in tough times; the more aggressive funds will show better relative performance in boom times.

One more thing. History clues you in about the consistency of performance. Is it erratic or does it always stay around the same level? Fidelity Magellan's figures are a 1-2-1-3, telling you performance was relatively strong until the last 2½ year period. Berger 100 Fund, a one-time highflier, is 1-1-3-3. No wonder the management company brought a new portfolio manager in last year.

In the bond fund Scoreboard, the relative performance is heavily influenced by the course of interest rates. Look at American Century-Benham Target Maturities 2020, a long-term zero-coupon bond fund. It's a top-drawer performer when rates go down, and a loser when rates go up. Now, for 1993, 1995, and 1997, periods in which rates went down, the fund is a first quartile performer. In 1994 and 1996, when rates went up, the fund was a fourth- or bottom-quartile performer. Strong Advantage Fund, an ultrashort-term bond fund, is just the opposite. It shines when long-term funds decline, and lags when they rally. Strong Advantage is a fourth-quartile performer in 1993, 1995, 1997—just the years the long-term fund leads the way, and it's a first-quartile fund when most others run into trouble.

Portfolio Data

The next set of data looks inside each fund's portfolio. The first column, "Turnover," is a measure of trading activity. To arrive at this number, we take the lesser of purchases or sales and divide it by average monthly assets. So if the lesser of the two is $50 million, and the average fund assets are $100 million, the turnover ratio is 50 percent—which happens to be a moderate figure. (A fund's prospectus will contain its exact turnover ratio.)

The funds are then ranked by those numbers in descending order. Next, the funds are assigned a rating from "very high" down to "very low," using a statistical distribution similar to that for the BUSINESS WEEK mutual fund ratings.

High turnover could mean higher expenses. High turnover could also mean higher taxes.

That's because mutual funds must distribute their net capital gains to shareholders, and funds that trade are presumably taking lots of gains. In contrast, low turnover funds tend to hold onto their winners and let them ride. There's no tax due until the fund sells the holdings. Funds with very high turnover tend to be small-cap growth, mid-cap growth, and even some large-cap blend funds. Funds with "very low" turnover are rather diverse, including precious metals, utilities, and, of course, all sorts of index funds.

While "Turnover" measures a fund characteristic over a period of time, the next three columns are snapshots of the portfolio. The item, "% Cash," shows the portion of the fund's portfolio that's not invested in stocks or bonds. A fund with a relatively low cash level, say 2 or 3 percent, is said to be "fully invested." If a fund has a double-digit cash level, it usually indicates the fund manager is wary of the market, or can't find the kinds of investment opportunities he or she likes. On occasion, this figure will be negative. That could mean one of two things. Funds that own stocks purchased on "margin"—that is, with borrowed funds—usually show a negative cash figure. But few funds actually buy on margin. More likely, the fund has just paid out a capital gains distribution.

Next comes "% Foreign." The idea in including this data is that many U.S. diversified funds do own a small measure of foreign stocks. Suppose you had chosen Putnam Diversified Equity B to fill in the mid-cap growth portion of your portfolio. By looking at this column, you will find the fund has 34 percent of its assets abroad, which could be enough to make you wonder if this fund is the optimal mid-cap growth fund for your portfolio. Likewise, this item of info is a way to check up on how international your international funds really are. SmallCap World, for instance, has only 40 percent of its assets abroad.

Then comes the "P–E Ratio," or price-to-earnings ratio. With equities, the p–e ratio is the price of the stock divided by the last 12 months' earnings per share. A stock that sells at 50 and has earned $2.50 per share has a p–e of 20. Another way to interpret the p–e is, "How many dollars do you have to pay for each $1 of earnings?" In that analysis, a 20 p–e tells you it costs $20 to "buy" every $1 of earnings.

Investment analysts use p–e's as a measure of value. Stocks with low p–e's are said to be "cheap," and high p–e's, "expensive." For the stock market as a whole, the average p–e over time is about 14; in bull markets, that average can climb over 20, as it is now, and in bear markets, it can dip into the single digits.

The price–earnings ratio for a mutual fund is simply the average of the p–e's of the stocks in the fund, weighted by the size of the holdings. Suppose a fund has just two stocks: $90 million of bank, with a p–e of 10, and $10 million worth of software company, with a p–e of 50. The average of the two numbers, 10 and 50, is 30. But 90 percent of the fund is in the stock with a p–e of 10, and 10 percent is in the stock with a lofty 50. So take 90 percent of 10, or 9, and add to it 10 percent of 50, or 5 percent. The weighted average p–e is 14.

Stocks with high p–e's often have no dividends or low dividends because the companies are growing so fast they need to reinvest all their profits. Low-growth companies, like automakers, utilities, and oil producers, pay relatively high dividends. High p–e funds are not going to generate a lot of dividends. Low p–e stocks are often a mainstay of growth and income and equity-income funds.

Stocks and funds with relatively high p–e's are considered riskier than those with low p–e's (Table 7-5). That's because Wall Street has high hopes for such companies and will be quick to dump them if they disappoint. If the investment world assigns a low p–e to a company's stock, expectations are already low. Funds with low p–e stocks are thought to be less risky than those with high p–e stocks.

A low p–e on a fund's stocks may make it look attractive, but these numbers require further analysis. For instance, in the 1998 Scoreboard, the much battered Asian funds show up with the lowest p–e's. How's that? The p–e is based on a current price and the last 12 months' earnings. In the case of many Asian stocks, that price will be much depressed because of all the recent market turmoil. Yet the earnings, the denominator in the ratio, are based on a level of earnings that will unlikely be repeated in the next 12 months as those nations go through dire financial and economic upheaval. If you could get a reasonable earnings estimate for the next 12 months and recalculate the p–e, you would probably find that it's much higher.

The next column, "Untaxed Gains," is also a revealing feature. This figure shows what percentage of the portfolio is unrealized capital gains and undistributed gains (see Chapter 6). Suppose a $500 million fund acquired its holdings at a cost of $400 million. There's $100 million in unrealized gains. All together, that's 20 percent of the port-

High p–e funds are riskier than low p–e funds.

TABLE 7-5

EQUITY FUNDS: PRICE–EARNINGS RATIOS

Fund HIGHEST	Price–earnings ratio*	Fund LOWEST	Price–earnings ratio*
TCW/DW MID-CAP EQUITY B	51	MATTHEWS ASIAN CONVERT.	9
PBHG SELECT EQUITY	50	GAM ASIAN CAPITAL A	9
STEIN ROE CAPITAL OPPORT.	47	LEXINGTON STRATEGIC INV.	9
JUNDT U.S. EMERGING GROWTH	47	IVY ASIA PACIFIC A	10
TCW/DW SMALL CAP GROWTH B	46	FIDELITY EMERGING MARKETS	11
IAI EMERGING GROWTH	46	FIDELITY HONG KONG & CHINA	12
DRESDNER RCM GLOBAL TECH.	44	COMPASS INTL. EMERGING INV.	12
DELAWARE AGGRESSIVE GROWTH A	43	GUINNESS FLIGHT ASIA BLUE CHIP	12
FIDELITY SELECT AMERICAN GOLD	43	WRIGHT EQUIFUND-HONG KONG	12
RYDEX PRECIOUS METALS	43	CAPSTONE NEW ZEALAND	12
PBHG EMERGING GROWTH	43	COLONIAL NEWPORT TIGER	12
LONGLEAF PARTNERS REALTY	43	LANDMARK EMERGING ASIAN MKTS.	12
BLANCHARD PRECIOUS METALS	43	BRUCE	12
IVY GLOBAL SCIENCE & TECHNOLOGY	43	OAKMARK INTL. SMALL CAP	13
STRONG GROWTH	42	VALLEY FORGE	13
MONTEREY OCM GOLD	42	GUINNESS FLIGHT CHINA	13
FIRST AMERICAN TECHNOLOGY	42	VISTA SOUTHEAST ASIAN A	13
VAN WAGONER POST-VENTURE	42	REMBRANDT ASIAN TIGERS INV.	14
JANUS ENTERPRISE	42	VAN ECK ASIA DYNASTY A	14
PUTNAM OTC & EMERGING GROWTH	42	GOVETT EMERGING MARKETS A	14

*1997   DATA: MORNINGSTAR INC.

folio. Suppose you buy the fund today, and the manager liquidates the entire portfolio tomorrow (that almost never happens). Twenty percent of the money that comes back to you will be capital gains on which you will owe tax.

Just because the figure may be high doesn't mean you should avoid the fund. The figure is very high for Century Shares, 77 percent, but that's because the fund is a long-term investor that holds on to stocks for years. A high potential gains figure is also a sign that the fund has been successful. A fast-growing fund will probably have a low figure because the fund assets will likely be increasing much faster than its portfolio profits.

Funds that have suffered large losses often have negative capital gains exposure. That's because although mutual funds have to distribute realized capital gains to shareholders, they're not permitted to distribute realized losses. Instead, the losses are retained within the fund, and used to offset or "shelter" capital gains. Buying a fund with large losses can be a smart move, if you think the fund is poised to make gains. Certainly, investors who bought high-yield bond funds in 1991 had the benefit of large losses incurred dur-

ing the 1989–1990 collapse of the junk bond market. And in 1993, many precious metals funds ran up big gains and sheltered them with losses built up over many years. But before buying a fund for the sheltering power of its capital losses, you should be convinced that the fund's fortunes are on the mend. Otherwise, you're just buying another money-losing fund. Going into 1998, various Asian funds are chockful of losses: Fidelity Southeast Asia Fund has losses amounting to 62 percent of its assets; at T. Rowe Price New Asia Fund, the figure is 50 percent. When those funds rebound—and they will someday—those losses will shelter some of those gains.

The column "Largest Holding" is also telling. Though most funds hold dozens, if not hundreds, of stocks, the largest holding often signals the investment style. If the largest holding is Exxon, Procter & Gamble, or General Electric, you know the fund likes large, strong, and well-established companies. If the largest holding is an obscure high-tech company you've never heard of, that's a tipoff, too. You can bet that the second, third, and other holdings are not Exxon, P&G, and GE.

Ask the fund to send a shareholder report that has the entire portfolio. Of course, that's only a snapshot of what the portfolio looked like on a particular day. In fact, a portfolio is dynamic. Even if the names don't change much, the numbers do, since the prices of the holdings can change every day. But the "personality" of the fund, as shown through the kind of investments it makes, doesn't change.

The "% Asset" that follows "Largest Holding" tells you how much of the fund is made up of this stock. If it's 10 percent (and that would be high), a 10 percent move in the underlying stock would, all things being equal, show up as a 1 percent move in the fund.

In the bond fund Scoreboard, there's an item called "Maturity." Like p–e's in the equity fund Scoreboard, maturity tells you something about the nature and risk profile of the fund. In the bond business maturity is simply the time until the bond matures or pays back the principal, or face amount. Maturity for a bond fund is simply the average of the maturities of the bonds in the fund, weighted according to the market value of those securities.

As a rule, the longer the maturity of a fund, the more volatile it is, and the greater the risk. Funds with longer maturities fare well when interest rates fall, but they're battered when rates rise. Shorter maturity funds do just the opposite. They may lose a bit when rates rise, but not nearly so much as the longer-term funds.

Keep in mind that there is one major difference between maturity of bonds and maturity of bond funds. The maturity of a bond is declining all the time. A 30-year bond issued 10 years ago is a 20-year bond today, and will be a 5-year security in 15 years. In that sense the riskiness of a bond declines as it gets closer to maturity.

A bond fund, on the other hand, never matures. The maturity does change, but does so by the decision of its portfolio manager. If the goal is to keep the fund's maturity at 15 years, for instance, the manager has to keep juggling the bonds and the mix of bonds so as to produce that average result.

I Risk

For our Scoreboard we define risk as the potential for losing money. There are other ways to define it, but for you as an investor it's the most significant way. If your mutual fund is volatile—if its net asset value is subject to sharp fluctuations—it's risky. You're probably not going to get too upset about sharp moves to the upside. But you're not going to like it when the NAV nosedives.

The BUSINESS WEEK ratings focus on downside risk. To determine a fund's risk, we first measure a fund's total return for each month in the five-year measurement period. Total return is the change in net asset value, plus any distributed dividends and capital gains. Suppose the net asset value of a fund drops from $12.50 per share to $12.25 during the month and there were no dividend or capital gains distributions. The fund's total return was –2 percent.

The next step is to calculate that month's Treasury bill rate of return—what you could have earned by taking on no risk at all. If the annualized T-bill rate was 3 percent, the one-month return is 3 percent divided by 12, or 0.25 percent. Then we take 2 percent away from 0.25 percent and get –1.75 percent.

When a fund earns less than the T-bill rate, the result will always be a negative number. Then all the negative numbers are added up and divided by the number of months in the period. So, suppose that in a 60-month period a fund underperforms in 24 months. The negative numbers for each of those months are added up and divided by 60.

The farther fund performance falls below the T-bill rate, the greater the average negative number will be. And the greater the number, the higher your risk of losing money in a mutual fund. This risk-of-loss factor is also subtracted from a fund's total return over the entire period to come up with the BUSINESS WEEK rating.

For the risk column, the Scoreboard translates these numbers into one of five categories of risk. The funds with the greatest risk-of-loss numbers get the "very high" designation. That classification is followed by "high," "average," "low," and "very low." The funds at each extreme—the very highest and very lowest—are highlighted in Tables 7-6 and 7-7.

We also have a feature in the risk column showing the best and worst quarters of the last five years or 20 calendar quarters. We only include this data for funds with five years of performance history. These figures can show you the range of quarterly results over the last five years, so you get a sense of how volatile the fund can be.

"Maturity" is an indicator of a bond fund's risk.

TABLE 7-6

RISKY BUSINESS
FUNDS WITH "VERY HIGH" RISK

ALGER SMALL CAPITALIZATION B	FONTAINE GLOBAL GROWTH	PIONEER GOLD A
AMERICAN CENT. GLOBAL GOLD	FORTIS ADVANT. CAPITAL APPR. A	PRUDENTIAL PACIFIC GROWTH B
AMERICAN CENT.–20TH CENT. GIFTRUST	FOUNDERS DISCOVERY	PUTNAM OTC & EMERGING GROWTH A
AMERICAN CENT.–20TH CENT. VISTA INV.	FRANKLIN GOLD I	REYNOLDS OPPORTUNITY
AMERICAN HERITAGE	FRONTIER EQUITY	ROBERTSON STEPHENS EMERGING GROWTH A
AMERICAN PERFORM. AGGR. GROWTH	GAM PACIFIC BASIN A	ROCKWOOD
APEX MID CAP GROWTH	GOVETT EMERGING MARKETS A	SCUDDER DEVELOPMENT
BLANCHARD PRECIOUS METALS	GOVETT SMALLER COMPANIES A	SCUDDER GOLD
BULL & BEAR GOLD INVESTORS	GT GLOBAL NEW PACIFIC A	SCUDDER LATIN AMERICA
BULL & BEAR SPECIAL EQUITIES	GT GLOBAL TELECOMMUNICATION A	SCUDDER PACIFIC OPPORT
BULL & BEAR U.S. & OVERSEAS	GT LATIN AMERICA GROWTH A	SELIGMAN COMMUNICATE & INFO A
CAPPIELLO-RUSHMORE EMERGING GROWTH	HANCOCK GLOBAL TECHNOLOGY A	SHELBY
CAPSTONE NEW ZEALAND	IAI EMERGING GROWTH	SMITH BARNEY NATURAL RESOURCES B
CAPSTONE NIKKO JAPAN	IDS PRECIOUS METALS A	SMITH BARNEY SPEC EQUITIES B
DAVIS GROWTH OPPORTUNITY B	INVESCO PACIFIC BASIN	STATE ST RESEARCH GLOBAL RESOURCES A
DEAN WITTER DEVELOPING GROWTH B	INVESCO STRAT GOLD	STEADMAN AMERICAN INDUSTRY
DEAN WITTER HEALTH SCIENCES B	IVY CANADA A	STEADMAN ASSOCIATED
DEAN WITTER PACIFIC GROWTH B	JAPAN	STEADMAN INVESTMENT
DEAN WITTER PREC. METALS & MINERALS B	KEMPER TECHNOLOGY A	STEADMAN TECHNOLOGY GROWTH
DOMINION INSIGHT GROWTH	LEXINGTON GOLDFUND	SUNAMERICA SMALL CO. GROWTH A
DREYFUS PREMIER AGGR. GROWTH A	LEXINGTON STRATEGIC INVESTMENTS	TCW/DW LATIN AMERICAN GROWTH B
EATON VANCE WLDWD DEV RES B	LEXINGTON STRATEGIC SILVER	TEMPLETON PACIFIC GROWTH I
EVERGREEN AGGRESSIVE GROWTH A	LEXINGTON WORLDWIDE EMERGING MARKETS	T. ROWE PRICE JAPAN
EVERGREEN PRECIOUS METALS B	MERRILL LYNCH DRAGON B	T. ROWE PRICE NEW ASIA
EVERGREEEN SMALL CO. GROWTH B	MERRILL LYNCH LATIN AMER B	UNITED GOLD & GOVERNMENT A
EXCELSIOR LATIN AMERICA	MERRILL LYNCH TECHNOLOGY B	USAA AGGRESSIVE GROWTH
EXCELSIOR PACIFIC/ASIA	MIDAS	USAA GOLD
FIDELITY EMERGING MARKETS	MONTEREY OCM GOLD	U.S. GLOBAL INV. GOLD SHARES
FIDELITY JAPAN	MONTGOMERY EMERGING MARKETS R	U.S. GLOBAL INV. WORLD GOLD
FIDELITY PACIFIC BASIN	NOMURA PACIFIC BASIN	VAN ECK GOLD/RESOURCES A
FIDELITY SELECT AIR TRANSPORT	OBERWEIS EMERGING GROWTH	VAN ECK INTL. INVEST. GOLD A
FIDELITY SELECT AMERICAN GOLD	OPPENHEIMER DISCOVERY A	VANGUARD INTL. EQUITY PACIFIC
FIDELITY SELECT BIOTECHNOLOGY	OPPENHEIMER GOLD & SPEC. MINERALS A	VANGUARD SPEC. GOLD & PREC. METALS
FIDELITY SELECT COMPUTERS	PACIFIC HORIZON AGGR. GROWTH A	WASATCH MID-CAP
FIDELITY SELECT DEVELOP. COMMUN.	PATHFINDER	WPG TUDOR
FIDELITY SELECT ELECTRONICS	PBHG GROWTH	WRIGHT EQUIFUND-HONG KONG
FIDELITY SELECT PREC. METALS & MINERALS	PIMCO OPPORTUNITY C	YORKTOWN CLASSIC VALUE
FIDELITY SELECT TECHNOLOGY	PIMCO PRECIOUS METALS C	
FLAG INV. EMERGING GROWTH A	PIN OAK AGGRESSIVE STOCK	

DATA: MORNINGSTAR INC.

Here's how you might use it. Consider Fidelity Low-Priced Stock Fund and Fidelity Magellan Fund. (It's easy to compare them because they're next to each other in the Scoreboard.) Fidelity Low-Priced Stock Fund's best quarter was the third of 1997, up 13 percent, and its worst, the fourth of 1994, down 1.3 percent. Fidelity Magellan Fund, on the other hand, had higher highs and lower lows: a 16.6 percent gain in the second quarter of 1997 and a 4.5 percent loss in the second quarter of 1994. The differences are pretty dramatic. You could also have surmised there was a difference by looking at the risk rating before the best quarter/worst quarter statistics. Fidelity Low-Priced Stock Fund has a "low" rating, while Fidelity Magellan Fund has an "average" rating.

The best/worst quarterly statistics could help you compare funds with the same risk ratings. Look at Fidelity Low-Priced Stock Fund and the Royce Micro-Cap Fund. Both are small-cap value funds and are low in risk. Royce Micro-Cap Fund has a 15.6 percent best quarter (not surprisingly, the third quarter of 1997 as well) and a –3.4 percent return in the third quarter of 1996. That's a little wider range of returns than the Fidelity fund, especially on the downside. If you are concerned about downside risk, there has been a little more in the Royce fund.

Specialized funds usually have bigger swings than the diversified funds. Look at Fidelity Select American Gold. Its best quarterly return was second quarter of 1993, up 32.5 percent; it's worst, the fourth quarter of 1997, down 32.1 percent. But funds that invest in emerging growth companies, characterized by high price-earnings ratios, can also have wide swings. Oppenheimer Discovery A, for instance, was up 18.5 percent in the second quarter of 1997 after being down 13 percent in the first quarter of the same year.

One thing these "worst quarter" figures don't show you is how the funds behaved in a bear market. There hasn't been one in the past five years. But as the statistics show, many funds went through some pretty ugly periods in 1992 and 1994, bad enough to give you a taste of the bear. Take each of your fund's worst quarter returns and double it. If you can live with that kind of one-quarter loss for one of your funds, you're ready for whatever the markets may give you.

TABLE 7-7

NOT SO RISKY BUSINESS
FUNDS WITH "VERY LOW" RISK

AIM ADV. FLEX C	GALAXY EQUITY INCOME RET. A	PEGASUS INTRINSIC VALUE A
ALLIANCE CONSERVATIVE INV. B	GATEWAY INDEX PLUS	PEGASUS MANAGED ASSETS CONSERV. A
ALLIANCE INCOME BUILDER C	GEORGE PUTNAM OF BOSTON A	PERMANENT PORTFOLIO
AMERICAN BALANCED	GREENSPRING	PHOENIX INCOME & GROWTH A
AMERICAN MUTUAL	HANCOCK SOVEREIGN BALANCED B	PIONEER BALANCED A
AMSOUTH BALANCED CLASSIC	HERITAGE INCOME-GROWTH A	PIPER BALANCED A
ANALYTIC OPTIONED EQUITY	HIGHMARK BALANCED RET.	PRIMARY INCOME
BERWYN INCOME	HOTCHKIS & WILEY BALANCED	PRINCIPAL BALANCED A
CALDWELL & ORKIN MARKET OPPORT.	IAA ASSET ALLOCATION	PUTNAM BALANCED RETIREMENT A
CAPITAL INCOME BUILDER	IDS DIVERSIFIED EQUITY-INCOME A	PUTNAM UTIL. GROWTH & INCOME A
CARILLON CAPITAL	IDS MUTUAL A	REA-GRAHAM BALANCED
COLUMBIA BALANCED	INCOME FUND OF AMERICA	RIGHTIME BLUE CHIP
COMPASS BALANCED INV. A	INVESCO TOTAL RETURN	RIGHTIME MIDCAP
COMPOSITE BOND & STOCK A	JANUS BALANCED	ROYCE PREMIER
CRABBE HUSON ASSET ALLOC. PRIM.	LINDNER DIVIDEND INVESTORS	SAFECO INCOME NO-LOAD
DELAWARE A	LONGLEAF PARTNERS	SCOUT REGIONAL
DODGE & COX BALANCED	LONGLEAF PARTNERS SMALL-CAP	SELIGMAN INCOME A
DREYFUS BALANCED	MAIRS & POWER BALANCED	SENTINEL BALANCED A
EATON VANCE INVESTORS A	MAP-EQUITY	SMITH BARNEY CONCERT SO. AWARE. A
ECLIPSE BALANCED	MAXUS EQUITY	SMITH BARNEY PREM. TOTAL RET. B
EVERGREEN BALANCED B	MAXUS INCOME	SMITH BARNEY PRIN. RET. 1998
EVERGREEN BALANCED II Y	MERGER	SOGEN INTERNATIONAL
FBL MANAGED	MERRILL LYNCH CAPITAL B	STAGECOACH BALANCED A
FBL VALUE GROWTH	MERRILL LYNCH GLOBAL ALLOCATION B	STELLAR INVESTMENT
FBP CONTRARIAN BALANCED	MERRIMAN GROWTH & INCOME	STRONG ASSET ALLOCATION
FEDERATED STOCK & BOND A	MFS TOTAL RETURN A	T. ROWE PRICE BALANCED
FIDELITY ASSET MANAGER: INCOME	MFS WORLD TOTAL RETURN A	T. ROWE PRICE CAPITAL APPRECIATION
FIDELITY LOW-PRICED STOCK	MOSAIC HILL BALANCED	T. ROWE PRICE DIVIDEND GROWTH
FIRST AMERICAN EQUITY-INCOME A	MUTUAL BEACON Z	T. ROWE PRICE EQUITY-INCOME
FIRST OMAHA EQUITY	MUTUAL DISCOVERY Z	T. ROWE PRICE SMALL-CAP VALUE
FLAG INV. VALUE BUILDER A	MUTUAL QUALIFIED Z	USAA GROWTH & TAX STRATEGY
FOUNDERS BALANCED	MUTUAL SHARES Z	VALLEY FORGE
FRANKLIN ASSET ALLOCATION	NEW CENTURY I	VANGUARD BALANCED INDEX
FRANKLIN BALANCE SHEET INVMT.	NEW ENGLAND BALANCED A	VANGUARD STAR
FRANKLIN EQUITY INCOME I	NORTH AMERICAN BALANCED C	VANGUARD/WELLESLEY INCOME
FRANKLIN INCOME I	OPPENHEIMER DISCIP. ALLOCATION A	VISTA BALANCED A
FUNDMANAGER MGD. T/R FIN. ADV.	OPPENHEIMER MULTIPLE STRAT. A	WESTWOOD BALANCED RET.
GABELLI EQUITY-INCOME	PARNASSUS INCOME BALANCED	ZWEIG APPRECIATION A
GALAXY ASSET ALLOC. RET. A	PAX WORLD	

DATA: MORNINGSTAR INC.

Are Four Great Years in a Row Really Possible?

At the beginning of 1997, most investment professionals did not have high expectations for the stock market. After all, how much better could things get? In 1995, the stock market had gone up 37.5 percent, the best annual performance in two decades, and 1996 wound up with a surprisingly strong 22.9 percent gain in the Standard & Poor's 500-stock index. Three in a row? C'mon.

But markets have a way of surprising. The Dow Jones industrial average breached 7000 in mid-February 1997 and 8000 by summer to reach a high of 8259 in August. Even with another October tremor—fallout from a financial collapse in Southeast Asia led to a 554-point one-day drop on October 27, 1997—the market recovered enough to finish the year on a high note. The final tally for 1997: the Dow up 1460 points, or 22.6 percent. The broader S&P 500 gained 31.3 percent in price, a smashing 33.4 percent return with dividends included. And investors in U.S. diversified equity mutual funds made out swimmingly. In the three-year period, they earned an average annual total return of 24.5 percent. That's a rate that doubles your money in just three years.

Now it's 1998. What happens to stock prices after three years of gains in excess of 20 percent? You can't find that in the record books because it's never happened before. The law of averages would suggest that stocks would have to have a subpar year soon, and logic would suggest the market would have to pull back and take a breather. All this is true, but stocks respond to and anticipate what's happening in the economy and in the corporate sector—and that's still fairly positive.

Start with the remarkable fact that the federal budget is balanced—indeed, it may even be running at a surplus. That lessens the need for the government to borrow and makes more funds available to the private sector and at a lower rate of interest. Indeed, by the end of 1997, long-term interest rates were at levels briefly seen in 1993 and not since the 1960s before that.

Perhaps even more important for stock prices is that the economy continues to grow at a good pace while inflation remains subdued. This is a remarkable environment that confounds many economists, since stronger economic growth in the past has led to higher inflation and higher interest rates. But the U.S. economy is global now, and competition is keen—especially from countries with lower labor costs.

U.S. companies, unable to boost profits by the traditional method of just raising prices, have learned to run leaner and meaner. They're making investments in technology that boosts productivity, and higher productivity allows companies to pay their employees and still make gains in profits. Sometimes the best way to cut overhead is through selling or shuttering operations, or seeking merger partners. Either form of corporate restructuring usually has a positive impact on stock prices. Indeed, 1997 was a record year for merger and acquisition activity.

As we look into 1998, it's clear that the four-year surge in corporate earnings that fueled this bull market is losing some of its strength. It's dropping from the 20-to-30 percent gains of a few years ago to a slower but more sustainable 8-to-10 percent pace. That's somewhat expected. But what's clouding 1998's earnings forecast—and creating much uncertainty about the stock market prospects—are the economic and financial crises in Asia. America sells plenty there—from computers to earthmovers to agricultural products. And as those countries' overheated and unstable economies sink into recession, it's bound to hurt U.S. companies conducting business there. Indeed, in 1998, the big question that investors ask of a company is "How much business has it done in Asia, and what's the prospect for that now?"

But the turmoil in Asia is not all bad for U.S. equity investors. For starters, investors worldwide have flocked to the United States. That bolsters our stock and bond markets and boosts the value of the dollar. The higher dollars give U.S. consumers more purchasing power around the world and help keep inflation down at home. No doubt part of the rally in bonds that drove long-term interest rates to record lows came from overseas buyers seeking a safe haven for their money. A generation ago, such people might have bought gold as a store of value. But now they want U.S. government securities. Indeed, for a host of reasons, gold now sells at an 18-year low.

Though many factors suggest a positive year for U.S. stocks, it's important to keep your expectations realistic. From 1995 through 1997 the S&P 500 delivered an average annual total return of 31.1 percent. That's nearly three times the long-term average; it's not the normal return from owning stocks or equity mutual funds, and investors should not expect that as an entitlement. In mid-1997, before the fourth quarter's market turmoil, one fund company's survey of investors revealed that investors had an expectation of 34 percent annual returns in the future. Get real, folks. If you're one with that sort of expectation, you're bound to be disappointed in years to come.

There's another lesson to learn from 1997's markets. If you make a long-term commitment to invest, you should basically stick with it for the long term, and not let short-term market forecasts push you out of the market.

Indeed, those who panicked out of the market in October 1997 may already regret it. By the end of February 1998, the Dow had climbed back over the August high and broke through 8500, and the S&P 500 leaped over the 1000 mark.

Equity Funds

During 1997, equity fund returns were absolutely great and relatively bad. U.S. domestic equity funds, which mainly invest in the United States and account for about two-thirds of equity fund assets, earned on average 24.1 percent. That's an absolutely great return. That's significantly better than 1996's 19.3 percent average return. But compared to the S&P 500—or the computer-run index funds that replicate the index—the stockpickers fell flat on their faces. For the fourth year in a row, they lagged the index—and this year, it was by 7 percentage points. In fact, the index was such a powerful performer in 1997 that it beat about 90 of the funds whose managers were picking stocks. And over the last five years, the index did almost as well, beating about 87 percent of the actively managed U.S. domestic funds.

Time to give up and put it all in index funds? Not yet. There's a strong case to be made that index funds, with their low expenses and portfolio turnover, should be in every equity fund investors' portfolio. But index funds are not a one-decision investment. The U.S. stock market has been in a bull market since late 1990, and the index is an ideal bull market investment. All the money is invested all the time, and when stocks are rising, that's an optimal strategy. When stocks decline, the index fund is still fully invested, which means there's no downside protection. A portfolio manager who can sell some vulnerable stocks, raise cash, or load up on defensive stocks like electric utilities can do a better job of conserving money in a difficult market.

In addition, though the S&P 500 index represents about 70 percent of the market value of the U.S. stock market, about 50 of the 500 stocks account for more than half its movement. The successes of Microsoft, Intel, General Electric, Coca-Cola, Gillette, and other giants are what's driving the index these days. In a period when small-to-mid-sized companies do better, as was the case in 1991, 1992, and 1993, many more mutual funds that compete against the S&P 500 actually beat it. In the 1991–1993 period, the stockpickers beat the index each year.

But these analyses don't account for risk-adjusted returns. BUSINESS WEEK rates mutual fund performance by starting with total return and adjusting that return for how much risk the fund took with the shareholders' money. To get a top overall fund rating from BW, a fund doesn't necessarily have to beat the S&P in absolute terms, but it has to beat it on a risk-adjusted basis.

That's why a good place to start your fund search is the list of 86 funds that earned A's, the highest rating for risk-adjusted total return over the last five years (Table 8-1). Many of these funds, like Babson Value, Fidelity Low-Priced Stock, T. Rowe Price Equity-Income, and the Mutual Series four—Mutual Beacon, Mutual Discovery, Mutual Qualified, and Mutual Shares funds—are familiar to BUSINESS WEEK readers. A few, like Longleaf Partners, the Merger Fund, Sequoia Fund, and T. Rowe Price Small-Cap Value Fund are closed to new investors. But there are scores of worthy funds with open doors including Mairs & Power Growth Fund, Oakmark Fund, Royce Premier Fund, Sound Shore Fund, Strong Schafer Value Fund, Torray Fund, and the Westwood Equity and Westwood Balanced funds.

The risk adjustment we perform on funds can bring a highflier down to earth or propel a steady

TABLE 8-1

TOP-PERFORMING EQUITY MUTUAL FUNDS

These equity mutual funds have earned A's
for delivering the best risk-adjusted total returns over the past five years.

Fund	Average annual total return*	Investment category	Risk	Fund	Average annual total return*	Investment category	Risk
AARP GROWTH & INCOME	20.2%	Large-cap Blend	Low	MAIRS & POWER BALANCED**	16.3%	Domestic Hybrid	Very low
AMERICAN CENT. EQUITY GROWTH INV.	21.0	Large-cap Value	Low	MAIRS & POWER GROWTH	23.7	Mid-cap Blend	Low
AMERICAN CENT. INCOME & GROWTH	20.4	Large-cap Value	Low	MAP-EQUITY**	18.7	Mid-cap Blend	Very low
AMERICAN MUTUAL	17.2	Large-cap Value	Very low	MAXUS EQUITY**	18.4	Mid-cap Value	Very low
BABSON VALUE	20.9	Large-cap Value	Low	MERGER	12.1	Mid-cap Blend	Very low
BERWYN INCOME	12.6	Domestic Hybrid	Very low	MERRILL LYNCH BASIC VALUE B	19.2	Large-cap Value	Low
CALDWELL & ORKIN MARKET OPPORT.**	16.9	Domestic Hybrid	Very low	MUTUAL BEACON Z	19.5	Mid-cap Value	Very low
DEAN WITTER EUROPEAN GROWTH B	22.1	Europe	Low	MUTUAL DISCOVERY Z	22.7	World	Very low
DODGE & COX BALANCED	16.1	Domestic Hybrid	Very low	MUTUAL QUALIFIED Z	20.0	Mid-cap Value	Very low
DODGE & COX STOCK	21.1	Large-cap Value	Low	MUTUAL SHARES Z	20.0	Mid-cap Value	Very low
DREYFUS BALANCED	13.6	Domestic Hybrid	Very low	OAKMARK	22.8	Large-cap Value	Low
ECLIPSE BALANCED**	14.9	Domestic Hybrid	Very low	PAINEWEBBER FINANCIAL SVCS. GR. A**	24.7	Financial	Low
EVERGREEN GROWTH & INCOME Y	20.3	Mid-cap Blend	Low	PEGASUS INTRINSIC VALUE A**	17.0	Mid-cap Value	Very low
EXCELSIOR VALUE & RESTRUCTURING A	27.2	Mid-cap Blend	Low	PELICAN	19.7	Large-cap Value	Low
FBL MANAGED**	12.7	Domestic Hybrid	Very low	PILGRIM AMERICA BANK & THRIFT A	28.7	Financial	Average
FIDELITY ADV. GROWTH OPPORTUNITY T	20.4	Large-cap Value	Low	PIMCO RENAISSANCE C	19.8	Large-cap Blend	Low
FIDELITY ASSET MANAGER: INCOME	10.0	Domestic Hybrid	Very low	T. ROWE PRICE CAPITAL APPRECIATION	14.8	Domestic Hybrid	Very low
FIDELITY DESTINY I	22.9	Large-cap Value	Low	T. ROWE PRICE DIVIDEND GROWTH	21.4	Large-cap Blend	Very low
FIDELITY DESTINY II	22.4	Large-cap Value	Low	T. ROWE PRICE EQUITY-INCOME	20.0	Large-cap Value	Very low
FIDELITY EQUITY-INCOME	20.3	Large-cap Value	Low	T. ROWE PRICE GROWTH & INCOME	18.0	Large-cap Blend	Low
FIDELITY GROWTH & INCOME	20.9	Large-cap Blend	Low	T. ROWE PRICE SMALL-CAP VALUE	20.2	Small-cap Value	Very low
FIDELITY LOW-PRICED STOCK	20.4	Small-cap Value	Very low	PUTNAM EQUITY INCOME A	19.5	Large-cap Value	Low
FIDELITY SELECT HOME FINANCE	32.0	Financial	Average	ROYCE PREMIER	15.2	Small-cap Value	Very low
FIDELITY VALUE	18.9	Mid-cap Value	Low	SAFECO EQUITY NO LOAD	22.9	Large-cap Blend	Low
FIRST AMERICAN EQUITY-INCOME A**	15.3	Large-cap Value	Very low	SAFECO INCOME NO LOAD	17.9	Large-cap Value	Very low
FIRST AMERICAN STOCK A**	20.1	Large-cap Value	Low	SALOMON BROS INVESTORS O	20.5	Large-cap Value	Low
FLAG INVESTORS VALUE BUILDER A	17.7	Domestic Hybrid	Very low	SCUDDER GROWTH & INCOME	19.9	Large-cap Blend	Low
FOUNDERS BALANCED	16.9	Domestic Hybrid	Very low	SEQUOIA	22.9	Large-cap Value	Average
FRANKLIN BALANCE SHEET INVESTMENT	19.7	Small-cap Value	Very low	SMITH BARNEY PREM. TOTAL RETURN B	15.8	Large-cap Value	Very low
FRANKLIN CALIFORNIA GROWTH I	25.0	Mid-cap Growth	Average	SOUND SHORE	21.5	Mid-cap Value	Low
FRANKLIN EQUITY INCOME I	16.2	Large-cap Value	Very low	STRATTON GROWTH**	19.5	Large-cap Value	Low
GABELLI ASSET	18.9	Mid-cap Blend	Low	STRONG SCHAFER VALUE	20.5	Mid-cap Value	Low
GABELLI EQUITY-INCOME**	18.2	Large-cap Value	Very low	THIRD AVENUE VALUE	19.4	Small-cap Value	Low
GREENSPRING	16.3	Domestic Hybrid	Very low	TORRAY	23.7	Large-cap Blend	Low
HANCOCK REGIONAL BANK B	28.4	Financial	Low	VANGUARD ASSET ALLOCATION	17.2	Domestic Hybrid	Low
HILLIARD LYONS GROWTH**	18.8	Large-cap Blend	Low	VANGUARD EQUITY-INCOME	19.0	Large-cap Value	Low
HOMESTEAD VALUE	19.5	Mid-cap Value	Low	VANGUARD STAR	14.9	Domestic Hybrid	Very low
HOTCHKIS & WILEY BALANCED**	13.1	Domestic Hybrid	Very low	VANGUARD/WINDSOR II	20.7	Large-cap Value	Low
INCOME FUND OF AMERICA	15.1	Domestic Hybrid	Very low	VISTA BALANCED A**	14.6	Domestic Hybrid	Very low
INVESCO TOTAL RETURN	15.9	Domestic Hybrid	Very low	VONTOBEL U.S. VALUE**	19.4	Large-cap Value	Low
JANUS BALANCED	14.6	Domestic Hybrid	Very low	WASHINGTON MUTUAL INVESTORS	20.8	Large-cap Value	Low
LONGLEAF PARTNERS	21.4	Mid-cap Blend	Very low	WESTWOOD BALANCED**	17.6	Domestic Hybrid	Very low
LONGLEAR PARTNERS SMALL-CAP	20.0	Small-cap Value	Very low	WESTWOOD EQUITY**	21.8	Large-cap Blend	Low

* 1993–97 pretax returns, appreciation plus reinvestment of dividends and capital gains.

** Fund data in Business Week Online.

DATA: MORNINGSTAR INC.

plodder to the top. That explains why the American Heritage Fund, up an eye-popping 75 percent in 1997, gets a big fat F rating in our Scoreboard. The fund's five-year return is an average of 1.1 percent. It was up 41.4 percent in 1993, but it had three negative years in a row: down 35.5 percent in 1994, 30.6 percent in 1995, and 5.1 percent in 1996. No wonder it's an F fund.

If you're concerned about buying into equity mutual funds after the market has had such a large run, you should appreciate this list of funds; 82 of the 86 A-list funds have either low or very low risk. The other four have average risk ratings. In addition, most of them practice a "value" investment style. They buy stocks with below-average price-to-earnings ratios and price-to-book ratios, as opposed to "growth" stocks, which have higher growth rates but higher p–e and p–b ratios.

These value funds don't grab the attention that dynamic growth funds sometimes command, but they have generally out-performed the growth funds over the past five years. Even more important, they often earn high ratings because they're less volatile than the growth funds. In that sense, they may make better investments. "Data shows that growth funds have higher long-term returns, but I suspect investors make more money in value funds," says John Rekenthaler, former publisher of *Morningstar Mutual Funds*, a biweekly publication that reports on mutual fund performance. "Because the funds are less volatile, investors tend to hold onto them longer and let the profits roll. With growth funds, they often buy when they've already gone up and sell when they're down."

The investor doesn't give up much in return when he or she invests in the best risk-adjusted funds. Over the last five years, the average annual total return of the funds on our A-list is 19.3 percent. True, that's 0.9 percentage point less than the return of the S&P 500. But 95 percent of the funds had low or very low risk relative to the S&P 500. That's an excellent trade-off. "When you look at funds by risk-adjusted returns, you are not necessarily looking at the most profitable, but the most comfortable funds," says Don Phillips, president of Morningstar. "Most of these funds can be considered all-weather investments."

They're the sorts of funds that can guide your money safely through rough waters. "We don't perform as well on days the market goes up," says David J. Williams, portfolio manager for the

Excelsior Value and Restructuring Fund. "But we hold like a rock when the market is down." And they're run by cool-headed managers who see market gyrations as opportunity. Williams invests in companies undergoing consolidations, selling assets, and refocusing their businesses. Restructuring, he says, is not a fad, but part of corporate life. When these companies are in the throes of restructuring, their stock price is much more influenced by what's going on in the company than by the vicissitudes of the stock market.

And some savvy managers say it's market volatility that gives them new opportunities. "Choppy markets are good for us," says Mutual Series' Michael Price. "That's when we find things to buy." In early 1998, as the Asian markets were reeling, Price dispatched a member of his investment team to Asia to look for deals.

Which of these A funds will work best for you depends on a number of variables, like your age, your stomach for risk, and even your tax bracket.

If you like an equity fund with dividends, some three dozen of the A-rated funds paid yields in 1997 that were higher than that of the S&P 500. Among them: Berwyn Income, with a 5.8 percent yield; Smith Barney Premium Total Return B, with a 5.3 percent yield; and Hotchkis & Wiley Balanced Fund, with a 4.6 percent yield. And though the rating dropped a notch last year, Lindner Dividend Fund is still a rich stew of high-dividend common stocks, convertible securities, and junk bonds that, when combined, produce a portfolio with very low risk and a relatively high yield of 5.7 percent.

But before you invest in a dividend-oriented fund, remember that the dividend income, like the interest you earn from a bank account, is taxable at your ordinary tax rate. So if you're in the 31 percent federal tax bracket, nearly a third (more perhaps, if you're also subject to state income tax) of what the fund pays to you in dividends eventually goes to the Internal Revenue Service.

That's why we include aftertax returns in the equity portion of the BW Mutual Fund Scoreboard. For instance, from the Scoreboard you learn that Lindner Dividend earned a 14.0 percent total return in 1997, which fell to 9.8 percent after taxes. Berwyn Income's 13.4 percent total return dropped to 10.2 percent after taxes. (The aftertax return is estimated using a 31 percent tax rate on dividends and a 28 percent rate on capital gains distributions.) Over five years, Berwyn's 12.6 percent total return shrank to 9.5 percent. Obviously, if you're in the 36 percent or

Most A-list funds have low risk.

39.6 percent tax brackets, you may want to avoid high-payout funds, even if they are highly rated. However, they make good investments for IRAs and 401(k) plans—steady income, low risk.

Still, there are other ways to invest for dividends. The T. Rowe Price Dividend Growth Fund takes a somewhat different approach to dividends. Instead of just choosing the stocks with the highest dividends now, this fund selects companies on their dividend-growth potential. "Our philosophy is to invest in companies with a regular pattern of raising their dividends," says William Stromberg, the fund's manager. "The only way a company can do that is to keep increasing their earnings, their cash flow." Stromberg's strict criteria narrow the list of fund-worthy companies to between 300 and 600. The fund has a little over 100 stocks. Adds Stromberg, "When you use this criteria, you end up with above average companies with above average management." And superior investment returns to boot.

The A-list is chockful of funds that are well suited to investors who need to earn equity-like rates of return but who have a hard time living with the day-to-day volatility of the stock market. Third Avenue Value Fund is a good example. Third Avenue Value's veteran "vulture" investor Martin J. Whitman and its returns are similar to those of Mutual Series funds. The main difference is that Whitman, with far less money to manage than Mutual Series, invests in much smaller companies, and with a higher bond component, ends up in the domestic hybrid category. But Whitman's not going to buy the kind of bonds that you'd find in a more traditional hybrid like Dodge & Cox Balanced. Through careful analysis, he looks for gems among the trash heap of distressed securities. Risky? Not really. When Whitman buys them, these securities are so cheap that there's little downside risk.

NEW FACES AMONG
THE TOP-RATED FUNDS

One of the most interesting things about the BW Scoreboard is that you sometimes find a little-known fund that rises to the top through our rigorous selection process. We have expanded our analysis to include 2300 equity funds. Data on the 885 largest of those funds are in the Scoreboard pages in the back of this book. Returns and ratings on those 885 and the 1400 smaller funds appear in the Interactive Mutual Fund Scoreboard at BUSINESS WEEK Online (www .businessweek.com). The advantage of the online

expansion is that we can cover about 2.5 times the number of funds we can in print. And with a much larger pool of funds to rate, we can uncover many excellent but relatively unknown funds. Of the 86 A-rated funds, 17 are smaller than the smallest in the printed Scoreboard and appear only online.

Two of the A-rated small-fry are Westwood Equity and Westwood Balanced Funds, both run by Susan M. Byrne. Her investment approach is to look for companies whose positive earnings surprises (the profit reports are better than had been expected) draw no reaction from investors. "That tells you Wall Street thinks the good news is a fluke, or nobody's paying attention," she says.

Working with those stocks, Byrne makes her own assessment of the company's prospects. One of her biggest hits was Dell Computer Corp., which she bought at a split-adjusted price of 4, selling the last shares at 76 for some hefty profits. Says Byrne: "If I'm right, I make a lot of money and if I'm wrong, the stock doesn't move. All I've lost is opportunity cost." The only difference between her two funds is that the equity fund is all-stock, while the balanced fund mixes those same stocks with bonds.

Another bantam-sized A-rated fund is Caldwell & Orkin Market Opportunity Fund. It's a fund that attempts to be "market neutral." A conventional equity fund is not market neutral because, with nearly all its money in stocks, it is sensitive to the direction of the overall stock market. Caldwell & Orkin tries to offset the market effect by balancing short sales off of the regular portfolio investments. On days the market declines, the regular or "long" positions tend to go down, while the short-sale stocks tend to go up. On days the market goes up, so does the long position, but the short position goes down. To make money, the fund manager has to be an exceptionally good stockpicker. The manager has to own stocks that on balance go up more than the market, and, perhaps more difficult, the manager has to sell short some stocks, which will beat the market on down days. All told, the strategy works well in this fund. The returns are excellent, and the fund's correlation with the stock market is only 11 on a scale of 1 to 100 (an S&P 500 index fund would be 100). Indeed, in the fourth quarter of 1997, when the S&P 500 was under pressure, this fund was actually up about 5.7 percent, 3 percentage points better than the index.

Other new names among larger funds are Flag Investors Value Builder A, another top-rated fund new to the list of top performers. The fund is

> One "market neutral" fund sells stocks short.

One fund
invests in
California
companies.

a domestic hybrid, so it blends stocks and bonds and chooses each with aplomb. "We'll go anyplace to invest our money if we can understand the company and how we can make money on it," says portfolio manager Hobart C. Buppert, who launched the fund in 1992. "I don't know of any value fund that would have Ford Motor and America Online, but I thought we could make money on both." His largest equity holding is the insurer Conseco, which, he says, is growing faster than most companies in the industry but sells at a lower p–e multiple.

On the bond side, Buppert doesn't take the easy route of stuffing the portfolio with U.S. Treasuries, which many managers use because they require no credit analysis. Instead, Buppert buys corporate bonds, but only after putting the issuers through the same rigid company analysis he gives stocks. "I stick with intermediate-term bonds," he adds. "If you're buying 20-year bonds, the risks are so great you might as well own stocks." The average annual return over the last five years is 17.7 percent, far surpassing the 12.9 percent average annual return for the domestic hybrid fund category.

The only A-rated fund to come from the "growth" side of the fund world is Franklin California Growth A, a mid-cap growth fund with a five-year average annual total return of 25 percent. A single-state bond fund, of course, can make a lot of investment sense, but a single-state equity fund? Of course, if the state is California, you've got 1400 public companies and a $1 trillion economy that's just slightly less than that of Great Britain.

Conrad Herrmann, the fund's portfolio manager, and his team of analysts are based in San Mateo, a short drive from Silicon Valley, and the Franklin investment pros tend to be friends and neighbors of those living and working in the high-tech industries. Herrmann says proximity can count in making investments. "When you drive by the company headquarters on a Sunday afternoon and the parking lot's filled, it's a clue something is up," jokes Herrmann. "But what you don't know is whether it's good or bad." While the state's heavy technology presence gives the fund a bias toward higher-growth, higher-risk companies, Herrmann balances that by diversifying in leading companies of more mundane industries such as energy, banking, and real estate.

TOP-RATED HOLDOVERS

A good chunk of the top-rated funds are holdovers from last year. Babson Value, Mairs &

Power Growth, Royce Premier, Scudder Growth & Income (and its sister fund, AARP Growth & Income), Strong Schaefer Value, and Sound Shore are among those that first emerged with top ratings in the 1997 Scoreboard and still retain them. Those ratings helped bring these funds to investors' attention as well, as evidenced by their remarkable asset growth. Babson Value Fund earned a 26.6 percent total return in 1997, but its assets were up 81 percent, mainly because of new cash inflows. Not bad for a fund that had been around since 1984. Mairs & Power Growth had also operated in obscurity until last year, when it earned a top rating. During 1997, its assets grew 165 percent, with 28.7 percent of that coming from investment returns. With the online expansion of the Scoreboard to reach smaller funds, Mairs & Power Growth's sister fund, Mairs & Power Balanced Fund now merits an A rating as well.

For phenomenal asset growth, look at the Sound Shore Fund. The fund, a sole offering from an institutional money manager, had been around for more than a decade when, at the start of 1997, the BW Scoreboard identified it as a top-rated fund. Since then, Sound Shore's assets ballooned $131.5 million to $1.3 billion. Sure some of that asset growth came from appreciation, since the fund was up a smart 36.4 percent in 1997. But the bulk of it came from new money pouring into the fund. Thus far, the fund does not seem to be strained by the asset load, but the situation bears watching. Berger 100 Fund ballooned in 1991, 1992, and 1993 and has been a mediocre performer since 1994. Even a change of portfolio manager in early 1997 doesn't seem to have helped much thus far.

CATEGORY RATINGS GIVE FUNDS ANOTHER LOOK

Since an investor looks at all his or her funds as one unified portfolio, there may be concern that some funds aren't getting good overall ratings. That's certainly been the case for the last few years with most international funds. Foreign markets have lagged the U.S. markets so most funds investing abroad have fared poorly when judged alongside funds that invest at home. Or consider the large-cap growth and small-cap growth fund categories. Not one fund from any of those categories earned an A in overall rating. Still, a diversified portfolio should contain some of those funds. But which ones?

That's why we also rate funds within their categories as well as against all funds (Table 8-2).

TABLE 8-2

THE BEST PERFORMERS IN THEIR CATEGORIES

Rating funds against their peers, these funds earn A's for five-year risk-adjusted total returns.
Not all categories have ratings, since some lack enough funds to perform a ratings review.

	Average annual total return*		Average annual total return*
LARGE-CAP GROWTH		**SMALL-CAP VALUE**	
DG EQUITY	18.3%	FIDELITY LOW-PRICED STOCK	20.4%
GABELLI GROWTH	19.4	FRANKLIN BALANCE SHEET INVESTMENT	19.7
PUTNAM INVESTORS A	20.7	LONGLEAF PARTNERS SMALL-CAP	20.0
VANGUARD INDEX GROWTH	19.5	**SMALL-CAP BLEND**	
VANGUARD U.S. GROWTH	17.6	GABELLI SMALL CAP GROWTH	17.9%
LARGE-CAP BLEND		T. ROWE PRICE SMALL CAP STOCK	19.9
AARP GROWTH & INCOME	20.2%	**SMALL-CAP GROWTH**	
COLUMBIA COMMON STOCK	18.7		
FIDELITY	20.6	BARON ASSET	24.0%
FIDELITY GROWTH & INCOME	20.9	MANAGERS SPECIAL EQUITY	19.1
GUARDIAN PARK AVENUE A	22.1	SMALLCAP WORLD	15.7
HILLIARD LYONS GROWTH**	18.8	**FOREIGN**	
PIMCO RENAISSANCE C	19.8	BT INVESTMENT INTERNATIONAL EQUITY	19.1%
T. ROWE PRICE DIVIDEND GROWTH	21.4	FIDELITY DIVERSIFIED INTERNATIONAL	17.3
T. ROWE PRICE GROWTH & INCOME	18.0	HARBOR INTERNATIONAL	19.8
SAFECO EQUITY NO LOAD	22.9	MANAGERS INTERNATIONAL EQUITY	15.4
SCUDDER GROWTH & INCOME	19.9	WADDELL & REED INTERNATIONAL GR. B**	9.4
SMITH BREEDEN EQUITY PLUS**	21.0	**WORLD**	
TORRAY	23.7		
WESTWOOD EQUITY**	21.8	JANUS WORLDWIDE	19.8%
		MUTUAL DISCOVERY Z	22.7
LARGE-CAP VALUE		TEMPLETON GROWTH I	17.5
FIDELITY DESTINY I	22.9%	**DOMESTIC HYBRID**	
FIDELITY DESTINY II	22.4	BERWYN INCOME	12.6%
FIRST AMERICAN EQUITY-INCOME A**	15.3	CALDWELL & ORKIN MARKET OPPORTUNITY**	16.9
GABELLI EQUITY-INCOME**	18.2	ECLIPSE BALANCED**	14.9
OAKMARK	22.8	FOUNDERS BALANCED	16.9
T. ROWE PRICE EQUITY-INCOME	20.0	GREENSPRING	16.3
SMITH BARNEY PREMIUM TOTAL RETURN B	15.8	INCOME FUND OF AMERICA	15.1
VONTOBEL U.S. VALUE**	19.4	INVESCO TOTAL RETURN	15.9
MID-CAP VALUE		JANUS BALANCED	14.6
		MAIRS & POWER BALANCED**	16.3
MUTUAL BEACON Z	19.5%	T. ROWE PRICE CAPITAL APPRECIATION	14.8
MUTUAL QUALIFIED Z	20.0	WESTWOOD BALANCED**	17.6
MUTUAL SHARES Z	20.0	**INTERNATIONAL HYBRID**	
SOUND SHORE	21.5	MERRILL LYNCH GLOBAL ALLOCATION B	12.5%
MID-CAP BLEND		**NATURAL RESOURCES**	
EVERGREEN GROWTH & INCOME Y	20.3%		
EXCELSIOR VALUE & RESTRUCTURING A	27.2	T. ROWE PRICE NEW ERA	14.9%
LONGLEAF PARTNERS	21.4	**PRECIOUS METALS**	
MAP-EQUITY**	18.7	LEXINGTON STRATEGIC SILVER**	11.3%
MERGER	12.1	**UNALIGNED**	
MID-CAP GROWTH		FIDELITY SELECT DEFENSE & AEROSPACE**	24.4%
FIDELITY NEW MILLENNIUM	24.0%	**UTILITIES**	
FRANKLIN CALIF. GROWTH I	25.0	PUTNAM UTILITIES GROWTH & INCOME A	15.3%
MERRILL LYNCH GROWTH B	22.0		
T. ROWE PRICE MID-CAP GROWTH	21.4		
RIGHTIME**	8.0		

*1993–97 pretax returns, appreciation plus reinvestment of dividends and capital gains.

**Fund data in Business Week Online.

DATA: MORNINGSTAR INC.

The same risk-adjustment methodology applies to these ratings. A fund needs five years of performance history to qualify for a rating, which runs the gamut from A to F. The difference, though, is that we need at least seven funds with five-year histories in a category to rate the category, so not all of our categories have category-rated funds. But all the major domestic and international categories do have ratings.

For instance, in the world category (international funds that can also invest in the United States), Janus Worldwide Fund, Templeton Growth Fund I, and Mutual Discovery earned A's. The Janus and Templeton funds are "bottom-up" international equity investors. What that means is the fund managers choose the stocks first rather than choosing the market or country where the stock trades or the company is domiciled. In the other strategy—"top down"—funds make allocation bets on various countries depending on their macroeconomic and market outlooks and buy stocks to fill in the allocations. Not that the country doesn't matter, of course, in the bottom-up strategy. It's just not the overriding concern.

The third fund, Mutual Discovery, one of the Mutual Series funds is a little different. Its prospectus does not describe it as a world fund, except that it's allowed to invest in value stocks without regard to country of domicile. Right now, the fund's about 58 percent invested abroad, mainly in Europe. But if the situation changed, and European holdings were sold off, the fund could become a domestic player once again. Mutual Discovery also has an A for an overall rating.

The foreign funds with A category ratings are BT Investment International Equity, Fidelity Diversified International, Harbor International, Managers International Equity, and Waddell & Reed International Growth B. The BT fund merits attention for two reasons: its returns, 19.1 percent average annual returns for the five-year period, are well beyond the category average of 12.1; and the fund is still relatively small—just $547.7 million—and thus should be more fleet of foot.

Managers International Equity is split between two managers. One, John Rensberg of Lazard Freres Asset Management, is a traditional bottom-up stockpicker. The other, William Holzer of Scudder, Stevens & Clark, takes an approach that's more like top-down managers. He first identifies important global trends and then finds the stocks that can capitalize on them. Harbor International is closed to new investors, but portfolio manager Haken Castegren also runs Ivy International, a load fund.

The category ratings will help you to identify the best of the large-cap and small-cap growth funds, none of which earned A's in overall ratings. Among the large-cap growth funds, there are five: DG Equity, Gabelli Growth, Putnam Investors A, Vanguard Index Growth, and Vanguard U.S. Growth Fund. The last two are not the same. Vanguard U.S. Growth is an actively managed fund, while Vanguard Index Growth is an index fund comprised of the "growth" stocks in the S&P 500, as defined by their price–earnings and price-to-book value ratios.

Among the small-cap growth funds, the top-rated funds are the Baron Asset Fund, Managers Special Equity Fund, and SmallCap World Fund. Baron Asset Fund is an exceptional fund, able to compete effectively in the small-cap growth arena without loading up on the volatile technology stocks. In fact, Baron Asset has only 2.5 percent of its portfolio in technology while the average small-cap growth fund has a 25 percent weighting. Baron Asset isn't immune to pullbacks in the small-cap sector. Still, the fund is resilient enough to stay well ahead of its peers. In 1997, it even beat the S&P 500, earning a 33.9 percent return. The average small-cap fund was up 13.4 percent (Table 8-3). Over the last five years, its 24 percent average annual return is 10 percentage points a year better than its peer group. No wonder the fund is taking in new investors by the bucket loads. Its assets swelled 186 percent last year to $3.8 billion.

Managers Special Equity Fund really is special. The portfolio is divided among three stock-pickers from three different investment firms. Gary Pilgrim, manager of the PBHG Growth Fund, practices an investment style of buying emerging growth stocks with a lot of "momentum." They also have high p–e ratios, and when they falter, a lot of downside risk. Timothy Ebright runs his portion as a micro-cap value fund, not unlike Charles Royce. The third manager, Andrew Knuth, is a "growth-at-a-price" investor among the larger small-cap stocks. "Growth-at-a-price" investors will pay up for growth, but not chase the shooting stars that Pilgrim and others do. The three different management approaches make the fund a good choice for an investor who wants just one small-cap growth fund in his or her portfolio.

SPECIALTY FUNDS: FINANCIAL, REAL ESTATE, AND UTILITIES SHINE

Mutual funds that invest in financial companies—like banks, thrifts, brokerage firms, and insurance companies—soared an average of 47.1 percent in 1997. The economic environment was tailor-made for these companies. The economy cruised along in the seventh year of an expansion, inflation remained low, and interest rates came down. The stock market soared, which helped brokers and investment management companies, and a wave of takeovers ran across the whole sector. Banks were bought at historically high prices, banks acquired investment banks and brokerage firms at rich valuation levels, and even the stuffy insurors started their own mergers and acquisition game. All of these factors were great for financial funds in 1997.

And frankly, most of those factors had been working on behalf of these funds for some time. Financial funds' five-year returns are an average 25.5 percent, beating the high-flying technology sector by 5.5 percentage points. Better yet, technology funds can be extremely volatile while financial funds have at most an average risk rating.

Some of those same forces, low interest rates and an expanding economy, also worked on behalf of the real estate funds. They followed an extremely strong 1996 (34 percent gain) with an impressive 22.4 percent total return in 1997. Real estate funds have only been around a few years. They scored big returns because, in part, of new demand for the real estate investment trusts (REITs). These trusts are not unlike mutual funds, except they own office buildings, shopping malls, nursing homes, hotels, apartments, and other sorts of properties. The income for REITs is rent, which the REITs pass on to shareholders after taking out operating and finance expenses. When a REIT's properties are doing well, the rental income goes up—and so do the dividends to shareholders. REITs benefit both from the growth in the value of the underlying properties and growth in rental income. Some REITs are diversified, but many specialize in one kind of real estate investment.

Among the real estate funds, Cohen & Steers Realty Shares and Fidelity Real Estate Investment Fund are REIT investors only, while Longleaf Realty Partners and CGM Realty take a more aggressive tack, investing in building and construction companies as well. Such funds usually have lower yields.

Most investors really don't need specialty funds, since buying a technology or health fund is usually duplicative of something that's already in the diversified funds they own. But not so with REITs, which are little owned by conventional

TABLE 8-3

EQUITY FUND PERFORMANCE

U.S. diversified funds woefully lagged the S&P 500 in 1997, but real returns were high nonetheless.

Category	Average annual total return*			
	1997	1995–97	1993–97	1988–97
FINANCIAL	47.1%	39.3%	25.6%	23.4%
LARGE-CAP BLEND	27.6	26.4	17.3	15.7
MID-CAP VALUE	27.0	24.9	16.6	15.2
LARGE-CAP GROWTH	26.9	25.9	16.2	16.9
LARGE-CAP VALUE	26.7	26.3	17.8	15.8
SMALL-CAP VALUE	26.6	23.6	16.4	14.9
COMMUNICATIONS	26.5	20.1	17.4	18.0
LATIN AMERICA	26.0	9.7	11.3	NA
UTILITIES	25.7	20.7	12.7	12.3
UNALIGNED	25.4	23.1	16.1	17.2
MID-CAP BLEND	23.5	23.3	15.7	15.5
SMALL-CAP BLEND	23.2	22.5	14.8	14.1
REAL ESTATE	22.4	22.4	13.4	10.8
HEALTH	21.2	25.9	16.7	21.3
DOMESTIC HYBRID	17.9	18.7	12.9	12.5
EUROPE	17.8	20.0	18.4	10.9
MID-CAP GROWTH	15.2	21.7	15.0	16.1
SMALL-CAP GROWTH	13.4	20.4	14.5	16.7
WORLD	10.0	14.2	14.2	11.4
TECHNOLOGY	9.9	23.5	20.0	19.4
INTERNATIONAL HYBRID	7.2	10.5	9.6	7.3
FOREIGN	5.0	8.8	12.1	9.0
NATURAL RESOURCES	3.9	18.3	15.4	11.1
DIV. EMERGING MKTS.	−5.3	0.1	6.2	7.0
JAPAN	−16.8	−9.8	0.7	0.9
DIV. PACIFIC/ASIA	−29.0	−9.1	3.1	3.3
PAC. EX-JAPAN	−33.9	−9.1	0.6	4.6
PRECIOUS METALS	−42.0	−14.1	0.7	−4.1
U.S. DIVERSIFIED FUNDS	24.1	24.5	16.4	15.7
ALL EQUITY FUNDS	17.5	19.7	14.9	14.2
S&P 500	33.4	31.1	20.2	18.0

*Pretax return, appreciation plus reinvestment of dividends and capital gains.
NA=Not available

DATA: MORNINGSTAR INC.

mutual funds. As such, real estate funds bring a diversification to a total fund portfolio. Real estate is also considered a hedge against inflation, though inflation has not been a serious problem for the last several years. Precious metals funds used to be considered an inflation hedge, but they're far more volatile and lack the dividend income the REITs offer. Even if inflation is not a problem, REITs can make money just from the normal course of the real estate business.

The utilities funds were the comeback kids of 1997. They scored a 25.7 percent total return and delivered the goods almost as no one was paying attention. In a runaway bull market, investors pay scant attention to utilities, since their growth rates are slow and their dividends are fully taxable. And in 1994 and 1996, as interest rates climbed, the yield-sensitive utility stocks were creamed. If that wasn't enough, regulators in many states began the arduous process of deregulation, busting up the monopolies as was done in the telephone industry in the 1980s.

But in 1997, several factors converged to help the utilities. Interest rates came down, which always gives these stocks a boost of performance. Then, shrewd investors started to come back to this overlooked sector, trying to invest in the companies that would survive the tectonic regulatory changes. Merger and acquisition fever hit this industry as well, as the less efficient producers realized they needed greater size and efficiencies to compete in the coming new world of deregulated power.

Finally, when market volatility surged in the fourth quarter, investors who had not bought utilities in years came back to these relatively staid stocks in droves. In the fourth quarter alone, the S&P Utilities Index was up 15 percent versus 2.4 percent for the S&P 500. Indeed, one reason the index continued to outperform the stockpickers in that volatile environment was that the utilities make up 3 percent of the S&P 500, but only about 2 percent of the average U.S. diversified equity fund.

INTERNATIONAL SECTORS

Among the international sector funds, the stars were Europe and Latin America. European stocks rallied along with the United States. In Great Britain, like the United States, corporate profits were strong and so was mergers and acquisition activity. The driver on the Continent was better earnings, lower interest rates, and industry consolidation as Europe gets ready for monetary union in 1999. Even in the face of a rising dollar, the European funds gave shareholders a 17.8 percent return for 1997 and a 20 percent return for the last three years.

Latin America, up 26 percent, is quite a different story. The last year was the continuation of a comeback from disastrous years in 1994 and 1995. Both Brazil and Mexico, the leading Latin American markets, were strong enough to withstand a near panic from emerging markets investors that resulted from the market implosions in Asia. Still, the Brazilian market finished 1997 up 44 percent, and the Mexican market, up 55 percent. However, because of a poor 1995, the three-year average annual total return for the Latin American funds is just 9.7 percent. That's a lot better than at the end of 1996, when the three-year average was negative.

The strength in Latin America—and in some of the tiny markets of Eastern Europe and Africa—wasn't enough to keep the diversified emerging markets funds in the black. Their total returns were negative, down 5.3 percent for the year. But Asia weighs heavily in emerging markets funds so the troubles there dragged the whole sector down. The long-suffering Japanese funds, down 16.8 percent on average last year, did not look all that bad compared to other categories. Diversified Pacific/Asia funds, which can include Japanese stocks, were down 29 percent. The Pacific ex-Japan category, which exclude Japanese stocks, were even worse, down 33.9 percent.

Bad as those numbers are, mutual fund investors as a whole have not lost much money. There has never been all that much money in those funds in the first place. International equity funds in total make up about 15 percent of all equity fund assets; diversified emerging markets funds comprise only 7 percent of that 20 percent, or 1.4 percent of the total. Southeast Asian or Japanese funds are even thinner slices of the mutual fund pie.

The funds that did worse than the Asian funds were precious metals funds, down 42 percent. Not even the crises in Asia could create any excitement here. Gold funds fell early in the year after the collapse of Bre-X Minerals, a Canadian company that had supposedly discovered an enormous gold source in Indonesia. The stock—and that of most of the other small gold exploration companies—collapsed when it was discovered that the big gold find had likely been a fraud. That hit mainly the gold shares. But then gold bullion itself started to slide, hurt by a strong dollar and low inflation. On top of that, many central banks, which in the aggregate hold about half the world's gold reserves, started selling, and two big holders, Switzerland and Australia, said they would lighten up their holdings as well. If the Swiss don't want to own gold, who does? The price of gold slipped to an 18-year low.

BIG IS BEAUTIFUL

In theory, at least, small funds should be better performers. They're fleet of foot, able to dart into and out of stocks without leaving tracks. Their shrewd managers have come and made their money before the rest of the crowd shows up. But 1997's results show you shouldn't underestimate the behemoths, either.

Sure big funds tend to invest in large-cap stocks, and so they did well because large-cap stocks did well. Still, some of the giants racked up impressive results nonetheless. Washington Mutual Investors, a $38 billion fund that's about as staid an equity fund as there is, delivered a 33.3 percent total return, one-tenth of a percentage point behind the S&P 500. Fidelity Growth & Income, $35.8 billion in assets, earned a 30.2 percent total return, besting the $63 billion Fidelity Magellan by 4 percentage points.

With Magellan now closed to new investors, Growth & Income seems set to step into the limelight as the company's new flagship. To keep risk under control, Growth & Income manager Steven Kaye balances the fund with both value and growth stocks, and downplays high technology. "I like getting a good night's sleep," says Kaye. Asian troubles, he says, might shave corporate profits some, but that damage should be offset by lower interest rates. His biggest bet now is health-care stocks: "The fundamentals are great, and I don't have to worry about the economy."

In the latest Scoreboard, 6 of the 25 largest equity funds earned A ratings for overall performance. They are Fidelity Advisor Growth Opportunity, Fidelity Equity-Income, Fidelity Growth & Income, Washington Mutual Investors, Vanguard/Windsor II, and Income Fund of America. And five of the top 25 earned B+, the second highest rating. They are Dean Witter Dividend Growth B, Fidelity Equity-Income II, Fidelity Puritan, Vanguard Index 500, and Vanguard/Wellington.

Bond Funds

Suppose the bond market staged a rally and nobody came. Well, that's sort of what happened during 1997. After a rocky start—rising interest rates caused bond fund losses in the first quarter—long-term interest rates trended downward for the remainder of the year. All told, bond funds, both taxable and tax-free, earned an average annual total return of 8.3 percent.

Yet the investment-grade bond funds, both government and municipal, that are best able to take advantage of a bond market rally were all but ignored by investors. Bond funds attracted their biggest cash flows in three years. But by and large, most of the money went toward high-yield bond funds.

Even with the drop in rates, investors who chose high-yield or "junk" bonds over investment-grade corporate and government funds did not make a mistake. High-yield funds, investing in the least creditworthy of all issuers, continued to earn high returns—13.2 percent total returns in 1997. That even beat the 13.1 percent total return earned by the average long-term government bond fund, the category of fund most sensitive to falling rates. The only category of bond fund to beat the high-yield category was the convertible, which logged a 17 percent gain.

It's not surprising that high-yields and convertibles continued to do so well. They are the sectors of the bond market most closely tied to the stock market. Convertibles' connection to stocks is obvious. Most of the companies that issue convertibles would probably be paying junk bond rates of interest if they issued straight debt. But by tying their bonds to their stock market fortunes, they're able to issue those bonds at a much lower interest rate. The bonds generally rise in value along with the underlying equity. As long as the stock is heading up, so does the convertible bond—though at a slower rate.

Perhaps less obvious is the high-yield bonds' connection to the stock market. These bonds are issued by less creditworthy companies, either start-ups without a long credit history or more mature companies with a lot of debt sitting atop a small cushion of equity.

High-yield bonds have a closer correlation with the stock market than the U.S. government bond market. That's because factors like rising corporate earnings improve the creditworthiness—and prices—for high-yield bonds. So does the ability to sell stock to the public. The more stock, or equity, on a company's balance sheet, the better the company's creditworthiness.

Given the strength of the stock market over the last five years, it's no wonder that the list of top-performing bond funds is dominated by the high-yield funds (Table 8-4). This list would put a

Bond funds rallied, but investors didn't notice.

TABLE 8-4

TOP-PERFORMING BOND MUTUAL FUNDS

These 83 funds stand out among all bond funds in the BUSINESS WEEK Mutual Fund Scoreboard.
They earned A's, meaning they achieved superior risk-adjusted returns over the past five years.

Fund	Average annual total return*	Investment category	Fund	Average annual total return*	Investment category
AIM HIGH-YIELD A	12.1%	High Yield	MERRILL LYNCH CORP. HI.-INC. B	10.3%	High Yield
AIM TAX-FREE INTERMEDIATE	5.7	Muni. Short	MERRILL LYNCH MUNI. LTD. MAT. B**	3.6	Muni. Short
AMERICAN CENT.-BEN. CA. MUNI. HY	8.2	Muni. S-S Long	MFS HIGH-INCOME A	11.6	High Yield
AMERICAN CENT.-BEN. CA. T/F LIM.**	4.5	Muni. Short	NICHOLAS INCOME	10.7	High Yield
AMERICAN HIGH-INCOME	11.3	High Yield	NORTHEAST INVESTORS	15.2	High Yield
CALVERT TAX-FR. RES. LTD.-TERM A	4.0	Muni. Short	NORTHSTAR HIGH-YIELD T	10.9	High Yield
COLONIAL HIGH-YIELD MUNI. B**	6.6	Muni. Natl. Long	NUVEEN MUNICIPAL BOND R	6.9	Muni. Natl. Long
COLONIAL HIGH-YIELD SECS. A	12.2	High Yield	OPPENHEIMER CHAMPION INCOME A	12.0	High Yield
COLORADO BONDSHARES**	8.3	Muni. S-S Interm.	OPPENHEIMER HIGH-YIELD A	11.6	High Yield
DAVIS CONVERTIBLE SECS. A	18.2	Convertibles	T. ROWE PRICE TAX-FREE HIGH-YIELD	7.8	Muni. Natl. Long
DAVIS TAX-FREE HIGH INCOME B	6.2	Muni. Short	T. ROWE PRICE T/F SHORT-INTERM.	4.8	Muni. Short
DELAWARE NATL. HI-YLD. MUNI. A**	7.8	Muni. Natl. Interm.	PRUDENTIAL CA. MUNI. CA. INCOME A	8.5	Muni. S-S Long
DREYFUS SHORT-INTRM. MUNI.	4.5	Muni. Short	PUTNAM HIGH YIELD A	11.5	High Yield
DUPREE KY. TAX-FREE SHORT-MED.**	4.4	Muni. Short	SAFECO HIGH-YIELD NO LOAD**	10.5	High Yield
EATON VANCE INCOME OF BOSTON	12.2	High Yield	SELIGMAN HIGH-YIELD BOND A	13.7	High Yield
ENTERPRISE HIGH-YIELD BOND A	11.8	High Yield	SELIGMAN MUNICIPAL CA. H-Y A**	7.0	Muni. S-S Interm.
EV MARATHON HIGH-INCOME	11.4	High Yield	SIT TAX-FREE INCOME	7.5	Muni. Short
EVERGREEN FL. HIGH-INC. MUNI. A**	8.8	High S-S Long	SMITH BARNEY HIGH-INCOME B	10.9	High Yield
EXCELSIOR SHORT-TM. T/E SECS.	4.1	Muni. Short	SMITH BARNEY MUNI. LTD. TERM A	6.1	Muni. Natl. Interm.
EXECUTIVE INVESTORS HI-YIELD**	11.5	High Yield	STATE ST. RESEARCH HIGH-INC. A	12.5	High Yield
FBL HIGH-YIELD BOND**	8.9	High Yield	STEIN ROE HIGH-YIELD MUNIS	7.3	Muni. Natl. Long
FEDERATED HIGH-YIELD	11.8	High Yield	STI CLASSIC INV. GR. T/E INV.**	8.0	Muni. Natl. Interm.
FEDERATED SH-TRM. MUNI. INST.	4.1	Muni. Short	STRONG ADVANTAGE	6.5	Ultrashort
FIDELITY ADV. HI-YIELD T	13.4	High Yield	THORNBURG INTERM. MUNI A	6.8	Muni. Natl. Interm
FIDELITY CAPITAL & INCOME	12.2	High Yield	THORNBURG LTD-TERM CA. A*	5.2	Muni. Short
FIDELITY SPARTAN HIGH-INCOME	14.7	High Yield	THORNBURG LTD.-TERM NATL. A	5.3	Muni. Short
FIDELITY SPARTAN SH.-INT. MUNI.	4.9	Muni. Short	U.S. GLOBAL INV. NEAR-TRM. T/F	5.4	Muni. Short
FIRST INVEST. FUND FOR INCOME A	12.3	High Yield	UNITED HIGH-INCOME A	11.3	High Yield
FIRST INVEST. HIGH-YIELD A	11.8	High Yield	UNITED HIGH-INCOME II A	11.2	High Yield
FORUM TAXSAVER BOND**	6.8	Muni. Natl. Interm.	UNITED MUNICIPAL HIGH-INC. A	8.9	Muni. Natl. Long
FRANKLIN AGE HIGH INCOME I	12.0	High Yield	USAA TAX-EXEMPT INTERM.-TERM	7.1	Muni. Natl. Interm.
FRANKLIN FED INT-TRM. T/F INCOME**	7.1	Muni. Natl. Interm.	USAA TAX-EXEMPT SHORT-TERM	4.9	Muni. Short
FRANKLIN FED TAX-FREE INCOME I	7.1	Muni. Natl. Long	VALUE LINE AGGRESSIVE INCOME	13.3	High Yield
FRANKLIN HIGH YIELD T/F INCOME I	8.6	Muni. Natl. Long	VAN KAMPEN AM CAP HI-INC. A	11.4	High Yield
FRANKLIN PA TAX-FREE INCOME I	7.1	Muni. S-S Long	VAN KAMPEN AM. CAP. HI-YIELD A	10.8	High Yield
FRANKLIN TX TAX-FREE INCOME I**	7.1	Muni. S-S Long	VAN KAMP. AM. CAP. HI-YLD MUNI. A	8.1	Muni. Natl. Interm.
HANCOCK HIGH-YIELD BOND B	11.9	High Yield	VANGUARD F/I HIGH-YIELD CORP.	11.2	High Yield
INVESCO HIGH-YIELD	11.6	High Yield	VANGUARD MUNI. INTERM.-TERM	6.7	Muni. Natl. Interm.
KEMPER HIGH-YIELD A	11.9	High Yield	VANGUARD MUNI. LIMITED-TERM	4.8	Muni. Short
KEY SBSF CONVERTIBLE SECS.	14.2	Convertibles	VANGUARD MUNI. SHORT-TERM	3.8	Muni. Short
LIMITED TERM NY MUNICIPAL A	6.4	Muni. Short	WARBURG PINCUS NY INT. MUNI.**	5.8	Muni. Short
MAINSTAY HI-YIELD CORP. BOND B	13.8	High Yield			

*1993–97 pretax returns, includes appreciation plus reinvestment of dividends and capital gains.
**For more data, see Business Week Online.

DATA: MORNINGSTAR INC.

big smile on the face of Michael R. Milken, the one-time junk bond king of Wall Street. The theory behind junk bonds is that while there's greater risk of default, higher yields more than make up for occasional bad bonds.

What's also noteworthy about the top performers' list is what's not on it: a government bond fund. How is that, especially since the fed-eral budget is now running at surplus for the first time in 30 years? Remember that the BUSINESS WEEK ratings are based on the last five years. Three of those years—1993, 1995, and 1997—were characterized by falling interest rates and rising bond prices. But 1996 showed mixed results, and 1994 was the bond market's worst year in six decades. That year lowered returns, and more significant in our rating system, raised risk. As such, government bond funds turn up only so-so ratings.

But even without 1994, government bond funds are not compelling. In the corporate or muni markets, smart credit research and good portfolio management can pay off. But in the government bond market, the most efficient securities market in the world, there are few inefficiencies to uncover and little value added by fund managers, especially after taking into account sales charges and ongoing fund expenses.

Still, if you want to invest in a government bond fund, we now have category ratings that will help you identify those that earned the highest risk-adjusted returns in each category. To derive these ratings, we go through the same process as with the equity fund category ratings.

The category ratings are particularly useful to the opportunistic investors. Suppose you are convinced that long-term interest rates will soon begin to fall, and fall hard. Under those circumstances, the best investment is a long-term government bond fund. But the best overall rating you will find for a long-term government fund is B, and most are D's and F's. But what if you rate the long-term government bond funds against each other instead of against all taxable funds. Checking the category ratings, you will find the Wasatch-Hoisington U.S. Treasury Fund with an A category rating. Table 8-5 lists the bond funds that are tops in their categories.

HIGH YIELD AND CONVERTS
LOOK GREAT, BUT . . .

Before you rush to high-yield funds, remember that you're viewing them under near ideal conditions. Over the past five years, the period for these ratings, junk bonds have had the wind at their backs. Interest rates fell, allowing many issuers to refinance; corporate cash flows swelled, improving issuers' ability to service their debt; and the economy, though slow at times, continued to grow and stayed clear of recession. And the default rate on junk bonds plummeted as well.

Managers of top-rated high-yield funds acknowledge that things have gone well since 1991 and are mindful that things might not always be so bright. And they acknowledge the linkage with the equity market may make these funds less attractive now. "We're starting to see some of the pressure that's on the equity market spill over to high-yields," says Thomas T. Sorviero,

portfolio manager of the A-rated Fidelity Spartan High-Income Fund. But Sorviero says he prepared for this by deemphasizing bonds from global industries such as paper, energy, and steel, and emphasizing the more domestic broadcasting, cable, and telecommunications issuers.

Still, if the high-yield bonds go into a bear market, it won't be as bad as the 1989–1990 period. Back then, the preponderance of bonds were issued by more leveraged companies and had higher interest rates. Now, the companies are less leveraged, more creditworthy, and, on average, paying lower interest rates than back then.

Indeed, interest rates on high-yield bonds have come down so much that they're now in the 8-to-9 percent range, and don't seem very high-yield at all. Some investment advisers ask if it's even worthwhile to invest in high-yields when the rates relative to government bonds are so low. But that's not the point. Because high-yield bonds don't have a strong correlation with bond funds in general, adding a high-yield fund to an income-oriented portfolio makes some sense.

High-yield bond funds can supplement and diversfy an equity fund portfolio as well. With the yield on stocks a measly 1.6 percent, a stock market investor who's looking for a little more income might find the high-yield funds a good alternative to stocks—more income and a little less appreciation. Any one of the high-yield funds on the top performers' list would make a good candidate for investment. The highest-rated of these highly rated funds are the three that received A category ratings: Fidelity Spartan High-Income, MainStay Hi-Yield Corporate Bond B, and Northeast Investors.

If the hyperbullish stock market slows to a snail's pace in 1998, will the convertible bond funds—bond-fund performance leaders for the last one-, three-, and five-year periods—get slammed (Table 8-6)? That depends on the degree to which stock prices slow or sink. Richard Janus, portfolio manager of the A-rated Key SBSF Convertible Securities, thinks converts are well-suited for today's environment. "In an equity market with a gentle upward or downward bias, we'll do just fine," he says. "And we'll lose less money than stocks in a bear market. But there's no way convertibles can keep up with the stock market when it's up 30 percent."

Well, Andrew Davis of top-drawer Davis Convertible Securities A came darn close. The fund earned a 27.8 percent total return versus 33.4

> High-yield bond funds diversify an equity portfolio.

TABLE 8-5

THE BEST PERFORMERS IN THEIR CATEGORIES

Rating bond funds by category, we awarded A's to these funds.
They delivered superior risk-adjusted returns when compared with their peers.

Fund	Average annual total return*	Fund	Average annual total return*
SHORT (GENERAL)		**MUNICIPAL SHORT**	
DREYFUS SHORT-TERM INCOME	6.9%	DAVIS TAX-FREE HIGH INCOME B	6.2%
HARBOR SHORT DURATION	5.4	**MUNICIPAL NATIONAL INTERMEDIATE**	
STRONG SHORT-TERM BOND	6.6	DELAWARE NATL. HI-YLD. MUNI. A**	7.8%
INTERMEDIATE (GENERAL)		STI CLASSIC INV. GR. T/E INV.**	8.0
CITIZENS INCOME**	7.7%	VAN KAMPEN AM. CAP. H-Y MUNI. A	8.1
FEDERATED BOND F	9.6	**MUNICIPAL NATIONAL LONG**	
FORUM INVESTORS BOND**	8.3	COLONIAL HIGH-YIELD MUNI. B**	6.6%
FPA NEW INCOME	8.2	FRANKLIN FED. TAX-FREE INC. I	7.1
STRONG CORPORATE BOND	11.3	FRANKLIN HIGH YLD. T/F INC. I	8.6
TIP: CLOVER FIXED-INCOME**	7.9	NUVEEN MUNICIPAL BOND R	6.9
WARBURG PINCUS FIXED-INCOME COM.	8.0	T. ROWE PRICE TAX-FR. EE HIGH-YIELD	7.8
LONG (GENERAL)		PRUDENTIAL MUNI. HIGH-YIELD B	7.3
FBL HIGH-GRADE BOND**	6.8%	STEIN ROE HIGH-YIELD MUNIS	7.3
INVESCO SELECT INCOME	9.2	UNITED MUNICIPAL HIGH-INCOME A	8.9
SHORT GOVERNMENT		**MUNICIPAL SINGLE-STATE INTERMEDIATE**	
FEDERATED ARMS INSTL. SVC.	4.9%	COLORADO BONDSHARES**	8.3%
MONTGOMERY SH. DUR. GOVT. R**	6.5	DELAWARE-VOYAGEUR T/F INT. A**	5.3
NEW ENGLAND ADJ. RATE U.S. GOVT. A	5.0	FRANKLIN CA INTERM.-TERM T/F**	7.1
SIT U.S. GOVERNMENT SECS.	6.7	IDAHO TAX-EXEMPT**	6.0
INTERMEDIATE GOVERNMENT		PUTNAM NY TAX EXEMPT OPPORT. A	6.9
ACCESSOR MORTGAGE SECURITIES	7.1%	SELIGMAN MUNICIPAL CA H/Y A**	7.0
AMER. CENT.-BEN. GNMA INV.	6.8	**MUNICIPAL SINGLE-STATE LONG**	
CARDINAL GOVT. OBLIGATIONS	6.4	AMERICAN CENT.-BEN. CA. MUNI. HIGH-YLD.	8.2%
DREYFUS BASIC GNMA**	7.6	EVERGREEN FL HIGH-INC. MUNI. A**	8.8
FIDELITY MORT. SECS. INIT.	7.9	FIDELITY SPARTAN PA MUNI. INC.	7.3
LEXINGTON GNMA INCOME	7.4	FRANKLIN AL TAX-FREE INC. I	7.2
SMITH BREEDEN INTERM. DUR. GOV.**	7.8	FRANKLIN AZ TAX-FREE INC. I	6.6
USAA GNMA	7.1	FRANKLIN CA TAX-FREE INC. I	6.9
VANGUARD F/I GNMA	7.2	FRANKLIN CO TAX-FREE INC. I	7.1
LONG GOVERNMENT		FRANKLIN FL TAX-FREE INC. I	7.0
WASATCH-HOISINGTON U.S. TREAS.**	8.0%	FRANKLIN GA TAX-FREE INC. I**	6.8
CONVERTIBLES		FRANKLIN IN TAX-FREE INCOME**	6.9
KEY SBSF CONVERTIBLE SECS.	14.2%	FRANKLIN LA TAX-FREE INC. I**	6.7
HIGH YIELD		FRANKLIN MA INS. T/F INC. I	6.8
FIDELITY SPARTAN HIGH-INCOME	14.7%	FRANKLIN MO TAX-FREE INC. I	7.3
MAINSTAY HI-YIELD CORP. BD. B	13.8	FRANKLIN NY TAX-FREE INC. I	6.9
NORTHEAST INVESTORS	15.2	FRANKLIN PA TAX-FREE INC. I	7.1
MULTISECTOR		FRANKLIN TX TAX-FREE INC. I	7.1
T. ROWE PRICE SPECTRUM INCOME	9.7%	FRANKLIN VA TAX-FREE INC. I	7.0
INTERNATIONAL		OCEAN STATE TAX-EXEMPT**	6.3
GLOBAL TOTAL RETURN A	10.3%	T. ROWE PRICE MD TAX-FREE**	7.1
PAYDEN & RYGEL GLOBAL F/I A	8.4	PRUDENTIAL CA MUNI. CA INC. A	8.5
PRUDENTIAL INTL. BOND A	10.6	SMITH BARNEY MUNI. FL A	7.7
		TAX-FREE FUND OF VT	5.8
		USAA VA BOND	7.3

*1993–97 pretax returns, includes appreciation plus reinvestment of dividends and capital gains.

**For more data, see Business Week Online.

DATA: MORNINGSTAR INC.

TABLE 8-6

BOND FUND PERFORMANCE

The best returns came from funds that track the stock market—convertibles and high-yield funds. Falling interest rates made long-term funds stand out as well.

	Average annual total return*		
	1997	1995–97	1993–97
CONVERTIBLES	17.0%	17.8%	12.6%
HIGH YIELD	13.2	14.4	11.4
LONG GOVERNMENT	13.1	12.1	8.4
LONG-TERM (CORP.)	10.4	11.3	7.9
MUNI. NATL. LONG	9.3	9.9	6.9
MUNI. S.S. LONG	8.9	9.7	6.8
INTERMEDIATE (GEN.)	8.7	9.7	7.0
INTERM GOVT.	8.4	9.2	6.2
MULTISECTOR	8.4	11.5	8.5
MUNI NATL. INTERM.	7.7	8.3	6.2
MUNI S.S. INTERM.	7.4	8.3	6.2
SHORT-TERM (GEN.)	6.6	7.4	5.5
SHORT GOVERNMENT	6.5	7.2	5.0
ULTRASHORT (GEN.)	5.5	5.8	4.7
MUNI. SHORT	5.3	5.8	5.0
INTERNATIONAL BOND	2.7	9.9	6.2
ALL BOND FUNDS	8.3	9.4	6.8
TAXABLE BOND FUNDS	8.3	9.8	7.1
TAX-FREE BOND FUNDS	8.3	9.1	6.6

*Pretax returns, appreciation plus reinvestment of dividends and capital gains.

DATA: MORNINGSTAR INC.

percent for the S&P 500 and 17 percent for convertible funds. His secret? "The 80-50 rule," says Davis. "I don't invest in a convert unless I believe it will give me at least 80 percent of the return of the common stock and no more than 50 percent of any losses on the common."

Investors looking to diversify away from the equity market should choose an investment-grade or even government bond fund, especially if they fear a slower economy ahead. You won't find those funds on the overall A list, but in the category ratings. In the general bond area, check out Dreyfus Short-Term Income, Strong Corporate Bond, and Invesco Select Income. For government funds, Sit U.S. Government Securities and Fidelity Mortgage Securities are among the highly rated.

INTERNATIONAL BONDS BITE BACK

Investment advisers usually recommend international bond funds as well as domestic funds for the same reasons as they tell people to invest in international equity funds: diversification and a chance for higher returns. That remains true for long periods of time, but it was certainly not true in the recent past. In 1997, international bond funds earned average annual returns of 2.7 percent.

Blame it on the emerging markets? Not really. True, the currency meltdowns in Thailand, Indonesia, and the Phillipines hurt the emerging markets debt funds—a big part of the international bond category—but not as much as you think. The majority of emerging markets bonds are dollar-denominated bonds, mainly issues from Latin America. Still, when the crisis hit in Asia, there were sympathetic sell-offs in all the emerging markets. But those funds managed to finish the year well in the black. Fidelity New Markets Income finished the year up 17.4 percent, with a 9.5 percent yield; T. Rowe Price Emerging Markets Bond, up 16.9 percent, with an 8.2 percent yield.

This time the trouble was in the investment grade international funds, and the main culprit was the U.S. dollar. When the dollar rises, other currencies fall in value. International bond funds, which invest in other currencies' securities, can get hit with capital losses. After all, a yen-denominated bond goes down in value as the dollar rises against the yen, and the yen interest payments also decline in value.

Most international bond funds have the ability to hedge their portfolios against some adverse currencies moves. But complete hedging costs too much, and the hedging job can be botched as well. In fact, few fund managers have done it well consistently. Besides, if you hedge the currency portion of the non-U.S. bond, you are taking away some of the benefit of diversification.

MUNI FUNDS PARTY— BUT NOBODY SHOWS

The story for municipal bond funds is much the same as it is for all but the high-yield bond funds. Investors just aren't interested. No matter that interest rates are down and credit quality is up— and muni bonds are one of the few tax-free instruments out there. The lure of the stock market is just too much.

But if investors start to see bond funds less as an income instrument and more as a way to diversify a portfolio, then they should consider muni bond funds. For sure, these funds are inappropriate for tax-deferred retirement accounts, but they are probably the bond fund of choice in all taxable accounts. They can't compete with high-yield corporate funds. (High-yield muni funds yield less than a percentage point more than conventional long-term funds.) But the muni funds can likely beat the aftertax returns of a government or investment-grade corporate fund in a taxable account.

Among the top-performing tax-free funds, Franklin funds rule. In part, that's because the company, with $49 billion in tax-free bond funds, is by far the largest in the business and thus has more funds to rate. Franklin Resources, Inc., based in San Mateo, California, has a huge asset base that affords it a large in-house research effort and gives the company a seat at the table when investment bankers and issuers are putting together a muni bond deal. Franklin buys about 90 percent of its muni bonds in the new issues market.

But that's not all. Thomas Kenny, who heads municipal bond research at Franklin, says the firm's managers stress income, not total return, in running their funds. As such, Franklin always buys current coupon bonds at or near par. In a falling rate environment, says Kenny, many other companies' fund managers buy lower-coupon discount bonds, which will rise in value if rates fall. "If the market rallies, we'll lag," Kenny admits. "But if rates rise, we won't be hurt as much. And we're still getting those higher yields."

Franklin's funds come at a price. They're broker-sold and have sales charges. But price-sensitive fund investors can find plenty of no-load fund managers, which also show they can deliver excellent risk-adjusted returns. For muni funds, good no-load alternatives include Dreyfus Short-Intermediate Muni, Fidelity Spartan Short-Intermediate Muni, T. Rowe Price Tax-Free High-Yield, Sit Tax-Free Income, Stein Roe High-Yield Munis, USAA Tax-Exempt Intermediate-Term, and three Vanguard Municipal offerings: Intermediate-Term, Limited-Term, and Short-Term.

Closed-End Funds

After the spectacular gains made in the stock market over the past year, a real bargain is hard to find—unless you shop among the closed-end funds. Many of these quirky funds, which invest like mutual funds but are bought and sold like stocks, have racked up impressive results in the last few years yet trade at prices that are discounts to their net asset values. (Remember what we said in Chapter 2: The price at which a closed-end fund trades is what the market will bear, not the value of its portfolio.) The closed-end fund market is the only place on Wall Street where you can buy $1 in assets for 90 cents.

But you have to shop carefully. For instance, were you thinking of playing a shrewd contrarian and snapping up some closed-end Asian equity funds while those markets are bleeding? Think twice. In early 1998, many of the funds traded at huge premiums to their bloodied net asset value. The Malaysia Fund traded at a 76.2 percent premium to NAV, the Indonesia Fund at a 114.7 percent premium, and the Thai Fund at a 145.5 percent premium. Put it this way, instead of getting $1 worth of assets for 90 cents, investing in shares of the Thai Fund at a 145.5 percent premium gets you 41 cents worth of assets for every dollar.

That battered funds sell for far more than they're worth doesn't make much sense. But this is the weird world of closed-end funds. There are several reasons for this phenomenon. For starters, the premium is the difference between the market price and the net asset value. And though investors and traders at the New York Stock Exchange can see the values in those country funds melting away, they don't have minute-by-minute information on the underlying stock as they do, say, the prices of General Electric or IBM. So the market prices of the fund shares don't fall in lockstep with the NAVs. "The net asset value of the fund collapses, but the share price doesn't collapse as much," says closed-end fund specialist Thomas J. Herzfeld of the Miami firm that bears his name. Still, the Asian meltdown started in mid-1997, and the fund shares have had more than enough time to catch up.

But in some cases, the premiums have actually increased. One reason is that traders sometimes buy the shares, betting on small upticks for quick in-and-out profits. "If you buy the fund at $3 and sell at $4, you've made a third on your money," says Herzfeld, who "flips" closed-end shares himself. Those who make such trades do so because they sense a short-term trading opportunity. They're not really concerned with the longer-term fundamentals. But Herzfeld cautions all but the trading pros from dabbling in high-premium closed-ends because of the "unfavorable risk-reward ratio."

These premiums will not persist. Indeed, if the Asian stock markets revive and the fund NAVs

Beaten-up Asian funds sell at premiums.

recover, the shares could eventually sell at discounts again. That's what happened to the Latin American funds, which three years ago were in much the same position as the Asian funds today. In 1997, the Mexico Fund was up 51.2 percent in NAV, but its shares gained only 45.5 percent in trading on the New York Stock Exchange. During the year, the fund discount ran as deep as 27.3 percent and as little as 15.3 percent.

Ironically, many of the closed-ends with the favorable risk-reward characteristics, those rated A, trade at discounts to their NAV. That makes them better investments for those with the longer-term view in mind (Table 8-7). The A-rated Salomon Brothers Fund, for instance, which earned an average of 30 percent a year on its portfolio over the last three years, trades at a discount of 9.6 percent. That's about midway in the range of discounts in which it traded during 1997. The fund shares a portfolio manager with the open-end Salomon Brothers Investors Fund. Both are large-cap blend funds and have near identical one- and three-year records. And the mutual fund charges loads, which can add as much as 5 percent to the cost.

Or look at Adams Express, another A-rated closed-end equity fund. It opened its doors just a few weeks before the 1929 stock market crash and has always made capital preservation a high priority. Not surprisingly, it's a low-risk fund. Yet Adams Express, with a large-cap blend investment style, still earns respectable returns: 30.6 percent NAV return in 1997, and an average 27.1 percent return for the 1995–1997 period. The discount in early 1998 was 15.5 percent.

Though buying Adams Express at a discount can be a smart move, don't buy it with the expectation that the discount will disappear. Gregg Wolper, closed-end fund editor for *Morningstar Mutual Funds*, says that many closed-ends, especially the older ones, are almost always at a discount. The discount can narrow or widen, but don't expect it to disappear. The reason to buy the fund, he says, is because you believe it will be a good investment for you.

That said, discounts on closed-end U.S. funds have been narrowing. Herzfeld data show they went from an average of about 10 percent in early 1997 to around 5 percent in early 1998. The reason? For starters, there's a growing interest by investors in these funds, and hence, greater demand. And Herzfeld believes some traders might be taking positions in the shares trading at a discount to NAV, figuring they can force the fund's board to convert to an open-end mutual fund, thereby instantly eliminating the discount. But though there have been a few conversions in the last few years—and more shareholder lobby-

TABLE 8-7

TOP-PERFORMING CLOSED-END FUNDS

These funds have earned A's for superior risk-adjusted returns.

	Average annual total return*		Average annual total return*
EQUITY FUNDS			
ADAMS EXPRESS	27.1%	HANCOCK BANK & THRIFT OPPORTUNITY	45.7%
DELAWARE DIVIDEND & INCOME	24.8	SALOMON BROTHERS FUND	30.0
DELAWARE GLOB. DIVIDEND & INCOME	21.0	SOURCE CAPITAL	22.8
FIRST FINANCIAL	44.0	SOUTHEASTERN THRIFT & BANK	43.5
BOND FUNDS			
APEX MUNICIPAL	10.9%	MUNICIPAL INCOME OPPORTUNITIES	9.3%
CIGNA HIGH-INCOME SHARES	18.1	MUNICIPAL INCOME OPPORTUNITIES II	10.5
CNA INCOME SHARES	17.2	MUNICIPAL INCOME OPPORTUNITIES III	10.5
COLONIAL INTERMEDIATE HIGH-INCOME	17.3	NEW AMERICA HIGH-INCOME	19.5
CORPORATE HIGH-YIELD	16.9	PREFERRED INCOME	17.4
ELLSWORTH CONVERTIBLE GRWTH. & INC.	24.1	PREFERRED INCOME MANAGEMENT	19.7
HANCOCK PATRIOT PREFERRED DIVIDEND	18.2	PREFERRED INCOME OPPORTUNITY	18.6
HIGH-YIELD PLUS	15.8	PUTNAM MGD. HIGH-YIELD	16.7
HIGHLANDER INCOME	15.5	PUTNAM TAX-FREE HEALTH CARE	10.9
MANAGED HIGH INCOME	15.6	SALOMON BROS. HIGH INCOME	17.3
MORGAN STANLEY HIGH-YIELD	20.6	VAN KAMP. AM. CAP. INTERMEDIATE HIGH-INC.	16.1
MUNIASSETS	12.6	VAN KAMP. AM. CAP. LTD.-TERM HIGH-INC.	16.4
MUNICIPAL HIGH-INCOME	10.9	ZENIX INCOME	19.5

*1995–97, pretax return based on appreciation of net asset value plus reinvestment of dividends and capital gains.

DATA: MORNINGSTAR INC.

ing for conversions—they are still not easy to effect. Again, if you're buying a closed-end, do it for the investment. Any profits from a conversion will be icing on the cake.

Among the closed-end bond funds, the discount and premium story has remained much the same all through 1997 and into 1998. The funds with the highest payouts generally trade at premiums to NAV. With interest rates having fallen so much, "Yield is scarce, and investors will pay up for it," says Morningstar's Wolper. And it's not only the drop in longer-term rates that have made the quest for yield so difficult. In 1997 especially, most of the rate drop was in the longer-term maturities, not in the short. By early 1998, there was little difference between short-term and long-term interest rates. That made it difficult for funds to boost yields by leveraging the portfolio. In that sort of transaction, the fund borrows money in the short-term market and buys longer-term bonds.

Buying any bond funds strictly on their yield can be a dangerous move. You have to look further: the fund could be taking on unreasonable credit or currency risk, or it may own bonds that could be called away and would have to be replaced with lower yielding securities. Still,

Wolper says, if the fund passes muster, it's okay to buy at a modest premium.

Take, for instance, the A-rated Van Kampen American Capital Intermediate-Term High Income, which in early 1998 sold at a 12.9 percent premium. Is it worth it? Start with its payout of 5.8 cents a month, or 70 cents a year (ask your broker or Van Kampen for the current distribution rate); then divide that figure by the market price of the shares—$7.25. That makes the current yield a plump 9.65 percent—4 percentage points over intermediate Treasuries. As long as you determine the portfolio is sound, there shouldn't be any problem in paying a modest premium for the fund.

Still, before paying a 10 percent premium for a high-yield closed-end fund, take another look at the high-yield bond mutual funds, especially the top-performing funds such as Northeast Investors or Fidelity Spartan High-Income. If you still want to consider closed-ends, consider the multi-sector bond funds. Some of these funds have a good portion of their assets in high-yield bonds, yet they trade at discounts to NAV. That translates into current yields that are nearly as high as those on the high-yield funds that sell at big premiums.

The BUSINESS WEEK
Mutual Fund Scoreboard

Equity Funds

MUTUAL FUND SCOREBOARD

How to Use the Tables

BUSINESS WEEK RATINGS
Overall ratings are based on five-year, risk-adjusted returns. They are calculated by subtracting a fund's risk-of-loss factor (see RISK) from historical pretax total return. To get a positive rating, the fund must beat the S&P 500 on a risk-adjusted basis. Category ratings are based on risk-adjusted returns of the funds in that category. The ratings are as follows:

A	SUPERIOR
B+	VERY GOOD
B	ABOVE AVERAGE
C	AVERAGE
C–	BELOW AVERAGE
D	POOR
F	VERY POOR

MANAGEMENT CHANGES
👤 indicates the fund's manager has held the job at least 10 years; 👤 indicates a new manager since Dec. 31, 1996.

S&P 500 COMPARISON
The pretax total returns for the S&P 500 are as follows: 1997, 33.4%; three-year average (1995-1997), 31.1%; five-year average (1993-97), 20.2%; 10-year average (1988-97), 18.0%.

CATEGORY
Each U.S. diversified fund is classified by market capitalization of the stocks in the portfolio and by the nature of those stocks. If the median market cap is greater than $5 billion, the fund is large-cap; from $1 billion to $5 billion, mid-

cap; and less than $1 billion, small-cap. "Value" funds are those whose stocks have price-to-earnings and price-to-book ratios lower than that of the S&P 500. "Growth" funds have higher than average p-e and p-b ratios. "Blend" funds are those in which the ratios are about average. Hybrids mix stocks and bonds, and possibly other assets. World funds generally include U.S. stocks; foreign funds do not. Sector and regional foreign funds are as indicated.

FUND	OVERALL RATING (COMPARES RISK-ADJUSTED PERFORMANCE OF EACH FUND AGAINST ALL FUNDS)	CATEGORY (COMPARES RISK-ADJUSTED PERFORMANCE OF FUND WITHIN CATEGORY)	RATING	SIZE ASSETS $MIL.	SIZE % CHG. 1996-97	FEES SALES CHARGE (%)	FEES EXPENSE RATIO (%)	1997 RETURNS (%) PRE-TAX	1997 RETURNS (%) AFTER-TAX	1997 RETURNS (%) YIELD
AARP BALANCED STOCK & BOND		Domestic Hybrid		635.7	43	No load	0.88	21.9	19.5	3.3
AARP CAPITAL GROWTH	C–	Large-cap Blend	D	1174.7	34	No load	0.90	35.1	32.8	0.6
AARP GROWTH & INCOME 👤	A	Large-cap Blend	A	6404.6	39	No load	0.69	31.0	27.9	2.0
ACORN 👤	C	Small-cap Blend	B	3618.5	27	No load	0.57	25.0	22.4	0.9
ACORN INTERNATIONAL	C	Foreign	B+	1690.1	–5	No load	1.17	0.2	–1.3	2.0
ACORN USA		Small-cap Blend		176.0	234	No load	1.79	32.3	31.6	0.0
AIM ADVISOR FLEX C (a)	B+	Domestic Hybrid	B+	602.8	23	1.00**	2.26†	23.6	22.4	1.4
AIM ADVISOR LARGE CAP VALUE C (b)	B	Large-cap Blend	C	172.1	25	1.00**	2.26†	30.7	27.8	0.0
AIM ADVISOR MULTIFLEX C (c)		Mid-cap Value		376.8	41	1.00**	2.45†	18.5	16.1	0.7
AIM AGGRESSIVE GROWTH	D	Small-cap Growth	B	3679.9	35	5.50‡	1.10†	12.2	11.4	0.0
AIM BALANCED A	B	Domestic Hybrid	C	683.8	105	4.75	1.15†	24.4	22.6	2.1
AIM BLUE CHIP A	C	Large-cap Growth	B+	569.9	261	5.50	1.26†	31.9	31.3	0.2
AIM CAPITAL DEVELOPMENT A		Small-cap Growth		590.4	86	5.50	1.35†	23.7	23.7	0.0
AIM CHARTER A	C	Large-cap Blend	C–	3531.6	26	5.50	1.12†	24.7	21.1	0.9
AIM CONSTELLATION A	D	Mid-cap Growth	C	13990.8	17	5.50	1.14†	12.9	11.2	0.0
AIM GLOBAL AGGRESSIVE GROWTH B		World		1198.6	29	5.00**	2.37†	3.5	3.5	0.0
AIM GLOBAL GROWTH B		World		228.2	60	5.00**	2.48†	13.3	12.6	0.0
AIM GLOBAL UTILITIES A	C	Utilities	C–	179.6	10	5.50	1.17†	23.7	22.6	2.5
AIM GROWTH B		Mid-cap Growth		356.3	27	5.00**	2.03†	18.5	15.6	0.0
AIM INTERNATIONAL EQUITY A	C–	Foreign	B	1601.7	31	5.50	1.57†	5.7	5.6	0.4
AIM SUMMIT	C–	Mid-cap Growth	B	1656.0	27	8.50	0.70	24.2	21.5	0.1
AIM VALUE B		Large-cap Blend		6828.9	40	5.00**	1.94†	23.0	19.7	0.0
AIM WEINGARTEN A 👤	C–	Mid-cap Blend	C–	5896.7	15	5.50	1.12†	26.0	21.5	0.0
ALGER CAPITAL APPRECIATION B (d)		Large-cap Growth		215.3	38	5.00**	2.45†	20.2	18.0	0.0
ALGER GROWTH B (e) 👤	C–	Large-cap Growth		283.2	–2	5.00**	2.07†	23.1	18.7	0.0
ALGER SMALL CAPITALIZATION B (f) 👤	D	Mid-cap Growth	D	571.2	–2	5.00**	2.13†	9.2	7.8	0.0
ALLIANCE A 👤	C	Large-cap Blend	D	1159.2	21	4.25	1.04†	36.0	26.4	0.0
ALLIANCE GROWTH & INCOME A	B	Large-cap Blend	C	821.5	40	4.25	0.97†	28.9	23.8	1.4
ALLIANCE GROWTH B 👤	B	Large-cap Blend	C	3758.3	38	4.00**	1.99†	26.2	24.2	0.0
ALLIANCE PREMIER GROWTH B	C–	Large-cap Blend	F	910.5	124	4.00**	2.32†	31.8	29.6	0.0
ALLIANCE QUASAR B	C–	Small-cap Growth	B+	550.6	239	4.00**	2.51†	16.3	14.8	0.0
ALLIANCE REAL ESTATE INVESTMENT B		Real Estate		293.2	778	4.00**	2.44†	22.2	20.9	3.1
ALLIANCE TECHNOLOGY B		Technology		1023.2	54	4.00**	2.44†	3.8	3.6	0.0
ALLIANCE WORLDWIDE PRIVATIZATION A		Foreign		480.2	–9	4.25	1.71†	13.2	9.9	1.4
AMCAP 👤	C	Large-cap Growth	B	4536.6	20	5.75	0.69†	30.6	26.3	0.6
AMCORE VINTAGE EQUITY	B	Large-cap Blend	C	381.6	51	No load	1.33†	30.1	27.4	0.1
AMERICAN BALANCED 👤	B+	Domestic Hybrid	B+	5035.9	28	5.75	0.67†	21.0	17.7	3.3
AMERICAN CENT. BALANCED (g)	C	Domestic Hybrid	D	925.3	5	No load	0.99	16.9	14.3	2.0
AMERICAN CENT. EQUITY GROWTH (h) 👤	A	Large-cap Value	B+	702.6	156	No load	0.63	36.1	31.2	1.1
AMERICAN CENT. EQUITY INCOME (i)		Mid-cap Value		287.7	54	No load	1.00	28.3	21.1	3.3
AMERICAN CENT. GLOBAL GOLD (j)	F	Precious Metals	D	225.3	–48	No load	0.62	–41.5	–42.2	1.4
AMERICAN CENT. INCOME & GROWTH (k) 👤	A	Large-cap Value	B+	1680.1	135	No load	0.62	34.3	30.3	1.4
AMERICAN CENT. STRAT. ALLOC.: MOD. (l)		Domestic Hybrid		201.1	201	No load	1.10	15.2	13.3	2.3
AMERICAN CENT. VALUE (m)		Mid-cap Value		2342.9	51	No load	1.00	26.0	19.8	1.5
AMERICAN CENT.-20THC. GIFTRUST (n)	F	Small-cap Growth	D	2342.9	168	No load	0.98	–1.2	–2.0	0.0

*Includes redemption fee. **Includes deferred sales charge. †12(b)-1 plan in effect. ‡Not currently accepting new accounts. §Less than 0.5% of assets. NA=Not available. NM=Not meaningful.
(a) Formerly Invesco Adv. Flex C. (b) Formerly Invesco Adv. Eq. C. (c) Formerly Invesco Adv. MultiFlex C. (d) Formerly Alger Cap. Apprec. (e) Formerly Alger Growth. (f) Formerly Alger Sm. Cap.

SALES CHARGE
The cost of buying a fund. Many funds take this "load" out of the initial investment, and for ratings purposes, returns are reduced by these charges. Loads may be levied on withdrawals.

EXPENSE RATIO
Expenses for 1997 as a percentage of average net assets, a measure of how much shareholders pay for management. Footnotes indicate if the ratio includes a 12(b)-1 plan, which spends shareholder money on marketing. The average is 1.21%.

PRETAX TOTAL RETURN
A fund's net gain to investors, including reinvestment of dividends and capital gains at month-end prices.

AFTERTAX TOTAL RETURN
Pretax return adjusted for federal taxes. Assumes ordinary income

and capital gains taxed at highest rate applicable in each year; uses 31% tax rate on income since 1992. Capital gains are assumed to be long-term.

YIELD
Income distributions as a percent of net asset value, adjusted for capital-gains distributions.

HISTORY
A fund's returns relative to all other funds for four periods, which from left to right are: Jan., 1988-June, 1990; July, 1990-Dec., 1992; Jan., 1993-June, 1995; July, 1995-Dec., 1997. The numbers designate which quartile the fund was in during the period: ▉ for the top quartile; ▉ for the second quartile; ▉ for the third quartile; ▉ for the bottom quartile. No number indicates no data for that period.

TURNOVER
Trading activity, the lesser of purchases or sales divided by average monthly assets.

% CASH
Portion of fund assets not invested in stocks or bonds. A negative number means the fund has borrowed to buy securities.

% FOREIGN
Portion of funds assets invested in non-U.S. securities.

PRICE-EARNINGS RATIO
The average, weighted price-earnings ratio of stocks in a fund's portfolio, based on last 12 months' earnings.

UNTAXED GAINS
Percentage of assets in portfolio that are unrealized and undistributed capital gains. A negative figure indicates losses that may offset future gains.

LARGEST HOLDING
Comes from the latest available fund reports.

RISK
Potential for losing money in a fund, or risk-of-loss factor. For each fund, the three-month Treasury bill return is subtracted from the monthly total return for each of the 60 months in the ratings period. When a fund has not performed as well as Treasury bills, the monthly result is negative. The sum of these negative numbers is divided by the number of months. The result is a negative number, and the greater its magnitude, the higher the risk of loss. This number is the basis for BW ratings, category ratings, and the RISK column.

BEST & WORST QUARTERS
The fund's highest and lowest quarterly returns of the past five years.

AVERAGE ANNUAL TOTAL RETURNS (%)						HISTORY	PORTFOLIO DATA							RISK						TELEPHONE
3 YEARS		5 YEARS		10 YEARS		RESULTS VS.	TURNOVER	CASH	FOREIGN	P-E	UNTAXED	LARGEST HOLDING		LEVEL		BEST		WORST		
PRETAX	AFTERTAX	PRETAX	AFTERTAX	PRETAX	AFTERTAX	ALL FUNDS		%	%	RATIO	GAINS (%)	COMPANY (% ASSETS)				QTR	%RET	QTR	%RET	
19.6	17.6	NA	NA	NA	NA	3	Low	9	16	21	22	Xerox (2)				NA		NA		800-322-2282
28.6	26.3	17.3	15.3	16.7	14.7	1331	Average	5	8	23	39	Compaq Computer (3)		High	II 97	20.8	I 94	-8.1		800-322-2282
28.1	25.5	20.2	18.0	16.9	14.9	3221	Low	3	20	22	37	Xerox (3)		Low	II 97	15.5	I 94	-3.3		800-322-2282
22.8	19.7	17.8	15.3	18.2	15.8	1122	Low	9	15	29	48	AES (3)		Average	III 97	13.7	I 94	-5.5		800-922-6769
9.6	8.8	13.6	13.0	NA	NA	14	Low	12	96	27	25	TT Tieto Cl. B (3)		Average	IV 93	14.6	IV 94	-7.0		800-922-6769
NA	NA	NA	NA	NA	NA		Low	8	NA	27	19	CalEnergy (5)				NA		NA		800-922-6769
21.4	19.8	14.7	13.0	NA	NA	233	Low	2	11	22	33	First Chicago NBD (2)		Very low	II 97	11.5	I 94	-3.9		800-554-1156
25.9	24.5	17.5	15.0	15.3	12.5	3322	Low	2	6	24	46	Textron (3)		Average	II 97	16.4	I 94	-3.0		800-554-1156
19.1	17.5	NA	NA	NA	NA	3	Average	6	27	23	24	Patriot American Hospitality (1)				NA		NA		800-554-1156
22.0	20.7	23.0	22.2	21.7	20.2	21113	Average	4	5	32	30	Brightpoint (1)		High	II 97	21.2	I 97	-13.9		800-347-4246
26.0	24.5	17.0	15.6	15.4	14.1	4132	Average	2	7	29	20	Compaq Computer (1)		Low	II 97	13.2	I 94	-3.8		800-347-4246
29.2	26.1	18.7	16.4	16.1	14.7	3331	Average	4	3	28	20	Philip Morris (2)		Average	II 97	18.2	I 94	-3.4		800-347-4246
NA	NA	NA	NA	NA	NA			8	5	31	23	Medical Manager (1)				NA				800-347-4246
26.5	23.0	16.2	13.6	16.5	14.2	2232	High	0	7	28	31	Philip Morris (2)		Average	II 97	17.6	IV 94	-3.1		800-347-4246
21.2	19.7	16.1	15.1	20.4	18.9	11113	Average	5	5	31	19	Dell Computer (1)		High	II 97	15.6	IV 97	-8.7		800-347-4246
18.6	18.6	NA	NA	NA	NA	3	Average	8	63	29	14	Fomento Econ. Mexicana B (1)				NA		NA		800-347-4246
20.5	20.0	NA	NA	NA	NA	3	Average	6	68	28	17	Rohm (1)				NA		NA		800-347-4246
21.7	20.4	12.4	10.9	NA	NA	242	Average	2	34	24	28	El Paso Natural Gas (3)		Average	II 97	10.5	I 94	-7.8		800-347-4246
22.8	20.5	NA	NA	NA	NA	3	High	8	5	30	30	Compuware (1)				NA		NA		800-347-4246
13.6	12.8	15.6	14.9	NA	NA	14	Average	5	99	27	18	Philips Electronics (1)		High	IV 93	13.9	IV 97	-7.9		800-347-4246
26.3	23.2	16.2	13.6	17.3	14.9	11132	High	5	4	28	37	Dell Computer (2)		High	II 97	17.3	II 94	-5.3		800-347-4246
23.1	20.8	NA	NA	NA	NA	3	High	10	15	25	27	WorldCom (5)				NA		NA		800-347-4246
25.9	21.2	15.1	11.5	16.7	14.5	1232	High	3	10	28	35	Service International (1)		High	II 97	16.8	II 94	-4.4		800-347-4246
34.7	33.4	NA	NA	NA	NA	2	High	4	4	31	23	Texas Instruments (3)				NA		NA		800-992-3863
24.2	21.5	17.8	15.3	18.1	16.3	11113	High	2	3	29	34	Texas Instruments (3)		High	II 95	17.5	I 94	-6.4		800-992-3863
19.2	16.0	12.8	10.2	19.7	17.2	11114	High	4	8	33	25	USA Waste Services (3)		Very high	II 95	22.8	I 97	-11.6		800-992-3863
29.2	22.3	19.2	13.4	17.7	13.1	2121	Average	0	5	30	40	Republic Industries (6)		High	III 97	20.8	I 94	-3.8		800-227-4618
30.2	25.5	18.4	14.6	16.1	11.7	2331	Average	3	2	23	30	Chase Manhattan (5)		Low	II 97	12.4	I 94	-4.0		800-227-4618
25.7	24.3	20.1	18.4	20.4	18.0	11112	Average	1	8	28	33	CUC International (6)		Average	II 97	17.2	I 97	-4.4		800-227-4618
33.3	30.6	19.5	17.5	NA	NA	21	High	5	7	29	27	MBNA (5)		High	II 97	21.3	I 94	-3.7		800-227-4618
30.9	25.5	18.9	14.3	NA	NA	31	High	12	7	30	14	Parker Drilling (3)		High	I 96	18.7	II 94	-8.0		800-227-4618
NA	NA	NA	NA	NA	NA		Low	3	NA	33	12	Starwood Lodging Trust (5)				NA		NA		800-227-4618
21.3	20.4	NA	NA	NA	NA	4	Low	6	6	33	25	Compaq Computer (7)				NA		NA		800-227-4618
13.3	10.8	NA	NA	NA	NA	3	Average	3	98	20	25	Deutsche Telekom (2)				NA		NA		800-227-4618
24.3	20.5	16.3	12.5	15.3	12.2	2232	Low	12	2	30	42	Medtronic (4)		Average	II 97	14.7	I 94	-3.0		800-421-4120
28.9	27.2	18.2	17.0	NA	NA	31	Low	0	1	29	48	Warner-Lambert (3)		Average	II 97	18.1	I 94	-3.2		800-438-6375
20.3	17.1	14.2	11.5	13.6	10.8	3233	Average	16	7	22	22	Alcoa (2)		Very low	II 97	10.0	I 94	-3.7		800-421-4120
16.9	13.8	11.4	9.1	NA	NA	343	High	5	7	33	25	Tyco Intl. (4)		Average	II 97	12.3	I 97	-2.6		800-345-2021
32.6	28.2	21.0	17.7	NA	NA	21	High	1	1	22	23	Ford Motor (4)		Low	II 97	15.3	I 94	-4.6		800-345-2021
27.0	21.8	NA	NA	NA	NA	1	High	2	1	21	20	Giant Food Cl. A (5)				NA		NA		800-345-2021
-14.7	-15.5	-1.3	-1.9	NA	NA	414	Average	2	70	33	-35	Barrick Gold (15)		Very high	II 93	34.3	IV 97	-31.4		800-345-2021
31.7	28.2	20.4	17.6	NA	NA	21	Average	1	4	22	23	Merck (3)		Low	II 97	15.7	I 94	-4.5		800-345-2021
NA	NA	NA	NA	NA	NA			2	33	28	7	Merrill Lynch (2)				NA		NA		800-345-2021
27.6	22.9	NA	NA	NA	NA	1	High	2	3	21	21	Giant Food Cl. A (5)				NA		NA		800-345-2021
13.1	11.4	16.6	14.4	20.6	18.5	11114	High	11	9	37	21	Jabil Circuit (3)		Very high	III 97	21.2	I 97	-20.8		800-345-2021

(g) Formerly 20th Cent. Balanced. (h) Formerly Benham Eq. Growth. (i) Formerly 20th Cent. Eq.-Inc. (j) Formerly Benham Global Gold. (k) Formerly Benham Inc. & Gr. (l) Formerly 20th Cent. Strat. Alloc.: Moder. (m) Formerly 20th Cent. Value. (n) Formerly 20th Century Giftrust.

DATA: MORNINGSTAR, INC., CHICAGO, IL.

181

MUTUAL FUND SCOREBOARD

FUND	OVERALL RATING (COMPARES RISK-ADJUSTED PERFORMANCE OF EACH FUND AGAINST ALL FUNDS)	CATEGORY (COMPARES RISK-ADJUSTED PERFORMANCE OF FUND WITHIN CATEGORY)	RATING	SIZE ASSETS $MIL.	SIZE % CHG. 1996-97	FEES SALES CHARGE (%)	FEES EXPENSE RATIO (%)	1997 RETURNS (%) PRE-TAX	1997 RETURNS (%) AFTER-TAX	1997 RETURNS (%) YIELD
AMERICAN CENT.-20THC. GROWTH (o) ⚖	D	Large-cap Growth	F	5172.3	11	No load	1.00	29.3	24.3	0.0
AMERICAN CENT.-20THC. HERITAGE (p)	C–	Mid-cap Growth	B	1311.7	17	No load	0.99	19.4	13.0	0.5
AMERICAN CENT.-20THC. INTL. DISC. (q)		Foreign		626.2	61	2.00*	1.88	17.5	16.1	0.2
AMERICAN CENT.-20THC. INTL. GROWTH (r)	C	Foreign	B	1723.7	26	No load	1.65	19.7	14.9	0.3
AMERICAN CENT.-20THC. SELECT (s)	C–	Large-cap Blend	F	4954.7	22	No load	1.00	32.2	26.3	0.4
AMERICAN CENT.-20THC. ULTRA (t) ⚖	D	Large-cap Growth	F	22204.5	21	No load	1.00	23.1	16.4	0.0
AMERICAN CENT.-20THC. VISTA (u)	F	Mid-cap Growth	F	1748.6	–22	No load	0.99	–8.7	–9.8	0.0
AMERICAN GAS INDEX	C	Natural Resources	B+	220.5	–4	No load	0.85	24.2	22.9	2.5
AMERICAN MUTUAL ⚖	A	Large-cap Value	B	9738.6	22	5.75	0.59†	26.4	23.4	2.5
AMERICAN NATIONAL GROWTH	C	Large-cap Blend	C–	178.1	17	5.75	1.15	22.2	18.8	1.0
AMERICAN NATIONAL INCOME	B	Large-cap Value	C	196.1	18	5.75	1.10	22.7	19.4	2.1
AMERICAN PERFORM. EQUITY	B	Large-cap Blend	C	184.3	88	4.00	1.06†	28.8	25.0	0.6
AMSOUTH BALANCED CLASSIC	B+	Domestic Hybrid	B	310.8	–11	4.50	0.98	20.4	17.8	2.9
AMSOUTH EQUITY CLASSIC	B	Large-cap Value	C–	901.7	124	4.50	1.02	32.3	30.4	1.1
ARIEL APPRECIATION	C	Mid-cap Value	C–	204.4	40	No load	1.33†	38.0	35.5	0.2
ARIEL GROWTH ⚖	C	Mid-cap Value	C–	174.2	45	No load	1.25†	36.4	34.1	0.3
ARTISAN INTERNATIONAL		Foreign		300.8	57	No load	1.61	3.5	0.5	1.5
ARTISAN SMALL CAP		Small-cap Blend		296.6	0	No load‡	1.41	22.7	17.6	0.0
ATLAS GROWTH & INCOME A	C	Large-cap Blend	C–	170.3	31	3.00	1.24†	26.0	21.8	0.5
BABSON ENTERPRISE ⚖	B+	Small-cap Blend	B	216.3	13	No load‡	1.08	32.4	29.1	0.3
BABSON GROWTH	B	Large-cap Blend	B	400.6	29	No load	0.83	28.0	25.6	0.5
BABSON VALUE ⚖	A	Large-cap Value	B+	1417.3	81	No load	0.96	26.6	25.2	1.1
BARON ASSET ⚖	B+	Small-cap Growth	A	3793.0	186	No load	1.30†	33.9	33.9	0.0
BARON GROWTH & INCOME		Small-cap Growth		415.1	70	No load	1.40†	31.1	31.0	0.1
BERGER 100 ⚖	D	Mid-cap Growth	C–	1777.4	–11	No load	1.42†	13.6	4.5	0.0
BERGER GROWTH & INCOME ⚖	C	Mid-cap Blend	C	344.8	7	No load	1.56†	22.7	18.3	0.5
BERGER SMALL COMPANY GROWTH		Small-cap Growth		775.2	–1	No load	1.68†	16.2	13.8	0.0
BERNSTEIN EMERGING MARKETS VALUE		Diversified Emerging Mkts.		339.0	9	2.00*	1.92	–23.8	–24.5	0.7
BERNSTEIN INTERNATIONAL VALUE	C	Foreign	B+	4697.8	34	No load	1.31	9.3	6.6	6.0
BERWYN INCOME	A	Domestic Hybrid	A	183.0	33	No load	0.68	13.4	10.2	5.8
BOSTON 1784 GROWTH (v)		Mid-cap Growth		294.7	221	No load	0.77†	13.9	12.6	0.0
BOSTON 1784 GROWTH & INCOME (w)		Large-cap Growth		504.2	34	No load	0.92†	19.7	19.0	0.6
BOSTON 1784 INTERNATIONAL EQUITY (x)		Foreign		438.5	1	No load	1.27†	–0.9	–1.5	1.2
BRANDYWINE ⚖	C–	Mid-cap Growth	B	9019.6	38	No load	1.04	12.0	7.1	0.0
BT INVESTMENT EQUITY 500 IDX.	B+	Large-cap Blend	B+	627.8	40	No load	0.25	33.0	31.3	1.4
BT INVESTMENT INTL. EQUITY	B	Foreign	A	547.7	160	No load	1.50†	17.4	16.5	0.1
BT INVESTMENT SMALL CAP		Small-cap Growth		228.7	22	No load	1.25†	13.2	9.7	0.0
CALVERT SOCIAL INV. MANAGED A	C	Domestic Hybrid	C–	621.1	3	4.75	1.26†	18.9	15.4	2.4
CALVERT WORLD VALUE INTL. EQ. A	C–	Foreign	C	201.2	0	4.75	1.81†	6.6	4.5	0.3
CAPITAL INCOME BUILDER	B+	Domestic Hybrid	B	7803.4	34	5.75	0.71†	23.3	20.9	3.9
CAPITAL WORLD GROWTH & INCOME		World		7358.8	41	5.75	0.85†	18.0	15.1	2.4
CARDINAL	C	Large-cap Value	D	296.7	25	4.50	0.75†	30.6	27.9	0.8
CENTURY SHARES ⚖	C	Financial	F	369.5	36	No load	0.82	50.1	48.5	0.8
CGM CAPITAL DEVELOPMENT ⚖	D	Mid-cap Blend	F	732.0	16	No load‡	0.82	22.3	14.0	0.0
CGM MUTUAL ⚖	C–	Domestic Hybrid	F	1218.0	6	No load	0.87	8.2	2.5	2.1
CGM REALTY		Real Estate		430.0	166	No load	1.00	26.7	22.2	4.2
CHESAPEAKE AGGRESSIVE GROWTH (y)	D	Mid-cap Blend	F	590.1	18	3.00‡	1.42	15.2	11.7	0.0
CHICAGO TRUST BALANCED (z)		Domestic Hybrid		191.1	18	No load	1.00†	20.9	18.5	2.5
CHICAGO TRUST GROWTH & INCOME		Large-cap Blend		283.6	32	No load	1.00†	26.7	24.9	0.3
CITISELECT FOLIO 200		Domestic Hybrid		184.9	80	No load	1.50†	8.3	7.1	2.0
CITISELECT FOLIO 300		Domestic Hybrid		349.6	80	No load	1.50†	9.9	8.7	1.2
CITISELECT FOLIO 400		Domestic Hybrid		469.6	87	No load	1.75†	10.3	9.3	0.7
CITISELECT FOLIO 500		International Hybrid		202.5	142	No load	1.75†	12.0	11.3	0.7
CITIZENS INDEX		Large-cap Growth		250.1	55	No load	1.59†	35.0	33.7	0.0
CLIPPER ⚖	B	Large-cap Value	C–	805.0	48	No load	1.08	30.4	26.9	1.6
COHEN & STEERS REALTY SHARES	B	Real Estate		3308.3	62	No load	1.08	21.2	18.6	3.6
COLONIAL A	B	Domestic Hybrid	C–	927.7	19	5.75	1.15†	26.1	22.3	1.4
COLONIAL GLOBAL UTILITIES A	C	Utilities	C	169.2	–2	5.75	1.38†	22.4	20.0	2.0
COLONIAL NEWPORT TIGER B		Pacific/Asia ex-Japan		390.0	–32	5.00**	2.49†	–34.4	–34.5	0.0
COLONIAL SELECT VALUE A (aa) ⚖		Mid-cap Blend	B	346.6	32	5.75	1.17†	33.2	30.8	0.0
COLONIAL SMALL CAP VALUE B (bb)	C	Small-cap Value	C–	266.9	106	5.00**	2.13†	23.0	21.3	0.0
COLONIAL U.S. STOCK B (cc)	B	Large-cap Blend	C	471.3	42	5.00**	2.20†	34.1	30.7	0.0
COLONIAL UTILITIES B	C	Utilities	C–	683.9	–5	5.00**	1.95†	27.3	26.1	2.5
COLUMBIA BALANCED	B+	Domestic Hybrid	B+	811.1	21	No load	0.66	18.8	15.4	3.6
COLUMBIA COMMON STOCK	B+	Large-cap Blend	A	783.5	46	No load	0.76	25.4	22.7	1.1
COLUMBIA GROWTH	C	Large-cap Blend	B+	1342.1	26	No load	0.71	26.3	23.1	0.4
COLUMBIA SPECIAL ⚖	C–	Mid-cap Growth	B+	1386.0	–13	No load	0.94	12.6	10.1	0.0
COMMERCE GROWTH INSTITUTIONAL		Large-cap Blend		366.1	63	3.50	1.08	28.1	26.3	0.5
COMMON SENSE GROWTH & INCOME 1	C	Large-cap Blend	C–	1097.5	27	8.50	0.91	24.5	19.1	1.3
COMMON SENSE GROWTH 1 ⚖	C	Large-cap Blend	C–	3547.8	25	8.50	0.93	27.7	22.1	0.8

*Includes redemption fee. **Includes deferred sales charge. †12(b)-1 plan in effect. ‡Not currently accepting new accounts. §Less than 0.5% of assets. NA=Not available. NM=Not meaningful. (o) Formerly 20th Cent. Growth. (p) Formerly 20th Cent. Heritage. (q) Formerly 20th Cent. Intl. Discovery. (r) Formerly 20th Cent. Intl. Equity. (s) Formerly 20th Cent. Select. (t) Formerly 20th Cent. Ultra Investors. (u) Formerly 20th Cent. Vista. (v) Formerly 1784 Growth. (w) Formerly 1784 Growth & Income. (x) Formerly 1784 Intl. Eq. (y) Formerly Chesapeake Growth. (z) Formerly Chicago Tr. Asset Alloc. (aa) Formerly Colonial Growth. (bb) Formerly Colonial Small Stock B. (cc) Formerly Colonial U.S. Fund for Growth B.

AVERAGE ANNUAL TOTAL RETURNS (%)						HISTORY	PORTFOLIO DATA						RISK		BEST		WORST		TELEPHONE
3 YEARS		5 YEARS		10 YEARS		RESULTS VS.	TURNOVER	CASH	FOREIGN	P-E	UNTAXED	LARGEST HOLDING	LEVEL						
PRETAX	AFTERTAX	PRETAX	AFTERTAX	PRETAX	AFTERTAX	ALL FUNDS		%	%	RATIO	GAINS (%)	COMPANY (% ASSETS)		QTR	%RET	QTR	%RET	
21.4	17.8	12.8	9.0	15.4	12.9	1 1 4 3	High	3	8	33	45	Compuware (4)	High	II 97	19.3	IV 95	−8.4	800-345-2021
20.4	16.7	14.5	11.6	15.5	13.2	1 3 2 3	High	3	8	31	38	Tosco (3)	High	II 97	16.3	IV 97	−8.7	800-345-2021
19.2	18.1	NA	NA	NA	NA	2	High	3	98	31	21	Marschollek Lautenschlager (3)			NA		NA	800-345-2021
15.3	12.5	15.8	13.4	NA	NA	2 3	High	1	99	30	21	Novartis (Reg) (4)	Average	IV 93	18.3	IV 94	−5.9	800-345-2021
24.6	20.0	15.3	11.3	14.2	11.4	2 4 4 2	High	3	4	31	38	General Electric (4)	Average	II 97	19.4	I 94	−5.1	800-345-2021
24.5	20.9	17.8	15.5	21.9	20.3	1 1 1 2	Average	2	8	30	43	General Electric (3)	High	II 97	19.1	IV 94	−8.3	800-345-2021
12.8	10.7	9.6	7.4	13.5	11.8	1 3 2 4	Average	12	4	35	29	USA Waste Services (3)	Very high	III 94	18.4	I 97	−18.9	800-345-2021
25.1	23.8	15.6	14.3	NA	NA	4 4 2	Very low	4	NA	22	39	Williams (5)	Average	I 93	15.1	IV 93	−7.0	800-343-3355
24.5	21.3	17.2	14.2	15.0	12.1	3 3 2 2	Low	23	3	23	39	Ameritech (2)	Very low	II 97	11.9	I 94	−3.2	800-421-4120
21.9	19.1	15.4	11.9	13.2	9.9	4 3 3 2	Low	11	5	25	39	Procter & Gamble (3)	Average	II 97	12.6	IV 97	−3.2	800-231-4639
22.7	20.0	15.1	11.9	14.3	11.1	3 2 3 2	Low	4	1	20	34	Schering-Plough (4)	Low	II 97	10.7	I 94	−4.1	800-231-4639
29.9	26.4	19.1	15.3	NA	NA	3 1	High	3	3	26	39	Intel (3)	Average	II 97	17.1	I 94	−4.4	800-762-7085
17.7	15.2	13.2	10.9	NA	NA	2 3	Low	1	2	25	29	Sara Lee (2)	Very low	II 97	9.2	I 94	−2.5	800-451-8379
24.9	22.7	18.3	16.3	NA	NA	3 2 2	Low	4	2	26	26	Washington Mutual (3)	Low	II 97	14.1	I 94	−2.8	800-451-8379
28.4	25.9	16.0	13.9	NA	NA	2 4 1	Low	7	NA	26	53	Northern Trust (5)	Average	II 97	14.6	I 94	−4.9	800-292-7435
25.9	22.6	15.8	13.0	16.3	14.2	1 3 4 1	Low	9	NA	26	53	Northern Trust (5)	Average	III 97	13.8	II 93	−5.6	800-292-7435
NA	NA	NA	NA	NA	NA		High	2	100	24	7	Novartis (Reg) (3)			NA		NA	800-344-1770
NA	NA	NA	NA	NA	NA	2	Average	2	2	24	30	Penn Treaty American (2)			NA		NA	800-344-1770
26.3	22.5	17.0	14.3	NA	NA	3 1	High	2	3	29	29	Tyco Intl. (2)	Average	II 97	13.7	II 94	−4.5	800-933-2852
23.2	18.9	17.4	13.7	18.4	15.2	1 1 3 2	Low	6	2	25	42	LS Starrett Cl. A (3)	Low	III 97	15.0	III 96	−4.2	800-422-2766
27.0	23.5	17.6	14.6	14.8	11.6	3 3 3 1	Low	5	1	31	55	Linear Technology (3)	Low	II 97	15.8	I 94	−3.1	800-422-2766
27.0	25.7	20.9	19.4	16.9	15.5	3 2 1 1	Very low	4	9	23	25	Tenet Healthcare (3)	Low	II 97	12.2	IV 94	−1.7	800-422-2766
30.2	30.2	24.0	23.5	19.9	19.0	1 3 1 1	Very low	6	3	33	24	Manor Care (7)	Average	II 97	19.3	I 97	−3.5	800-992-2766
36.7	36.3	NA	NA	NA	NA	1	Low	1	2	31	27	Choice Hotels International (12)			NA		NA	800-992-2766
16.2	10.8	12.1	9.0	17.9	15.4	1 1 3 3	High	14	2	28	40	Household International (3)	High	III 97	13.5	II 94	−10.8	800-333-1001
20.7	17.5	14.6	12.6	14.5	12.8	4 1 3 2	High	13	4	30	36	McKesson (3)	Average	III 97	13.9	IV 94	−6.2	800-333-1001
22.0	20.6	NA	NA	NA	NA	2	Average	9	5	39	43	Fairfield Communities (2)			NA		NA	800-333-1001
NA	NA	NA	NA	NA	NA		Very low	4	100	15	−15	Yapi Ve Kredi Bankasi (3)			NA		NA	212-756-4097
11.5	9.6	14.2	12.6	NA	NA	2 3	Low	2	100	23	13	Telecom Italia (3)	Average	I 93	15.5	IV 97	−6.7	212-756-4097
16.1	12.9	12.6	9.5	13.0	9.8	4 1 2 4	Low	1	11	16	12	Unicom (2)	Very low	III 97	8.6	IV 94	−2.5	800-992-6757
NA	NA	NA	NA	NA	NA		Average	4	15	37	31	JD Wetherspoon (4)			NA		NA	800-252-1784
24.5	23.9	NA	NA	NA	NA	2	Very low	7	20	31	38	Pizza Express (4)			NA		NA	800-252-1784
8.5	7.8	NA	NA	NA	NA	4	Low	3	100	27	12	Ahold (3)			NA		NA	800-252-1784
23.9	20.0	18.4	15.0	20.3	17.5	1 1 1 3	Very high	3	2	29	8	Bristol-Myers Squibb (3)	High	III 97	19.0	IV 97	−14.1	800-656-3017
30.9	29.6	19.9	18.7	NA	NA	2 1	Very low	2	3	27	38	General Electric (4)	Average	II 97	17.5	I 94	−3.8	800-730-1313
18.8	17.5	19.1	18.0	NA	NA	1 3	Average	6	100	25	17	Credito Italiano (2)	Average	II 97	15.3	IV 97	−6.6	800-730-1313
24.3	21.1	NA	NA	NA	NA	3	High	9	3	35	24	E Trade Group (2)			NA		NA	800-730-1313
17.7	13.8	10.5	7.7	10.8	8.5	4 3 4 3	High	7	3	31	22	Cisco Systems (2)	Low	II 97	11.1	I 94	−3.4	800-368-2748
10.1	8.8	10.3	9.0	NA	NA	3 4	High	2	99	25	15	Zurich Insurance (3)	Average	II 97	12.1	IV 97	−7.8	800-368-2748
22.0	19.6	15.4	13.3	14.8	12.7	4 1 3 2	Low	11	37	21	28	American Home Products (2)	Very low	IV 96	9.8	I 94	−5.8	800-421-4120
20.3	17.9	NA	NA	NA	NA	2	Low	13	64	22	25	ING Groep (2)			NA		NA	800-421-4120
25.7	21.4	15.3	11.9	14.7	11.9	3 2 4 1	Average	7	4	27	45	General Electric (4)	Average	II 97	16.8	IV 94	−4.3	800-848-7734
33.5	31.7	17.9	16.1	19.1	16.8	1 1 4 1	Very low	1	1	21	77	Progressive (9)	Average	II 97	19.9	IV 93	−8.6	800-321-1928
30.3	24.2	17.0	11.9	19.8	15.5	4 1 4 1	Very high	1	23	23	41	Southdown (3)	High	III 97	19.5	IV 94	−14.8	800-345-4048
18.5	14.0	12.8	9.4	13.2	10.1	4 1 3 3	Very high	0	20	26	28	Warner-Lambert (6)	Average	IV 96	12.8	IV 97	−10.1	800-345-4048
29.8	26.4	NA	NA	NA	NA	1	Average	1	NA	33	25	Felcor Suite Hotels (10)			NA		NA	800-345-4048
18.5	15.7	18.9	17.1	NA	NA	1 4	High	3	5	27	36	Jones Apparel Group (3)	High	II 97	19.5	IV 97	−15.1	800-525-3863
NA	NA	NA	NA	NA	NA		Low	9	4	31	24	Norwest (2)			NA		NA	800-992-8151
29.2	28.0	NA	NA	NA	NA	1	Low	5	4	29	35	Royal Dutch Petroleum (NY) (4)			NA		NA	800-992-8151
NA	NA	NA	NA	NA	NA			31	19	24	8	Ford Motor Credit (1)			NA		NA	800-846-5200
NA	NA	NA	NA	NA	NA			17	23	23	10	General Electric (1)			NA		NA	800-846-5200
NA	NA	NA	NA	NA	NA			17	33	23	11	LTV (1)			NA		NA	800-846-5200
NA	NA	NA	NA	NA	NA			14	38	23	10	Akzo Nobel (1)			NA		NA	800-846-5200
NA	NA	NA	NA	NA	NA	1	Low	0	1	31	38	Microsoft (6)			NA		NA	800-223-7010
31.3	27.9	19.7	16.4	17.7	15.0	3 1 2 1	Low	28	NA	23	36	FHLMC (10)	Average	II 97	14.2	I 94	−4.8	800-776-5033
23.1	21.0	19.1	17.0	NA	NA	2 1	Low	2	1	32	22	Vornado Realty Trust (6)	Average	I 93	20.5	IV 93	−6.9	800-437-9912
23.7	20.3	16.2	13.4	15.1	12.5	3 2 2 2	Low	4	17	20	36	Textron (3)	Low	II 97	15.6	I 94	−2.4	800-426-3750
17.6	15.9	11.8	10.0	NA	NA	4 3	Low	0	51	25	23	AES (3)	Low	II 97	9.6	I 94	−4.4	800-426-3750
NA	NA	NA	NA	NA	NA	4	Very low	2	100	15	−23	Hong Kong & China Gas (7)			NA		NA	800-426-3750
30.3	26.8	18.8	15.4	17.8	14.4	1 3 3 1	High	3	NA	27	32	Omnicom Group (4)	Average	II 97	14.8	IV 94	−2.6	800-426-3750
25.6	23.8	19.8	18.8	NA	NA	1 2	Average	12	1	21	23	Fremont General (2)	Average	II 97	17.8	I 97	−5.8	800-426-3750
27.0	23.9	18.1	15.7	NA	NA	2 2	Average	6	NA	23	36	Philip Morris (3)	Average	II 97	16.7	I 94	−4.1	800-426-3750
21.5	20.2	11.6	10.3	NA	NA	4 2	Very low	1	2	23	13	Bell Atlantic (8)	Average	IV 97	14.6	I 94	−9.2	800-426-3750
18.4	15.3	13.6	11.1	NA	NA	3 3	High	1	4	29	18	FHLMC (2)	Very low	II 97	9.4	I 94	−2.5	800-547-1707
25.6	22.0	18.7	16.0	NA	NA	2 1	High	3	4	28	24	Fred Meyer (3)	Low	II 97	13.2	I 94	−2.6	800-547-1707
26.6	22.3	17.9	14.3	16.9	13.4	2 2 2 2	Average	2	1	31	31	Warnaco Group Cl. A (3)	Average	II 97	16.8	I 94	−3.4	800-547-1707
18.1	13.6	15.4	11.3	19.1	15.8	1 2 1 3	High	6	4	30	15	American Stores (3)	High	II 97	12.1	IV 97	−5.1	800-547-1707
29.7	27.5	NA	NA	NA	NA	1	Low	4	3	23	33	Mobil (4)			NA		NA	800-305-2140
26.1	21.1	16.2	12.0	15.0	12.3	2 3 3 2	High	3	14	25	32	Texaco (2)	Average	II 97	14.6	I 94	−3.9	800-544-5445
26.3	21.6	16.6	12.8	16.0	13.2	2 2 2 2	Very high	7	6	24	34	V. Kamp. Am. Cap. Sm. Cap. (3)	Average	II 97	14.7	I 94	−2.8	800-544-5445

DATA: MORNINGSTAR, INC., CHICAGO, IL.

MUTUAL FUND SCOREBOARD

FUND	OVERALL RATING (COMPARES RISK-ADJUSTED PERFORMANCE OF EACH FUND AGAINST ALL FUNDS)	CATEGORY (COMPARES RISK-ADJUSTED PERFORMANCE OF FUND WITHIN CATEGORY)	RATING	SIZE ASSETS $MIL.	% CHG. 1996-97	FEES SALES CHARGE (%)	EXPENSE RATIO (%)	1997 RETURNS (%) PRE-TAX	AFTER-TAX	YIELD
COMPOSITE BOND & STOCK A	B+	Domestic Hybrid	B	312.2	17	4.50	0.98†	19.9	16.2	3.0
COMPOSITE GROWTH & INCOME A	B	Large-cap Blend	B	306.4	58	4.50	1.03†	29.5	27.0	0.5
COMPOSITE NORTHWEST A	C-	Mid-cap Blend	C-	263.3	38	4.50	1.08†	32.9	29.0	0.0
CRABBE HUSON EQUITY PRIM.	B	Mid-cap Blend	B	377.6	-7	No load	1.37†	25.7	19.1	0.2
CRABBE HUSON SPECIAL PRIM.	C	Small-cap Blend	C	352.7	-19	No load	1.37†	11.3	8.4	1.0
DAVIS FINANCIAL A	B+	Financial	C	287.8	168	4.75	1.15†	44.5	44.0	0.5
DAVIS N.Y. VENTURE A	B	Large-cap Value	C-	4655.5	75	4.75	0.89†	33.7	32.3	1.0
DEAN WITTER AMERICAN VALUE B (dd) ⚖	C-	Large-cap Growth	C	3977.5	28	5.00**	1.53†	31.6	25.0	0.0
DEAN WITTER CAPITAL APPREC B. (ee)		Small-cap Growth		365.5	12	5.00**	NA†	5.9	5.1	0.0
DEAN WITTER CAPITAL GROWTH B (ff)	D	Mid-cap Growth	C	520.7	4	5.00**	1.89†	25.2	20.2	0.0
DEAN WITTER DEVELOPING GROWTH B (gg)	D	Mid-cap Growth	C-	804.3	4	5.00**	1.69†	13.3	10.9	0.0
DEAN WITTER DIVIDEND GROWTH B (hh) ⚖	B+	Large-cap Blend	B+	15422.9	27	5.00**	1.31†	25.7	24.7	1.5
DEAN WITTER EUROPEAN GROWTH B (ii)	A	Europe	B+	1714.6	25	5.00**	2.13†	14.5	12.1	0.9
DEAN WITTER GLOBAL DIV. GROWTH B (jj)		World		3566.5	22	5.00**	1.75†	15.6	11.4	0.8
DEAN WITTER GLOBAL UTILITIES B (kk)		Utilities		365.5	3	5.00**	1.87†	18.8	17.3	1.0
DEAN WITTER HEALTH SCIENCES B (ll)	F	Health	F	403.9	-14	5.00**	2.25†	5.5	3.8	0.0
DEAN WITTER INCOME BUILDER B (mm)		Domestic Hybrid		388.6	99	5.00**	NA†	24.0	20.9	3.3
DEAN WITTER INFORMATION B (nn)		Communications		229.2	-17	5.00**	NA†	15.8	15.8	0.0
DEAN WITTER MID-CAP GROWTH B (oo)		Mid-cap Growth		564.2	55	5.00**	2.05†	30.8	28.3	0.0
DEAN WITTER NATURAL RES. DEV. B (pp) ⚖	C	Natural Resources	B	287.6	22	5.00**	1.84†	14.0	10.7	0.0
DEAN WITTER PACIFIC GROWTH B (qq)	F	Diversified Pacific/Asia	F	687.8	-58	5.00**	2.39†	-38.8	-39.1	1.7
DEAN WITTER SPECIAL VALUE B (rr)		Small-cap Value		295.8	47	5.00**	NA†	26.4	23.7	0.0
DEAN WITTER STRATEGIST B (ss)	C	Domestic Hybrid	C-	1480.0	8	5.00**	1.58†	15.8	14.5	1.7
DEAN WITTER UTILITIES B (tt)	C	Utilities	C	2356.5	-12	5.00**	1.64†	25.8	22.6	2.7
DEAN WITTER VALUE-ADDED MKT. EQ. B (uu)	B	Mid-cap Value	C-	1471.9	32	5.00**	1.51†	26.7	25.5	0.4
DEAN WITTER WORLDWIDE INVMT. B (vv)	D	World	F	310.3	-34	5.00**	2.41†	2.6	0.5	0.0
DELAWARE A	B	Domestic Hybrid	C	568.3	12	4.75	0.99†	24.5	20.8	2.5
DELAWARE DECATUR INCOME A	B+	Large-cap Value	B	1907.0	21	4.75	0.85†	29.7	25.1	2.6
DELAWARE DECATUR TOTAL RETURN A	B+	Large-cap Value	C	862.6	31	4.75	1.11†	31.2	27.8	1.4
DELAWARE DELCAP A	D	Mid-cap Growth	C-	733.5	-15	4.75	1.35†	14.0	9.6	0.0
DELAWARE SMALL CAP VALUE A (ww) ⚖	B+	Small-cap Value	B	268.2	33	4.75	1.45†	33.0	31.0	0.5
DELAWARE TREND A	D	Small-cap Growth	C	465.4	-3	4.75	1.34†	19.4	16.9	0.0
DG EQUITY	B	Large-cap Growth	A	648.8	42	3.50	0.92	35.9	35.5	0.5
DODGE & COX BALANCED	A	Domestic Hybrid	B+	5415.4	49	No load	0.56	21.2	18.8	3.2
DODGE & COX STOCK	A	Large-cap Value	B+	3999.4	78	No load	0.59	28.4	26.1	1.5
DOMINI SOCIAL EQUITY	B	Large-cap Blend	B	267.9	132	No load	0.98†	36.2	36.0	0.4
DREYFUS ⚖	C-	Large-cap Value	F	2614.8	-4	No load	0.73	10.8	5.5	0.7
DREYFUS APPRECIATION	C	Large-cap Growth	B+	1978.8	126	No load	0.91	27.9	27.5	0.8
DREYFUS BALANCED ⚖	A	Domestic Hybrid	B+	372.0	27	No load	0.96	17.4	12.9	2.4
DREYFUS CORE VALUE INV. ⚖	B+	Large-cap Value	C	585.7	20	No load	1.13†	25.2	18.0	0.6
DREYFUS DISC. STOCK (xx) ⚖	B+	Large-cap Blend	B+	1645.6	88	No load	0.90	32.4	28.6	1.0
DREYFUS GROWTH & INCOME ⚖	C	Large-cap Blend	D	1944.0	-3	No load	1.03	16.0	10.8	1.5
DREYFUS GROWTH OPPORTUNITY	C-	Large-cap Value	F	499.9	8	No load	1.06	15.1	10.0	0.6
DREYFUS MIDCAP INDEX	C	Mid-cap Blend	C	257.3	40	1.00*	0.50	31.5	29.0	0.8
DREYFUS NEW LEADERS	C	Small-cap Blend	B	866.1	9	1.00*	1.17	19.5	17.1	0.0
DREYFUS PREMIER AGGRES. GROWTH A (yy)	F	Small-cap Growth	F	305.4	-35	5.75	1.50	-13.0	-13.0	0.0
DREYFUS PREMIER VALUE A (zz)	C-	Large-cap Value	F	206.0	-7	5.75	1.19	16.4	11.4	0.5
DREYFUS PREMIER WRLDWD. GROWTH B (aaa)		Large-cap Blend		297.8	217	4.00**	2.00†	22.8	22.8	0.0
DREYFUS S&P 500 INDEX	B+	Large-cap Blend	B	1430.9	119	1.00*	0.57	32.6	31.7	1.0
DREYFUS SMALL COMPANY VALUE		Small-cap Value		402.3	1593	No load	1.27	26.1	25.3	0.1
DREYFUS THIRD CENTURY	C-	Large-cap Growth	C	804.1	43	No load	1.03	29.4	26.7	0.2
EATON VANCE GROWTH A (bbb)	C-	Large-cap Blend	F	173.7	27	4.75	0.98†	28.5	25.7	0.2
EATON VANCE INVESTORS A (ccc)	B	Domestic Hybrid	C	266.7	19	4.75	0.93†	21.6	18.2	2.1
EATON VANCE TAX-MGD. GROWTH B (ddd)		Large-cap Blend		643.0	217	5.00**	1.63†	31.0	31.0	0.0
EATON VANCE TOTAL RETURN A (eee)	C-	Utilities	F	366.4	-8	4.75	1.23	16.4	11.0	3.4
ECLIPSE EQUITY ⚖	B	Small-cap Value	C	192.9	13	No load	1.15	33.3	27.6	0.8
ENTERPRISE GROWTH A ⚖	C	Large-cap Growth	B+	410.8	109	4.75	1.53†	31.8	31.2	0.0
EUROPACIFIC GROWTH ⚖	C	Foreign	B+	18853.5	20	5.75	0.90†	9.2	7.0	1.6
EVERGREEN BALANCED B (fff) ⚖	B	Domestic Hybrid	C	1615.7	3	4.00**	1.69†	19.0	15.8	2.4
EVERGREEN BALANCED II Y (ggg)	B+	Domestic Hybrid		812.4	9	No load	0.68	21.2	15.7	3.4
EVERGREEN BLUE CHIP B (hhh)	C	Large-cap Blend	C	321.3	21	4.00**	1.56†	30.5	26.3	0.5
EVERGREEN FOUNDATION Y	B+	Domestic Hybrid	B	993.5	23	No load	1.00	25.7	24.0	2.5
EVERGREEN GLOBAL OPPORT. B (iii)		World		203.8	-42	5.00**	2.61†	0.4	-1.0	0.0
EVERGREEN GROWTH & INCOME Y ⚖	A	Mid-cap Blend	A	680.4	54	No load	1.21	31.3	30.0	0.7
EVERGREEN INCOME & GROWTH Y (jjj) ⚖	B	Mid-cap Value	C-	907.0	6	No load	1.18	25.6	22.2	4.2
EVERGREEN SMALL CO. GROWTH B (kkk)	D	Mid-cap Growth	D	1363.6	-24	4.00**	1.73†	13.4	9.6	0.0
EVERGREEN STRATEGIC GROWTH B (lll)	C-	Large-cap Growth	C	882.6	71	4.00**	1.18†	31.7	28.4	0.1
EVERGREEN VALUE A	B	Large-cap Value	C-	381.6	16	4.75	0.92†	25.7	23.9	1.5
EVERGREEN Y ⚖	B	Mid-cap Blend	B	1080.6	23	No load	1.15	30.3	29.4	0.6
EXCELSIOR BLENDED EQUITY A (mmm)	C	Large-cap Blend	C-	542.2	76	No load	1.01	29.8	27.8	0.5

*Includes redemption fee. **Includes deferred sales charge. †12(b)-1 plan in effect. ‡Not currently accepting new accounts. §Less than 0.5% of assets. NA=Not available. NM=Not meaningful. (dd) Formerly Dean Witter Amer. Val. (ee) Formerly Dean Witter Cap. Apprec. (ff) Formerly Dean Witter Cap. Gr. (gg) Formerly Dean Witter Dev. Gr. (hh) Formerly Dean Witter Dvd. Gr. (ii) Formerly Dean Witter Euro. Gr. (jj) Formerly Dean Witter Glob. Dvd. Gr. (kk) Formerly Dean Witter Glob. Util. (ll) Formerly Dean Witter Health Sci. (mm) Formerly Dean Witter Inc. Bldr. B. (nn) Formerly Dean Witter Info. (oo) Formerly Dean Witter Mid-Cap Gr. (pp) Formerly Dean Witter Nat. Res. Dev. (qq) Formerly Dean Witter Pac. Gr. (rr) Formerly Dean Witter Spec. Val. (ss) For-

3 YEARS PRETAX	3 YEARS AFTERTAX	5 YEARS PRETAX	5 YEARS AFTERTAX	10 YEARS PRETAX	10 YEARS AFTERTAX	RESULTS VS. ALL FUNDS	TURNOVER	CASH %	FOREIGN %	P-E RATIO	UNTAXED GAINS (%)	LARGEST HOLDING COMPANY (% ASSETS)	RISK LEVEL	BEST QTR	BEST %RET	WORST QTR	WORST %RET	TELEPHONE
21.3	18.2	13.8	11.3	12.7	10.3	4 2 3 3	Average	1	6	23	26	Columbia/HCA Healthcare (1)	Very low	II 97	9.6	I 94	-3.5	800-543-8072
28.2	25.7	18.2	15.9	15.1	12.9	4 2 3 1	Average	1	8	25	31	General Electric (2)	Low	II 97	16.2	IV 94	-1.5	800-543-8072
27.3	24.6	15.8	14.0	18.0	16.9	1 2 4 1	Low	3	NA	29	51	Microsoft (4)	High	II 97	19.8	IV 97	-4.5	800-543-8072
20.3	16.5	17.4	14.6	NA	NA	1 1 3	High	8	6	25	35	LCI International (3)	Low	II 97	18.8	II 97	-3.0	800-541-9732
9.3	7.4	14.4	12.8	16.1	13.1	2 1 1 4	Low	36	8	38	24	Tellabs (7)	Average	IV 93	13.6	II 97	-8.6	800-541-9732
42.0	39.6	25.7	23.4	NA	NA	2 1	Low	13	6	22	37	BankAmerica (5)	Average	II 97	17.1	I 94	-5.9	800-279-0279
33.5	31.3	22.0	20.0	21.1	18.4	1 1 1 1	Low	10	7	24	34	IBM (4)	Average	II 97	16.7	I 94	-3.4	800-279-0279
27.4	22.6	18.0	14.7	17.7	15.1	3 1 2 2	Very high	4	11	33	27	Lehman Brothers Holdings (2)	High	III 97	16.1	II 94	-7.2	800-869-6397
NA	NA	NA	NA	NA	NA			1	6	34	NA	Smart Modular Tech. (2)			NA		NA	800-869-3326
22.1	18.4	9.9	7.2	NA	NA	2 4 2	Low	1	5	32	38	Washington Mutual (3)	High	II 97	17.1	II 93	-7.3	800-869-3863
23.4	19.6	18.6	15.9	15.1	13.8	2 4 1 3	High	4	7	31	24	Saville Systems (ADR) (1)	Very high	III 97	18.2	I 97	-13.1	800-869-6397
26.4	25.4	17.5	16.6	16.2	14.9	2 3 2 2	Very low	3	5	23	48	IBM (2)	Low	II 97	15.7	IV 97	-2.2	800-869-3863
22.5	20.0	22.1	19.9	NA	NA	4 1 2	Average	3	100	25	30	Philips Electronics (2)	Low	III 93	11.9	IV 97	-2.2	800-869-3863
17.5	14.4	NA	NA	NA	NA	3	Low	2	70	21	17	Minnesota Mining & Mfg (1)			NA		NA	800-869-3863
15.4	14.5	NA	NA	NA	NA	3	Low	3	67	26	27	Australian Gas Light (3)			NA		NA	800-869-3863
20.1	17.8	11.4	10.1	NA	NA	4 3	Average	2	5	40	33	Agouron Pharm. (3)	Very high	IV 95	19.0	I 93	-17.8	800-869-3863
NA	NA	NA	NA	NA	NA			1	1	18	NA	Occidental Petrol. (144A) (2)			NA		NA	800-869-6397
NA	NA	NA	NA	NA	NA			6	18	41	NA	Chancelor Media (2)			NA		NA	800-869-3863
28.4	25.4	NA	NA	NA	NA	1	Very high	5	6	34	22	Dekalb Genetics Cl. B (2)			NA		NA	800-869-3863
21.4	17.9	15.8	12.7	12.5	10.2	2 4 3 2	High	1	19	25	18	Exxon (2)	Average	III 97	14.7	IV 97	-9.3	800-869-6397
-12.6	-13.1	1.4	0.6	NA	NA	1 4	Average	3	100	19	-52	Hutchison Whampoa (7)	Very high	IV 93	35.6	IV 97	-28.6	800-869-3863
NA	NA	NA	NA	NA	NA			13	5	25	NA	Tracor (3)			NA		NA	800-869-6397
18.4	15.6	11.9	9.7	NA	NA	2 4 3	Very high	9	1	26	21	Pier 1 Imports (2)	Low	I 97	9.8	I 94	-2.5	800-869-3863
19.3	17.2	11.5	9.7	NA	NA	2 4 3	Very low	1	11	22	38	SBC Communications (3)	Average	IV 97	13.2	I 94	-6.5	800-869-3863
24.1	23.2	16.6	15.9	15.1	14.3	3 3 2 2	Very low	4	2	24	40	Texas Utilities (§)	Average	II 97	14.3	I 94	-2.7	800-869-3863
4.5	3.0	8.3	6.9	7.0	5.3	4 4 3 4	Average	2	76	27	10	Hutchison Whampoa (1)	High	II 97	11.5	IV 94	-7.8	800-869-3863
21.3	17.6	14.0	10.9	14.8	11.9	2 3 4 2	Average	1	4	24	25	Tyco Intl. (3)	Very low	II 97	11.2	I 94	-2.1	800-523-4640
27.5	22.5	18.9	14.6	14.9	11.4	3 4 2 1	High	1	11	25	24	Pitney Bowes (3)	Low	II 97	13.7	I 94	-3.8	800-523-4640
29.1	24.8	19.7	15.8	16.7	13.6	2 3 2 1	Average	1	11	25	26	Pitney Bowes (3)	Low	II 97	15.3	I 94	-3.9	800-523-4640
19.0	14.5	12.3	9.0	14.7	12.7	1 3 4 3	Average	6	4	34	45	CompUSA (3)	High	II 97	14.9	II 94	-8.3	800-523-4640
26.1	22.8	17.3	15.2	18.7	16.9	1 1 4 1	Average	8	NA	21	32	Keystone International (2)	Low	II 97	15.3	I 94	-4.9	800-523-4640
23.5	20.7	15.7	12.7	20.3	17.2	1 1 2 3	High	8	2	35	30	Platinum Technology (2)	High	III 97	20.2	II 94	-7.2	800-523-4640
29.2	28.0	18.3	17.3	NA	NA	3 1	Very high	7	NA	31	43	Compaq Computer (4)	Average	II 97	18.1	I 94	-3.8	800-748-8500
21.2	19.1	16.1	14.1	14.6	12.6	3 3 2 3	Low	4	10	20	21	General Motors (2)	Very low	II 97	11.0	I 94	-1.2	800-621-3979
27.9	25.9	21.1	19.2	17.0	15.2	2 3 1 1	Very low	10	9	20	31	General Motors (3)	Low	II 97	15.4	IV 97	-1.5	800-621-3979
30.9	30.5	19.0	18.4	NA	NA	3 1	Very low	2	0	28	31	Microsoft (6)	Average	II 97	17.3	I 94	-3.9	800-762-6814
16.7	9.9	10.1	5.4	11.0	7.6	3 3 4 4	Very high	4	8	20	21	Ingersoll-Rand (2)	Average	II 97	11.5	IV 97	-6.3	800-373-9387
30.4	29.9	18.3	17.7	17.1	16.0	2 2 3 1	Very low	1	9	26	30	Pfizer (5)	Average	II 97	16.4	I 94	-5.2	800-373-9387
17.9	14.6	13.6	11.0	NA	NA	2 3	Very high	-1	3	22	19	General Signal (2)	Very low	I 97	8.2	I 94	-2.5	800-373-9387
27.3	21.3	19.2	14.5	14.8	10.8	2 4 2 1	Average	1	19	21	28	Philips Electronics (ADR) (3)	Average	II 97	15.3	IV 94	-2.4	800-373-9387
31.3	28.5	20.2	18.0	18.3	16.4	2 2 2 1	Average	2	6	25	28	General Electric (3)	Average	II 97	17.3	I 94	-3.4	800-373-9387
18.4	14.2	13.3	10.5	NA	NA	3 3	High	14	5	22	18	Carnival Cl A (2)	Average	II 97	11.9	IV 94	-3.7	800-373-9387
21.8	16.7	11.5	6.0	12.2	8.7	3 2 4 3	High	5	8	20	21	CNF Transportation (2)	High	II 97	12.2	IV 97	-7.0	800-373-9387
26.7	24.3	17.2	15.2	NA	NA	3 2	Very low	4	0	27	36	Midcap 400 Index (Fut.) (4)	Average	III 97	16.0	I 94	-3.8	800-373-9387
22.1	19.4	16.3	13.5	17.1	14.6	1 2 2 2	High	6	3	25	36	Global Industries (2)	Average	II 97	17.8	I 97	-6.8	800-373-9387
-2.0	-2.8	0.1	-1.7	5.5	3.5	4 2 4 4	High	1	20	27	5	Teva Pharmaceutical (ADR) (7)	Very high	II 97	15.8	IV 97	-21.3	800-554-4611
19.3	14.5	12.0	8.3	11.5	8.6	4 2 4 3	High	3	10	21	25	Watson Pharmaceuticals (3)	High	II 97	11.1	I 94	-7.1	800-554-4611
24.0	23.9	NA	NA	NA	NA	2	Very low	3	40	26	18	Intel (4)			NA		NA	800-554-4611
30.4	29.1	19.6	17.7	NA	NA	2 2 1	Very high	4	3	26	30	S&P 500 (Fut.) (4)	Average	II 97	17.3	I 94	-3.9	800-373-9387
32.0	29.2	NA	NA	NA	NA	1	Very high	11	3	25	15	Young Broadcasting Cl. A (2)			NA		NA	800-373-9387
29.8	26.0	16.3	12.7	16.2	13.5	1 2 4 1	Average	2	NA	31	35	Schlumberger (3)	Average	II 97	17.6	II 94	-5.3	800-373-9387
25.2	22.7	12.9	10.7	13.7	11.1	2 3 4 2	High	6	17	28	36	Sofamor/Danek Group (6)	High	II 97	16.9	II 93	-5.5	800-225-6265
21.5	17.8	14.4	11.1	13.1	9.8	4 3 3 3	Average	7	16	26	36	Sofamor/Danek Group (4)	Very low	II 97	11.2	I 94	-2.8	800-225-6265
NA	NA	NA	NA	NA	NA		Very low	1	7	30	14	Merck (8)			NA		NA	800-225-6265
16.7	12.3	8.8	5.6	11.6	8.4	3 1 4 3	High	2	16	25	19	ACC (6)	Average	I 93	10.5	I 94	-7.7	800-225-6265
27.5	22.0	18.2	13.6	15.2	12.1	4 2 4 1	Average	1	1	19	1	US Airways Group (1)	Average	III 97	17.3	I 94	-6.2	800-872-2710
34.7	33.3	21.8	20.1	18.5	16.2	3 1 2 1	Low	4	2	35	35	Cisco Systems (5)	Average	II 97	21.2	II 94	-4.2	800-432-4320
13.5	11.8	14.9	13.4	13.8	12.2	1 4 1 4	Low	12	99	24	5	Novartis (Reg) (3)	Average	II 97	12.2	IV 97	-7.5	800-421-4120
20.6	18.1	13.0	10.8	12.0	9.7	4 3 4 3	Average	1	3	26	40	General Electric (4)	Very low	II 97	10.4	I 94	-4.4	800-343-2898
19.8	15.5	13.2	10.1	NA	NA	3 3	Low	5	4	28	23	General Electric (2)	Very low	II 97	9.3	I 94	-2.9	800-343-2898
27.7	23.0	16.6	12.9	14.0	11.0	3 4 4 1	High	4	6	29	35	General Electric (4)	Average	II 97	16.3	I 94	-4.7	800-343-2898
22.0	20.3	15.8	14.0	NA	NA	1 2 3	Very low	10	0	25	24	Intel (2)	Low	II 97	11.5	I 94	-3.7	800-343-2898
8.2	7.1	NA	NA	NA	NA	4		4	34	31	14	ACC (2)			NA		NA	800-343-2898
29.3	28.1	20.3	18.7	18.3	16.3	2 2 2 1	Very low	20	1	26	31	Webster Financial (2)	Low	II 97	15.6	I 94	-4.2	800-343-2898
20.7	18.2	13.2	10.5	12.3	9.8	4 3 4 3	High	1	14	20	15	PP&L Resources (4)	Low	II 97	10.7	I 94	-6.8	800-343-2898
15.9	12.2	14.4	10.8	17.0	14.1	2 1 1 4	Average	0	1	33	35	Astoria Financial (4)	Very high	II 97	16.6	I 97	-11.3	800-343-2898
23.8	19.8	15.8	12.1	15.1	11.9	2 3 2 2	High	4	3	31	33	General Electric (4)	High	II 97	16.6	II 94	-4.2	800-343-2898
25.4	21.9	17.0	14.1	15.9	13.2	2 3 2 2	Average	7	6	23	28	CoreStates Financial (3)	Low	II 97	11.7	I 94	-2.8	800-343-2898
28.1	26.9	17.6	15.4	15.7	13.5	3 2 3 1	Very low	17	1	25	47	Clear Channel Communs. (3)	Low	II 97	14.1	IV 94	-2.2	800-343-2898
26.1	23.6	18.5	16.6	17.2	15.6	2 2 2 2	Low	2	2	27	30	General Electric (4)	Average	II 97	16.5	I 94	-5.6	800-446-1012

merly Dean Witter Strat. (tt) Formerly Dean Witter Util. (uu) Formerly Dean Witter Val.-Ad. Mkt. (vv) Formerly Dean Witter World Wide (ww) Formerly Delaware Val. A. (xx) Formerly Dreyfus Disc. Stk. R. (yy) Formerly Premier Aggres. Gr. A. (zz) Formerly Premier Val. A. (aaa) Formerly Premier Gr. B. (bbb) Formerly EV Trad. Gr. (ccc) Formerly EV Trad. Inv. (ddd) Formerly EV Marathon Tax-Mgd. Gr. (eee) Formerly EV Trad. T/R. (fff) Formerly Keystone Bal. K-1. (ggg) Formerly Evergreen Bal. Y. (hhh) Formerly Keystone Gr.-Inc. S-1. (iii) Formerly Keystone Glbl. Opport. B. (jjj) Formerly Evergreen T/R Y. (kkk) Formerly Keystone Sm. Co. Gr. S-4. (lll) Formerly Keystone Strat. Gr. K-2. (mmm) Formerly Excelsior Eq. A.   DATA: MORNINGSTAR, INC., CHICAGO, IL.

MUTUAL FUND SCOREBOARD

FUND	OVERALL RATING (COMPARES RISK-ADJUSTED PERFORMANCE OF EACH FUND AGAINST ALL FUNDS)		CATEGORY (COMPARES RISK-ADJUSTED PERFORMANCE OF FUND WITHIN CATEGORY)	RATING	SIZE		FEES		1997 RETURNS (%)		
					ASSETS $MIL.	% CHG. 1996-97	SALES CHARGE (%)	EXPENSE RATIO (%)	PRE-TAX	AFTER-TAX	YIELD
EXCELSIOR INTERNATIONAL	C–		Foreign	C	177.7	61	No load	1.40	9.3	8.4	0.5
EXCELSIOR VALUE & RESTRUCT. A (nnn)	A		Mid-cap Blend	A	230.0	103	No load	0.91	33.6	33.0	0.5
FAM VALUE ⬚	B		Small-cap Value	C	331.8	31	No load	1.27	39.1	38.2	0.2
FEDERATED AMERICAN LEADERS A	B		Large-cap Value	C–	1256.7	108	5.50	1.17	32.0	28.1	0.7
FEDERATED EQUITY-INCOME B ⬚			Large-cap Blend		834.7	168	5.50**	1.87†	24.2	22.2	1.4
FEDERATED GROWTH STRAT. A	C–		Mid-cap Growth	B	487.2	24	5.50	1.13	27.1	21.5	0.0
FEDERATED MAX-CAP INSTL.	B+		Large-cap Blend		1233.9	29	No load	0.31	32.7	31.3	1.5
FEDERATED SMALL CAP STRAT. B			Small-cap Blend		192.4	327	5.50**	2.10†	13.4	13.4	0.0
FEDERATED STOCK	B+		Large-cap Value	B	1216.4	45	No load	0.99	34.4	29.4	0.9
FEDERATED UTILITY A	C		Utilities	C	781.6	3	5.50	1.15	26.6	22.5	2.5
FIDELITY	B+		Large-cap Blend	A	6335.5	42	No load	0.59	32.1	29.3	1.0
FIDELITY ADVISOR BALANCED T (ooo)	C		Domestic Hybrid	D	2995.2	4	3.50	1.25†	22.3	19.3	2.8
FIDELITY ADVISOR EQUITY GROWTH T ⬚	C		Large-cap Growth	B	4206.3	22	3.50	1.34†	23.9	20.7	0.0
FIDELITY ADVISOR EQUITY INCOME T	B+		Large-cap Value	B	2255.4	36	3.50	1.26†	25.9	23.9	0.9
FIDELITY ADVISOR GROWTH OPPORT. T ⬚	A		Large-cap Value	B+	20408.6	35	3.50	1.34†	28.6	26.5	1.1
FIDELITY ADVISOR MID CAP T			Mid-cap Blend		326.5	71	3.50	1.60†	27.3	23.3	0.0
FIDELITY ADVISOR NATURAL RES. T ⬚	C–		Natural Resources	B	528.3	–19	3.50	1.44†	–0.8	–4.5	0.0
FIDELITY ADVISOR OVERSEAS T	C–		Foreign	B	1096.8	6	3.50	1.60†	11.3	9.5	0.9
FIDELITY ADVISOR STRAT. OPPORT. T	C		Mid-cap Value	D	529.3	–6	3.50	1.27†	26.0	22.0	0.0
FIDELITY ASSET MANAGER	B		Domestic Hybrid	C	11890.5	8	No load	0.78	22.3	19.4	3.1
FIDELITY ASSET MANAGER: GROWTH	B		Domestic Hybrid	C	4530.9	34	No load	0.86	26.5	23.2	2.0
FIDELITY ASSET MANAGER: INCOME	A		Domestic Hybrid	B+	687.3	17	No load	0.76	12.4	10.2	4.4
FIDELITY BALANCED ⬚	B		Domestic Hybrid	C–	4283.9	9	No load	0.74	23.5	19.6	3.4
FIDELITY BLUE CHIP GROWTH	B		Large-cap Blend	B	13166.0	38	3.00	0.78	27.0	25.4	0.6
FIDELITY CAPITAL APPRECIATION	B		Mid-cap Blend	B	2046.9	25	No load	0.80	26.5	21.9	0.4
FIDELITY CONTRAFUND	B		Large-cap Blend	B	30263.0	27	3.00	0.79	23.0	19.7	0.7
FIDELITY DESTINY I ⬚	A		Large-cap Value	A	6034.5	23	8.67	0.38	30.9	27.9	1.8
FIDELITY DESTINY II ⬚	A		Large-cap Value	A	3693.2	32	8.67	0.53	29.6	27.0	1.7
FIDELITY DISCIPLINED EQUITY	C		Large-cap Blend	C–	2451.5	17	No load	0.64	33.3	29.0	0.9
FIDELITY DIVERSIFIED INTL.	C		Foreign	A	1496.7	98	No load	1.27	13.7	12.6	1.2
FIDELITY DIVIDEND GROWTH ⬚			Large-cap Blend		4368.9	86	No load	0.92	27.9	24.5	0.6
FIDELITY EMERGING GROWTH ⬚	D		Mid-cap Growth	C	1977.9	7	3.75*	1.09	19.5	13.4	0.0
FIDELITY EMERGING MARKETS ⬚	F		Diversified Emerging Mkts.		463.1	–60	4.50*	1.35	–40.8	–41.2	2.4
FIDELITY EQUITY-INCOME	A		Large-cap Value	B+	21177.7	49	No load	0.66	30.0	28.0	1.8
FIDELITY EQUITY-INCOME II	B+		Large-cap Value	C	16977.5	11	No load	0.72	27.2	23.6	1.5
FIDELITY EUROPE	B+		Europe	B	926.0	20	4.00*	1.18	22.9	20.5	1.2
FIDELITY EUROPE CAPITAL APPREC.			Europe		368.8	95	4.00*	1.07	25.0	20.2	1.0
FIDELITY FIFTY			Large-cap Blend		171.4	16	3.00	0.84	23.0	19.9	0.3
FIDELITY GROWTH & INCOME	A		Large-cap Blend	A	35785.6	50	No load	0.71	30.2	28.7	1.1
FIDELITY GROWTH COMPANY ⬚	C		Large-cap Growth	C	10523.8	13	No load	0.85	18.9	16.2	0.5
FIDELITY HONG KONG & CHINA			Pacific/Asia ex-Japan		178.8	–9	4.50*	1.62	–22.1	–22.2	0.5
FIDELITY INTL. GROWTH & INCOME	C		International Hybrid	C–	1024.2	–5	No load	1.14	7.1	5.6	1.8
FIDELITY INTL. VALUE			Foreign		383.9	44	No load	1.26	7.9	7.3	0.5
FIDELITY JAPAN	F		Japan		230.9	–10	4.50*	1.14	–10.7	–11.2	1.8
FIDELITY LATIN AMERICA			Latin America		826.7	55	4.50*	1.32	32.9	32.4	1.2
FIDELITY LOW-PRICED STOCK	A		Small-cap Value	A	10459.3	85	4.50*	1.01	26.7	24.5	1.1
FIDELITY MAGELLAN	C		Large-cap Blend	C–	63035.4	17	3.00‡	0.64	26.6	24.5	1.2
FIDELITY MID-CAP STOCK ⬚			Mid-cap Blend		1700.6	0	No load	0.96	27.1	24.2	0.1
FIDELITY NEW MILLENNIUM	C		Mid-cap Growth	A	1529.9	22	3.00‡	1.03	24.6	20.5	0.0
FIDELITY OTC	C–		Mid-cap Growth	B	3956.8	17	3.00	0.84	9.9	8.0	0.0
FIDELITY OVERSEAS	C–		Foreign	B	3683.9	13	No load	1.12	10.9	9.7	1.0
FIDELITY PACIFIC BASIN	F		Diversified Pacific/Asia	C	227.7	–49	4.00*	1.24	–15.1	–15.6	2.0
FIDELITY PURITAN ⬚	B+		Domestic Hybrid	B+	22821.8	23	No load	0.66	22.4	19.8	3.3
FIDELITY REAL ESTATE INVESTMENT ⬚	C		Specialty-Real Estate		2375.9	38.0	0.8*	0.90	21.4	19.1	3.8
FIDELITY RETIREMENT GROWTH	C		Large-cap Blend	D	4017.7	–1	No load	0.70	18.5	14.2	0.6
FIDELITY SEL. AMERICAN GOLD ⬚	F		Precious Metals	B	262.0	–26	3.75*	1.42	–39.4	–40.4	0.0
FIDELITY SEL. BIOTECHNOLOGY ⬚	F		Health	D	616.1	–3	3.75*	1.56	15.4	12.0	0.0
FIDELITY SEL. BROKERAGE & INVMT. ⬚	C		Financial	D	509.0	357	3.75*	1.93	62.3	61.5	0.2
FIDELITY SEL. COMPUTERS ⬚	D		Technology	D	660.0	–1	3.75*	1.44	–1.1	–9.9	0.0
FIDELITY SEL. DEVELOP. COMMUN. ⬚	F		Communications		221.6	–20	3.75*	1.62	5.6	–0.6	0.0
FIDELITY SEL. ELECTRONICS	C–		Technology	B+	2549.1	63	3.75*	1.29	14.2	4.6	0.0
FIDELITY SEL. ENERGY ⬚	C–		Natural Resources	C	185.6	–23	3.75*	1.55	10.5	5.4	0.4
FIDELITY SEL. ENERGY SERVICE	C		Natural Resources	B+	1625.3	189	3.75*	1.45	51.9	48.4	0.0
FIDELITY SEL. FINANCIAL SERVICES	C		Financial	C–	457.6	36	3.75*	1.43	42.0	37.8	0.6
FIDELITY SEL. FOOD & AGRICULTURE	B		Unaligned	B+	218.8	–13	3.75*	1.50	30.3	26.3	0.7
FIDELITY SEL. HEALTH CARE ⬚	B		Health	B+	1569.3	26	3.75*	1.32	31.1	25.2	0.2
FIDELITY SEL. HOME FINANCE	A		Financial	B	1493.0	88	3.75*	1.34	45.9	41.1	0.5
FIDELITY SEL. REGIONAL BANKS	B		Financial	C	1047.5	105	3.75*	1.45	45.5	44.3	0.7
FIDELITY SEL. SOFTWARE & COMPUTERS ⬚	D		Technology	C	433.9	8	3.75*	1.51	14.9	10.5	0.0
FIDELITY SEL. TECHNOLOGY	D		Technology	C	547.9	12	3.75*	1.44	10.4	2.7	0.0

*Includes redemption fee. **Includes deferred sales charge. †12(b)-1 plan in effect. ‡Not currently accepting new accounts. §Less than 0.5% of assets. NA=Not available. NM=Not meaningful.
(nnn) Formerly Excelsior Business & Industrial A. (ooo) Formerly Fidelity Advisor Income & Growth T.

3 YEARS PRETAX	3 YEARS AFTERTAX	5 YEARS PRETAX	5 YEARS AFTERTAX	10 YEARS PRETAX	10 YEARS AFTERTAX	RESULTS VS. ALL FUNDS	TURNOVER	CASH %	FOREIGN %	P-E RATIO	UNTAXED GAINS (%)	LARGEST HOLDING COMPANY (% ASSETS)	RISK LEVEL	BEST QTR	BEST %RET	WORST QTR	WORST %RET	TELEPHONE
8.0	7.2	11.3	10.3	7.6	6.7	3424	Low	4	98	23	12	Siebe (3)	High	II 97	12.7	IV 97	-6.7	800-446-1012
32.4	31.3	27.2	26.4	NA	NA	11	Average	3	9	26	31	Texas Instruments (2)	Low	II 97	18.7	IV 94	-4.1	800-446-1012
22.8	21.9	14.7	13.8	19.1	18.1	1142	Very low	4	NA	21	49	Reliastar Financial (7)	Low	III 97	17.0	I 94	-3.9	800-932-3271
29.2	26.3	19.3	17.0	15.8	13.1	4221	Average	3	6	23	22	Sun (3)	Average	II 97	14.0	IV 94	-2.8	800-341-7400
26.0	23.8	NA	NA	NA	NA	2	Average	2	6	24	16	Mellon Bank (3)			NA		NA	800-341-7400
29.9	23.9	15.6	11.8	17.0	13.7	1341	Average	3	3	32	34	General Electric (2)	High	III 97	17.6	IV 97	-5.9	800-341-7400
30.6	27.5	19.8	17.5	NA	NA	21	Very low	5	3	26	37	General Electric (3)	Average	II 97	17.4	I 94	-3.9	800-341-7400
NA	NA	NA	NA	NA	NA		Average	4	1	23	14	Frontier Insurance Group (1)			NA		NA	800-341-7400
30.2	25.8	19.9	16.7	15.8	12.7	4221	Average	1	6	23	38	Dayton Hudson (3)	Low	II 97	14.6	IV 94	-3.4	800-341-7400
21.1	18.2	13.5	11.1	NA	NA	142	Average	6	6	23	27	CMS Energy (3)	Low	IV 97	12.9	I 94	-7.2	800-341-7400
28.1	25.0	20.6	17.3	17.4	14.5	2323	High	3	6	26	28	General Electric (4)	Low	II 97	17.4	I 94	-2.5	800-544-8888
14.8	12.9	11.4	9.8	13.9	11.7	2143	Very high	2	13	25	24	Citicorp (2)	Low	II 97	12.6	I 94	-3.1	800-522-7297
26.1	23.9	17.9	16.2	NA	NA	12	Average	7	5	30	32	Philip Morris (4)	Average	II 97	17.2	II 94	-4.0	800-522-7297
24.1	22.4	19.2	17.8	NA	NA	12	Average	2	6	22	28	British Petroleum (ADR) (4)	Low	II 97	15.7	I 94	-2.5	800-522-7297
26.3	24.6	20.4	18.8	21.1	19.1	1112	Low	7	10	23	32	Philip Morris (7)	Low	II 97	14.4	IV 94	-1.0	800-522-7297
NA	NA	NA	NA	NA	NA			3	2	30	18	Evergreen Media Cl. A (1)			NA		NA	800-522-7297
18.6	15.9	17.6	15.6	15.6	13.2	1413	High	4	28	25	15	Total (ADR) (4)	High	III 97	14.2	IV 97	-13.2	800-522-7297
10.8	9.5	14.5	13.6	NA	NA	414	Average	7	96	27	20	Alcatel Alsthom (2)	Average	I 93	13.9	IV 97	-6.7	800-522-7297
20.9	17.9	14.6	12.0	15.2	12.7	2223	High	6	11	26	31	Whole Foods Market (9)	Average	III 97	18.1	I 94	-6.5	800-522-7297
17.7	15.4	13.4	11.4	NA	NA	133	Average	11	8	24	28	Fannie Mae (5)	Low	II 97	11.3	I 94	-4.8	800-544-8888
21.3	19.0	15.9	14.1	NA	NA	32	Average	9	8	23	18	Fannie Mae (6)		II 97	13.7	IV 94	-5.1	800-544-8888
12.2	10.1	10.0	8.1	NA	NA	34	High	33	4	23	11	Fannie Mae (2)	Very low	I 93	6.5	I 94	-2.0	800-544-8888
15.8	13.4	11.9	9.7	12.7	10.2	3243	Average	0	9	22	16	General Electric (2)	Low	II 97	11.3	I 94	-3.3	800-544-8888
23.5	20.9	20.8	18.0	20.2	18.6	1112	Average	4	3	29	24	General Electric (3)	Average	II 97	16.7	I 97	0.0	800-544-8888
20.0	16.6	18.8	15.4	16.1	13.2	1413	Very high	2	6	28	28	Microsoft (5)	Average	II 97	17.5	IV 94	-3.4	800-544-8888
26.9	23.5	19.7	17.1	23.0	20.8	1112	High	8	16	28	30	Schlumberger (2)	Average	II 95	13.8	II 94	-3.2	800-544-8888
28.6	25.4	22.9	18.8	20.6	16.9	2111	Low	4	10	23	47	Fannie Mae (7)	Low	II 97	15.4	IV 94	-0.6	800-752-2347
27.6	25.1	22.4	19.4	21.1	17.9	1112	Low	5	9	24	40	Fannie Mae (6)	Low	II 97	14.6	IV 94	-0.7	800-752-2347
25.6	21.9	18.4	15.5	NA	NA	122	High	7	0	23	24	General Electric (4)	Average	II 97	15.2	I 94	-1.5	800-544-8888
17.2	15.8	17.3	16.2	NA	NA	13	High	6	97	23	17	Novartis (Reg) (2)	Average	I 93	14.4	IV 97	-4.3	800-544-8888
31.8	29.3	NA	NA	NA	NA	1	High	6	6	25	19	Schering-Plough (4)			NA		NA	800-544-8888
23.4	20.6	17.6	14.5	NA	NA	13	High	1	5	34	36	Microsoft (3)	High	II 95	19.6	II 94	-10.2	800-544-8888
-14.2	-14.8	-1.2	-1.6	NA	NA	14	Average	5	100	11	-91	Telebras (ADR) (6)	Very high	IV 93	39.7	IV 97	-22.6	800-544-8888
27.5	25.1	20.3	18.0	16.7	14.3	3211	Low	4	13	22	34	General Electric (3)	Low	II 97	14.8	I 94	-3.3	800-544-8888
24.0	21.5	18.5	16.1	NA	NA	22	Average	3	10	25	34	General Electric (4)	Low	II 97	15.9	IV 94	-2.2	800-544-8888
22.4	20.2	19.9	18.5	12.9	11.8	2412	Average	3	100	25	31	Shell Trans. & Trad. (Reg) (3)	Average	II 97	9.4	II 94	-2.3	800-544-8888
21.7	18.6	NA	NA	NA	NA	2	Very high	6	100	27	12	Rhone-Poulenc Cl. A (4)			NA		NA	800-544-8888
23.5	20.4	NA	NA	NA	NA	3	High	1	3	29	20	Russell 2000 Futures (7)			NA		NA	800-544-8888
28.4	26.5	20.9	18.9	19.8	17.3	1111	Low	5	8	27	30	General Electric (3)	Low	II 97	16.8	I 94	-2.7	800-544-8888
24.7	22.6	17.1	14.9	19.6	17.6	1113	Average	5	5	31	32	General Electric (2)	High	II 95	16.0	II 94	-4.0	800-544-8888
NA	NA	NA	NA	NA	NA		High	3	100	12	-6	HSBC Holdings (HK) (21)			NA		NA	800-544-8888
10.7	9.4	12.2	11.2	9.1	8.3	3424	High	7	100	26	18	Honda Motor (1)	Average	I 93	11.4	IV 97	-5.2	800-544-8888
10.4	9.6	NA	NA	NA	NA	4	Average	13	95	26	10	Alcatel Alsthom (2)			NA		NA	800-544-8888
-8.1	-8.3	1.7	1.2	NA	NA	34	Average	4	99	32	-26	Toyota Motor (5)	Very high	II 97	23.5	IV 97	-15.5	800-544-8888
13.2	12.7	NA	NA	NA	NA	1	Average	7	100	19	4	Telebras (ADR) (7)			NA		NA	800-544-8888
26.2	23.3	20.4	17.1	NA	NA	111	Average	18	25	20	23	Canadian Nat'l. Railway (1)	Very low	III 97	13.0	IV 94	-1.3	800-544-8888
24.6	21.1	18.8	15.8	18.9	15.8	1213	Average	4	9	27	8	General Electric (3)	Average	II 97	16.6	II 94	-4.5	800-544-8888
26.2	23.4	NA	NA	NA	NA	2	High	5	1	28	24	Keane (1)			NA		NA	800-544-8888
32.7	29.7	24.0	22.0	NA	NA	11	High	3	9	29	36	Global Marine (3)	High	III 97	19.4	IV 97	-8.8	800-544-8888
23.4	20.3	14.7	11.9	17.9	15.0	1123	High	5	6	30	25	Intel (7)	High	II 97	16.4	IV 97	-11.0	800-544-8888
11.0	9.6	14.2	13.1	8.2	6.7	4414	Average	10	96	26	21	Alcatel Alsthom (2)	Average	II 97	12.5	IV 97	-6.8	800-544-8888
-8.1	-8.4	4.3	3.3	1.4	0.7	4414	Average	5	100	27	-32	Toyota Motor (6)	Very high	II 97	19.1	IV 97	-17.2	800-544-8888
19.6	16.6	16.2	13.0	15.0	12.0	3223	Average	4	13	25	19	General Electric (3)	Low	II 97	12.3	IV 94	-1.8	800-544-8888
22.4	20.4	16.1	14.3	14.9	13.1	4141	Average	4	1	30	27	Equity Resident. Ppty. Tr. (5)	Average	IV 96	19.0	IV 93	-5.6	800-544-8888
16.9	14.8	14.3	10.5	15.6	12.4	1223	Very high	3	15	27	22	Wal-Mart Stores (4)	Average	II 97	15.3	IV 97	-5.4	800-544-8888
-6.9	-7.6	4.1	3.6	-0.2	-0.4	4413	Average	5	63	43	-13	Getchell Gold (10)	Very high	II 93	32.5	IV 97	-32.1	800-544-8888
22.0	19.3	8.4	7.0	19.2	17.4	1143	Low	6	2	37	30	Genentech (10)	Very high	III 97	14.6	I 93	-19.3	800-544-8888
41.0	39.0	28.2	26.5	22.3	21.3	3111	Very low	10	9	18	31	Morg. St., Dean Wit., Disc. (7)	High	II 97	26.0	I 94	-13.9	800-544-8888
25.4	19.4	25.1	20.8	19.4	17.2	4114	Very high	11	4	25	28	Compaq Computer (10)	Very high	III 97	30.2	IV 97	-25.8	800-544-8888
12.4	7.5	16.6	12.3	NA	NA	1114	Very high	13	14	30	21	Vitesse Semiconductor (7)	Very high	II 97	22.9	I 97	-15.5	800-544-8888
40.0	33.4	33.5	28.4	23.4	21.0	3212	Very high	7	12	26	22	Compaq Computer (8)	Very high	II 95	36.3	IV 97	-22.3	800-544-8888
21.1	18.0	16.3	14.0	12.6	10.9	1422	Average	6	31	23	31	Total Cl. B (ADR) (7)	High	I 93	16.3	IV 93	-9.5	800-544-8888
47.2	45.0	31.2	29.5	17.4	16.6	1411	High	11	12	32	36	Cooper Cameron (6)	High	III 97	36.9	IV 93	-12.1	800-544-8888
40.3	37.6	25.6	22.4	22.0	19.8	4111	Average	7	0	20	36	Barnett Banks (7)	High	II 97	17.9	IV 94	-6.3	800-544-8888
26.4	23.3	18.4	15.6	21.5	18.8	1122	Average	6	3	30	28	Philip Morris (4)	Low	II 97	10.5	I 94	-2.4	800-544-8888
30.2	25.4	22.4	19.0	23.2	20.0	1112	Average	6	11	34	34	American Home Products (9)	Average	II 97	21.3	I 93	-13.1	800-544-8888
45.2	42.2	32.0	28.6	27.6	25.5	4111	Average	5	NA	23	35	Washington Mutual (5)	Average	II 97	19.4	IV 94	-10.6	800-544-8888
42.6	40.7	26.4	23.3	26.0	23.4	3121	Average	4	4	21	33	BankAmerica (7)	Average	II 97	15.4	IV 94	-7.2	800-544-8888
26.9	22.7	22.2	17.9	20.8	18.0	3112	Very high	5	5	37	26	Microsoft (10)	High	III 94	21.6	II 94	-17.5	800-544-8888
22.4	17.0	21.3	16.9	19.0	16.5	4114	Very high	9	13	31	17	Compaq Computer (10)	Very high	II 95	22.1	IV 97	-19.9	800-544-8888

DATA: MORNINGSTAR, INC., CHICAGO, IL.

MUTUAL FUND SCOREBOARD

FUND	OVERALL RATING (COMPARES RISK-ADJUSTED PERFORMANCE OF EACH FUND AGAINST ALL FUNDS)	CATEGORY (COMPARES RISK-ADJUSTED PERFORMANCE OF FUND WITHIN CATEGORY)	RATING	SIZE ASSETS $MIL.	SIZE % CHG. 1996-97	FEES SALES CHARGE (%)	FEES EXPENSE RATIO (%)	1997 RETURNS (%) PRE-TAX	1997 RETURNS (%) AFTER-TAX	1997 RETURNS (%) YIELD
FIDELITY SEL. TELECOMMUNICATIONS	C	Communications		423.7	–3	3.75*	1.47	25.8	22.1	0.0
FIDELITY SEL. UTILITIES GROWTH ⚲	C	Utilities	C	250.2	–2	3.75*	1.46	30.4	26.1	1.0
FIDELITY SMALL CAP SELECTOR (ppp)		Small-cap Blend		944.8	76	3.75*	0.90	27.3	25.2	0.8
FIDELITY SOUTHEAST ASIA		Pacific/Asia ex-Japan		276.2	–64	4.50*	1.12	–38.9	–39.0	0.6
FIDELITY SPARTAN MARKET INDEX (qqq)	B+	Large-cap Blend	B+	3697.9	131	0.50*	0.44	33.0	31.8	1.4
FIDELITY STOCK SELECTOR	C	Large-cap Blend	D	1876.2	17	No load	0.84	28.9	25.7	1.1
FIDELITY TREND ⚲	D	Mid-cap Blend	F	1497.7	12	No load	0.66	8.5	5.8	0.1
FIDELITY UTILITIES ⚲	B	Utilities	B+	1708.7	35	No load	0.81	31.6	27.6	2.0
FIDELITY VALUE	A	Mid-cap Value	B+	7942.6	12	No load	0.66	21.1	17.7	0.8
FIDELITY WORLDWIDE	C	World	B	1117.2	21	No load	1.18	12.1	10.3	0.6
FIRST EAGLE FUND OF AMERICA ⚲	B+	Mid-cap Value	B	268.9	57	No load	1.80	29.5	24.0	0.0
FIRST INVESTORS BLUE CHIP A ⚲	C	Large-cap Blend	C–	350.7	46	6.25	1.44†	26.1	23.8	0.3
FIRST INVESTORS GLOBAL A	C–	World	C–	277.2	5	6.25	1.83†	8.0	5.2	0.4
FIRST INVESTORS GROWTH & INCOME A		Large-cap Blend		211.1	75	6.25	1.31†	27.2	26.3	0.3
FIRST INVESTORS SPECIAL SITUATIONS A	D	Small-cap Growth	C	194.1	23	6.25	1.59†	16.2	14.1	0.0
FIRST OMAHA EQUITY	B+	Large-cap Blend	B+	287.3	12	No load	1.04†	19.3	16.8	1.9
FIRST PRIORITY GROWTH INVMT.	C	Large-cap Growth	B	264.4	56	7.75**	1.05†	27.2	24.2	0.4
FLAG INVESTORS TELEPHONE INCOME A ⚲	C	Communications		622.8	23	4.50	1.14†	37.4	34.3	1.9
FLAG INVESTORS VALUE BUILDER A	A	Domestic Hybrid	B+	408.4	63	4.50	1.27†	22.7	21.4	2.2
FORTIS CAPITAL A ⚲	C–	Large-cap Growth	D	336.5	12	4.75	1.18†	23.8	18.9	0.0
FORTIS GROWTH A ⚲	D	Mid-cap Growth	D	715.3	3	4.75	1.07†	13.7	10.5	0.0
FOUNDERS BALANCED	A	Domestic Hybrid	A	966.3	145	No load	1.10†	18.9	15.4	2.5
FOUNDERS BLUE CHIP	B	Large-cap Blend	B	548.1	2	No load	1.15†	19.4	12.2	1.6
FOUNDERS DISCOVERY ⚲	D	Small-cap Growth	C–	254.5	2	No load	1.58†	12.0	8.4	0.0
FOUNDERS FRONTIER	D	Mid-cap Growth	C	231.4	–34	No load	1.52†	6.2	1.1	0.0
FOUNDERS GROWTH	C	Large-cap Growth	B	1730.1	68	No load	1.19†	26.6	21.5	0.4
FOUNDERS SPECIAL ⚲	C	Mid-cap Growth	C	323.7	–11	No load	1.34†	16.4	12.0	0.0
FOUNDERS WORLDWIDE GROWTH	C–	World	C	313.7	–8	No load	1.53†	10.6	7.2	0.2
FOUNTAIN SQ. MID CAP A	C–	Mid-cap Blend	C–	210.2	48	4.50	1.00†	32.6	29.5	0.1
FOUNTAIN SQ. QUALITY GROWTH A	C	Large-cap Blend	C–	448.4	63	4.50	0.99†	32.7	30.1	0.3
FPA CAPITAL ⚲	B+	Mid-cap Value	B	730.9	29	6.50‡	0.84	17.7	14.7	1.1
FPA PARAMOUNT ⚲	C–	Domestic Hybrid	F	699.2	1	6.50	0.86	–1.8	–7.3	1.8
FRANKLIN BALANCE SHEET INVESTMENT	A	Small-cap Value	A	1244.6	75	1.50‡	1.08†	26.0	23.9	1.3
FRANKLIN CALIF. GROWTH I	A	Mid-cap Growth	A	559.2	197	4.50	1.08†	15.7	14.3	0.6
FRANKLIN DYNATECH I ⚲	C–	Technology	B+	183.1	51	4.50	1.04†	14.6	13.1	1.0
FRANKLIN EQUITY I	C	Large-cap Growth	B+	519.4	26	4.50	0.91†	27.4	23.8	1.1
FRANKLIN EQUITY INCOME I	A	Large-cap Value	B	370.2	37	4.50	0.98†	27.2	24.7	3.2
FRANKLIN GLOBAL HEALTH I	D	Health	C–	185.1	19	4.50	1.14†	10.2	8.0	0.5
FRANKLIN GLOBAL UTILITIES I	C	Utilities	B	195.7	14	4.50	1.00†	27.0	23.0	2.1
FRANKLIN GOLD I ⚲	F	Precious Metals	B+	200.9	–41	4.50	1.05†	–35.7	–35.9	1.3
FRANKLIN GROWTH I ⚲	B	Large-cap Blend	C	1481.8	33	4.50	0.89†	18.6	17.8	1.7
FRANKLIN INCOME I ⚲	B+	Domestic Hybrid	B	7828.6	11	4.25	0.72†	16.9	13.9	7.0
FRANKLIN MICROCAP VALUE I		Small-cap Value		192.3	52	4.50‡	1.24†	27.7	26.1	0.0
FRANKLIN REAL ESTATE SEC. I		Real Estate		286.0	192	4.50	0.98†	19.9	18.9	2.4
FRANKLIN RISING DIVIDENDS I ⚲	C	Mid-cap Value	D	407.1	35	4.50	1.41†	32.4	28.8	0.6
FRANKLIN SMALL CAP GROWTH I	C–	Small-cap Growth	B+	2652.1	232	4.50	0.92†	15.8	14.7	0.4
FRANKLIN UTILITIES I ⚲	C–	Utilities	D	2043.0	–12	4.25	0.75†	24.9	22.3	4.6
FREMONT GLOBAL	C	International Hybrid	C	661.6	11	No load	0.87	9.9	7.6	3.3
FUNDAMENTAL INVESTORS ⚲	B+	Large-cap Blend	B+	10464.6	46	5.75	0.66†	26.7	23.2	1.4
GABELLI ASSET ⚲	A	Mid-cap Blend	B+	1334.2	23	No load	1.34†	38.1	34.5	0.2
GABELLI GROWTH	B	Large-cap Growth	A	951.5	53	No load	1.43†	42.6	37.8	0.0
GABELLI SMALL CAP GROWTH	B+	Small-cap Blend	A	293.0	35	No load	1.58†	36.5	32.4	0.0
GABELLI VALUE	B+	Mid-cap Blend	B+	596.7	29	5.50	1.40†	48.2	43.2	0.0
GALAXY ASSET ALLOC. RET. A	B+	Domestic Hybrid	B	194.5	57	3.75	1.42	19.8	17.0	2.4
GALAXY EQUITY GROWTH RET. A	B	Large-cap Blend	C	241.2	41	3.75	1.40	30.4	26.2	0.2
GALAXY EQUITY INCOME RET. A	B+	Large-cap Blend	B+	183.2	36	3.75	1.40	25.5	22.8	1.4
GALAXY EQUITY VALUE RET. A	B+	Large-cap Value	C	193.6	40	3.75	1.45	27.7	22.5	0.6
GALAXY II LARGE CO. INDEX RET.	B+	Large-cap Blend	B	547.0	55	No load	0.40	32.8	30.9	1.5
GALAXY II SMALL CO. INDEX RET.	C	Mid-cap Blend	C	379.3	16	No load	0.40	23.6	14.3	1.2
GAM INTERNATIONAL A	B	International Hybrid	B	1667.1	65	5.00	1.56†	29.1	27.3	3.1
GATEWAY INDEX PLUS	B+	Large-cap Blend	B+	254.5	31	No load	1.14	12.4	10.2	0.9
GINTEL ⚲	C–	Mid-cap Value	F	174.1	18	No load	1.80	29.2	27.3	0.7
GLOBAL UTILITY B	C	Utilities	B	179.5	–6	5.00**	1.96†	23.4	19.9	2.0
GOLDMAN SACHS CAPITAL GRTH A ⚲	C	Large-cap Blend	C	1215.1	38	5.50	1.40†	35.3	30.1	0.1
GOLDMAN SACHS CORE U.S. EQ. A (rrr)	B	Large-cap Blend	C	384.9	84	5.50	1.29†	31.8	28.9	0.4
GOLDMAN SACHS GROWTH & INC. A		Large-cap Value		1167.3	104	5.50	1.22†	27.9	24.7	0.4
GOLDMAN SACHS INTL. EQTY. A	C–	Foreign	C	686.9	32	5.50	1.69†	4.5	2.4	1.5
GOLDMAN SACHS SM. CAP VAL. A (sss)	C–	Small-cap Value	F	367.4	79	5.50	1.60†	30.2	26.9	0.0
GRADISON ESTABLISHED VALUE (ttt) ⚲	B+	Mid-cap Value	B	516.6	24	No load	1.12†	22.7	20.1	1.4
GREENSPRING ⚲	A	Domestic Hybrid	A	180.9	98	No load	1.04	24.0	21.9	3.3

*Includes redemption fee. **Includes deferred sales charge. †12(b)-1 plan in effect. ‡Not currently accepting new accounts. §Less than 0.5% of assets. NA=Not available. NM=Not meaningful. (ppp) Formerly Fidelity Small Cap Stock. (qqq) Formerly Fidelity Market Index. (rrr) Formerly Goldman Sachs Select Equity A. (sss) Formerly Goldman Sachs Small Capital Eqty A. (ttt) Formerly Gradison-McDonald Established Value.

Equity Funds

3 YEARS PRETAX	3 YEARS AFTERTAX	5 YEARS PRETAX	5 YEARS AFTERTAX	10 YEARS PRETAX	10 YEARS AFTERTAX	HISTORY RESULTS VS. ALL FUNDS	TURNOVER	CASH %	FOREIGN %	P-E RATIO	UNTAXED GAINS (%)	LARGEST HOLDING COMPANY (% ASSETS)	RISK LEVEL	BEST QTR	BEST %RET	WORST QTR	WORST %RET	TELEPHONE
19.7	16.0	18.4	15.0	18.9	16.8	1213	Very high	6	24	37	26	WorldCom (14)	Average	II 97	24.3	I 97	–7.0	800-544-8888
25.0	22.1	15.3	12.3	16.1	13.6	2141	Low	11	1	29	34	SBC Communications (10)	Average	II 97	13.8	IV 93	–6.2	800-544-8888
22.3	20.4	NA	NA	NA	NA	3	Very high	6	9	20	26	Ross Stores (4)			NA		NA	800-544-8888
–8.9	–9.5	NA	NA	NA	NA	4	High	13	100	17	–62	Hutchison Whampoa (5)			NA		NA	800-544-8888
30.7	29.4	19.9	18.7	NA	NA	321	Very low	0	3	26	5	General Electric (3)	Average	II 97	17.4	I 94	–3.9	800-544-8888
27.2	23.9	18.8	16.1	NA	NA	2	Very high	4	14	22	32	Intel (5)	Average	II 97	15.2	I 93	–1.4	800-544-8888
15.7	12.0	11.5	8.2	14.6	12.0	1134	High	3	19	28	28	Anchor Gaming (4)	High	I 97	19.5	IV 97	–13.5	800-544-8888
24.2	21.5	16.0	13.4	15.3	12.7	3142	Average	3	2	24	38	GTE (5)	Low	IV 97	12.3	IV 93	–4.0	800-544-8888
21.6	18.5	18.9	16.2	17.5	15.4	2212	Average	3	8	24	–13	Wal-Mart Stores (3)	Low	II 97	13.7	IV 97	–4.2	800-544-8888
12.6	11.4	14.9	13.7	NA	NA	414	Average	6	76	20	21	Honda Motor (1)	Average	I 93	11.8	IV 97	–7.7	800-544-8888
31.7	27.2	22.5	18.2	18.2	14.9	2321	Average	2	NA	22	32	Aavid Thermal Tech. (4)	Average	II 97	14.2	IV 94	–5.2	800-451-3623
26.8	24.6	16.3	13.9	NA	NA	332	Average	7	6	28	34	General Electric (3)	Average	I 97	14.0	I 94	–3.5	800-423-4026
13.3	10.4	11.5	9.5	10.4	8.9	1434	Average	6	73	25	22	Canadian Pacific (2)	Average	II 97	11.3	IV 97	–6.6	800-423-4026
25.8	24.9	NA	NA	NA	NA	2	Low	4	3	26	28	General Electric (3)			NA		NA	800-423-4026
17.1	15.3	13.3	11.6	NA	NA	23	High	10	9	26	30	Rite Aid (1)	High	III 97	17.0	IV 97	–8.0	800-423-4026
20.5	17.7	15.8	13.5	NA	NA	23	Low	19	NA	23	30	Motorola (4)	Very low	II 97	12.3	I 94	–2.8	800-662-4203
24.6	22.1	14.7	12.8	NA	NA	42	Average	1	1	32	30	General Electric (6)	Average	II 97	20.0	I 94	–2.3	800-433-2829
27.7	24.5	18.1	15.7	18.1	15.6	1231	Low	1	5	35	51	SBC Communications (18)	Average	II 97	19.6	I 94	–5.7	800-767-3524
26.6	25.2	17.7	16.4	NA	NA	22	Very low	9	6	25	32	Conseco (4)	Very low	II 97	10.5	I 94	–2.6	800-767-3524
21.3	18.2	13.5	10.8	14.7	12.4	2233	Average	7	3	34	55	Microsoft (5)	High	II 97	18.0	I 97	–3.3	800-800-2638
18.7	15.9	11.1	9.0	15.2	13.3	1143	Low	10	6	36	56	WorldCom (4)	High	II 97	16.8	II 94	–12.3	800-800-2638
22.3	18.5	16.9	13.7	14.2	11.5	3322	High	0	31	24	11	US West Commun. Group (4)	Very low	II 97	10.1	IV 94	–1.9	800-525-2440
24.2	18.0	17.2	11.9	15.5	11.1	4214	Very high	1	32	25	27	US West Commun. Group (4)	Low	II 97	12.6	I 94	–2.8	800-525-2440
21.2	16.8	12.7	10.1	NA	NA	143	High	13	6	37	30	Fairfield Communities (3)	Very high	III 97	22.2	I 97	–12.6	800-525-2440
18.5	13.7	13.5	10.3	18.1	15.7	1123	Average	8	9	35	43	Watson Pharmaceuticals (4)	High	II 97	15.4	I 97	–12.0	800-525-2440
29.0	24.6	21.1	17.9	18.2	15.3	2211	High	6	8	30	25	General Electric (3)	High	II 97	17.9	II 94	–10.3	800-525-2440
19.1	14.4	13.2	9.2	16.6	12.8	2123	Very high	16	29	28	30	USA Waste Services (3)	High	II 97	15.9	II 94	–8.6	800-525-2440
15.0	12.9	14.1	12.5	NA	NA	214	Average	11	80	25	26	Sony (3)	Average	IV 93	15.3	I 94	–5.1	800-525-2440
25.3	23.0	15.2	13.8	NA	NA	42	Average	5	3	26	28	Adaptec (6)	Average	III 97	17.1	II 93	–4.8	800-334-0483
29.3	27.6	16.4	15.3	NA	NA	41	Low	2	NA	27	28	Intel (6)	Average	II 97	20.1	II 93	–4.2	800-334-0483
30.9	27.9	23.7	20.7	22.1	19.0	1111	Low	20	NA	19	38	Green Tree Financial (6)	Average	II 95	16.1	IV 95	–3.6	800-982-4372
12.7	8.6	13.6	9.6	14.4	9.9	2214	High	39	10	22	10	Newmont Mining (6)	Average	I 96	11.0	IV 97	–11.0	800-982-4372
24.4	21.9	19.7	17.6	NA	NA	212	Low	22	10	21	23	USLife (2)	Very low	II 97	11.5	IV 94	–4.3	800-342-5236
30.6	28.1	25.0	22.3	NA	NA	11	Average	14	3	29	17	Atlantic Richfield (2)	Average	III 97	16.1	I 97	–7.0	800-342-5236
23.0	21.8	16.1	14.7	16.4	14.9	1323	Very low	38	1	30	38	Intel (14)	Average	II 95	15.5	IV 97	–5.7	800-342-5236
27.7	24.9	17.4	14.2	14.6	12.1	2432	Average	5	9	33	42	Intel (2)	Average	II 97	16.9	IV 97	–3.5	800-342-5236
21.7	19.3	16.2	13.8	NA	NA	222	Low	5	14	20	22	Atlantic Richfield (2)	Very low	II 97	9.1	I 94	–4.7	800-342-5236
25.7	23.5	19.2	17.3	NA	NA	21	Average	15	17	38	19	Access Health (4)	High	III 95	22.2	I 93	–12.4	800-342-5236
23.0	19.7	17.4	14.9	NA	NA	22	Average	5	41	26	23	Tel. Argentina Cl. B (ADR) (4)	Average	II 97	12.3	I 94	–6.7	800-342-5236
–13.8	–14.9	1.2	0.2	–0.9	–1.9	4414	Very low	11	76	33	–16	Newmont Mining (11)	Very high	II 93	27.3	IV 97	–28.0	800-342-5236
24.2	23.5	16.1	15.5	14.3	13.5	3322	Very low	32	1	26	40	Schering-Plough (3)	Low	II 97	11.3	I 94	–6.5	800-342-5236
16.1	13.1	12.2	9.2	12.5	9.0	4133	Low	4	7	17	11	Philip Morris (2)	Very low	I 93	8.0	I 94	–5.2	800-342-5236
NA	NA	NA	NA	NA	NA			4	2	23	26	Video Lottery Technology (3)			NA		NA	800-342-5236
23.3	22.1	NA	NA	NA	NA	1	Very low	10	3	30	16	Patriot American Hospitality (4)			NA		NA	800-342-5236
28.6	26.2	14.3	12.7	15.3	14.1	3141	Low	3	1	22	43	Family Dollar Stores (3)	Low	II 97	14.2	I 94	–7.1	800-342-5236
27.9	25.9	22.7	20.6	NA	NA	12	Average	14	5	30	20	Scor (3)	High	II 97	18.7	I 97	–9.1	800-342-5236
18.5	15.8	10.4	8.1	12.1	9.7	4143	Very low	2	2	19	23	FPL Group (4)	Average	IV 97	15.0	I 94	–9.9	800-342-5236
14.3	10.9	11.4	9.0	NA	NA	334	Average	7	33	21	7	Exxon (1)	Low	II 97	9.4	I 94	–5.6	800-548-4539
26.8	23.9	19.6	16.6	17.2	14.2	2312	Low	6	16	23	33	Atlantic Richfield (3)	Low	II 97	14.0	I 94	–2.6	800-421-4120
25.1	21.8	18.6	16.5	17.6	15.3	1222	Very low	6	11	26	54	Time Warner (3)	Low	II 97	16.5	I 94	–2.9	800-422-3554
31.2	26.5	19.4	15.7	20.6	18.1	1231	Average	4	2	28	45	First Data (5)	Average	II 97	19.4	I 97	–5.9	800-422-3554
24.1	20.7	17.9	15.3	NA	NA	22	Very low	16	5	25	47	United Television (3)	Low	II 97	16.3	I 94	–3.6	800-422-3554
25.4	21.6	22.5	18.1	NA	NA	311	Low	1	7	26	46	Media General Cl. A (15)	Average	II 97	21.3	I 94	–6.0	800-422-3554
21.6	19.5	13.6	12.1	NA	NA	33	Average	10	NA	31	23	Home Depot (3)	Very low	II 97	10.2	I 94	–3.1	800-628-0414
28.8	26.0	17.8	15.9	NA	NA	31	Low	10	1	29	43	Schlumberger (2)	Low	II 97	16.2	I 94	–3.6	800-628-0414
24.8	22.0	16.3	14.1	NA	NA	32	Average	18	NA	27	28	Ford Motor (4)	Very low	II 97	13.3	I 94	–3.4	800-628-0414
25.5	21.1	18.6	15.1	NA	NA	322	High	4	2	22	30	S&P 500 Dep. Rec. (4)	Low	II 97	15.6	I 94	–1.8	800-628-0414
30.7	29.0	19.8	18.3	NA	NA	21	Very low	17	3	26	39	General Electric (2)	Average	II 97	17.4	I 94	–3.9	800-628-0414
25.3	20.8	16.1	12.9	NA	NA	32	Very low	16	1	25	47	Safeway (1)	Average	III 97	15.9	I 94	–3.7	800-628-0414
22.3	21.1	24.2	21.2	17.1	14.3	2413	Average	6	100	22	21	HSBC Holdings (HK) (4)	Average	IV 93	28.2	I 94	–10.6	800-426-4685
11.3	10.3	9.4	7.9	11.8	9.8	3444	Low	5	1	26	23	General Electric (7)	Very low	III 94	4.6	I 94	–2.6	800-354-6339
30.4	27.6	13.6	11.3	15.1	13.0	1341	Average	18	NA	17	46	Checkfree (20)	High	II 97	17.3	I 94	–9.5	800-243-5808
19.5	16.8	13.7	11.6	NA	NA	33	Very low	3	56	25	38	SBC Communications (3)	Low	IV 96	9.2	I 94	–5.7	800-225-1852
27.4	22.1	18.5	14.2	NA	NA	121	Average	2	2	29	38	BankAmerica (3)	Average	II 97	19.3	IV 94	–5.0	800-526-7384
29.3	27.4	19.8	17.4	NA	NA	21	Low	4	3	28	28	General Electric (4)	Average	II 97	16.7	I 94	–2.3	800-526-7384
29.1	26.1	NA	NA	NA	NA	1	Average	7	2	18	27	Lear (4)			NA			800-526-7384
13.8	12.0	10.7	9.3	NA	NA	44	Low	6	97	24	18	Novartis (Br.) (4)	High	II 97	11.9	IV 97	–8.1	800-526-7384
19.9	18.3	14.0	12.4	NA	NA	42	High	16	9	24	22	Movado Group (4)	High	II 96	15.6	IV 94	–13.4	800-526-7384
22.8	20.0	17.5	15.2	14.1	12.1	4312	Low	27	3	19	38	Compaq Computer (4)	Low	II 97	12.4	II 94	–3.5	800-869-5999
21.8	19.6	16.3	13.7	13.5	11.0	4322	Average	17	3	19	23	Castle Energy (3)	Very low	II 97	8.9	IV 94	–1.3	800-366-3863

DATA: MORNINGSTAR, INC., CHICAGO, IL.

MUTUAL FUND SCOREBOARD

FUND	OVERALL RATING (COMPARES RISK-ADJUSTED PERFORMANCE OF EACH FUND AGAINST ALL FUNDS)	CATEGORY (COMPARES RISK-ADJUSTED PERFORMANCE OF FUND WITHIN CATEGORY)	RATING	SIZE: ASSETS $MIL.	SIZE: % CHG. 1996-97	FEES: SALES CHARGE (%)	FEES: EXPENSE RATIO (%)	1997 RETURNS (%): PRE-TAX	1997 RETURNS (%): AFTER-TAX	1997 RETURNS (%): YIELD
GRIFFIN GROWTH & INCOME A		Large-cap Value		235.6	87	4.50	0.72†	26.0	22.7	0.9
GROWTH FUND OF AMERICA	C	Large-cap Blend	D	12247.8	27	5.75	0.72†	26.9	23.7	0.6
GT GLOBAL AMER. MID CAP GR. A (uuu)	C–	Mid-cap Growth	B	257.6	–25	4.75	1.36†	14.1	10.1	0.0
GT GLOBAL DEVELOP. MKTS. A		International Hybrid		231.2	–54	4.75	1.82†	–8.5	–9.8	5.0
GT GLOBAL EUROPE GROWTH A	C–	Europe	F	438.4	–7	4.75	1.82†	11.2	11.2	0.0
GT GLOBAL GROWTH & INCOME B	B	International Hybrid	B	470.6	18	5.00**	2.24†	17.5	16.2	2.2
GT GLOBAL HEALTH CARE A	D	Health	D	420.5	–19	4.75	1.80†	8.0	1.1	0.0
GT GLOBAL TELECOMMUN. A	D	Communications		861.7	–21	4.75	1.74†	13.2	11.7	0.0
GUARDIAN PARK AVENUE A	B+	Large-cap Blend	A	2249.0	61	4.50	0.79†	34.9	31.9	0.8
GUINNESS FLIGHT CHINA		Pacific/Asia ex-Japan		242.8	–21	1.00*	1.96	–20.3	–22.1	1.4
HANCOCK EMERGING GROWTH B	D	Small-cap Growth	C	454.6	0	5.00**	2.05†	14.5	9.5	0.0
HANCOCK FINANCIAL INDUSTRIES A		Financial		460.3	4566	5.00	NA†	37.8	37.4	0.7
HANCOCK GLOBAL TECHNOLOGY A	D	Technology	C–	180.0	4	5.00	1.57†	6.7	4.8	0.0
HANCOCK GROWTH & INCOME B	C	Large-cap Blend	C–	284.0	94	5.00**	1.90†	35.8	33.2	0.1
HANCOCK GROWTH A	D	Large-cap Growth	D	310.3	13	5.00	1.48†	16.7	12.8	0.0
HANCOCK REGIONAL BANK B	A	Financial	B+	5043.2	77	5.00**‡	2.07†	52.8	52.2	0.6
HANCOCK SOVEREIGN INVESTORS A	B	Large-cap Blend	C	1703.8	19	5.00	1.13†	29.1	26.0	1.3
HANCOCK SPECIAL EQUITIES B		Small-cap Growth		909.6	–9	5.00**	2.16†	4.1	4.1	0.0
HANCOCK SPECIAL OPPORTUNITIES B		Mid-cap Growth		197.9	–22	5.00**	2.29†	1.6	–1.3	0.0
HANCOCK SPECIAL VALUE B		Small-cap Value		256.4	1060	5.00**	1.69†	24.4	22.7	0.0
HARBOR CAPITAL APPRECIATION	C–	Large-cap Growth	C	2906.3	73	No load	0.75	31.5	27.5	0.2
HARBOR INTERNATIONAL	C	Foreign	A	5276.6	22	No load‡	0.99	15.5	14.5	1.1
HARBOR INTERNATIONAL GROWTH		Foreign		943.8	46	No load	1.10	3.6	2.6	0.7
HARBOR VALUE	B+	Large-cap Value	C	174.8	50	No load	0.83	31.2	25.2	1.7
HARTFORD CAP. APPREC. A (vvv)		Small-cap Blend		233.0	2488	5.50	NA†	55.1	53.3	0.0
HEARTLAND SMALL CAP CONTRARIAN		Small-cap Value		296.1	13	No load‡	1.30†	13.7	9.8	0.3
HEARTLAND VALUE	B	Small-cap Value	C	2192.1	35	No load‡	1.23†	23.2	19.9	0.5
HEARTLAND VALUE PLUS		Domestic Hybrid		306.6	360	No load	1.45†	30.6	26.6	2.8
HERITAGE SMALL CAP STOCK A		Small-cap Blend		234.2	114	4.75	1.41†	29.3	27.4	0.0
HOMESTEAD VALUE	A	Mid-cap Value	B+	367.0	58	No load	0.73	26.7	25.5	1.4
HOTCHKIS & WILEY EQUITY-INCOME	B	Large-cap Value	C–	196.9	–3	No load	0.88	31.2	26.5	2.0
HOTCHKIS & WILEY INTERNATIONAL	C	Foreign	B+	1041.9	100	No load	1.00	5.3	4.3	3.2
IAI EMERGING GROWTH	F	Mid-cap Growth	D	324.7	–47	No load	1.19	–2.9	–5.7	0.0
IAI REGIONAL	C	Mid-cap Blend	C	501.7	–11	No load	1.21	18.9	15.9	0.0
ICAP EQUITY		Large-cap Value		371.4	149	No load	0.80	29.1	25.7	1.0
IDEX GLOBAL A	C	World	B+	218.8	48	5.50	2.06†	20.4	17.4	0.0
IDEX GROWTH T		Large-cap Growth		644.3	12	8.50	1.17	17.1	13.4	0.1
IDS BLUE CHIP ADVANTAGE A	B	Large-cap Blend	C	1136.3	84	5.00	0.89	26.2	21.8	0.9
IDS DISCOVERY A	D	Mid-cap Growth	C–	940.2	17	5.00	1.13	18.8	14.8	0.0
IDS DIVERSIFIED EQUITY-INCOME A	B+	Large-cap Value	B	1815.4	31	5.00	0.93	20.1	15.8	3.4
IDS EMERGING MARKETS A		Diversified Emerging Mkts.		248.9	1352	5.00	NA	6.3	5.5	0.0
IDS EQUITY SELECT A	C	Mid-cap Blend	C	976.3	21	5.00	0.84	29.9	24.7	0.4
IDS EQUITY VALUE B	B	Large-cap Value	C	1709.0	16	5.00**	1.64†	23.1	17.7	1.6
IDS GLOBAL GROWTH A	D	Foreign	D	884.9	–6	5.00	1.37	7.2	6.3	0.9
IDS GROWTH A	C–	Large-cap Growth	C–	3094.6	31	5.00	1.04	20.8	20.0	0.1
IDS INTERNATIONAL A	D	Foreign	D	831.8	–11	5.00	1.31	1.9	1.0	1.2
IDS MANAGED ALLOCATION A	C–	Large-cap Blend	F	2546.2	2	5.00	0.80	14.6	9.8	2.6
IDS MUTUAL A	B	Domestic Hybrid	C	3243.1	12	5.00	0.87	18.8	14.2	3.6
IDS NEW DIMENSIONS A	C	Large-cap Growth	B	8787.6	30	5.00	0.94	24.6	22.4	0.7
IDS PROGRESSIVE A	B+	Small-cap Value	B	484.7	25	5.00	1.04	25.3	22.3	0.8
IDS RESEARCH OPPORTUNITIES A		Large-cap Blend		247.6	191	5.00	NA	26.2	23.0	0.0
IDS SMALL COMPANY INDEX A		Small-cap Blend		344.3	351	5.00	1.00	23.1	22.6	0.0
IDS STOCK A	C	Large-cap Blend	C	2876.5	19	5.00	0.80	25.2	20.7	1.4
IDS STRATEGY AGGRESSIVE B	C–	Mid-cap Growth	C	791.8	–4	5.00**	1.85†	14.7	9.8	0.0
IDS UTILITIES INCOME A	C	Utilities	B+	817.9	18	5.00	0.89	29.0	24.2	2.7
INCOME FUND OF AMERICA	A	Domestic Hybrid	A	20220.8	25	5.75	0.61†	22.2	18.6	4.3
INDEPENDENCE ONE EQUITY PLUS		Large-cap Blend		186.7	16	No load	0.39	28.7	27.1	1.3
INTERACTIVE INV. TECH. VALUE		Technology		194.4	454	No load	1.81	6.5	4.0	0.0
INVESCO DYNAMICS	C	Mid-cap Growth	B+	1120.5	31	No load	1.16†	24.9	20.5	0.0
INVESCO EUROPEAN	C	Europe	D	331.4	2	No load	1.36	15.2	10.1	0.5
INVESCO GROWTH	C	Large-cap Growth	C	753.3	16	No load	1.07†	27.2	18.5	0.1
INVESCO INDUSTRIAL INCOME	B+	Large-cap Blend	B+	4858.9	13	No load	0.95†	26.5	22.6	2.2
INVESCO SMALL COMPANY GROWTH (www)	D	Small-cap Growth	C	313.6	17	No load	1.52†	18.3	10.6	0.0
INVESCO STRAT. ENERGY	D	Natural Resources	C–	212.1	–9	No load	1.30	19.1	12.2	0.4
INVESCO STRAT. FINANCIAL SVCS	B	Financial	C–	1307.2	110	No load	1.11	44.8	40.0	0.8
INVESCO STRAT. HEALTH SCIENCE	D	Health	C–	945.8	1	No load	0.98	18.5	14.7	0.3
INVESCO STRAT. LEISURE	C	Unaligned	C	222.7	–6	No load	1.30	26.5	23.6	0.1
INVESCO STRAT. TECHNOLOGY	C–	Technology	B	1021.3	22	No load	1.08	8.9	2.5	0.4
INVESCO STRAT. UTILITIES	B	Utilities	B+	212.5	35	No load	1.17	24.4	22.8	2.4
INVESCO TOTAL RETURN	A	Domestic Hybrid	A	2160.7	76	No load	0.86	25.0	23.6	2.5

*Includes redemption fee. **Includes deferred sales charge. †12(b)-1 plan in effect. ‡Not currently accepting new accounts. §Less than 0.5% of assets. NA=Not available. NM=Not meaningful.
(uuu) Formerly GT Global America Growth A. (vvv) Formerly ITT Hartford Capital Appreciation A. (www) Formerly Invesco Emerging Growth.

3 YEARS PRETAX	3 YEARS AFTERTAX	5 YEARS PRETAX	5 YEARS AFTERTAX	10 YEARS PRETAX	10 YEARS AFTERTAX	RESULTS VS. ALL FUNDS	TURNOVER	CASH %	FOREIGN %	P-E RATIO	UNTAXED GAINS (%)	LARGEST HOLDING COMPANY (% ASSETS)	RISK LEVEL	BEST QTR	BEST %RET	WORST QTR	WORST %RET	TELEPHONE
28.3	25.6	NA	NA	NA	NA	1	Average	5	12	22	21	Philips Electronics (ADR) (3)			NA		NA	800-676-4450
23.6	20.9	16.7	14.6	16.7	14.4	1213	Low	15	10	27	14	Time Warner (4)	Average	III 97	14.0	I 94	-2.5	800-421-4120
17.6	14.0	15.3	11.9	17.7	15.1	1314	Very high	2	3	41	27	HFS (5)	High	III 97	16.8	I 97	-15.0	800-824-1580
4.2	2.6	NA	NA	NA	NA	4	High	4	99	18	-18	Asustek Computer (GDR) (3)			NA		NA	800-824-1580
13.5	13.2	12.1	11.7	8.1	7.5	1433	High	3	100	24	7	Telecom Italia (4)	High	IV 93	8.7	I 95	-4.4	800-824-1580
16.0	14.8	13.7	12.5	NA	NA	33	Low	1	74	20	29	Bristol-Myers Squibb (3)	Low	II 96	8.1	I 94	-5.0	800-824-1580
22.3	17.2	13.5	10.1	NA	NA	242	High	14	3	31	35	Protein Design Labs (7)	High	III 94	14.9	I 93	-14.9	800-824-1580
9.0	7.0	12.8	11.1	NA	NA	14	Low	2	63	34	24	Nokia Cl. A (5)	Very high	II 97	17.7	IV 97	-12.7	800-824-1580
31.8	28.4	22.1	19.4	19.2	16.3	2111	Average	7	2	23	36	General Electric (3)	Low	II 97	17.2	I 94	-2.9	800-221-3253
8.9	7.5	NA	NA	NA	NA	4	Low	4	100	13	-6	HSBC Holdings (HK) (12)			NA		NA	800-915-6565
22.5	20.4	15.1	14.0	18.4	17.6	1123	Average	0	4	35	64	Heftel Broadcasting Cl. A (1)	High	III 97	21.2	IV 97	-10.5	800-225-5291
NA	NA	NA	NA	NA	NA			10	11	21	NA	General Re (2)			NA		NA	800-225-5291
20.7	18.7	20.6	18.0	14.1	11.8	4414	Average	4	4	35	51	Computer Associates Intl. (6)	Very high	II 95	24.7	IV 97	-14.2	800-225-5291
30.8	28.4	17.2	15.6	NA	NA	41	Average	7	1	28	35	Progressive (4)	Average	II 97	18.2	I 94	-6.5	800-225-5291
21.4	18.3	13.3	10.7	14.1	11.6	2333	Average	1	2	31	44	Applied Materials (2)	High	II 97	13.9	II 94	-7.8	800-225-5291
42.5	41.7	28.4	27.2	26.1	24.0	3111	Very low	10	0	23	39	Washington Mutual (1)	Low	III 97	15.1	IV 94	-9.3	800-225-5291
25.2	22.8	15.3	13.5	15.1	12.8	3242	Average	7	NA	24	38	DuPont (3)	Low	II 97	14.0	I 94	-4.1	800-225-5291
17.0	16.7	NA	NA	NA	NA	4	Average	3	4	38	29	Chancelor Media (5)			NA		NA	800-225-5291
20.1	16.7	NA	NA	NA	NA	3	Very high	1	3	28	28	Suiza Foods (4)			NA		NA	800-225-5291
19.2	16.9	NA	NA	NA	NA	3	Average	1	5	25	13	Tejon Ranch (4)			NA		NA	800-225-5291
29.5	27.6	20.3	18.6	19.7	17.3	2112	Average	1	9	33	34	Pfizer (4)	High	II 97	19.8	II 94	-4.8	800-422-1050
17.2	16.2	19.8	18.8	17.7	16.4	1413	Very low	4	100	22	39	Lukoil (144A) (ADR) (4)	Average	IV 93	13.9	IV 97	-5.0	800-422-1050
19.3	18.5	NA	NA	NA	NA	3	Average	3	100	27	11	Granada Group (6)			NA		NA	800-422-1050
28.7	23.4	18.4	13.9	16.1	12.7	1431	High	3	3	22	24	General Signal (2)	Low	II 97	13.9	I 94	-5.0	800-422-1050
NA	NA	NA	NA	NA	NA			8	11	26	NA	CP Clare (5)			NA		NA	888-843-7824
NA	NA	NA	NA	NA	NA	3	Average	5	11	22	23	ICN Pharmaceuticals (4)			NA		NA	800-432-7856
24.6	22.0	18.5	16.4	18.8	16.6	3112	Low	22	5	19	35	ICN Pharmaceuticals (6)	Average	III 97	14.8	IV 97	-5.9	800-432-7856
29.5	26.3	NA	NA	NA	NA	1	Average	14	8	17	15	Core Capital REIT (Units) (3)			NA		NA	800-432-7856
31.1	28.9	NA	NA	NA	NA	1	Average	5	5	24	29	Precision Drilling Cl. A (2)			NA		NA	800-421-4184
26.0	24.5	19.5	18.3	NA	NA	12	Very low	8	3	20	32	Southwest Airlines (3)	Low	II 97	13.5	IV 94	-2.1	800-258-3030
27.4	23.3	18.3	15.1	15.9	13.3	3221	Average	3	4	19	38	AT&T (4)	Average	II 97	12.9	I 94	-4.7	800-346-7301
14.3	13.3	16.1	15.1	NA	NA	14	Low	6	100	19	10	Swiss Reinsurance (Reg) (2)	Average	IV 93	15.3	IV 97	-7.2	800-346-7301
15.8	12.7	12.3	9.9	NA	NA	24	Average	2	6	46	28	HNC Software (3)	Very high	II 97	20.1	I 97	-20.6	800-945-3863
22.2	17.7	14.9	11.2	15.9	12.4	1332	Average	0	0	27	30	Snap-On (4)	Average	III 97	17.0	IV 97	-6.5	800-945-3863
31.3	28.6	NA	NA	NA	NA	1	High	2	26	23	22	Philips Electronics (ADR) (5)			NA		NA	888-221-4227
22.4	19.7	19.3	17.5	NA	NA	12	High	5	88	30	27	Philips Electronics (3)	Average	IV 93	16.6	IV 95	-3.5	800-851-9777
NA	NA	NA	NA	NA	NA		Average	4	8	32	41	Microsoft (6)			NA		NA	800-851-9777
27.9	24.7	18.9	15.9	NA	NA	321	High	4	5	27	20	Royal Dutch Petrol. (ADR) (3)	Average	II 97	16.8	I 94	-3.1	800-328-8300
20.6	15.0	12.2	8.7	15.9	13.4	1142	High	2	5	29	27	Tech Data (3)	High	II 97	22.1	I 97	-11.2	800-328-8300
20.8	17.8	16.6	13.7	NA	NA	22	Average	25	13	22	16	Thomas & Betts (1)	Very low	II 97	9.6	IV 94	-4.0	800-328-8300
NA	NA	NA	NA	NA	NA			19	100	21	NA	China Merchant Hldgs. (144A) (4)			NA		NA	612-671-3733
27.5	22.9	16.9	13.3	15.8	12.7	2241	Average	4	6	28	41	Tyco International (3)	Average	II 97	16.0	I 94	-5.8	800-328-8300
23.6	19.9	16.3	13.1	15.9	12.7	2232	Average	20	15	22	35	Gannett (2)	Low	II 97	12.0	I 94	-3.8	800-328-8300
9.4	7.9	11.0	9.9	NA	NA	424	High	2	72	24	3	Telebras (ADR) (2)	High	IV 93	12.8	IV 94	-9.6	800-328-8300
28.5	27.3	18.9	16.8	19.0	15.3	1121	Low	2	6	32	46	Tellabs (4)	High	II 97	21.8	IV 97	-6.7	800-328-8300
7.2	5.9	9.8	8.4	7.7	6.2	3434	Average	9	98	23	11	Philips Electronics (4)	High	IV 93	11.0	IV 97	-8.4	800-328-8300
15.3	11.3	10.9	7.5	14.3	11.1	1144	High	23	34	28	18	General Electric (1)	Average	II 97	10.6	I 94	-6.0	800-328-8300
19.0	15.7	13.4	10.2	12.7	9.4	4233	Average	13	16	23	23	Gannett (1)	Very low	II 97	8.8	I 94	-3.8	800-328-8300
28.1	26.3	18.4	16.7	18.7	16.6	2121	Average	11	8	30	42	General Electric (4)	Average	II 97	15.5	I 94	-3.3	800-328-8300
22.3	19.5	15.7	13.1	13.1	10.7	4332	Average	17	10	21	32	Allied Group (3)	Low	II 97	12.5	I 94	-2.6	800-328-8300
NA	NA	NA	NA	NA	NA			1	NA	NA	NA				NA		NA	800-328-8300
NA	NA	NA	NA	NA	NA		Average	1	2	25	NA	Corrections Corp. of Amer. (1)			NA		NA	800-328-8300
23.4	20.4	16.3	13.0	15.5	11.9	2232	Average	3	24	27	35	General Electric (2)	Average	II 97	13.4	IV 94	-3.6	800-328-8300
22.3	19.2	13.0	10.5	14.7	12.9	1242	High	3	6	37	45	HBO (4)	High	III 95	12.9	I 97	-9.5	800-328-8300
22.2	19.3	15.0	12.2	NA	NA	242	Average	4	23	20	30	Ameritech (4)	Low	IV 97	13.7	I 94	-6.4	800-328-8300
22.0	18.8	15.1	12.2	14.4	11.5	3232	Low	13	15	19	25	Atlantic Richfield (3)	Very low	II 97	8.0	I 94	-4.5	800-421-4120
NA	NA	NA	NA	NA	NA			2	1	25	35	General Electric (7)			NA		NA	800-334-2292
40.2	37.3	NA	NA	NA	NA	1	Average	2	NA	37	9	PMC Sierra (9)			NA		NA	888-883-3863
25.7	21.4	18.3	14.0	18.6	15.6	3122	Very high	3	9	31	27	Cooper Cameron (2)	High	III 97	17.1	I 97	-8.2	800-525-8085
21.2	17.3	16.5	14.1	11.5	10.0	2422	Average	2	99	31	31	Novartis (Reg) (3)	Average	IV 96	10.1	II 94	-3.5	800-525-8085
25.9	19.2	15.6	11.4	15.7	12.2	2341	Very high	1	8	29	2	Merck (5)	Average	II 97	18.4	II 94	-4.7	800-525-8085
23.4	20.3	16.1	13.1	16.9	14.0	1132	Average	5	5	25	39	Warner-Lambert (2)	Low	II 97	13.3	I 94	-2.1	800-525-8085
19.8	16.4	15.3	11.8	NA	NA	23	Very high	16	12	31	30	Primark (1)	High	II 97	20.0	I 97	-10.4	800-525-8085
25.6	21.9	16.5	14.3	9.5	8.3	2441	Very high	7	7	25	31	Baker Hughes (5)	High	III 97	28.2	IV 97	-13.8	800-525-8085
38.2	34.1	24.1	20.0	25.5	22.6	1131	High	6	9	22	29	American Intl. Group (4)	Average	II 97	18.8	I 94	-5.7	800-525-8085
28.0	23.6	14.2	11.8	22.5	20.3	1141	Average	6	15	38	36	Warner-Lambert (10)	High	III 95	19.5	I 93	-22.0	800-525-8085
16.9	14.1	15.0	13.0	19.9	17.2	1113	Average	6	21	27	36	Time Warner (4)	Average	III 93	19.8	I 94	-5.6	800-525-8085
24.6	18.3	18.5	13.8	22.2	19.0	1113	Very high	12	14	32	25	Schlumberger (4)	High	III 97	17.2	IV 97	-12.9	800-525-8085
20.7	18.4	13.9	11.1	13.9	11.3	3242	High	2	10	22	15	Bell Atlantic (4)	Low	IV 97	11.1	I 94	-6.3	800-525-8085
22.1	20.6	15.9	14.5	14.3	12.5	4223	Very low	7	12	22	24	Compaq Computer (2)	Very low	II 97	11.9	I 94	-3.0	800-525-8085

MUTUAL FUND SCOREBOARD

FUND	OVERALL RATING	CATEGORY	RATING	SIZE		FEES		1997 RETURNS (%)		
(COMPARES RISK-ADJUSTED PERFORMANCE OF EACH FUND AGAINST ALL FUNDS)		(COMPARES RISK-ADJUSTED PERFORMANCE OF FUND WITHIN CATEGORY)		ASSETS $MIL.	% CHG. 1996-97	SALES CHARGE (%)	EXPENSE RATIO (%)	PRE-TAX	AFTER-TAX	YIELD
INVESCO VALUE EQUITY	B	Large-cap Value	C	379.1	51	No load	1.04	28.0	25.6	0.8
INVESTMENT CO. OF AMERICA ⚖	B	Large-cap Blend	B	39717.7	29	5.75	0.59†	29.8	26.9	1.6
IVY GROWTH A	C–	Mid-cap Blend	D	322.9	12	5.75	1.45†	11.7	9.3	0.8
IVY INTERNATIONAL A ⚖	C	Foreign	B+	1673.0	76	5.75‡	1.65†	10.4	10.0	0.5
JANUS ⚖	B	Large-cap Blend	C	19280.2	21	No load	0.85	22.7	17.4	NA
JANUS BALANCED	A	Domestic Hybrid	A	389.4	77	No load	1.21	21.8	18.0	NA
JANUS ENTERPRISE	C–	Small-cap Growth	B	573.1	–21	No load	1.12	10.8	9.4	NA
JANUS GROWTH & INCOME ⚖	C	Large-cap Growth	B	2004.5	82	No load	1.03	34.7	31.3	NA
JANUS MERCURY		Mid-cap Growth		1911.5	–7	No load	1.00	11.9	8.4	NA
JANUS OLYMPUS ⚖		Large-cap Growth		629.2	52	No load	1.15	26.7	25.2	0.2
JANUS OVERSEAS		Foreign		3240.9	239	No load	1.23	18.2	17.1	NA
JANUS SPECIAL SITUATIONS		Mid-cap Blend		389.4	383	No load	NA	46.0	44.0	0.0
JANUS TWENTY ⚖	C–	Large-cap Growth	C–	6003.7	47	No load	0.92	29.7	25.2	NA
JANUS VENTURE ⚖	C–	Small-cap Growth	B	1234.3	–28	No load‡	0.88	13.1	8.1	NA
JANUS WORLDWIDE	B	World	A	10567.8	109	No load	1.01	20.5	18.2	NA
JAPAN	F	Japan		297.4	–23	No load	1.16	–14.4	–15.8	5.4
KAUFMANN ⚖	C–	Small-cap Growth	B+	6028.5	13	0.20*	1.93†	12.6	11.9	0.0
KEMPER-DREMAN HIGH RET. EQ. A (xxx)	B+	Large-cap Value	C	1380.8	261	5.75	1.21†	31.9	29.8	1.7
KEMPER BLUE CHIP A	C	Large-cap Blend	D	321.0	49	5.75	1.26	26.2	21.5	0.9
KEMPER GROWTH A ⚖	D	Large-cap Growth	D	1832.5	2	5.75	1.07	16.8	12.4	0.0
KEMPER INTERNATIONAL A	C–	Foreign	C	403.0	8	5.75	1.64†	9.0	7.8	0.6
KEMPER SMALL CAP EQUITY A ⚖	D	Small-cap Growth	C	683.5	8	5.75	1.08	20.5	17.7	0.0
KEMPER SMALL CAP VALUE A (yyy)	C	Small-cap Value	D	735.0	413	5.75	1.31†	20.0	19.1	0.0
KEMPER TECHNOLOGY A	D	Technology	C–	1061.6	5	5.75	0.89	7.1	3.4	0.0
KEMPER TOTAL RETURN A	C	Domestic Hybrid	F	2130.8	12	5.75	1.05	19.1	14.4	2.8
KEYPREMIER EST GROWTH		Large-cap Blend		214.2	35	4.50	0.44	26.2	25.7	1.0
LANDMARK BALANCED A	C	Domestic Hybrid	D	227.0	–2	4.75	1.02†	20.9	16.1	2.3
LANDMARK EQUITY A	C	Large-cap Growth	B	260.7	14	4.75	1.05†	31.4	22.6	0.2
LEGG MASON AMER. LEADING PRIM.		Large-cap Blend		170.5	87	No load	1.95†	23.8	21.0	0.0
LEGG MASON INTL EQUITY PRIM.		Foreign		226.1	35	No load	2.25†	1.7	0.7	0.7
LEGG MASON SPEC INVMNT PRIM. ⚖	C–	Small-cap Blend	D	1345.2	39	No load	1.92†	22.1	20.8	0.0
LEGG MASON TOTAL RETURN PRIM.	B+	Mid-cap Value	B	555.2	61	No load	1.93†	37.5	34.0	1.6
LEGG MASON VALUE PRIM. ⚖	B+	Large-cap Value	B	3604.8	82	No load	1.77†	37.1	35.5	0.1
LEXINGTON CORPORATE LEADERS	B+	Large-cap Value	C	526.8	34	No load	0.63	23.1	16.8	10.7
LEXINGTON GROWTH & INCOME	B	Large-cap Blend	B	228.1	14	No load	1.13†	30.4	25.1	1.4
LINDNER DIVIDEND INV. ⚖	B+	Domestic Hybrid	B	1815.6	–20	No load	0.60	14.0	9.8	5.7
LINDNER GROWTH INV. ⚖	C	Small-cap Value	D	1425.1	–5	No load	0.44	8.7	5.3	1.3
LKCM SMALL CAP EQUITY		Small-cap Value		276.3	39	No load	1.00	23.1	18.0	0.4
LONGLEAF PARTNERS ⚖	A	Mid-cap Blend	A	2930.5	27	No load‡	0.95	28.3	25.2	0.7
LONGLEAF PARTNERS REALTY		Real Estate		737.3	373	No load	1.50	29.7	28.5	0.7
LONGLEAF PARTNERS SMALL-CAP	A	Small-cap Value	A	915.3	263	No load‡	1.23	29.0	28.0	0.8
LORD ABBETT AFFILIATED A	B+	Large-cap Value	C	7683.5	22	5.75	0.66†	25.2	21.9	2.0
LORD ABBETT DEVELOPING GR. A	C–	Small-cap Growth	B+	432.6	43	5.75	1.10†	30.8	27.7	0.0
LORD ABBETT MID-CAP VALUE A	B	Mid-cap Value	C	326.4	27	5.75	1.22†	31.5	23.1	1.4
LORD ABBETT RESEARCH SMALL CAP A		Small-cap Value		201.9	1441	5.75	NA†	36.7	36.0	0.0
MAINSTAY CAPITAL APPREC. B	C–	Large-cap Growth	C	1845.8	38	5.00**	1.60†	23.5	22.6	0.0
MAINSTAY EQUITY INDEX A	B	Large-cap Blend	C	417.2	85	3.00	0.80†	35.4	34.6	1.0
MAINSTAY TOTAL RETURN B ⚖	C	Domestic Hybrid	D	1195.3	16	5.00**	1.60†	17.7	15.3	1.3
MAINSTAY VALUE B	B+	Large-cap Value	C	1358.2	33	5.00**	1.60†	21.3	18.3	0.6
MAIRS & POWER GROWTH ⚖	A	Mid-cap Blend	B+	398.3	165	No load	0.89	28.7	27.7	1.1
MANAGERS INTL. EQUITY	C	Foreign	A	376.0	39	No load	1.53	10.8	9.1	1.4
MANAGERS SPECIAL EQUITY ⚖	C	Small-cap Growth	A	686.4	154	No load	1.43	24.5	23.4	0.1
MARKETVEST EQUITY		Large-cap Value		568.4	11	4.75	1.05†	29.4	26.0	1.1
MARKETWATCH EQUITY		Large-cap Blend		333.0	44	4.50	1.35†	32.5	30.8	0.6
MARSHALL EQUITY-INCOME		Large-cap Value		526.3	127	No load	0.98	27.5	24.7	2.0
MARSHALL INTERNATIONAL STOCK		Foreign		225.3	33	No load	1.35†	10.9	9.8	1.7
MARSHALL LARGE-CAP GR. & INC. (zzz)	C–	Large-cap Blend	F	288.5	22	No load	0.97	26.2	24.0	0.6
MARSHALL MID-CAP GROWTH (aaaa)		Mid-cap Growth		216.1	34	No load	1.01	22.7	19.2	0.0
MARSHALL MID-CAP VALUE (bbbb) ⚖		Mid-cap Value		184.5	5	No load	0.98	23.4	19.4	0.9
MASTERS' SELECT EQUITY		Large-cap Growth		296.7	154	No load	NA	29.1	25.8	0.2
MENTOR GROWTH B ⚖	C–	Small-cap Growth	B	483.5	24	4.00**	2.03†	17.7	16.2	0.0
MENTOR STRATEGY B		Domestic Hybrid		282.3	–7	4.00**	2.19†	7.5	3.5	1.6
MERGER	A	Mid-cap Blend	A	460.1	–3	No load‡	4.29†	11.7	9.4	0.2
MERIDIAN ⚖	C	Mid-cap Blend	C–	336.8	–11	No load	0.96	19.2	15.6	0.9
MERRILL LYNCH BASIC VALUE B	A	Large-cap Value	B+	4320.6	14	4.00**	1.58†	28.2	26.3	1.1
MERRILL LYNCH CAPITAL B	B+	Domestic Hybrid	B	5420.4	5	4.00**	1.57†	20.2	18.0	2.1
MERRILL LYNCH DEV. CAP. MKTS. B		Diversified Emerging Mkts.		286.1	–7	4.00**	2.56†	–7.8	–8.8	1.0
MERRILL LYNCH DRAGON B	F	Pacific/Asia ex-Japan		428.2	–63	4.00**	2.36†	–41.4	–43.5	0.0
MERRILL LYNCH EUROFUND B ⚖	B	Europe	C	799.6	4	4.00**	2.13†	23.5	18.4	6.7
MERRILL LYNCH FUND FOR TOMORROW D		Large-cap Blend		241.1	8	5.25	1.25†	21.5	16.6	1.8

*Includes redemption fee. **Includes deferred sales charge. †12(b)-1 plan in effect. ‡Not currently accepting new accounts. §Less than 0.5% of assets. NA=Not available. NM=Not meaningful. (xxx) Formerly Kemper-Dreman High Return. (yyy) Formerly Kemper-Dreman Small Cap Value A. (zzz) Formerly Marshall Stock. (aaaa) Formerly Marshall Mid-Cap Stock. (bbbb) Formerly Marshall Value Equity.

3 Years PRETAX	3 Years AFTERTAX	5 Years PRETAX	5 Years AFTERTAX	10 Years PRETAX	10 Years AFTERTAX	HISTORY RESULTS VS. ALL FUNDS	TURNOVER	CASH %	FOREIGN %	P-E RATIO	UNTAXED GAINS (%)	LARGEST HOLDING COMPANY (% ASSETS)	RISK LEVEL	BEST QTR %RET	WORST QTR %RET	TELEPHONE
25.6	23.8	17.9	15.7	15.8	13.6	3 2 2 2	Low	6	4	23	37	Electronic Data Systems (2)	Low	II 97 16.1	I 94 −2.8	800-525-8085
26.5	23.9	17.7	15.4	16.3	13.9	2 2 3 1	Low	11	12	24	46	Philip Morris (3)	Low	II 97 14.9	I 94 −3.7	800-421-4120
18.6	15.9	12.7	10.1	13.1	10.4	3 3 3 3	Average	10	31	27	31	Cisco Systems (1)	High	II 97 14.1	IV 97 −5.5	800-456-5111
14.2	13.6	18.1	17.3	14.5	13.7	1 4 1 3	Very low	4	100	19	16	Lukoil (144A) (ADR) (3)	Average	IV 93 12.9	IV 97 −6.6	800-456-5111
23.9	19.9	15.8	13.0	18.3	15.6	1 1 3 2	High	5	17	32	32	Monsanto (4)	Low	II 97 13.2	I 94 −2.6	800-525-8983
21.4	17.9	14.6	12.1	NA	NA	3 2	High	3	17	27	17	Dionex (2)	Very low	II 97 10.6	I 94 −0.7	800-525-8983
16.3	14.6	14.7	13.2	NA	NA	2 3	High	3	15	42	32	Fastenal (7)	High	II 97 16.6	I 97 −13.5	800-525-8983
32.3	28.3	18.6	16.2	NA	NA	4 1	High	7	8	35	30	Warner-Lambert (4)	Average	II 97 18.9	II 94 −3.8	800-525-8983
20.5	16.3	NA	NA	NA	NA	3	Very high	2	21	35	21	Warner-Lambert (5)		NA	NA	800-525-8983
NA	NA	NA	NA	NA	NA		Very high	4	14	40	22	Pfizer (6)		NA	NA	800-525-8983
23.0	22.1	NA	NA	NA	NA	1	Average	10	98	30	14	Electrolux Cl. B (3)		NA	NA	800-525-8983
NA	NA	NA	NA	NA	NA			1	17	26	NA	Federal-Mogul (7)		NA	NA	800-525-8983
31.2	25.2	16.9	13.4	21.1	18.7	1 1 4 1	High	10	1	36	29	Schlumberger (6)	High	II 97 17.8	II 94 −6.4	800-525-8983
15.6	11.4	12.2	8.7	16.7	13.9	1 1 2 4	High	6	6	38	40	Camco International (2)	High	III 95 14.7	I 97 −12.0	800-525-8983
22.9	20.8	19.8	17.9	NA	NA	1 2	Average	5	80	31	19	Philips Electronics (ADR) (3)	Average	IV 93 12.7	IV 97 −4.2	800-525-8983
−11.5	−12.2	−1.2	−2.5	−1.0	−3.4	4 4 4 4	Average	3	100	34	−23	Orix (4)	Very high	II 97 25.6	I 97 −18.1	800-535-2726
23.1	22.0	19.1	18.4	26.5	26.0	1 1 1 2	Average	9	9	36	35	HFS (2)	High	II 97 16.5	I 97 −9.8	800-237-0132
35.6	33.9	22.0	20.7	NA	NA	1 3 1	Very low	6	5	18	14	Philip Morris (7)	Average	II 97 14.0	IV 94 −5.3	800-621-1048
28.5	23.2	15.8	12.3	13.7	11.4	4 2 4 1	High	2	4	25	19	American Home Products (2)	Average	II 97 14.2	I 94 −4.1	800-621-1048
21.5	15.5	11.4	7.5	15.5	12.9	1 1 4 3	High	3	5	29	9	United HealthCare (3)	High	II 97 16.3	I 94 −7.4	800-621-1048
13.0	11.6	13.4	12.0	9.6	7.9	3 4 2 4	High	4	100	27	22	Bank of Ireland (3)	Average	III 93 12.0	IV 97 −6.0	800-621-1048
21.7	17.8	15.3	12.2	16.1	13.4	3 1 2 3	Average	6	6	32	39	Precision Drilling Cl. A (2)	High	II 97 21.4	IV 94 −8.3	800-621-1048
30.6	29.0	18.3	16.7	NA	NA	2 2	Low	9	1	18	12	S&P Midcap 400 SPDR (3)	Average	III 95 16.4	IV 94 −6.4	800-621-1048
22.7	17.3	18.1	13.5	15.5	11.4	3 3 1 3	High	6	5	32	35	Compaq Computer (5)	Very high	III 97 20.1	IV 97 −13.8	800-621-1048
20.3	15.8	12.0	8.5	13.2	10.3	3 2 4 3	Average	3	3	26	21	General Electric (2)	Average	II 97 13.1	I 94 −5.5	800-621-1048
NA	NA	NA	NA	NA	NA			3	3	27	46	Unifi (4)		NA	NA	800-766-3960
16.8	13.7	11.1	8.9	NA	NA	4 3	Very high	2	NA	33	23	General Electric (4)	Low	II 97 12.3	I 94 −3.7	800-721-1899
24.0	19.8	16.4	13.6	NA	NA	3 2	Average	4	NA	31	38	General Electric (5)	Average	II 97 19.5	I 94 −4.1	800-721-1899
25.0	23.5	NA	NA	NA	NA	1	Average	6	NA	25	30	Conseco (5)		NA	NA	800-577-8589
NA	NA	NA	NA	NA	NA	4	Average	3	100	20	9	Lloyds TSB Group (2)		NA	NA	800-577-8589
24.4	23.0	15.7	14.8	18.2	16.9	1 1 4 2	Low	3	9	22	8	America Online (7)	High	II 97 15.8	IV 97 −8.2	800-577-8589
33.0	30.6	20.0	17.9	16.8	15.2	4 2 3 1	Low	4	13	19	34	IBM (6)	Low	III 97 13.8	IV 94 −8.6	800-577-8589
38.7	36.6	24.7	23.3	19.0	17.8	2 3 2 1	Very low	3	8	22	11	Dell Computer (6)	High	II 97 18.1	IV 97 −3.6	800-577-8589
28.0	24.9	19.6	16.8	17.0	13.9	2 3 2 1		1	2	23	21	Chevron (6)	Average	II 97 13.5	I 94 −5.1	800-526-0056
26.4	22.4	17.3	13.5	14.6	11.4	3 3 4 1	High	3	1	28	36	FHLMC (4)	Low	II 97 14.1	IV 94 −3.7	800-526-0056
15.6	12.3	11.4	8.3	13.2	10.0	4 1 3 4	Low	2	10	15	14	Enserch Exploration (2)	Very low	I 93 6.9	IV 94 −2.7	314-727-5305
16.4	12.8	13.4	10.4	13.0	10.4	2 3 2 3	Low	11	18	22	39	NorAm Energy (4)	Average	III 97 13.3	IV 97 −9.2	314-727-5305
27.7	24.8	NA	NA	NA	NA	1	Average	10	2	26	21	Kirby (3)		NA	NA	817-332-3235
25.5	22.8	21.4	18.8	19.9	17.5	1 1 1 2	Low	2	23	27	36	Knight-Ridder (12)	Very low	III 97 14.8	IV 94 −4.9	800-445-9469
NA	NA	NA	NA	NA	NA			7	4	43	16	Host Marriott (11)		NA	NA	800-445-9469
26.0	23.8	20.0	18.3	NA	NA	4 2 1	Low	11	7	30	19	US West Media Group (5)	Very low	II 97 9.7	II 94 −3.7	800-445-9469
25.6	21.7	18.4	14.9	15.5	12.1	3 3 2 2	Average	1	4	24	36	Deere (3)	Low	II 97 13.4	I 94 −3.5	800-874-3733
32.6	26.9	22.8	18.3	16.7	14.1	4 3 1 1	Low	3	4	26	44	CellStar (4)	High	III 97 21.8	I 94 −8.1	800-874-3733
26.2	20.4	17.3	12.5	15.5	12.1	3 2 3 1	Low	4	4	24	35	Snap-On (3)	Low	II 97 13.8	IV 94 −4.5	800-874-3733
NA	NA	NA	NA	NA	NA			12	NA	23	17	Rogers (2)		NA	NA	800-874-3733
25.5	25.1	17.3	16.8	18.8	17.5	3 1 2 2	Low	2	3	34	40	Tyco Intl. (3)	High	II 97 17.8	II 94 −6.2	800-624-6782
30.8	29.3	19.3	18.1	NA	NA	3 1	Very low	11	3	27	24	General Electric (3)	Average	II 97 17.2	I 94 −4.2	800-624-6782
19.3	17.8	12.9	11.6	12.9	11.4	4 2 3 3	Very high	1	3	34	35	Guidant (2)	Average	II 97 12.5	I 94 −4.2	800-624-6782
23.4	21.0	16.3	14.3	16.9	14.8	3 1 3 2	Average	4	3	20	27	AT&T (3)	Low	II 97 11.2	IV 94 −4.3	800-624-6782
34.4	33.2	23.7	22.4	20.5	18.8	2 1 1 1	Very low	5	NA	27	20	Emerson Electric (4)	Low	II 97 19.0	I 94 −3.8	800-304-7404
13.3	11.7	15.4	14.3	11.2	10.1	4 4 1 4	Low	8	99	27	18	Viag (2)	Average	IV 93 10.5	IV 97 −5.1	800-835-3879
27.6	24.9	19.1	16.6	19.5	16.6	1 1 3 1	Average	12	2	29	21	XTRA (2)	Average	II 97 18.4	I 97 −7.1	800-835-3879
NA	NA	NA	NA	NA	NA		Low	5	7	23	30	Compaq Computer (2)		NA	NA	800-658-8378
30.2	29.0	NA	NA	NA	NA	1	Very low	0	NA	23	35	Intel (3)		NA	NA	800-232-9091
27.5	24.9	NA	NA	NA	NA	1	Average	9	4	21	24	Philip Morris (3)		NA	NA	800-236-8560
14.0	12.0	NA	NA	NA	NA	4	Low	10	98	18	19	BTR (3)		NA	NA	800-236-8560
24.5	21.0	13.4	11.4	NA	NA	4 2	High	5	6	26	32	General Electric (3)	Average	II 97 15.4	I 94 −4.9	800-236-8560
25.6	22.4	NA	NA	NA	NA	2	Very high	2	7	37	28	Kohl's (4)		NA	NA	800-236-8560
20.8	16.4	NA	NA	NA	NA	3	Average	7	11	24	24	Darden Restaurants (3)		NA	NA	800-236-8560
NA	NA	NA	NA	NA	NA			NA	NA	NA	NA	NA		NA	NA	800-960-0188
25.7	21.8	17.0	13.8	16.6	14.2	3 1 3 2	High	8	3	32	25	Markel (2)	High	II 97 19.5	I 97 −11.0	800-382-0016
16.9	14.4	NA	NA	NA	NA	3	High	11	NA	27	5	CellStar (1)		NA	NA	800-382-0016
11.9	9.4	12.1	9.6	NA	NA	3 2 4	Very high	−5	8	29	12	Equitable of Iowa (7)	Very low	II 93 5.5	IV 94 0.0	800-343-8959
17.5	14.8	13.0	11.1	17.3	15.3	1 1 3 3	Low	22	NA	31	24	Quorum Health Group (3)	Average	III 95 11.2	I 94 −3.9	800-446-6662
25.3	23.3	19.2	17.3	NA	NA	3 1 2	Very low	13	13	19	40	IBM (3)	Low	II 97 14.2	I 94 −2.1	800-637-3863
20.8	17.7	14.7	11.9	NA	NA	3 2 3	Average	2	21	24	23	Williams (2)	Very low	II 97 10.2	I 94 −2.1	800-637-3863
−0.4	−1.9	NA	NA	NA	NA	4	Average	4	100	16	−3	Telebras (ADR) (3)		NA	NA	800-637-3863
−11.1	−12.2	1.8	0.7	NA	NA	1 4	Low	5	100	14	−4	HSBC Holdings (HK) (8)	Very high	IV 93 41.6	IV 97 −30.2	800-637-3863
19.7	15.1	18.3	14.6	12.1	10.1	3 4 1 3	Average	12	100	24	26	Novartis (Reg) (3)	Average	IV 93 10.6	II 94 −1.6	800-637-3863
20.7	16.4	NA	NA	NA	NA	3	Low	7	20	27	35	IBM (4)		NA	NA	800-637-3863

DATA: MORNINGSTAR, INC., CHICAGO, IL.

MUTUAL FUND SCOREBOARD

FUND (COMPARES RISK-ADJUSTED PERFORMANCE OF EACH FUND AGAINST ALL FUNDS)	OVERALL RATING	CATEGORY (COMPARES RISK-ADJUSTED PERFORMANCE OF FUND WITHIN CATEGORY)	RATING	SIZE ASSETS $MIL.	SIZE % CHG. 1996-97	FEES SALES CHARGE (%)	FEES EXPENSE RATIO (%)	1997 RETURNS (%) PRE-TAX	1997 RETURNS (%) AFTER-TAX	1997 RETURNS (%) YIELD
MERRILL LYNCH FUNDAMENTAL GR. B		Large-cap Growth		268.4	88	4.00**	2.16†	30.6	26.6	0.0
MERRILL LYNCH GLOBAL ALLOC. B	B+	International Hybrid	A	9771.2	9	4.00**	1.87†	10.3	6.9	6.5
MERRILL LYNCH GLOBAL UTILITIES B	C	Utilities	C−	301.5	−9	4.00**	1.61†	23.1	20.7	1.8
MERRILL LYNCH GLOBAL VALUE B ♟		World		878.3	14	4.00**	NA†	22.8	21.4	3.9
MERRILL LYNCH GROWTH B ♟	C	Mid-cap Growth	A	4487.1	45	4.00**	1.82†	17.4	15.6	0.9
MERRILL LYNCH HEALTHCARE B	C−	Health	C	181.5	−10	4.00**	2.44†	28.1	20.8	4.6
MERRILL LYNCH INTL. EQUITY B		Foreign		435.2	−43	4.00**	2.14†	−6.0	−9.4	3.3
MERRILL LYNCH LATIN AMER. B	F	Latin America		527.5	3	4.00**	2.54†	24.1	24.1	0.0
MERRILL LYNCH PACIFIC B	D	Diversified Pacific/Asia	B	875.4	−28	4.00**	1.90†	−7.3	−10.6	4.0
MERRILL LYNCH PHOENIX B	C−	Small-cap Value	D	313.8	−18	4.00**	2.29†	18.6	12.1	3.5
MERRILL LYNCH SPEC. VALUE B		Small-cap Value	D	533.3	45	4.00**	2.13†	24.0	19.9	0.0
MERRILL LYNCH TECHNOLOGY B	F	Technology	F	352.7	−19	4.00**	2.35†	−4.4	−10.2	0.0
MFS EMERGING GROWTH B ♟	C−	Mid-cap Growth	C	5124.8	44	4.00**	2.00†	19.7	19.6	0.0
MFS GROWTH OPPORTUNITIES A	C−	Large-cap Growth	C−	930.2	14	5.75	0.84†	23.3	20.1	0.0
MFS LARGE CAP GROWTH B (cccc) ♟	C	Large-cap Blend	C−	432.4	1	4.00**	2.13†	23.7	18.7	0.0
MFS MANAGED SECTORS A		Mid-cap Blend		286.5	24	5.75	1.43†	25.5	19.7	0.0
MFS MASS. INV. A (dddd)	B+	Large-cap Blend	B+	4218.5	57	5.75	0.74†	31.7	29.4	1.0
MFS MASS. INV. GROWTH A (eeee)	C−	Large-cap Growth	C	1760.8	42	5.75	0.72†	48.3	42.7	0.2
MFS RESEARCH A	C	Large-cap Blend	C	2287.4	89	5.75	0.91†	20.5	19.1	0.4
MFS TOTAL RETURN A	B+	Domestic Hybrid	B	3225.1	19	4.75	0.93†	20.7	17.1	3.5
MFS VALUE A	B+	Mid-cap Blend	B	610.4	40	5.75	1.32†	26.5	22.6	0.2
MFS WORLD EQUITY B	C	World	B	258.6	29	4.00**	2.45†	15.5	14.2	0.0
MFS WORLD GROWTH B		World		306.2	7	4.00**	2.39†	12.8	10.4	0.0
MONTAG & CALDWELL GROWTH N		Large-cap Growth		548.6	180	No load	1.28†	31.9	31.6	0.0
MONTGOMERY EMERGING MARKETS R	F	Diversified Emerging Mkts.		988.6	8	No load	1.67	−3.1	−4.0	1.2
MONTGOMERY GROWTH R		Mid-cap Blend		1364.4	37	No load	1.27	24.2	21.0	0.6
MONTGOMERY MICRO CAP R		Small-cap Blend		368.1	23	No load‡	1.71	27.1	25.6	0.0
MONTGOMERY SELECT 50 R		Mid-cap Growth		230.8	159	No load	1.82	29.4	26.1	0.0
MONTGOMERY SMALL CAP OPPORT. R		Small-cap Growth		243.9	22	No load	1.50	16.5	15.9	0.0
MONTGOMERY SMALL CAP R	D	Small-cap Growth	C	207.7	−6	No load‡	1.20	23.9	20.3	0.0
MORGAN (J.P.) U.S. EQUITY (ffff)	B	Large-cap Blend	C	398.5	20	No load	0.80	28.4	22.9	0.7
MORGAN (J.P.) U.S. SMALL CO. (gggg)	C−	Small-cap Blend	C	264.2	17	No load	0.90	22.8	18.9	0.5
MUTUAL BEACON Z ♟	A	Mid-cap Value	A	5686.9	15	No load‡	0.73	23.0	19.6	3.5
MUTUAL DISCOVERY Z	A	World	A	3854.4	30	No load‡	0.96	22.9	19.7	4.0
MUTUAL QUALIFIED Z ♟	A	Mid-cap Value	A	5180.1	4	No load‡	0.75	24.9	21.8	3.3
MUTUAL SHARES Z ♟	A	Mid-cap Value	A	7848.7	29	No load‡	0.70	26.4	23.4	2.4
NATIONWIDE ♟	B+	Large-cap Blend	B+	1516.0	52	4.50	0.61	39.6	37.7	1.1
NATIONWIDE GROWTH ♟	C	Large-cap Blend	C−	824.4	20	4.50	0.64	26.2	22.9	0.7
NEUBERGER & BERMAN FOCUS	C	Large-cap Value	F	1368.9	16	No load	0.89	24.2	20.6	0.2
NEUBERGER & BERMAN GENESIS	B+	Small-cap Value	B+	1246.4	317	No load	1.28	34.9	34.5	0.0
NEUBERGER & BERMAN GUARDIAN ♟	C	Large-cap Value	D	5987.3	9	No load	0.82	17.9	14.3	0.6
NEUBERGER & BERMAN MANHATTAN ♟	D	Mid-cap Blend	D	571.3	7	No load	0.98	29.2	21.8	0.0
NEUBERGER & BERMAN PARTNERS	B+	Mid-cap Blend	B	3230.4	46	No load	0.84	29.2	23.2	0.6
NEW ECONOMY ♟	C	Large-cap Blend	D	4985.0	21	5.75	0.84†	28.9	26.5	0.6
NEW ENGLAND BALANCED A	B	Domestic Hybrid	C	233.7	6	5.75	1.33†	17.5	13.7	2.1
NEW ENGLAND GROWTH A ♟	C−	Large-cap Blend	F	1461.1	12	5.75	1.18†	23.5	14.9	0.0
NEW ENGLAND GROWTH OPPORT. A	B	Large-cap Blend	C	220.5	32	5.75	1.30†	33.4	27.4	0.3
NEW ENGLAND STAR ADVISERS B		Mid-cap Growth		462.2	26	5.00**	2.43†	19.3	13.7	0.0
NEW ENGLAND VALUE A		Large-cap Value	C−	350.0	17	5.75	1.31†	21.0	17.3	0.1
NEW PERSPECTIVE ♟	C	World	B+	16202.7	26	5.75	0.79†	15.0	13.0	1.4
NICHOLAS ♟	B	Mid-cap Blend	B	5082.6	28	No load	0.72	37.0	34.9	0.4
NICHOLAS-APPLEGATE EMG. GROWTH C		Small-cap Growth		215.0	−4	1.00**	2.35†	10.6	7.8	0.0
NICHOLAS-APPLEGATE GROWTH EQ. B	D	Mid-cap Growth	C	284.7	−10	5.00**	2.23†	16.5	10.0	0.0
NICHOLAS II	B	Mid-cap Blend	B	1004.6	28	No load	0.61	37.0	33.0	0.2
NICHOLAS LIMITED EDITION	B	Small-cap Blend	B+	316.4	36	No load	0.86	33.0	30.6	0.0
NORTHERN GROWTH EQUITY		Large-cap Growth		422.0	46	No load	1.00	30.1	27.3	0.3
NORTHERN SMALL CAP		Small-cap Value		336.5	74	No load	1.00	29.8	28.4	0.3
NUVEEN GROWTH & INCOME STOCK A		Large-cap Value		683.5	44	5.25	1.20†	27.1	24.6	1.0
OAKMARK	A	Large-cap Value	A	6907.6	65	No load	1.08	32.6	30.9	0.9
OAKMARK INTERNATIONAL	C−	Foreign	C	1306.2	6	No load	1.26	3.3	−1.9	3.7
OAKMARK SELECT		Mid-cap Value		624.1	1142	No load	1.12	55.0	54.5	0.0
OAKMARK SMALL CAP		Small-cap Value		1446.3	357	No load‡	1.37	40.5	38.9	0.0
OLSTEIN FINANCIAL ALERT		Mid-cap Value		217.6	73	2.50**	2.38†	34.8	28.2	0.0
ONE GROUP EQUITY INDEX B		Large-cap Blend		230.1	176	5.00**	1.30†	31.7	30.7	0.6
ONE GROUP INCOME EQUITY B		Large-cap Blend		230.1	403	5.00**	2.00†	31.2	28.3	0.6
ONE GROUP LARGE CO. GROWTH B		Large-cap Blend		176.6	115	5.00**	2.00†	31.5	27.7	0.0
111 CORCORAN EQUITY		Large-cap Blend		199.9	35	4.50	1.25†	30.3	28.7	0.4
OPPENHEIMER CAPITAL APPREC. A	C	Large-cap Growth	B	1212.7	31	5.75	1.09†	26.3	23.2	0.4
OPPENHEIMER DISCIP. ALLOC. A	B	Domestic Hybrid	C	247.1	5	5.75	1.11†	17.9	14.3	2.8
OPPENHEIMER DISCIP. VALUE A ♟	B	Large-cap Value	C	385.2	103	5.75	1.13†	24.0	20.9	0.5

*Includes redemption fee. **Includes deferred sales charge. †12(b)-1 plan in effect. ‡Not currently accepting new accounts. §Less than 0.5% of assets. NA=Not available. NM=Not meaningful. (cccc) Formerly MFS Capital Growth B. (dddd) Formerly Massachusetts Investor A. (eeee) Formerly Massachusetts Investors Growth Stock A. (ffff) Formerly JPM Pierpont Equity. (gggg) Formerly JPM Pierpont Capital Appreciation.

3 YEARS PRETAX	3 YEARS AFTERTAX	5 YEARS PRETAX	5 YEARS AFTERTAX	10 YEARS PRETAX	10 YEARS AFTERTAX	HISTORY RESULTS VS. ALL FUNDS	TURNOVER	CASH %	FOREIGN %	P-E RATIO	UNTAXED GAINS (%)	LARGEST HOLDING COMPANY (% ASSETS)	RISK LEVEL	BEST QTR	BEST %RET	WORST QTR	WORST %RET	TELEPHONE
26.8	24.2	NA	NA	NA	NA	1	Average	4	14	32	27	Compaq Computer (4)			NA		NA	800-637-3863
15.8	12.6	12.5	10.0	NA	NA	2 3 3	Average	16	47	24	15	Noble Drilling (1)	Very low	II 95	9.1	IV 94	−3.0	800-637-3863
19.7	17.6	13.5	11.9	NA	NA	4 3	Very low	2	64	24	34	Telefonica de Espana (4)	Average	IV 96	9.6	I 94	−7.5	800-637-3863
NA	NA	NA	NA	NA	NA			6	68	19	NA	Guinness (5)			NA		NA	609-282-2800
26.9	24.1	22.0	19.3	18.6	16.6	1 3 1 2	Low	19	8	23	36	Ensco International (8)	Average	III 97	19.2	IV 97	−9.4	800-637-3863
28.1	23.4	14.0	10.9	NA	NA	4 4 1	High	11	23	37	26	Novartis (Reg) (6)	High	II 97	18.1	I 93	−12.1	800-637-3863
1.4	−0.3	NA	NA	NA	NA	4	Average	14	100	26	9	China Overseas Land & Invest. (2)			NA		NA	800-637-3863
5.2	4.9	9.8	9.4	NA	NA	4 3	Average	3	99	15	−13	Tel. de Mexico A (ADR) (7)	Very high	IV 93	32.6	I 95	−29.9	800-637-3863
1.5	−0.8	7.2	5.6	NA	NA	4 2 4	Very low	6	100	25	11	HSBC Holdings (HK) (7)	High	II 97	17.7	IV 97	−19.0	800-637-3863
17.9	13.8	14.3	10.3	NA	NA	2 2 3	Average	11	7	26	7	Novell (4)	Average	III 97	15.3	I 94	−7.0	800-637-3863
22.6	18.6	16.4	13.0	NA	NA	3 3 2	High	9	3	26	25	Vivus (3)	Average	II 97	19.1	IV 94	−10.7	800-637-3863
1.1	−2.4	9.4	4.9	NA	NA	1 4	Very high	45	27	20	−10	Creative Technology (24)	Very high	III 95	24.6	IV 97	−33.5	800-637-3863
24.1	23.9	19.8	19.4	21.3	20.9	1 1 1 2	Low	2	2	40	36	HFS (6)	High	II 97	17.2	II 94	−9.2	800-637-2929
26.4	22.2	17.6	13.9	14.8	11.2	3 3 2 2	Average	1	2	33	41	HFS (4)	High	II 97	17.4	I 94	−5.6	800-637-2929
26.1	19.7	15.7	11.3	15.6	12.8	2 2 4 2	High	6	10	31	22	ADT (5)	Average	II 97	14.1	II 93	−3.6	800-637-2929
25.1	19.3	NA	NA	NA	NA	2	High	3	1	32	36	Tyco Intl. (8)			NA		NA	800-637-2929
32.2	28.8	20.3	16.4	17.9	13.8	1 3 3 1	Average	5	3	26	37	Bristol-Myers Squibb (3)	Low	II 97	17.4	I 94	−1.8	800-637-2929
32.7	26.0	20.1	14.5	18.1	13.8	2 2 3 1	High	3	7	35	37	Microsoft (7)	High	II 97	22.9	I 94	−8.3	800-637-2929
27.6	25.7	20.4	17.8	17.2	14.4	3 2 1 1	Average	4	3	31	20	Bristol-Myers Squibb (3)	Average	II 97	16.3	IV 94	−4.1	800-637-2929
20.6	17.0	14.5	11.7	13.8	11.1	3 3 3 3	High	4	9	21	26	British Petroleum (ADR) (1)	Very low	II 97	9.3	I 94	−2.8	800-637-2929
28.6	25.0	21.1	17.4	17.9	14.3	2 3 1 1	High	0	18	27	21	Tyco Intl. (10)	Average	III 95	13.7	IV 94	−6.2	800-637-2929
17.4	15.4	15.0	12.8	10.4	9.0	4 4 2 3	Average	7	66	26	23	Powergen (5)	Average	II 97	13.7	IV 94	−3.4	800-637-2929
13.6	11.2	NA	NA	NA	NA	3	High	2	62	31	22	Computer Associates Intl. (2)			NA		NA	800-637-2929
34.4	34.2	NA	NA	NA	NA	1	Low	2	2	34	24	Intel (5)			NA		NA	800-992-8151
−0.4	−0.7	7.7	7.0	NA	NA	1 4	Average	4	99	20	−1	Tel. de Mexico L (ADR) (5)	Very high	IV 93	29.1	IV 97	−17.1	800-572-3863
22.7	18.9	NA	NA	NA	NA	2	Average	20	12	25	32	Avid Technology (4)			NA		NA	800-572-3863
24.9	23.4	NA	NA	NA	NA	2	Average	7	1	23	40	Moog Cl. A (3)			NA		NA	800-572-3863
NA	NA	NA	NA	NA	NA		High	9	41	26	20	Tatneft (ADR) (144A) (6)			NA		NA	800-572-3863
NA	NA	NA	NA	NA	NA		High	5	2	30	23	Cooper (4)			NA		NA	800-572-3863
25.7	21.2	17.3	13.8	NA	NA	3 1	Average	2	6	28	43	ICG Communications (5)	High	II 97	20.1	I 97	−11.7	800-572-3863
27.2	22.7	17.9	13.8	17.6	14.5	1 1 2 1	High	2	0	27	24	Warner-Lambert (3)	Average	II 97	14.6	IV 94	−2.8	800-221-7930
25.0	20.9	14.8	10.8	15.5	13.3	2 2 4 2	High	5	2	25	25	Dekalb Genetics Cl. B (2)	Average	III 97	15.3	II 94	−6.7	800-221-7930
23.4	19.8	19.5	16.5	17.2	14.4	2 2 1 2	High	16	34	23	29	Chase Manhattan (2)	Very low	III 97	9.6	IV 94	−3.3	800-342-5236
25.5	22.4	22.7	20.0	NA	NA	1 2	Average	18	58	22	25	Pacific Forest Products (2)	Very low	I 93	12.3	IV 94	−3.3	800-342-5236
24.2	20.3	20.0	16.5	17.4	14.0	3 2 1 2	Average	16	29	24	31	Sunbeam (144A) (3)	Very low	III 95	9.7	I 94	−1.6	800-342-5236
25.4	21.0	20.0	16.3	17.4	13.9	2 2 1 2	Average	17	19	24	36	Chase Manhattan (5)	Very low	III 95	11.1	I 94	−2.8	800-553-3014
31.0	28.5	19.3	16.6	17.6	14.8	1 2 4 1	Low	2	NA	26	52	Warner-Lambert (7)	Low	II 97	18.5	I 94	−3.7	800-848-0920
23.8	20.3	16.5	14.0	15.0	12.7	3 2 2 2	Low	2	2	27	43	Cendant (2)	Average	II 97	18.3	I 94	−3.8	800-848-0920
25.3	22.8	18.2	15.7	17.3	14.5	2 1 1 2	Low	3	2	19	49	Compaq Computer (5)	High	II 97	17.0	IV 97	−6.0	800-877-9700
30.7	29.6	20.1	18.6	NA	NA	2 3 1	Low	7	0	22	27	Thiokol (2)	Average	III 97	20.1	IV 97	−3.8	800-877-9700
22.5	19.9	16.2	14.3	17.5	15.1	2 1 1 3	Low	8	3	19	40	Compaq Computer (5)	Average	III 97	12.7	IV 94	−7.5	800-877-9700
23.0	18.1	14.5	10.2	15.6	12.2	2 1 3 3	Average	1	9	34	41	Dura Pharmaceuticals (3)	High	II 97	14.1	II 94	−5.8	800-877-9700
30.3	25.3	20.4	16.2	17.2	13.8	3 2 2 1	High	5	11	22	35	Allstate (2)	Average	II 97	14.0	I 94	−4.4	800-877-9700
21.9	19.6	16.8	14.5	17.5	14.6	1 2 2 2	Low	10	27	28	37	Fannie Mae (3)	Average	II 97	15.2	I 94	−8.0	800-421-4120
20.3	16.8	14.1	11.4	11.9	9.8	4 2 3 3	Average	3	5	22	19	Philips Electronics (ADR) (2)	Very low	II 97	10.1	I 94	−3.2	800-225-7670
27.3	21.3	16.4	11.9	15.1	11.7	3 2 2 2	Very high	0	10	27	9	Pfizer (6)	High	II 95	20.8	IV 97	−5.0	800-225-7670
28.3	22.1	18.2	14.2	16.0	12.4	3 2 3 1	High	0	3	23	19	IBM (3)	Average	II 97	17.5	I 94	−3.7	800-225-7670
23.4	19.5	NA	NA	NA	NA	2	High	7	10	28	9	Philip Morris (2)			NA		NA	800-225-7670
26.4	22.2	18.1	14.8	13.4	10.8	4 3 2 2	Average	1	4	22	28	Philips Electronics (ADR) (3)	Average	II 97	13.2	I 94	−2.9	800-421-4120
17.5	15.6	16.3	14.3	14.0	11.8	2 4 1 3	Low	11	60	25	24	Novartis (Reg) (2)	Average	II 97	12.0	IV 97	−4.9	800-225-7670
30.5	27.7	18.0	15.6	17.7	15.8	2 1 4 1	Very low	3	2	26	55	Mercury General (5)	Low	II 97	16.0	I 94	−4.7	800-227-5987
20.4	18.0	NA	NA	NA	NA	3	High	−1	4	36	37	Network Appliance (1)			NA		NA	800-551-8043
20.5	16.1	13.4	9.9	NA	NA	3 3	High	2	8	36	35	Health Mgmt. Assoc. Cl. A (3)	High	III 97	15.0	I 97	−7.6	800-225-1852
28.1	24.4	17.7	14.7	16.1	14.0	3 2 4 1	Low	2	9	29	48	Health Mgmt. Assoc. Cl. A (5)	Average	II 97	14.6	I 94	−2.9	800-227-5987
28.3	24.1	17.4	14.1	18.5	16.2	1 1 4 1	Low	4	5	31	47	Heartland Express (4)	Average	II 97	17.9	I 94	−3.5	800-227-5987
24.6	22.9	NA	NA	NA	NA	2	Average	4	5	34	33	State Street (4)			NA		NA	800-595-9111
23.7	21.7	NA	NA	NA	NA	2	Low	5	4	22	28	Argonaut Group (1)			NA		NA	800-595-9111
NA	NA	NA	NA	NA	NA		High	0	20	25	19	Philips Electronics (NV) (4)			NA		NA	800-351-4100
27.5	25.6	22.8	20.9	NA	NA	1 1	Low	11	5	25	29	Philip Morris (7)	Low	II 97	15.2	I 94	−4.2	800-625-6275
12.7	9.8	14.9	12.4	NA	NA	1 4	Low	6	100	15	−20	Cordiant (6)	High	I 93	18.4	IV 97	−13.7	800-625-6275
NA	NA	NA	NA	NA	NA			8	8	19	18	Tele-Comm. Lbty. Media Cl. A (15)			NA		NA	800-625-6275
NA	NA	NA	NA	NA	NA		Low	8	5	24	15	Peoples Bank (CT) (7)			NA		NA	800-625-6275
NA	NA	NA	NA	NA	NA		High	30	NA	22	31	Coachmen Industries (3)			NA		NA	914-397-7565
29.4	28.2	NA	NA	NA	NA	1	Very low	4	3	27	27	S&P 500 (Futures) (4)			NA		NA	800-480-4111
26.5	24.3	NA	NA	NA	NA	1	Low	0	3	25	34	Bristol-Myers Squibb (3)			NA		NA	800-480-4111
24.3	22.3	NA	NA	NA	NA	2	Average	2	2	32	27	General Electric (5)			NA		NA	800-480-4111
26.9	25.7	NA	NA	NA	NA	1	Average	2	3	23	19	Fannie Mae (5)			NA		NA	800-422-2080
29.7	25.8	17.9	14.7	18.4	16.3	1 1 3 1	Average	18	3	27	41	Travelers Group (3)	Average	II 97	16.2	II 94	−2.8	800-525-7048
17.0	13.5	12.7	9.6	13.2	10.2	3 2 3 3	Average	7	NA	20	18	Columbia Gas System (2)	Very low	II 97	9.4	I 94	−2.5	800-525-7048
26.0	22.9	19.2	16.1	18.0	15.0	1 2 1 2	Average	9	NA	18	25	Textron (3)	Low	II 97	13.5	I 94	−2.3	800-525-7048

DATA: MORNINGSTAR, INC., CHICAGO, IL.

MUTUAL FUND SCOREBOARD

FUND	OVERALL RATING (COMPARES RISK-ADJUSTED PERFORMANCE OF EACH FUND AGAINST ALL FUNDS)	CATEGORY (COMPARES RISK-ADJUSTED PERFORMANCE OF FUND WITHIN CATEGORY)	RATING	SIZE ASSETS $MIL.	% CHG. 1996-97	FEES SALES CHARGE (%)	EXPENSE RATIO (%)	1997 RETURNS (%) PRE-TAX	AFTER-TAX	YIELD
OPPENHEIMER DISCOVERY A	D	Small-cap Growth	C−	1251.2	13	5.75	1.22†	10.4	9.9	0.0
OPPENHEIMER EQUITY-INCOME A	B+	Domestic Hybrid	B	2988.3	27	5.75	0.89†	29.7	26.9	3.3
OPPENHEIMER GLOBAL A	C	World	B	3239.4	24	5.75	1.17†	21.8	18.2	1.8
OPPENHEIMER GLOBAL GR. & INC. A	C	International Hybrid	C	187.3	52	5.75	1.52†	28.3	25.3	3.5
OPPENHEIMER GROWTH A ⚖	C	Large-cap Blend	C−	1585.6	21	5.75	1.01†	18.1	15.1	1.7
OPPENHEIMER MAIN ST. INC. & GR. A	B	Large-cap Blend	B	4849.4	35	5.75	0.99†	26.6	24.3	1.1
OPPENHEIMER MULTIPLE STRAT. A (hhhh)	B+	Domestic Hybrid	B	693.3	153	5.75	1.21†	17.8	14.6	3.3
OPPENHEIMER QUEST CAP. VAL. A ⚖	C−	Mid-cap Blend	D	277.7	−58	5.75	NA	15.2	7.5	0.3
OPPENHEIMER QUEST GLOB. VAL. A ⚖	B	World	B+	266.4	37	5.75	1.88†	14.6	13.6	0.1
OPPENHEIMER QUEST OPPORT. A	B+	Large-cap Value	B	1958.9	92	5.75	1.62†	20.1	19.3	0.5
OPPENHEIMER QUEST SM. CAP A	C	Small-cap Value	D	194.4	77	5.75	1.90†	24.3	22.2	0.0
OPPENHEIMER QUEST VALUE A	B	Large-cap Value	C	751.4	67	5.75	1.71†	26.5	25.2	0.5
OPPENHEIMER TOTAL RETURN A	C	Large-cap Blend	C	2237.0	23	5.75	0.90†	27.4	24.2	1.1
PACIFIC HORIZON AGGRES. GRTH A ⚖	D	Small-cap Growth	D	211.9	1	4.50	1.42	14.2	12.2	0.0
PACIFIC HORIZON BLUE CHIP A		Large-cap Blend		247.0	90	4.50	1.28	33.7	29.8	1.2
PAINEWEBBER BALANCED A	C	Domestic Hybrid	C−	180.5	11	4.50	1.34†	24.6	20.3	1.7
PAINEWEBBER GLOBAL EQUITY A	C−	World	C−	289.4	−9	4.50	1.48†	6.3	3.5	0.0
PAINEWEBBER GROWTH & INCOME A	C	Large-cap Blend	D	523.9	69	4.50	1.15†	31.7	29.2	0.7
PAINEWEBBER GROWTH A ⚖	C−	Mid-cap Growth	C	210.8	−1	4.50	1.27†	17.0	10.8	0.0
PAINEWEBBER TACTICAL ALLOC. C	B	Large-cap Blend	C	272.3	162	1.00**	1.95†	31.0	30.8	0.0
PAPP AMERICA-ABROAD	C	Large-cap Growth	B+	288.2	873	No load	1.25	29.9	29.8	0.1
PARKSTONE SMALL CAP INV. A		Small-cap Growth		196.2	20	4.50	1.57†	−6.3	−7.2	0.0
PARNASSUS ⚖	D	Small-cap Value	F	353.4	32	3.50	1.10	29.7	23.4	8.9
PAX WORLD ⚖	B	Domestic Hybrid	C	608.1	17	No load	0.89†	25.1	21.8	2.5
PAYDEN & RYGEL GROWTH & INC. A		Large-cap Value		173.2	513	No load	NA	26.9	26.3	1.4
PBHG CORE GROWTH		Mid-cap Growth		192.3	−58	No load	1.36	−9.7	−9.7	0.0
PBHG EMERGING GROWTH		Small-cap Growth		1516.2	0	No load	1.28	−3.7	−3.7	0.0
PBHG GROWTH ⚖	D	Mid-cap Growth	D	5463.5	−8	No load	1.25	−3.4	−3.4	0.0
PBHG LIMITED		Small-cap Growth		172.1	−14	No load‡	1.42	16.1	15.0	0.0
PBHG SELECT EQUITY		Mid-cap Growth		348.6	−40	No load	1.26	6.8	6.8	0.0
PBHG TECHNOLOGY & COMMUN.		Technology		551.0	−2	No load	1.33	3.3	1.8	0.0
PEGASUS EQUITY INDEX A	B	Large-cap Blend	B	193.7	450	3.00	0.37†	33.1	31.6	1.5
PEGASUS MID CAP OPPORT. A	C	Mid-cap Value	C−	234.0	156	5.00	0.93†	27.6	25.4	0.0
PELICAN	A	Large-cap Value	B+	200.0	7	No load	1.10	26.5	22.2	2.1
PENNSYLVANIA MUTUAL INV. ⚖	B	Small-cap Value	C	507.7	11	1.00*	0.99	25.0	21.9	0.7
PHOENIX-ENGEMANN GROWTH A (iiii) ⚖	D	Large-cap Growth	F	393.7	−8	5.50	1.60	16.0	11.5	0.0
PHOENIX-ENGEMANN NIFTY FIFTY A (jjjj)	C−	Large-cap Growth	C−	176.9	22	5.50	1.70	19.2	17.4	0.0
PHOENIX AGGRESSIVE GROWTH A ⚖	C−	Mid-cap Growth	B	248.2	6	4.75	1.20†	19.4	11.9	0.0
PHOENIX BALANCED A	C	Domestic Hybrid	D	1689.0	−8	4.75	1.01†	18.3	12.6	2.6
PHOENIX EQUITY OPPORT. A ⚖	D	Mid-cap Growth	C−	182.0	−10	4.75	1.23†	9.1	3.2	0.0
PHOENIX GROWTH A	C	Large-cap Blend	C−	2495.6	5	4.75	1.17†	23.3	17.4	0.4
PHOENIX INCOME & GROWTH A ⚖	B	Domestic Hybrid	C	459.7	−2	4.75	1.18†	17.1	12.4	3.7
PHOENIX MID CAP A ⚖	D	Mid-cap Growth	C	352.6	−18	4.75	1.35†	13.2	10.6	0.1
PHOENIX SMALL CAP A		Small-cap Growth		192.4	7	4.75	1.37†	9.5	3.1	0.0
PHOENIX STRAT ALLOCATION A	C	Domestic Hybrid	C−	308.5	0	4.75	1.21†	20.7	14.1	1.6
PILGRIM AMERICA BANK & THRIFT A ⚖	A	Financial	B+	363.6	NA	5.75	1.01†	64.2	59.8	1.7
PILGRIM AMERICA MAGNACAP A	B	Large-cap Blend	B	310.9	21	5.75	1.46†	27.7	14.3	0.4
PIMCO GROWTH C (kkkk)	C−	Large-cap Growth	C	1544.9	4	1.00**	1.86†	21.8	16.9	0.0
PIMCO INNOVATION C (llll)		Technology		175.9	14	1.00**	2.03†	8.1	6.2	0.0
PIMCO OPPORTUNITY C (mmmm)	F	Small-cap Growth	D	597.7	−19	1.00**‡	1.97†	−4.8	−6.1	0.0
PIMCO RENAISSANCE C (nnnn)	A	Large-cap Value	A	363.6	42	1.00**	1.97†	34.9	27.8	0.1
PIMCO TARGET C (oooo)	C	Mid-cap Growth	B+	981.8	−1	1.00**	1.94†	15.4	7.0	0.0
PIONEER A ⚖	B+	Large-cap Blend	B	3931.8	36	5.75	0.99†	38.5	36.5	0.8
PIONEER BALANCED A (pppp) ⚖	B	Domestic Hybrid	C	277.4	0	4.50	1.08†	13.9	9.3	3.5
PIONEER CAPITAL GROWTH A ⚖	B	Small-cap Value	C	1605.8	15	5.75	1.00†	17.5	14.6	0.5
PIONEER EQUITY-INCOME A	B+	Large-cap Value	C	479.6	36	5.75	1.18†	34.9	33.2	1.9
PIONEER GROWTH A	C−	Large-cap Growth	C	539.2	94	5.75	1.13†	43.8	42.8	0.0
PIONEER II A	C	Mid-cap Value	C−	7148.7	19	5.75	0.90†	23.7	20.1	0.6
PIONEER INTERNATIONAL GROWTH A		Foreign		395.9	5	5.75	1.77†	5.8	−0.3	5.7
PIONEER MID-CAP A	D	Mid-cap Growth	C−	944.3	−7	5.75	0.88†	7.2	3.0	0.0
PIONEER SMALL COMPANY B ⚖		Small-cap Blend		261.6	15	4.00**‡	2.23†	18.2	13.8	0.0
PIONEER WORLD EQUITY A		World		272.3	4450	5.75	1.75†	5.8	5.5	0.0
PIPER EMERGING GROWTH A	C−	Mid-cap Growth	B	262.0	−12	4.00	1.18†	23.3	20.6	0.0
PIPER GROWTH A	C−	Large-cap Blend	F	191.1	4	4.00	1.24†	23.1	20.4	0.0
PREFERRED GROWTH	C−	Large-cap Growth		501.6	31	No load	0.84	31.9	26.5	0.0
PREFERRED INTERNATIONAL	C	Foreign	B+	233.1	11	No load	1.25	6.8	5.1	1.6
PREFERRED VALUE	B+	Large-cap Value	C	399.3	30	No load	0.85	28.0	27.7	1.0
T. ROWE PRICE BALANCED	B+	Domestic Hybrid	B	1231.7	41	No load	0.87	19.0	17.6	3.2
T. ROWE PRICE BLUE CHIP GROWTH		Large-cap Blend		2141.6	297	No load	1.12	27.6	27.3	0.5
T. ROWE PRICE CAPITAL APPREC.	A	Domestic Hybrid	A	1053.8	10	No load	0.76	16.2	12.3	3.1

*Includes redemption fee. **Includes deferred sales charge. †12(b)-1 plan in effect. ‡Not currently accepting new accounts. §Less than 0.5% of assets. NA=Not available. NM=Not meaningful. (hhhh) Formerly Oppenheimer Asset Allocation A. (iiii) Formerly Pasadena Growth A. (jjjj) Formerly Pasadena Nifty Fifty A. (kkkk) Formerly PIMCo Advisors Growth C. (llll) Formerly PIMCo Advisors Innovation C. (mmmm) Formerly PIMCo Advisors Opportunity C. (nnnn) Formerly PIMCo Advisors Equity-Income C. (oooo) Formerly PIMCo Advisors Target B. (pppp) Formerly Pioneer Income A.

AVERAGE ANNUAL TOTAL RETURNS (%)						HISTORY	PORTFOLIO DATA						RISK					TELEPHONE
3 YEARS		5 YEARS		10 YEARS		RESULTS VS. ALL FUNDS	TURNOVER	CASH %	FOREIGN %	P-E RATIO	UNTAXED GAINS (%)	LARGEST HOLDING COMPANY (% ASSETS)	LEVEL	BEST		WORST		
PRETAX	AFTERTAX	PRETAX	AFTERTAX	PRETAX	AFTERTAX									QTR	%RET	QTR	%RET	
20.1	18.0	12.7	10.9	17.4	15.8	2 1 4 3	Average	14	7	39	28	Saville Systems (ADR) (2)	Very high	II 97	18.5	I 97	–13.0	800-525-7048
25.8	23.1	17.3	14.9	14.0	11.6	3 3 3 1	Average	11	4	22	37	First Union (3)	Low	II 97	11.3	I 94	–3.7	800-525-7048
18.6	16.1	18.2	15.2	15.3	12.9	1 4 1 3	High	5	77	30	33	Nintendo (4)	Average	IV 93	16.5	IV 94	–5.3	800-525-7048
20.2	16.9	18.2	15.3	NA	NA	1 2	Very high	6	68	31	23	Porsche (6)	Average	IV 93	13.6	IV 94	–5.0	800-525-7048
25.3	21.5	15.7	12.6	16.8	14.6	2 1 3 2	Low	47	3	24	22	Compaq Computer (2)	Average	II 97	11.7	IV 94	–4.3	800-525-7048
24.2	22.2	20.6	18.6	NA	NA	1 1 2	High	8	9	27	26	S&P 500 (Futures) (5)	Average	III 93	14.4	II 94	–5.2	800-525-7048
19.2	16.1	14.2	11.4	12.7	10.4	4 3 3 3	Low	17	23	23	10	Intel (2)	Very low	II 97	9.1	I 94	–3.2	800-525-7048
20.4	17.6	13.4	11.7	21.1	20.0	1 1 2 4		9	26	19	NA	Countrywide Credit Ind. (8)	High	II 97	14.0	I 97	–5.8	800-525-7048
17.2	15.4	15.9	13.8	NA	NA	4 1 3	Average	8	58	26	29	Wells Fargo (4)	Low	II 97	11.9	IV 97	–4.6	800-525-7048
28.0	27.1	18.9	17.9	NA	NA	1 1 2	Low	18	2	25	22	Wells Fargo (6)	Low	II 95	14.5	I 94	–0.7	800-525-7048
18.6	15.7	14.5	12.1	NA	NA	1 3 2	Average	17	4	22	25	Wang Laboratories (4)	Average	II 97	16.6	I 94	–4.3	800-525-7048
29.6	27.5	18.5	16.5	17.0	15.0	3 1 2 1	Low	22	13	18	32	ACE (6)	Low	II 97	13.5	I 94	–2.5	800-525-7048
25.7	21.9	17.3	14.4	16.1	13.1	3 1 3 2	High	6	2	29	32	Travelers Group (2)	Average	II 97	13.5	I 94	–5.5	800-525-7048
23.1	16.8	12.1	7.1	15.7	12.4	2 1 4 3	High	6	14	31	19	NICE-Systems (ADR) (3)	Very high	III 95	19.4	I 97	–9.5	800-332-3863
31.0	28.9	NA	NA	NA	NA	1	Average	2	1	25	21	Microsoft (3)		NA		NA		800-332-3863
20.8	16.8	12.9	9.2	NA	NA	4 3	High	2	5	23	28	Travelers Group (1)	Low	II 97	11.8	I 94	–5.8	800-647-1568
11.5	9.7	12.1	10.4	NA	NA	1 4	Low	1	77	28	18	AirTouch Communications (3)	Average	II 97	12.2	IV 97	–7.0	800-647-1568
29.5	26.1	14.8	12.3	15.1	13.4	2 2 4 1	Average	7	5	23	25	Allstate (2)	Average	II 97	16.3	I 93	–4.8	800-647-1568
21.3	17.1	13.6	10.9	16.0	13.9	1 2 4 2	Average	6	8	34	24	HFS (2)	High	III 97	12.7	I 94	–7.0	800-647-1568
28.5	27.4	17.7	16.3	NA	NA	3 1	Very low	0	3	27	24	General Electric (3)	Average	II 97	17.1	I 94	–4.2	800-647-1568
31.5	30.6	19.6	18.9	NA	NA	2 1	Very low	2	9	26	22	State Street (6)	Average	II 97	21.5	II 93	–5.2	800-421-4004
17.5	13.8	NA	NA	NA	NA	3	Average	8	2	41	33	Sanmina (3)		NA		NA		800-451-8377
13.4	10.7	13.9	11.0	16.5	14.2	2 1 1 4	Average	7	NA	27	35	Electro Scientific Inds. (8)	High	III 97	21.9	IV 97	–13.3	800-999-3505
21.3	18.5	12.6	10.5	13.0	10.5	2 3 4 2	Low	24	NA	31	25	AirTouch Communications (5)	Very low	II 97	11.3	I 94	–3.7	800-767-1729
NA	NA	NA	NA	NA	NA			2	NA	18	NA	S&P 500 Dep. Rec. SPDR (50)		NA		NA		800-572-9336
NA	NA	NA	NA	NA	NA		Average	3	3	41	–21	Varco International (3)		NA		NA		800-433-0051
18.7	17.8	NA	NA	NA	NA	3	Average	6	4	43	15	Legato Systems (2)		NA		NA		800-433-0051
16.9	16.9	19.7	19.6	19.5	16.7	2 1 1 4	Average	8	8	41	16	Citrix Systems (3)	Very high	III 93	18.9	I 97	–19.8	800-433-0051
NA	NA	NA	NA	NA	NA		Average	11	4	36	25	Applied Voice Technology (3)		NA		NA		800-433-0051
NA	NA	NA	NA	NA	NA	1	Average	1	11	50	14	PeopleSoft (6)		NA		NA		800-433-0051
NA	NA	NA	NA	NA	NA		Very high	3	17	40	17	Electronics for Imaging (4)		NA		NA		800-433-0051
30.9	29.4	20.0	18.5	NA	NA	2 1	Very low	0	3	27	18	General Electric (3)	Average	II 97	17.2	I 94	–3.9	800-688-3350
24.1	21.8	18.1	16.0	NA	NA	2 2	Low	3	NA	22	25	Charter One Financial (3)	Average	II 97	17.4	IV 94	–2.9	800-688-3350
25.6	22.7	19.7	16.9	NA	NA	3 1 2	Low	1	7	21	38	Waste Management (3)	Low	II 97	12.1	I 94	–2.5	617-330-7500
18.7	14.0	13.1	9.2	13.8	10.8	2 2 3 3	Low	11	3	20	54	Penn Engineering & Mfg. (2)	Low	III 97	12.7	II 94	–2.2	800-221-4268
21.8	19.1	10.4	8.9	17.0	16.0	1 1 4 3	Average	1	7	33	59	Gillette (5)	High	II 97	17.0	I 97	–6.6	800-648-8050
24.6	23.2	14.2	13.5	NA	NA	4 2	Average	1	5	32	45	Gillette (5)	High	II 97	17.3	I 94	–4.9	800-648-8050
26.2	20.0	16.6	11.9	13.7	10.3	4 3 2 2	Very high	3	5	39	23	Immunex (4)	High	III 97	16.1	I 97	–7.7	800-243-4361
16.6	12.1	10.0	6.9	11.6	8.7	4 2 4 3	Very high	6	4	30	19	IBM (2)	Low	II 97	10.2	I 94	–3.7	800-243-4361
17.7	13.0	12.1	7.0	13.7	9.8	2 3 3 4	Very high	0	3	39	23	Immunex (4)	High	II 97	17.3	I 97	–12.7	800-243-4361
23.7	18.6	14.2	10.8	14.2	11.2	3 2 4 2	High	4	11	29	29	Philips Electronics (ADR) (5)	Low	II 97	14.7	I 94	–3.1	800-243-4361
17.7	14.0	11.8	8.4	13.0	9.9	3 2 4 3	High	5	13	27	19	Perkin-Elmer (2)	Very low	II 97	8.7	I 94	–4.0	800-243-4361
17.2	13.2	11.2	8.3	NA	NA	1 4 4	Very high	2	NA	31	23	Comverse Technology (4)	High	III 97	14.0	I 97	–6.6	800-243-4361
NA	NA	NA	NA	NA	NA		Very high	5	5	37	23	Jabil Circuit (3)		NA		NA		800-243-4361
15.8	11.3	10.9	7.8	14.8	8.7	4 1 4 1	Very high	2	8	30	20	IBM (3)	Low	III 97	9.1	I 94	–2.5	800-243-4361
50.3	45.7	28.7	24.9	23.8	20.9	4 1 3 1	Low	4	NA	21	NA	Comerica (4)	Average	II 97	15.9	IV 94	–8.7	800-334-3444
27.0	22.0	18.4	14.4	15.7	13.0	2 3 2 1	Average	6	3	24	44	Charter One Financial (4)	Low	II 97	13.6	II 93	–1.4	800-334-3444
22.2	17.5	14.9	11.1	15.9	13.0	1 2 3 3	High	2	2	33	31	HBO (4)	Average	II 97	14.8	I 97	–3.7	800-426-0107
24.1	22.9	NA	NA	NA	NA	3	High	3	13	34	28	Motorola (6)		NA		NA		800-426-0107
14.5	9.9	14.3	10.7	19.2	16.5	1 1 1 4	Average	6	4	33	27	Veritas DGC (4)	Very high	II 94	16.6	I 97	–20.5	800-426-0107
28.9	23.9	19.8	16.5	NA	NA	3 3 1	Very high	8	11	22	24	McKesson (3)	Low	II 97	16.3	IV 94	–4.1	800-426-0107
20.3	14.5	17.4	13.9	NA	NA	1 3	High	7	NA	29	25	Sunbeam (4)	High	II 97	15.1	IV 97	–6.5	800-426-0107
28.0	25.1	19.0	16.4	15.8	13.0	3 3 2 1	Low	0	4	24	51	Schering-Plough (3)	Low	II 97	18.3	I 94	–2.8	800-225-6292
15.2	12.0	10.0	7.1	10.7	7.9	4 3 4 4	Low	4	3	23	21	Chase Manhattan (3)	Very low	III 97	8.6	I 94	–3.0	800-225-6292
19.7	17.0	18.1	15.3	NA	NA	1 3	Low	6	7	25	14	20th Century Industries (3)	Low	II 97	11.6	IV 94	–5.6	800-225-6292
26.2	24.3	17.5	15.7	NA	NA	3 1	Average	0	NA	22	30	Schering-Plough (4)	Low	II 97	13.8	I 94	–3.4	800-225-6292
33.3	30.1	20.2	15.8	20.0	17.0	1 3 4 1	High	2	4	31	33	Dell Computer (6)	High	II 97	24.1	II 94	–12.8	800-225-6292
24.3	20.7	17.5	13.8	15.0	11.7	2 4 2 2	Average	0	12	21	39	AMBAC (4)	Average	II 97	15.5	I 94	–5.9	800-225-6292
8.2	5.2	NA	NA	NA	NA	4	Very high	5	100	21	13	SK Telecom (2)		NA		NA		800-225-6292
13.2	9.6	9.8	6.6	13.5	10.7	2 1 3 4	Average	1	NA	29	38	NA	High	III 97	16.8	I 97	–10.6	800-225-6292
NA	NA	NA	NA	NA	NA		Average	8	6	24	22	Bally Total Fitness Hldg. (4)		NA		NA		800-225-6292
NA	NA	NA	NA	NA	NA		Average	5	80	23	4	Telebras (ADR) (1)		NA		NA		800-225-6292
24.3	21.1	16.7	14.9	NA	NA	1 2 2	Average	5	5	32	43	FINOVA Group (3)	High	II 97	18.3	II 94	–8.2	800-866-7778
23.3	18.4	13.7	10.9	16.3	14.5	1 1 4 2	Low	2	3	28	38	Schlumberger (5)	Average	III 97	14.1	I 94	–4.3	800-866-7778
26.2	22.2	18.2	15.9	NA	NA	1 2	Average	0	8	34	47	Cisco Systems (4)	High	II 97	18.6	II 94	–6.3	800-662-4769
11.2	10.0	15.0	13.8	NA	NA	1 4	Very low	5	100	21	21	Tesco (UK) (3)	Average	IV 93	16.0	IV 97	–9.1	800-662-4769
30.2	29.1	19.3	18.3	NA	NA	2 1	Very low	5	7	24	48	Travelers Group (5)	Low	II 97	14.7	I 94	–2.5	800-662-4769
19.4	17.8	13.6	12.4	13.3	11.1	4 2 3 3	Low	1	24	26	24	General Electric (1)	Very low	II 97	10.3	I 94	–3.9	800-638-5660
31.0	30.6	NA	NA	NA	NA	1	Low	9	5	28	16	AlliedSignal (1)		NA		NA		800-638-5660
18.5	15.1	14.8	12.0	14.5	11.5	2 3 2 3	Average	12	4	26	28	Centerior Energy (4)	Very low	II 97	8.3	IV 94	–1.2	800-638-5660

DATA: MORNINGSTAR, INC., CHICAGO, IL.

MUTUAL FUND SCOREBOARD

FUND	OVERALL RATING (COMPARES RISK-ADJUSTED PERFORMANCE OF EACH FUND AGAINST ALL FUNDS)	CATEGORY (COMPARES RISK-ADJUSTED PERFORMANCE OF FUND WITHIN CATEGORY)	RATING	SIZE ASSETS $MIL.	% CHG. 1996-97	FEES SALES CHARGE (%)	EXPENSE RATIO (%)	PRE-TAX	AFTER-TAX	YIELD
T. ROWE PRICE DIVIDEND GROWTH	A	Large-cap Blend	A	684.4	227	No load	1.10	30.8	28.5	2.1
T. ROWE PRICE EQUITY-INCOME ⚖	A	Large-cap Value	A	12324.6	58	No load	0.81	28.8	25.3	2.3
T. ROWE PRICE EQUITY INDEX	B+	Large-cap Blend	B+	1833.5	127	0.50*	0.40	32.9	31.9	1.3
T. ROWE PRICE EUROPEAN STOCK	B	Europe	C	998.8	31	No load	1.12	17.0	15.3	1.2
T. ROWE PRICE GROWTH & INC ⚖	A	Large-cap Blend	A	3358.2	35	No load	0.82	23.5	21.7	2.1
T. ROWE PRICE GROWTH STOCK ⚖	B+	Large-cap Blend	B+	3980.2	16	No load	0.77	26.6	22.8	0.6
T. ROWE PRICE HEALTH SCIENCE		Health		269.9	39	No load	1.35	19.4	17.0	0.0
T. ROWE PRICE INTL DISCOVERY	D	Foreign	D	238.5	−26	2.00*	1.45	−5.7	−6.0	0.0
T. ROWE PRICE INTL STOCK ⚖	C−	Foreign	C	9842.6	5	No load	0.88	2.7	1.3	1.4
T. ROWE PRICE LATIN AMERICA		Latin America		410.6	95	2.00*	1.66	31.9	31.4	1.1
T. ROWE PRICE MID-CAP GROWTH	B+	Mid-cap Growth	A	1750.6	71	No load	1.04	18.3	18.0	0.0
T. ROWE PRICE MID-CAP VALUE		Mid-cap Value		177.6	261	No load	1.25	27.1	26.5	0.6
T. ROWE PRICE NEW AMERICA GROWTH	C	Mid-cap Growth	B+	1705.5	18	No load	1.01	21.1	19.6	0.0
T. ROWE PRICE NEW ASIA	F	Pacific/Asia ex-Japan		842.9	−61	No load	1.11	−37.1	−37.4	1.4
T. ROWE PRICE NEW ERA ⚖	C	Natural Resources	A	1551.0	6	No load	0.76	9.8	7.1	1.3
T. ROWE PRICE NEW HORIZONS ⚖	C−	Mid-cap Growth	B+	5016.0	15	No load‡	0.90	9.8	9.2	0.0
T. ROWE PRICE PERSONAL STRAT. BAL.		Domestic Hybrid		277.8	55	No load	1.05	17.8	16.1	2.9
T. ROWE PRICE SCIENCE & TECH.	D	Technology	C	3737.1	14	No load	0.97	1.7	−0.7	0.0
T. ROWE PRICE SMALL-CAP VAL.	A	Small-cap Value	B+	2057.8	46	1.00*‡	0.94	27.9	25.7	0.8
T. ROWE PRICE SMALL CAP STOCK (qqqq)	B+	Small-cap Blend	A	779.2	87	No load	1.07	28.8	27.2	0.2
T. ROWE PRICE SPECTRUM GROWTH	B+	Large-cap Blend	B+	2558.7	22	No load	0.00	17.4	14.8	1.1
T. ROWE PRICE VALUE		Mid-cap Value		508.7	157	No load	1.10	29.3	25.2	1.1
PRINCIPAL CAPITAL VALUE A (rrrr) ⚖	B	Large-cap Blend	C	509.5	10	4.75	0.69†	28.7	25.8	1.6
PRINCIPAL GROWTH A (ssss) ⚖	C	Large-cap Blend	C−	328.1	33	4.75	1.08†	28.4	27.4	0.6
PRINCIPAL INTERNATIONAL A (tttt)	C	Foreign	B+	283.5	52	4.75	1.45†	12.2	11.3	1.1
PRINCIPAL MIDCAP A (uuuu) ⚖	B	Small-cap Blend	B+	347.3	39	4.75	1.32†	22.9	22.3	0.1
PRUDENTIAL BALANCED B (vvvv)	C	Domestic Hybrid	D	583.7	36	5.00**	1.92†	13.5	8.9	1.9
PRUDENTIAL EQUITY-INCOME B ⚖	B+	Mid-cap Value	B	1285.2	31	5.00**	1.73†	35.3	32.0	1.5
PRUDENTIAL EQUITY B	B+	Large-cap Value	B	3124.0	19	5.00**	1.64†	23.1	21.1	1.0
PRUDENTIAL JENN GROWTH B		Large-cap Growth		423.1	66	5.00**	1.84†	30.4	28.0	0.0
PRUDENTIAL MULTI-SECTOR A	C	Mid-cap Blend	C−	257.3	16	5.00	1.23†	16.1	9.7	0.0
PRUDENTIAL SMALL CO. VAL. B (wwww)	B	Small-cap Value	C	642.1	64	5.00**	1.96†	32.6	29.2	0.0
PRUDENTIAL UTILITY A	C	Utilities	C	2413.6	19	5.00	0.86†	27.8	24.1	2.4
PRUDENTIAL WORLD GLOBAL B	C−	World	C	327.8	−3	5.00**	2.12†	4.3	1.4	0.1
PUTNAM ASIA PACIFIC GROWTH A	D	Diversified Pacific/Asia	B+	463.3	89	5.75	1.50†	−15.0	−15.2	0.8
PUTNAM ASSET ALLOC.: BAL. A		Domestic Hybrid		725.3	95	5.75	1.27†	16.2	13.4	2.2
PUTNAM ASSET ALLOC.: CONS. A		Domestic Hybrid		313.8	38	5.75	1.38†	11.8	9.5	2.9
PUTNAM ASSET ALLOC.: GROWTH A ⚖		Large-cap Blend		540.7	120	5.75	1.39†	18.4	16.2	1.0
PUTNAM BALANCED RETIREMENT A	B+	Domestic Hybrid	B	600.5	19	5.75	1.20†	18.5	15.0	3.7
PUTNAM CAPITAL APPREC. A		Mid-cap Blend		1036.0	265	5.75	1.29†	29.8	28.9	0.4
PUTNAM DIVERSIFIED EQUITY B		Large-cap Blend		306.7	41	5.00**	2.09†	22.6	19.0	0.4
PUTNAM EQUITY INCOME A	A	Large-cap Value	B+	898.1	55	5.75	1.09†	26.5	24.5	1.7
PUTNAM EUROPE GROWTH A	B	Europe	B	418.1	122	5.75	1.45†	21.9	19.6	1.9
PUTNAM FUND FOR GR. & INC. A	B	Large-cap Value	C	17297.8	41	5.75	0.92†	24.2	20.4	2.1
PUTNAM (GEORGE) OF BOSTON A	B+	Domestic Hybrid	B	2871.8	57	5.75	1.06†	21.0	18.0	3.1
PUTNAM GLOBAL GROWTH A	C	World	C	2657.2	15	5.75	1.27†	13.4	8.3	2.1
PUTNAM GLOBAL NATURAL RES. A	C−	Natural Resources	C	235.2	19	5.75	1.23†	16.2	14.1	1.0
PUTNAM GROWTH & INCOME II B		Large-cap Value		1272.4	64	5.00**	1.84†	24.0	20.9	1.0
PUTNAM HEALTH SCIENCES A ⚖	C	Health	B	1908.3	48	5.75	1.08†	32.4	29.3	1.0
PUTNAM INTL. GR. & INC. B		Foreign		291.6	555	5.00**	2.21†	19.5	18.0	1.0
PUTNAM INTL. GROWTH A	C	Foreign	B+	1102.2	264	5.75	1.59†	17.7	15.8	1.4
PUTNAM INTL. NEW OPPORT. B		Foreign		941.8	34	5.00**	2.50†	0.9	−1.7	0.0
PUTNAM INVESTORS A	B	Large-cap Growth	A	1942.6	47	5.75	1.03†	34.5	31.9	0.3
PUTNAM NEW OPPORTUNITIES A	C−	Mid-cap Growth	B	8457.5	42	5.75‡	1.06†	22.6	22.0	0.0
PUTNAM NEW VALUE A		Large-cap Value		481.1	145	5.75	1.22†	19.0	17.0	0.8
PUTNAM OTC & EMERGING GROWTH A	D	Mid-cap Growth	C−	2276.6	24	5.75	1.16†	10.2	10.2	0.0
PUTNAM UTILITIES GR. & INC. A	B	Utilities	A	746.8	19	5.75	1.05†	26.8	23.4	3.3
PUTNAM VISTA A	C−	Mid-cap Growth	B+	2797.2	67	5.75	1.10†	23.2	21.3	0.0
PUTNAM VOYAGER A	C−	Mid-cap Growth	B+	11755.4	36	5.75	1.03†	26.0	24.4	0.0
PUTNAM VOYAGER II A		Mid-cap Growth		532.4	52	5.75	1.44†	23.4	23.4	0.0
RAINIER CORE EQUITY		Large-cap Blend		481.7	119	No load	1.22†	33.9	28.6	0.3
RAINIER SMALL/MID CAP EQUITY		Mid-cap Value		323.9	160	No load	1.40†	32.2	28.4	0.0
RIGHTIME BLUE CHIP ⚖	C	Large-cap Blend	C	260.7	−10	4.75	2.17†	4.0	4.0	0.1
ROBERTSON STEPHENS CONTRARIAN A		World		501.9	−53	No load	2.46†	−29.5	−29.6	0.4
ROBERTSON STEPHENS EMG. GROWTH A	D	Small-cap Growth	C−	254.7	21	No load	1.60†	18.5	10.9	0.0
ROBERTSON STEPHENS GROWTH & INCOME A		Mid-cap Blend		300.0	−3	No load	1.71†	22.3	15.6	0.2
ROBERTSON STEPHENS PARTNER A		Small-cap Value		212.3	67	No load	1.93†	18.1	16.6	0.7
ROBERTSON STEPHENS VALUE + GROWTH A	C−	Large-cap Growth	C−	803.4	25	No load	1.51†	13.9	9.0	0.0
ROYCE MICRO-CAP	B	Small-cap Value	B	199.5	41	1.00*	1.79	24.7	22.5	0.0
ROYCE PREMIER	A	Small-cap Value	B+	533.6	68	1.00*	1.25	18.4	16.9	1.0

*Includes redemption fee. **Includes deferred sales charge. †12(b)-1 plan in effect. ‡Not currently accepting new accounts. §Less than 0.5% of assets. NA=Not available. NM=Not meaningful. (qqqq) Formerly T. Rowe Price Over-the-Counter Secs. (rrrr) Formerly Princor Capital Accumulation A. (ssss) Formerly Princor Growth A. (tttt) Formerly Princor World A. (uuuu) Formerly Princor Emerging Growth A. (vvvv) Formerly Prudential Allocation Balanced B. (wwww) Formerly Prudential Small Companies B.

3 YEARS PRETAX	3 YEARS AFTERTAX	5 YEARS PRETAX	5 YEARS AFTERTAX	10 YEARS PRETAX	10 YEARS AFTERTAX	RESULTS VS. ALL FUNDS	TURNOVER	CASH %	FOREIGN %	P-E RATIO	UNTAXED GAINS (%)	LARGEST HOLDING COMPANY (% ASSETS)	RISK LEVEL	BEST QTR %RET	WORST QTR %RET	TELEPHONE
29.3	27.1	21.4	19.4	NA	NA	2 1	Average	10	14	24	17	Fannie Mae (2)	Very low	II 97 12.1	I 94 −3.0	800-638-5660
27.4	24.6	20.0	17.2	17.0	14.4	3 2 2 1	Low	9	8	23	28	Mellon Bank (2)	Very low	II 97 11.4	I 94 −2.8	800-638-5660
30.8	29.4	19.8	18.6	NA	NA	3 2 1	Very low	3	4	27	27	General Electric (3)	Average	II 97 17.4	I 94 −3.9	800-638-5660
21.5	20.2	18.9	18.0	NA	NA	4 1 2	Very low	4	100	27	33	Royal Dutch Petrol. (Neth.) (3)	Average	IV 93 9.4	I 94 −1.8	800-638-5660
26.7	24.4	18.0	16.0	16.5	14.3	2 2 3 1	Very low	9	7	26	36	Corning (3)	Low	II 97 12.9	I 94 −4.0	800-638-5660
26.4	23.4	18.7	15.9	15.6	13.1	3 3 2 1	Average	6	23	29	51	Berkshire Hathaway (3)	Low	II 97 16.0	I 94 −4.1	800-638-5660
NA	NA	NA	NA	NA	NA		High	5	16	33	16	Warner-Lambert (4)		NA	NA	800-638-5660
0.9	0.6	7.3	6.7	NA	NA	4 2 4	Average	6	94	26	5	Reserve Investment Fund (6)	High	IV 93 15.1	IV 97 −10.8	800-638-5660
9.9	8.8	13.0	11.7	10.6	8.8	2 4 1 4	Very low	4	100	26	20	Royal Dutch Petrol. (Neth.) (3)	High	IV 93 12.1	IV 97 −7.5	800-638-5660
9.8	9.4	NA	NA	NA	NA	2	Low	4	100	20	1	Tel. de Mexico L (ADR) (6)		NA	NA	800-638-5660
27.7	26.7	21.4	20.5	NA	NA	1 1	Low	10	5	29	18	ACE (2)	Average	II 97 13.7	I 97 −6.6	800-638-5660
NA	NA	NA	NA	NA	NA		Very low	13	6	22	15	Unifi (2)		NA	NA	800-638-5660
28.0	25.7	17.9	16.2	19.3	18.2	1 1 3 1	Low	6	1	30	42	Franklin Resources (3)	Average	III 95 15.5	I 94 −5.5	800-638-5660
−9.5	−9.8	1.4	0.4	NA	NA	1 4	Average	9	100	15	−50	Hutchison Whampoa (8)	Very high	IV 93 33.9	IV 97 −27.1	800-638-5660
18.1	15.4	14.9	12.4	11.3	9.0	4 4 2 3	Low	7	21	26	43	Mobil (4)	Average	III 97 11.3	IV 97 −10.4	800-638-5660
25.9	23.1	19.6	16.2	18.3	15.6	2 1 1 2	Low	4	3	33	33	Paychex (2)	High	III 95 17.9	I 97 −11.5	800-638-5660
19.9	18.2	NA	NA	NA	NA	3	Average	0	28	25	11	Delta Air Lines (1)		NA	NA	800-638-5660
21.8	17.8	21.1	17.7	22.8	19.8	1 1 1 4	High	9	4	35	21	BMC Software (5)	High	II 95 20.1	I 97 −14.0	800-638-5660
27.3	25.3	20.2	18.3	NA	NA	2 1 1	Very low	12	1	21	37	Suiza Foods (2)	Very low	III 97 14.9	IV 94 −3.2	800-638-5660
27.8	24.6	19.9	16.6	16.8	13.3	2 3 2 1	Low	9	4	26	31	Harleysville Group (2)	Low	II 97 15.5	I 97 −3.5	800-638-5660
22.5	19.9	17.7	15.1	NA	NA	3 1 2	Very low	7	30	27	27	T. Rowe Price Gr. Stock (23)	Low	II 97 13.1	I 94 −3.2	800-638-5660
32.4	29.0	NA	NA	NA	NA	1	Average	8	8	24	19	Newmont Mining (2)		NA	NA	800-638-5660
28.0	24.0	17.7	14.6	14.7	12.1	4 2 3 1	Average	1	NA	24	32	American Greetings Cl. A (3)	Low	II 97 13.3	I 94 −4.0	800-451-5447
24.4	23.3	16.4	15.1	16.9	15.2	3 1 2 2	Very low	13	4	28	41	Microsoft (3)	Average	II 97 13.9	I 93 −2.8	800-451-5447
15.7	14.2	16.5	15.3	12.0	11.0	3 4 1 3	Low	4	98	19	24	Novartis (Reg) (2)	Average	IV 93 15.3	IV 97 −7.2	800-451-5447
25.3	24.2	17.9	17.2	18.2	17.2	2 1 2 2	Very low	8	2	27	38	EVI (5)	Average	II 97 14.7	IV 97 −4.8	800-451-5447
15.3	12.1	11.0	8.4	10.7	8.3	4 3 3 4	High	10	9	26	20	Novartis (ADR) (3)	Low	II 97 10.9	I 94 −3.9	800-225-1852
25.5	22.7	18.8	16.3	16.0	14.0	3 3 2 1	Low	2	8	20	37	Equity Residential Ppty. Tr. (5)	Low	II 97 16.3	IV 94 −3.6	800-225-1852
23.5	20.8	18.3	15.9	16.7	14.4	2 2 1 2	Low	23	7	21	36	Loews (3)	Low	II 97 11.2	I 94 −3.0	800-225-1852
NA	NA	NA	NA	NA	NA		Average	1	9	32	21	Pfizer (3)		NA	NA	800-225-1852
18.8	13.8	16.4	11.9	NA	NA	3 1 3	High	0	14	27	25	Novartis (ADR) (4)	Average	II 97 17.8	I 97 −7.4	800-225-1852
26.2	22.4	18.1	14.9	17.5	15.3	2 1 2 1	Average	11	3	17	18	Universal Health Svcs Cl. B (2)	Average	III 97 15.8	I 94 −5.3	800-225-1852
25.2	22.1	16.0	13.2	NA	NA	3 4 1	Low	4	26	19	35	Sonat (5)	Average	IV 96 12.4	I 94 −4.8	800-225-1852
12.1	9.6	14.5	12.9	7.8	6.7	4 4 1 4	Average	4	79	28	28	Microsoft (2)	High	IV 93 14.7	IV 97 −9.7	800-225-1852
−2.5	−3.4	8.6	7.8	NA	NA	1 4	Average	9	97	25	−13	Sony (3)	High	IV 93 21.8	IV 97 −15.0	800-225-1581
19.2	16.7	NA	NA	NA	NA	3	High	3	22	29	17	DAX Index (Futures) (3)		NA	NA	800-225-1581
14.4	12.2	NA	NA	NA	NA	4	Very high	4	26	28	11	DAX Index (Futures) (3)		NA	NA	800-225-1581
20.9	18.9	NA	NA	NA	NA	2	High	3	21	29	18	S&P 500 Index (Futures) (4)		NA	NA	800-225-1581
19.6	16.4	13.7	11.0	13.6	10.4	3 2 3 3	High	2	7	23	20	SBC Communications (1)	Very low	II 97 8.6	I 94 −3.1	800-225-1581
31.5	29.9	NA	NA	NA	NA	1	Average	5	10	24	22	Warner-Lambert (2)		NA	NA	800-225-1581
22.1	19.4	NA	NA	NA	NA	2	Average	4	34	29	24	Computer Associates Intl. (2)		NA	NA	800-225-1581
27.4	26.0	19.5	18.2	15.4	12.7	3 3 2 1	Average	4	7	23	19	SBC Communications (2)	Low	II 97 11.8	I 94 −3.5	800-225-1581
22.0	19.9	20.4	19.0	NA	NA	1 2	Average	3	100	21	18	Total Cl. B (3)	Average	IV 93 11.6	IV 97 −1.8	800-225-1581
27.3	24.0	18.7	15.8	16.7	13.7	2 2 2 1	Low	2	4	24	27	Pharmacia & Upjohn (2)	Low	II 97 12.8	I 94 −4.0	800-225-1581
22.3	19.2	15.1	12.3	13.9	10.9	3 3 3 2	High	3	7	23	19	SBC Communications (1)	Very low	II 97 9.6	I 94 −3.7	800-225-1581
14.9	11.7	14.7	12.4	11.2	9.5	3 4 2 3	Average	2	66	30	22	General Electric (2)	Average	II 97 14.2	IV 97 −5.6	800-225-1581
20.0	18.1	13.8	11.1	12.9	10.7	1 4 3 3	Low	1	14	22	23	Schlumberger (4)	High	I 93 11.9	IV 93 −9.9	800-225-1581
NA	NA	NA	NA	NA	NA	2	Average	3	5	22	19	IBM (2)		NA	NA	800-225-1581
29.8	28.0	20.3	19.0	19.8	17.6	1 2 2 1	Average	5	9	36	48	Eli Lilly (5)	High	II 97 20.3	I 93 −9.7	800-225-1581
NA	NA	NA	NA	NA	NA			3	99	22	6	B.A.T. Industries (2)		NA	NA	800-225-1581
16.0	14.9	17.6	16.7	NA	NA	1 3	Average	8	98	23	10	Philips Electronics (NV) (2)	Average	IV 93 16.4	IV 97 −5.4	800-225-1581
NA	NA	NA	NA	NA	NA		High	6	99	27	4	Smithkline Beecham (3)		NA	NA	800-225-1581
31.0	26.8	20.7	16.6	17.4	13.8	2 3 2 1	High	4	NA	33	34	General Electric (3)	Average	II 97 18.5	I 94 −3.8	800-225-1581
25.7	25.4	22.2	21.8	NA	NA	1 2	Average	1	7	38	26	HFS (2)	High	II 97 19.3	I 97 −8.3	800-225-1581
25.4	23.3	NA	NA	NA	NA	2	Average	4	9	24	15	Kmart (2)		NA	NA	800-225-1581
21.6	19.3	19.4	16.8	17.9	15.8	1 2 1 2	High	3	5	42	23	Compuware (3)	Very high	IV 97 22.3	I 97 −16.1	800-225-1581
24.3	21.3	15.3	12.7	NA	NA	4 2	Average	5	7	23	25	SBC Communications (4)	Very low	IV 97 12.2	I 94 −6.9	800-225-1581
28.1	25.4	18.9	16.7	17.9	15.0	3 1 2 1	High	2	2	32	26	TJX (2)	High	II 97 17.9	I 97 −6.2	800-225-1581
25.8	23.7	18.8	17.1	19.1	17.0	2 1 2 2	Average	2	9	34	33	Computer Associates Intl. (2)	High	II 97 17.3	I 94 −6.3	800-225-1581
25.9	25.6	NA	NA	NA	NA	2	Average	1	11	36	18	American Express (1)		NA	NA	800-225-1581
34.4	30.3	NA	NA	NA	NA	1	High	1	2	25	23	Microsoft (3)		NA	NA	800-248-6314
33.7	30.1	NA	NA	NA	NA	1	High	1	1	24	21	Cadence Design Systems (2)		NA	NA	800-248-6314
14.2	12.3	10.3	7.9	10.0	7.9	4 3 3 4	Low	2	3	26	17	S&P 400 (Futures) (5)	Very low	II 95 8.9	II 97 −1.9	800-242-1421
3.9	3.7	NA	NA	NA	NA	4	Average	−9	64	29	5	Royal Group Technologies (14)		NA	NA	800-766-3863
20.1	14.8	14.9	11.1	18.8	15.8	1 1 4 2	Very high	11	10	41	29	800-JR Cigar (2)	Very high	II 97 22.9	I 97 −14.0	800-766-3863
NA	NA	NA	NA	NA	NA		Very high	0	5	25	35	Vans (2)		NA	NA	800-766-3863
NA	NA	NA	NA	NA	NA		High	24	20	22	21	Kaiser Aluminum (5)		NA	NA	800-766-3863
22.8	20.2	22.6	20.8	NA	NA	1 4	Very high	0	6	29	38	Compaq Computer (5)	High	II 95 22.0	II 95 −14.7	800-766-3863
19.7	17.9	17.1	15.0	NA	NA	1 3	Average	12	4	23	28	Sevenson Environ. Svcs. (2)	Low	III 97 15.6	III 96 −3.4	800-221-4268
18.1	15.9	15.2	13.6	NA	NA	2 3	Low	13	2	21	24	CalMat (3)	Very low	II 97 13.3	IV 97 −5.5	800-221-4268

MUTUAL FUND SCOREBOARD

FUND	OVERALL RATING	CATEGORY	RATING	ASSETS $MIL.	% CHG. 1996-97	SALES CHARGE (%)	EXPENSE RATIO (%)	PRE-TAX	AFTER-TAX	YIELD
	(COMPARES RISK-ADJUSTED PERFORMANCE OF EACH FUND AGAINST ALL FUNDS)	(COMPARES RISK-ADJUSTED PERFORMANCE OF FUND WITHIN CATEGORY)								
RYDEX NOVA		Large-cap Blend		776.9	116	No load	1.16	42.3	42.3	0.0
RYDEX OTC ♑		Large-cap Growth		206.1	18	No load	1.27	21.9	21.7	0.5
RYDEX URSA		Large-cap Blend		379.9	27	No load	1.34	–21.0	–21.1	0.4
SAFECO EQUITY NO LOAD	A	Large-cap Blend	A	1480.2	74	No load	0.79	24.2	22.4	1.1
SAFECO GROWTH NO LOAD	C–	Small-cap Blend	C	638.6	226	No load	1.02	50.0	44.9	0.0
SAFECO INCOME NO LOAD	A	Large-cap Value	B+	402.0	38	No load	0.86	26.4	22.8	2.5
SALOMON BROS. CAPITAL O	C	Large-cap Value	F	174.1	27	4.75	1.38†	26.8	21.4	0.0
SALOMON BROS. INVESTORS O	A	Large-cap Value	B	592.6	14	No load‡	0.76	26.5	23.0	0.8
SALOMON BROS. OPPORTUNITY ♑	B+	Large-cap Value	C	199.7	26	No load	1.16	33.0	32.0	0.7
SCHRODER INTERNATIONAL INV. ♑	C–	Foreign	C	174.1	–8	No load	0.99	3.3	1.0	1.6
SCHWAB 1000 INV.	B	Large-cap Blend	B	2823.1	48	0.50*	0.47	31.9	31.5	1.0
SCHWAB ASSET-HIGH GROWTH		Large-cap Blend		184.0	63	No load	0.89	21.0	19.0	1.2
SCHWAB INTERNATIONAL INDEX INV.		Foreign		317.8	22	0.75*	0.69	7.3	6.9	1.2
SCHWAB S&P 500 INV.		Large-cap Blend		1032.4	253	No load	0.49	32.5	32.1	0.9
SCHWAB SMALL CAP INDEX INV.		Small-cap Blend		410.5	76	0.50*	0.59	25.7	25.6	0.4
SCOUT STOCK ♑	B	Mid-cap Value	C	198.5	11	No load	0.86	21.0	18.9	2.1
SCUDDER DEVELOPMENT	D	Small-cap Growth	C–	862.7	–11	No load	1.36	6.9	4.9	0.0
SCUDDER EMERGING MARKETS GROWTH		Diversified Emerging Mkts.		203.4	105	2.00*	2.00	3.6	3.4	0.4
SCUDDER GLOBAL ♑	C	World	B+	1554.2	10	No load	1.34	17.2	13.1	2.7
SCUDDER GLOBAL DISCOVERY	C	World	C	334.9	–8	No load	1.60	9.9	7.5	3.0
SCUDDER GREATER EUROPE GROWTH		Europe		200.2	33	No load	1.50	24.0	21.6	2.5
SCUDDER GROWTH & INCOME ♑	A	Large-cap Blend	A	6715.8	60	No load	0.78	30.3	27.2	2.0
SCUDDER INTERNATIONAL ♑	C–	Foreign	B	2632.0	0	No load	1.15	8.0	5.6	0.5
SCUDDER LARGE COMPANY GROWTH (xxxx)	C–	Large-cap Growth	C–	299.4	37	No load	1.07	32.8	31.2	0.0
SCUDDER LARGE COMPANY VALUE (yyyy)	C	Large-cap Value	D	2197.2	24	No load	0.93	32.5	30.5	0.8
SCUDDER LATIN AMERICA	F	Latin America		907.5	42	No load	1.96	31.3	29.8	0.9
SCUDDER PATHWAY BALANCED		Domestic Hybrid		206.6	811	No load	NA	13.7	12.3	2.9
SCUDDER SMALL COMPANY VALUE		Small-cap Value		198.9	252	1.00*	1.50	37.0	36.6	0.1
SCUDDER VALUE	B+	Large-cap Value	B	332.1	224	No load	1.25	35.4	33.0	1.0
SECURITY EQUITY A ♑	B	Large-cap Blend	B	745.2	20	5.75	1.03	29.7	27.1	0.3
SELECTED AMERICAN	B	Large-cap Value	C–	2218.1	61	No load	1.03†	37.3	34.7	0.7
SELIGMAN CAPITAL A	D	Mid-cap Growth	C–	284.2	10	4.75	1.07†	22.3	19.2	0.0
SELIGMAN COMMON STOCK A	C	Large-cap Blend	C–	734.6	12	4.75	1.15†	23.6	19.9	1.8
SELIGMAN COMMUNICATIONS & INFO. A	D	Technology	C	3107.5	29	4.75	1.68†	23.0	16.8	0.0
SELIGMAN FRONTIER A	C–	Small-cap Growth	B	546.2	10	4.75	1.56†	17.8	15.3	0.0
SELIGMAN GROWTH A	C–	Large-cap Growth	D	732.8	9	4.75	1.20†	18.1	15.3	0.0
SELIGMAN HENDERSON GLOBAL SM. A	C	World	B	434.4	15	4.75	1.75†	3.6	2.5	0.0
SELIGMAN HENDERSON GLOBAL TECH A		Technology		583.3	6	4.75	1.75†	11.8	7.3	0.0
SELIGMAN INCOME A	B	Domestic Hybrid	C	270.7	–9	4.75	1.14†	14.1	10.3	4.6
SENTINEL BALANCED A ♑	B	Domestic Hybrid	C	314.9	9	5.00	1.20†	20.6	18.1	2.7
SENTINEL COMMON STOCK A	B	Large-cap Blend	C	1510.3	20	5.00	1.06†	27.9	24.7	1.3
SEQUOIA ♑	A	Large-cap Value	B	3468.0	34	No load‡	1.00	42.3	42.2	0.1
SIERRA GROWTH & INCOME A	C	Large-cap Blend	C	178.2	14	5.75	1.53†	28.6	21.5	0.1
SIFE TRUST A-I	B+	Financial	C	1051.8	37	5.00	1.20	45.1	42.1	3.4
SIT MID CAP GROWTH ♑	D	Mid-cap Growth	C	381.6	2	No load	0.92	17.7	14.8	0.0
SKYLINE SPECIAL EQUITIES ♑	B+	Small-cap Value	B	455.8	108	No load‡	1.51	35.4	32.2	0.0
SMALLCAP WORLD	C	Small-cap Growth	A	8667.0	23	5.75	1.07†	11.8	9.5	0.4
SMITH BARNEY AGGRES. GROWTH A ♑	D	Mid-cap Growth	C	331.6	23	5.00	1.21†	28.6	27.3	0.0
SMITH BARNEY APPRECIATION A ♑	B	Large-cap Blend	C	2419.4	17	5.00	1.00†	26.5	22.4	1.2
SMITH BARNEY CONC. BALANCED B		Domestic Hybrid		177.1	71	5.00**	1.35†	11.5	9.6	3.5
SMITH BARNEY CONC. GROWTH B		Domestic Hybrid		315.4	67	5.00**	1.35†	13.8	12.3	1.6
SMITH BARNEY CONC. HIGH GR. A		Large-cap Blend		241.4	75	5.00	0.60†	12.5	11.5	1.0
SMITH BARNEY CONCERT SO. AW. A (zzzz)	B+	Domestic Hybrid	B	193.5	9	5.00	1.28†	21.3	18.1	2.5
SMITH BARNEY EQUITY INCOME A ♑	B	Large-cap Value	C–	724.0	12	5.00	0.95†	27.9	25.0	1.8
SMITH BARNEY FUNDAMENTAL VALUE B	B	Large-cap Value	C–	879.7	13	5.00**	1.90†	14.3	13.1	0.2
SMITH BARNEY INTL EQUITY A ♑	D	Foreign	D	443.5	–14	5.00	1.29†	1.9	1.9	0.0
SMITH BARNEY MANAGED GROWTH B		Small-cap Value		557.0	15	5.00**	2.03†	12.8	11.1	0.0
SMITH BARNEY PREM. TOTAL RET. B	A	Large-cap Value	A	3001.4	27	5.00**	1.62†	24.6	22.0	5.3
SMITH BARNEY SECURITY & GROWTH		Domestic Hybrid		213.7	–10	4.00‡	0.99	11.1	5.7	2.5
SMITH BARNEY SPEC EQUITIES B	F	Mid-cap Growth	F	277.7	–23	5.00**	1.91†	–6.4	–6.4	0.0
SMITH BARNEY UTILITIES B	C	Utilities	C–	866.6	–28	5.00**	1.52†	20.3	17.6	4.4
SOGEN INTERNATIONAL ♑	B+	International Hybrid	B+	3997.9	6	3.75	1.21†	8.5	5.8	5.1
SOGEN OVERSEAS		Foreign		963.5	13	3.75	1.27†	3.0	0.0	6.4
SOUND SHORE ♑	A	Mid-cap Value	A	1303.5	891	No load	1.15	36.4	35.4	0.4
SOUTHTRUST VULCAN STOCK	C	Large-cap Value	D	348.4	44	4.50	0.87	27.5	24.3	0.9
SSGA EMERGING MARKETS ♑		Diversified Emerging Mkts.		241.1	63	No load	1.25†	–8.8	–9.5	1.5
SSGA MATRIX EQUITY	B	Large-cap Blend	B	465.0	48	No load	0.58†	34.2	28.0	1.1
SSGA S&P 500 INDEX	B+	Large-cap Blend	B+	1776.7	106	No load	0.16†	33.1	31.4	1.5
SSGA SMALL CAP	C	Small-cap Blend	B	257.2	237	No load	1.00†	23.6	21.3	0.2
STAGECOACH ASSET ALLOC. A	B	Domestic Hybrid	C	1194.7	10	4.50	0.92†	22.0	19.0	3.2

*Includes redemption fee. **Includes deferred sales charge. †12(b)-1 plan in effect. ‡Not currently accepting new accounts. §Less than 0.5% of assets. NA=Not available. NM=Not meaningful.
(xxxx) Formerly Scudder Quality Growth. (yyyy) Formerly Scudder Capital Growth. (zzzz) Formerly Smith Barney Strategic Investors A.

AVERAGE ANNUAL TOTAL RETURNS (%)						HISTORY	PORTFOLIO DATA						RISK					TELEPHONE
3 YEARS		5 YEARS		10 YEARS		RESULTS VS.	TURNOVER	CASH	FOREIGN	P-E	UNTAXED	LARGEST HOLDING	LEVEL	BEST		WORST		
PRETAX	AFTERTAX	PRETAX	AFTERTAX	PRETAX	AFTERTAX	ALL FUNDS		%	%	RATIO	GAINS (%)	COMPANY (% ASSETS)		QTR	%RET	QTR	%RET	
39.0	38.0	NA	NA	NA	NA	1	Very low	0	NA	NA	20	S&P 500 10/97 (Opt.) Call (21)			NA		NA	800-820-0888
35.1	34.5	NA	NA	NA	NA	1	Very high	0	NA	35	9	Microsoft (20)			NA		NA	800-820-0888
−17.9	−18.2	NA	NA	NA	NA	4	Very low	0	NA	NA	−44	S&P 500 12/97 (Opt) Call 400 (124)			NA		NA	800-820-0888
24.8	21.1	22.9	19.6	19.8	16.9	1312	Average	3	7	23	26	Chase Manhattan (5)	Low	II 97	14.2	I 94	−0.6	800-426-6730
32.5	25.2	22.8	17.7	18.5	14.5	1421	High	5	2	24	36	Micros Systems (5)	High	II 97	19.0	I 94	−4.7	800-426-6730
26.9	22.7	17.9	14.8	14.8	12.2	3331	Average	3	2	23	31	American Home Products (4)	Very low	II 97	13.1	IV 94	−3.0	800-426-6730
31.6	25.4	18.0	13.0	14.5	10.9	3341	Very high	6	9	24	31	Sears Roebuck (3)	Average	II 97	13.4	I 94	−9.3	800-725-6666
30.6	26.3	20.5	16.0	16.8	12.7	3321	Average	7	12	24	44	Tyco Intl. (3)	Low	II 97	14.1	I 94	−2.5	800-725-6666
29.0	27.4	19.6	17.7	16.4	14.5	3221	Very low	10	13	22	71	Chubb (12)	Average	II 97	16.1	I 94	−1.7	800-725-6666
8.2	4.2	13.0	9.7	9.1	7.0	2414	Average	7	100	26	18	Novartis (Reg.) (4)	High	IV 93	13.2	IV 97	−7.9	800-344-8332
29.9	29.4	19.1	18.6	NA	NA	21	Very low	0	0	27	37	General Electric (3)	Average	II 97	16.7	I 94	−4.1	800-435-4000
NA	NA	NA	NA	NA	NA			2	28	28	20	Schwab Intl. Index (20)			NA		NA	800-435-4000
10.2	9.8	NA	NA	NA	NA	4	Very low	1	100	28	17	Royal Dutch Petrol. (Neth.) (2)			NA		NA	800-435-4000
NA	NA	NA	NA	NA	NA			2	3	27	17	General Electric (3)			NA		NA	800-435-4000
22.8	22.7	NA	NA	NA	NA	2	Low	1	1	26	28	Dell Computer (1)			NA		NA	800-435-4000
17.0	14.5	12.8	10.1	12.4	10.1	3333	Low	18	0	24	24	SBC Communications (1)	Low	II 97	10.8	I 94	−1.7	800-422-2766
21.0	17.8	12.8	9.9	15.7	13.2	2123	Average	1	6	33	46	AccuStaff (4)	Very high	II 95	17.7	I 97	−15.5	800-225-2470
NA	NA	NA	NA	NA	NA			13	96	22	9	Telebras (2)			NA		NA	800-225-2470
17.1	14.5	15.1	13.2	14.2	12.6	1423	Low	9	75	26	35	IBM (2)	Average	II 97	13.6	IV 94	−4.4	800-225-2470
16.3	14.4	15.0	13.7	NA	NA	23	Average	9	49	35	30	Bank of Ireland (4)	Average	II 97	12.5	IV 94	−4.9	800-225-2470
26.1	24.9	NA	NA	NA	NA	1	Low	5	99	27	26	Misys (2)			NA		NA	800-225-2470
27.8	25.3	19.9	17.3	17.0	14.3	3221	Low	4	15	22	34	Xerox (2)	Low	II 97	15.3	I 94	−3.3	800-225-2470
11.6	9.7	13.0	11.3	10.6	8.7	1424	Low	5	100	28	31	Skandia Foersaekrings (2)	Average	II 97	12.6	IV 97	−6.2	800-225-2470
27.7	25.6	15.5	13.6	NA	NA	41	Average	2	6	36	37	General Electric (5)	High	II 97	22.9	I 94	−4.1	800-225-2470
27.8	23.8	17.7	14.4	17.4	14.4	1231	Average	2	9	20	37	Bell Atlantic (3)	Average	II 97	15.7	I 94	−8.7	800-225-2470
15.0	14.3	19.1	18.4	NA	NA	21	Low	5	100	21	18	YPF (ADR) (6)	Very high	IV 93	27.0	I 95	−23.2	800-225-2470
NA	NA	NA	NA	NA	NA			3	NA	26	NA	Scudder Income (26)			NA		NA	800-225-2470
NA	NA	NA	NA	NA	NA		Low	6	NA	17	25	SPX (1)			NA		NA	800-225-2470
29.4	26.8	19.7	17.8	NA	NA	21	Average	18	16	19	23	S&P 500 Index (Futures) (15)	Low	II 97	15.2	I 94	−2.9	800-225-2470
30.1	27.0	19.7	16.0	18.5	15.2	1221	Average	6	4	27	36	Tyco Intl. (2)	Average	II 97	17.0	I 94	−3.6	800-888-2461
35.4	33.2	20.4	17.2	18.6	15.7	2131	Low	4	5	24	43	Hewlett-Packard (4)	Average	II 97	18.1	I 94	−3.8	800-243-1575
25.2	21.0	13.8	10.0	16.3	12.9	2142	High	5	5	31	41	Travelers Group (3)	High	II 97	14.2	I 94	−11.6	800-221-2783
22.3	18.8	15.6	12.4	14.3	11.1	3323	Average	7	2	25	39	General Electric (2)	Average	II 97	15.4	I 94	−4.7	800-221-2783
25.4	21.7	29.3	24.8	23.3	19.0	1114	High	4	5	28	32	EMC (4)	Very high	II 95	29.8	IV 95	−14.4	800-221-2783
21.4	19.4	19.3	15.9	19.0	16.4	2113	Average	7	0	30	23	AccuStaff (3)	High	II 97	20.3	I 97	−9.9	800-221-2783
22.5	19.2	13.4	9.6	14.7	11.4	2242	Low	2	NA	31	43	Pfizer (4)	High	II 97	14.2	IV 94	−5.3	800-221-2783
15.0	13.3	18.6	17.3	NA	NA	14	Average	1	57	25	10	Ceridian (2)	Average	III 95	14.4	IV 97	−7.1	800-221-2450
22.8	20.4	NA	NA	NA	NA	4	Average	6	42	30	27	Novellus Systems (3)			NA		NA	800-221-2783
14.2	11.4	10.3	7.8	11.3	8.5	4134	High	8	27	23	16	Natl. Australia Bank (ADR) (1)	Very low	II 95	7.3	I 94	−4.0	800-221-2783
19.2	17.0	12.4	10.5	12.1	10.0	4343	Average	6	4	22	31	Pfizer (1)	Very low	II 97	9.6	I 94	−3.7	800-282-3863
27.6	23.9	17.5	14.6	15.9	13.1	3231	Low	7	4	22	54	Parker-Hannifin (3)	Low	II 97	13.9	I 94	−4.7	800-282-3863
34.8	33.7	22.9	21.2	19.4	17.2	2121	Low	5	NA	32	66	Berkshire Hathaway (31)	Average	II 97	21.5	II 96	−2.1	800-686-6884
27.0	21.9	17.9	13.6	NA	NA	321	High	2	4	25	31	Exxon (3)	Average	II 97	14.8	I 94	−2.5	800-222-5852
40.3	34.8	24.4	20.6	20.8	17.7	4121	High	16	0	20	49	Bankers Trust New York (5)	Average	II 97	15.3	IV 94	−8.5	800-524-7433
24.2	19.9	15.7	12.5	17.2	14.9	1142	Low	3	10	33	47	Mercury General (4)	High	II 97	20.3	I 97	−10.1	800-332-5580
26.2	22.2	19.5	15.3	22.3	18.8	1131	High	10	2	19	29	Furon (2)	Low	II 97	19.3	IV 97	−4.2	800-458-5222
18.0	14.8	15.7	13.1	NA	NA	313	Average	10	40	28	12	Fletcher Challenge Energy (1)	Average	II 97	12.8	IV 97	−7.0	800-421-4120
21.5	19.6	16.4	15.1	16.3	14.8	1313	Very low	0	1	26	51	Intel (11)	High	III 97	21.8	IV 97	−9.7	800-451-2010
25.0	21.1	15.9	13.0	15.3	13.1	2332	Average	17	5	23	44	Allstate (3)	Low	II 97	13.2	I 94	−2.8	800-451-2010
NA	NA	NA	NA	NA	NA		Very low	NA	NA	23	9	Smith Barney Dvr. Strat. Inc. A (15)			NA		NA	800-451-2010
NA	NA	NA	NA	NA	NA		Very low	NA	NA	23	11	Smith Barney Aggres. Gr. A (10)			NA		NA	800-451-2010
NA	NA	NA	NA	NA	NA		Very low	NA	NA	25	11	Smith Barney Aggres. Gr. A (20)			NA		NA	800-451-2010
19.4	16.5	14.1	11.3	NA	NA	23	Average	6	6	25	29	American Express (2)	Very low	II 97	10.7	I 94	−2.0	800-451-2010
25.5	21.6	17.1	14.0	14.7	11.8	3332	Average	9	7	23	35	Bristol-Myers Squibb (3)	Low	II 97	15.3	I 94	−4.5	800-451-2010
19.9	18.2	15.7	13.4	NA	NA	13	Average	15	8	22	24	Adobe Systems (4)	Low	II 95	9.0	IV 97	−4.2	800-451-2010
5.9	5.8	10.6	10.4	11.6	10.8	1414	Average	1	98	27	24	Novartis (Reg) (3)	High	IV 93	19.2	IV 97	−10.1	800-451-2010
NA	NA	NA	NA	NA	NA	4	Low	13	6	27	20	Forest Laboratories Cl. A (4)			NA		NA	800-451-2010
22.2	19.5	15.8	13.3	16.2	13.2	2132	Average	14	24	21	6	SLM Holding (5)	Very low	II 97	10.2	I 94	−0.8	800-451-2010
NA	NA	NA	NA	NA	NA	4	Average	1	8	20	31	Quantum (6)			NA		NA	800-451-2010
12.5	11.9	12.0	11.5	10.8	10.0	4414	High	8	10	34	45	Starbucks (6)	Very high	III 93	20.3	I 97	−14.0	800-451-2010
17.0	14.6	10.7	7.6	NA	NA	244	Average	4	NA	20	1	FPL Group (5)	Average	II 97	10.7	I 94	−7.4	800-334-2143
12.4	10.0	13.0	11.1	12.0	9.8	3314	Very low	20	56	24	9	Buderus (1)	Very low	I 93	7.9	IV 97	−5.1	800-334-2143
9.7	7.3	NA	NA	NA	NA	4	Very low	15	98	22	10	Buderus (2)			NA		NA	800-334-2143
33.2	30.1	21.5	18.7	18.9	16.0	2221	Average	4	5	17	16	Toys 'R' Us (4)	Low	II 97	16.2	IV 94	−1.5	800-551-1980
28.9	26.1	16.7	14.9	NA	NA	41	Low	4	3	22	33	Intel (3)	Average	II 97	13.2	I 94	−5.1	800-239-7470
−1.2	−1.8	NA	NA	NA	NA	4	Very low	5	99	17	−7	Telebras (4)			NA		NA	800-647-7327
28.6	23.8	19.8	16.7	NA	NA	21	High	0	NA	23	22	Intel (3)	Average	II 97	17.1	I 94	−3.8	800-647-7327
30.8	28.6	20.0	18.3	NA	NA	21	Very low	6	3	27	31	S&P 500 Index (Fut.) 9/97 (4)	Average	II 97	17.5	I 94	−3.7	800-647-7327
31.2	29.2	20.4	18.2	NA	NA	21	High	2	1	23	19	FIRSTPLUS Financial Group (2)	Average	II 97	19.1	I 97	−6.2	800-647-7327
20.7	17.9	14.5	11.6	13.0	11.4	4223	Very low	0	3	27	22	General Electric (2)	Low	II 97	10.5	I 94	−4.2	800-222-8222

MUTUAL FUND SCOREBOARD

FUND	OVERALL RATING (COMPARES RISK-ADJUSTED PERFORMANCE OF EACH FUND AGAINST ALL FUNDS)	CATEGORY (COMPARES RISK-ADJUSTED PERFORMANCE OF FUND WITHIN CATEGORY)	RATING	SIZE ASSETS $MIL.	% CHG. 1996-97	FEES SALES CHARGE (%)	EXPENSE RATIO (%)	1997 RETURNS (%) PRE-TAX	AFTER-TAX	YIELD
STAGECOACH DIVERS EQ. INCOME A (aaaaa)	B	Large-cap Blend	C	182.9	21	5.25	1.10†	20.2	18.5	1.5
STAGECOACH EQUITY INDEX A (bbbbb)	B	Large-cap Blend	B	510.6	29	No load	0.97†	31.9	30.9	0.7
STAGECOACH GROWTH A (ccccc)	C−	Large-cap Blend	F	282.5	1	5.25	1.14†	19.1	15.4	0.4
STAGECOACH LIFEPATH 2040 A		Large-cap Blend		211.2	21	No load	1.20†	26.5	23.8	0.8
STATE ST RESEARCH CAPITAL B ♟		Mid-cap Growth		501.8	33	5.00**	2.01†	5.4	5.2	0.0
STATE ST RESEARCH INVESTMENT B		Large-cap Blend		540.3	107	5.00**	1.50†	27.8	24.7	0.2
STATE ST RESEARCH MGD. ASSETS B		Domestic Hybrid		318.7	31	5.00**	2.00†	15.4	11.6	1.2
STEIN ROE BALANCED	B	Domestic Hybrid	C	280.8	9	No load	1.05	17.5	15.0	2.6
STEIN ROE CAPITAL OPPORT.	D	Mid-cap Growth	C	988.0	−31	No load	1.22	6.2	6.2	0.0
STEIN ROE GROWTH & INCOME	B+	Large-cap Blend	B+	337.2	40	No load	1.18	25.7	24.1	1.2
STEIN ROE GROWTH STOCK	C−	Large-cap Growth	C	606.4	37	No load‡	1.08	31.6	30.0	0.0
STEIN ROE SPECIAL ♟	C	Mid-cap Blend	C	1277.1	11	No load	1.18	25.9	23.2	0.0
STEIN ROE SPECIAL VENTURE		Small-cap Blend		229.1	45	No load	1.25	9.7	6.9	0.0
STEIN ROE YOUNG INVESTOR		Large-cap Growth		496.3	83	No load	1.21	26.3	25.9	0.0
STI CLASSIC CAPITAL GROWTH INV.	C	Large-cap Blend	D	242.5	23	3.75	1.80†	30.3	24.5	0.0
STI CLASSIC VAL. INC. STOCK INV.		Large-cap Value		187.3	30	3.75	1.30†	26.6	20.0	1.6
STRONG ASSET ALLOCATION	B	Domestic Hybrid	C	278.6	3	No load	1.10	16.7	12.2	3.1
STRONG COMMON STOCK	B+	Mid-cap Blend	B+	1541.9	24	No load‡	1.20	24.0	18.4	0.2
STRONG DISCOVERY ♟	D	Mid-cap Growth	C−	398.7	−22	No load	1.40	10.9	6.8	0.0
STRONG GROWTH		Mid-cap Growth		1617.1	24	No load	1.30	19.1	13.6	0.0
STRONG GROWTH & INCOME		Large-cap Blend		237.3	389	No load	1.90	30.4	28.5	0.4
STRONG OPPORTUNITY	B+	Mid-cap Blend	B+	1916.2	8	No load	1.30	23.5	18.6	0.2
STRONG SCHAFER VALUE ♟	A	Mid-cap Value	B+	1436.3	179	No load	1.27	29.3	28.1	0.5
STRONG SMALL CAP		Small-cap Growth		187.1	19	No load	1.50	−4.5	−4.7	0.9
STRONG TOTAL RETURN	C	Large-cap Growth	B	847.7	12	No load	1.10	24.2	16.0	0.6
SUNAMERICA BALANCED ASSETS B ♟	C	Domestic Hybrid	C−	174.2	3	4.00**	2.11†	23.4	20.7	0.9
TCW/DW CORE EQUITY B (ddddd)	C−	Large-cap Blend	F	820.3	6	5.00**	1.73†	21.9	18.1	0.0
TCW/DW LATIN AMERICAN GROWTH B (eeeee)	F	Latin America		300.1	21	5.00**	2.98†	30.6	30.6	0.0
TCW/DW MID-CAP EQUITY B (fffff)		Mid-cap Growth		174.5	−12	5.00**	NA†	11.0	11.0	0.0
TCW/DW SMALL CAP GROWTH B (ggggg)		Small-cap Growth		328.7	8	5.00**	2.57†	10.6	10.6	0.0
TEMPLETON CAPITAL ACCUMULATOR	C	World	B	179.3	36	9.00	1.00	11.2	10.0	1.7
TEMPLETON DEVELOPING MKTS. I	D	Diversified Emerging Mkts.		3605.4	9	5.75	2.03†	−9.8	−11.3	1.1
TEMPLETON FOREIGN I ♟	C	Foreign	B+	14033.7	27	5.75	1.08†	6.6	4.0	3.0
TEMPLETON GLOBAL OPPORT. I	C−	World	C	801.6	26	5.75	1.45†	14.1	11.6	2.3
TEMPLETON GLOBAL SMALL CO. I ♟	C	World	B	1737.0	4	5.75	1.30†	7.0	5.1	1.4
TEMPLETON GROWTH I ♟	B	World	A	12405.9	29	5.75	1.08†	16.1	12.1	2.5
TEMPLETON WORLD I	B	World	B+	8504.8	19	5.75	1.03†	19.1	15.2	2.3
THIRD AVENUE VALUE	A	Small-cap Value	B+	1676.0	160	No load	1.21	23.9	23.3	1.3
TORRAY	A	Large-cap Blend	A	531.8	356	No load	1.25	37.1	36.5	0.4
TOWER CAPITAL APPRECIATION A	B	Large-cap Blend	B	294.3	54	4.50	1.24†	31.6	28.8	0.5
TWEEDY, BROWNE AMERICAN VALUE		Mid-cap Value		643.0	132	No load	1.39	38.9	37.8	0.8
TWEEDY, BROWNE GLOBAL VALUE		World		1932.2	60	No load	1.58	23.0	20.3	5.2
UNITED ACCUMULATIVE A ♟	C	Large-cap Blend	C−	1567.3	22	5.75	0.83†	29.4	23.4	0.9
UNITED CONTINENTAL INCOME A	C	Domestic Hybrid	C−	582.6	14	5.75	0.93†	17.3	14.0	2.9
UNITED INCOME A ♟	C	Large-cap Blend	C−	6169.8	27	5.75	0.86†	27.2	24.7	0.7
UNITED INTERNATIONAL GROWTH A	C−	Foreign	C	1002.9	18	5.75	1.28†	17.3	13.3	0.5
UNITED NEW CONCEPTS A	C−	Mid-cap Growth	B	650.6	19	5.75	1.27†	16.7	14.3	0.1
UNITED RETIREMENT SHARES A	B	Domestic Hybrid	C−	753.6	17	5.75	0.92†	18.1	15.0	2.7
UNITED SCIENCE & TECHNOLOGY A ♟	D	Technology	D	1033.4	5	5.75	0.98†	7.2	3.0	0.0
UNITED VANGUARD A ♟	C−	Large-cap Growth	C−	1416.5	10	5.75	1.09†	19.6	14.5	0.7
USAA AGGRESSIVE GROWTH	D	Small-cap Growth	C−	749.6	5	No load	0.74	7.6	5.9	0.0
USAA CORNERSTONE STRATEGY	B+	Mid-cap Value	C	1390.7	19	No load	1.06	15.6	13.1	2.4
USAA EMERGING MARKETS		Diversified Emerging Mkts.		261.3	371	No load	1.81	−3.5	−3.9	0.0
USAA GROWTH	C−	Large-cap Blend	F	1416.3	8	No load	0.97	3.7	1.1	0.5
USAA GROWTH & INCOME		Large-cap Value		866.2	69	No load	0.89	26.0	24.5	1.2
USAA GROWTH & TAX STRATEGY	B+	Domestic Hybrid	B+	203.8	18	No load	0.74	16.2	14.1	3.2
USAA GROWTH STRATEGY		Mid-cap Growth		235.1	65	No load	1.31	9.1	8.4	0.9
USAA INCOME STOCK	B+	Large-cap Value	B	2333.7	21	No load	0.68	27.0	24.0	3.8
USAA INTERNATIONAL	C−	Foreign	B	582.4	14	No load	1.09	9.0	6.8	0.6
USAA S&P 500 INDEX		Large-cap Blend		595.4	234	No load	0.18	33.0	32.4	1.4
USAA WORLD GROWTH	C	World	C	326.1	22	No load	1.20	12.9	11.1	0.5
VALUE LINE		Mid-cap Growth	B+	391.5	12	No load	0.80	21.6	17.2	0.6
VALUE LINE LEVERAGED GROWTH INV.	C−	Large-cap Growth	C	433.0	17	No load	0.88	23.8	21.6	0.0
VAN ECK INTL. INVEST. GOLD A	F	Precious Metals	B	256.4	−40	5.75	1.43	−36.0	−36.2	1.2
VAN KAMPEN AM. CAP COMSTOCK A	B	Large-cap Value		1484.6	20	5.75	1.00†	29.9	24.1	1.3
VAN KAMPEN AM. CAP EMERG GR A	D	Mid-cap Growth	C	2021.2	24	5.75	1.05†	21.3	19.0	0.0
VAN KAMPEN AM. CAP ENTERPR. A	C	Large-cap Blend	D	1702.0	33	5.75	1.01†	28.6	25.3	0.3
VAN KAMPEN AM. CAP EQ.-INC. B	B+	Domestic Hybrid	C	892.6	41	5.00**	1.74†	23.2	18.9	1.4
VAN KAMPEN AM. CAP GR. & INC. A	B	Large-cap Blend	C	769.5	33	5.75	1.04†	24.5	20.2	1.2
VAN KAMPEN AM. CAP. PACE A	C	Large-cap Blend	C−	3217.4	20	5.75	0.97†	30.2	24.5	0.9

*Includes redemption fee. **Includes deferred sales charge. †12(b)-1 plan in effect. ‡Not currently accepting new accounts. §Less than 0.5% of assets. NA=Not available. NM=Not meaningful. (aaaaa) Formerly Stagecoach Diversified Income A. (bbbbb) Formerly Stagecoach Corporate Stock A. (ccccc) Formerly Stagecoach Growth & Income A. (ddddd) Formerly TCW/DW Core Equity. (eeeee) Formerly TCW/DW Latin American Growth. (fffff) Formerly TCW/DW Mid-Cap Equity. (ggggg) Formerly TCW/DW Small Capitalization Growth.

3 YR PRETAX	3 YR AFTERTAX	5 YR PRETAX	5 YR AFTERTAX	10 YR PRETAX	10 YR AFTERTAX	RESULTS VS. ALL FUNDS	TURNOVER	CASH %	FOREIGN %	P-E RATIO	UNTAXED GAINS (%)	LARGEST HOLDING COMPANY (% ASSETS)	RISK LEVEL	BEST QTR	BEST %RET	WORST QTR	WORST %RET	TELEPHONE
24.1	21.9	16.5	14.8	NA	NA	3 2	Average	4	4	21	24	Household International (4)	Low	II 97	13.6	I 94	-3.2	800-222-8222
29.7	28.5	19.0	17.7	16.7	15.9	2 3 2 1	Very low	1	3	27	60	General Electric (3)	Average	II 97	17.2	I 94	-4.0	800-222-8222
23.2	20.2	15.1	13.0	NA	NA	3 2	Average	0	13	30	22	LM Ericsson Tel. (ADR) (5)	Average	II 97	13.8	I 94	-3.6	800-222-8222
25.6	23.4	NA	NA	NA	NA	2	Low	1	23	26	30	Daimler Benz (ADR) (2)			NA		NA	800-222-8222
13.8	12.8	NA	NA	NA	NA	4	Very high	1	3	31	12	HFS (4)			NA		NA	800-882-0052
26.5	21.8	NA	NA	NA	NA	1	Average	3	8	28	37	DuPont (3)			NA		NA	800-882-0052
18.8	15.8	NA	NA	NA	NA	3	High	5	24	27	20	Seagull Energy (1)			NA		NA	800-882-0052
19.0	16.0	12.7	10.1	12.5	9.7	4 2 4 3	Average	1	25	25	30	General Electric (3)	Low	II 97	9.9	IV 94	-3.2	800-338-2550
24.4	23.9	19.7	19.4	14.3	13.3	4 4 1 2	Low	10	8	47	19	Paychex (5)	High	II 97	21.4	I 97	-18.4	800-338-2550
25.8	23.4	17.6	15.4	16.5	14.6	2 2 3 1	Very low	16	3	29	34	Warner-Lambert (3)	Low	II 97	14.2	I 94	-3.2	800-338-2550
29.2	25.2	16.4	13.4	16.6	14.3	2 1 4 1	Low	4	9	36	47	Motorola (4)	High	II 97	20.1	I 94	-5.8	800-338-2550
21.1	18.3	15.6	13.0	17.3	14.7	1 2 3 2	Low	11	12	28	51	Harley-Davidson (3)	Average	II 97	18.7	I 94	-6.7	800-338-2550
21.5	18.7	NA	NA	NA	NA	2	Average	9	4	26	20	AVX (3)			NA		NA	800-338-2550
33.6	32.5	NA	NA	NA	NA	1	High	5	3	33	18	AT&T (2)			NA		NA	800-338-2550
26.6	21.7	15.3	12.1	NA	NA	4 1	High	8	2	28	33	General Electric (3)	Average	II 97	16.8	IV 94	-4.3	800-428-6970
26.9	21.3	NA	NA	NA	NA	1	High	3	3	24	7	ITT Industries (2)			NA		NA	800-428-6970
16.3	12.3	12.1	8.8	10.6	7.6	4 3 3 3	Very high	4	1	30	14	General Electric (2)	Very low	II 97	8.1	I 94	-2.1	800-368-1030
25.5	20.2	19.8	15.9	NA	NA	1 1 2	Average	8	5	24	30	Sybase (2)	Average	II 97	15.1	IV 97	-4.7	800-368-1030
14.9	11.2	11.8	8.5	16.2	12.8	1 1 2 4	Very high	11	3	29	19	Budget Group (3)	High	III 97	16.4	I 97	-10.1	800-368-1030
26.1	23.5	NA	NA	NA	NA	2	Very high	10	3	42	29	Kohl's (2)			NA		NA	800-368-1030
NA	NA	NA	NA	NA	NA		Very high	0	6	27	14	Schlumberger (1)			NA		NA	800-368-1030
22.9	19.2	18.3	15.4	15.9	13.8	3 2 1 2	High	11	11	26	34	Comcast Special Cl. A (2)	Low	III 97	14.9	IV 94	-2.8	800-368-1030
28.8	27.4	20.5	19.0	19.3	16.8	2 1 1 1	Low	2	20	18	23	Reading & Bates (3)	Low	II 97	15.7	IV 94	-3.7	800-368-1030
NA	NA	NA	NA	NA	NA		Very high	6	6	38	1	Gulf Island Fabrication (2)			NA		NA	800-368-1030
21.6	16.2	16.8	13.5	12.4	9.7	4 3 2 2	Very high	6	4	30	24	Schlumberger (2)	Average	II 97	13.8	I 94	-2.9	800-368-1030
19.3	16.1	13.5	10.5	12.1	9.4	4 3 3 3	High	3	5	28	24	Summit Bancorp (3)	Low	II 97	11.0	I 94	-5.0	800-858-8850
21.8	19.5	14.7	13.4	NA	NA	2 3	Average	1	3	28	95	Intel (5)	High	II 97	17.5	I 94	-5.3	800-526-3143
8.3	8.3	7.3	7.1	NA	NA	4 2	Average	4	99	21	-4	Tel. de Mexico L (ADR) (5)	Very high	IV 93	33.6	I 95	-29.6	800-526-3143
NA	NA	NA	NA	NA	NA			2	3	51	NA	Romac International (6)			NA		NA	800-526-3143
26.3	26.3	NA	NA	NA	NA	2	High	4	4	46	34	Safeskin (3)			NA		NA	800-526-3143
16.2	15.1	17.6	16.4	NA	NA	1 3	Very low	13	79	22	22	Philips Electronics (2)	Average	IV 93	11.2	IV 97	-8.2	800-292-9293
3.5	2.2	12.1	10.9	NA	NA	1 4	Very low	3	100	17	8	Electricidad de Caracas (3)	High	IV 93	21.2	IV 97	-25.2	800-292-9293
11.8	9.7	13.9	11.9	13.4	11.0	1 4 1 4	Low	23	100	18	5	Philips Electronics (NV) (2)	Average	IV 93	10.9	IV 97	-8.3	800-292-9293
16.9	14.6	16.2	13.5	NA	NA	3 1 3	Low	20	75	20	29	Peregrine Invmt. Hldgs. (2)	Average	II 97	11.8	IV 97	-10.0	800-292-9293
15.4	11.9	14.1	11.7	13.6	10.2	2 4 1 4	Low	11	76	18	23	News (2)	Average	I 93	10.9	IV 97	-9.8	800-292-9293
18.8	15.3	17.5	14.3	15.5	12.4	2 4 1 3	Average	14	66	20	15	Philips Electronics (2)	Low	II 97	11.6	IV 97	-5.2	800-292-9293
20.7	16.6	18.8	14.9	14.6	11.1	3 4 1 3	Low	18	68	21	19	Morg. Stanley/Dean Witter (2)	Average	II 97	13.2	IV 97	-6.1	800-292-9293
25.8	24.9	19.4	18.5	NA	NA	1 2	Very low	38	13	28	24	Tejon Ranch (4)	Low	I 93	14.4	IV 97	-5.0	800-443-1021
38.6	37.6	23.7	22.6	NA	NA	2 1	Low	2	NA	24	19	AT&T (7)	Low	II 97	16.1	I 94	-3.4	800-443-3036
30.7	27.5	20.0	17.2	NA	NA	3 2 1	Average	1	1	25	38	Microsoft (3)	Average	II 97	16.9	I 94	-4.3	800-999-0124
32.3	31.4	NA	NA	NA	NA	1	Very low	9	13	20	28	Chase Manhattan (3)			NA		NA	800-432-4789
17.8	15.9	NA	NA	NA	NA	2	Low	8	79	23	23	Nestle (Reg) (4)			NA		NA	800-432-4789
25.0	20.1	16.4	12.1	15.0	11.5	2 3 3 2	Very high	4	11	23	27	Novartis (ADR) (4)	Average	II 97	14.2	I 94	-2.1	800-366-5465
17.1	13.9	12.6	10.0	12.6	10.4	3 3 3 3	Low	11	9	25	24	BankAmerica (2)	Low	II 97	9.5	IV 94	-1.8	800-366-5465
25.7	23.6	17.8	16.0	16.7	14.6	1 3 2 2	Low	2	6	28	53	Intel (3)	Average	II 97	18.7	IV 94	-2.5	800-366-5465
14.5	11.8	17.5	14.6	11.0	9.0	4 4 1 3	High	7	98	27	14	Credit Suisse Group (Reg) (4)	High	IV 93	17.4	I 95	-7.4	800-366-5465
17.9	16.2	15.1	13.4	16.4	15.3	4 1 1 3	Low	27	2	37	38	America Online (4)	High	II 97	17.3	I 97	-9.0	800-366-5465
17.3	14.0	12.6	9.9	13.9	11.6	2 2 3 3	Low	15	9	23	24	BankAmerica (2)	Low	II 97	9.8	I 94	-2.0	800-366-5465
21.9	19.1	16.6	14.1	16.3	13.8	3 1 1 3	Low	12	4	37	46	America Online (3)	High	I 95	19.1	I 97	-15.2	800-366-5465
17.2	12.9	14.3	11.0	12.8	10.0	3 4 1 4	High	5	10	25	33	Applied Materials (6)	High	II 97	13.7	II 94	-3.2	800-366-5465
23.5	21.9	15.1	13.2	14.1	12.0	3 2 3 2	Average	2	4	35	34	Cisco Systems (2)	Very high	II 97	18.6	I 97	-12.7	800-382-8722
17.3	15.1	14.6	12.4	11.4	9.7	4 4 2 3	Low	2	33	26	26	Bristol-Myers Squibb (1)	Low	I 93	10.1	I 94	-2.4	800-382-8722
5.3	4.3	NA	NA	NA	NA	4	Average	6	100	20	-6	Panamerican Beverages (2)			NA		NA	800-382-8722
17.3	13.4	12.4	8.3	13.1	10.5	3 2 2 4	Average	0	5	29	13	Cadbury Schweppes (ADR) (5)	High	III 94	12.1	IV 97	-16.1	800-382-8722
26.8	25.3	NA	NA	NA	NA	1	Very low	3	4	24	24	Boeing (4)			NA		NA	800-382-8722
16.6	15.0	11.9	10.4	NA	NA	3 3 3	Very high	1	4	24	21	Halliburton (4)	Very low	II 97	8.4	I 94	-3.5	800-382-8722
NA	NA	NA	NA	NA	NA		Average	1	23	30	15	Pharmacia & Upjohn (2)			NA		NA	800-382-8722
24.7	21.7	16.5	13.9	16.0	13.5	2 2 3 2	Low	2	NA	20	24	Bankers Trust New York (4)	Low	III 97	10.0	I 94	-4.0	800-382-8722
12.1	10.8	15.1	13.7	NA	NA	4 1 4	Average	4	96	27	21	Akzo Nobel (2)	Average	IV 93	13.8	IV 97	-9.3	800-382-8722
NA	NA	NA	NA	NA	NA		Very low	4	4	27	17	General Electric (3)			NA		NA	800-382-8722
14.9	13.2	13.6	12.4	NA	NA	2 3	Average	5	71	28	24	Elf Aquitaine (ADR) (1)	Average	II 97	12.0	IV 97	-7.0	800-382-8722
25.3	21.5	15.0	11.2	16.5	13.0	2 1 4 2	Average	14	1	30	48	Transocean Offshore (3)	High	II 97	15.0	II 94	-5.6	800-223-0818
27.6	24.2	18.4	16.0	16.5	13.6	2 2 2 2	Low	3	2	33	57	Dell Computer (4)	High	II 97	18.4	I 97	-6.1	800-223-0818
-19.2	-19.7	2.2	1.3	-3.5	-4.6	4 4 1 4	Very low	27	66	27	4	Barrick Gold (6)	Very high	II 93	39.1	IV 97	-25.0	800-826-1115
29.4	23.2	17.9	11.9	16.6	12.4	2 3 3 1	Very high	1	8	21	27	Tele-Comm. TCI Group Cl. A (3)	Low	III 97	12.8	I 94	-3.8	800-421-5666
27.4	24.7	19.0	16.8	19.1	17.2	2 1 1 2	Average	4	3	35	36	Dell Computer (3)	High	II 97	19.0	I 97	-8.3	800-421-5666
28.6	24.7	18.7	15.1	17.6	14.2	2 2 2 1	High	2	3	27	38	Philip Morris (5)	Average	II 97	16.3	I 94	-3.2	800-421-5666
22.9	19.7	15.8	13.1	NA	NA	2 2	High	4	15	24	24	BankAmerica (2)	Low	II 97	12.6	I 94	-3.7	800-421-5666
25.9	22.3	17.9	14.2	15.3	12.3	3 3 2 2	High	3	16	25	26	Philip Morris (2)	Low	II 97	14.7	I 94	-3.1	800-421-5666
27.8	22.5	17.4	12.5	15.3	11.5	2 3 3 1	High	1	8	24	37	Philip Morris (2)	Average	II 97	15.9	I 94	-3.6	800-421-5666

DATA: MORNINGSTAR, INC., CHICAGO, IL.

MUTUAL FUND SCOREBOARD

FUND	OVERALL RATING	CATEGORY	RATING	SIZE		FEES		1997 RETURNS (%)		
(COMPARES RISK-ADJUSTED PERFORMANCE OF EACH FUND AGAINST ALL FUNDS)		(COMPARES RISK-ADJUSTED PERFORMANCE OF FUND WITHIN CATEGORY)		ASSETS $MIL.	% CHG. 1996-97	SALES CHARGE (%)	EXPENSE RATIO (%)	PRE-TAX	AFTER-TAX	YIELD
VAN WAGONER EMERGING GROWTH		Mid-cap Growth		313.2	–51	No load	1.95†	–20.0	–20.0	0.0
VANGUARD ASSET ALLOCATION	A	Domestic Hybrid	B+	3984.3	53	No load	0.49	27.3	24.6	3.4
VANGUARD BALANCED INDEX	B+	Domestic Hybrid	B	1211.2	47	No load	0.20	22.2	20.7	3.2
VANGUARD EQUITY-INCOME	A	Large-cap Value	B+	2029.2	42	No load	0.45	31.2	28.9	2.9
VANGUARD EXPLORER	C–	Small-cap Blend	C–	2516.2	11	No load	0.62	14.6	12.1	0.4
VANGUARD GROWTH & INCOME (hhhhh) ♁	B+	Large-cap Blend	C	2077.0	62	No load	0.38	35.6	30.6	1.4
VANGUARD HORIZON AGGRES. GROWTH		Mid-cap Value		457.5	199	1.00*	0.38	26.1	23.5	0.9
VANGUARD INDEX EXTENDED MARKET ♁	C	Mid-cap Blend	C	2715.5	29	No load	0.25	26.7	24.4	1.1
VANGUARD INDEX 500 ♁	B+	Large-cap Blend	B+	48264.6	59	No load	0.20	33.2	32.4	1.5
VANGUARD INDEX GROWTH	B	Large-cap Growth	A	2280.8	190	No load	0.20	36.3	35.4	1.0
VANGUARD INDEX SMALL CAP. STOCK	C	Small-cap Blend	C	2623.4	53	No load	0.25	24.6	22.9	1.1
VANGUARD INDEX TOTAL STOCK MKT.	B	Large-cap Blend	B	4887.9	38	No load	0.22	31.0	30.0	1.4
VANGUARD INDEX VALUE	B+	Large-cap Value	B	1728.1	70	No load	0.20	29.8	27.7	1.7
VANGUARD INTERNATIONAL VALUE (iiiii)	D	Foreign	C–	833.4	–9	No load	0.50	–4.6	–8.0	2.7
VANGUARD INTL. EQ. EMG. MKT.		Diversified Emerging Mkts.		684.5	7	No load	0.60	–16.7	–17.3	2.3
VANGUARD INTL. EQ. EUROPEAN	B	Europe	C	2340.1	47	No load	0.35	24.2	23.4	1.8
VANGUARD INTL. EQ. PACIFIC	F	Japan		887.4	–9	No load	0.35	–25.7	–25.9	1.2
VANGUARD INTL. GROWTH ♁	C–	Foreign	B	6843.3	23	No load	0.57	4.1	3.0	1.2
VANGUARD LIFESTRATEGY CONS. GROWTH		Domestic Hybrid		772.9	67	No load	0.00	16.8	14.9	4.1
VANGUARD LIFESTRATEGY GROWTH		Large-cap Blend		1126.5	79	No load	0.00	21.8	20.5	2.3
VANGUARD LIFESTRATEGY INCOME		Domestic Hybrid		234.4	55	No load	0.00	14.2	12.2	5.0
VANGUARD LIFESTRATEGY MOD. GROWTH		Large-cap Blend		1306.1	58	No load	0.00	19.8	18.1	3.3
VANGUARD SELECTED VALUE		Small-cap Value		190.7	81	No load	0.74	17.4	16.1	0.4
VANGUARD SPEC. ENERGY ♁	C–	Natural Resources	C	1197.0	41	1.00*	0.39	14.9	13.0	1.3
VANGUARD SPEC. GOLD & PREC. METALS	F	Precious Metals	B	287.4	–42	1.00*	0.50	–38.9	–39.3	1.9
VANGUARD SPEC. HEALTH CARE ♁	B+	Health	B+	4383.9	65	1.00*	0.38	28.6	27.2	1.1
VANGUARD SPEC. UTILITIES INC.	C	Utilities	B	645.0	–2	No load	0.40	25.1	23.0	3.9
VANGUARD SPECIAL REIT INDEX		Real Estate		1216.2	159	1.00*	0.36	18.8	16.8	5.1
VANGUARD STAR	A	Domestic Hybrid	B+	7234.6	23	No load	0.00	21.2	18.2	3.2
VANGUARD STAR TOTAL INTL. ♁		Foreign		869.2	210	No load	0.00	–0.8	–1.4	1.7
VANGUARD TAX-MGDL CAP APPREC.		Large-cap Growth		866.8	68	2.00*	0.20	27.3	27.1	0.6
VANGUARD TAX-MGD. GROWTH & INCOME		Large-cap Blend		549.3	134	2.00*	0.20	33.3	32.7	1.3
VANGUARD U.S. GROWTH ♁	C	Large-cap Growth	A	7912.8	43	No load	0.42	25.9	24.8	0.9
VANGUARD/MORGAN GROWTH	C	Large-cap Blend	C–	2739.7	33	No load	0.51	30.8	26.2	0.8
VANGUARD/PRIMECAP ♁	B+	Mid-cap Blend	B+	8063.7	92	No load	0.59	36.8	35.5	0.5
VANGUARD/TRUSTEES' EQUITY U.S.	C	Large-cap Blend	C	170.6	8	No load	0.49	29.5	21.4	0.9
VANGUARD/WELLESLEY INCOME ♁	B+	Domestic Hybrid	B	7616.4	9	No load	0.31	20.2	16.5	5.2
VANGUARD/WELLINGTON	B+	Domestic Hybrid	B+	21340.3	32	No load	0.31	23.2	20.5	3.6
VANGUARD/WINDSOR	B	Large-cap Value	C	20836.6	24	No load‡	0.27	22.0	17.2	1.6
VANGUARD/WINDSOR II ♁	A	Large-cap Value	B+	23545.0	50	No load	0.37	32.4	29.4	2.1
VICTORY BALANCED A		Domestic Hybrid		348.7	24	5.75	1.27	19.5	17.2	2.6
VICTORY DIVERSIFIED STOCK A	B	Large-cap Blend	B	796.1	34	5.75	1.05	28.3	25.2	0.8
VICTORY GROWTH		Large-cap Growth		197.4	28	5.75	1.33	31.3	29.5	0.1
VICTORY SPECIAL VALUE A		Mid-cap Value		443.5	48	5.75	1.37	27.8	25.5	0.6
VICTORY STOCK INDEX		Large-cap Blend		506.9	66	5.75	0.57	32.4	30.1	1.5
VICTORY VALUE		Large-cap Value		496.3	26	5.75	1.33	27.5	25.1	0.8
VISTA CAPITAL GROWTH A	C	Mid-cap Value	C–	861.1	10	4.75	1.37†	23.4	19.9	0.2
VISTA GROWTH & INCOME A	B	Large-cap Value	C–	1537.6	–6	4.75	1.32†	29.5	24.8	0.6
VISTA SMALL CAP EQUITY A		Small-cap Blend		173.3	14	4.75‡	1.50†	17.8	17.0	0.0
WADDELL & REED GROWTH B	C–	Domestic Hybrid	F	256.6	5	3.00**	2.12†	21.1	19.9	0.0
WADDELL & REED TOTAL RET. B	C	Large-cap Blend	C–	408.7	40	3.00**	1.95†	24.6	23.7	0.0
WARBURG PINCUS CAP APPREC. COMM.	B	Large-cap Blend	B	623.4	34	No load	1.03	31.4	24.7	0.4
WARBURG PINCUS EMG. GR. COMM.	C–	Small-cap Growth	B+	1578.0	37	No load	1.27	21.3	19.4	0.0
WARBURG PINCUS GR. & INC. COMM. ♁	C	Large-cap Value	D	616.4	34	No load	1.21	30.3	23.9	1.0
WARBURG PINCUS INTL. EQ. COMM.	D	Foreign	C–	1956.2	–34	No load	1.37	–4.4	–7.7	1.5
WARBURG PINCUS SMALL VAL. COMM.		Small-cap Value		200.6	66	No load	1.75†	19.2	15.5	0.0
WASATCH AGGRESSIVE EQUITY ♁	C–	Small-cap Growth	B+	172.2	–21	No load‡	1.50	19.2	15.6	0.0
WASHINGTON MUTUAL INVESTORS ♁	A	Large-cap Value	B	38246.0	51	5.75	0.64†	33.3	31.0	1.9
WEITZ VALUE	B+	Mid-cap Value	B+	366.0	40	No load	1.29	38.9	34.2	1.1
WESTCORE MIDCO GROWTH ♁	D	Mid-cap Growth	C	649.9	14	No load	1.14	14.9	11.5	0.0
WHITE OAK GROWTH STOCK	C–	Large-cap Growth	C	391.9	870	No load	0.95	24.3	24.2	0.1
WILLIAM BLAIR GROWTH	C	Mid-cap Growth	B+	591.4	18	No load	0.79	20.1	18.8	0.0
WINTHROP SMALL COMPANY VAL. A (jjjjj)	B	Small-cap Value	C	283.0	19	4.75	1.47†	26.2	24.3	0.3
WPG TUDOR ♁	D	Small-cap Growth	C–	170.7	–6	No load	1.25	11.1	7.7	0.0
WRIGHT INTL BLUE CHIP EQUITY	C–	Foreign	B	212.7	–21	No load	1.30†	1.5	–0.0	1.0
WRIGHT SELECTED BLUE CHIP EQ ♁	B	Mid-cap Value	C	259.5	26	No load	1.04†	32.7	25.7	0.6
YACKTMAN	C	Mid-cap Blend	C	1082.1	43	No load	0.90†	18.3	15.1	1.4
ZWEIG APPRECIATION A	B+	Mid-cap Value	B	289.9	5	5.50	1.62†	23.8	22.0	0.5
ZWEIG MANAGED ASSETS C		International Hybrid		409.3	–4	1.25**	2.34†	14.1	9.7	0.0
ZWEIG STRATEGY C	B	Mid-cap Value	C	588.8	–5	1.25**	1.98†	17.4	14.9	0.5

*Includes redemption fee. **Includes deferred sales charge. †12(b)-1 plan in effect. ‡Not currently accepting new accounts. §Less than 0.5% of assets. NA=Not available. NM=Not meaningful. (hhhhh) Formerly Vanguard Quantitative. (iiiii) Formerly Vanguard/Trustees' Equity Intl. (jjjjj) Formerly Winthrop Aggressive Growth A.

3 YEARS PRETAX	3 YEARS AFTERTAX	5 YEARS PRETAX	5 YEARS AFTERTAX	10 YEARS PRETAX	10 YEARS AFTERTAX	HISTORY RESULTS VS. ALL FUNDS	TURNOVER	CASH %	FOREIGN %	P-E RATIO	UNTAXED GAINS (%)	LARGEST HOLDING COMPANY (% ASSETS)	RISK LEVEL	BEST QTR	BEST %RET	WORST QTR	WORST %RET	TELEPHONE
NA	NA	NA	NA	NA	NA		High	0	4	36	-17	Avant! (9)			NA		NA	800-228-2121
25.9	22.9	17.2	14.7	NA	NA	2 2 2	Very low	10	3	27	27	General Electric (1)	Low	II 97	12.5	I 94	-4.6	800-662-7447
21.5	19.9	14.2	12.8	NA	NA	3 3	Low	4	1	27	24	General Electric (1)	Very low	II 97	11.5	I 94	-3.5	800-662-7447
28.4	26.1	19.0	16.8	NA	NA	3 2 1	Low	6	3	23	41	Bell Atlantic (3)	Low	II 97	12.2	I 94	-6.6	800-662-7447
18.3	15.8	13.9	11.3	15.3	13.4	3 1 2 3	Average	11	2	27	17	Air Express Intl. (2)	High	III 97	14.8	I 97	-7.5	800-662-7447
31.4	27.7	20.7	17.5	18.3	15.9	1 2 2 1	Average	4	2	24	33	Compaq Computer (4)	Average	II 97	16.9	I 94	-4.1	800-662-7447
NA	NA	NA	NA	NA	NA		High	1	0	22	20	Smart Modular Technologies (2)			NA		NA	800-662-7447
25.9	23.7	17.5	16.0	16.4	15.1	3 2 2 2	Low	4	1	27	37	Berkshire Hathaway Cl. A (2)	Average	II 97	15.7	I 97	-3.4	800-662-7447
31.0	30.1	20.1	19.2	17.8	16.6	2 3 2 1	Very low	2	3	27	36	General Electric (3)	Average	II 97	17.4	I 94	-3.8	800-662-7447
32.6	31.8	19.5	18.7	NA	NA	3 1	Low	0	2	32	23	General Electric (6)	Average	II 97	20.2	I 94	-4.4	800-662-7447
23.7	21.7	17.5	15.6	15.8	13.9	3 2 2 2	Low	4	0	25	26	U.S. Office Products (§)	Average	II 97	17.3	I 97	-5.0	800-662-7447
29.1	28.1	18.9	18.0	NA	NA	2 1	Very low	6	0	27	31	General Electric (2)	Average	II 97	16.8	I 94	-3.7	800-662-7447
29.4	27.5	20.5	18.9	NA	NA	1 1	Low	0	5	21	25	Exxon (4)	Average	II 97	14.5	I 94	-3.2	800-662-7447
4.9	0.4	9.6	6.4	7.6	4.6	2 4 1 4	Average	5	99	25	19	Groupe Danone (3)	High	II 97	11.2	IV 97	-12.8	800-662-7447
-1.0	-1.6	NA	NA	NA	NA	4	Very low	5	100	16	-17	Eletrobras-Centrais Ele Bras (3)			NA		NA	800-662-7447
22.6	21.7	19.4	18.5	NA	NA	4 1 2	Very low	2	100	24	32	Royal Dutch Petrol. (Neth.) (3)	Average	II 97	9.6	I 94	-2.1	800-662-7447
-11.0	-11.3	1.5	1.2	NA	NA	4 1 4	Very low	1	100	33	-19	NTT (4)	Very high	II 93	19.3	IV 97	-20.7	800-662-7447
11.1	9.9	14.9	14.0	9.2	7.9	3 4 1 4	Low	5	100	28	18	Novartis (Reg) (4)	Average	II 97	13.9	IV 97	-9.4	800-662-7447
17.0	15.1	NA	NA	NA	NA	3	Very low	0	NA	27	11	Vanguard Bond Idx Total Bd. (30)			NA		NA	800-662-7447
22.0	20.6	NA	NA	NA	NA	2	Very low	0	NA	27	18	Vanguard Index Total Mkt. (50)			NA		NA	800-662-7447
14.8	12.7	NA	NA	NA	NA	4	Low	0	NA	26	8	Vanguard Bond Idx. Total Bd. (50)			NA		NA	800-662-7447
20.0	18.3	NA	NA	NA	NA	3	Very low	0	NA	27	15	Vanguard Idx. Total Stk. Mkt. (35)			NA		NA	800-662-7447
NA	NA	NA	NA	NA	NA		Low	7	4	20	9	Canandaigua Brands Cl. A (5)			NA		NA	800-662-7447
24.5	23.0	19.1	17.3	15.9	14.0	1 4 1 2	Very low	9	29	24	34	Amerada Hess (4)	High	I 93	21.3	IV 93	-8.9	800-662-7447
-16.7	-17.1	1.2	0.6	-2.2	-3.0	4 4 1 4	Low	10	78	31	-32	Newmont Mining (8)	Very high	II 93	31.3	IV 97	-28.8	800-662-7447
31.3	29.9	22.6	20.7	23.1	21.0	1 1 1 1	Very low	12	22	33	35	Warner-Lambert (5)	Average	II 97	19.1	I 93	-7.9	800-662-7447
20.9	19.0	13.2	11.1	NA	NA	4 3	Low	3	10	20	19	New Eng. Electric System (4)	Low	IV 97	13.1	I 94	-7.0	800-662-7447
NA	NA	NA	NA	NA	NA			2	NA	28	13	Crescent Real Estate Eq. (4)			NA		NA	800-662-7447
21.9	18.8	14.9	12.3	14.1	11.5	3 2 3 3	Low	13	NA	22	28	Vanguard/Windsor II (28)	Very low	II 97	10.1	I 94	-3.1	800-662-7447
NA	NA	NA	NA	NA	NA			0	100	26	0	Vanguard Intl. Eq. European (53)			NA		NA	800-662-7447
27.4	27.2	NA	NA	NA	NA	2	Very low	0	0	29	30	General Electric (3)			NA		NA	800-662-7447
31.2	30.4	NA	NA	NA	NA	1	Very low	0	3	27	25	General Electric (3)			NA		NA	800-662-7447
30.0	28.1	17.6	16.4	18.2	17.3	1 2 3 1	Low	3	5	34	36	Intel (5)	Average	II 97	16.7	I 93	-3.0	800-662-7447
29.9	25.8	18.3	14.9	17.1	13.9	1 2 3 1	Average	8	6	26	38	Home Depot (2)	Average	II 97	16.1	I 94	-4.1	800-662-7447
29.9	28.7	23.6	22.4	19.0	17.6	2 3 1 1	Very low	10	9	24	42	Texas Instruments (5)	Average	III 97	19.7	IV 97	-5.6	800-662-7447
27.9	22.3	18.7	14.9	15.6	12.4	3 3 2 1	High	1	NA	27	35	General Electric (4)	Average	II 97	17.3	II 94	-5.2	800-662-7447
19.2	16.1	13.2	10.3	13.3	10.4	3 2 3 3	Low	2	6	21	20	First Union (2)	Very low	II 95	8.5	I 94	-4.5	800-662-7447
23.9	21.3	16.5	14.3	14.7	12.3	3 3 2 2	Low	1	9	21	31	Allstate (2)	Low	II 97	12.2	I 94	-3.9	800-662-7447
26.1	21.7	19.0	15.2	16.2	12.6	3 3 1 2	Average	4	12	19	17	Citicorp (5)	Average	II 95	11.4	IV 97	-3.4	800-662-7447
31.7	28.9	20.7	18.3	18.2	15.7	2 2 2 1	Low	7	4	20	33	Chase Manhattan (3)	Low	II 97	14.7	I 94	-4.5	800-662-7447
20.0	17.9	NA	NA	NA	NA	3	Average	3	10	24	24	Texaco (2)			NA		NA	800-539-3863
29.4	25.4	19.9	15.9	NA	NA	3 2 1	High	1	0	24	30	IBM (4)	Average	II 97	13.4	I 94	-3.4	800-539-3863
29.2	27.4	NA	NA	NA	NA	1	Low	1	NA	31	43	General Electric (4)			NA		NA	800-539-3863
24.5	22.3	NA	NA	NA	NA	2	Average	4	3	23	29	Warnaco Group Cl. A (2)			NA		NA	800-539-3863
30.2	28.4	NA	NA	NA	NA	1	Very low	12	3	27	31	General Electric (4)			NA		NA	800-539-3863
27.8	25.6	NA	NA	NA	NA	1	Low	2	3	24	39	Mobil (3)			NA		NA	800-539-3863
23.3	20.2	17.3	15.2	21.8	20.0	1 1 2 2	Average	2	0	23	35	Tenet Healthcare (3)	Average	II 97	13.4	I 97	-3.5	800-348-4782
25.4	21.9	16.6	14.3	24.1	21.4	1 1 3 2	Average	4	5	23	43	Dow Chemical (2)	Low	II 97	14.3	I 94	-2.7	800-348-4782
32.7	32.0	NA	NA	NA	NA	1	Average	8	5	30	32	Stage Stores (2)			NA		NA	800-348-4782
17.9	16.9	18.1	17.2	NA	NA	1 3	Low	15	4	34	28	America Online (5)	High	II 97	18.9	I 97	-10.5	913-236-2000
24.0	23.6	16.3	16.1	NA	NA	2 2	Low	8	3	27	34	Gillette (3)	Average	II 97	17.1	IV 94	-2.2	913-236-2000
30.8	25.5	20.3	16.2	17.4	14.7	2 3 2 1	Very high	1	8	24	30	Warner-Lambert (4)	Average	II 97	14.3	I 94	-5.6	800-927-2874
24.9	23.5	17.8	16.6	NA	NA	1 1 2	Average	8	3	35	29	Maxim Integrated Products (3)	High	III 95	17.1	I 97	-6.7	800-927-2874
15.7	13.0	17.8	14.2	NA	NA	3 1 4	High	6	8	20	32	British Petroleum (ADR) (3)	Average	III 93	17.9	III 96	-5.2	800-927-2874
5.3	3.3	12.1	10.5	NA	NA	4 1 4	Low	3	100	25	8	Orix (2)	High	IV 93	17.3	IV 97	-15.0	800-927-2874
NA	NA	NA	NA	NA	NA			7	5	19	22	Terra Nova (Berm) Hldg. Cl. A (3)			NA		NA	800-927-2874
17.1	15.1	15.7	13.5	16.5	15.0	2 1 1 4	Average	4	1	27	49	National Health Investors (7)	High	II 97	20.3	I 97	-7.0	800-551-1700
31.3	28.5	20.8	18.4	17.6	15.3	2 3 2 1	Low	4	0	22	41	Atlantic Richfield (3)	Low	II 97	14.4	I 94	-5.0	800-421-4120
31.7	28.3	19.8	17.4	17.1	14.9	3 2 3 1	Low	14	0	30	34	Redwood Trust (6)	Low	II 97	14.1	I 94	-6.7	800-232-4161
19.6	16.4	14.8	12.2	17.8	14.8	2 1 2 3	Average	6	6	35	42	WorldCom (5)	High	II 97	20.8	I 97	-10.0	800-392-2673
35.9	35.8	21.6	21.5	NA	NA	2 1	Very low	8	NA	29	16	Cisco Systems (6)	High	II 97	22.1	IV 97	-8.1	888-462-5386
22.3	20.9	17.6	15.5	17.0	13.8	2 1 1 3	Average	3	6	33	37	Automatic Data Processing (4)	Average	II 97	18.2	I 97	-6.8	800-742-7272
20.2	18.8	16.0	14.3	17.2	14.1	3 1 2 3	Low	9	NA	20	33	Carlisle (2)	Low	II 97	14.5	IV 94	-3.6	800-225-8011
23.1	17.9	13.8	9.1	14.8	10.8	2 2 4 2	High	4	9	36	39	Qualcom (2)	Very high	III 97	17.0	I 97	-12.1	800-223-3332
11.7	10.3	11.9	11.0	NA	NA	4 1 4	Low	-1	100	22	26	Loblaw (3)	Average	IV 93	10.9	IV 94	-4.8	800-888-9471
27.1	22.4	15.1	12.2	15.5	12.2	2 2 4 1	Average	0	NA	18	34	A.G. Edwards (2)	Low	II 97	14.2	I 94	-3.0	800-888-9471
24.8	21.0	14.6	12.2	NA	NA	4 2	Average	16	3	24	24	Philip Morris (14)	Average	IV 96	11.4	II 93	-6.9	800-525-8258
21.0	18.0	14.8	12.5	NA	NA	3 2	Average	8	10	17	36	Popular (1)	Very low	III 97	13.1	IV 94	-1.7	800-444-2706
12.8	9.7	NA	NA	NA	NA	4	Very high	17	59	24	19	MCI Communications (1)			NA		NA	800-444-2706
17.8	15.4	13.3	10.4	NA	NA	2 3	Very high	3	22	16	24	S&P 500 Index (Futures) (15)	Low	II 95	11.2	IV 93	-2.7	800-444-2706

DATA: MORNINGSTAR, INC., CHICAGO, IL.

Bond Funds

MUTUAL FUND SCOREBOARD

How to Use the Tables

BUSINESS WEEK RATING
Ratings measure risk-adjusted performance. This shows how well a fund performed relative to other funds and relative to the level of risk it took. Risk-adjusted performance is determined by subtracting a fund's risk-of-loss factor (see below) from its historic total return. Performance calculations are based on the five-year time period between Jan. 1, 1993, and Dec. 31, 1997. For BW ratings, funds are divided into taxable and tax-exempt funds. Funds are also rated against others in their category. Ratings are based on a normal statistical distribution within each group and awarded as follows:

A	SUPERIOR
B+	VERY GOOD
B	ABOVE AVERAGE
C	AVERAGE
C−	BELOW AVERAGE
D	POOR
F	VERY POOR

RISK
The risk-of-loss factor is the potential for losing money in a fund, calculated as follows: The monthly Treasury bill return is subtracted from the fund's total return for each of the 60 months in the rating period. When a fund has not performed as well as Treasury bills, the result is negative. The sum of these negative numbers is then divided by the number of months in the period. The result is a negative number, and the greater its magnitude, the higher a shareholder's risk of loss.

PERFORMANCE COMPARISON
The tables provide performance data over three time periods. Here are equivalent total returns for the Lehman Brothers bond indexes during those periods:

	GOVT./CORP.	MUNI.
1997	9.8%	9.2%
3-year average (1995-97)	10.4%	10.2%
5-year average (1993-97)	7.6%	7.4%

FUND CATEGORIES
General bond funds are classified long-term (CL), intermediate-term (CI), short-term (CS) and ultra-short (UB); government funds, long (GL), intermediate (GI) and short (GS); municipal funds, national long (ML), national intermediate (MI), single-state long (SL), single-state intermediate (SI) and short-term (MS); specialized funds, convertible (CV), high-yield (HY), international (IB), and multisector (MU).

SALES CHARGE
The cost of buying a fund, commonly called the "load." Many funds take loads out of initial investments, and for ratings purposes, performance is reduced by these charges. Loads on withdrawals can take two forms. Deferred charges decrease over time. Redemption fees are imposed whenever investors sell shares. Funds with none of these charges are called "no-load."

EXPENSE RATIO
Fund expenses for 1997 as a percentage of average net assets. The measures show how much shareholders pay for fund management. Footnotes indicate 12(b)-1 plans, which allocate shareholder money for marketing costs. The average expense ratio is 1.01% for taxable funds, 0.85% for tax-free funds.

TOTAL RETURN
A fund's net gain to investors, including reinvestment of dividends and capital gains at month-end prices.

YIELD
Income distributions during 1997 expressed as a percent of net asset value, adjusted for capital gains.

MATURITY
The average maturity of the securities in a fund's portfolio, weighted by market value.

HISTORY
A fund's relative performance during the five 12-month periods from Jan. 1, 1993, to Dec. 31, 1997. The numbers designate which quartile the fund was in during the period: ■ for the top quartile; ■ for the second quartile; ■ for the third quartile; ■ for the bottom quartile. No number indicates no data for that period.

TELEPHONE NUMBERS
See index on page 216.

FUND (COMPARES RISK-ADJUSTED PERFORMANCE OF EACH FUND AGAINST ALL FUNDS)	RATING	CATEGORY (RATING COMPARES FUND WITHIN CATEGORY)	RATING	SIZE ASSETS $MIL.	SIZE % CHG. 1996-97	FEES SALES CHARGE (%)	FEES EXPENSE RATIO (%)	TOTAL RETURN (%) 1 YR.	TOTAL RETURN (%) 3 YR.	TOTAL RETURN (%) 5 YR.	PORTFOLIO YIELD (%)	PORTFOLIO MATURITY (YEARS)	HISTORY RESULTS VS. ALL FUNDS
TAXABLE													
AARP GNMA & U.S. TREASURY	B	GS	C	4565.5	−5	No load	0.64	8.0	8.4	5.8	6.5	NA	4 1 4 2 3
AARP HIGH-QUALITY BOND	C−	CI	C	4513.7	799	No load	0.91	7.8	9.1	6.6	5.7	9.2	3 2 2 4 3
ACCESSOR MORTGAGE SECURITIES	B	GI	A	108.0	46	No load	0.95	9.5	10.1	7.1	5.7	7.2	4 1 3 1 1
ADVANCE CAPITAL I RETIREMENT INCOME	B	CL	B	197.2	15	No load	0.82 †	12.2	13.0	9.2	7.0	16.4	1 3 1 2 1
AIM HIGH-YIELD A	A	HY	B	1787.8	41	4.75	0.97 †	12.5	14.9	12.1	8.9	7.4	1 1 2 1 1
AIM INCOME A	C	MU	F	339.2	19	4.75	0.97 †	11.9	14.3	9.7	6.5	12.8	1 4 1 1 1
AIM INTERMEDIATE GOVERNMENT A	C−	GI	C	166.8	−4	4.75	1.00 †	9.1	9.1	6.1	6.7	6.8	4 2 2 4 2
AIM LTD. MATURITY TREASURY RET.	B	GS	B+	384.9	2	1.00	0.54 †	6.0	6.7	5.0	5.4	1.6	4 1 4 1 4
ALLIANCE BOND CORPORATE BOND B		CL		573.7	37	3.00 **	1.82 †	11.1	15.6	NA	7.9	20.1	4 1 1 1
ALLIANCE BOND U.S. GOVERNMENT B	D	GI	D	432.5	−23	3.00 **	1.73 †	7.8	7.4	5.1	6.9	5.0	4 3 3 4 3
ALLIANCE GLOBAL DOLLAR GOVERNMENT B		IB		94.3	14	3.00 **	2.26 †	8.4	23.0	NA	8.8	13.0	1 1 3
ALLIANCE MORTGAGE SECURITIES INCOME A	C−	GI	C	372.2	−9	4.25	1.03 †	8.4	9.2	6.1	6.6	NA	3 3 3 2 3
ALLIANCE MULTI-MARKET STRATEGY A	F	IB	C−	96.0	41	4.25	1.64 †	6.7	9.5	4.9	9.4	3.5	3 4 4 1 4
ALLIANCE NORTH AMER. GOVT. INCOME B	F	IB	F	1393.2	6	3.00 **	3.05 †	14.2	22.1	8.2	11.2	11.4	1 4 1 1 1
ALLIANCE SHORT-TERM MULTI-MARKET A	D	IB		431.5	11	4.25	1.29 †	5.3	7.9	4.4	7.9	1.3	4 4 4 1 4
AMCORE VINTAGE FIXED-INCOME	C	CI	C	103.8	15	No load	1.20 †	7.1	8.0	5.9	5.1	5.1	3 2 3 4 3
AMERICAN CENT.-BENHAM BOND INV. (a)	C	CI	C	127.4	−7	No load	0.79	8.7	10.2	7.1	6.1	9.5	3 2 1 4 2
AMERICAN CENT.-BENHAM GNMA INV. (b)	B	GI	A	1224.8	8	No load	0.55	8.7	9.8	6.8	6.5	22.0	4 1 3 1 2
AMERICAN CENT.-BENHAM INTERM. TREAS. (c)	C	GI	B+	361.3	7	No load	0.51	8.3	8.6	6.2	5.6	6.0	4 1 3 2 3
AMERICAN CENT.-BENHAM INTL. BOND (d)	F	IB	C−	179.2	−29	No load	0.83	−5.9	7.6	7.7	0.3	NA	1 1 1 1 4
AMERICAN CENT.-BENHAM LONG TREAS. (e)	F	GL	C−	125.2	3	No load	0.60	14.7	13.5	9.3	5.6	20.9	4 1 4 1 4
AMERICAN CENT.-BENHAM S/T GOVT. INV. (f)	B	GS	C	513.3	49	No load	0.70	6.0	6.8	4.8	5.5	3.8	4 1 4 2 4
AMERICAN CENT.-BENHAM TARGET 2000 (g)	D	GI	C−	245.3	−8	No load	0.56	7.1	9.5	6.9	0.0	2.5	1 4 1 4 4
AMERICAN CENT.-BENHAM TARGET 2005 (h)	F	GL	D	297.2	23	No load	0.57	11.6	13.1	8.8	0.0	7.5	1 4 1 4 1
AMERICAN CENT.-BENHAM TARGET 2010 (i)	F	GL	D	145.8	33	No load	0.62	16.8	16.7	11.5	0.0	12.5	1 4 1 4 1

*Includes redemption fee. **Includes deferred sales charge. †12(b)-1 plan in effect. ‡Not currently accepting new accounts or deposits. NA=Not available. NM=Not meaningful.
(a) Prev. Twentieth Cent. L-T Bd. (b) Prev. Benham GNMA Income. (c) Prev. Benham Treasury Note. (d) Prev. Benham European Government Bond. (e) Prev. Benham Long-Term Treasury & Agency. (f) Prev. 20th C. U.S. Govts. S-T. (g) Prev. Benham Target Maturities 2000. (h) Prev. Benham Target Maturities 2005. (i) Prev. Benham Target Maturities 2010.
DATA: MORNINGSTAR, INC., CHICAGO, IL.

MUTUAL FUND SCOREBOARD — Bond Funds

FUND (COMPARES RISK-ADJUSTED PERFORMANCE OF EACH FUND AGAINST ALL FUNDS)	RATING	CATEGORY	RATING (RATING COMPARES FUND WITHIN CATEGORY)	SIZE ASSETS $MIL.	SIZE % CHG. 1996-97	FEES SALES CHARGE (%)	FEES EXPENSE RATIO (%)	TOTAL RETURN (%) 1 YR.	TOTAL RETURN (%) 3 YR.	TOTAL RETURN (%) 5 YR.	YIELD (%)	MATURITY (YEARS)	HISTORY RESULTS VS. ALL FUNDS
AMERICAN CENT.-BENHAM TARGET 2015 (j)	F	GL	F	127.6	8	No load	0.61	22.9	20.6	12.5	0.0	17.5	1 4 1 4 1
AMERICAN CENT.-BENHAM TARGET 2020 (k)	F	GL	F	601.5	−32	No load	0.53	28.6	23.7	15.4	0.0	22.5	1 4 1 4 1
AMERICAN CENT.-BENHAM TARGET 2025 (l)		GL		150.4	230	No load	0.62	30.1	NA	NA	0.0	27.5	1
AMERICAN HIGH-INCOME	A	HY	C−	2194.2	31	4.75	0.82 †	11.6	15.3	11.3	7.6	5.3	1 3 1 1 1
AMSOUTH BOND CLASSIC	C−	CL	B	304.0	128	3.00	0.75	9.2	9.9	7.1	5.8	8.6	3 2 1 4 2
AMSOUTH LIMITED MATURITY CLASSIC	C	CS	D	118.6	181	3.00	0.76	6.7	7.7	5.5	5.6	3.4	4 1 4 3 4
ARMADA BOND INSTITUTIONAL (m)		GI		94.3	5	4.00	0.83 †	8.0	8.4	NA	5.8	10.0	3 3 3
ASSET MGMT. ADJUSTABLE RATE	B+	UB	B	762.0	2	No load	0.47 †	6.6	7.2	5.6	6.1	3.5	4 1 4 1 4
ASSET MGMT. SHORT U.S. GOVT. SEC.	B	GS	B	105.8	−40	No load	0.48 †	6.3	7.1	5.4	6.0	2.2	4 1 4 3 4
ATLAS U.S. GOVT. & MORTGAGE A	C	GI		199.3	−11	3.00	1.02 †	7.9	9.2	6.2	6.2	NA	4 2 3 2 3
BABSON BOND L	C	CI	B	131.9	−4	No load	0.97	9.3	9.3	7.0	6.2	10.4	3 2 3 3 2
BERNSTEIN GOVT. SHORT DURATION	B	GS	B+	144.6	8	No load	0.69	5.9	6.6	5.0	5.6	1.7	4 1 4 1 4
BERNSTEIN INTERM. DURATION	C	CI	B	2136.6	34	No load	0.63	7.7	9.5	7.0	6.3	7.0	3 2 2 3 3
BERNSTEIN SHORT DURATION PLUS	B+	CS	B	597.2	9	No load	0.65	5.6	6.7	5.2	6.1	1.7	4 1 4 1 4
BLAIR (WILLIAM) INCOME	B	CS	C	160.1	7	No load	0.70	8.0	8.4	6.4	6.3	4.5	4 1 3 3 3
BLANCHARD FLEXIBLE INCOME	B	MU	C−	151.3	−14	No load	1.59 †	9.4	10.1	7.5	6.0	4.6	1 3 3 1 2
BLANCHARD SHORT-TERM FLEXIBLE INCOME		CS		125.0	−17	No load	1.44 †	7.2	7.7	NA	5.6	1.8	1 4 1 3
BOND FUND OF AMERICA	B	CI	B+	8176.1	17	4.75	0.71 †	9.3	11.3	8.4	7.0	6.7	1 3 1 1 2
BOSTON 1784 INCOME (n)		CI		376.8	17	No load	0.80 †	7.9	9.3	NA	6.1	12.1	2 4 3
BOSTON 1784 SHORT-TERM INCOME (o)		CS		193.7	33	No load	0.65 †	6.3	7.3	NA	5.7	2.1	4 2 4
BOSTON 1784 U.S. GOVT. MEDIUM-TERM (p)		GS		240.5	22	No load	0.79 †	8.1	8.5	NA	6.0	7.1	2 3 4 3
CAPITAL WORLD BOND	C	IB	B	710.0	−13	4.75	1.07 †	−0.4	8.8	8.2	5.4	6.9	1 1 1 1 4
CARDINAL GOVERNMENT OBLIGATION	B	GI	A	125.0	−6	4.50	0.78	9.0	9.6	6.4	6.9	23.1	4 1 3 1 2
CHICAGO TRUST BOND		CI		126.0	49	No load	0.80 †	9.0	10.0	NA	6.0	8.2	2 2 2 2
COLONIAL FEDERAL SECURITIES A	D	GL	B	864.9	−13	4.75	1.18 †	9.9	10.2	7.1	6.1	10.9	2 3 1 4 1
COLONIAL HIGH-YIELD SECURITIES A	A	HY	B+	589.0	13	4.75	1.20 †	13.1	14.3	12.2	7.8	8.2	1 1 2 1 1
COLONIAL INCOME A	C−	CL	C	119.7	−8	4.75	1.10 †	8.6	10.6	7.8	6.8	11.1	2 2 1 3 2
COLONIAL INTERM. U.S. GOVT. A (q)	C	GI	C	708.6	−19	4.75	1.11 †	8.3	8.6	5.8	5.9	6.9	4 2 3 1 3
COLONIAL STRATEGIC INCOME B	B+	MU	C	827.9	5	5.00 **	1.93 †	7.2	11.8	9.0	6.8	9.8	1 2 1 1 3
COLUMBIA FIXED-INCOME SECURITIES	C	CI	B	377.8	6	No load	0.64	9.6	10.4	7.5	6.3	5.4	3 2 1 3 1
COMMERCE BOND INSTITUTIONAL		CI		244.0	59	3.50	0.84	9.0	10.0	NA	6.0	NA	1 4 2
COMMON SENSE GOVERNMENT 1	D	GI	F	239.8	−14	6.75	0.84	8.9	9.0	5.9	5.8	NA	4 3 2 4 2
COMPOSITE U.S. GOVT. SECURITIES A	C−	GI	C−	108.2	−22	4.00	0.97 †	9.9	10.4	6.7	5.7	10.6	4 3 1 4 1
DAVIS CONVERTIBLE SECURITIES A	A	CV	B+	89.8	110	4.75	1.05 †	28.7	28.3	18.2	2.8	8.6	1 4 1 1 1
DEAN WITTER CONVERTIBLE B (r)	B+	CV	C	317.1	29	5.00 **	1.89 †	16.4	18.0	13.0	3.8	7.9	1 2 1 1 1
DEAN WITTER DIVERSIFIED INCOME B (s)	B+	MU	C	942.6	21	5.00 **	1.44 †	6.0	9.0	7.0	7.7	NA	3 1 4 1 4
DEAN WITTER FEDERAL SECURITIES B (t)	D	GI	D	616.1	−12	5.00 **	1.52 †	8.9	9.3	6.2	6.3	NA	3 3 1 4 2
DEAN WITTER INTERM. INCOME B (u)	C	CI	C	154.7	−20	5.00 **	1.63 †	6.4	7.6	5.6	5.5	NA	4 2 4 3 4
DEAN WITTER SHORT-TERM U.S. TREAS.	C	GS	C	280.5	−6	No load	0.83 †	6.1	6.6	4.6	5.4	NA	4 1 4 2 4
DEAN WITTER U.S. GOVT. SECURITIES B (v)	C	GI	C	5414.6	−16	5.00 **	1.25 †	8.6	9.3	6.2	6.1	8.0	4 2 2 3 2
DEAN WITTER WORLDWIDE INCOME B (w)	C	IB	B	90.3	−19	5.00 **	1.93 †	3.3	11.1	7.6	7.5	NA	3 2 1 1 4
DELAWARE DELCHESTER A	B+	HY	D	1023.4	2	4.75	1.04 †	13.7	13.3	10.1	8.7	7.9	1 2 3 1 1
DELAWARE LIMITED-TERM GOVT. A	C	GS	C−	356.8	−23	3.00	0.93 †	5.1	5.8	4.1	6.8	12.7	4 1 4 3 4
DELAWARE U.S. GOVT. A	D	GI	D	144.3	−7	4.75	1.16 †	8.3	8.2	5.2	6.8	20.0	4 3 3 4 3
DG GOVERNMENT INCOME	C−	CI	C−	262.1	9	2.00	0.70	8.8	9.2	6.6	5.5	7.9	3 2 2 4 2
DODGE & COX INCOME	B	CI	B+	693.0	30	No load	0.50	10.0	11.1	8.2	6.0	12.5	3 2 1 3 1
DREYFUS 100% U.S. TREAS. INTERM. TERM	C	GI	C	187.7	−2	No load	0.70	7.6	8.7	6.5	7.2	6.9	3 2 3 3 3
DREYFUS 100% U.S. TREAS. LONG TERM	D	GL	C	133.8	−2	No load	0.80	11.7	12.1	8.3	6.1	18.8	1 4 1 4 1
DREYFUS 100% U.S. TREAS. SHORT TERM	B	GS	B	194.6	4	No load	0.70	6.1	7.2	5.6	6.3	2.8	4 1 4 2 4
DREYFUS A BONDS PLUS	C	CI	C	633.3	5	No load	0.96	9.4	10.6	7.8	5.9	14.8	1 3 1 4 1
DREYFUS GNMA	B	GI	B+	1199.1	−8	No load	0.96 †	8.8	9.4	6.4	6.1	22.2	4 2 3 2 2
DREYFUS HIGH-YIELD SECURITIES		HY		139.3	249	1.00 *	0.29	16.7	NA	NA	11.2	7.4	1
DREYFUS PREMIER GNMA A (x)	C	GI	B	94.9	−15	4.50	1.04	8.9	9.4	6.6	5.8	22.0	4 2 3 2 2
DREYFUS SHORT-INTERM. GOVT.	B	GS	B	477.5	−15	No load	0.74	6.1	7.5	5.8	6.2	4.4	4 1 4 2 4
DREYFUS SHORT-TERM HIGH-YIELD		HY		156.0	409	No load	NA	12.6	NA	NA	9.2	2.8	1
DREYFUS SHORT-TERM INCOME	B+	CS	A	294.5	37	No load	0.80	8.2	8.5	6.9	7.1	3.8	3 1 4 1 3
DREYFUS STRATEGIC INCOME	B	MU	C	277.0	−6	No load	1.04	11.2	12.7	9.1	6.8	13.9	1 3 1 1 1
EATON VANCE GOVT. OBLIGATIONS A (y)	C	GS	C	276.8	−9	3.75	1.86 †	7.3	8.5	6.5	7.6	3.5	3 1 3 2 3
EATON VANCE INCOME OF BOSTON	A	HY	B	209.2	36	3.75	1.07 †	16.4	15.2	12.2	9.0	6.5	1 1 3 1 1
EATON VANCE SHORT-TERM TREASURY	B+	UB	C	476.7	292	No load	0.60 †	5.0	5.5	4.5	1.8	NA	4 1 4 1 4
EATON VANCE STRATEGIC INCOME B (z)	B	MU	D	133.5	2	5.00 **	2.17 †	8.7	13.7	9.1	8.4	NA	3 3 3 1 2
EATON VANCE MARATHON HIGH-INCOME	A	HY	B	657.6	11	5.00 **	1.77 †	15.4	14.3	11.4	8.1	6.5	1 1 3 1 1
EVERGREEN DIVERSIFIED BOND B (aa)	C	CI	C	445.1	−19	4.00 **	1.87 †	11.1	10.6	7.5	5.9	12.9	1 4 3 1 1
EVERGREEN HIGH-YIELD BOND B (bb)	C−	HY	F	527.7	−11	4.00 **	1.95 †	13.0	11.1	8.7	7.4	6.3	1 4 4 1 1
EVERGREEN QUALITY BOND B (cc)	D	CL	C−	177.9	−17	4.00 **	1.98 †	7.9	8.5	5.7	5.1	11.2	4 3 2 4 3
EVERGREEN STRATEGIC INCOME B (dd)		MU		117.3	−3	5.00 **	2.02 †	7.9	9.4	NA	6.4	9.5	4 4 1 3
EVERGREEN U.S. GOVERNMENT B		GI		143.4	−8	5.00 **	1.73 †	7.9	8.5	NA	5.7	9.2	2 3 4 3
EXCELSIOR INTERM.-TERM MGD. INCOME	C	CI	C	91.4	20	No load	0.63	8.5	9.7	6.6	5.7	7.3	4 2 1 4 2
EXCELSIOR MANAGED INCOME	C−	CL	C	197.6	5	No load	0.90	9.8	10.6	7.5	5.5	20.9	2 3 1 4 1
FEDERATED ADJ. RATE U.S. GOVT. F	B	GS	B+	186.5	−17	1.00 **	1.02 †	5.9	6.5	5.0	5.6	0.8	4 1 4 1 4

*Includes redemption fee. **Includes deferred sales charge. †12(b)-1 plan in effect. ‡Not currently accepting new accounts or deposits. NA=Not available. NM=Not meaningful.
(j) Prev. Benham Tar. Mat. 2015. (k) Prev. Ben. T. M. 2020. (l) Prev. Benham T. M. 2025. (m) Prev. Armada Interm. Govt. Instl. (n) Prev. 1784 Inc. (o) Prev. 1784 S-T Inc. (p) Prev. 1784 U.S. Govt. M-T Inc. (q) Prev. Colonial U.S. Govt. A. (r) Prev. DW Conv. Prev. DW Divers. Inc. (t) Prev. DW Fed. (u) Prev. DW Intrmd. Inc. (v) Prev. DW U.S. Govt. (w) Prev. DW Wwde. Inc. (x) Prev. Premier GNMA A. (y) Prev. EV Tradl. Govt. Oblig. (z) Prev. EV Mar. Strat. Inc. B. (aa) Prev. Keystone Div. Bd. B-2. (bb) Prev. Keyston Hi-Inc. B-4. (cc) Prev. Keystone Qual. Bd. B-1. (dd) Prev. Keystone Strat. Inc. B.   DATA: MORNINGSTAR, INC., CHICAGO, IL.

MUTUAL FUND SCOREBOARD

Bond Funds

FUND (COMPARES RISK-ADJUSTED PERFORMANCE OF EACH FUND AGAINST ALL FUNDS)	RATING	CATEGORY	RATING (RATING COMPARES FUND WITHIN CATEGORY)	SIZE ASSETS $MIL.	% CHG. 1996-97	FEES SALES CHARGE (%)	FEES EXPENSE RATIO (%)	PERFORMANCE TOTAL RETURN (%) 1 YR.	3 YR.	5 YR.	PORTFOLIO YIELD (%)	MATURITY (YEARS)	HISTORY RESULTS VS. ALL FUNDS
FEDERATED ARMS INSTITUTIONAL	B+	GS	A	112.4	15	No load	0.80 †	6.1	7.0	4.9	5.8	0.6	4 1 4 1 4
FEDERATED BOND F	B+	CI	A	353.4	26	2.00 **	1.08	10.9	12.0	9.6	7.0	11.0	1 2 1 1 1
FEDERATED FUND FOR U.S. GOVT. A	C	GI	B	1164.4	−5	4.50	0.95	8.5	8.9	5.9	6.5	NA	4 1 3 2 2
FEDERATED GOVT. INCOME SECURITIES F	C	GI	B	1477.7	−20	2.00 **	0.96	9.5	9.3	6.1	6.9	NA	4 1 3 2 1
FEDERATED HIGH-INCOME BOND B		HY		853.9	91	5.50 **	1.99 †	12.4	14.4	NA	7.8	5.4	1 1 1
FEDERATED HIGH-YIELD	A	HY	B	1121.3	26	No load	0.88	13.3	15.0	11.8	8.6	5.2	1 1 1 1 1
FEDERATED INCOME INSTL.	B	GI	B+	759.2	−10	No load	0.58	8.9	9.6	6.5	6.5	NA	4 1 3 1 2
FEDERATED INTERM. INCOME INSTL.		CI		152.6	23	No load	0.55	8.7	10.5	7.4	6.3	9.3	1 1 3 2
FEDERATED INTL. INCOME A	F	IB	C	171.6	−12	4.50	1.30 †	−5.0	7.4	8.4	6.1	7.9	1 2 2 1 4
FEDERATED LTD. TERM A	B	CS	C	91.2	−18	1.00	1.10 †	7.1	7.9	5.9	5.9	2.4	4 1 4 1 4
FEDERATED SHORT-TERM INCOME INSTL.	B+	CS	B	199.1	−13	No load	0.56	6.4	7.5	5.5	6.1	1.8	4 1 4 1 4
FEDERATED STRATEGIC INCOME B		MU		323.7	145	5.50 **	1.80 †	7.7	NA	NA	7.6	6.8	1 3
FIDELITY ADV. EMERG. MKTS. T		IB		85.1	9	3.50	1.48 †	16.4	20.5	NA	7.8	17.6	4 1 1
FIDELITY ADV. GOVT. INVMNT. T	C−	GI	C−	148.4	−31	3.50	0.99 †	8.7	9.3	6.6	5.8	8.3	3 2 2 4 2
FIDELITY ADV. HIGH-YIELD T	A	HY	B+	2268.1	28	3.50	1.11 †	17.0	16.5	13.4	8.3	7.7	1 1 1 1 1
FIDELITY ADV. INTERM. BOND T	C	CS	C−	279.8	7	2.75	0.96 †	7.0	7.5	6.2	5.8	5.7	3 1 4 3 4
FIDELITY ADV. SHORT FIXED-INCOME T	B	CS	C	357.8	−11	1.50	0.88 †	6.2	6.8	5.2	6.1	2.2	3 2 4 1 4
FIDELITY ADV. STRATEGIC INCOME T		MU		115.0	17	3.50	1.22 †	9.2	14.6	NA	7.0	7.2	1 1 2
FIDELITY CAPITAL & INCOME	A	HY	C	2096.1	−3	1.50 *	0.86	14.7	14.3	12.2	6.8	7.5	1 2 2 1 1
FIDELITY CONVERTIBLE SECURITIES	C	CV	C−	1029.1	−8	No load	0.83	14.5	16.3	12.7	3.6	NA	1 1 1 1 1
FIDELITY GINNIE MAE	B	GI	B+	862.5	9	No load	0.75	8.7	10.0	6.7	6.5	6.1	4 1 2 1 2
FIDELITY GOVERNMENT SECURITIES	C−	GI	C	1164.9	20	No load	0.72	8.9	9.5	6.9	6.2	8.0	2 3 2 4 2
FIDELITY INTERMEDIATE BOND	B	CS	C	3193.4	4	No load	0.69	7.6	8.0	6.7	6.4	5.3	2 1 4 3 3
FIDELITY INVESTMENT GRADE BOND	C	CI	B	1649.6	13	No load	0.75	8.9	9.0	7.4	6.2	8.9	1 3 3 3 2
FIDELITY MORTGAGE SECURITIES INITIAL (ee)	B+	GI	A	488.3	−6	No load ‡	0.73	9.0	10.4	7.9	6.2	5.9	4 1 2 1 2
FIDELITY NEW MARKETS INCOME		IB		371.3	21	1.00 *	1.09	17.4	21.5	NA	9.5	15.7	4 4 1 1
FIDELITY SHORT-INTERM. GOVT.	B	GS	C	123.4	2	No load	0.81	6.6	7.5	5.2	6.1	3.6	4 1 4 2 4
FIDELITY SHORT-TERM BOND	B	CS	C	876.1	−12	No load	0.70	6.2	6.9	5.1	6.3	6.1	3 2 4 1 4
FIDELITY SPARTAN GINNIE MAE	B	GI	B+	593.7	34	No load	0.51	9.0	10.1	6.9	6.7	6.1	4 1 2 1 2
FIDELITY SPARTAN GOVT. INCOME	C	GI	C	279.8	1	No load	0.60	9.2	9.8	6.5	6.2	8.7	4 2 1 4 2
FIDELITY SPARTAN HIGH-INCOME	A	HY	A	2446.9	42	1.00 *	0.80	16.9	16.5	14.7	7.7	8.2	1 1 1 1 1
FIDELITY SPARTAN INVESTMENT GRADE BOND	C	CI	B	658.3	83	No load	0.48	9.3	10.2	8.0	6.2	8.4	1 3 1 3 2
FIDELITY SPARTAN LTD. MAT. GOVT.	B	GS	B	758.1	6	No load	0.38	7.7	8.5	6.1	7.0	4.5	4 1 3 2 3
FIDELITY SPARTAN SHORT-TERM BOND	B	CS	C	284.1	−11	No load	0.65	6.5	7.2	5.1	6.5	2.3	3 2 4 1 4
FIRST INVESTORS FUND FOR INCOME A	A	HY	B+	434.0	1	6.25	1.16 †	12.6	14.6	12.3	8.5	5.3	1 1 2 1 1
FIRST INVESTORS GOVERNMENT A	D	GI	D	170.1	−9	6.25	1.39 †	8.4	8.7	5.3	5.8	27.3	4 2 3 3 3
FIRST INVESTORS HIGH-YIELD A	A	HY	B	208.7	3	6.25	1.37 †	11.9	14.2	11.8	8.7	5.3	1 1 2 1 1
FIRST PRIORITY FIXED-INCOME INVESTMENT	C−	CI	D	185.6	25	7.75 **	1.02 †	8.0	9.1	5.9	5.6	6.1	4 3 3 3 3
FORTIS ADVANTAGE HIGH-YIELD A	B	HY	F	119.5	1	4.50	1.19 †	9.5	11.0	10.0	10.0	5.3	1 2 4 1 1
FORTIS U.S. GOVT. SECURITIES E	D	GI	C−	307.4	−14	4.50 ‡	0.81	8.9	9.3	5.9	6.1	7.0	4 3 3 3 2
FOUNTAIN SQ. QUALITY BOND A	D	CI	F	97.2	9	4.50	0.75 †	8.2	8.7	5.8	5.6	7.1	4 2 2 4 3
FPA NEW INCOME	B+	CI	A	563.2	50	4.50	0.59	8.3	9.9	8.2	6.0	7.7	3 1 3 1 3
FRANKLIN ADJ. U.S. GOVT. SECURITIES	C	GS	C−	321.9	−16	2.25	0.69 †	7.0	7.5	4.3	5.8	NA	4 1 4 1 4
FRANKLIN AGE HIGH INCOME I	A	HY	B	3003.3	21	4.25	0.71 †	12.1	15.0	12.0	8.9	8.4	1 1 1 1 1
FRANKLIN CONVERTIBLE SECURITIES I	B+	CV	B	222.5	60	4.50	1.02 †	20.3	20.2	15.6	4.3	NA	1 1 1 1 1
FRANKLIN GLOBAL GOVT. INCOME I	C−	IB	C	116.4	−15	4.25	0.85 †	2.8	10.4	8.0	7.3	NA	1 4 1 1 4
FRANKLIN SHORT-INTERM. GOVT. I	C	GS	C−	187.0	−6	2.25	0.74 †	6.1	7.0	5.3	5.6	NA	4 1 4 2 4
FRANKLIN STRATEGIC INCOME		MU		102.0	346	4.25	0.23 †	10.0	15.2	NA	8.0	NA	1 1 1
FRANKLIN U.S. GOVT. SECURITIES I	C	GI	B+	9287.8	−7	4.25	0.64 †	9.5	10.2	6.8	6.9	6.2	4 1 2 1 1
FREMONT BOND		CI		109.4	50	No load	0.68	9.1	11.5	NA	5.7	7.1	2 1 1 2
GALAXY II U.S. TREAS. INDEX RET.	C	GI	B	115.5	1	No load	0.40	9.3	9.7	7.0	6.0	8.3	3 2 2 4 2
GE GOVERNMENT B (ff)	D	GI	F	489.4	−30	5.00 **	1.69 †	8.6	8.0	4.3	6.0	7.7	4 4 4 4 2
GLOBAL TOTAL RETURN A	B+	IB	A	190.1	−17	4.00	1.33 †	4.6	14.1	10.3	8.3	7.4	1 4 1 1 4
GOLDMAN SACHS GLOBAL A	B	IB	B+	168.3	−16	4.50	1.16 †	9.6	12.2	8.6	7.3	NA	2 3 2 1 1
GRADISON GOVT. INCOME (gg)	C	GI	B	155.5	−5	No load	0.90 †	8.3	9.5	6.4	5.9	4.8	4 2 2 3 3
GRIFFIN U.S. GOVT. INCOME A		GI		84.5	77	4.50	0.46 †	8.8	9.3	NA	6.1	6.8	1 2 4 2
GT GLOBAL GOVT. INCOME A	F	IB	C−	144.3	−38	4.75	1.34 †	3.4	8.2	6.5	5.9	8.6	1 4 3 1 4
GT GLOBAL HIGH-INCOME B	F	IB	C−	220.1	−18	5.00 **	2.34 †	11.2	21.7	16.9	8.5	14.5	1 4 1 1 1
GT GLOBAL STRAT. INCOME B	D	IB	C	274.1	−19	5.00 **	2.03 †	6.2	14.1	10.8	6.3	11.2	1 4 2 1 4
GUARDIAN INVEST. QUAL. BOND A		CI		97.3	92	4.50	0.75 †	8.4	9.1	NA	5.9	8.2	3 2 4 3
HANCOCK GOVERNMENT INCOME A		GI		353.3	−8	4.50	1.17 †	9.5	9.8	NA	6.9	12.1	1 1 4 1
HANCOCK HIGH-YIELD BOND B	A	HY	C	583.9	108	5.00 **	1.82 †	16.9	15.5	11.9	8.9	7.8	1 3 3 1 1
HANCOCK SOVEREIGN BOND A	C	CI	B	1354.1	−4	4.50	1.14 †	9.6	10.9	8.1	6.9	13.4	1 2 1 2 1
HANCOCK SOVEREIGN U.S. GOVT. A	D	GI	D	302.1	−7	4.50	1.15 †	9.3	9.5	6.6	6.4	9.7	3 2 1 4 2
HANCOCK STRATEGIC INCOME A	B+	MU	B+	444.9	9	4.50	1.00 †	12.7	14.3	10.5	8.3	8.2	1 2 1 1 1
HARBOR BOND	B	CI	B+	384.6	33	No load	0.70	9.4	11.0	8.2	5.7	8.9	2 2 1 1 1
HARBOR SHORT DURATION	B+	CS	A	165.5	−7	No load	1.59	6.3	6.7	5.4	6.4	2.0	4 1 4 1 4
HOMESTEAD SHORT-TERM BOND	B+	CS	B+	108.6	34	No load	0.75	6.6	7.5	5.8	5.7	2.8	4 1 4 1 4
HOTCHKIS & WILEY LOW DUR.		CS		194.1	14	No load	0.58	7.8	8.9	NA	6.8	3.1	1 4 1 3
IDS BOND A	B	CI	B+	2679.3	2	5.00	0.84	10.2	12.1	9.3	6.7	15.0	1 2 1 1 1

*Includes redemption fee. **Includes deferred sales charge. †12(b)-1 plan in effect. ‡Not currently accepting new accounts or deposits. NA=Not available. NM=Not meaningful. (ee) Prev. Fid. Mort. Sec. (ff) Prev. Inv. Tr. Govt. B. (gg) Prev. Grad.-McD.d Govt. Inc.

MUTUAL FUND SCOREBOARD — Bond Funds

FUND	RATING (COMPARES RISK-ADJUSTED PERFORMANCE OF EACH FUND AGAINST ALL FUNDS)	CATEGORY	RATING (RATING COMPARES FUND WITHIN CATEGORY)	SIZE ASSETS $MIL.	% CHG. 1996-97	FEES SALES CHARGE (%)	EXPENSE RATIO (%)	TOTAL RETURN (%) 1 YR.	3 YR.	5 YR.	YIELD (%)	MATURITY (YEARS)	HISTORY RESULTS VS. ALL FUNDS
IDS EXTRA INCOME A	B+	HY	C-	2910.9	21	5.00	0.94	13.0	16.3	11.8	8.3	7.6	1 4 1 1 1
IDS FEDERAL INCOME A	B	GS	C	1351.6	16	5.00	0.91	7.9	8.6	6.2	6.0	12.5	4 1 3 2 3
IDS GLOBAL BOND A	C-	IB	B	742.6	4	5.00	1.20	3.1	9.9	8.3	4.4	11.2	1 3 1 1 4
IDS SELECTIVE A	C-	CI	C-	1261.2	-8	5.00	0.89	8.3	10.4	7.8	6.2	17.2	2 2 1 4 3
INTERMEDIATE BOND FUND OF AMERICA	C	CI	C	1327.7	-6	4.75	0.82†	7.1	8.3	6.1	6.5	4.0	3 2 3 2 4
INVESCO HIGH-YIELD	A	HY	C	588.3	34	No load	1.00†	17.1	16.4	11.6	8.3	5.8	1 3 2 1 1
INVESCO SELECT INCOME	B+	CL	A	331.8	23	No load	1.03†	11.7	12.2	9.2	6.6	8.9	3 1 1 1 1
ISI TOTAL RETURN U.S. TREAS.	D	GL	B+	294.9	57	4.45	0.81†	10.6	10.5	8.0	6.3	NA	1 2 1 4 1
IVY BOND A	B	CL	B+	103.8	7	4.75	1.56†	11.9	12.4	9.5	6.9	13.5	1 2 2 1 1
JANUS FLEXIBLE INCOME	B+	MU	B+	766.4	23	No load	0.87	10.7	12.8	10.0	NA	10.3	1 2 1 1 1
JANUS HIGH-YIELD		HY		357.4	50	No load	1.00	15.4	NA	NA	7.8	6.2	1 1
KEMPER DIVERSIFIED INCOME A	B+	MU	B	569.6	9	4.50	1.03	8.3	12.1	10.4	7.6	7.3	1 2 1 1 3
KEMPER HIGH-YIELD A	A	HY	C	3662.4	21	4.50	0.88	11.5	14.1	11.9	8.7	7.7	1 1 2 1 1
KEMPER INCOME & CAP. PRES. A	C	CI	C	523.9	6	4.50	0.96	8.6	10.4	7.7	6.7	9.5	2 2 1 4 2
KEMPER SHORT-INTERM. GOVT. B	C-	GS	D	107.8	-31	4.00 **	1.97†	4.8	5.8	4.0	5.4	3.3	4 1 4 4 4
KEMPER U.S. GOVT. SECURITIES A	C	GI	C	3484.8	-12	4.50	0.77	9.0	9.9	6.5	7.1	7.9	4 2 1 4 2
KEMPER U.S. MORTGAGE A	C-	GI	C	1767.4	-5	4.50	0.97	8.9	9.7	6.1	7.2	7.9	4 2 2 4 2
KEY SBSF CONVERTIBLE SECURITIES	A	CV	A	100.8	59	No load	1.31	16.7	20.0	14.2	4.1	6.7	1 3 1 1 1
KEYPREMIER INTERM. INCOME		CI		230.6	22	4.50	0.37	8.1	NA	NA	6.3	8.6	3
KIEWIT INTERMEDIATE-TERM BOND		CI		247.5	111	No load	0.50	8.1	8.5	NA	6.0	5.5	3 3
KIEWIT SHORT-TERM GOVERNMENT		GS		255.5	82	No load	0.30	6.2	6.6	NA	5.7	1.8	4 2 4
LEGG MASON GLOBAL GOVT. PRIM.		IB		136.7	-15	No load	1.86†	-1.7	8.8	NA	5.5	7.0	1 1 1 4
LEGG MASON HIGH-YIELD PRIM.		HY		380.4	63	No load	1.50†	15.9	16.3	NA	8.2	NA	2 1 1
LEGG MASON INVESTMENT GRADE PRIM.	C	CI	B	121.7	33	No load	0.88†	10.0	11.3	7.9	5.9	15.6	3 3 1 2 1
LEGG MASON U.S. GOVT. I/T PRIM.	B	GS	C	300.3	2	No load	0.90†	6.7	8.4	5.9	5.6	7.0	4 1 3 2 4
LEXINGTON GNMA INCOME	B+	GI	A	157.6	18	No load	1.05	10.2	10.5	7.4	6.2	NA	4 1 3 1 1
LORD ABBETT BOND-DEBENTURE A	B+	HY	D	2031.0	16	4.75	0.89†	12.7	13.8	10.4	8.2	8.3	1 2 2 1 1
LORD ABBETT GLOBAL INCOME A	C-	IB	C	145.1	-25	4.75	1.04†	4.0	9.2	6.9	7.0	8.7	3 2 2 1 4
LORD ABBETT U.S. GOVT. SECURITIES A	D	GI	F	2081.3	-18	4.75	0.88†	8.9	8.6	5.9	7.7	6.9	4 2 3 4 2
MAINSTAY CONVERTIBLE B	B+	CV	B	868.3	9	5.00 **‡	2.10†	10.7	14.9	13.2	3.5	8.6	1 1 1 1 1
MAINSTAY GOVERNMENT B	C-	GI	C	638.5	-19	5.00 **	1.60†	8.5	8.3	5.5	5.5	10.2	4 2 3 4 2
MAINSTAY HIGH-YIELD CORP. BOND B	A	HY	A	3339.6	37	5.00 **	1.60†	11.6	15.6	13.8	8.1	5.3	1 1 1 1 1
MARKETVEST INTERM. U.S. GOVT.		GI		263.5	3	3.50	0.85†	6.7	NA	NA	7.0	8.7	4
MARKETVEST SHORT-TERM BOND		CS		136.3	-7	3.50	0.90†	5.7	NA	NA	5.7	6.7	4
MARKETWATCH INTERM. FIXED-INC.		CI		94.9	-4	4.50	1.09†	8.7	8.5	NA	5.4	9.4	2 3 4 2
MARQUIS GOVT. SECURITIES A		GI		147.3	-8	3.50	0.70	8.0	8.5	NA	5.5	5.9	1 3 2 3
MARSHALL GOVERNMENT INCOME	C	GI	B	219.1	39	No load	0.86	8.4	9.3	6.1	6.6	8.0	4 2 2 3 3
MARSHALL INTERMEDIATE BOND	C	CS	F	554.2	28	No load	0.72	7.2	8.2	5.6	6.2	4.4	4 2 3 4 3
MARSHALL SHORT-TERM INCOME	B+	CS	B+	150.4	45	No load	0.51	6.4	6.8	5.2	6.4	2.1	4 1 4 1 4
MCM INTERMEDIATE FIXED-INCOME		CI		107.8	21	No load	0.50	7.9	8.9	NA	5.7	4.2	3 2 3
MERRILL LYNCH ADJ. RATE SEC. B	B	GS	B	91.9	-23	4.00 **	1.65†	5.5	6.6	4.5	5.3	3.4	4 1 4 1 4
MERRILL LYNCH AMERICAS INCOME B		IB		84.5	-46	4.00 **	2.10†	1.1	19.2	NA	5.9	10.0	4 1 1 4
MERRILL LYNCH CORP. HIGH-INCOME B	A	HY	C-	5526.8	22	4.00 **	1.28†	10.6	13.2	10.3	8.4	6.5	1 2 2 1 1
MERRILL LYNCH CORP. INTERM.-TERM B	C	CI	C	149.2	-30	1.00 **	1.11†	7.6	9.1	6.8	5.8	5.3	2 2 2 4 3
MERRILL LYNCH CORP. INVMT. GRADE B	C-	CI	D	575.0	-19	4.00 **	1.32†	7.5	9.1	6.4	5.8	10.6	2 3 1 4 3
MERRILL LYNCH FEDERAL SECURITIES D		GI	B	928.4	-2	4.00	0.90†	8.4	9.3	6.2	6.3	5.8	4 2 3 2 3
MERRILL LYNCH GLOBAL BOND B	F	IB	C	168.2	-52	4.00 **	1.65†	0.4	6.1	4.7	5.1	11.8	2 3 4 1 4
MERRILL LYNCH SHORT-TERM GLOB. B	C	IB	B	166.3	-31	4.00 **	1.74†	3.1	4.6	3.3	4.6	NA	4 2 4 2 4
MERRILL LYNCH WORLD INCOME B	B	MU	C-	658.8	-33	4.00 **	1.52†	5.3	10.0	7.5	6.4	6.7	1 3 3 1 4
MFS BOND A	C	CI	B	627.7	12	4.75	1.02†	10.4	11.7	8.7	6.8	12.9	1 2 1 2 1
MFS GOVERNMENT LTD. MATURITY A	C	GS	C	193.5	-14	2.50	0.84†	6.3	6.5	5.1	6.2	4.1	4 1 4 3 4
MFS GOVERNMENT MORTGAGE A	C	GI	B	628.6	20	4.75	1.09†	8.5	9.2	6.3	6.4	8.7	4 1 2 3 2
MFS GOVERNMENT SECURITIES A	C-	GI	C	289.2	-4	4.75	0.84†	9.2	9.6	6.9	6.3	4.8	3 2 1 4 2
MFS HIGH-INCOME A	A	HY	C	705.3	10	4.75	1.02†	12.9	14.2	11.6	8.5	7.8	1 1 2 1 1
MFS INTERMEDIATE INCOME B	C-	MU	F	119.6	-28	4.00 **	2.24†	4.9	7.8	5.1	6.6	6.7	3 3 3 2 4
MFS LIMITED MATURITY A	B	CS	C	93.9	-5	2.50	0.89†	5.4	7.3	5.6	6.8	3.9	4 1 4 1 4
MFS WORLD GOVERNMENTS A	D	IB	C	187.2	-31	4.75	1.42†	0.3	6.9	6.2	4.0	7.3	1 4 3 1 4
MORGAN (J.P.) BOND (hh)	C	CI	B	176.6	19	No load	0.66	9.1	10.0	7.2	6.3	12.9	3 2 1 3 2
MORGAN STANLEY WRLDWD. HIGH INCOME A		IB		101.6	61	4.75	1.52†	15.6	20.5	NA	7.9	NA	1 1 1
NATIONWIDE BOND	D	CL	D	125.9	-4	4.50	0.70	9.3	11.3	7.0	6.7	7.6	3 4 1 4 2
NEUBERGER & BERMAN LTD. MAT.	B	CS	B	252.4	5	No load	0.70	6.9	7.3	5.6	6.3	2.5	4 1 4 2 4
NEW ENGLAND ADJ. RATE U.S. GOVT. A	B+	GS	A	197.8	-11	1.00	0.70†	6.1	6.9	5.0	5.7	0.7	4 1 4 1 4
NEW ENGLAND BOND INCOME A	C	CI	C	193.5	2	4.50	1.05†	11.0	11.9	8.5	6.6	8.5	2 2 1 1 1
NEW ENGLAND GOVT. SECURITIES A	D	GL	B	104.5	-14	4.50	1.32†	10.3	10.1	6.6	5.4	13.7	4 3 1 4 1
NEW ENGLAND LTD. TERM U.S. GOVT. A	C	GS	D	222.4	-19	3.00	1.25†	7.3	7.4	5.2	6.2	5.2	4 1 4 4 3
NEW ENGLAND STRATEGIC INCOME B		MU		145.9	57	4.00 **	1.71†	8.5	NA	NA	6.7	18.9	1 2
NICHOLAS INCOME	A	HY	B+	254.2	37	No load	0.55	13.1	13.9	10.7	7.9	7.3	2 1 3 1 1
NORTHEAST INVESTORS	A	HY	A	2161.0	60	No load	0.66	13.9	17.1	15.2	8.2	7.7	1 1 2 1 1
NORTHERN FIXED-INCOME		CI		163.7	43	No load	0.90	9.3	10.0	NA	5.7	12.0	1 4 2
NORTHERN INCOME EQUITY		CV		103.7	46	No load	1.00	20.8	19.9	NA	3.2	NA	1 1 1

*Includes redemption fee. **Includes deferred sales charge. †12(b)-1 plan in effect. ‡Not currently accepting new accounts or deposits. NA=Not available. NM=Not meaningful.
(hh) Prev. JPM Pierpont Bd.

DATA: MORNINGSTAR, INC., CHICAGO, IL.

MUTUAL FUND SCOREBOARD — Bond Funds

FUND (COMPARES RISK-ADJUSTED PERFORMANCE OF EACH FUND AGAINST ALL FUNDS)	RATING	CATEGORY (RATING COMPARES FUND WITHIN CATEGORY)	RATING	SIZE ASSETS $MIL.	% CHG. 1996-97	FEES SALES CHARGE (%)	EXPENSE RATIO (%)	PERFORMANCE TOTAL RETURN (%) 1 YR.	3 YR.	5 YR.	PORTFOLIO YIELD (%)	MATURITY (YEARS)	HISTORY RESULTS VS. ALL FUNDS
NORTHERN U.S. GOVERNMENT		GS		214.5	25	No load	0.90	7.3	7.6	NA	5.3	4.9	4 3 3
NORTHSTAR GOVERNMENT SECURITIES T	F	GI	F	91.2	−19	4.00 **‡	1.30†	7.4	9.8	7.2	6.3	23.0	1 4 1 4 3
NORTHSTAR HIGH TOTAL RET. B		HY		569.1	42	5.00 **	2.23†	10.7	15.2	NA	9.1	8.0	1 1 1
NORTHSTAR HIGH-YIELD T	A	HY	C	110.3	−11	4.00 **‡	1.31†	10.9	13.0	10.9	8.0	8.1	1 1 3 1 1
111 CORCORAN BOND	C	CI	C	84.0	−6	4.50	0.32	8.6	10.4	7.5	6.4	6.7	2 2 1 2 2
OPPENHEIMER BOND A	C	CI	C	189.9	−1	4.75	1.26†	10.1	10.5	7.4	7.0	7.3	3 2 2 1 1
OPPENHEIMER BOND FOR GROWTH B		CV		362.2	77	5.00 **	1.75†	17.9	NA	NA	3.7	7.1	1 1
OPPENHEIMER CHAMPION INCOME A	A	HY	B+	527.8	35	4.75	1.17†	11.9	13.3	12.0	8.4	7.2	1 1 3 1 1
OPPENHEIMER HIGH-YIELD A	A	HY	C	1224.0	7	4.75	1.03†	11.9	13.7	11.6	8.4	8.8	1 1 3 1 1
OPPENHEIMER INTL. BOND B		IB		124.0	75	5.00 **	NA†	1.7	NA	NA	9.4	7.3	1 4
OPPENHEIMER LTD.-TERM GOVT. A	B	GS	B+	561.4	30	3.50	0.87†	7.6	7.6	6.2	7.0	3.0	4 1 4 1 3
OPPENHEIMER STRAT. INCOME A	B+	MU	B	4013.0	9	4.75	0.97†	8.4	12.1	10.0	8.5	6.0	1 2 3 1 3
OPPENHEIMER U.S. GOVT. A	C	GI	B+	499.0	4	4.75	1.08†	10.4	9.8	7.1	6.9	5.7	4 1 3 2 1
PACIFIC HORIZON CAPITAL INCOME A	B+	CV	B	385.0	32	4.50	1.18	22.0	21.8	15.9	3.0	3.6	1 3 1 1 1
PAINEWEBBER GLOBAL INCOME A	C	IB	B+	488.8	−9	4.00	1.27†	3.8	8.0	6.7	6.7	6.0	1 2 4 1 4
PAINEWEBBER HIGH-INCOME A	C	HY	F	272.3	12	4.00	0.96†	13.0	13.7	9.8	8.8	8.6	1 1 3 1 1
PAINEWEBBER INVMT. GRADE INCOME A		CL	B	212.5	−5	4.00	0.94†	12.1	11.7	8.3	6.9	14.6	1 3 1 2 1
PAINEWEBBER LOW DUR. U.S. GOVT. C		GS		91.7	−22	0.75 **	1.80†	6.6	7.1	NA	5.1	NA	3 4 1 4
PAINEWEBBER U.S. GOVT. INCOME A	F	GI	F	291.5	−12	4.00	0.94†	9.4	8.8	4.2	5.9	14.2	4 4 2 4 2
PAYDEN & RYGEL GLOBAL FIXED INCOME A	B+	IB	A	493.6	−25	No load	0.53	9.1	10.8	8.4	9.3	7.3	2 2 2 1 2
PAYDEN & RYGEL INTERM. BOND A		CS		110.1	279	No load	0.45	7.5	8.2	NA	5.6	4.4	2 3 4 3
PAYDEN & RYGEL INVMT. QUALITY BOND A		CI		119.2	223	No load	0.00	9.0	9.9	NA	5.9	6.5	2 1 4 2
PAYDEN & RYGEL LIMITED MATURITY A		UB		138.4	161	No load	0.30	5.5	5.9	NA	5.4	0.6	4 1 4
PEGASUS BOND A	C	CI	C	125.5	168	4.50	0.78†	9.6	12.5	8.1	6.0	6.1	3 4 1 1 1
PERMANENT PORTFOLIO TREASURY BILL	B	UB	D	93.3	−12	No load	0.90	4.1	4.4	3.8	4.1	0.2	4 1 4 2 4
PHOENIX CONVERTIBLE A	B	CV	C	197.8	−5	4.75	1.17†	13.9	15.5	10.2	2.8	6.4	3 2 1 1 1
PHOENIX HIGH-YIELD A	B+	HY	D	664.9	27	4.75	1.17†	13.6	16.2	11.9	8.8	7.1	1 4 2 1 1
PHOENIX MULTI-SECTOR FIXED INCOME A	C	MU	D	174.7	−1	4.75	1.07†	8.9	14.0	9.8	7.2	12.9	1 4 1 1 2
PHOENIX U.S. GOVT. SECURITIES A	C−	GI	C−	100.9	−50	4.75	1.03†	9.2	9.3	6.4	5.9	11.6	4 2 2 4 2
PIONEER AMERICA INCOME A	C−	GI	C	137.1	−5	4.50	1.00†	8.3	8.8	6.1	6.3	7.9	3 2 3 4 3
PIONEER BOND A	C−	CI	C−	106.0	6	4.50	1.18†	9.2	9.6	7.0	6.6	8.3	3 2 1 4 2
PIPER ADJ. RATE MORTGAGE SECURITIES	D	GS	F	170.1	−27	1.50	0.81†	6.3	4.7	3.1	5.8	1.1	3 1 2 3 2
PREFERRED FIXED-INCOME	B	CI	B	147.1	12	No load	0.74	8.5	9.5	7.2	6.2	13.3	3 1 2 3 2
PRICE (T. ROWE) EMERG MKTS. BOND		IB		113.4	185	No load	1.25	16.9	26.2	NA	8.2	19.0	1 1 1
PRICE (T. ROWE) GNMA	B	GI	B+	1063.3	15	No load	0.74	9.5	10.0	6.8	6.7	8.4	4 1 2 3 1
PRICE (T. ROWE) HIGH-YIELD	B+	HY	D	1571.7	19	1.00 *	0.84	14.5	13.9	10.6	8.7	9.6	1 4 3 1 1
PRICE (T. ROWE) INTL. BOND	D	IB	C	825.8	−15	No load	0.87	−3.2	7.7	8.0	5.5	8.5	1 1 1 1 4
PRICE (T. ROWE) NEW INCOME	C	CI	B	1945.0	15	No load	0.74	9.3	9.9	7.2	6.3	11.5	3 1 1 4 2
PRICE (T. ROWE) SHORT-TERM BOND	C	CS	C−	344.9	−23	No load	0.74	6.3	6.6	4.6	5.9	2.3	4 2 4 2 4
PRICE (T. ROWE) SHORT-TERM U.S.	B	GS	C	102.1	7	No load	0.70	6.7	7.3	4.8	6.0	2.8	4 1 4 2 4
PRICE (T. ROWE) SPECTRUM INCOME	B+	MU	A	2022.2	49	No load	0.00	12.2	13.0	9.7	6.0	9.0	2 1 1 1 1
PRICE (T. ROWE) U.S. TREAS. INTERM.	C	GI	B	199.5	3	No load	0.64	8.2	8.7	6.3	5.9	5.1	4 1 3 4 3
PRICE (T. ROWE) U.S. TREAS. LONG-TERM	D	GL	C	206.8	183	No load	0.80	14.7	12.9	8.9	5.6	23.4	2 3 1 4 1
PRINCIPAL BOND A (ii)	C−	CL	C	127.7	13	4.75	0.95†	11.0	11.5	8.4	6.5	11.2	2 2 1 4 1
PRINCIPAL GOVT. SECURITIES INCOME A (jj)	C−	GL	B+	248.9	−3	4.75	0.81†	9.7	10.7	7.1	6.0	9.6	3 3 1 2 1
PRUDENTIAL DIVERSIFIED BOND B		CI		153.4	13	5.00 **	1.39†	7.3	NA	NA	6.7	12.1	1 3
PRUDENTIAL GLOBAL LTD. MAT. A	C−	IB	B	83.0	2	3.00	1.32†	3.7	8.4	5.6	6.8	NA	4 2 4 1 4
PRUDENTIAL GOVT. INCOME A	C−	GI	C−	829.0	−7	4.00	0.90†	9.3	9.9	6.6	6.4	NA	4 2 1 4 2
PRUDENTIAL GOVT. SHORT-INTERM. A	C	GS		149.4	−17	No load	1.01†	6.9	7.9	5.6	5.2	NA	4 1 4 2 4
PRUDENTIAL HIGH-YIELD B	B+	HY	C−	2612.4	1	5.00 **	1.32†	12.1	13.8	10.8	8.4	9.0	1 2 2 1 1
PRUDENTIAL INTL. GLOBAL INCOME A	B	IB	B+	143.9	−13	3.00	1.40†	4.4	12.7	9.1	6.3	6.5	1 4 1 1 4
PRUDENTIAL INTL. BOND A (kk)	B+	IB	A	100.9	−20	4.00	1.48†	3.7	13.9	10.6	5.0	7.9	1 3 1 1 4
PRUDENTIAL MORTGAGE INCOME A	C	GI	C	89.9	−4	4.00	1.12†	8.6	9.3	6.1	6.2	NA	4 1 3 2 2
PUTNAM AMERICAN GOVT. INCOME A	C−	GI	C−	1528.9	−12	4.75	0.97†	9.2	9.8	6.4	5.9	6.6	4 2 1 4 2
PUTNAM CONVERT INCOME-GROWTH A	B+	CV	B+	1187.6	26	5.75	1.06†	19.6	20.4	14.9	4.1	6.9	1 1 1 1 1
PUTNAM DIVERSIFIED INCOME B		MU		2336.5	5	5.00 **	1.74†	7.3	11.0	NA	6.1	9.6	3 2 1 3
PUTNAM FEDERAL INCOME A	D	GI	C−	343.5	−7	4.75	1.15†	8.3	9.6	6.0	6.2	8.1	4 2 1 4 3
PUTNAM GLOBAL GOVT. INCOME A	F	IB	C−	298.5	−12	4.75	1.29†	−0.4	8.1	5.3	6.7	8.3	1 4 3 1 4
PUTNAM HIGH YIELD A	A	HY	C−	3279.9	1	4.75 ‡	0.96†	14.7	15.1	11.5	9.4	6.3	1 2 1 1 1
PUTNAM HIGH YIELD ADV. M		HY		2191.5	230	3.25	1.36†	13.1	13.9	NA	9.0	6.0	1 1 1
PUTNAM INCOME A	C	CI	C	1318.2	26	4.75	1.05†	8.4	10.6	7.9	6.2	10.9	2 2 1 2 3
PUTNAM INTERM. U.S. GOVT. INC. A		GS		135.1	−5	3.25	1.22†	7.5	8.7	NA	5.7	6.7	1 3 2 3
PUTNAM U.S. GOVT. INCOME A	C	GI	C	2106.6	−12	4.75	0.89†	8.7	9.5	6.2	6.3	7.5	4 1 3 2 2
SALOMON BROS. HIGH-YIELD BOND B		HY		312.7	196	5.00 **	1.99†	12.2	NA	NA	8.9	10.6	1 1
SCHWAB SHORT-TERM BOND MKT. INDEX (ll)	C	GS	C	138.1	5	No load	0.49	6.9	7.2	5.2	5.9	2.7	4 2 4 2 4
SCUDDER EMERGING MKTS. INCOME		IB		345.7	7	No load	1.44	13.1	22.1	NA	8.3	11.2	4 1 1 1
SCUDDER GLOBAL BOND	D	IB	C	131.7	−35	No load	1.00	0.2	3.6	3.3	6.2	6.3	4 1 4 3 4
SCUDDER GNMA	C	GI	B	387.7	−4	No load	0.96	8.0	9.5	6.2	6.1	7.0	4 2 2 2 3
SCUDDER HIGH-YIELD BOND		HY		152.1	188	1.00 *	NA	14.6	NA	NA	8.7	6.6	1
SCUDDER INCOME	C	CI	B	682.8	18	No load	0.98	8.7	10.1	7.5	5.9	10.1	2 2 1 2 2

*Includes redemption fee. **Includes deferred sales charge. †12(b)-1 plan in effect. ‡Not currently accepting new accounts or deposits. NA=Not available. NM=Not meaningful.
(ii) Prev. Princor Bond A. (jj) Prev. Princor Govt. Sec. Inc. A. (kk) Prev. Glob. Govt. Pl. A. (ll) Prev. Schwab S/I Govt. Bd.

DATA: MORNINGSTAR, INC., CHICAGO, IL.

MUTUAL FUND SCOREBOARD — Bond Funds

FUND (COMPARES RISK-ADJUSTED PERFORMANCE OF EACH FUND AGAINST ALL FUNDS)	RATING	CATEGORY	RATING (RATING COMPARES FUND WITHIN CATEGORY)	SIZE ASSETS $MIL.	% CHG. 1996-97	FEES SALES CHARGE (%)	EXPENSE RATIO (%)	PERFORMANCE TOTAL RETURN (%) 1 YR.	3 YR.	5 YR.	PORTFOLIO YIELD (%)	MATURITY (YEARS)	HISTORY RESULTS VS. ALL FUNDS
SCUDDER INTERNATIONAL BOND	F	IB	D	187.0	−48	No load	1.36	−4.3	2.5	2.6	5.5	NA	1 4 4 3 4
SCUDDER SHORT-TERM BOND	B	CS	C−	1185.1	−19	No load	0.80	6.0	6.8	5.0	5.9	4.4	4 2 4 2 4
SELIGMAN HIGH-YIELD BOND A	A	HY	B+	750.5	84	4.75	1.16†	14.1	16.6	13.7	9.1	8.6	1 1 1 1 1
SENTINEL BOND A	C−	CI	D	88.6	−9	4.00	0.99†	8.6	9.9	7.2	6.2	8.3	2 3 1 4 2
SIERRA CORPORATE INCOME A	F	CL	D	172.4	−31	4.50	1.18†	12.0	12.8	8.4	7.0	20.4	1 4 1 4 1
SIERRA U.S. GOVERNMENT A	D	GI	C−	222.9	−31	4.50	0.98†	9.7	9.8	5.9	6.6	7.8	4 3 2 3 1
SIT U.S. GOVERNMENT SECURITIES	B+	GS	A	94.5	46	No load	0.80	8.1	8.2	6.7	5.9	4.9	4 1 4 1 3
SMITH BARNEY ADJ. RATE GOVT. A	B+	GS	B+	121.4	−16	No load	1.58†	5.7	6.3	4.8	5.3	NA	4 1 4 1 4
SMITH BARNEY DIVERS. STRAT. INCOME B	B+	MU	B	2382.8	−3	4.50 **	1.51†	7.1	10.6	8.1	7.8	6.0	2 2 3 1 4
SMITH BARNEY GLOBAL GOVT. A	B	IB	B+	91.2	−12	4.50	1.24†	8.2	10.3	9.0	7.2	NA	1 2 3 1 3
SMITH BARNEY GOVT. SECURITIES A	D	GI	D	361.6	−7	4.50	0.93†	11.2	8.6	6.7	6.2	NA	3 2 4 4 1
SMITH BARNEY HIGH-INCOME B	A	HY	C	723.1	16	4.50 **	1.55†	12.5	14.1	10.9	8.7	6.6	1 4 1 4 1
SMITH BARNEY INVESTMENT GRADE BOND B	F	CL	F	249.3	−4	4.50 **	1.54†	16.4	15.8	10.7	5.6	NA	1 4 1 4 1
SMITH BARNEY MANAGED GOVT. A	C−	GI	C	391.0	−11	4.50	1.04†	9.5	8.8	6.7	6.3	NA	3 1 4 3 1
SMITH BARNEY U.S. GOVT. SECURITIES A	C	GI	B	271.9	−13	4.50	1.09†	9.7	9.9	6.9	6.4	10.0	4 1 2 2 1
SMITH BREEDEN SHORT DUR. U.S. GOVT.	B+	UB	C	89.9	−52	No load	0.78	6.3	6.2	5.4	5.2	0.5	4 1 4 1 4
SOUTHTRUST VULCAN BOND	C−	CI	D	105.5	18	3.50	0.87	9.5	9.1	6.5	5.9	9.9	3 2 3 4 1
SSGA BOND MARKET		CI		107.9	163	No load	0.54†	8.9	NA	NA	5.5	6.0	2
SSGA YIELD PLUS	B+	UB	B	701.2	−30	No load	0.38†	5.5	5.9	5.0	5.5	0.6	4 1 4 1 4
STAGECOACH U.S. GOVT. INCOME A (mm)	D	GI	D	100.8	30	4.50	0.89†	8.5	8.9	6.4	5.9	19.2	3 3 1 4 2
STAGECOACH VAR. RATE GOVT. A (nn)	C	GS	D	276.3	−30	3.00	0.88†	5.2	5.8	3.6	5.3	18.7	4 2 4 2 4
STAR STRATEGIC INCOME		MU		177.6	57	5.00 **	1.36†	9.5	9.3	NA	7.1	9.9	4 1 1
STAR U.S. GOVERNMENT INCOME		GI		136.3	−2	3.50	0.92†	9.0	8.7	NA	5.7	11.1	2 3 4 2
STATE ST. RESEARCH GOVT. INCOME A	C	GI	B	523.1	−8	4.50	1.09†	9.1	9.8	7.2	6.4	8.4	3 3 2 3 2
STATE ST. RESEARCH HIGH-INCOME A	A	HY	B	693.8	3	4.50	1.10†	14.4	14.5	12.5	9.2	4.9	1 1 4 1 1
STEIN ROE INCOME	B	CI	B+	421.5	25	No load	0.82	9.4	11.2	8.4	6.8	9.6	1 2 1 1 1
STEIN ROE INTERMEDIATE BOND	B	CI	B+	392.5	26	No load	0.70	9.0	10.0	7.2	6.3	12.1	3 1 2 1 2
STRONG ADVANTAGE	A	UB	B+	2041.0	44	No load	0.80	6.5	6.9	6.5	6.2	0.7	4 1 4 1 4
STRONG CORPORATE BOND	B+	CI	A	560.5	84	No load	1.00	11.9	14.0	11.3	6.8	14.7	1 1 1 1 1
STRONG GOVERNMENT SECURITIES	B	CI	B+	907.4	38	No load	0.90	9.1	10.4	7.9	6.0	6.7	2 2 1 4 2
STRONG HIGH-YIELD BOND		HY		568.9	101	No load	NA	16.0	NA	NA	8.6	7.6	1 1
STRONG SHORT-TERM BOND	B+	CS	A	1320.7	12	No load	0.90	7.0	8.6	6.6	6.9	2.5	3 1 4 1 4
STRONG SHORT-TERM GLOBAL BOND		MU		106.8	38	No load	0.90	9.4	9.0	NA	8.6	2.1	4 1 4
SUNAMERICA HIGH-INCOME B		HY		107.5	−2	4.00 **	2.11†	12.8	13.4	NA	7.3	NA	4 4 1 1
SUNAMERICA U.S. GOVT. SECURITIES B	C	GI	B	233.3	−33	4.00 **	2.18†	7.0	7.9	5.2	4.6	13.0	4 1 3 4 4
TCW/DW NORTH AMERICA GOVT. INCOME	F	IB	C−	200.6	−36	No load	1.59†	7.9	9.2	3.5	5.0	NA	4 4 3 2 3
TEMPLETON GLOBAL BOND I	C	IB	B	198.5	2	4.25	1.15†	1.8	10.2	7.3	6.1	4.2	3 2 1 1 4
THORNBURG LTD.-TERM U.S. A	C	GS	C−	130.5	−6	2.50	0.97†	6.6	7.9	5.5	5.9	4.0	4 1 4 2 4
U.S. GOVERNMENT SECURITIES	C−	GI	C−	1121.5	−6	4.75	0.80†	8.4	8.8	6.3	6.5	6.6	3 2 3 4 3
UNITED BOND A	C−	CI	D	520.7	0	5.75	0.77†	9.8	10.9	7.8	6.3	10.6	2 3 1 3 1
UNITED GOVERNMENT SECURITIES A	C−	GI	C	128.5	−5	4.25	0.91†	9.1	9.8	7.0	6.0	NA	3 2 1 4 2
UNITED HIGH-INCOME A	A	HY	C	1063.4	7	5.75	0.89†	14.3	14.6	11.3	8.3	5.5	1 2 2 1 1
UNITED HIGH-INCOME II A	A	HY	C−	410.4	10	5.75	0.93†	15.0	14.6	11.2	8.2	5.7	1 2 2 1 1
USAA GNMA	B	GI	A	340.8	11	No load	0.30	9.5	9.6	7.1	6.6	8.4	4 1 2 1 1
USAA INCOME	C−	CL	C	1707.2	−11	No load	0.39	11.1	11.9	7.9	6.5	11.2	3 3 1 4 1
USAA SHORT-TERM BOND		CS		140.9	26	No load	0.50	7.2	8.2	NA	6.1	2.3	1 4 1 3
VALUE LINE AGGRESSIVE INCOME	A	HY	B+	129.7	75	No load	1.10	13.8	17.8	13.3	8.3	7.6	1 2 1 1 1
VALUE LINE CONVERTIBLE	B+	CV	B	83.0	23	No load	1.01	17.0	20.0	13.4	4.6	7.4	1 3 1 1 1
VALUE LINE U.S. GOVERNMENT	D	GI	D	191.4	−6	No load	0.65	9.2	9.1	5.0	6.5	9.3	3 4 3 2 2
VAN KAMPEN AM. CAP. CORP. BOND A	C−	CI	C−	163.9	−2	4.75	1.13†	10.7	11.3	8.1	6.9	14.5	2 2 1 4 1
VAN KAMPEN AM. CAP. GOVT. SECURITIES A	D	GI	C−	1937.6	−11	4.75	1.06†	9.2	9.1	6.1	6.4	5.9	4 2 2 4 2
VAN KAMPEN AM. CAP. HARBOR A	C−	CV	D	389.1	4	5.75	1.09†	16.9	17.1	11.3	4.4	NA	1 3 1 1 1
VAN KAMPEN AM. CAP. HIGH-INCOME A	A	HY	C	500.3	14	4.75	1.08†	11.9	14.3	11.4	9.2	7.3	1 2 2 1 1
VAN KAMPEN AM. CAP. HIGH-YIELD A	A	HY	C−	292.5	4	4.75	1.31†	11.0	13.6	10.8	8.7	6.4	1 2 2 1 1
VAN KAMPEN AM. CAP. U.S. GOVT. INC. B	D	GI	D	120.0	−17	4.00 **	1.94†	7.3	7.7	4.7	6.0	4.8	4 3 3 4 3
VAN KAMPEN AM. CAP. U.S. GOVT. A	C−	GI	C	2304.1	−10	4.75	0.92†	8.5	9.9	6.4	7.0	6.7	4 3 2 2 2
VANGUARD BOND INDEX INTERM.-TERM		CI		684.3	50	No load	0.20	9.4	10.7	NA	6.5	7.0	1 4 1
VANGUARD BOND INDEX LONG-TERM		CL		87.3	99	No load	0.20	14.3	13.9	NA	6.3	21.7	1 4 1
VANGUARD BOND INDEX SHORT-TERM		CS		438.3	34	No load	0.20	7.0	8.1	NA	6.0	2.4	4 2 4
VANGUARD BOND INDEX TOTAL	B	CI	B+	5010.0	70	No load	0.20	9.4	10.2	7.4	6.4	8.6	3 1 1 3 1
VANGUARD CONVERTIBLE SECURITIES	D	CV	D	186.7	12	No load	0.69	16.4	16.2	10.9	4.2	7.0	1 4 1 1 1
VANGUARD F/I GNMA	B	GI	A	8725.2	18	No load	0.27	9.5	10.5	7.2	6.9	7.6	4 1 2 1 1
VANGUARD F/I HIGH-YIELD CORP.	A	HY	B	4543.9	28	1.00 *	0.29	11.9	13.5	11.2	8.5	8.2	1 1 1 1 1
VANGUARD F/I INTERM.-TERM CORP.		CI		860.1	39	No load	0.25	8.9	10.8	NA	6.4	6.7	2 1 4 2
VANGUARD F/I INTERM.-TERM U.S.	C−	GI	C	1498.5	18	No load	0.25	9.0	10.2	7.4	6.1	6.6	3 2 1 4 2
VANGUARD F/I L/T CORP. BOND	C−	CL	C	3599.2	5	No load	0.28	13.8	13.3	9.6	6.6	22.2	1 3 1 4 1
VANGUARD F/I L/T U.S. TREAS.	D	GL	C	1030.2	12	No load	0.25	13.9	13.5	9.7	6.1	19.7	1 4 1 4 1
VANGUARD F/I SHORT-TERM CORP.	B+	CS	B+	4595.5	0	No load	0.25	7.0	8.1	6.2	6.1	2.4	4 1 4 1 4
VANGUARD F/I SHORT-TERM FED.	B	GS	B+	1413.6	6	No load	0.25	6.5	7.8	5.8	6.1	2.1	4 1 4 1 4
VANGUARD F/I SHORT-TERM U.S. TREAS.	B	GS	B	993.8	3	No load	0.25	6.5	7.6	5.7	5.9	1.9	4 1 4 2 4

*Includes redemption fee. **Includes deferred sales charge. †12(b)-1 plan in effect. ‡Not currently accepting new accounts or deposits. NA=Not available. NM=Not meaningful.
(mm) Prev. Overland Exp. U.S. Govt. Inc. A. (nn) Prev. Overland Exp. Var. Rate Govt. A.

DATA: MORNINGSTAR, INC., CHICAGO, IL.

FUND (COMPARES RISK-ADJUSTED PERFORMANCE OF EACH FUND AGAINST ALL FUNDS)	RATING	CATEGORY (RATING COMPARES FUND WITHIN CATEGORY)	RATING	SIZE ASSETS $MIL.	% CHG. 1996-97	FEES SALES CHARGE (%)	EXPENSE RATIO (%)	PERFORMANCE TOTAL RETURN (%) 1 YR.	3 YR.	5 YR.	PORTFOLIO YIELD (%)	MATURITY (YEARS)	HISTORY RESULTS VS. ALL FUNDS
VANGUARD PREFERRED STOCK	B	CL	B+	329.5	11	No load	0.37	13.0	15.6	9.9	6.4	29.3	2 4 1 1 1
VICTORY GOVERNMENT MORTGAGE	C	GI	B	103.7	−15	5.75	0.89	8.8	9.3	6.7	6.3	9.2	4 1 3 2 2
VICTORY INTERMEDIATE INCOME		CS		245.1	−9	5.75	0.94	7.1	8.0	NA	5.8	4.7	1 3 3 4
VICTORY INVESTMENT QUALITY BOND		CI		184.6	20	5.75	1.01	8.5	9.0	NA	5.8	8.3	1 2 4 2
VIRTUS U.S. GOVT. SECURITIES INVMT.	C	GS	D	99.8	−14	2.00 **	1.14 †	6.3	7.5	5.2	5.9	5.0	4 2 3 4 4
WARBURG PINCUS FIXED INC. COMM.	B+	CI	A	312.1	97	No load	0.75	8.8	10.0	8.0	5.9	5.5	3 1 3 1 2
WARBURG PINCUS GLOBAL FIXED-INC.	B	IB	B+	174.5	22	No load	0.95 †	2.2	9.2	8.1	6.8	4.4	1 3 3 1 4
WESTERN ASSET INTL. SECURITIES		IB		175.0	−34	No load	0.28	7.7	10.9	NA	10.4	6.5	4 3 1 3
WPG GOVERNMENT SECURITIES	D	CI	F	107.7	−16	No load	0.81	7.4	8.1	4.7	5.4	4.9	4 4 4 2 3
WRIGHT U.S. TREAS. NEAR TERM	C	GS	C−	102.4	−23	No load	0.80 †	5.9	7.2	5.2	5.7	1.9	4 2 4 2 4

TAX EXEMPT

FUND	RATING	CATEGORY	RATING	ASSETS $MIL.	% CHG. 1996-97	SALES CHARGE (%)	EXPENSE RATIO (%)	1 YR.	3 YR.	5 YR.	YIELD (%)	MATURITY (YEARS)	HISTORY
AARP INSURED T/F GENERAL BOND	C	ML	C	1699.9	−2	No load	0.66	8.7	9.4	6.7	4.5	11.0	2 3 3 3 2
AIM MUNICIPAL BOND A	B	MI	C	317.7	14	4.75	0.80 †	7.3	8.0	6.2	5.1	13.0	2 2 4 2 3
AIM TAX-FREE INTERMEDIATE	A	MS	C−	193.2	132	1.00	0.56	7.3	7.1	5.7	4.6	7.9	3 1 4 2 3
ALLIANCE MUNI INCOME CALIF. A	C	SL	C	482.8	5	4.25	0.77 †	10.9	12.8	7.8	5.2	25.0	2 4 1 2 1
ALLIANCE MUNI INCOME NATL. A	C−	ML	C	336.3	4	4.25	0.69 †	10.0	12.0	7.5	5.3	24.9	1 4 1 2 1
ALLIANCE MUNI INCOME N.Y. A	D	SL	C−	189.0	6	4.25	0.64 †	11.2	12.0	7.3	5.4	25.7	2 4 1 2 1
ALLIANCE MUNI INSURED NATL. A	F	ML	F	175.4	6	4.25	1.02 †	9.7	12.0	7.6	4.9	22.5	2 4 1 1 1
AMERICAN CENT.-BENHAM CALIF. MUNI H-Y (oo)	A	SL	A	213.9	35	No load	0.50	10.5	11.4	8.2	5.4	19.6	2 3 1 1 1
AMERICAN CENT.-BENHAM CALIF. T/F INS. (pp)	C	SL	C	196.0	2	No load	0.48	9.3	10.5	7.4	4.9	18.3	1 4 1 3 2
AMERICAN CENT.-BENHAM CALIF. T/F INTERM. (qq)	B+	SI	B+	434.6	−1	No load	0.48	7.4	8.3	6.3	4.6	8.2	3 2 4 2 3
AMERICAN CENT.-BENHAM CALIF. T/F LONG (rr)	B	SL	B+	309.5	4	No load	0.48	9.7	10.8	7.7	5.1	19.5	1 3 1 3 1
AMERICAN HIGH-INCOME MUNI BOND		MI		364.7	47	4.75	0.87 †	10.4	11.8	NA	5.2	7.9	1 1 1
ATLAS CALIF. MUNICIPAL BOND A	C−	SL	C	176.5	0	3.00	0.93 †	7.9	8.8	6.6	4.6	19.6	1 3 3 2 3
BERNSTEIN CALIF. MUNICIPAL	B+	SI	B+	429.5	38	No load	0.68	6.4	7.8	5.6	4.2	7.2	4 2 3 3 4
BERNSTEIN DIVERSIFIED MUNI	B+	MI	B	1185.9	33	No load	0.66	6.7	7.7	5.7	4.4	6.5	4 1 4 3 4
BERNSTEIN N.Y. MUNICIPAL	B+	SI	B+	705.3	24	No load	0.66	6.6	7.5	5.7	4.4	6.0	4 1 4 3 4
BOSTON 1784 MASS. T/E INCOME (ss)		SI		184.3	41	No load	0.79 †	8.9	8.6	NA	4.5	8.3	3 3 3 2
BOSTON 1784 T/E MED.-TERM INC. (tt)		MI		287.1	24	No load	0.80 †	9.1	9.2	NA	4.6	9.1	2 3 2 2
CALIFORNIA INVMT. TAX-FEE INCOME	C−	SL	C−	212.9	2	No load	0.59	9.3	10.8	7.3	4.5	13.1	1 4 1 3 2
CALVERT TAX-FREE RES. LTD.-TERM A	A	MS	B	566.2	11	1.00	0.70	4.1	4.5	4.0	3.9	0.9	4 1 4 2 4
CHURCHILL TAX-FREE OF KY. A	B+	SI	B+	224.8	1	4.00	0.74 †	7.8	8.5	6.7	5.0	17.3	2 2 3 2 3
COLONIAL CALIF. TAX-EXEMPT A	D	SL	D	253.0	−6	4.75	0.88 †	9.2	10.6	6.8	4.4	18.4	3 4 1 3 2
COLONIAL MASS. TAX-EXEMPT A	C−	SL	C	180.5	−5	4.75	0.90 †	8.5	9.8	6.9	4.6	16.5	2 3 1 3 2
COLONIAL TAX-EXEMPT A	D	ML	D	2551.5	−7	4.75	0.99 †	9.1	9.7	6.5	4.9	19.1	3 3 2 4 2
COLONIAL TAX-EXEMPT INSURED A	F	ML	F	181.6	−10	4.75	1.05 †	9.0	9.4	6.4	4.2	18.6	3 3 2 4 2
COLUMBIA MUNICIPAL BOND	B+	SI	B+	404.5	8	No load	0.56	8.4	8.7	6.3	4.8	13.9	3 2 3 2 3
COMPOSITE TAX-EXEMPT BOND A	D	ML	D	187.0	−8	4.00	0.75 †	8.5	9.6	6.7	4.6	13.8	2 4 1 4 2
DAVIS TAX-FREE HIGH INCOME B	A	MS	A	179.7	65	4.00 **	2.10 †	7.0	6.8	6.2	5.9	16.6	4 1 4 1 4
DEAN WITTER CALIF. TAX-FREE INCOME B (uu)	C	SL	C	912.5	−6	5.00 **	1.33 †	7.5	8.4	5.9	4.4	19.8	3 3 3 3 3
DEAN WITTER N.Y. TAX-FREE INC. B (vv)	C−	SL	C−	169.5	−12	5.00 **	1.41 †	8.4	9.1	6.0	4.2	16.3	2 4 2 4 3
DELAWARE TAX-FREE PA. A	B	SL	B+	923.5	−3	4.75	0.91 †	7.6	8.5	6.4	5.2	21.4	3 2 3 3 3
DELAWARE TAX-FREE U.S.A. A	B	MI	C	605.7	−11	4.75	0.94 †	8.2	7.4	6.1	5.2	24.0	2 2 4 4 3
DELAWARE-VOYAGEUR MINN. INS. A (ww)	C	SL	C	288.1	−5	3.75	0.92 †	8.4	9.7	6.8	4.9	19.7	1 4 2 2 3
DELAWARE-VOYAGEUR T/F ARIZ. INS. A (xx)	C	SL	C	186.6	−11	3.75	0.82 †	8.8	10.5	7.1	4.7	17.9	2 4 1 2 2
DELAWARE-VOYAGEUR T/F COLO. A (yy)	C	SL	B	358.0	−11	3.75	0.78 †	11.3	11.8	7.6	5.1	21.6	1 4 1 2 1
DELAWARE-VOYAGEUR T/F FLA. INS. A (zz)	D	SL	C−	162.2	−16	3.75	0.73 †	10.3	11.2	7.2	4.8	22.3	2 4 1 4 1
DELAWARE-VOYAGEUR T/F MINN. A (aaa)	C	SL	B	417.1	−3	3.75	0.92 †	9.5	10.0	6.9	4.9	20.6	2 4 2 3 1
DREYFUS CALIF. INTERMEDIATE MUNI	B	SI	B	203.0	−8	No load	0.78	7.6	8.2	6.5	4.3	9.3	1 3 4 3 3
DREYFUS CALIF. TAX-EXEMPT BOND	C−	SL	C−	1333.0	−5	No load	0.73	8.3	8.5	5.8	4.8	19.8	2 4 3 3 3
DREYFUS FLA. INTERMEDIATE MUNI	C	SI	C−	349.4	−9	1.00 *	0.80	6.4	7.8	6.1	4.4	7.2	2 3 3 3 4
DREYFUS INSURED MUNI BOND	F	ML	F	195.1	−5	No load	0.80 †	8.4	8.6	5.7	4.8	22.8	2 4 3 4 3
DREYFUS INTERMEDIATE MUNI	B+	MI	C	1372.4	−4	No load	0.73	7.6	8.5	6.3	4.9	9.0	2 3 3 2 3
DREYFUS MASS. TAX-EXEMPT BOND	C	SI	C	156.1	0	No load	0.79	9.1	9.4	6.7	5.1	21.1	2 3 3 2 3
DREYFUS MUNI BOND	C	ML	C	3414.7	−5	No load	0.71	8.0	9.0	6.3	5.2	20.5	2 4 3 3 3
DREYFUS N.J. INTERM. MUNI BOND	C	SI	C	215.5	−4	No load	0.78	6.9	8.0	6.1	4.3	7.5	2 3 3 3 4
DREYFUS N.J. MUNI BOND	B	SL	B+	594.3	0	1.00 *	0.80 †	8.8	9.1	6.6	5.1	18.0	2 3 3 3 2
DREYFUS N.Y.TAX-EXEMPT BOND	C−	SL	C−	1681.6	−5	1.00 *	0.74	9.1	9.1	6.4	4.8	16.6	2 4 2 4 2
DREYFUS N.Y. TAX-EXEMPT INTERM. BOND	B	SI		363.5	0	1.00 *	0.80 †	8.2	8.7	6.4	4.8	8.7	3 3 3 3 3
DREYFUS PREMIER CALIF. MUNI BOND A (bbb)	C−	SL	C	153.4	−8	4.50	0.92	7.9	9.6	7.1	4.7	20.0	1 3 2 2 3
DREYFUS PREMIER MUNI BOND A (ccc)	B	ML	B	448.6	−6	4.50	0.91	9.6	10.2	7.4	5.4	21.2	1 3 2 2 1
DREYFUS PREMIER STATE MUNI CONN. A (ddd)	C	SL	B	315.1	−8	4.50	0.93	9.3	9.7	7.0	5.1	20.6	2 3 2 2 3
DREYFUS PREMIER STATE MUNI FLA. A (eee)	D	SL	C−	181.2	−13	4.50	0.92	4.9	8.1	6.2	4.9	23.0	2 2 2 3 4
DREYFUS PREMIER STATE MUNI MD. A (fff)	B	SL	B+	265.5	−3	4.50	0.90	9.5	9.9	7.1	5.1	22.7	3 3 3 2 1
DREYFUS PREMIER STATE MUNI MICH. A (ggg)	B	SL	B	155.9	−4	4.50	0.91	8.5	9.6	7.4	5.1	17.6	1 2 2 3 2
DREYFUS PREMIER STATE MUNI OHIO A (hhh)	B	SL	B+	240.9	−4	4.50	0.91	8.2	9.1	7.0	5.1	17.9	2 2 3 2 3
DREYFUS PREMIER STATE MUNI PA. A (iii)	C	SL	B	200.6	−4	4.50	0.92	9.8	10.3	7.5	5.0	21.2	2 3 2 2 1
DREYFUS SHORT-INTERM. MUNI BOND	A	MS	B	288.2	−8	No load	0.80 †	5.2	5.5	4.5	4.2	2.8	4 1 4 2 4
DUPREE KY. TAX-FREE INCOME	B+	SI	B+	348.2	11	No load	0.63	8.0	8.5	7.0	5.2	16.8	2 2 3 3 3

*Includes redemption fee. **Includes deferred sales charge. †12(b)-1 plan in effect. ‡Not currently accepting new accounts or deposits. NA=Not available. NM=Not meaningful. (oo) Prev. Benham Ca. Muni. H-Y. (pp) Prev. Benham Ca. T-F Ins. (qq) Prev. Benham Ca. T-F I/T. (rr) Prev. Benham Ca. T-F L/T. (ss) Prev. 1784 Mass. T-E Inc. (tt) Prev. 1784 T-E M/T Inc. (uu) Prev. DW Calif. T-F Inc. (vv) Prev. DW N.Y. T-F Inc. (ww) Prev. Voyageur Minn. Ins. A. (xx) Prev. Voyageur Ariz. Ins. T-F A. (yy) Prev. Voyageur Colo. T-F A. (zz) Prev. Voyageur Fla. Ins. T-F A. (aaa) Prev. Voyageur Minn. T-F A. (bbb) Prev. Premier Calif. A. (ccc) Prev. Premier Muni. Bd. A. (ddd) Prev. Premier Conn. A. (eee) Prev. Premier Fla. A. (fff) Prev. Premier Md. A. (ggg) Prev. Premier Mich. A. (hhh) Prev. Premier Ohio A. (iii) Prev. Premier Pa. A.   DATA: MORNINGSTAR, INC., CHICAGO, IL.

FUND	RATING (COMPARES RISK-ADJUSTED PERFORMANCE OF EACH FUND AGAINST ALL FUNDS)	CATEGORY (RATING COMPARES FUND WITHIN CATEGORY)	RATING	SIZE ASSETS $MIL.	SIZE % CHG. 1996-97	FEES SALES CHARGE (%)	FEES EXPENSE RATIO (%)	PERF. 1 YR.	PERF. 3 YR.	PERF. 5 YR.	PORT. YIELD (%)	PORT. MATURITY (YEARS)	HISTORY RESULTS VS. ALL FUNDS
EATON VANCE CALIF. MUNICIPALS B (jjj)	D	SL	D	317.2	-9	5.00**	1.65†	10.8	10.5	6.4	4.5	21.4	3 4 1 4 1
EATON VANCE CONN. MUNICIPALS B (kkk)	F	SL	F	167.0	-8	5.00**	1.57†	8.5	9.5	5.8	4.2	20.1	2 4 2 4 2
EATON VANCE FLA. MUNICIPALS B (lll)	F	SL	F	495.0	-17	5.00**	1.52†	7.7	9.0	5.9	4.4	22.9	2 4 1 4 3
EATON VANCE MASS. MUNICIPALS B (mmm)	D	SL	D	236.7	-9	5.00**	1.58†	9.6	9.5	6.0	4.5	22.2	2 4 2 4 1
EATON VANCE NATL. MUNICIPAL B (nnn)	B	ML	B	2073.8	-1	5.00**	1.54†	12.9	11.9	8.1	5.2	23.4	1 4 1 3 1
EATON VANCE N.J. MUNICIPALS B (ooo)	C-	SL	C-	333.9	-10	5.00**	1.56†	9.4	9.2	6.1	4.5	24.0	2 4 3 4 1
EATON VANCE N.Y. MUNICIPALS B (ppp)	F	SL	D	508.2	-12	5.00**	1.51†	9.3	9.8	6.4	4.4	19.7	1 4 2 4 2
EATON VANCE OHIO MUNICIPALS B (qqq)	D	SL	D	265.0	-7	5.00**	1.61†	8.6	9.6	6.3	4.4	19.4	2 4 2 4 2
EATON VANCE PA. MUNICIPALS B (rrr)	D	SL	C-	379.5	-10	5.00**	1.54†	8.9	9.7	6.0	4.7	20.7	2 4 2 3 2
EATON VANCE VA. MUNICIPALS B (sss)	F	SL	F	157.5	-10	5.00**	1.53†	8.1	9.2	5.8	4.3	21.8	3 4 2 4 3
EATON VANCE MARATHON HIGH-YLD. MUNIS		ML		182.9	23	5.00**	0.88†	13.2	NA	NA	5.3	24.3	1 1
EVERGREEN TAX-FREE B (ttt)	C	ML	C	1370.6	-12	4.00**	0.86†	8.2	9.2	6.0	5.1	19.0	3 4 2 3 3
EXCELSIOR INTERM.-TERM TAX-EXEMPT	B+	MI	B	253.5	-27	No load	0.58	7.3	8.8	6.4	4.3	8.0	3 2 3 2 3
FEDERATED INTERMEDIATE MUNI	B	MI	C	213.2	-4	No load	0.57	6.9	7.4	5.5	5.0	6.6	3 2 4 2 4
FEDERATED MUNICIPAL OPPORT. F	C	ML	B	327.6	-12	2.00**	1.08†	9.8	9.0	6.3	5.1	20.5	3 3 3 4 1
FEDERATED MUNICIPAL SECURITIES A	C	ML	C	595.1	-3	4.50	0.93	9.1	7.5	5.7	4.8	19.2	3 2 4 4 2
FEDERATED PA. MUNI INCOME A	C	SL	B	217.6	160	4.50	0.75†	9.3	10.9	7.5	5.3	10.7	2 3 2 1 2
FEDERATED SHORT-TERM MUNI INST.	A	MS	C	177.9	-14	No load	0.47	4.5	5.5	4.1	4.3	3.0	4 1 4 2 4
FIDELITY ADV. MUNI INCOME T (uuu)	C	ML	C	388.1	-15	3.50	0.89†	10.1	9.8	6.7	4.8	14.2	1 4 2 3 1
FIDELITY LIMITED-TERM MUNI INCOME	B+	MI	B	911.8	1	No load	0.56	8.2	9.1	6.8	4.9	7.5	2 3 3 2 3
FIDELITY MUNI BOND INITIAL	C	ML	C	924.8	-2	No load ‡	0.56	9.0	10.3	6.8	4.6	11.6	2 4 1 2 2
FIDELITY N.Y. INSURED MUNI INCOME	C-	SL	C	302.7	-5	No load	0.60	8.8	10.2	6.8	4.6	10.8	2 4 1 2 2
FIDELITY N.Y. MUNICIPAL INCOME	C	SL	C	444.6	8	No load	0.59	9.7	10.8	7.2	4.9	15.1	2 4 1 2 1
FIDELITY SPARTAN AGGRES. MUNI (vvv)	B+	ML	B+	954.6	12	1.00*	0.63	9.8	9.3	6.9	4.9	13.7	1 3 3 3 1
FIDELITY SPARTAN CALIF. MUNI INC. (www)	C	SL	B	1209.7	151	No load	0.57	9.8	11.1	7.2	4.8	14.2	1 4 1 1 1
FIDELITY SPARTAN CONN. MUNI INC.	C	SL	B	344.1	4	0.50*	0.52	9.1	10.0	7.0	4.8	12.1	2 4 2 2 2
FIDELITY SPARTAN FLA. MUNI INC.	B	SL	B	419.0	7	0.50*	0.54	8.8	10.3	7.5	4.7	13.1	1 4 1 2 2
FIDELITY SPARTAN INS. MUNI INC. (xxx)	C	ML	C	331.4	0	No load	0.60	9.5	10.5	7.2	4.7	13.0	1 4 1 3 1
FIDELITY SPARTAN INTERM. MUNI		MI		196.8	-7	No load	0.55	8.0	8.9	NA	4.6	8.0	3 3 1 3
FIDELITY SPARTAN MASS. MUNI INC. (yyy)	B	SL	B+	1210.3	6	No load	0.56	9.3	10.2	7.2	5.0	14.1	2 3 2 2 2
FIDELITY SPARTAN MICH. MUNI INC. (zzz)	C	SL	C	456.2	1	No load	0.59	9.1	9.2	6.5	4.9	14.5	1 4 3 3 2
FIDELITY SPARTAN MINN. MUNI INC. (aaaa)	B	SL	B+	295.9	1	No load	0.60	8.9	9.4	6.7	4.9	14.5	2 3 3 2 2
FIDELITY SPARTAN MUNI INC. (bbbb)	B	ML	B	2347.1	31	No load	0.56	9.2	10.0	6.9	4.8	12.2	2 4 3 1 2
FIDELITY SPARTAN N.J. MUNI INC.	B	SL	B+	363.7	4	0.50*	0.52	8.4	9.2	6.8	4.9	12.8	2 3 3 2 3
FIDELITY SPARTAN N.Y. MUNI INC.	C	SL	B	314.0	0	0.50*	0.54	10.0	11.0	7.3	4.8	14.9	1 4 1 2 1
FIDELITY SPARTAN OHIO MUNI INC. (cccc)	B	SL	B+	387.8	2	No load	0.59	8.7	9.7	7.0	4.7	12.2	2 3 2 2 2
FIDELITY SPARTAN PA. MUNI INC.	B+	SL	A	263.7	-3	0.50*	0.53	8.3	9.8	7.3	4.6	12.1	2 3 2 2 3
FIDELITY SPARTAN SHORT-INTERM. MUNI	A	MS	C	699.5	-5	No load	0.55	5.5	5.9	4.9	4.2	3.1	4 1 4 2 4
FIRST INVESTORS INSURED T/E A	D	ML	D	1192.1	-5	6.25	1.14†	8.4	8.8	6.0	4.9	17.0	3 3 3 4 3
FIRST INVESTOS N.Y. INSURED T/F A	D	SL	C-	195.3	-4	6.25	1.23†	7.8	8.5	5.9	4.8	19.0	3 3 3 3 3
FOUNTAIN SQ. OHIO TAX-FREE BOND A		SI		173.2	-1	4.50	0.74†	6.9	8.0	NA	4.2	7.1	2 2 3 4
FRANKLIN ALA. TAX-FREE INCOME I	B+	SL	A	213.0	12	4.25	0.71†	9.0	9.7	7.2	5.4	21.3	2 2 3 1 2
FRANKLIN ARIZ. TAX-FREE INCOME I	B+	SL	A	789.4	5	4.25	0.62†	8.3	8.9	6.6	5.4	18.7	3 2 3 2 3
FRANKLIN CALIF. HIGH YIELD MUNI I		SL		314.8	81	4.25	0.34†	11.7	12.2	NA	5.9	23.3	3 1 1 1
FRANKLIN CALIF. INS. TAX-FREE INCOME I	B	SL	B+	1683.7	3	4.25	0.60†	8.3	9.5	7.0	5.2	21.1	2 3 2 2 3
FRANKLIN CALIF. TAX-FREE INCOME I	B+	SL	A	14681.1	7	4.25	0.56†	8.8	9.4	6.9	5.8	20.6	3 2 3 1 2
FRANKLIN COLO. TAX-FREE INCOME I	B+	SL	A	265.6	13	4.25	0.71†	8.9	9.8	7.1	5.3	20.1	2 3 3 1 2
FRANKLIN CONN. TAX-FREE INCOME I	B	SL	B+	200.2	11	4.25	0.72†	8.5	9.0	6.6	5.4	17.6	2 3 3 2 2
FRANKLIN FED. TAX-FREE INCOME I	A	ML	A	7096.2	1	4.25	0.58†	9.0	9.5	7.1	5.7	19.6	3 2 3 1 2
FRANKLIN FLA. TAX-FREE INCOME I	B+	SL	A	1664.9	15	4.25	0.60†	8.1	9.0	7.0	5.7	19.7	3 3 3 2 2
FRANKLIN HIGH YIELD TAX-FREE INCOME I	A	ML	A	5226.5	21	4.25	0.62†	10.7	11.0	8.6	6.0	20.1	1 1 2 1 1
FRANKLIN INSURED TAX-FREE INCOME I	B+	ML	B+	1683.4	1	4.25	0.60†	8.2	8.6	6.7	5.4	19.9	2 2 3 2 2
FRANKLIN MD. TAX-FREE INCOME I	B+	SL	B+	211.6	16	4.25	0.73†	8.6	9.8	7.1	5.2	20.2	2 3 2 2 2
FRANKLIN MASS. INSURED TAX-FREE INC. I	B+	SL	A	343.1	11	4.25	0.68†	8.9	8.9	6.8	5.2	20.7	2 2 3 2 2
FRANKLIN MICH. INSURED TAX-FREE INC. I	B+	SL	B+	1138.2	2	4.25	0.62†	8.2	8.7	6.5	5.3	19.7	2 2 3 2 2
FRANKLIN MINN. INSURED TAX-FREE INC. I	B+	SL	B+	490.1	1	4.25	0.66†	7.7	8.1	6.2	5.3	18.1	3 2 4 3 3
FRANKLIN MO. TAX-FREE INCOME I	B+	SL	A	302.7	14	4.25	0.70†	9.2	9.8	7.3	5.3	18.8	1 3 3 1 2
FRANKLIN N.J. TAX-FREE INCOME I	B	SL	B+	628.6	10	4.25	0.64†	8.4	9.2	6.5	5.4	20.0	3 3 3 2 3
FRANKLIN N.Y. INSURED TAX-FREE INC. I	C-	SL	C	261.0	0	4.25	0.65†	8.8	10.4	7.1	5.0	23.5	1 4 1 2 2
FRANKLIN N.Y. TAX-FREE INCOME I	B+	SL	A	4826.6	1	4.25	0.59†	9.5	9.0	6.9	5.5	20.2	2 2 4 1 1
FRANKLIN N.C. TAX-FREE INCOME I	B	SL	B+	292.2	14	4.25	0.70†	8.9	9.6	6.8	5.2	19.1	2 3 3 2 2
FRANKLIN OHIO INS. TAX-FREE INCOME I	B+	SL	B+	733.9	5	4.25	0.64†	8.2	8.9	6.8	5.2	20.8	2 2 3 2 3
FRANKLIN ORE. TAX-FREE INCOME I	B+	SL	B+	419.0	10	4.25	0.66†	8.3	9.1	6.5	5.3	18.3	3 3 3 2 3
FRANKLIN PA. TAX-FREE INCOME I	A	SL	A	704.4	8	4.25	0.64†	9.0	9.2	7.1	5.3	18.9	2 2 3 2 2
FRANKLIN P.R. TAX-FREE INCOME I	B+	SL	B+	205.1	7	4.25	0.73†	8.8	9.4	6.8	5.3	20.3	3 2 3 1 2
FRANKLIN VA. TAX-FREE INCOME I	B+	SL	A	325.8	15	4.25	0.69†	8.5	9.3	7.0	5.4	21.4	2 2 3 2 2
GENERAL CALIF. MUNICIPAL BOND	C	SL	B	294.0	-3	0.10*	0.76	8.8	10.2	7.2	5.1	19.7	1 4 2 3 3
GENERAL MUNICIPAL BOND	C	ML	C	654.1	-19	0.10*	0.88†	8.1	9.3	6.5	5.2	19.9	1 4 2 3 3
GENERAL N.Y. MUNICIPAL BOND	C	SL	C	317.4	1	No load	0.91†	9.6	9.6	6.9	4.8	20.7	1 4 2 3 1
HANCOCK CALIF. TAX-FREE INCOME A	C	SL	C	292.6	-1	4.50	0.75†	10.1	11.9	7.6	5.2	21.6	1 4 1 2 1

*Includes redemption fee. **Includes deferred sales charge. †12(b)-1 plan in effect. ‡Not currently accepting new accounts or deposits. NA=Not available. NM=Not meaningful.
(jjj) Prev. EV Mara. Ca. Muni. (kkk) Prev. EV M. Conn. Muni. (lll) Prev. EV M. Fla. Muni. (mmm) Prev. EV M. Mass. Muni. (nnn) Prev. EV M. Natl. Muni. (ooo) Prev. EV M. N.J. Muni. (ppp) Prev. EV M. N.Y. Muni. (qqq) Prev. EV M. Ohio Muni. (rrr) Prev. EV M. Pa. Muni. (sss) Prev. EV M. Va. Muni. (ttt) Prev. Keystone T-F. (uuu) Prev. Fid. Adv. Hi-Inc. Muni T. (vvv) Prev. Fid. Aggres. Muni. (www) Prev. Fid. Calif. Muni. Inc. (xxx) Prev. Fid. Ins. Muni. Inc. (yyy) Prev. Fid. Mass. Muni. Inc. (zzz) Prev. Fid. Mich. Muni. Inc. (aaaa) Prev. Fid. Minn. Muni. Ince. (bbbb) Prev. Fid. Muni. Inc. (cccc) Prev. Fid. Ohio Mun. Inc.　　　DATA: MORNINGSTAR, INC., CHICAGO, IL.

MUTUAL FUND SCOREBOARD — Bond Funds

FUND	RATING (COMPARES RISK-ADJUSTED PERFORMANCE OF EACH FUND AGAINST ALL FUNDS)	CATEGORY	RATING (RATING COMPARES FUND WITHIN CATEGORY)	SIZE ASSETS $MIL.	% CHG. 1996-97	FEES SALES CHARGE (%)	EXPENSE RATIO (%)	1 YR.	3 YR.	5 YR.	YIELD (%)	MATURITY (YEARS)	HISTORY RESULTS VS. ALL FUNDS
HANCOCK TAX-FREE BOND A	C–	ML	C–	595.5	–2	4.50	0.85 †	9.8	11.2	7.5	5.3	19.0	1 4 1 2 1
HAWAIIAN TAX-FREE A	C	SL	B	651.9	–1	4.00	0.73 †	7.6	8.9	6.3	5.0	14.6	3 2 3 2 3
IDS CALIF. TAX-EXEMPT A	C–	SL	C	238.3	1	5.00	0.77	8.0	8.8	6.5	5.5	21.5	2 3 3 3 3
IDS HIGH-YIELD TAX-EXEMPT A	B	ML	B	5773.1	–3	5.00	0.70	9.3	9.7	6.6	5.7	20.2	3 3 2 4 2
IDS INSURED TAX-EXEMPT A	D	ML	D	464.7	–3	5.00	0.74	7.6	8.7	6.5	5.3	21.6	1 3 2 4 3
IDS MINN. TAX-EXEMPT A	C	SL	B	381.8	–1	5.00	0.75	8.5	8.9	6.6	5.6	21.3	3 2 3 3 2
IDS TAX-EXEMPT BOND A	D	ML	D	1005.0	–4	5.00	0.73	9.8	10.0	6.9	5.0	19.1	2 4 1 4 1
INVESCO TAX-FREE LONG-TERM BOND	C	ML	C	220.3	–8	No load	0.91 †	8.7	8.8	6.4	4.0	19.4	2 3 3 4 2
KEMPER MUNICIPAL BOND A	C–	ML	C–	3146.8	–3	4.50	0.66	9.4	10.2	7.4	5.1	19.7	1 3 1 3 2
KEMPER STATE TAX-FREE INCOME CALIF. A	C–	SL	C	998.4	–3	4.50	0.78	8.6	10.1	7.3	4.9	17.7	2 3 1 3 2
KEMPER STATE TAX-FREE INCOME N.Y. A	C	SL	C	271.1	–7	4.50	0.83	8.9	9.8	7.3	4.9	15.9	2 3 2 3 2
KIEWIT TAX-EXEMPT		MS		157.3	15	No load	0.50	6.3	6.6	NA	4.4	9.4	4 3 4
LIMITED TERM N.Y. MUNICIPAL A	A	MS	B+	771.8	21	3.50	0.89 †	7.9	7.6	6.4	5.2	12.6	3 1 4 1 3
LIMITED TERM TAX-EXEMPT BOND AMER.		MS		207.9	–1	4.75	0.75 †	7.3	8.0	NA	4.5	5.5	2 4 2 3
LORD ABBETT TAX-FREE INCOME CALIF. A	F	SL	F	256.9	–6	4.75	0.75 †	8.7	9.7	6.1	5.0	18.8	1 4 2 3 2
LORD ABBETT TAX-FREE INCOME NATL. A	D	ML	D	600.0	–4	4.75	0.90 †	9.9	10.4	6.9	5.0	21.0	2 4 2 2 1
LORD ABBETT TAX-FREE INCOME N.J.	C	SI	C–	185.4	0	4.75	0.79 †	8.6	9.9	7.1	4.8	20.6	1 4 2 2 2
LORD ABBETT TAX-FREE INCOME N.Y. A	F	SL	F	292.2	–5	4.75	0.81 †	8.2	9.2	5.9	5.0	19.3	2 4 3 3 3
MAINSTAY TAX-FREE BOND B	C	ML	C	477.1	–4	5.00 **	1.20 †	8.8	8.9	6.0	4.8	24.6	3 3 3 3 2
MARKETVEST PA. INTERM. MUNI BOND		SL		197.6	–11	3.50	0.83 †	6.6	NA	NA	4.3	7.2	4
MERRILL LYNCH CALIF. MUNI BOND B	C–	SL	C–	364.6	–18	4.00 **	1.14 †	8.2	9.6	6.4	4.8	21.4	2 4 2 2 3
MERRILL LYNCH MUNI INSURED B	D	ML	D	532.9	–20	4.00 **	1.19 †	7.9	8.9	6.0	4.6	19.0	2 4 2 4 3
MERRILL LYNCH MUNI NATL. B	C	ML	C	408.1	3	4.00 **	1.31 †	8.5	9.8	6.5	4.8	20.3	3 4 2 2 2
MERRILL LYNCH N.Y. MUNI BOND B	F	SL	F	271.1	–27	4.00 **	1.16 †	9.0	9.0	5.6	4.6	21.1	3 4 3 4 2
MFS CALIF. MUNICIPAL BOND A	D	SL	C–	224.3	–10	4.75	0.66 †	9.8	10.1	6.7	5.0	15.5	2 4 2 3 1
MFS MASS. MUNICIPAL BOND A	C	SL	C	236.8	–3	4.75	1.12 †	8.8	9.1	6.4	5.1	17.1	3 3 3 4 2
MFS MUNICIPAL BOND A	D	ML	D	1682.1	–9	4.75	0.60	8.9	9.1	6.7	4.8	16.5	1 3 2 4 2
MFS MUNICIPAL HIGH-INCOME A	B+	ML	B+	1089.9	10	4.75	0.93	8.7	9.2	6.8	6.3	21.1	3 2 3 3 2
MFS MUNICIPAL INCOME B	C	ML	C	190.4	–26	4.00 **	2.11 †	8.8	8.4	6.0	4.8	17.7	3 3 3 4 2
MFS N.C. MUNICIPAL BOND A	C–	SL	C–	376.1	–5	4.75	1.08 †	9.0	9.5	6.4	4.8	18.8	3 3 2 3 2
MFS VA. MUNICIPAL BOND A	D	SL	D	374.4	–5	4.75	1.08 †	8.9	8.9	6.0	4.9	16.7	3 4 2 4 2
MORGAN (J.P.) TAX-EXEMPT BOND (dddd)	B+	MI	C	390.3	7	No load	0.64	7.4	8.0	6.1	4.5	8.0	3 2 4 3 3
NATIONWIDE TAX-FREE INCOME	C–	ML	C–	258.8	–2	5.00 **	0.96 †	8.6	9.8	6.3	4.7	18.9	2 4 2 3 2
NEW ENGLAND MUNICIPAL INCOME A	C–	ML	C–	177.2	–2	4.50	0.92 †	8.6	10.0	6.3	5.2	11.0	2 4 2 1 2
NORTHERN INTERMEDIATE TAX-EXEMPT		MS		290.6	14	No load	0.85	5.8	7.0	NA	3.9	5.4	4 3 4
NORTHERN TAX-EXEMPT		ML		154.1	17	No load	0.85	8.7	9.5	NA	4.5	14.7	2 4 2
NUVEEN FLAGSHIP ALL-AMER. A (eeee)	B	ML	B+	224.6	5	4.20	0.87 †	10.8	10.7	7.9	5.2	22.0	1 3 2 2 1
NUVEEN FLAGSHIP CONN. MUNI A (ffff)	C	SL	C	215.2	2	4.20	0.73 †	8.8	9.7	6.9	5.2	19.6	2 3 2 2 2
NUVEEN FLAGSHIP FLA. MUNI A (gggg)	C–	SL	C	297.0	–4	4.20	0.82 †	8.5	9.0	6.7	5.1	21.2	1 3 2 4 2
NUVEEN FLAGSHIP KY. MUNI A (hhhh)	C	SL	B	445.3	4	4.20	0.75 †	9.1	9.9	7.1	5.2	20.9	2 3 2 3 2
NUVEEN FLAGSHIP LTD.-TERM MUNI A (iiii)	B+	MS	D	430.5	–6	2.50	0.80 †	6.9	7.1	5.6	4.6	7.1	3 1 4 2 4
NUVEEN FLAGSHIP MICH. MUNI A (jjjj)	C	SL	B	262.7	3	4.20	0.85 †	8.8	9.5	6.9	5.1	18.4	2 3 2 3 2
NUVEEN FLAGSHIP MO. MUNI A (kkkk)	C	SL	C	234.8	5	4.20	0.86 †	9.4	9.7	7.1	5.0	10.9	1 3 2 2 2
NUVEEN FLAGSHIP N.C. MUNI A (llll)	C	SL	C	187.1	1	4.20	0.93 †	8.9	9.0	6.4	5.0	19.7	3 3 3 3 2
NUVEEN FLAGSHIP OHIO MUNI A (mmmm)	C	SL	B	476.8	6	4.20	0.89 †	8.3	8.9	6.5	5.2	19.3	3 2 3 3 3
NUVEEN FLAGSHIP TENN. MUNI A (nnnn)	C	SL	C	271.3	5	4.20	0.85 †	9.1	9.3	6.8	5.1	19.0	2 3 3 3 2
NUVEEN MUNICIPAL BOND R	A	ML	A	2965.4	5	No load ‡	0.57	9.1	9.5	6.9	5.1	20.0	4 1 3 2 2
OPPENHEIMER CALIF. MUNICIPAL A	C	SL	C	298.7	2	4.75	0.97 †	9.7	11.3	7.3	5.1	22.6	2 4 1 1 1
OPPENHEIMER MUNICIPAL BOND A	C–	ML	C–	585.9	–1	4.75	0.92 †	9.4	10.8	7.0	5.2	18.5	1 4 1 1 1
OPPENHEIMER N.Y. MUNICIPAL A	D	SL	C–	634.4	–5	4.75	0.91 †	9.2	10.2	6.7	5.3	17.4	2 4 2 2 2
PACIFIC HORIZON CALIF. T/E BOND A	C–	SL	C	217.8	–1	4.50	0.90	8.5	9.5	6.8	4.7	16.2	2 3 2 3 2
PAINEWEBBER NATL. TAX-FREE INCOME A	F	MI	F	229.5	–18	4.00	0.91 †	9.3	9.0	6.1	4.6	19.2	2 4 3 4 2
PIONEER TAX-FREE INCOME A	C	ML	C	411.4	–7	4.50	0.90 †	8.8	9.6	6.9	4.6	20.8	2 3 3 3 2
PRICE (T. ROWE) CALIF. TAX-FREE BOND	B	SL	B+	188.1	20	No load	0.62	9.1	10.2	7.3	5.0	17.0	2 3 2 2 2
PRICE (T. ROWE) MD. TAX-FREE	B+	SL	A	908.4	12	No load	0.54	8.7	9.5	7.1	5.1	15.8	2 3 2 2 2
PRICE (T. ROWE) N.Y. TAX-FREE	B	SL	B+	171.1	21	No load	0.65	9.5	10.0	7.3	5.1	20.6	1 3 2 2 1
PRICE (T. ROWE) TAX-FREE HIGH-YIELD	A	ML	A	1199.5	16	No load	0.74	10.2	10.5	7.8	5.5	18.8	2 2 1 1 1
PRICE (T. ROWE) TAX-FREE INCOME	B	ML	B	1384.5	3	No load	0.57	9.3	9.9	7.2	5.2	17.2	2 3 2 3 2
PRICE (T. ROWE) TAX-FREE SHORT-INTERM.	A	MS	C	439.2	0	No load	0.56	5.3	5.8	4.8	4.2	3.8	4 1 4 2 4
PRICE (T. ROWE) VA. TAX-FREE	B	SL	B+	226.9	20	No load	0.65	9.0	9.7	7.2	5.0	17.5	2 3 2 2 2
PRINCIPAL TAX-EXEMPT BOND A (oooo)	C–	ML	C–	195.2	3	4.75	0.78 †	9.2	11.3	7.0	4.9	18.0	2 4 1 1 2
PRUDENTIAL CALIF. MUNI CALIF. INCOME A	A	SL	A	161.1	5	3.00	0.73 †	10.3	10.9	8.5	4.9	19.5	1 2 1 2 1
PRUDENTIAL MUNI HIGH-YIELD B	B+	ML	A	670.1	–4	5.00 **	1.04 †	10.4	9.8	7.3	5.9	10.0	3 2 2 3 1
PRUDENTIAL MUNI INSURED B	D	ML	D	266.7	–20	5.00 **	1.08 †	8.4	8.9	6.3	4.3	15.8	3 3 2 4 3
PRUDENTIAL MUNICIPAL N.Y. A	C	SL	C	172.1	–2	3.00	0.68 †	9.2	9.6	6.9	5.0	17.0	2 3 2 2 2
PRUDENTIAL NATL. MUNICIPALS A	C–	ML	C	487.9	–3	3.00	0.68 †	9.8	9.7	6.9	5.0	17.6	2 3 2 4 1
PUTNAM CALIF. TAX-EXEMPT INCOME A	C	SL	C	3102.3	–2	4.75	0.74 †	8.7	10.3	7.2	5.0	21.5	2 4 1 3 2
PUTNAM FLA. TAX-EXEMPT INCOME A	D	SL	C–	244.1	–3	4.75	0.96 †	9.0	9.6	6.5	5.1	19.6	3 3 3 3 2
PUTNAM MASS. TAX-EXEMPT INCOME A	C	SL	B	289.8	6	4.75	0.96 †	8.9	10.2	7.1	5.4	19.8	2 3 1 2 2
PUTNAM MUNICIPAL INCOME A	C	ML	C	826.0	1	4.75	0.96 †	9.6	10.3	7.1	5.5	18.7	2 3 1 3 1

*Includes redemption fee. **Includes deferred sales charge. †12(b)-1 plan in effect. ‡Not currently accepting new accounts or deposits. NA=Not available. NM=Not meaningful. (dddd) Prev. JPM Pierpont T-E Bond. (eeee) Prev. Flagship All-Amer. T-E A. (ffff) Prev. Flagship Conn. Double T-E A. (gggg) Prev. Flagship Fla. Double T-E A. (hhhh) Prev. Flagship Ky. Triple T-E A. (iiii) Prev. Flagship L-T T-E A. (jjjj) Prev. Flagship Mich. Triple T-E A. (kkkk) Prev. Flagship Mo. Double T-E A. (llll) Prev. Flagship N.C Double T-E A. (mmmm) Prev. Flagship Ohio Double T-E A. (nnnn) Prev. Flagship Tenn. Double T-E A. (oooo) Prev. Princor T-E Bond A.　　　DATA: MORNINGSTAR, INC., CHICAGO, IL.

MUTUAL FUND SCOREBOARD — Bond Funds

FUND	RATING (COMPARES RISK-ADJUSTED PERFORMANCE OF EACH FUND AGAINST ALL FUNDS)	CATEGORY (RATING COMPARES FUND WITHIN CATEGORY)	RATING	SIZE ASSETS $MIL.	% CHG. 1996-97	FEES SALES CHARGE (%)	EXPENSE RATIO (%)	PERFORMANCE 1 YR.	3 YR.	5 YR.	PORTFOLIO YIELD (%)	MATURITY (YEARS)	HISTORY RESULTS VS. ALL FUNDS
PUTNAM N.J. TAX-EXEMPT INCOME A	C–	SL	C	225.9	–2	4.75	0.96†	8.8	9.5	6.7	4.9	18.7	2 3 2 3 2
PUTNAM N.Y. TAX-EXEMPT INCOME A	F	SL	D	1732.3	–6	4.75	0.81†	9.0	9.2	6.4	5.1	10.7	1 4 3 3 2
PUTNAM N.Y. TAX-EXEMPT OPPORT. A	B+	SI	A	166.7	1	4.75	0.96†	8.9	9.6	6.9	5.3	18.2	3 2 2 2 2
PUTNAM OHIO TAX-EXEMPT INCOME A	C	SL	B	185.2	–2	4.75	0.98†	8.5	9.2	6.6	5.0	17.3	3 3 3 3 2
PUTNAM PA. TAX-EXEMPT INCOME A	C	SL	B	191.1	1	4.75	0.98†	8.7	9.6	7.1	5.2	17.9	2 3 2 3 2
PUTNAM TAX-EXEMPT INCOME A	D	ML	D	2054.0	–3	4.75	0.78†	9.6	9.9	6.8	5.2	9.9	1 4 2 3 1
PUTNAM TAX-FREE HIGH YIELD B	B	ML	B	1227.3	–15	5.00**	1.50†	8.5	8.9	6.4	5.0	18.9	2 3 3 3 2
PUTNAM TAX-FREE INSURED B	C–	ML	C–	337.0	–4	5.00**	1.58†	8.2	9.1	6.2	5.0	18.3	3 3 2 4 3
ROCHESTER FUND MUNICIPALS A	B	SL	B	2847.2	23	4.75	0.82†	10.2	11.2	7.7	5.9	21.9	1 4 1 1 1
SAFECO MUNICIPAL BOND NO LOAD	C–	ML	C–	503.0	4	No load	0.54	10.6	11.5	7.5	5.0	23.5	2 4 1 3 1
SCUDDER CALIF. TAX-FREE	C	SL	B	310.1	5	No load	0.78	10.1	10.7	7.4	4.6	11.0	1 4 1 3 1
SCUDDER HIGH-YIELD TAX-FREE	B+	ML	B+	324.8	11	No load	0.91	11.9	11.7	7.8	5.1	10.0	1 4 1 2 1
SCUDDER MASS. TAX-FREE	B	SL	B+	356.0	8	No load	0.76	8.4	10.0	7.4	4.8	9.0	1 3 2 3 2
SCUDDER MANAGED MUNI BONDS	B	ML	B	719.2	–2	No load	0.63	9.2	10.0	7.2	4.9	10.2	1 3 2 2 2
SCUDDER MEDIUM-TERM TAX-FREE	B+	MI	B	651.7	0	No load	0.72	7.6	8.5	6.5	4.4	6.5	3 2 3 2 3
SCUDDER N.Y. TAX-FREE	D	SL	C–	189.1	1	No load	0.83	9.5	10.1	6.9	4.2	10.7	2 4 2 3 1
SELIGMAN MUNICIPAL OHIO A	C	SI	C–	154.3	–3	4.75	0.77†	8.4	9.0	6.6	5.0	19.1	2 3 3 3 2
SIERRA CALIF. MUNICIPAL A	C	SL	C	312.8	–13	4.50	0.97†	10.3	10.8	7.2	5.2	19.7	1 4 1 2 1
SIERRA NATIONAL MUNICIPAL A	C	ML	C	161.6	–23	4.50	1.04†	9.0	9.6	7.1	5.4	18.8	1 4 3 2 2
SIT TAX-FREE INCOME	A	MS	B+	445.2	46	No load	0.79	9.7	9.4	7.5	5.2	18.0	3 1 4 1 1
SMITH BARNEY CALIF. MUNICIPALS A	B	SL	B+	650.0	13	4.00	0.71†	11.1	12.8	8.6	4.9	21.1	2 4 1 1 1
SMITH BARNEY INTERM. MAT. CALIF. A	B	SI	B	258.3	945	2.00	0.77†	7.5	8.6	6.3	4.6	7.3	3 3 3 2 3
SMITH BARNEY MANAGED MUNIS A	B+	ML	B+	2306.4	17	4.00	0.68†	10.9	12.1	9.3	5.4	24.0	1 2 1 1 1
SMITH BARNEY MUNI HIGH INCOME B (pppp)	B	ML	B	532.9	–15	4.50**	1.32†	9.1	9.5	6.5	4.9	22.4	2 3 1 1 2
SMITH BARNEY MUNI LTD. TERM A	A	MI	B+	253.9	–32	2.00	0.75†	8.1	7.7	6.1	5.0	8.5	3 1 4 3 3
SMITH BARNEY MUNI NATIONAL A	B+	ML	B+	365.4	0	4.00	0.70†	10.6	10.9	7.8	5.6	21.4	1 3 1 3 1
SMITH BARNEY MUNI N.Y. A	B	SL	B+	553.3	1	4.00	0.75†	10.3	10.8	7.6	5.3	24.0	2 3 1 2 1
SMITH BARNEY N.J. MUNICIPALS A	C	SL	C	154.2	4	4.00	0.76†	9.3	10.0	6.9	5.2	20.5	2 4 2 2 2
STAGECOACH CALIF. TAX-FREE BOND A (qqqq)	B	SL	B+	219.8	–8	4.50	0.71†	8.9	9.7	7.4	4.8	15.3	2 2 2 2 2
STATE ST. RESEARCH TAX-EXEMPT A	C–	ML	C–	207.5	–7	4.50	1.04†	10.2	9.8	6.7	4.6	10.4	2 4 2 3 1
STEIN ROE HIGH-YIELD MUNIS	A	ML	A	323.1	10	No load	0.77	9.2	10.3	7.3	5.4	20.3	3 2 2 2 2
STEIN ROE INTERMEDIATE MUNIS	B+	MI	C	200.1	0	No load	0.70	7.2	8.1	6.2	4.5	8.9	3 2 4 2 3
STEIN ROE MANAGED MUNICIPALS	B	ML	B	591.7	–3	No load	0.73	9.0	9.7	6.8	4.8	15.3	3 3 2 2 2
STRONG HIGH-YIELD MUNI BOND		ML		443.6	81	No load	0.70	13.9	11.7	NA	5.8	10.5	1 3 1 1
STRONG MUNICIPAL ADVANTAGE		MS		925.2	85	No load	0.00	4.9	NA	NA	4.4	9.3	1 4
STRONG MUNICIPAL BOND	B	MI	C–	240.9	3	No load	0.80	12.1	8.6	6.4	5.2	9.1	2 2 4 4 1
STRONG SHORT-TERM MUNI BOND	B+	MS	D	180.7	24	No load	0.70	6.9	5.7	4.5	4.8	2.9	4 1 4 1 4
TAX-EXEMPT BOND OF AMERICA	B	ML	B+	1666.0	10	4.75	0.68†	9.0	10.2	7.3	5.1	8.7	2 3 2 1 2
TAX-EXEMPT FUND OF CALIF.	B	SL	B+	314.9	20	4.75	0.72†	8.1	9.9	7.3	4.6	8.9	2 3 2 2 3
TAX-FREE FUND OF COLO. A	B	SI	B	214.0	0	4.00	0.69†	7.3	8.0	6.1	4.9	8.3	3 2 4 2 3
TAX-FREE TRUST OF ARIZ. A	C	SI	C–	393.7	0	4.00	0.72†	8.4	9.0	6.4	5.0	14.9	3 3 3 3 3
TAX-FREE TRUST OF ORE. A	B	SI	C	312.8	3	4.00	0.72†	7.4	8.3	6.1	5.0	14.5	3 2 3 3 3
THORNBURG INTERM. MUNI A	A	MI	B+	315.9	28	3.50	1.00†	7.2	8.2	6.8	4.8	7.5	2 1 4 2 3
THORNBURG LTD.-TERM NATL. A	A	MS	C–	856.2	–6	2.50	0.96†	5.5	6.4	5.3	4.6	3.6	4 1 4 2 4
UNITED MUNICIPAL BOND A	C	ML	C	995.6	2	4.25	0.67†	10.2	11.3	7.9	5.0	17.7	1 4 1 2 1
UNITED MUNICIPAL HIGH-INCOME A	A	ML	A	482.0	18	4.25	0.78†	11.8	11.7	8.9	5.9	22.0	2 2 2 1 1
USAA CALIF. BOND	B	SL	B+	498.6	14	No load	0.41	10.4	12.3	7.7	5.4	19.9	2 4 1 1 1
USAA TAX-EXEMPT INTERM.-TERM	A	MI	B+	1936.0	13	No load	0.37	9.4	9.6	7.1	5.4	9.7	3 2 3 2 1
USAA TAX-EXEMPT LONG-TERM	B	ML	B+	1995.4	7	No load	0.37	10.4	11.0	7.2	5.6	22.4	2 4 1 2 1
USAA TAX-EXEMPT SHORT-TERM	A	MS	B+	878.3	12	No load	0.41	5.9	6.1	4.9	4.5	2.8	4 1 4 2 4
USAA VA. BOND	B+	SL	B+	324.7	14	No load	0.46	9.5	10.4	7.3	5.4	20.8	2 3 2 1 1
VALUE LINE TAX-EXEMPT HIGH-YIELD	C	ML	C	187.5	–7	No load	0.60	8.6	9.5	6.4	4.7	17.7	3 4 2 3 2
VAN KAMPEN AM. CAP. HIGH-YIELD MN. A	A	MI	A	778.1	27	4.75‡	1.01†	11.0	10.2	8.1	6.3	21.0	3 1 3 1 1
VAN KAMPEN AM. CAP. INS. TAX-FREE A	D	ML	D	1288.6	0	4.75	0.95†	7.7	9.5	6.7	4.9	19.5	2 3 2 3 3
VAN KAMPEN AM. CAP. MUNI INCOME A	C–	ML	C	794.1	–1	4.75	0.94†	9.1	9.5	6.6	5.2	18.9	2 3 3 2 2
VAN KAMPEN AM. CAP. PA. T/F A	C–	SL	C	222.0	–2	4.75	1.09†	8.6	9.6	7.0	5.0	19.3	1 3 2 2 2
VAN KAMPEN AM. CAP. T/F HIGH A	B+	ML	B+	697.0	4	4.75	0.99†	9.1	9.7	7.4	6.0	21.1	1 3 3 3 2
VANGUARD CALIF. TAX-FREE INS. INTERM.		SI		622.9	78	No load	0.19	7.7	8.7	NA	4.7	6.0	4 1 3
VANGUARD CALIF. TAX-FREE INS. LONG-TERM	C	SL	B	1225.6	17	No load	0.19	8.9	10.7	7.6	5.1	10.1	2 3 1 1 2
VANGUARD FLA. INSURED TAX-FREE	B	SL	B	687.8	26	No load	0.19	8.9	10.1	7.6	4.9	9.7	1 2 2 2 2
VANGUARD MUNI HIGH-YIELD	B	ML	B+	2292.3	12	No load	0.19	9.2	10.5	7.6	5.5	9.2	2 3 1 2 2
VANGUARD MUNI INSURED LONG-TERM	C	ML	C	2075.3	6	No load	0.19	8.7	10.3	7.4	5.3	9.7	2 3 1 2 2
VANGUARD MUNI INTERMEDIATE-TERM	A	MI	B+	6849.4	12	No load	0.19	7.1	8.2	6.7	5.0	6.7	3 1 4 2 4
VANGUARD MUNI LIMITED-TERM	A	MS	C	2020.1	13	No load	0.19	5.1	5.9	4.8	4.4	3.4	4 1 4 2 4
VANGUARD MUNI LONG-TERM	B	ML	B	1282.0	12	No load	0.19	9.3	10.7	7.7	5.2	10.5	1 3 1 2 2
VANGUARD MUNI SHORT-TERM	A	MS	B	1494.7	3	No load	0.19	4.1	4.6	3.8	4.0	1.2	4 1 4 3 4
VANGUARD N.J. TAX-FREE INS. LONG-TERM	C	SL	B	965.1	15	No load	0.20	8.6	9.5	7.1	5.1	9.2	1 3 2 3 2
VANGUARD N.Y. INSURED LONG-TERM (rrrr)	C	SL	B	1161.0	23	No load	0.20	8.7	10.0	7.3	5.1	8.4	2 3 2 2 2
VANGUARD OHIO TAX-FREE INS. LONG-TERM	B	SL	B+	258.5	20	No load	0.20	8.5	9.7	7.2	5.0	7.9	2 3 2 2 2
VANGUARD PA. TAX-FREE INS. LONG-TERM	B+	SL	B+	1771.9	9	No load	0.19	8.3	9.6	7.2	5.3	7.4	2 2 2 2 3

*Includes redemption fee. **Includes deferred sales charge. †12(b)-1 plan in effect. ‡Not currently accepting new accounts or deposits. NA=Not available. NM=Not meaningful. (pppp) Prev. Smith Barney T-E Inc. B. (qqqq) Prev. Overland Express Calif. T-F Bond A. (rrrr) Prev. Vanguard N.Y. Insured Tax-Free.

DATA: MORNINGSTAR, INC., CHICAGO, IL.

AARP INVESTMENT PROGRAM
800-322-2282

ADVANCE CAPITAL I GROUP
800-345-4783

AIM FUNDS
800-347-4246

ALLIANCE CAPITAL GROUP
800-227-4618

AMCORE VINTAGE MUTUAL FUNDS
800-438-6375

AMERICAN CENTURY INVESTMENTS
800-345-2021

AMERICAN FUNDS GROUP
800-421-4120

AMERISTAR FUNDS
800-824-3741

AMSOUTH FUNDS
800-451-8379

AQUILA GROUP
800-872-5859

ARMADA FUNDS
800-342-5734

ASSET MANAGEMENT FUND (AMF)
800-527-3713

ATLAS FUNDS
800-933-2852

BABSON FUND GROUP
800-422-2766

BERNSTEIN (SANFORD C.) FUND
212-756-4097

BLAIR (WILLIAM) MUTUAL FUNDS
800-742-7272

BLANCHARD GROUP OF FUNDS
800-829-3863

BOND FUND OF AMERICA
See American Funds Group

BOSTON 1784 FUNDS
800-252-1784

CALIFORNIA INVESTMENT TRUST GRP.
800-225-8778

CALVERT GROUP
800-368-2748

CAPITAL WORLD BOND
See American Funds Group

CARDINAL GROUP
800-848-7734

CHICAGO TRUST BOND FUNDS
800-992-8151

CHURCHILL FUNDS
800-872-5859

COLONIAL GROUP
800-426-3750

COLUMBIA FUNDS
800-547-1707

COMMERCE FUNDS
800-305-2140

COMMON SENSE TRUST
800-544-5445

COMPOSITE GROUP OF FUNDS
800-543-8072

DAVIS FUNDS
800-279-0279

DEAN WITTER FUNDS
800-869-3863

DELAWARE GROUP
800-523-4640

DG INVESTOR SERIES
800-748-8500

DODGE & COX GROUP
800-621-3979

DREYFUS GROUP
800-373-9387

DREYFUS PREMIER FUNDS
800-554-4611

DUPREE MUTUAL FUNDS
800-866-0614

EATON VANCE GROUP
800-225-6265

EVERGREEN KEYSTONE FUNDS
800-343-2829

EXCELSIOR FUNDS
800-446-1012

FEDERATED FUNDS
800-341-7400

FIDELITY ADVISOR FUNDS
800-522-7297

FIDELITY GROUP
800-544-8888

FIRST INVESTORS GROUP
800-423-4026

FIRST OMAHA FUNDS
800-662-4203

FIRST PRIORITY FUNDS
800-433-2829

FORTIS FUNDS
800-800-2638

FOUNTAIN SQUARE FUNDS
800-334-0483

FPA FUNDS
800-982-4372

FRANKLIN GROUP OF FUNDS
800-342-5236

FREMONT FUNDS
800-824-1580

FUNDAMENTAL FUNDS
800-322-6864

GALAXY FUNDS
800-628-0414

GE FUNDS
800-656-6626

GENERAL CA MUNICIPAL BOND
See Dreyfus Group

GENERAL MUNICIPAL BOND
See Dreyfus Group

GENERAL N. Y. MUNICIPAL BOND
See Dreyfus Group

GLOBAL GOVERNMENT PLUS
See Prudential Mutual Funds

GLOBAL TOTAL RETURN A
See Prudential Mutual Funds

GOLDMAN SACHS ASSET MGMT. GRP.
800-526-7384

GRADISON MUTUAL FUNDS
800-869-5999

GT GLOBAL GROUP OF FUNDS
800-824-1580

GUARDIAN FUNDS
800-221-3253

HANCOCK JOHN FUNDS
800-225-5291

HARBOR FUNDS
800-422-1050

HAWAIIAN TAX-FREE A
See Aquila Group

HOMESTEAD FUNDS
800-258-3030

HOTCHKIS & WILEY FUNDS
800-346-7301

IDS GROUP
800-328-8300

INTERMEDIATE BOND FD. AMERICA
See American Funds Group

INVESCO FUNDS
800-525-8085

INVESTORS TRUST
800-656-6626

ISI FUNDS
800-955-7175

IVY/MACKENZIE GROUP OF FUNDS
800-456-5111

JANUS GROUP
800-525-8983

KEMPER FUNDS
800-621-1048

KEY FUNDS
See Victory Group

KEYPREMIER FUNDS
800-766-3960

KEYSTONE FUNDS
See Evergreen Keystone Funds

KIEWIT MUTUAL FUND
800-254-3948

LEGG MASON FUNDS
800-577-8589

LEXINGTON GROUP
800-526-0056

LIMITED TERM TAX-EX. BD. AMER
See American Funds Group

LORD ABBETT FUNDS
800-874-3733

MAINSTAY FUNDS
800-624-6768

MARKETVEST FUNDS
800-658-8378

MARKETWATCH FUNDS
800-232-9091

MARQUIS FUNDS
800-462-9511

MARSHALL FUNDS
800-236-8560

MCM FUNDS
800-788-9485

MERRILL LYNCH GROUP
800-637-3863

MFS FUNDS
800-637-2929

MORGAN (J. P.) FUNDS
800-225-7670

MORGAN STANLEY FUNDS
800-282-4404

NATIONWIDE FUNDS
800-848-0920

NEUBERGER & BERMAN GROUP
800-877-9700

NEW ENGLAND FUND GROUP
800-225-7670

NICHOLAS GROUP
800-227-5987

NORTHEAST INVESTORS GROUP
800-225-6704

NORTHERN FUNDS
800-595-9111

NORTHSTAR FUNDS
800-595-7827

NUVEEN MUTUAL FUNDS
800-621-7227

111 CORCORAN FUNDS
800-422-2080

OPPENHEIMER FUNDS
800-525-7048

OVERLAND EXPRESS FUNDS
800-552-9612

PACIFIC HORIZON FUNDS
800-332-3863

PAINEWEBBER MUTUAL FUNDS
800-647-1568

PAYDEN & RYGEL INVESTMENT GRP.
800-572-9336

PERMANENT PORTFOLIO FUNDS
800-531-5142

PHOENIX FUNDS
800-243-4361

PIONEER GROUP
800-225-6292

PIPER FUNDS
800-866-7778

PREFERRED GROUP
800-662-4769

PRICE (T. ROWE) FUNDS
800-638-5660

PRINCOR FUNDS
800-451-5447

PRUDENTIAL MUTUAL FUNDS
800-225-1852

PUTNAM FUNDS
800-225-1581

ROCHESTER FUNDS
716-383-1300

SAFECO MUTUAL FUNDS
800-426-6730

SALOMON BROTHERS GROUP
800-725-6666

SCHWAB FUNDS
800-526-8600

SCUDDER FUNDS
800-225-2470

SELIGMAN GROUP
800-221-2783

SENTINEL GROUP
800-282-3863

SIERRA TRUST FUNDS
800-222-5852

SIT GROUP
800-332-5580

SMITH BARNEY GROUP
800-451-2010

SMITH BREEDEN FUNDS
800-221-3138

SOUTHTRUST VULCAN FUNDS
800-239-7470

SSGA FUNDS
800-647-7327

STAGECOACH FUNDS
800-222-8222

STAR FUNDS
800-677-3863

STATE STREET RESEARCH GROUP
800-882-0052

STEIN ROE MUTUAL FUNDS
800-338-2550

STRONG FUNDS
800-368-1030

SUNAMERICA FUNDS
800-858-8850

TAX-EXEMPT BOND OF AMERICA
See American Funds Group

TAX-FREE FUND OF COLO. A
See Aquila Group

TAX-FREE TRUST OF ARIZ. A
See Aquila Group

TAX-FREE TRUST OF ORE. A
See Aquila Group

TCW/DW FUNDS
800-526-3143

TEMPLETON GROUP
800-292-9293

THORNBURG FUNDS
800-847-0200

U.S. GOVERNMENT SECURITIES
See American Funds Group

UNITED GROUP
800-366-5465

USAA GROUP
800-382-8722

VALUE LINE MUTUAL FUNDS
800-223-0818

VAN ECK GLOBAL FUNDS
800-826-1115

VAN KAMPEN AMER. CAPITAL FDS.
800-421-5666

VANGUARD GROUP
800-662-7447

VICTORY GROUP
800-539-3863

VIRTUS FUNDS
800-723-9512

VISTA MUTUAL FUNDS
800-648-4782

WARBURG PINCUS FUNDS
800-927-2874

WESTERN ASSET TRUST
818-584-4300

WPG MUTUAL FUNDS
800-223-3332

WRIGHT MANAGED INVESTMENT COS.
800-888-9471

MUTUAL FUND SCOREBOARD

Closed-End Equity Funds

FUND	RATING	CATEGORY	RISK	SIZE ASSETS $MIL.	FEES EXPENSE RATIO (%)	NAV. RET. (%) 1 YR.	3 YRS.	SHARES RET. (%) 1 YR.	3 YRS.	YIELD (%)	HISTORY RESULTS VS. ALL FUNDS	PREMIUM/DISCOUNT DIFFERENCE FROM NAV 1997 HIGH	LOW	1/30/98
ADAMS EXPRESS	A	Large-cap Blend	Low	1424.2	0.34	30.6	27.1	33.1	26.1	1.7	1 1 1	-13.5	-18.1	-15.5
ALLIANCE ALL-MARKET ADVANTAGE	B	Large-cap Blend	Average	76.2	2.43	43.4	33.2	59.2	38.1	0.0	1 1 1	0.2	-20.3	-4.8
ARGENTINA	C-	Latin America	High	150.6	1.90	22.0	13.2	11.6	4.8	1.9	4 1 1	-5.3	-19.2	-16.8
ASA LIMITED	D	Precious Metals	High	201.1	0.49	-34.3	-23.3	-38.3	-19.7	5.8	4 4 4	17.1	-1.5	5.3
ASIA PACIFIC	D	Pacific ex-Japan	High	240.3	1.57	-39.6	-11.9	-37.8	-15.6	2.5	4 2 4	-10.5	-20.8	2.1
ASIA TIGERS	C-	Pacific ex-Japan	High	184.0	NA	-32.8	-8.6	-31.0	-6.8	0.0	4 2 4	-15.4	-21.4	-5.5
AUSTRIA	C	Europe	Average	136.3	1.71	6.5	10.9	18.9	10.7	3.6	4 1 4	-15.6	-24.8	-18.3
BAKER FENTRESS	B	Mid-cap Growth	Low	783.7	0.73	15.9	21.9	25.2	24.4	2.6	1 1 1	-13.4	-22.6	-17.0
BERGSTROM CAPITAL	B	Large-cap Growth	Average	158.9	0.76	21.2	25.5	27.9	26.6	0.3	1 1 1	-8.5	-17.5	-9.1
BLUE CHIP VALUE	B+	Large-cap Value	Low	149.0	1.05	30.0	29.6	39.3	40.1	0.8	1 1 1	10.9	-10.9	6.7
BRAZIL	C-	Latin America	High	429.3	1.60	19.1	5.3	9.6	-4.7	2.2	4 1 1	-13.3	-24.9	-19.5
BRAZILIAN EQUITY	C-	Latin America	High	68.4	NA	11.4	3.7	7.9	-7.5	0.0	4 1 2	-14.0	-25.8	-15.7
CENTRAL EUROPEAN EQUITY	B	Europe	Average	226.7	1.08	27.9	25.0	31.7	26.4	6.6	4 1 1	-11.5	-22.6	-18.3
CENTRAL FUND OF CANADA	C	Precious Metals	Average	77.7	0.89	-4.2	-2.9	-12.5	-5.9	0.3	4 4 4	4.2	-15.3	-6.5
CENTRAL SECURITIES	B+	Mid-cap Value	Low	425.4	0.55	26.1	28.8	34.9	34.5	1.9	1 1 1	15.6	-5.4	6.5
CHILE	C-	Latin America	Average	305.4	1.48	15.1	2.1	2.2	-0.2	1.2	4 4 1	-6.1	-21.6	-17.8
CHINA	C-	Pacific ex-Japan	Average	157.5	2.56	-7.2	6.8	-2.7	0.8	4.1	4 1 4	-14.4	-25.6	-8.9
CLEMENTE GLOBAL GROWTH	C	World	Average	61.4	1.53	25.3	11.7	38.1	12.9	0.0	4 1 1	-15.7	-25.5	-17.9
COHEN & STEERS REALTY INCOME	B+	Real Estate	Very Low	32.1	1.45	22.5	23.0	14.0	23.8	5.3	4 1 1	23.6	-2.7	10.9
COHEN & STEERS TOTAL RETURN REALTY	B	Real Estate	Low	129.6	NA	21.6	21.4	26.0	24.8	4.9	4 1 1	3.7	-4.7	11.7
CZECH REPUBLIC	C	Europe	Average	88.2	2.00	-2.1	7.4	-8.4	4.1	0.7	4 1 4	-8.1	-23.7	-20.1
DELAWARE GROUP DIV. & INC.	A	Dom. Hybrid	Very Low	256.7	0.87	29.3	24.8	31.1	31.2	8.2	2 1 1	10.9	-0.3	3.2
DELAWARE GROUP GLOBAL DIV. & INC.	A	Dom. Hybrid	Very Low	253.6	1.71	18.2	21.0	30.0	30.0	8.7	2 1 1	10.2	-2.5	6.0
DUFF & PHELPS UTILITIES INCOME	B	Utilities	Low	1915.4	1.18	27.4	21.0	27.5	18.5	7.4	1 4 1	11.6	0.3	7.0
EMERGING GERMANY	C	Europe	Average	176.4	NA	26.4	13.1	48.4	17.8	0.5	4 1 1	-15.7	-25.9	-17.2
EMERGING MARKETS INFRASTRUCTURE	C	Div. Emg. Mkts.	Average	235.2	1.81	10.0	4.8	9.5	5.7	0.3	4 1 3	-15.0	-23.8	-15.2
EMERGING MARKETS TELECOM.	C	Div. Emg. Mkts.	Average	138.8	1.90	18.2	9.1	13.0	4.3	0.1	4 2 1	-12.9	-21.7	-13.8
EMERGING MEXICO	C-	Latin America	High	145.9	1.64	51.3	14.3	44.1	-3.5	0.0	4 1 1	-14.2	-25.1	-19.0
ENGEX	C-	Small-cap Growth	High	15.4	3.32	-21.8	9.2	-14.4	13.5	0.0	1 4 4	-19.0	-34.0	-23.5
EQUUS II	C	Dom. Hybrid	Average	140.9	13.2	27.0	28.1	44.3	32.4	2.2	3 1 1	-17.2	-36.6	-13.4
EUROPE	B+	Europe	Low	210.8	1.42	20.0	25.6	21.5	27.6	0.8	2 1 1	-8.4	-20.9	-15.6
EUROPEAN WARRANT	C	Europe	Average	180.4	1.85	64.8	46.4	79.3	46.3	0.0	2 1 1	-13.1	-25.3	-20.4
FIDELITY ADVISOR EMERGING ASIA	C-	Pacific ex-Japan	High	112.6	NA	-33.1	-7.8	-33.1	-7.2	1.1	4 1 4	-11.1	-20.1	-8.7
FIDELITY ADVISOR KOREA	F	Pacific ex-Japan	Very High	45.3	1.88	-66.7	-38.6	-58.5	-34.3	0.0	4 1 4	38.4	-15.7	23.3
FIRST AUSTRALIA	C	Pacific ex-Japan	Average	188.4	1.41	-12.5	0.6	-12.9	-1.6	2.1	4 2 4	-16.1	-24.0	-17.2
FIRST FINANCIAL	A	Financial	Low	303.6	1.04	35.8	44.0	40.4	53.3	0.6	1 1 1	24.5	-5.5	11.8
FIRST IBERIAN	B	Europe	Average	108.6	1.92	27.7	27.8	47.9	33.4	0.2	3 1 1	-8.4	-24.1	-9.6
FIRST ISRAEL	C	Foreign	Average	82.1	2.26	29.6	19.9	23.9	13.9	7.0	2 2 1	-8.5	-24.9	-17.4
FIRST PHILIPPINE	D	Pacific ex-Japan	Very High	105.2	1.75	-60.5	-28.1	-55.0	-26.3	0.0	4 1 1	8.5	-21.6	18.9
FOREIGN & COLONIAL EMERG. MIDDLE EAST	B	Foreign	Low	54.9	3.16	32.0	16.7	34.8	13.5	1.3	4 1 1	-10.0	-20.8	-9.2
FRANCE GROWTH	C	Europe	Average	218.7	1.54	15.8	18.1	19.5	16.6	5.2	4 1 1	-17.6	-23.9	-19.0
GABELLI EQUITY	B+	Mid-cap Blend	Very Low	1201.8	1.18	30.5	19.7	37.5	18.8	0.6	3 2 1	0.8	-9.4	0.9
GABELLI GLOBAL MULTIMEDIA	B	Communication	Low	92.4	1.87	35.3	18.4	40.6	13.8	0.1	4 2 1	-14.7	-21.1	-14.1
GENERAL AMERICAN INVESTORS	B+	Large-cap Blend	Low	702.6	1.05	31.7	24.8	42.2	27.0	0.7	2 1 1	-9.8	-17.6	-10.7
GERMANY	C	Europe	Average	219.2	1.26	30.1	23.6	42.6	25.8	3.7	4 1 1	-14.7	-21.4	-18.8
GLOBAL SMALL CAP	C	World	Average	61.1	1.53	10.9	9.6	14.0	9.9	0.0	4 1 3	-14.6	-24.1	-20.0
GREATER CHINA	C-	Pacific ex-Japan	High	211.7	2.07	-7.3	10.9	-7.7	7.6	3.0	4 1 4	-14.9	-26.4	-7.1
GROWTH FUND OF SPAIN	C	Europe	Average	294.4	1.25	20.2	25.1	40.5	29.3	0.6	2 1 1	-7.3	-21.9	-8.9
GT GLOBAL EASTERN EUROPE	C	Europe	Average	127.7	1.87	24.2	17.3	34.7	19.3	0.0	4 1 1	-8.6	-19.6	-11.2
H&Q HEALTHCARE INVESTORS	C	Health	Average	178.3	1.62	12.2	24.2	-5.1	17.3	0.0	1 2 2	-11.3	-25.4	-16.4

NA = Not available.

DATA: MORNINGSTAR, INC., CHICAGO, IL.

How to Use the Tables

Closed-end funds are publicly traded investment companies. Their results are measured two ways: one, by the change in net asset value (NAV), which is generated by the fund's manager; the other, by the change in the shares' market price. Total returns, which include dividends and capital gains, are shown for one- and three-year periods. The three-year figure is an average annual return. All returns are pretax.

BUSINESS WEEK RATING
Ratings are based on three-year risk-adjusted performance of the fund's portfolio. A rating is calcu-lated by subtracting a fund's risk-of-loss factor from total return. Equity funds are rated against each other, and to earn an above-average rating, must beat the S&P 500 on a risk-adjusted basis. For ratings, municipal bond funds are separated from other bond funds.

A	SUPERIOR
B+	VERY GOOD
B	ABOVE AVERAGE
C	AVERAGE
C-	BELOW AVERAGE
D	POOR
F	VERY POOR

RISK
For each fund, the monthly Treasury bill return is subtracted from the monthly NAV return in each month of the rating period. When a fund has underperformed Treasury bills, this monthly result is negative. The sum of these negative numbers is then divided by the number of months. The result is a negative number, and the greater its magnitude, the higher the risk of loss.

EXPENSE RATIO
Fund expenses for 1997 as a percent of average net assets. Ratio may include interest expense.

YIELD
Income earned during 1997, as a percentage of yearend NAV per share, adjusted for capital gains.

MATURITY
The average maturity of the securities in a bond fund, weighted according to their market value.

HISTORY
A fund's relative performance during 1995, 1996, and 1997. From left to right, the numbers designate which quartile the fund was in for each period: **1** for the top quartile; **2** for the second quartile; **3** for the third quartile; and **4** for the bottom quartile.

PREMIUM/DISCOUNT
The market price of closed-end funds is either less than the value of their securities, a discount, or more, a premium, to their NAVs.

FUND	RATING	CATEGORY	RISK	SIZE ASSETS $MIL.	FEES EXPENSE RATIO (%)	NAV. RET. (%) 1 YR.	3 YRS.	SHARES RET. (%) 1 YR.	3 YRS.	YIELD (%)	HISTORY RESULTS VS. ALL FUNDS	1997 HIGH	LOW	1/30/98
H&Q LIFE SCIENCES INVESTORS	C	Health	Average	112.8	1.61	2.1	20.4	-0.2	19.5	0.0	1 4 4	-12.9	-21.4	-17.8
HANCOCK (JOHN) BANK & THRIFT OPPORT.	A	Financial	Very Low	1137.2	1.50	60.8	45.7	100.2	60.8	0.9	1 1 1	8.3	-17.1	1.0
HERZFELD CARIBBEAN BASIN	B	World	Low	9.1	3.32	26.1	12.8	14.4	-2.1	0.0	4 2 1	3.4	-20.3	-2.5
INDIA	D	Pacific ex-Japan	High	275.8	NA	7.3	-16.4	-3.3	-11.4	0.0	4 4 4	10.2	-18.4	-14.8
INDIA GROWTH	D	Pacific ex-Japan	High	103.0	2.23	2.3	-17.8	-17.8	-19.1	0.0	4 4 4	14.7	-16.7	-13.3
INDONESIA	F	Pacific ex-Japan	Very High	16.5	1.91	-66.6	-27.0	-52.6	-27.2	0.0	4 1 4	49.1	-12.9	114.7
INVESCO GLOBAL HEALTH SCIENCES	C	Health	Average	480.8	1.21	17.5	31.3	31.0	35.9	0.0	1 1 1	-8.3	-21.3	-9.4
IRISH INVESTMENT	B+	Europe	Low	98.2	1.63	20.3	28.4	33.8	32.6	0.4	1 1 1	-6.9	-21.6	-20.4
ITALY	C	Europe	Average	116.8	1.42	22.5	12.8	23.1	10.6	0.2	4 1 1	-13.9	-22.8	-18.4
JAKARTA GROWTH	F	Pacific ex-Japan	Very High	14.2	1.94	-70.2	-30.6	-57.2	-26.1	0.6	4 2 4	26.6	-15.0	84.4
JAPAN EQUITY	D	Japan	High	61.1	0.90	-36.5	-19.9	-31.6	-17.2	0.0	4 4 4	23.8	5.5	27.6
JAPAN OVER-THE-COUNTER EQUITY	D	Japan	High	48.2	1.47	-38.7	-24.7	-27.0	-20.7	1.7	4 4 4	19.5	-7.7	16.2
JARDINE FLEMING CHINA REGION	C-	Pacific ex-Japan	High	164.4	2.18	-17.1	-1.6	-13.0	-4.2	0.4	4 1 4	-14.1	-29.5	-9.1
JARDINE FLEMING INDIA	D	Pacific ex-Japan	Very High	93.2	2.83	13.7	-16.7	-0.9	-17.0	0.0	4 4 2	12.1	-18.4	-14.2
KOREA	F	Pacific ex-Japan	Very High	661.5	1.63	-66.7	-37.8	-53.8	-30.3	0.0	4 4 4	38.9	-17.7	26.8
KOREA EQUITY	F	Pacific ex-Japan	Very High	17.3	1.89	-66.2	-40.6	-52.0	-30.4	0.0	4 4 4	43.6	-19.1	43.1
KOREAN INVESTMENT	F	Pacific ex-Japan	Very High	21.9	2.11	-65.1	-42.4	-50.8	-33.1	0.0	4 4 4	44.6	-17.4	33.6
LATIN AMERICA EQUITY	C-	Latin America	Average	148.1	1.69	14.5	3.3	9.8	-3.8	1.1	4 2 1	-11.3	-23.6	-17.8
LATIN AMERICA GROWTH	C	Latin America	Average	49.0	2.20	6.1	-0.8	3.3	-4.9	3.2	4 2 4	-14.6	-23.2	-14.4
LATIN AMERICA INVESTMENT	C-	Latin America	Average	143.1	1.70	13.1	3.2	7.9	-2.4	1.3	4 2 2	-12.5	-23.9	-19.4
LATIN AMERICAN DISCOVERY	C-	Latin America	High	236.3	1.81	42.0	15.4	48.0	6.5	0.0	4 1 1	-2.6	-15.9	-7.2
LIBERTY ALL-STAR EQUITY	B	Large-cap Blend	Low	1150.4	1.03	23.3	25.6	31.0	29.8	0.3	1 1 1	2.3	-8.2	1.6
LIBERTY ALL-STAR GROWTH	B	Large-cap Blend	Low	166.7	1.35	27.2	19.9	43.3	23.6	0.2	4 1 1	-1.5	-18.8	-0.7
MALAYSIA	F	Pacific ex-Japan	Very High	49.6	1.29	-72.7	-30.1	-61.2	-22.2	0.0	4 1 4	50.7	-14.0	76.2
MEXICO	D	Latin America	High	1314.3	1.00	51.2	15.1	45.5	1.9	1.7	4 1 1	-15.3	-27.3	-18.5
MEXICO EQUITY AND INCOME	C-	Latin America	High	214.8	1.49	60.9	22.9	53.1	4.0	1.4	4 1 1	-15.4	-25.0	-16.6
MFS SPECIAL VALUE	B	Small-cap Blend	Low	89.1	1.14	15.8	23.2	30.2	32.4	8.2	1 1 1	35.6	18.2	32.9
MORGAN FUNSHARES	B	Large-cap Growth	Low	7.4	NA	21.6	21.5	27.8	18.2	0.0	1 1 1	-7.6	-24.1	-13.2
MORGAN GRENFELL SMALLCAP	C	Small-cap Growth	Average	105.0	1.76	12.2	25.3	26.3	27.4	0.0	1 1 2	-0.6	-18.2	-5.8
MORGAN STANLEY AFRICA INVESTMENT	C	Foreign	Average	223.2	1.79	4.1	12.9	2.6	13.1	2.2	1 2 4	-7.6	-23.6	-18.9
MORGAN STANLEY ASIA-PACIFIC	C-	Div. Pacific	High	628.2	1.39	-26.4	-8.3	-23.5	-12.3	0.3	4 4 4	-14.1	-22.4	-10.6
MORGAN STANLEY EMERGING MARKETS	C-	Div. Emg. Mkts.	Average	354.2	1.87	-1.2	-1.7	-5.8	-9.7	0.1	4 2 4	-5.2	-18.1	-6.3
MORGAN STANLEY INDIA INVESTMENT	D	Pacific ex-Japan	High	315.0	2.10	0.2	-14.3	-11.8	-9.4	0.0	4 4 4	18.1	-12.9	-7.2
NAIC GROWTH	B+	Large-cap Blend	Low	17.3	NA	24.6	27.6	57.6	50.0	0.7	1 1 1	63.8	4.8	36.8
NATIONS BALANCED TARGET MATURITY	B+	Dom. Hybrid	Very Low	56.6	1.18	18.6	19.9	25.5	24.8	3.9	1 2 1	-4.3	-14.5	-9.0
NEW GERMANY	C	Europe	Average	545.4	1.01	11.9	14.7	18.9	16.4	8.7	4 1 2	-17.7	-25.6	-21.2
NEW SOUTH AFRICA	C-	Foreign	Average	63.2	1.98	-0.3	-1.1	-2.0	-2.3	0.9	2 4 4	-14.8	-23.2	-16.8
PAKISTAN INVESTMENT	F	Pacific ex-Japan	Very High	69.8	NA	26.3	-19.1	-4.7	-18.4	0.2	4 4 1	9.1	-23.2	-18.1
PETROLEUM AND RESOURCES	B	Nat. Resources	Low	556.5	0.63	19.1	23.8	12.0	21.1	2.0	1 1 1	-2.6	-14.1	-9.1
PORTUGAL	B	Europe	Average	103.4	1.62	40.5	20.4	45.0	13.6	0.1	4 1 1	-15.3	-24.5	-21.0
ROC TAIWAN	D	Pacific ex-Japan	High	313.8	2.29	13.8	0.4	9.9	-1.7	16.1	4 1 2	6.6	-29.0	-11.0
ROYCE GLOBAL	B	Int. Hybrid	Low	30.9	1.91	20.5	12.3	21.6	16.2	10.5	4 3 1	-12.6	-21.6	-13.1
ROYCE MICRO-CAP	B	Small-cap Value	Low	142.4	0.85	27.1	22.1	34.6	22.2	9.9	2 1 1	-3.7	-19.1	-6.7
ROYCE VALUE	B	Small-cap Value	Low	434.2	0.60	27.5	21.5	29.0	20.8	8.0	3 1 1	-6.9	-18.5	-11.2
SALOMON BROTHERS FUNDS	A	Large-cap Blend	Low	1708.8	0.51	24.2	30.0	28.1	37.1	0.9	1 1 1	-2.0	-15.2	-9.6
SCHRODER ASIAN GROWTH	D	Div. Pacific	High	136.6	1.57	-38.3	-12.7	-33.2	-7.9	0.0	4 2 4	-3.8	-14.4	-4.9
SCUDDER NEW ASIA	C-	Div. Pacific	High	151.2	1.87	-25.4	-9.1	-21.7	-11.8	0.3	4 4 4	-11.8	-20.2	-4.2
SCUDDER NEW EUROPE	B	Europe	Low	317.0	1.51	20.5	24.4	25.4	24.3	0.5	3 1 1	-16.4	-23.1	-20.3
SINGAPORE	D	Pacific ex-Japan	High	66.5	1.85	-44.9	-16.0	-39.4	-17.6	0.0	4 4 4	10.3	-12.8	8.0
SOURCE CAPITAL	A	Mid-cap Value	Very Low	371.3	0.89	25.5	22.8	27.3	25.2	11.9	3 1 1	4.0	-8.8	4.1
SOUTHEASTERN THRIFT & BANK	A	Financial	Very Low	102.6	1.13	59.7	43.5	85.7	48.9	0.4	1 1 1	4.9	-17.3	6.2
SOUTHERN AFRICA	C	Foreign	Average	93.0	2.04	10.6	11.4	6.7	12.7	2.8	1 4 3	-15.7	-20.9	-17.2
SPAIN	C	Europe	Average	162.5	1.73	30.0	27.1	49.4	28.6	2.6	4 1 1	-13.4	-22.7	-16.7
SWISS HELVETIA	C	Europe	Average	406.0	1.22	39.8	24.6	41.4	18.2	0.5	1 4 1	-15.4	-23.4	-21.0
TAIWAN EQUITY	D	Pacific ex-Japan	High	61.5	2.29	12.8	-0.2	12.3	-0.5	0.0	4 1 2	-13.6	-29.2	-19.8
TAIWAN	D	Pacific ex-Japan	High	325.1	2.24	-1.4	1.5	-4.7	-1.6	0.0	4 1 4	-8.0	-29.2	-12.3
TCW/DW EMERG. MKTS. OPPORT.	C	Div. Emg. Mkts.	Average	286.8	1.72	1.8	3.0	19.9	8.1	1.1	4 1 4	-4.6	-19.4	0.8
TEMPLETON CHINA WORLD	C-	Pacific ex-Japan	Average	208.5	1.65	-28.7	2.1	-30.0	-0.3	2.9	4 1 4	-8.8	-30.1	-4.2
TEMPLETON DRAGON	C	Pacific ex-Japan	Average	713.3	1.50	-22.9	5.9	-24.7	4.0	2.9	4 1 4	-12.5	-25.8	-1.9
TEMPLETON EMERGING MARKETS	C	Div. Emg. Mkts.	Average	257.5	1.67	0.4	6.6	4.7	7.2	1.4	4 1 4	20.3	3.1	22.0
TEMPLETON EMERG. MKTS. APPREC.	C	Int. Hybrid	Average	56.2	1.83	1.6	12.1	20.0	12.7	5.1	4 1 4	-6.5	-15.6	0.2
TEMPLETON VIETNAM OPPORTUNITIES	C-	Pacific ex-Japan	High	58.2	1.47	-44.1	-13.7	-36.0	-11.6	0.4	4 2 4	-3.8	-21.5	-4.2
THAI	F	Pacific ex-Japan	Very High	46.0	1.43	-77.0	-47.2	-67.1	-34.7	2.1	4 4 4	81.1	6.7	145.5
THAI CAPITAL	F	Pacific ex-Japan	Very High	18.1	2.22	-70.0	-41.2	-62.5	-31.5	0.0	4 4 4	66.7	3.8	88.0
TRI-CONTINENTAL	B+	Large-cap Blend	Low	3391.8	0.62	24.4	25.9	27.4	25.6	1.5	1 1 1	-15.9	-20.0	-17.8
TURKISH INVESTMENT	C-	Foreign	High	60.0	2.07	65.8	24.1	36.7	11.8	1.9	4 1 1	2.8	-19.4	-16.0
UNITED KINGDOM	B	Europe	Low	62.7	1.55	11.5	18.0	22.9	20.3	4.9	3 1 2	-10.6	-20.8	-12.0
Z-SEVEN	B	World	Low	21.4	NA	14.0	13.6	15.2	26.7	6.5	3 2 1	21.9	-2.4	6.3
ZWEIG	B+	Dom. Hybrid	Low	666.4	1.18	21.8	18.2	34.5	19.9	9.1	3 1 1	8.4	-6.1	10.8
ZWEIG TOTAL RETURN	B+	Dom. Hybrid	Very Low	677.1	1.03	14.1	12.6	29.7	16.6	8.9	3 2 1	11.2	-2.7	10.8

NA=Not available.

DATA: MORNINGSTAR, INC., CHICAGO, IL.

FUND	RATING	CATEGORY	RISK	SIZE ASSETS $MIL.	FEES EXPENSE RATIO (%)	NAV RET. (%) 1 YR.	NAV RET. (%) 3 YRS.	SHARES RET. (%) 1 YR.	SHARES RET. (%) 3 YRS.	YIELD (%)	MAT. (YRS.)	TREND 3-YEAR ANALYSIS	1996 HIGH	LOW	1/31/97
ACM GOVT. INCOME	F	Multisector	Very High	605.7	1.18	13.9	19.5	19.7	18.3	7.3	16.2	1 1 2	5.5	-4.2	12.0
ACM GOVT. OPPORT.	F	Multisector	Very High	112.6	1.27	10.2	14.2	20.7	11.8	7.1	11.9	1 2 3	-4.3	-14.6	-4.6
ACM GOVT. SECS.	D	Multisector	Very High	814.7	1.16	15.0	20.4	24.1	19.1	8.2	16.2	1 1 1	0.4	-10.5	-2.0
ACM GOVT. SPECTRUM	F	Multisector	Very High	267.9	1.17	10.6	12.6	13.8	8.1	9.2	15.8	2 2 3	-0.1	-10.3	-7.5
ACM MANAGED DOLLAR INCOME	C	International	Very High	173.6	1.01	19.6	29.7	33.6	29.8	9.8	15.2	1 1 1	-2.5	-11.0	2.5
ACM MANAGED INCOME	B+	Multisector	High	210.7	1.05	18.7	21.6	17.2	19.3	9.3	10.7	1 2 1	16.2	2.8	7.8
ACM MUNI. SECS. INCOME	B	Muni. Ntl. Long	Average	145.2	1.53	13.3	14.9	25.1	22.4	6.1	26.0	2 2 2	8.0	-0.5	9.5
ALL AMERICAN	B+	Interm. (Gen.)	Low	204.8	1.18	11.3	13.3	18.6	14.9	7.4	7.9	3 2 3	-6.9	-12.3	-6.2
ALLIANCE WORLD DOLLAR GOVT.	B	International	Very High	129.2	NA	15.0	32.3	26.4	27.2	8.7	18.2	1 1 1	-0.9	-12.6	4.9
ALLIANCE WORLD DOLLAR GOVT. II	F	International	Very High	962.1	1.29	14.9	24.1	28.5	30.0	11.5	21.1	2 1 1	-0.3	-11.1	7.8
ALLMERICA SECS.	C-	Interm. (Gen.)	Average	101.6	0.75	11.5	11.6	13.6	13.0	7.8	11.8	3 3 2	0.0	-11.7	-7.6
AMERICAN GOVT. INCOME	B	Interm. Govt.	Average	93.8	1.11	9.2	13.9	10.8	6.0	6.8	9.7	1 2 3	-4.0	-11.2	-7.8
AMERICAN GOVT. INCOME	B	Interm. Govt.	Low	127.2	1.31	9.5	13.6	12.4	5.9	6.7	10.3	2 2 3	-5.0	-11.1	-9.1
AMERICAN MUNI. INCOME	C-	Muni. Ntl. Long	High	71.2	0.78	12.1	17.4	15.9	15.2	5.7	19.1	1 3 2	-7.2	-13.7	-11.2
AMERICAN MUNI.	C	Muni. Ntl. Long	Low	97.3	0.64	6.3	9.7	8.9	11.5	5.6	14.8	3 4 4	-0.9	-7.1	-0.0
AMERICAN MUNI. II	C	Muni. Ntl. Long	Low	84.1	0.64	7.7	10.8	12.5	12.5	5.4	19.4	3 3 4	-1.9	-7.9	-2.7
AMERICAN MUNI. III	C-	Muni. Ntl. Long	Average	58.3	0.69	10.5	13.4	11.9	15.3	5.2	20.0	1 3 3	-3.7	-7.6	-3.8
AMERICAN OPPORT. INCOME	B	Interm. Govt.	Average	113.1	1.42	10.1	14.0	10.9	5.1	7.2	10.9	2 2 3	-5.1	-11.1	-9.3
AMERICAN SELECT	B+	Interm. (Gen.)	Low	152.9	1.03	12.9	14.3	20.1	14.1	9.3	5.1	2 2 2	-6.1	-14.9	-7.0
AMERICAN STRAT. INCOME	B	Interm. (Gen.)	Low	60.8	NA	12.2	13.0	18.8	9.1	8.2	12.6	3 2 2	-6.6	-13.9	-8.9
AMERICAN STRAT. INCOME II	B+	Interm. (Gen.)	Very Low	232.4	2.39	11.1	13.4	17.8	10.8	8.5	13.7	2 2 3	-8.4	-14.9	-8.5
AMERICAN STRAT. INCOME III	B+	Interm. (Gen.)	Very Low	297.5	1.34	11.9	12.9	16.2	13.4	9.3	12.5	3 2 2	-6.6	-13.7	-6.6
AMERICAS INCOME	F	International	Very High	58.3	1.27	12.2	14.9	18.4	9.3	7.9	11.8	4 1 2	-8.5	-20.3	-11.5
APEX MUNI.	A	Muni. Ntl. Long	Very Low	205.1	0.90	11.7	10.9	21.3	14.0	6.2	21.0	4 2 2	-0.5	-9.0	-1.2
BANCROFT CONV.	B+	Convertibles	High	94	1.20	22.2	23.0	24.7	23.6	5.8	6.6	1 1 1	-4.1	-16.2	-1.9
BEA INCOME	B	Interm. (Gen.)	Average	291.2	0.94	12.6	13.9	24.3	20.0	7.5	9.7	3 2 2	4.0	-6.0	3.4
BEA STRAT. INCOME	B+	Multisector	Low	92.9	NA	11.8	14.2	20.2	16.0	7.5	8.6	3 2 2	-4.7	-12.1	-4.3
BLACKROCK 1998	C	Interm. (Gen.)	Very Low	584.1	NA	5.4	9.2	9.1	12.7	4.7	7.1	4 2 4	-1.8	-6.2	-1.7
BLACKROCK 1999	B	Interm. (Gen.)	Very Low	212.5	NA	7.1	10.9	9.9	13.3	3.9	10.1	3 2 4	-2.8	-8.5	-5.5
BLACKROCK 2001	C	Interm. (Gen.)	Low	1326.4	0.64	9.8	11.4	13.9	12.6	4.7	9.5	3 3 3	-8.1	-13.5	-7.2
BLACKROCK ADV.AGE	C-	Long (Gen.)	High	100.7	NA	11.9	13.7	16.2	14.5	6.7	9.9	2 3 2	-11.0	-16.1	-11.1
BLACKROCK BROAD INVMT. GR. 2009	C	Multisector	High	42.7	1.12	16.5	16.4	20.2	16.9	7.8	11.3	1 3 1	-12.8	-19.0	-11.9
BLACKROCK CALIF. INS. MUNI. 2008	C	Muni. S.S. Long	Average	171.5	NA	10.8	13.0	9.8	14.5	5.1	14.8	2 3 3	-6.5	-12.5	-8.1
BLACKROCK CALIF. INVMT. QUAL. MUNI.	C	Muni. S.S. Long	High	7.5	1.42	12.1	16.1	18.6	18.8	5.7	19.8	1 3 2	5.1	-2.7	1.8
BLACKROCK FLA. INS. MUNI. 2008	C-	Muni. S.S. Long	Average	141.1	NA	9.5	11.7	12.2	16.3	5.4	13.9	2 3 3	0.5	-6.2	-1.0
BLACKROCK FLA. INVMT. QUAL. MUNI.	D	Muni. S.S. Long	High	8.3	1.46	13.1	15.5	16.8	16.4	5.3	22.1	1 4 2	-6.0	-13.4	-8.6
BLACKROCK INCOME	B	Long (Gen.)	Low	508.2	1.08	15.9	14.5	20.1	14.9	8.0	13.6	2 2 1	-11.2	-19.0	-12.0
BLACKROCK INS. MUNI. 2008	C-	Muni. Ntl. Long	Average	450.2	NA	11.4	12.9	10.9	14.0	5.2	13.4	2 3 3	-6.6	-11.0	-7.1
BLACKROCK INS. MUNI.	C	Muni. Ntl. Long	Low	287	NA	9.3	11.3	15.2	15.8	5.7	13.3	3 3 3	-1.3	-7.6	-0.6
BLACKROCK INVMT. QUAL. MUNI.	C	Muni. Ntl. Long	Average	256.9	1.12	13.4	16.7	18.7	18.3	5.6	22.7	1 2 2	-9.1	-14.0	-9.0
BLACKROCK INVMT. QUAL.	C-	Long (Gen.)	Average	347.9	0.91	12.0	13.2	18.3	14.6	7.4	12.6	2 4 2	-10.7	-17.0	-11.3
BLACKROCK MUNI. TARGET	C	Muni. Ntl. Long	Low	280	0.91	8.4	10.5	13.7	14.2	5.6	9.6	3 3 4	-1.1	-7.7	-0.6
BLACKROCK N.J. INVMT. QUAL. MUNI.	C-	Muni. S.S. Long	High	6.8	1.57	12.5	14.8	19.2	13.8	5.3	20.9	1 4 2	-7.6	-14.4	-5.3
BLACKROCK N.Y. INS. MUNI. 2008	C-	Muni. S.S. Long	Average	97.8	NA	10.8	12.6	10.9	14.7	5.4	13.1	2 4 3	-1.7	-5.6	-3.9
BLACKROCK N.Y. INVMT. QUAL. MUNI.	C-	Muni. S.S. Long	High	9.7	1.37	14.3	16.8	27.1	21.1	5.4	19.0	1 3 1	-1.5	-12.0	-2.1
BLACKROCK N. AMER. GOVT. INC.	B	International	High	446.8	0.97	9.4	18.1	14.2	17.3	8.0	13.2	1 2 3	-13.2	-19.7	-13.3
BLACKROCK STRAT.	C	Interm. Govt.	Average	546.6	NA	9.9	12.7	12.3	13.2	5.6	9.3	2 3 3	-11.2	-15.3	-11.1
BLACKROCK TARGET	C-	Interm. Govt.	Average	945.2	NA	6.7	10.5	11.5	12.0	6.1	7.4	3 2 3	-5.4	-11.0	-6.3
BULL & BEAR GLOBAL INC.	F	International	Very High	24.1	2.18	2.6	7.3	NA	NA	9.0	NA	4 2 4	6.7	-17.8	3.1
BULL & BEAR U.S. GOVT. SECS.	F	Interm. Govt.	High	11	2.10	7.2	7.0	8.5	NA	6.7	NA	4 4 4	-11.1	-17.1	-10.8
CASTLE CONV.	B+	Convertibles	Very Low	62.1	1.00	14.1	18.1	18.8	17.5	5.5	9.0	2 1 2	-8.9	-17.3	-9.9
CIGNA HIGH-INC. SHARES	A	High Yield	Low	295.5	1.07	16.2	18.1	11.5	18.8	10.2	8.2	2 1 1	18.9	7.2	6.7
CIM HIGH-YIELD SECS.	B	High Yield	Average	46.2	1.10	14.3	14.9	13.1	16.5	9.7	8.0	4 1 1	8.4	-1.6	8.2
CIRCLE INCOME SHARES	C	Interm. (Gen.)	Average	33.5	0.89	9.7	11.4	14.1	15.4	7.4	10.5	3 3 3	2.3	-11.2	1.7
CNA INCOME SHARES	A	Interm. (Gen.)	Low	83.8	NA	15.0	17.2	28.0	20.4	8.0	12.6	3 1 1	13.8	-1.0	11.2
COLONIAL HIGH-INC. MUNI.	B+	Muni. Ntl. Long	Very Low	262	1.00	9.0	9.7	13.3	15.7	6.3	22.5	4 3 3	2.1	-5.9	3.6
COLONIAL INTERMKT. INC. I	B	Multisector	Low	126	0.95	9.6	13.1	12.4	12.8	8.6	8.9	3 2 3	-2.7	-8.1	-5.8
COLONIAL INTERM. HIGH-INC.	A	High Yield	Very Low	108.4	0.98	14.8	17.3	17.4	18.8	8.9	8.2	3 1 1	6.9	0.5	4.3
COLONIAL INVMT. GR. MUNI.	C	Muni. Ntl. Long	Average	128.9	NA	11.4	11.2	9.4	11.0	6.0	23.6	3 3 2	-0.6	-8.1	-5.6
COLONIAL MUNI. INCOME	B	Muni. Ntl. Long	Very Low	203.4	NA	8.7	8.9	15.6	13.7	6.7	23.0	4 3 4	6.4	-3.2	5.5
CORPORATE HIGH-YIELD	A	High Yield	Low	328.2	NA	12.7	16.9	16.3	21.5	9.7	7.0	1 2 2	9.2	-1.0	6.4
CORPORATE HIGH-YIELD II	B+	High Yield	Average	117.6	NA	12.0	16.3	15.2	17.1	9.7	9.6	2 2 2	5.7	-1.8	2.6
CURRENT INCOME SHARES	D	Long (Gen.)	High	45.8	NA	10.5	12.3	15.3	13.4	7.0	12.9	2 4 3	-5.9	-15.6	-8.6
DEAN WITTER GOVT. INCOME	C	Interm. Govt.	Low	422.9	0.73	10.0	10.8	10.6	11.2	7.1	9.4	3 2 3	-6.9	-11.1	-7.8
DREYFUS CALIF. MUNI. INC.	B+	Muni. S.S. Long	Very Low	44.1	1.06	7.8	11.0	32.5	15.5	5.8	23.0	3 2 4	8.8	-11.4	7.7
DREYFUS MUNI. INCOME	B	Muni. Ntl. Long	Low	195.3	0.83	5.8	8.9	13.5	13.2	6.1	23.8	2 3 3	11.9	0.4	10.4
DREYFUS N.Y. MUNI. INC.	B+	Muni. S.S. Interm.	Very Low	37.8	1.03	7.3	7.8	17.9	13.6	5.7	19.8	4 4 4	8.3	-2.3	5.7
DREYFUS STRAT. GOVT. INC.	C-	Multisector	Average	152.8	0.90	11.7	12.5	19.5	13.4	12.5	8.3	3 2 2	-8.9	-14.7	-8.7
DREYFUS STRAT. MUNI. BOND	B+	Muni. Ntl. Long	Very Low	449.5	0.82	7.3	9.9	19.6	15.8	6.2	22.5	3 3 4	12.2	2.5	13.5
DREYFUS STRAT. MUNI.	B	Muni. Ntl. Long	Very Low	584.5	0.86	8.2	9.4	17.8	13.6	6.3	22.7	4 3 4	8.0	-0.9	9.2

NA=Not available.

DATA: MORNINGSTAR, INC., CHICAGO, IL.

MUTUAL FUND SCOREBOARD — Closed-End Bond Funds

FUND	RATING	CATEGORY	RISK	SIZE ASSETS $MIL.	FEES EXPENSE RATIO (%)	NAV. RET. (%) 1 YR.	NAV. RET. (%) 3 YRS.	SHARES RET. (%) 1 YR.	SHARES RET. (%) 3 YRS.	YIELD (%)	MAT. (YRS.)	TREND 3-YEAR ANALYSIS	1996 HIGH	LOW	1/31/97
DUFF & PHELPS UTILITIES T-F INC.	C–	Muni. Ntl. Long	Average	129.7	NA	11.1	12.2	12.4	16.2	5.8	21.6	2 4 3	3.0	–1.8	3.1
DUFF & PHELPS UTILITY & CORP. BOND	F	Long (Gen.)	Very High	507.7	0.80	14.3	15.3	22.2	18.7	8.2	19.9	1 4 1	0.8	–5.8	1.8
1838 BOND-DEBENTURE TRADING	F	Long (Gen.)	High	81.4	0.86	13.7	12.5	11.4	10.6	7.4	23.0	2 4 2	–3.5	–10.2	–5.9
ELLSWORTH CONV. GR. & INC.	A	Convertibles	Very Low	90.3	1.20	24.3	24.1	26.8	26.0	5.0	7.5	1 1 1	–7.1	–17.5	–10.3
EMERGING MKTS. FLOATING RATE	F	International	Very High	72.6	1.52	12.6	21.2	11.0	26.5	9.1	16.2	3 1 2	5.4	–6.2	7.2
EMERGING MKTS. INCOME	F	International	Very High	58.7	NA	15.6	32.0	21.4	34.4	10.4	15.4	1 1 1	2.6	–13.3	5.8
EMERGING MKTS. INCOME II	F	International	Very High	337.4	1.37	15.5	32.3	19.2	32.2	9.8	16.0	1 1 1	1.2	–10.3	2.7
EXCELSIOR INCOME SHARES	C–	Interm. (Gen.)	Average	40.1	NA	9.1	11.0	14.2	12.5	7.0	10.9	3 4 3	–9.2	–15.3	–8.7
FIRST AUSTRALIA PRIME INC.	F	International	Very High	1194.6	1.29	–13.4	6.1	–9.8	6.9	11.1	6.8	4 1 4	1.4	–10.1	–1.8
FIRST COMMONWEALTH	F	International	Very High	96.7	NA	–0.6	12.3	8.9	14.7	8.2	8.5	3 1 4	–6.9	–16.4	–9.0
FORT DEARBORN INC. SECS.	F	Long (Gen.)	High	145.8	0.75	13.1	13.5	14.8	15.6	6.9	19.1	2 4 2	–3.4	–10.1	–6.3
FORTIS SECS.	C	Interm. (Gen.)	Low	120.7	0.80	13.4	12.6	24.8	13.9	8.0	15.3	3 2 2	–1.9	–10.1	–0.6
FRANKLIN MULTI-INC.	B+	Multisector	High	68.4	3.21	23.2	20.8	21.1	21.6	7.0	9.1	1 2 1	–8.3	–14.0	–7.2
FRANKLIN PRINCIPAL MATURITY	B+	Multisector	Average	207.2	3.06	15.0	17.0	18.2	20.3	5.8	4.6	3 1 1	–3.8	–12.0	–4.8
FRANKLIN UNIVERSAL	B+	Multisector	Average	378.5	2.17	18.0	18.6	23.5	20.5	7.8	8.4	1 2 1	–2.2	–9.9	–3.0
GABELLI CONV. SECS.	B+	Convertibles	Very Low	109.2	1.45	8.0	10.4	16.2	NA	3.7	8.7	4 2 4	–10.8	–16.4	–8.2
GLOBAL HIGH INC. DOLLAR	C	International	Very High	353	1.43	11.8	19.9	15.2	20.1	9.4	17.0	2 1 2	–12.7	–17.4	–11.9
GLOBAL PARTNERS INCOME	B	International	Very High	226.4	1.32	15.5	27.7	19.1	30.0	10.7	13.2	1 1 1	–1.9	–9.7	1.8
GREENWICH ST. CALIF. MUNI.	C–	Muni. S.S. Long	High	51.1	1.15	12.1	14.5	15.4	15.7	4.6	23.6	1 3 2	–2.0	–9.9	–9.2
GREENWICH ST. MUNI.	F	Muni. Ntl. Long	High	235.4	1.06	6.8	10.1	6.6	12.5	5.6	22.6	2 4 4	2.0	–5.7	–0.9
HANCOCK INCOME SECS.	C–	Interm. (Gen.)	Average	173.9	0.84	10.3	11.6	21.6	15.6	7.2	12.7	3 3 3	0.3	–8.3	1.5
HANCOCK INVESTORS	C–	Interm. (Gen.)	Average	167.1	NA	10.3	11.7	22.1	16.2	7.2	12.6	3 3 3	2.5	–8.7	3.5
HANCOCK PATRIOT GLOBAL DIV.	B+	Long (Gen.)	Average	127.2	1.27	17.9	19.1	14.8	19.5	7.9	NA	1 2 1	–8.4	–13.9	–12.5
HANCOCK PATRIOT PREF. DIV.	A	Long (Gen.)	Low	103.8	NA	15.1	18.2	17.4	22.0	8.0	NA	1 2 1	4.7	–4.1	1.8
HANCOCK PATRIOT PREM. DIV. I	B+	Long (Gen.)	High	158.6	2.20	21.6	20.3	7.2	18.5	7.5	NA	1 2 1	4.3	–9.8	–3.6
HANCOCK PATRIOT PREM. DIV. II	B+	Long (Gen.)	High	200.1	NA	21.5	21.6	14.7	19.9	7.6	NA	1 2 1	–4.2	–11.5	–10.1
HANCOCK PATRIOT SEL. DIV.	B+	Long (Gen.)	High	167.1	1.25	19.8	20.0	19.0	19.8	8.7	NA	1 2 1	–2.7	–9.4	–8.9
HATTERAS INCOME SECS.	D	Interm. (Gen.)	Average	54.2	NA	9.3	10.6	11.1	8.2	7.7	14.1	3 4 3	–7.6	–11.7	–5.7
HERITAGE U.S. GOVT. INCOME	D	Interm. Govt.	High	37.7	NA	9.6	10.8	11.0	13.4	8.9	8.8	3 4 3	1.5	–9.8	–5.4
HIGH INCOME ADV.	C	High Yield	Low	152.2	0.92	8.9	11.0	9.9	15.0	10.8	7.5	4 2 4	25.5	16.3	19.6
HIGH INCOME ADV. II	C	High Yield	Low	203.9	0.91	9.9	11.6	10.9	15.5	11.7	7.0	4 2 3	17.4	9.1	15.3
HIGH INCOME ADV. III	C	High Yield	Average	79.7	0.98	9.8	11.2	14.9	15.1	10.5	7.0	4 2 3	22.6	11.4	18.3
HIGH INCOME OPPORT.	B+	High Yield	Low	8696.1	1.21	12.6	15.1	19.2	19.9	8.9	8.4	3 2 2	2.4	–3.7	3.6
HIGH-YIELD INCOME	B+	High Yield	Average	85.8	2.89	14.5	16.1	11.9	15.9	9.3	7.9	3 2 1	10.1	1.2	4.3
HIGH-YIELD PLUS	A	High Yield	Low	98.2	1.08	12.9	15.8	12.8	20.6	8.8	8.0	2 2 2	7.5	2.0	7.2
HIGHLANDER INCOME	A	Multisector	Low	29.1	1.44	13.0	15.5	17.0	11.9	8.4	9.2	2 2 2	–5.1	–14.8	–9.4
HYPERION 1999	F	Interm. Govt.	High	444.8	NA	9.7	5.8	12.4	9.2	8.4	10.1	4 4 3	–4.2	–9.6	–4.3
HYPERION 2002	D	Long Govt.	High	290.4	3.40	14.3	13.5	17.7	15.3	6.1	15.2	2 4 1	–10.4	–15.1	–11.7
HYPERION 2005 INVMT. GR. OPPORT.	C–	Long Govt.	High	100.9	NA	18.7	15.3	21.4	15.4	7.2	18.4	2 4 1	–11.4	–17.3	–9.8
HYPERION TOTAL RETURN	C	Multisector	Average	248.5	3.42	12.4	14.6	12.9	16.5	8.2	13.7	2 2 2	–4.9	–14.9	–11.4
INA INVMT. SECS.	D	Interm. (Gen.)	Average	91.8	NA	10.2	10.4	16.1	12.0	7.1	12.3	3 4 3	–9.0	–15.4	–7.3
INCOME OPPORTUNITIES 1999	B+	Interm. (Gen.)	Very Low	425.2	0.65	8.4	13.0	12.1	15.6	6.0	13.4	2 2 4	–4.1	–8.9	–4.1
INCOME OPPORTUNITIES 2000	C	Interm. (Gen.)	Average	111	NA	8.6	12.8	14.4	16.8	6.7	17.0	2 2 4	–4.6	–10.6	–6.0
INDEPENDENCE SQUARE INCOME	D	Interm. (Gen.)	High	33.3	0.68	10.4	11.9	17.9	13.0	7.3	19.7	2 4 3	–3.8	–11.7	–5.5
INSURED MUNI. INCOME	F	Muni. Ntl. Long	Very High	168.2	1.33	9.4	14.7	20.6	17.0	5.7	27.1	1 4 3	–9.1	–17.3	–10.9
INTERCAPITAL CALIF. INS. MUNI. INC.	D	Muni. S.S. Long	Very High	184.7	NA	12.7	15.7	20.5	14.2	5.6	24.7	1 3 2	–4.4	–11.2	–6.9
INTERCAPITAL CALIF. QUAL. MUNI.	D	Muni. S.S. Long	Very High	155.6	NA	14.3	17.7	22.6	18.3	5.4	25.5	1 3 1	–5.1	–15.1	–6.8
INTERCAPITAL INCOME SECS.	D	Long (Gen.)	High	218.9	0.65	14.0	12.9	20.2	12.2	7.7	22.2	3 2 2	–8.2	–12.3	–4.4
INTERCAPITAL INS. CALIF. MUNI.	C–	Muni. S.S. Long	Average	0.3	NA	10.0	12.4	12.3	16.1	5.4	25.6	2 3 3	–1.9	–8.5	–4.9
INTERCAPITAL INS. MUNI. BOND	B	Muni. Ntl. Long	Low	79.9	NA	8.0	10.3	22.2	12.5	5.9	22.8	3 3 4	5.8	–5.8	5.9
INTERCAPITAL INS. MUNI. INC.	C–	Muni. Ntl. Long	High	435.3	NA	14.1	16.4	23.9	15.2	5.8	24.8	1 3 2	–7.2	–15.5	–9.2
INTERCAPITAL INS. MUNI.	C–	Muni. Ntl. Long	Average	139.2	NA	10.5	12.5	18.7	14.8	5.6	24.6	2 3 3	–4.4	–12.8	–4.7
INTERCAPITAL INS. MUNI.	C	Muni. Ntl. Long	Average	357	NA	7.7	11.3	13.7	14.3	5.7	25.6	2 3 4	1.2	–6.8	–0.4
INTERCAPITAL N.Y. QUAL. MUNI.	C–	Muni. S.S. Long	High	72.2	NA	14.8	16.8	22.6	18.3	5.4	22.6	1 3 1	–9.9	–16.0	–8.9
INTERCAPITAL QUAL. MUNI. INC.	B	Muni. Ntl. Long	Average	534.1	0.68	10.6	13.2	15.7	18.2	6.3	20.1	2 3 3	–1.2	–7.0	–4.0
INTERCAPITAL QUAL. MUNI. INVMT.	B	Muni. Ntl. Long	Low	279.7	NA	10.0	11.5	19.6	15.3	6.1	22.3	3 3 3	0.5	–6.0	1.1
INTERCAPITAL QUAL. MUNI.	C–	Muni. Ntl. Long	High	267.4	NA	14.9	17.7	22.9	18.5	5.7	21.7	1 3 1	–10.9	–16.6	–9.9
INVESTMENT GRADE MUNI.	B	Muni. Ntl. Long	Average	95.4	1.34	9.9	13.5	20.5	15.5	5.8	25.6	2 2 3	–8.4	–17.3	–9.6
KEMPER HIGH-INCOME	B+	High Yield	Low	222.6	1.59	11.4	14.7	11.7	18.6	8.1	8.0	3 1 2	11.3	2.9	7.1
KEMPER INTERM. GOVT.	D	Short Govt.	Average	267.2	0.95	8.5	9.5	13.8	11.7	8.4	10.8	3 4 4	–1.1	–9.0	–2.1
KEMPER MULTI-MARKET INC.	C	Multisector	Average	219.2	0.99	8.8	12.4	2.2	13.1	7.7	10.6	3 2 4	2.7	–6.9	–5.6
KEMPER MUNI. INCOME	B	Muni. Ntl. Long	Low	476	1.04	8.9	10.6	15.5	19.4	6.1	22.9	3 3 3	15.2	6.0	15.2
KEMPER STRAT. INCOME	C–	Multisector	Very High	53.4	1.23	11.5	21.9	17.8	30.5	8.4	10.2	1 1 2	34.7	13.0	30.2
KEMPER STRAT. MUNI. INC.	B+	Muni. Ntl. Interm.	Very Low	131.8	0.74	9.0	9.2	12.7	13.2	6.2	19.5	4 2 3	11.9	9	9.2
KLEINWORT BENSON AUSTRALIAN INC.	F	International	Very High	109.2	1.22	–7.6	7.4	–7.3	6.4	9.7	6.8	4 1 4	–7.3	–13.4	–9.1
LIBERTY 1999	C–	Interm. Govt.	Low	38.8	0.90	9.5	9.3	11.8	11.2	5.1	10.7	4 3 3	–4.3	–8.5	–5.2
LINCOLN NATIONAL CONV. SECS.	F	Convertibles	Very High	135.8	1.05	12.4	18.2	20.0	21.5	5.0	6.9	3 1 2	–1.7	–14.0	–3.9
LINCOLN NATIONAL INCOME	C	Long (Gen.)	Average	95.5	NA	11.7	15.0	17.1	19.0	9.1	12.4	1 2 2	0.5	–8.6	1.6
MANAGED HIGH-INCOME	A	High Yield	Low	488	1.20	13.2	15.6	20.2	21.1	8.9	8.4	3 1 2	3.9	–1.8	4.2
MANAGED HIGH-YIELD	B	High Yield	Average	86.1	1.25	13.5	15.0	20.1	17.5	8.8	8.2	4 1 2	0.6	–6.1	0.1

NA=Not available.

DATA: MORNINGSTAR, INC., CHICAGO, IL.

FUND	RATING	CATEGORY	RISK	SIZE ASSETS $MIL.	FEES EXPENSE RATIO (%)	NAV. RET. (%) 1 YR.	3 YRS.	SHARES RET. (%) 1 YR.	3 YRS.	YIELD (%)	MAT. (YRS.)	TREND 3-YEAR ANALYSIS	1996 HIGH	LOW	1/31/97
MANAGED MUNIS	D	Muni. Ntl. Long	Average	428.9	1.00	10.1	11.1	12.1	14.5	5.2	23.8	3 4 3	0.5	−7.2	−2.4
MANAGED MUNIS II	D	Muni. Ntl. Long	Average	138.5	1.10	8.1	10.6	6.9	11.7	5.5	25.2	3 4 4	−1.3	−7.2	−0.0
MASS. HEALTH & EDUC. T-E	C	Muni. S.S. Long	Average	21.5	NA	13.1	13.6	21.7	17.1	5.3	21.5	2 3 2	2.2	−7.3	1.7
MENTOR INCOME	D	Interm. Govt.	High	121.2	1.13	9.3	11.9	18.8	15.6	8.8	17.1	2 3 3	−4.7	−11.7	−4.8
MFS CHARTER INCOME	C	Multisector	Low	723.4	0.93	10.2	12.4	10.7	13.4	8.1	8.6	3 2 3	−6.7	−11.1	−8.9
MFS GOVT. MKTS. INCOME	C−	Multisector	Average	526.5	1.00	7.1	10.4	5.2	10.8	7.6	11.4	3 3 4	−7.4	−13.0	−11.0
MFS INTERM. INCOME	C	Multisector	Low	1097.4	0.97	7.0	10.6	5.8	12.7	8.1	7.9	3 2 4	−5.2	−12.0	−4.4
MFS MULTIMARKET INCOME	C	Multisector	Average	733.2	1.11	9.9	13.2	7.3	13.7	8.7	10.7	3 2 3	−5.0	−11.9	−7.5
MFS MUNI. INCOME	B+	Muni. Ntl. Long	Very Low	331.9	1.24	7.6	7.6	6.3	9.9	6.9	18.5	4 4 4	17.3	6.5	11.3
MINNESOTA MUNI. INCOME	C−	Muni. S.S. Long	High	61.4	0.82	8.7	17.0	14.8	16.2	5.6	19.6	1 2 4	−3.7	−12.0	−5.9
MINNESOTA MUNI.	B	Muni. S.S. Long	Low	65.5	0.98	7.3	10.2	12.5	12.8	5.5	17.4	3 3 4	−0.4	−7.5	1.0
MINNESOTA MUNI. II	B	Muni. S.S. Long	Low	37.8	1.06	8.3	11.3	10.8	14.0	5.5	17.3	2 3 4	0.3	−6.5	−1.9
MONTGOMERY STREET INC. SECS.	C	Long (Gen.)	Average	207.3	NA	12.2	13.2	21.2	16.1	7.4	11.8	2 2 2	−4.0	−12.0	−4.5
MORGAN STANLEY EMG. MKTS.	D	International	Very High	354.2	1.38	21.3	32.2	40.3	35.4	6.7	10.6	2 1 1	0.1	−12.2	6.6
MORGAN STANLEY GLOBAL OPPORT.	C−	International	Very High	57.1	NA	18.3	23.3	14.8	20.6	8.3	8.4	3 1 1	4.8	−12.1	0.6
MORGAN STANLEY HIGH-YIELD	A	High Yield	Average	133	1.12	18.4	20.6	23.6	24.9	8.2	11.2	1 1 1	3.6	−3.4	5.7
MUNIASSETS	A	Muni. Ntl. Long	Very Low	151.3	0.55	12.1	12.6	21.0	15.6	6.0	21.0	3 2 2	−3.4	−12.7	−3.0
MUNICIPAL ADVANTAGE	C−	Muni. Ntl. Long	High	108.3	NA	13.0	15.5	23.8	19.4	5.8	21.3	1 3 2	−6.9	−15.5	−8.3
MUNICIPAL HIGH-INC.	A	Muni. Ntl. Long	Very Low	874	0.77	9.8	10.9	17.7	15.6	6.2	22.2	3 2 3	3.3	−4.6	2.9
MUNICIPAL INCOME	C	Muni. Ntl. Long	Low	303.5	0.63	9.2	9.3	17.3	10.0	5.3	20.1	4 3 3	−2.3	−10.1	−4.5
MUNICIPAL INCOME II	B	Muni. Ntl. Long	Low	275.1	NA	9.3	9.4	12.3	9.1	5.3	20.3	4 3 3	−4.4	−10.8	−5.6
MUNICIPAL INCOME III	C	Muni. Ntl. Long	Low	63.4	NA	8.7	8.9	12.7	8.2	5.4	20.3	4 4 4	−2.2	−9.1	−4.2
MUNICIPAL INCOME OPPORTUNITIES	A	Muni. Ntl. Long	Very Low	181.8	1.07	10.0	9.3	14.3	12.8	6.1	18.2	4 2 3	6.6	−0.8	4.5
MUNICIPAL INCOME OPPORTUNITIES II	A	Muni. Short	Very Low	178.8	1.01	10.1	10.5	11.6	14.3	6.7	19.5	4 2 3	3.1	−5.2	−0.7
MUNICIPAL INCOME OPPORTUNITIES III	A	Muni. Short	Very Low	105.1	1.06	9.6	10.5	9.7	17.6	6.8	21.1	4 2 3	8.4	−3.3	6.0
MUNICIPAL PARTNERS	B+	Muni. Ntl. Long	Average	84.2	NA	13.0	16.2	21.8	18.4	5.9	28.8	1 3 2	−7.6	−15.9	−7.3
MUNICIPAL PARTNERS II	B	Muni. Ntl. Long	High	85	1.44	13.3	16.8	20.9	19.3	5.8	26.0	1 3 2	−8.7	−16.0	−7.6
MUNICIPAL PREM. INCOME	C	Muni. Ntl. Long	Low	253	1.14	9.4	11.1	15.9	12.7	6.0	20.4	1 3 2	−3.6	−11.1	−3.9
MUNIENHANCED	D	Muni. Ntl. Long	High	350.5	0.68	10.2	12.2	20.2	16.3	5.9	21.8	2 4 3	−2.3	−10.4	−0.5
MUNIINSURED	C	Muni. Ntl. Long	Average	81	NA	10.0	10.8	20.3	11.7	5.4	23.2	3 3 3	−4.4	−13.9	−3.5
MUNIVEST	C	Muni. Ntl. Long	Average	607.3	0.93	10.8	12.9	17.9	17.4	6.2	21.5	2 3 3	−0.3	−8.5	−0.6
MUNIVEST II	C	Muni. Ntl. Long	Average	289.5	NA	11.1	13.8	22.7	19.4	6.1	21.7	2 3 3	−2.4	−10.7	−2.0
MUNIVEST FLA.	C−	Muni. S.S. Long	Average	82.8	NA	10.7	12.8	12.7	17.1	5.6	23.5	2 3 3	0.2	−7.4	−1.1
MUNIVEST MICH. INS.	C−	Muni. S.S. Long	High	102.9	NA	9.4	13.0	18.9	15.5	5.8	20.6	1 4 3	−1.4	−10.5	−6.1
MUNIVEST N.J.	C−	Muni. S.S. Long	Average	78.1	NA	10.1	12.8	18.4	16.2	5.7	22.1	2 4 3	−1.2	−9.8	−0.3
MUNIVEST PA. INS.	D	Muni. S.S. Long	High	53.2	NA	12.0	12.6	19.5	16.0	5.6	21.3	2 4 2	−3.4	−11.5	−5.0
MUNIYIELD	B	Muni. Ntl. Long	Average	597	0.64	11.9	13.6	17.3	18.8	6.0	23.2	2 2 2	2.4	−5.4	0.4
MUNIYIELD ARIZ.	C−	Muni. S.S. Long	High	60.2	NA	12.1	14.0	15.9	13.3	5.6	18.2	1 4 2	−2.2	−10.2	−3.7
MUNIYIELD CALIF.	B	Muni. S.S. Long	Average	268.2	0.67	10.2	13.5	17.1	20.0	5.7	21.7	2 2 3	1.2	−5.1	0.4
MUNIYIELD CALIF. INS.	C−	Muni. S.S. Long	High	247.5	NA	11.4	13.9	15.6	18.5	5.7	23.9	1 4 2	1.7	−5.5	−2.1
MUNIYIELD CALIF. INS. II	D	Muni. S.S. Long	High	282.3	NA	11.5	13.7	14.3	17.1	5.7	22.9	1 4 2	−0.4	−6.7	−2.3
MUNIYIELD FLA.	D	Muni. S.S. Long	Average	122.6	NA	9.8	11.7	15.2	17.2	5.5	23.3	2 3 3	2.6	−4.9	2.1
MUNIYIELD FLA. INS.	F	Muni. S.S. Long	High	129.1	NA	10.5	12.2	15.9	18.2	5.4	21.9	2 4 3	1.1	−7.0	0.6
MUNIYIELD INS.	C−	Muni. Ntl. Long	Average	913.3	NA	11.1	13.3	21.6	17.8	5.9	23.4	2 3 3	−2.1	−9.0	−4.2
MUNIYIELD MICH.	C	Muni. S.S. Long	Average	120.1	NA	9.1	11.9	18.7	15.2	5.7	19.6	2 3 3	−0.2	−9.3	0.3
MUNIYIELD MICH. INS.	D	Muni. S.S. Long	High	114.3	NA	9.2	12.1	13.4	15.2	5.6	21.0	2 4 3	−3.9	−11.1	−5.3
MUNIYIELD N.J.	C	Muni. S.S. Long	Average	137.7	NA	9.0	11.2	15.6	17.8	5.6	20.6	2 4 3	2.9	−4.1	2.8
MUNIYIELD N.J. INS.	D	Muni. S.S. Long	Average	130	NA	9.4	11.4	14.2	16.9	5.7	22.6	2 4 3	6.1	−3.3	4.7
MUNIYIELD N.Y. INS.	D	Muni. S.S. Long	High	191.7	NA	10.2	11.8	16.8	16.7	5.6	23.0	2 4 3	4.0	−5.8	2.5
MUNIYIELD N.Y. INS. II	D	Muni. S.S. Long	High	319.8	NA	11.8	12.4	26.4	16.3	5.4	20.9	2 4 2	0.7	−12.5	−3.8
MUNIYIELD PA.	C	Muni. S.S. Long	Average	90.6	NA	11.9	12.5	16.3	15.8	5.8	21.3	2 4 2	−0.3	−8.3	0.8
MUNIYIELD QUAL.	B	Muni. Ntl. Long	Average	459.7	NA	12.1	13.3	22.7	16.9	6.1	22.1	2 4 2	−1.8	−11.7	−2.9
MUNIYIELD QUAL II	B	Muni. Ntl. Long	Average	340.1	NA	12.2	14.2	20.1	18.0	6.0	22.5	2 3 2	−2.0	−9.9	−3.4
NATIONS GOVT. INCOME 2003	B	Long Govt.	High	140.9	0.27	13.1	18.0	18.0	18.0	6.7	13.0	1 2 2	−3.6	−13.0	−9.3
NATIONS GOVT. INCOME 2004	B	Interm. Govt.	Average	124.2	NA	12.6	17.2	18.2	17.3	7.0	11.4	1 2 2	−4.0	−13.4	−8.6
NEW AMERICA HIGH-INC.	A	High Yield	Average	243.6	0.73	14.2	19.5	25.9	25.3	8.0	8.2	1 1 1	12.7	−5.8	5.6
N.Y. TAX-EXEMPT INCOME	B+	Muni. S.S. Interm.	Very Low	2.4	NA	7.5	8.9	14.8	13.4	5.7	22.7	4 3 4	12.0	2.1	14.6
NUVEEN ARIZ. PREM. INC. MUNI.	C−	Muni. S.S. Long	Average	66.5	0.90	10.2	13.2	22.8	18.2	5.3	18.3	1 4 3	4.9	−7.8	4.2
NUVEEN CALIF. INVMT. QUAL.	B+	Muni. S.S. Long	Low	211.2	0.81	8.2	10.3	12.0	13.7	5.8	21.2	3 3 4	8.5	1.8	5.3
NUVEEN CALIF. MUNI. MKT. OPPORT.	B	Muni. S.S. Long	Average	130.3	0.82	9.1	11.3	11.5	16.5	5.8	23.2	2 4 3	9.2	1.7	6.2
NUVEEN CALIF. MUNI. VALUE	B	Muni. S.S. Interm.	Very Low	258.7	0.77	8.3	8.2	2.5	7.4	5.8	20.5	4 3 4	4.0	−7.0	−4.6
NUVEEN CALIF. PERF. PLUS MUNI.	B+	Muni. S.S. Interm.	Low	200.6	0.80	8.3	10.3	10.3	17.9	5.9	21.8	3 3 4	12.9	4.2	10.0
NUVEEN CALIF. PREM. INC. MUNI.	C	Muni. S.S. Long	High	80.4	1.41	11.6	16.6	14.8	19.5	5.4	20.3	1 3 2	−1.0	−8.7	2.5
NUVEEN CALIF. QUAL. INC. MUNI.	B+	Muni. S.S. Long	Low	348.2	0.79	9.8	12.7	13.3	18.7	5.8	21.1	2 2 3	6.1	−1.2	3.1
NUVEEN CALIF. SELECT QUAL. MUNI.	B	Muni. S.S. Long	Low	359.4	0.79	9.2	11.9	11.0	17.8	5.9	22.8	2 3 3	7.8	0.8	4.9
NUVEEN CONN. PREM. INC. MUNI.	C−	Muni. S.S. Long	High	74.8	0.89	12.0	14.8	16.2	19.5	5.2	20.6	1 4 2	9.1	−2.2	9.0
NUVEEN FLA. INVMT. QUAL. MUNI.	C	Muni. S.S. Interm.	Low	256	NA	8.0	7.5	9.4	17.2	5.5	21.4	4 4 3	13.0	2.6	11.7
NUVEEN FLA. QUAL. INC. MUNI.	C	Muni. S.S. Long	Average	225.7	0.82	8.6	11.0	14.5	17.5	5.5	22.0	3 3 4	6.1	−2.7	3.1
NUVEEN GA. PREM. INC. MUNI.	C−	Muni. S.S. Long	High	54.2	0.91	12.5	15.5	16.9	19.1	5.3	21.4	1 4 2	5.1	−4.5	2.2
NUVEEN INS. CALIF. PREM. INC. MUNI.	F	Muni. S.S. Long	Very High	103.1	1.29	12.7	15.3	16.7	15.8	5.3	24.3	1 4 2	−1.1	−8.5	−3.9

NA=Not available.

DATA: MORNINGSTAR, INC., CHICAGO, IL.

FUND	RATING	CATEGORY	RISK	SIZE ASSETS $MIL.	FEES EXPENSE RATIO (%)	NAV RET.(%) 1 YR.	NAV RET.(%) 3 YRS.	SHARES RET.(%) 1 YR.	SHARES RET.(%) 3 YRS.	YIELD (%)	MAT. (YRS.)	TREND 3-YEAR ANALYSIS	1996 HIGH	LOW	1/31/97
NUVEEN INS. CALIF. PREM. INC. MUNI. 2	D	Muni. S.S. Long	High	183.6	1.31	11.7	15.5	15.2	17.5	5.4	21.7	1 3 2	-1.2	-9.2	-4.2
NUVEEN INS. CALIF. SEL. T-F INC.	C	Muni. S.S. Long	Average	95.3	0.44	8.8	10.6	10.4	11.5	5.5	21.4	3 3 4	-0.8	-5.5	-3.4
NUVEEN INS. FLA. PREM. INC. MUNI.	F	Muni. S.S. Long	High	221.2	0.81	11.7	14.3	18.7	17.6	5.2	21.8	1 4 2	-2.4	-7.3	-2.8
NUVEEN INS. MUNI. OPPORT.	C	Muni. Ntl. Long	Average	1276.8	NA	8.9	11.6	15.2	17.6	6.0	23.9	2 3 3	4.2	-1.9	2.9
NUVEEN INS. N.Y. PREM. INC. MUNI.	D	Muni. S.S. Long	High	125.6	0.86	11.4	14.7	15.8	18.5	5.4	23.4	1 4 3	1.3	-4.5	0.5
NUVEEN INS. N.Y. SEL. T-F INC.	C	Muni. S.S. Long	Low	58.4	0.48	8.5	10.0	14.9	13.1	5.3	20.5	3 3 4	1.3	-7.4	4.5
NUVEEN INS. PREM. INC. MUNI. 2	D	Muni. Ntl. Long	High	515.5	NA	11.4	15.0	18.7	17.0	5.6	19.5	1 4 2	-5.4	-12.3	-5.5
NUVEEN INS. QUAL. MUNI.	C-	Muni. Ntl. Long	Average	596.2	NA	8.8	10.7	15.8	15.9	5.9	23.4	3 3 4	3.4	-3.0	0.9
NUVEEN INVMT. QUAL. MUNI.	C	Muni. Ntl. Interm.	Low	566.5	0.78	9.7	10.5	17.7	14.3	6.2	21.3	3 4 3	0.8	-6.2	3.0
NUVEEN MD. PREM. INC. MUNI.	C	Muni. S.S. Long	Average	150.8	0.87	11.0	14.9	14.9	19.8	5.2	19.0	1 4 3	3.2	-3.5	2.2
NUVEEN MASS. PREM. INC. MUNI.	B	Muni. S.S. Long	Average	68.9	0.88	11.9	14.8	24.1	19.1	5.2	20.4	1 4 2	8.4	-1.2	8.5
NUVEEN MICH. PREM. INC. MUNI.	C	Muni. S.S. Long	Average	117.4	0.87	11.7	14.4	21.3	19.3	5.4	18.7	1 4 2	-2.2	-12.2	-1.0
NUVEEN MICH. QUAL. INC. MUNI.	C	Muni. S.S. Long	Average	181.3	0.83	9.3	11.3	14.3	16.7	5.5	22.4	2 4 3	10.3	0.5	6.8
NUVEEN MO. PREM. INC. MUNI.	C-	Muni. S.S. Long	High	30.9	1.01	11.3	15.1	18.9	16.1	5.2	18.2	1 4 3	1.1	-10.5	-1.9
NUVEEN MUNI. ADV.	B	Muni. Ntl. Interm.	Low	669.7	0.78	8.8	10.4	13.9	14.0	6.4	22.3	3 3 4	3.3	-3.9	3.1
NUVEEN MUNI. INCOME	B+	Muni. Ntl. Interm.	Very Low	94.7	0.80	8.1	8.9	12.1	11.1	6.2	22.1	4 3 4	6.8	-3.4	2.6
NUVEEN MUNI. MKT. OPPORT.	B	Muni. Ntl. Interm.	Low	716	0.77	8.6	10.3	16.9	14.7	6.4	21.6	3 3 4	2.8	-5.1	2.8
NUVEEN MUNI. VALUE	B	Muni. Ntl. Long	Low	2000.6	0.69	9.3	9.3	15.1	8.5	5.9	21.1	4 3 3	-3.5	-10.7	-4.1
NUVEEN N.J. INVMT. QUAL. MUNI.	B	Muni. S.S. Long	Low	309.2	0.81	8.6	10.2	14.0	15.5	5.7	18.3	3 3 4	8.6	1.4	9.6
NUVEEN N.J. PREM. INC. MUNI.	B	Muni. S.S. Long	Average	182.5	0.86	11.5	13.2	20.2	18.1	5.6	18.3	2 4 2	2.0	-6.3	0.2
NUVEEN N.Y. INVMT. QUAL. MUNI.	B	Muni. S.S. Interm.	Very Low	276.6	0.82	8.1	8.4	11.9	16.0	6.0	22.2	3 4 4	16.2	5.0	12.2
NUVEEN N.Y. MUNI. VALUE	B+	Muni. S.S. Interm.	Very Low	154.5	0.83	7.1	7.2	7.6	7.8	5.8	20.5	4 4 4	6.4	-0.3	3.3
NUVEEN N.Y. PERF. PL. MUNI.	B	Muni. S.S. Interm.	Very Low	238.6	0.82	6.4	8.6	14.1	15.3	6.0	22.7	4 4 4	16.8	5.1	15.3
NUVEEN N.Y. QUAL. INC. MUNI.	C	Muni. S.S. Long	Average	373.3	0.79	8.5	10.9	17.1	17.1	5.6	22.6	3 4 4	7.3	-1.1	3.6
NUVEEN N.Y. SEL. QUAL. MUNI.	C	Muni. S.S. Long	Low	365.7	0.80	6.8	9.5	16.3	16.3	5.7	22.5	3 4 4	9.0	-0.6	7.0
NUVEEN N.C. PREM. INC.	D	Muni. S.S. Long	High	90.2	0.88	13.2	15.1	19.9	17.1	5.4	21.0	1 4 2	8.8	-2.1	9.8
NUVEEN OHIO QUAL. INC. MUNI.	C	Muni. S.S. Long	Average	155.8	0.87	10.0	12.5	19.8	18.4	5.3	21.0	2 3 3	10.1	0.4	8.6
NUVEEN PA. INVMT. QUAL. MUNI.	B	Muni. S.S. Long	Low	254.5	NA	7.3	9.6	14.4	14.9	5.9	20.9	3 3 4	7.6	-1.1	9.7
NUVEEN PA. PREM. INC. MUNI. 2	C	Muni. S.S. Long	Average	233.3	0.84	11.4	15.1	20.8	17.2	5.5	21.3	1 3 2	-5.1	-10.9	-5.3
NUVEEN PERF. PLUS MUNI.	B	Muni. Ntl. Interm.	Very Low	913.2	0.78	8.6	9.6	14.5	13.6	6.4	21.8	4 3 4	2.8	-2.9	3.6
NUVEEN PREM. INS. MUNI. INC.	C-	Muni. Ntl. Long	Average	305.7	NA	9.2	11.4	17.3	16.3	5.8	21.2	2 4 3	1.8	-4.8	1.1
NUVEEN PREM. MUNI. INC.	B+	Muni. Ntl. Long	Low	311.5	0.81	9.2	11.5	19.6	18.7	6.1	19.9	3 2 3	6.6	-2.3	7.5
NUVEEN PREM. INC. MUNI.	C	Muni. Ntl. Long	Low	983.9	NA	9.9	10.7	14.8	11.9	6.3	22.6	3 3 3	-1.9	-8.2	-2.8
NUVEEN PREM. INC. MUNI. 2	B	Muni. Ntl. Long	Average	648.2	NA	11.4	14.6	17.0	20.7	5.8	23.0	1 3 2	0.2	-4.8	0.4
NUVEEN PREM. INC. MUNI. 4	B	Muni. Ntl. Long	Average	606.7	NA	11.8	14.5	18.3	18.5	5.8	19.8	1 3 2	-4.6	-9.5	-1.1
NUVEEN QUAL. INC. MUNI.	B+	Muni. Ntl. Interm.	Low	845.1	0.77	9.1	11.2	18.7	17.8	6.2	21.8	3 3 3	7.0	-2.9	7.8
NUVEEN SEL. MAT. MUNI.	C	Muni. Ntl. Long	Low	148.3	0.63	8.4	9.3	13.5	11.7	5.4	14.7	4 3 4	-2.0	-8.1	-1.2
NUVEEN SEL. QUAL. MUNI.	B	Muni. Ntl. Interm.	Low	525.2	0.78	10.0	11.1	18.0	16.1	6.1	22.5	3 3 3	3.7	-3.3	4.5
NUVEEN SEL. T-F INCOME	B+	Muni. Ntl. Long	Very Low	257.3	0.36	9.0	10.5	13.8	12.4	5.7	20.4	3 3 3	0.8	-4.5	1.0
NUVEEN SEL. T-F INCOME 2	B+	Muni. Ntl. Long	Very Low	272.1	0.42	8.5	10.3	11.1	12.5	5.8	20.5	3 3 3	0.5	-5.3	1.1
NUVEEN SEL. T-F INCOME 3	B+	Muni. Ntl. Long	Low	193.9	0.44	9.5	11.1	13.2	13.9	5.6	21.2	3 3 3	-0.4	-7.5	0.0
NUVEEN TEX. QUAL. INC. MUNI.	C	Muni. S.S. Long	Average	150.4	0.83	10.7	12.2	13.4	17.9	5.9	20.9	2 3 3	2.1	-4.2	0.7
NUVEEN VA. PREM. INC. MUNI.	C-	Muni. S.S. Long	High	127.5	0.87	12.3	15.4	22.0	20.6	5.2	23.4	1 3 2	7.7	-2.5	11.0
NUVEEN WASH. PREM. INC. MUNI.	C-	Muni. S.S. Long	High	34.9	0.94	13.1	14.8	15.4	16.2	5.5	22.5	1 4 2	-5.8	-13.2	-7.7
OPPENHEIMER MULTI-SECTOR INC.	B	Multisector	Low	309.8	1.04	8.7	12.3	15.1	11.8	8.6	8.2	4 2 4	0.3	-8.2	-2.7
OPPENHEIMER WORLD BOND	C	Multisector	Low	55.3	NA	6.1	11.4	19.1	13.9	8.5	9.1	4 2 4	-2.6	-13.8	-3.6
PACIFIC AMER. INC. SHARES	C	Interm. (Gen.)	Average	150.1	0.72	10.4	13.4	22.0	17.0	7.3	15.2	2 2 3	0.3	-7.6	1.7
PILGRIM AMER. PRIME RATE	C	Ultrashort	Very Low	1027.8	1.13	8.3	7.7	16.1	15.3	8.2	5.8	4 2 4	10.6	3.1	12.2
PIMCO COMMERCIAL MORT. SECS.	B	Interm. (Gen.)	Average	154.6	0.99	10.6	13.9	16.4	17.3	9.0	18.9	2 2 3	-0.5	-6.7	-0.1
PIONEER INTEREST SHARES	C-	Interm. (Gen.)	Average	101.5	NA	11.1	11.4	17.8	14.9	7.7	18.3	3 2 3	3.7	-4.6	5.7
PREFERRED INCOME	A	Long (Gen.)	Low	161.6	1.51	15.5	17.4	19.2	20.0	7.3	NA	2 2 1	-2.4	-9.8	-4.3
PREFERRED INC. MGMT.	A	Long (Gen.)	Low	152.1	1.84	17.5	19.7	19.5	23.8	7.4	NA	1 1 1	0.1	-7.7	-2.9
PREFERRED INCOME OPPORT.	A	Long (Gen.)	Low	150.1	1.71	17.2	18.6	22.3	20.8	7.2	NA	2 2 1	-2.7	-9.7	-6.2
PROSPECT ST. HIGH-INC.	B+	High Yield	Low	155.2	1.55	12.8	15.7	14.7	16.9	10.5	7.5	4 1 2	11.5	-5.5	1.3
PUTNAM CALIF. INVMT. GR. MUNI.	B	Muni. S.S. Long	Average	56.1	1.15	10.2	12.8	15.6	18.6	5.8	23.5	2 3 3	5.2	-1.6	3.6
PUTNAM CONV. OPPORT. & INC.		Convertibles		100.1	NA	17.2	NA	27.4	NA	6.7	8.4	1 1	-0.6	-11.3	-1.4
PUTNAM DIV. INCOME	B+	Long (Gen.)	Low	65.3	1.46	13.9	13.7	15.4	14.6	7.4	NA	3 2 2	-6.3	-14.4	-11.6
PUTNAM HIGH INC. CONV. & BOND	B	Convertibles	Average	131.8	0.97	13.1	15.3	22.3	19.9	7.3	7.9	3 2 2	13.4	0.0	13.6
PUTNAM HIGH YIELD MUNI.	B+	Muni. Ntl. Long	Very Low	158.6	1.12	8.4	10.2	17.8	16.7	6.3	23.1	3 2 4	18.6	7.3	18.2
PUTNAM INTERM. GOVT. INC.	D	Multisector	Average	527.6	NA	4.1	8.9	8.2	10.0	8.0	8.3	3 3 4	-7.9	-12.8	-6.4
PUTNAM INVMT. GR. MUNI.	C-	Muni. Ntl. Long	Average	111.4	1.49	10.7	9.9	19.4	16.1	6.5	21.5	3 4 3	26.1	14.6	27.0
PUTNAM INVMT. GR. MUNI. II	C	Muni. Ntl. Long	Low	129.4	1.23	10.8	10.0	15.2	18.3	6.2	21.8	3 4 3	8.5	1.5	7.1
PUTNAM INVMT. GR. MUNI. III	C	Muni. Ntl. Long	Low	44.1	NA	9.9	10.1	14.1	15.0	6.1	20.9	3 4 3	0.2	-9.3	0.1
PUTNAM MGD. HIGH YIELD	A	High Yield	Low	110.8	1.04	15.6	16.7	19.7	21.3	8.7	8.0	3 2 1	6.1	0.5	5.2
PUTNAM MGD. MUNI. INC.	C	Muni. Ntl. Long	Low	459.3	1.24	8.5	10.2	13.3	16.0	6.4	20.4	3 4 4	20.0	9.4	20.6
PUTNAM MASTER INC.	B	Multisector	Low	490.7	NA	8.7	12.8	19.6	16.0	8.1	9.0	3 2 4	-3.3	-10.8	-4.3
PUTNAM MASTER INTM. INC.	B	Multisector	Low	332	1.01	7.9	12.0	21.1	16.7	7.8	8.4	3 2 4	-4.5	-15.4	-5.3
PUTNAM MUNI. OPPORTUNITIES	C	Muni. Ntl. Long	Average	107.7	1.05	9.5	12.0	13.6	15.8	6.4	24.3	2 3 3	6.0	0.6	5.2
PUTNAM N.Y. INVMT. GR. MUNI.	C	Muni. S.S. Long	Low	30.3	1.28	9.8	9.7	17.7	12.5	5.8	24.1	3 4 3	3.8	-9.0	4.1
PUTNAM PREMIER INCOME	B	Multisector	Low	1239.1	0.82	8.9	13.0	22.1	17.2	8.2	10.0	3 2 4	-1.1	-11.8	-0.5

NA=Not available.

DATA: MORNINGSTAR, INC., CHICAGO, IL.

MUTUAL FUND SCOREBOARD — Closed-End Bond Funds

FUND	RATING	CATEGORY	RISK	SIZE ASSETS $MIL.	FEES EXPENSE RATIO (%)	NAV. RET. (%) 1 YR.	NAV. RET. (%) 3 YRS.	SHARES RET. (%) 1 YR.	SHARES RET. (%) 3 YRS.	YIELD (%)	MAT. (YRS.)	TREND 3-YEAR ANALYSIS	1996 HIGH	LOW	1/31/97
PUTNAM T-F HEALTH CARE	A	Muni. Ntl. Long	Very Low	207.3	0.90	10.4	10.9	16.7	12.4	6.1	19.9	4 2 3	0.0	−6.0	0.8
RCM STRAT. GLOBAL GOVT. INC.	C−	International	Average	183	1.25	9.1	11.6	16.5	14.1	8.2	12.5	3 2 3	−3.6	−12.6	−6.9
SALOMON BROS. 2008 WWIDE DOL.	B+	International	Very High	377.5	NA	20.3	28.4	22.8	25.3	9.7	18.4	1 1 1	−2.8	−12.3	−6.2
SALOMON BROS. HIGH INC.	A	High Yield	Low	73.2	NA	13.9	17.3	20.2	21.2	8.4	9.6	3 1 2	13.2	4.5	13.6
SALOMON BROS. WWIDE INC.	D	International	Very High	210.3	NA	15.7	32.9	16.8	29.6	10.9	13.7	1 1 1	−2.5	−14.4	−0.1
SCUDDER GLOBAL HIGH INC.	F	International	Very High	77.9	1.79	11.6	29.4	25.4	30.1	9.2	14.4	3 1 2	3.1	−11.1	8.8
SELIGMAN QUAL. MUNI.	C	Muni. Ntl. Long	Average	71.6	1.64	10.1	12.4	17.8	18.2	6.0	25.1	2 3 3	3.4	−5.9	3.8
SELIGMAN SELECT MUNI.	C	Muni. Ntl. Long	Average	200.5	NA	9.6	10.2	20.5	18.5	6.0	23.1	3 3 3	12.1	2.3	10.3
SENIOR HIGH-INC.	B+	High Yield	Very Low	491.1	0.75	11.5	12.3	19.4	16.2	9.0	6.9	4 2 2	9.3	1.9	8.5
SMITH BARNEY INTM. MUNI.	B	Muni. Ntl. Interm.	Very Low	88.2	0.77	7.5	8.4	12.4	9.8	5.5	9.7	4 3 4	1.2	−8.1	1.6
SMITH BARNEY MUNI.	B	Muni. Ntl. Long	Low	63.2	NA	8.7	10.2	9.5	12.5	5.7	12.2	3 4 4	−3.6	−9.4	−3.7
STRATEGIC GLOBAL INCOME	C	International	Average	300.4	1.21	6.9	13.9	12.6	15.2	8.9	14.6	3 1 4	−10.7	−17.3	−11.2
TAURUS MUNI CALIF. HLDG.	C−	Muni. S.S. Long	Average	61.4	NA	10.3	13.1	20.9	19.0	5.7	20.1	2 3 3	3.4	−7.6	3.6
TAURUS MUNI N.Y. HLDG.	D	Muni. S.S. Long	High	82.9	NA	11.7	12.2	35.7	21.5	5.2	22.9	2 3 2	9.7	−8.6	−2.0
TCW CONV. SECS.	C−	Convertibles	Very High	355.1	0.77	19.0	18.9	14.7	19.8	9.0	6.7	2 2 1	13.5	−1.2	6.2
TCW/DW 2000	B	Interm. (Gen.)	High	466.4	NA	13.4	18.0	20.7	15.9	5.5	16.5	1 2 2	−5.2	−10.6	−4.9
TCW/DW 2002	B	Long (Gen.)	High	429.3	0.79	14.6	19.9	18.9	12.9	7.1	16.4	1 2 1	−5.5	−12.6	−6.5
TCW/DW 2003	C	Long (Gen.)	Very High	938.2	0.74	16.4	20.2	25.0	17.1	7.0	14.1	1 2 1	−7.9	−16.7	−8.9
TEMPLETON EMG. MKTS. INC.	D	International	Very High	648	1.09	11.0	18.1	11.2	18.3	10.1	11.2	3 1 3	−4.3	−11.8	−5.9
TEMPLETON GLOBAL GOVT. INC.	C−	International	Average	180.2	0.96	2.3	10.6	13.2	13.3	8.2	7.5	3 2 4	−3.8	−13.1	−4.7
TEMPLETON GLOBAL INC.	C−	International	Average	996.9	0.72	3.1	10.6	12.1	13.3	8.0	5.8	3 2 4	−8.1	−17.6	−7.4
TRANSAMERICA INC. SHARES	D	Long (Gen.)	High	160.1	0.62	11.2	12.6	16.1	15.4	7.6	16.7	2 4 3	1.7	−5.3	2.9
TWO THOUSAND TWO TARGET	C	Long Govt.	Average	118.1	NA	10.3	12.9	16.2	16.2	6.3	17.4	2 2 3	−8.5	−14.5	−9.7
USF&G PACHOLDER	C	High Yield	Average	126.3	1.80	15.2	15.3	13.9	14.6	9.3	7.7	4 1 1	5.2	−5.9	2.3
USLIFE INCOME	C	Long (Gen.)	Average	60.3	1.17	15.7	13.8	16.1	13.8	7.9	22.5	3 2 1	−7.1	−12.0	−8.0
VAN KAMP. AM. CAP. ADV. MUNI. INC.	C	Muni. Ntl. Long	Average	318.3	1.72	12.7	13.7	17.7	13.7	6.2	22.2	2 3 2	−5.6	−10.9	−6.3
VAN KAMP. AM. CAP. ADV. MUNI. INC. II	D	Muni. Ntl. Long	High	117.6	NA	12.5	13.9	20.5	15.8	5.8	21.6	2 3 2	−8.9	−15.6	−9.3
VAN KAMP. AM. CAP. ADV. PA. MUNI. INC.	C−	Muni. S.S. Long	High	76.1	NA	10.3	12.8	13.8	18.0	5.7	21.2	2 4 3	−0.9	−9.6	−0.3
VAN KAMP. AM. CAP. BOND	C−	Interm. (Gen.)	High	237.5	0.68	11.1	12.6	20.0	16.4	7.4	20.1	2 4 3	−2.3	−8.0	0.0
VAN KAMP. AM. CAP. CALIF. MUNI. INC.	C	Muni. S.S. Long	Average	−999	1.58	10.7	11.6	12.3	17.3	5.9	19.9	3 4 3	22.2	11.2	17.1
VAN KAMP. AM. CAP. CALIF. QUAL. MUNI	B+	Muni. S.S. Long	Average	169.3	1.61	12.6	14.4	9.5	17.7	5.8	21.0	2 3 2	0.3	−6.1	0.5
VAN KAMP. AM. CAP. CALIF. VAL. MUNI. INC.	C	Muni. S.S. Long	High	98.3	NA	13.4	16.0	25.2	19.3	5.2	16.7	1 3 2	−7.6	−15.0	−5.0
VAN KAMP. AM. CAP. CONV. SECS.	B+	Convertibles	Very Low	53.7	NA	19.5	18.6	20.3	20.1	4.9	9.7	2 2 1	−9.4	−19.1	−11.3
VAN KAMP. AM. CAP. FLA. MUNI. OPPORT.	D	Muni. S.S. Long	High	25.3	NA	12.2	14.7	15.2	18.4	5.3	20.4	1 4 2	−6.5	−11.4	−4.5
VAN KAMP. AM. CAP. FLA. QUAL. MUNI.	C−	Muni. S.S. Long	Average	111.4	1.64	8.2	10.5	6.1	12.2	6.0	20.5	3 4 4	5.7	−0.5	1.8
VAN KAMP. AM. CAP. INC.	B+	Long (Gen.)	Very Low	123.1	1.00	11.4	13.1	17.1	17.2	9.0	10.3	3 2 2	−1.4	−7.5	1.1
VAN KAMP. AM. CAP. INTM. HI-INC.	A	High Yield	Low	88.7	NA	12.3	16.1	20.4	22.2	9.5	6.6	2 2 2	16.6	7.7	12.9
VAN KAMP. AM. CAP. INVMT. GR. MUNI.	D	Muni. Ntl. Long	Average	51.7	1.51	8.6	8.3	9.2	8.4	6.4	20.8	4 4 4	5.0	−0.1	5.2
VAN KAMP. AM. CAP. LTD. HI-INC.	A	High Yield	Low	68.4	NA	12.0	16.4	15.5	21.4	9.8	6.5	2 2 2	21.3	10.2	17.5
VAN KAMP. AM. CAP. MASS. VAL. MUNI INC.	C	Muni. S.S. Long	Average	41.8	NA	12.1	15.1	23.8	16.1	5.3	18.4	1 3 2	−2.5	−13.6	−4.3
VAN KAMP. AM. CAP. MUNI.	C	Muni. Ntl. Long	Average	619.9	1.61	11.9	13.0	24.3	15.1	5.9	20.1	2 3 2	−4.8	−13.7	−5.2
VAN KAMP. AM. CAP. MUNI. INC.	C−	Muni. Ntl. Long	Average	293.6	1.28	10.7	11.3	11.4	11.3	6.6	19.8	3 3 3	10.4	2.4	6.0
VAN KAMP. AM. CAP. MUNI. OPPORT.	C	Muni. Ntl. Long	High	266.1	1.66	13.4	13.8	22.0	14.0	5.8	19.6	2 3 2	−8.7	−15.0	−8.9
VAN KAMP. AM. CAP. MUNI. OPPORT. II	D	Muni. Ntl. Long	High	172.8	NA	12.3	14.1	24.7	16.8	5.6	21.1	1 3 2	−8.6	−16.6	−7.6
VAN KAMP. AM. CAP. N.J. VAL. MUNI. INC.	C	Muni. S.S. Long	High	38.6	NA	12.8	15.2	23.3	18.0	5.3	19.6	1 3 2	−4.4	−15.0	−6.8
VAN KAMP. AM. CAP. N.Y. QUAL. MUNI.	C	Muni. S.S. Long	Average	97.4	1.68	10.4	11.5	10.0	13.2	5.9	18.6	2 4 3	−2.3	−7.1	−3.6
VAN KAMP. AM. CAP. N.Y. VAL. MUNI. INC.	D	Muni. S.S. Long	High	67.5	NA	14.4	15.7	25.7	17.8	5.1	17.7	1 4 1	−10.0	−18.2	−9.3
VAN KAMP. AM. CAP. OHIO QUAL. MUNI.	B	Muni. S.S. Long	Low	74	1.78	8.9	11.9	17.0	15.4	5.4	18.7	2 3 4	6.9	−1.5	6.1
VAN KAMP. AM. CAP. OHIO VAL. MUNI. INC.	C−	Muni. S.S. Long	High	26	NA	11.7	13.7	23.7	12.6	4.9	18.9	2 3 2	−12.1	−19.6	−10.8
VAN KAMP. AM. CAP. PA. QUAL. MUNI.	B	Muni. S.S. Long	Low	141.2	NA	9.5	11.4	8.4	13.9	6.0	17.8	2 4 3	3.5	−2.8	2.2
VAN KAMP. AM. CAP. PA. VAL. MUNI. INC.	C−	Muni. S.S. Long	High	70.4	NA	11.4	14.6	16.5	14.9	5.5	17.3	1 3 2	−8.4	−18.1	−10.4
VAN KAMP. AM. CAP. SEL. SECT. MUNI.	C−	Muni. Ntl. Long	Average	64.8	1.55	12.6	13.6	20.7	14.4	5.7	21.4	2 3 2	−10.2	−17.9	−8.0
VAN KAMP. AM. CAP. STRAT. SECT. MUNI.	D	Muni. Ntl. Long	High	158	1.67	12.9	13.3	20.1	13.7	5.9	20.9	2 4 2	−6.3	−14.6	−8.0
VAN KAMP. AM. CAP. INS. MUNI.	C−	Muni. Ntl. Long	Average	166	NA	11.1	12.2	13.3	16.6	6.0	21.2	2 4 3	4.2	−1.5	−0.4
VAN KAMP. AM. CAP. MUNI.	C	Muni. Ntl. Long	Average	473.7	NA	12.5	13.5	14.1	13.8	6.3	22.2	2 3 2	−5.2	−9.1	−5.1
VAN KAMP. AM. CAP. CALIF. MUNI.	C	Muni. S.S. Long	Average	79.6	NA	12.4	14.0	15.8	18.2	5.7	20.8	2 3 2	1.0	−6.7	−1.5
VAN KAMP. AM. CAP. FLA. MUNI.	D	Muni. S.S. Long	High	73.8	NA	9.3	11.9	16.8	17.4	5.5	20.4	2 4 3	0.6	−6.3	−0.3
VAN KAMP. AM. CAP. N.J. MUNI.	C−	Muni. S.S. Long	High	70.1	NA	11.4	13.0	20.6	15.9	5.6	19.2	2 4 2	−3.9	−11.1	−3.7
VAN KAMP. AM. CAP. N.Y.	C	Muni. S.S. Long	Average	108.9	NA	11.6	13.5	22.1	16.7	5.4	20.4	2 4 2	−4.5	−12.5	−3.7
VAN KAMP. AM. CAP. PA.	C−	Muni. S.S. Long	Average	131	NA	10.2	12.4	11.7	15.7	5.9	21.0	2 4 3	−4.1	−9.4	−3.0
VAN KAMP. AM. CAP. VAL. MUNI. INC.	D	Muni. Ntl. Long	High	363.4	1.77	12.1	13.7	22.2	15.6	5.8	19.9	2 3 2	−8.0	−16.3	−8.0
VESTAUR SECURITIES	D	Interm. (Gen.)	Average	98.3	0.90	10.3	11.6	20.9	17.1	7.2	18.2	2 4 3	−2.0	−6.6	0.2
VOYAGEUR ARIZ. MUNI. INC.	D	Muni. S.S. Long	High	44.7	0.78	11.8	15.5	20.9	17.0	5.4	19.1	1 4 2	−1.8	−9.3	−0.9
VOYAGEUR COLO. INS. MUNI. INC.	F	Muni. S.S. Long	High	32.5	0.75	12.9	14.1	12.7	14.3	5.3	19.5	1 4 2	−1.8	−8.7	−2.9
VOYAGEUR FLA. INS. MUNI. INC.	F	Muni. S.S. Long	Very High	36.9	0.80	13.4	16.0	18.6	18.4	5.3	22.9	1 4 2	−3.9	−11.4	−2.8
VOYAGEUR MINN. MUNI. INC.	C	Muni. S.S. Long	Average	25.3	0.82	10.8	12.8	12.0	12.4	6.0	21.1	2 4 3	3.1	−1.8	−0.4
VOYAGEUR MINN. MUNI. INC. II	C	Muni. S.S. Long	High	107.1	0.77	12.8	15.4	17.3	15.7	5.9	23.1	1 4 2	−3.0	−10.7	−2.9
VOYAGEUR MINN. MUNI. INC. III	C	Muni. S.S. Long	High	39.8	0.81	12.5	15.2	18.8	15.7	5.9	23.8	1 3 2	−2.3	−10.3	−4.1
WORLDWIDE DOLLARVEST	B	International	Very High	104.2	0.80	8.4	31.4	18.8	32.4	10.7	13.7	1 1 4	−6.2	−17.4	−2.0
ZENIX INCOME	A	High Yield	Average	104.1	NA	16.6	19.5	28.6	23.3	9.0	8.4	1 1 1	22.3	8.0	18.5

NA=Not available.

DATA: MORNINGSTAR, INC., CHICAGO, IL.

About the Author

Jeffrey M. Laderman is a senior writer at BUSINESS WEEK specializing in finance. He helped launch the annual BUSINESS WEEK Mutual Fund Scoreboard, writes the accompanying cover stories, and reports on the stock market and mutual funds. He also helped create the Interactive Mutual Fund Scoreboard and is a regular contributor to Business Week Online. Mr. Laderman is a graduate of Rutgers University and has a master's degree in journalism from Columbia University. He is a Chartered Financial Analyst and a member of the New York Society of Security Analysts and the Association for Investment Management and Research.